Presidential Elections

Presidential Elections

Contemporary Strategies
of
American Electoral Politics

EIGHTH EDITION

Nelson W. Polsby
Aaron Wildavsky

THE FREE PRESS
A Division of Macmillan, Inc.
NEW YORK

Maxwell Macmillan Canada
TORONTO

Maxwell Macmillan International
NEW YORK   OXFORD   SINGAPORE   SYDNEY

The Free Press
A Division of Macmillan, Inc.
866 Third Avenue, New York, N.Y. 10022

Maxwell Macmillan Canada, Inc.
1200 Eglinton Avenue East
Suite 200
Don Mills, Ontario M3C 3N1

Macmillan, Inc. is part of the Maxwell Communication
Group of Companies.

Printed in the United States of America

printing number

1 2 3 4 5 6 7 8 9 10

Library of Congress Cataloging-in-Publication Data

Polsby, Nelson W.
    Presidential elections: contemporary strategies of American
electoral politics / Nelson W. Polsby, Aaron Wildavsky.—8th ed.
        p.   cm.
    Includes bibliographical references and index.
    ISBN 0-02-922785-2.—ISBN 0-02-922786-0 (pbk.)
    1. Presidents—United States—Election.   I. Wildavsky, Aaron B.
II. Title.
JK528.P63   1991
324.973—dc20   91–26954
                                                   CIP

To our children
Lisa, Emily, and Daniel Polsby
Adam, Sara, Ben, and Dan Wildavsky

Contents

Preface

The central purpose of this book is to provide what for want of a better name might be called civic education. We think people are entitled to information about the choices they make—not merely about the alternatives presented, but also about the processes that produce alternatives. We also think that Americans owe it to themselves and to their community to seek out and evaluate information about the choices that will be important in their lives. Presidential elections in the United States involve significant choices for millions of Americans and in one way or another affect nearly everyone else on earth. Thus, it has seemed to us worthwhile to offer a discussion of the entire presidential election process, a discussion that is unsentimental, nonpartisan, and as clear as we can make it about how and why things happen as they do. Ideally, this should help people follow events and, if they choose, participate in them. It should also help to minimize false expectations, by supplying an antidote to the unrealistic and cynical views of politics that tend to develop when people do not understand why things turn out less well than they had hoped.

We think that civic education plays an important part in the risky business of self-government. Among other things, it alerts people to changes that are likely to affect their lives. Over the past twenty years, changes in presidential elections have had such effects. For example, between 1972 and 1976 the Democratic party forbade unit voting and made it easier for more than one candidate to come into the national convention with a chance to win. This attempt to increase political competition was largely nullified by the national television networks. The networks, following their own need to generate excitement over early nomination coverage, stimulated delegates and party leaders to decide on their preferences early in the election season and consequently started bandwagons. Thus, a rule change that made it more difficult for a single candidate to sew up the nomination before the nominating convention was overwhelmed by the gradual growth of tele-

xi

vision's focus on the candidates who led early in the selection processes. Between 1976 and 1984, the Democrats made some more changes. This time they required the states to choose their delegates during a more restricted period of three months. Here again, the attempt was to keep the networks from focusing on just one contest by making sure that more than one state's delegate selection would take place on each of the Tuesdays set aside for that purpose. But what happened was that the set of candidates was winnowed sharply after the earliest delegate-selecting events, in Iowa and New Hampshire, and all other prospective candidates were eliminated.

In 1988, media effects were also strong. Although Richard Gephardt won in the first-in-the-nation Iowa Democratic caucuses, he failed to get much favorable notice in the news media because something more interesting to journalists occurred that night on the Republican side, namely an unexpectedly strong showing by the Reverend Pat Robertson. Without an adequate media bounce, Gephardt could not overcome the natural geographic advantage of Massachusetts Governor Michael Dukakis in the New Hampshire primary, the next event of the election year.

For most of this century many academics and a few politicians have called for responsible party government. The idea was that the centrifugal tendencies of the separation of powers would be overcome by establishing strong political parties. These parties would at once be ideologically consistent—proposing a coherent set of policies across the board—and compelling—enforcing these views on presidents and legislators. In our book we give reasons for believing that such parties of advocacy would be unwise and, likely, unworkable. These views may be about to be tested. Party activists, unlike the general run of the citizenry, are becoming more ideological. This has occurred primarily because southern conservatives are less likely than heretofore to be Democrats and more likely to add strength to the right wing of the Republican party. Meanwhile, the northeastern liberal component of the Republican party is shrinking. Democratic party activists, augmented by the increased pressure of strong feminists and leaders from the African-American community, are becoming more left, liberal, and egalitarian than Democratic voters at large and Republican party activists are more right-wing, socially conservative and hierarchical, and economically individualistic and market oriented than rank-and-file Republican members. Whether these internal party changes will have the effects they are supposed to have on public policy without antagonizing voters is an important question of our time.

It is now clear that the changes in the nominating process of the past few elections add up to a fundamentally different role for political parties. This should be understood and debated before these changes accumulate into an inexorable and inevitable pattern. The question is whether our parties will seek office by maintaining and nurturing consensus or will become organizations purely of factional advocacy. Every party must do—and does—some of each: reconciling conflicting views and advancing the interests of factions. But how much of each? The balance has been altered in favor of factionalism to the detriment of consensus building. There would be no great difficulty in this if it were not that sometimes the policy positions advocated by party activists tend to be unpopular with most other people. Thus, it is possible for the nominating process to produce candidates who appeal to the people who become delegates but not to voters. This happened to the Democrats in 1972 and to the Republicans in 1964. In 1976 a Democratic president was elected who could boast that he owed nothing to anybody—certainly not to the leaders of his own party. In 1980, he failed to be reelected, the first such failure of an elected incumbent since Herbert Hoover lost in 1932, in the middle of the Great Depression. Though Ronald Reagan was in many ways a single-minded ideologue, he achieved broad popular appeal in the later months of his presidency, after the Iran-Contra scandal blew over, and while relations with the Soviet bloc relaxed dramatically. This momentarily obscured the extent to which partisan polarization was taking place. But if our national parties no longer aspire to perform the integrative function of keeping the country together, what agencies will do so? This is one question that we must keep in mind while pondering the real functions of such mechanisms as the formulas for financing the elections and the methods for allocating delegates on the basis of votes in primaries.

Another way of approaching the role of political parties in presidential elections is to ask whether their purpose is to express shades of opinion among their own activists or to govern the nation. If their purpose is expression, then rules maximizing the most minute differences are in order. If their purpose is to govern, then rules for maximizing cohesion are appropriate. Evidently, both the capacity to express differences and the ability to govern effectively are necessary. The issue is one of proportion. As our system is presently structured, we think the danger is that expressiveness will overwhelm effectiveness. Yet the need for effectiveness does not seem to have abated, judging from widespread complaints about the activities of the so-called single-issue special-interest groups. Crises over such issues as the federal budget suggest that there is still a need for institutions whose functions are to moderate opinions and structure difficult issues so that they can be resolved. Political parties have traditionally been those institutions. As the California Committee for Party Renewal says:

> Only political parties can compromise and incorporate the wishes of a wide range of citizens in programs that encompass a multitude of issues and stretch across a greater span of time than a brief term of office that may or may not be renewed. Only political parties can marshal the resources and develop the strategy to recruit, train, support and guide a succession of highly qualified individuals to advance those programs during their terms in office. Only political parties can provide an effective means of holding elected representatives accountable to the people who elect them on the basis of such programs, by being ready to deny their resources to unworthy incumbents seeking reelection. Only political parties can put forward a broad panel of spokespersons in defense of such programs informing and educating the citizenry in a debate which extends beyond the short-range electoral prospects of particular candidates. In short, only political parties can provide us with the cohesion, continuity and accountability necessary to make democracy work.[1]

We agree.

We have tried in this book not merely to keep up with changes in the rules governing candidate selection, political campaign contributions, party delegate participation, voting eligibility, and the like, but in addition to organize and synthesize these into the general view of political resources and political strategies that has informed our approach to presidential elections from the beginning. As always, we are confident that our understanding of these matters is imperfect and the unfolding of events will make this only too clear. We have, however, attempted to stay abreast of political life in America and to shift our gaze toward those elements that seem most important in shaping the strategies and outcomes of politics in the 1990s, just as earlier editions attempted the same tasks for the 1960s, 1970s, and 1980s. We only hope that what we say in this edition is sufficiently interesting so that four years hence it will still seem worthwhile for us to try again, in another edition, to come nearer to the mark.

Twenty-eight years is a long useful life for a book—especially a book about something as volatile as American politics. When we wrote the first edition of *Presidential Elections*, in the 1960s, the rules and practices of the presidential nomination and election process had not changed for decades. Since then, they have changed a lot. Anyone who claims that there is no such thing as real or fundamental change in American politics need only glance at the necessary amendments we have made to our account of what has happened over the years. Procedures for making nominating decisions, the kinds of people who are influential in making them, the roles of the news media, the methods and objectives of nomination and election campaigns, the characteristics of convention delegates, and their basic dispositions toward politics have all undergone drastic alterations. Our one confident expectation is that the growth industry of chronicling changes from one edition of *Presidential Elections* to the next will not suffer decline.

For over a decade, from the Second Edition in 1968 to the Fifth Edition in 1980, we argued, with as much cogency as we could muster and as much passion as propriety would permit, that the party system was in trouble. The worst wounds, we felt, were self-inflicted: changes in rules that drove out deliberation by party leaders in favor of choice through a large number of primaries that involved more people but in a less consequential way. The results of primaries were added together and early primaries, magnified by the coverage of the news media, had an enormous impact on later decisions. It thus became evident that national nominating conventions were losing their decision-making ability, ratifying rather than actually choosing presidential candidates. By the 1980 conventions, which were even drearier than usual, the choices were foregone conclusions. The preferences of political scientists, reporters, and other professional observers began to change. They, too, became worried about the decline of deliberative party decision making. The result was a number of serious proposals to bring party professionals and public officials back into the nominating conventions in significant numbers. The body of this book contains the story. Here, in our preface, we wish to observe that if this Eighth Edition contains less advocacy, that is because the main lines of our earlier thinking have become much more commonly accepted. We do not claim that our views now prevail, however. Rival conceptions of representation continue to be reflected in contention over basic rules of the nominating process.

As changes have mounted up through the years, a few features of the system have remained. The professional party regulars of the First Edition, who wanted party unity in order to win the presidential election, are still here and active. Their numbers were modestly augmented by the rules that gave members of Congress and governors and other party officials delegate status. Professionals are outnumbered by the amateur activists purists of the Second and Third Editions, who would rather be right and remain a minority than compromise and attract a majority; circumstances, however, themselves a product in part of rule changes, have altered the position of party activists. On the one hand, they agree more on issues than before. On the other hand, the dominance of primaries in the delegate selection process means that the nomination is essentially determined before the convention. This makes ideological purism at the conventions moot. There is no point in arguing about a nomination that has already been decided. Activists, therefore, do want to win with their party's candidate, but their views on that subject no longer matter by the time they get to the convention. State primaries and state conventions are still around, but candidates whose delegates are selected in primaries—especially the early primaries—have a dominant voice. Money is still, as the late Jesse Unruh said, the mother's milk of politics, but it is now raised differently than it once was, and it must be spent earlier and in different and more dispersed feedings. State caucuses and candidate organizations still matter a great deal at the conventions, but increasingly they must ally themselves with organized caucuses of young people, women, African-Americans, Mexican-Americans, and other groups organized on demographic lines. All this change means that we have had to take account of the ways in which the nomination and election of presidents have evolved in our time; thus there is much history in this book along with contemporary analysis.

It would be fair to say, since we last wrote, that concern over the effectiveness and the cohesion of American government has increased. Perhaps the rise of unease has something to do with the decline of political parties. And perhaps the decline of parties has something to do with the way in which nomination and election to the presidency, once celebrated as the central source of party unity, has begun to contribute to the problem instead of the solution. The polarization of party activists on ideological lines only adds urgency to this quest. In this edition, therefore, we pay even more attention than in the past to the prospects of the American party system, not only to what has been but also to what it is becoming and what it ought to be.

We are pleased to acknowledge that now, as in the past, our work relies heavily upon the contributions of our colleagues in the profession of political science, who have done so much to increase knowledge about parties, voters, and elections. We have acknowledged their work, as scholars do, in the notes at the end of this book, where curious readers can also find a great deal of the technical detail that sustains many of our statements, as well as ideas for further reading. Some of our colleagues have given us direct aid and comfort. We continue to be grateful for the work that has stood the test of time that Bill Cavala, Byron Shafer, and Duane Oldfield put into earlier editions. The sizeable effort that we have made to update this book was greatly facilitated by the help of Jonathan Bernstein, John Gerring, Kim Jolliff, Russell Paulsen, Jesse Malkin, Christine Trost, Eunice Baek, Ben Highton, Beth Reingold, Paul S. Edwards and Robert Lopez. Friends and colleagues who have read parts or all of this new edition or supplied us with information include Merrill Shanks, Warren E. Miller, and Herbert Alexander.

Finally, we acknowledge that our families have been uppermost in our minds as we wrote this revision. Now that most of our children have reached voting age, and beyond, it gives us special pleasure to dedicate this book to them.

Berkeley California   N. W. P.
April 1, 1991   A. W.

Introduction: Political Strategies and Presidential Elections

This book is about the winning of the presidential office. Although many writers have alleged that the president occupies a great and lonely eminence, the presidential office exists within a cultural and political tradition that shapes the ways in which it is won and, later, the ways in which presidential power is exercised. We will, however, not speak further here about the exercise of executive power, except as it is affected by the processes of selection. Rather, the task before us is to describe the context within which the battle for presidential office is waged, to discuss the strategies of contending parties, and, if possible, to explain why some strategies are used by some contestants and other strategies by others. In this way we hope to elucidate a significant area of our common political life.

Our thesis is a simple one: that strategies of participants in a presidential election make sense once we understand the web of circumstances in which they operate. This principle applies to candidates and their managers, to delegates at nominating conventions, to party workers, and to voters. Strategies are courses of action consciously pursued toward well-understood goals. Watching strategies helps us to learn how leaders use the constraints and opportunities of their environment to achieve their goals.

Both the political strategies of participants in presidential elections and the circumstances that give rise to them are relatively stable, persistent features of our political system. We have had a two-party political system with the same two major parties for well over a hundred years. Presidential nominees have been formally selected in national party conventions for an even longer period.[1] Presidential candidates have always been faced with such problems as deciding whether more or less emphasis on their party affiliation will help them gain votes. So long as party preferences were not distributed evenly among the electorate, it has made sense for the strategy of Democratic candidates to emphasize their party label, while Republicans have been more inclined to minimize their connection with their party. The growth of identification with the Republican party over the last decade has weakened the force of this strategic imperative in recent years, and Democrats have had to worry whether turning out Democratic identifiers would be enough to win.

Political strategies that persist over a period of time are reasonably easy to identify, even when they are colored by the distinctive styles and personalities of particular candidates. We hope, therefore, to achieve a level of discussion that goes beyond the special circumstances of 1992 or any other year, and say something about American presidential elections in general. This task is not made easier by the undeniable fact that the rules of the game themselves have undergone changes over time, but it has not been made impossible. Our intention is to show how changes in the rules affect how politicians behave in presidential election politics. In fact, the very rapidity with which the rules have recently changed makes clearer than ever that the importance politicians ascribe to them is not accidental. Their disagreements over the rules reveal that real differences in outcomes are at stake depending upon whether the game is played by one set of rules or another.

In large measure, a description and analysis such as ours is possible because of the efforts of dozens of scholars who have reported upon and with ever-increasing detail and accuracy investigated the component parts of the American political system. The purpose of this book is to synthesize these reports for the enlightenment and use of interested citizens. But we cannot forecast the outcome of any particular election, and we have no desire (at least, not here) to advise people how to vote.

In the first two chapters we identify the characteristics of the American political system that make up the strategic environment within which the pursuit of the presidency takes place. The would-be president must come to terms with voters and political activists, who enter each election period as complex bundles of already formed habits, attitudes, and loyalties. Candidates must deal with interest groups and parties that activate these habits. And they must pay attention to the rules by which votes are counted. In the second chapter, we discuss the comparative availability to candidates of certain key resources, such as money and control over information.

These two chapters lay out a framework for much that follows in the third and fourth chapters. These deal, successively, with the various steps of the nomination and election processes. At this point in the book, we discuss a variety of classic strategic "moves," such as entering or delaying entry in primaries, the manipulation of interpretations of primary results so as to gain momentum from one primary to the next, the starting and stopping of bandwagons before and at national party conventions, the selection of areas of the country in which to campaign, and the choice of issues to emphasize. In Chapters 3 and 4, we relate those moves to their necessary preconditions in terms of resources and also relate them to their probable consequences.

In the fifth chapter, we discuss significant reforms that have altered the strategic framework of presidential elections, as well as reform proposals that would in some respects reconstitute the party system and redistribute resources among presidential candidates. Reforms and reform proposals are often debated rather abstractly on their presumed merits, without being related to any concrete consequences. We hope to provoke insight into the subject by looking at reforms in the light of the distributions of benefits and handicaps which we believe they allocate to various participants in presidential elections. We are interested, for example, in the on-again, off-again emergence of a regional primary in the South. If successful, this may well lead to a demand for national primaries, which, in turn, could spur a reconsideration of the electoral college.

Finally, in Chapter 6, we state in general terms the properties of political parties as they are emerging in the framework provided by contemporary presidential elections. In particular we juxtapose the emerging parties of advocacy with the persisting fact that in our system public officials receive a few specific and meaningful policy directives from the electorate. We show that while our political system discourages both strict application of majority rule and mandates on specific policies, it is still meaningful to speak of our form of government as democratic, open, and responsive—as well as flexible, tough, stable, and resourceful. Whether these qualities will persist, however, depends on the maintenance of major political parties that continue to reconcile divergent interests. The capacity of parties to mediate between citizen and government and among sectors of society is now under severe strain. Insofar as there is a tendency for activists identified with the two major parties to grow further apart, not only from each other, but from the bulk of citizens who identify with party labels, it is worthwhile considering whether parties ameliorate, reflect, or in fact exacerbate differences. Activists who care mostly about programmatic and ideological correctness coexist with those who care mostly about political cohesion and winning elections in the presidential nominating process. The final chapter assesses the balance of power between these groups within the parties, and considers whether popular attitudes toward the entire process are becoming so negative as to give advantage to politicians and candidates who oppose the whole fabric of representative government in the United States.

There is evidence that political parties have in fact not declined in some ways. The national party committees have grown strong in important respects and party cohesion is growing in Congress. But there can be little doubt that important functions parties once performed, especially in presidential elections, now have to be shared with other forces.[2] Once upon a time, political parties virtually monopolized election campaigns. Now they share with or relinquish to candidates and their entourages of professional specialists the jobs of recruiting people to run the campaign, ascertaining popular preferences, and communicating with voters. The financing of elections, the raising of issues, the recruitment and advertising of candidates now belong to a variety of interest groups, media people, and self-starting candidates, all of whom compete as well as cooperate with political parties. Although the financial base and training capacity of national parties has improved, so has the ability of rival institutions. Thus the traditional division of labor—public officials and interest groups making policies and political parties nominating and electing candidates—has become complicated. Interest groups have become much more important at the electoral level, in which they once participated only sporadically, because the focus of their activities was at the policy level. Parties, by contrast, have diminished in electoral importance. They are consequently less important in the coordination of public policy and are less effective at keeping certain issues out of politics and mobilizing support for opposition to others. The crucial connections between electoral politics and policy politics have diminished.

Nevertheless, the most active members of the parties have increasingly developed coherent views on public policy. Democrats are more unambiguously liberal and Republicans more conservative than they were twenty or thirty years ago. While parties are more closely identified with public policies, consequently, they may be less effective in implementing them.

Presidential elections are important to us as citizens. They constitute a major (though, of course, not the only) means of guiding our future and remind us of our heritage of political responsibility and freedom.

1

The Strategic Enviroment: Participants

Political strategies are worked out within a framework of circumstances that are in part subject to manipulation but in greater part are "given." This fact of life also applies to the strategies of aspirants to the presidency, who must construct extremely complex plans of action within a context of hundreds of relevant circumstances, most of which lie beyond their control. Some of these circumstances are contingent upon and relate to the strategies and resources of other participants in the election process. Other circumstances are more stable and have to do with features of the American political system that are in place before the contest starts. These features provide advantages and handicaps differently to Democrats and Republicans, to incumbent presidents and challengers, to household names and newcomers. In this chapter and the next, we shall deal with these "givens" of the political system to show how they shape the decisions of presidential election strategists.

Voters

Voters vary in their party loyalties, the strength of their commitment to their views, and their interest in politics. Most of them are not interested in most public issues most of the time.[1] In a society like ours, it apparently is quite possible to live comfortably without being politically concerned. Political activity is costly and eats up time and energy at an astounding rate. To be informed and politically active on issues like control of nuclear arms or on the operations of a municipal electric plant is not a matter of a few moments of reflection. One must attend meetings, listen to or participate in discussion, read books and articles, attempt to

I

persuade or be persuaded by others, and engage in other time-consuming labor. This means foregoing other activities, like devoting extra time to the job, playing with the children, and watching TV. So far as we can tell it is these other activities rather than public affairs that are the primary concerns of most people, and the costs of participation in public affairs appear, for most people, to be greater than the returns. Only a few people receive financial rewards or hold jobs or are acclaimed in the public arena, considerations that might lead them to devote the time and effort required to participate. It is only when issues strike close to home, as prolonged unemployment might do, or rapid inflation or sudden and sharp tax increases, that most citizens would find it worthwhile to attend to politics rather than do other things.

Even so, there are a few people who are continuously interested in a wide variety of issues. These are usually public officials, interest-group leaders, newspaper editors, and academics—all people whose occupations require political interest. There is a larger number who have specialized interests in specific policy areas. These may include all of the above, as well as members of civic organizations and interest groups, citizens who are directly affected, and a sprinkling of others who make a hobby of being interested, including seekers after causes and people who like to get their names on letterheads. These political activists, who may or may not themselves be leaders, are different from ordinary voters, as we shall see.

The fact that individuals vary enormously in their degree of interest has profound implications for political life. For ordinary citizens, interest is a necessary condition for influence. The interested tend to go to meetings where public affairs are discussed and decided. They tend to belong to political parties and to work in various ways to help the party of their choice. They cultivate their access to public officials. They tend to care more about the outcomes of public policies and to communicate their concerns to decision makers. And so they become more influential.

Differences in interest also influence voting behavior: people who are interested in politics tend to vote, and those who are uninterested tend not to vote.[2] Who are included in these two groups? In general, the better-educated people are more active and interested in public affairs. They also tend to be better off financially and more settled in their communities.[3] This is also the population from which the Republican party draws disproportionate support, which consequently gives it a substantial advantage among voters who tend to turn out most reliably for presidential elections. On the other hand, the low-turnout groups, frequently Democratic, tend to be numerically greater than the high-turnout groups. Furthermore, traditionally Democratic groups may be clustered in a way that maximizes their strength in presidential elections by being located in areas that are favored by the Electoral College system of vote counting. We shall return to this topic later.

How do voters make up their minds whom to support? Most people vote according to their habitual party affiliation.[4] In other words, because they always support a particular party, many people will have made up their minds how to vote in 1992 before the candidates are even chosen. These party regulars are likely to be more interested and active in politics and have more political knowledge than people who call themselves political "independents."[5] But they rarely change their minds. They tend to listen mostly to their own side of political arguments and to agree with the policies espoused by their party. They even go so far as to ignore information that they perceive to be unfavorable to the party of their choice.[6]

If party is so important in giving a structure to voters' pictures of reality and in helping them choose their preferred presidential candidate before the candidate is even nominated, we had best inquire where people get their party affiliations. There seems to be no simple answer to this. The party affiliations of most voters seem to be governed by a number of forces. An individual lives in a social context and inherits a social identity that often contains a political component. People are Democrats or Republicans, in part, because their families and the other people with whom they interact are Democrats or Republicans.[7] Most individuals come into close contact with affiliates of only one party.[8] And just as people tend to share characteristics with their friends and families, such as income and educational level, religious affiliation, area of residence, and so on, so they also tend to share party loyalties with them.[9]

Of course, we all know of instances where people do not share various status-giving characteristics with their parents and at least some of their friends, so it should come as no surprise that sometimes children do not share the politics of their parents. No doubt political differences tend to run together with the other kinds of differences. But by and large, voters retain the party loyalties of the primary groups of which they are a part.

The overall result is to give each of the major political parties reservoirs of voting strength they can count on from year to year. Republicans traditionally do well in the small towns and rural areas of New England, the Middle Atlantic states, and the Midwest. They draw their support from people who are richer and better educated than Democratic supporters, occupy managerial or professional positions or run small businesses, live in or move into the well-to-do suburban areas, and are predominantly Protestant. Democrats draw great support from the large cities. Wage earners, union members, Catholics, African-American voters, and many of the descendants of the great waves of immigrants who entered this country in the latter half of the nineteenth century—Jews, Irish, Poles—all contribute disproportionately to the Democratic vote.[10]

One may ask how these particular groups came to have these particular loyalties. We must turn to history to find answers to this question. Enough is known about a few groups to make it possible to speculate about what kinds of historical events tend to align groups with a political party.

Let us take a few examples. We all know about the "Solid South," which from the Civil War until the era of George Wallace and Barry Goldwater was predominantly Democratic in its presidential voting. For all those years, resentment against the harsh Reconstruction period under the leadership of the Republican party was reflected in the election returns. Less well known is the fact that the South was not unanimous in its enthusiasm for the Civil War or in its resentment of Reconstruction. In many states of the Old South there were two kinds of farms: plantations on the flat land, which grew cash crops, used slaves, and, in general, prospered before the Civil War; and subsistence farms in the uplands, which had a few or no slaves and, in general, were run by poorer white people. This latter group formed the historical core of mountain areas that year after year, well into the latter half of the twentieth century, voted Republican in presidential elections. These areas were located in western Virginia and North Carolina, eastern Tennessee and Kentucky, and southeastern West Virginia.[11] More recently, through a combination of white Republicans migrating in, black Democrats migrating out, and conversion from Democratic to Republican of conservative white southerners, the once-solidly Democratic South has become far more competitive—a lot less Democratic and a lot more Republican.[12]

The voting habits of African-American citizens, where they have voted, have been shaped by several traumas. The Civil War freed them and made them Lincoln Republicans. The reaction to Reconstruction in the South disenfranchised them, and the growth of American industry brought them north, where a crushing burden of economic destitution was added to racial discrimination. The severe effects of the Great Depression of 1929 on African-American voters in the North brought them into the New Deal coalition, and the Northern African-American voter has remained Democratic ever since.[13] As these voters have observed Democratic politicians espousing causes in which they believe, they have increased their already high levels of support.

If, for some people, the historical events of the Civil War and the depression of the late 1920s and early 1930s shaped their political heritage, for others the critical forces seem less dramatic and more diffuse. It is possible to see why the poor become Democrats, since the Democratic party since the 1930s has been so welfare-minded; but why do the rich lean toward the Republicans? Undoubtedly, in part, this is a reaction to the redistributive aspirations of some New Deal programs and the inclination of Democratic presidents to expand the role of government in the economy. But in all probability it is also a response to the record of the congressional wing of the Republican party, which so thoroughly dominated the post–Civil War era of industrial expansion. In this era, Republican policies vigorously encouraged—and to a degree underwrote—risk taking by private businessmen, granted them federal aid in a variety of forms, and withheld federal regulation from private enterprises.

Sometimes party affiliation coincides with ethnic identification because of the political and social circumstances surrounding the entry of ethnic groups into the country. In southern New England, politics was dominated by the Republican party and by "Yankees" of substance and high status during the decades following the Civil War. During these decades, thousands of Irish people streamed into this area. The Democratic party welcomed them; the Republicans did not. Soon the Democratic percentage of the two-party vote began to increase, and Irish politicians took over the Democratic party.[14] In the Midwest, events such as American involvement in two wars against Germany under Democratic auspices seem to have shaped the political preferences of Americans of German descent toward the Republicans.[15]

These are a few examples of the ways in which group membership and historical circumstances have given voters special ties with particular parties. Once voters have such ties, a great deal follows. Merely to list the functions that party identification performs for voters—reducing their costs of acquiring political information, telling them what side they are on, organizing their information by ordering their preferences, letting them know what is of prime importance—is to suggest the profound significance of parties for voting behavior. Politics is complex; there are many possible issues, relevant political personalities, and choices to be made on election day. Voters who follow their party identification, however, can simplify their choices and reduce to manageable proportions the time and effort they spend on public affairs simply by voting for their party's candidate. Voters with strong party identifications need not puzzle over each and every issue. They can, instead, listen to the pronouncements of their party leaders, who inform them what issues are important, what information is most relevant to those issues, and what position they ought to take. Of course, citizens with greater interest in public affairs will want to investigate matters for themselves. Even so, their party identification provides them with important guides in learning about the issues that interest them as well as for the many matters on which they

cannot possibly be well informed. All of us, including full-time participants like the president, have to find ways to cut information costs on
some issues.[16] For most people who vote, identification with one of the
two major political parties performs that indispensable function most of
the time.

Another method of reducing the costs of information might be for
voters to have a set of internally consistent beliefs, sometimes known as
an "ideology." There are three ways in which ideologies might structure
political beliefs. Voters or party activists might be conscious of having an
ideology, they might use ideological labels as a shortcut in decision
making, or they might think of one issue as related to another. There is
some evidence that a minority of voters use consistent ideological thinking, a larger minority make use of various forms of group references
when expressing preferences for a particular candidate, and an even larger
group makes use of ideological labels.[17] Labels such as left and right and
liberal and conservative, while commonly used in political discourse,
sometimes work and sometimes do not in structuring attitudes. If we talk
about social welfare or economic redistributive issues, these labels serve
reasonably well. But some social issues are harder to sort out. What
would be the "conservative" position on abortion, for example, when
conservative libertarians are pro-choice and conservative authoritarians
pro-life?[18]

Specific candidates of special attractiveness or unattractiveness may
under certain circumstances sway voters to leave the party of their choice.
The extraordinary elections of President Eisenhower are one example of
this. His appeal to Democrats was quite amazing. But this was possible
partially because these Democrats did not perceive Eisenhower as a partisan figure, but rather as a nonpartisan war hero. It is not surprising,
then, that his personal popularity did not greatly aid other Republicans
who ran with him, or the Republican party, once he no longer headed the
ticket. The candidacy of George McGovern had the opposite effect; it
propelled Democrats out of their party. So did Jimmy Carter in 1980.
While Ronald Reagan was avowedly partisan, he did his best to identify
with past Democratic heroes—Franklin Delano Roosevelt and Harry S.
Truman. Reagan's personal popularity, both in 1980 and 1984, was far
greater than his party's.[19]

Most of the time issues have much the same sporadic and peripheral
effect on voters' loyalties as candidates. Let us see why. We can say to
begin with that at least three preconditions must be satisfied for a voter's
opinion about an issue to change his or her vote.[20] First, voters must
know about the issue; second, they must care about it at least a little; and
third, they must be able to distinguish the positions of the parties and their

candidates on the issue. Data from public opinion polls tell us that most people are not well informed about the content of issues most of the time.[21] All but major public issues are thus eliminated for most people. And even these major issues may enter the consciousness of most people in only the most rudimentary way.

Once a voter has some grasp of the content of a public policy and learns to prefer one outcome over another, he must also find public leaders to espouse his point of view. Finding differences on policy issues between parties is not always easy. Party statements on policy may be vague because leaders have not decided what to do. Leaders may deliberately obfuscate an issue for fear of alienating interested publics. They may try to hold divergent factions in their parties together by glossing over disagreements on many specific issues. Even when real party differences on policy exist, many voters may not be aware of them. The subject may be highly technical, or the time required to master the subject may be more than most people are willing to expend. By the time we get down to those who know and care about and can discriminate between party positions on issues, we usually have a small proportion of the electorate. The proportion of ideologically sophisticated voters appears to be no larger than 30 percent.[22] What can we say about these people?

Their most obvious characteristic is interest in and concern about issues and party positions. But these are precisely the people who are most likely to be strong party identifiers. Party loyalty thus works against the possibility that voters will shift allegiance just because of a disagreement on one or two issues.[23] The number of issue-oriented "independents" who are left is very small, especially if we consider that most people who call themselves independents actually lean toward one or another of the two major parties.[24] It is not unlikely that purely issue-oriented people are distributed in sufficiently small numbers on both sides of major policy questions, that the total number of votes changed by the impact of any specific issue is bound to be minute.

We still have some preconditions to satisfy, however, before even these changes can be accepted as certain. One is that there must not be other issues that are also highly salient to voters and that work the other way. For if voters were willing to change their votes on one particular issue, why should they not switch their support back because of another? There usually are many issues in a campaign; only if all or most of the issues pointed voters in the same direction would they be likely to switch their votes. But what is the likelihood that parties will arrange their policies along a broad front, forcing large numbers of "independent" voters from or into the fold? It is low, but not impossible. In 1964 the Republicans, led by Barry Goldwater, may have done so. And in 1972 the Democratic candidate, George McGovern, "was perceived as so far left on the issues that his Republican opponent, Richard Nixon, was generally closer to the electorate's average issue position . . . on 11 out of 14 separate issues."[25]

Although it is true that the less knowledge a person has about public affairs, the more likely he is to vote for a candidate of the opposite party, it is important to distinguish between those who only have a little knowledge and those who have none at all. The voter who is utterly without any contact with the political world, except at the polls, has no reason whatsoever to change his or her customary party vote. Thus changes in vote from one party to another are likely to be concentrated among those who receive a little but not a great deal of information about parties, issues, and candidates.[26]

The complex relationship between issues and electoral outcomes was illustrated by two issues in the especially heated 1968 election: the war in Vietnam and what was delicately called the "social issue"—racial conflict, crime, and law and order. Both issues had enormous public exposure and excited the passions of the politically aware. Yet the most sensitive and sophisticated analysis we have of how these issues related to public opinion shows that party identification had "fifty times the net impact of the Vietnam issue"[27] in determining whether voters favored Nixon or Humphrey for president. Party was so powerful that it cannot be considered on the same scale with other forces. Figure 1.1, which sum-

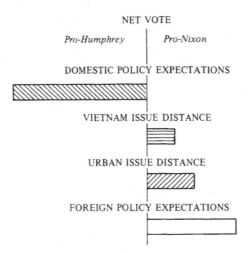

FIGURE 1.1   *Domestic Policy More Important Than Vietnam and Urban Issues Combined: Issue Forces and the Presidential Vote, 1968*
Source: Richard A. Brody et al., "Vietnam, the Urban Crisis and the 1968 Presidential Election: A Preliminary Analysis," prepared for delivery at the 1969 meeting of the American Sociological Association, September, 1969.

marizes the impact of various issues on the 1968 presidential vote, shows that domestic policy issues (the bread-and-butter matters of social welfare, employment, and prosperity) were considerably more important than Vietnam and social issues combined. Like other Democrats before him, presidential candidate Hubert Humphrey gained on domestic policy because voters saw themselves as closer to him than to his Republican opponent. Richard Nixon gained on the foreign policy side because of the Democratic image as the party of war.

Why was the Vietnam issue so unimportant? Most voters found something wrong with most of the Democrats who ran for the presidency in 1968: Senators Robert Kennedy and Eugene McCarthy were too "dovish" for their taste and Governor George Wallace was much too "hawkish." The candidates of the major parties were rather close to the voters' preferences, with Nixon coming a little closer than Humphrey. Vietnam, Page and Brody argue, was an extremely "hot" issue. But the candidates managed to convince much of the electorate that their positions differed little, while those respondents who saw a difference tended to make that perception fit their preexisting bias—Democrats feeling closer to Humphrey and Republicans to Nixon, regardless of their own personal opinions.[28] It is difficult for an issue to have a major impact on an election outcome when the voters do not differentiate greatly among the candidates with respect to that issue. So, once again, we come back to party as the more important organizer of voters' ideas and sentiments.

Issues that arouse deep feelings can alter voting patterns but this usually occurs when one party gets very far out of step with the preferences of most voters. In the 1930s and 1940s this happened to the Republicans on the issue of welfare programs; in the 1970s and 80s, Democratic leaders lost ground on crime, tending to see society more at fault than criminals. More common is voting based on performance evaluations. But when voters perceive a vast chasm separating them from one of the candidates, as they did with George McGovern in 1972, the importance of issues relative to party is bound to grow. The research group at the Michigan Center for Political Studies estimates that in 1972, party identification and issue differences each accounted for approximately one-third of the total vote. In this election Nixon received almost all Republican votes (94 percent), two-thirds of independents' votes (66 percent), and nearly half the votes of people calling themselves Democrats (42 percent). This was a better showing among Democrats than Dwight D. Eisenhower managed in his landslide year of 1956, when he got 28 percent of the Democratic vote. Why did this happen? Because "McGovern was seen as quite distant from the population's policy preferences. . . ." The Michigan group concluded that "a candidate such as

McGovern who may represent only one segment of the national policy preference spectrum may capture control of a political party that shares his policy preferences but cannot go on to win an electoral victory under contemporary conditions of polarization."[29] This suggests that if most voters agree with a candidate, and know they disagree with him, they are likely to vote against him.

When voters wish to reject the current presidential administration, yet they are not sure the other party's policies are better, they may nevertheless decide to "throw the rascals out." Stung by "stagflation," the hitherto unheard of combination of high inflation and unemployment, and dismayed over what they perceived to be President Carter's lack of leadership, many voters in 1980 chose Ronald Reagan despite uneasiness about his conservative issue positions. They may have thought that in the light of uncertainty about then current economic wisdom, a new administration would do better. When unemployment rose in 1981 and 1982 President Reagan's popularity dropped and Republican congressional candidates suffered. Economic recovery brought Reagan renewed support and a resounding victory in 1984. Figure 1.2 shows how well the vote for the President's party tracks the performance of the economy. While the voters' judgments concerning administration performance fluctuated dramatically, their issue positions changed less. One important study shows that in 1984 voters were largely acquiescent in their judgments of the status quo, and gave more acceptance to President Reagan's policies. Those who wanted policy change wanted more liberal policies.[30]

Thus far we have considered factors that cause voters to deviate from

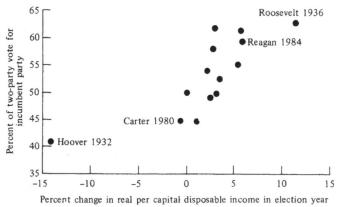

FIGURE 1.2   *Economic Performance and Vote for the Incumbent President's Party*
Source: Economic data from Thomas Ferguson and Joel Rogers," The Myth of America's Turn to the Right," *Atlantic Monthly*, May 1986, p. 50; election data from *CQ Guide to Elections*, 2nd ed.

their underlying party allegiance. How do voters come to this allegiance? Under what conditions do they change their party identification?

The prevailing model of party identification—which holds that it begins early in life, is remarkably stable, resists short-lived political forces, and changes only through reaction to long-lasting and powerful political events, like the great depression of the 1930s—has been challenged.[31] The essence of the old model, authoritatively propounded in *The American Voter,* was that party identification, with its strong emotional bonding, was "firm but not immovable."[32] Challengers lay greater emphasis on issue-related voting. One study seeks to demonstrate that there is considerable issue content in the citizens's behavior at the polls by showing that those who change party from one election to the next generally are sympathetic to some key policies of their new party. "Standpatters," on the other hand, are in general sympathy with major policies of their party.[33] Whether the citizen is taught what to believe by his party or finds a party in accordance with his beliefs cannot be determined from evidence now available.

How effectively does the new model criticize the old? Not very, we think. A revisionist, Charles Franklin, recognizes "that there is substantial continuity in partisanship from one point in time to the next," and that the prevailing model "can be interpreted as the individual's accumulated evaluation of the parties."[34] How different is this from the accepted view? Only a little but that little is useful.

In addition to massive tidal waves that change the party preferences of large numbers of voters, there are also squalls that affect the life experiences of individuals and lead a relatively few voters to alter their party identification from time to time. Since these flows and eddies lack a common origin, they largely cancel one another out in their net effects. Thus the picture of relatively stable partisanship overall can be reconciled with a more sophisticated picture of occasional individual change. Both the thinking and feeling individuals who change parties ever-so-slowly and the large masses of people who are caught up in infrequent movements away from or toward certain parties are galvanized by their reactions to shared experiences. Thus individuals whose partisanship is not firmly fixed early on, perhaps because politics was seldom discussed in the home, may develop party identifications in their twenties or thirties. They adjust their party to their policy preferences. But they do not make the adjustments often. As Franklin tells us, ". . . citizens remain open to change throughout life, though as experience with the parties accumulates, it is accorded greater weight."[35]

Is party identification a durable standing decision to vote a certain way, as the authors of *The American Voter* put it, or, as Morris Fiorina says, a "running tally of retrospective evaluations of party promises and performance?"[36] Donald Kinder finds that citizen assessment of party performance on major dimensions of public policy—war and peace, employment, inflation, race—do matter.[37] However, most changes of party identification involved switching in and out of the independent category rather than between the parties.[38] As Kinder sums up:

> [P]arty identification is not immovable: it both influences and is influenced by the performance of government, by policy disagreements, and by the emergence of new candidates. . . . The loyalty citizens invest in party is at least partly a function of what governments and parties do, and what they fail to do. . . . We should not press this too far, however. Although party identification does respond to political events, it does so sluggishly. It is one thing for Republicans to feel less enthusiastic toward their party after a period of sustained national difficulty presided over by a Republican administration; it is quite another to embrace the opposition. The later seldom happens. In this respect the running balance sheet metaphor is quite misleading. The strongest message of the evidence reviewed here may be the durability of party identification, how difficult it is to budge people from their commitment to party.[39]

Has there been a decline in party identification? From 1952 to 1964, the overall level of party identification among voters remained stable. From 1964 onward, many more Americans identified themselves as independents. Indeed, by 1974, self-styled independents outnumbered Republicans five to three and came near to the number of Democrats. It is important to distinguish, however, between pure independents, who exhibit no party feeling, and partisan independents, who lean toward the Democratic or Republican party. Almost two out of every three people who call themselves "independents" say that they are closer to one party than the other.[40] These partisan independents (as compared with independents who do not lean) are far more knowledgeable and participate much more actively in politics; they also evidence a far greater tendency to vote, and they give large proportions of their vote to the party toward which they lean.[41]

Partisan independents—leaners—vote their party preferences less frequently than strong party identifiers but more frequently than weak ones, and pure independents do not vote very much at all. Party identification was considered strong in 1952; at that time 23 percent of the voting public declared themselves to be independents: 10 percent leaning to Democrats, 7 percent leaning to Republicans, and 6 percent pure independents. By 1980 the proportion of self-styled independents had risen to 37 percent—13 percent pure, 11 percent Democratic, and 13 percent Republican. Thus while the number of pure independents has doubled, they are still not a large fraction of the voting population. It is easy to overstate the political impact of the decline in party identifiers, in view of the fact that the increase among independents is divided between two-thirds hidden party supporters and one-third general nonvoters.[42]

People are a lot more stable in their party identifications than in the policy preferences that are sometimes held to underlie party allegiances.[43] However, there have been massive defections of identifiers from the major parties in presidential voting in recent elections. From 1952 to 1968, Democrats defected about twice as often as Republicans (19 percent to 10 percent). Since 1972, Republican defection rates have stayed about the same, but Democratic defections have increased (to a mean of 24 percent), and they remained at high levels through 1988.[44]

Do defections such as these mean a long-term drop in party identification, or are they a short-term response to particular events and specific candidates? No one can say for sure. What might challenge or supplant parties as organizers of issues, presenters of alternatives, and publicizers of public affairs? The personal efforts of candidates may substitute for party leadership, and so may the mass media. Presumably an indicator of the contemporary weakness of parties is the decline in partisan identification among voters.[45]

While fewer party identifiers may mean that parties are weaker, this does not mean that because they are dissatisfied with parties people are less likely to give themselves a party label. Some people undoubtedly like to call themselves independents because being independent is valued in our political culture. As we have seen, about two-thirds of the people who claim that status actually vote rather steadily for one party or the other.[46] There has also been a long-term increase, from about 2.1 percent in 1964 to 9.7 percent in 1980, in survey respondents who do not call themselves independents but also have no party preference. These people are presumably indifferent to the parties. What evidence we have suggests that they are not "turned off" by the parties, but have "tuned out."[47]

A source of confusion about the condition of the major political parties is the fact that the term "party" refers to more than one thing. So far, we have been talking about party-in-the-electorate. But there are also party organizations. At the federal level, the national party committees, especially the Republican one, have undergone revival. They do a lot to finance, educate, and even promote promising candidates. In this sense, the major parties are stronger than they recently have been. Party organizations in Congress are also stronger than they used to be. The state and local organizational picture is mixed, varying from much improved to nearly nonexistent. It is the drop in party identification among the citizenry and the displacement of state party leaders from leading roles in the presidential nominating process, as we shall see, that has caused most of the concern about the decline of American parties.

Amid these subtleties in the analysis of party identification, what may we safely conclude? We can begin by saying that party as a value and an orientation point is less important than it once was, but it is still very important. Most people—especially most voters, since those without any preference are not likely to vote—identify with or lean towards one party or the other. There are always defections, however, and the parties cannot automatically count on all their identifiers to give them unqualified support in every election. Party identification does not translate automatically into party-line voting. Voters may tend to be loyal, but they can also be driven away.

This, more or less, explains the direction of voting. But why do people turn out to vote at all? Clearly, some people vote and some people do not. In the last few presidential elections only about 54 percent of those eligible by virtue of age actually voted.[48] And of course the numbers are even lower for midterm national elections for Congress, where there is no presidential contest.

"What if they gave an election and everybody came?" asked *New York Times* reporter E. J. Dionne, Jr. George Bush would have been elected by a somewhat larger margin. How come? Nonvoters are generally poorer, have not attended college, and are younger. Such people, especially the younger voters, would have given Bush a considerably larger margin. Indeed, young people who did not vote were more strongly in favor of Bush than those who did.[49]

So why didn't they vote? "By far the most important reason, given by 37 percent, was that they could not vote because they were not registered." Another big difference was that people who moved in the past two years were much less likely to vote (35 to 16 percent, nonvoters to voters). As we see from the chart below, people are less inclined to vote who identify weakly or not at all with a political party, who believe that there are no important differences between the parties, who are fatalistic

TABLE 1.1   *Turnout in Presidential Elections, 1968–1984 (Percent of Age-Eligible Voters)*

1968	1972	1976	1980	1984	1988
60.9%	55.2%	53.5%	52.6%	53.1%	50.2%

Source: U.S. Bureau of the Census, *Statistical Abstract of the United States* (Washington, D.C. 1990), p. 265.

about the effects of political action, and who do not care a lot about who wins. It is also possible of course that the line of causality runs at least partly the other way in that people who do not expect to vote don't pay much attention to the campaign and don't see differences among the parties because they don't want to look for them.

While there are attitudes people hold toward government and society that cannot be changed, at least in the short run, there are aspects of the voting process that might make a difference. In a number of European countries, as Raymond E. Wolfinger points out, the law requires voters to report their new addresses to the government, which registers them to vote in their new domiciles. Once we realize that something like 85

TABLE 1.2   *Who Were the Voters and Nonvoters?*

	Percent of Voters Who:	*Percent of Nonvoters Who:*
Demographic Characteristics		
Were under 30 years of age	24	42
Reported annual household income under $25,000	38	49
Have not attended college	58	75
Are black	11	11
Moved in the last two years	16	35
Partisanship and Candidate Preferences		
Preferred Bush for President	53	50
Preferred Dukakis for President	45	34
Have a favorable opinion now of at least one of the Presidential candidates	83	64
Say there are important differences in what the Democratic and Republican parties stand for	64	44
Identify strongly with a party	39	20
Describe themselves as independent, or decline to identify with a party	27	50
Civic Attitudes		
Say things to go on as before no matter who is elected	23	31
Trust government in Washington to do what is right always or most of the time	45	41
Say people in the government waste a lot of the money paid in taxes	73	67
Say government is run by a few big interests looking out for themselves	57	59
Paid a lot of attention to campaign	50	26
Say they cared a good deal who would win this year	83	57

Source: The New York Times/CBS News Poll. Based on telephone interviews with 1,627 respondents November 10–16, 1988. Respondents were also interviewed November 2–4, 1988.

percent of those registered actually vote, making registration easier, especially for people who have recently moved, would make a considerable difference. That done, we would know that it was not procedural obstacles but other aspects of political life that were responsible for nonvoting.[50]

It is estimated that as much as 14 percent of voting is affected by cumbersome registration requirements.[51] Greg W. Smith has shown that strength of party organization is related to whether a voter is registered and turns out to vote. County party organizations that are well organized, i.e. fill their leadership positions, engage in campaign activity, recruit people to run for office, are a central part of campaign organizations, and otherwise show signs of strength, produce significantly higher voter turnout than counties where party organization is weak.[52]

Although there has been a considerable overall decline in the trust citizens feel for government, that decline is not related to turnout. A sense of efficacy in politics on the other hand, does encourage a person who is registered to vote. Though there had been no reported decline in the sense of efficacy among voters until 1988, Carole Uhlaner argues that if one compares people with the highest to people with the lowest sense of efficacy there is a decline of around one-quarter in registration and 27 percent in turnout.[53] The most comprehensive study, published in November 1990 by the General Accounting Office, concludes

> . . . that the comparatively low and declining American voter turnout is not the consequence of political alienation among citizens. . . . The evidence points to election procedures as the source of voter-turnout disparities among the Western democracies. . . . Voter turnout . . . has been declining for the last three decades. . . . The decline . . . is associated with the weakening of party identification and a lowering of the public's sense of governmental responsiveness and efficacy.

Moreover the sizeable disparities among states in registration and turnout, the GAO report continues, are a consequence of different population characteristics (such as the age and education of the electorate, the least educated and youngest being least likely to vote), and the rules for holding elections, ". . . the closing date of registration being the most important electoral role influencing turnout."[54]

In order to vote, people must register as voters according to regulations and procedures that vary somewhat from state to state. Voting itself takes place not on a holiday, as in some countries, or over a weekend, but on a regular workday, customarily the first Tuesday after the first Monday in November. The number of people voting in an enormous political system like the United States is usually so large that, as one observer calculated, it is less likely that an individual vote will decisively affect an electoral outcome than that the voter will be struck by lightning on his way to the polling place.[55] So it is doubtful that people vote because they know—or even mistakenly believe—they can affect the outcome of a presidential election.

Since there are barriers to voting, since the link between one's vote and a policy result is tenuous, and since the variety of choices on an American ballot can be overwhelming, we should not be surprised that some people do not vote. There is, however, something to be explained in the decline since 1960 in voting rates. One possible explanation, building upon observations in the early voting literature, is that decline in party identification contributes to a decline in voting.[56] Another relates decline in voting to a sense that the system will not respond anyway, a phenomenon that we would argue may also be related to party weakness.[57] Party strength can also be important for voting participation in a way not related to voters' attitudes: strong party organizations knock on doors and get out the vote.

Party feeling is not, however, the sole source of the impulse to vote. The socioeconomic status and general educational level of voters, both of which correlate with a voter's general level of social connectedness, also matter. The sense of membership in society gives people a stake in events and increases the likelihood that they will be part of a group that is particularly interested in current politics. The younger the population of voters, therefore, the less likely they are to vote. As people get older their ties to their social environment become stronger and more numerous, and they tend to vote in greater numbers. When people move about, their ties loosen and they vote less conscientiously; but as they settle down, they vote more frequently. Because one cannot vote unless one is registered, and registration lapses when one moves, the high residential mobility of Americans leads to considerably lower voting rates than elsewhere.[58] Thus the aging of the electorate, a consequence of a lower birth rate, the spread of higher education, and easier registration procedures should increase turnout, whereas the lowering of the voting age to eighteen and the increased physical mobility of the population would tend to decrease turnout.

The more educated people are, the more varied connections they maintain with the outside world in the form of membership in voluntary organizations, the more likely they are to vote. Group membership, then, is a factor in voting rates and other forms of participation. Naturally one's group affiliations also influence one's voting choice. Therefore it is useful to consider more thoroughly the strategic role of interest groups in presidential elections.

Interest Groups and Voting Blocs

Interest groups are collections of people who are similarly situated with respect to one or more policies of government and who organize to do something about it. The interest groups most significant for elections in our society are those having one or more of the following characteristics:

1. They have a mass base, that is, are composed of many members.
2. They are concentrated geographically, rather than dispersed over the entire map, or they are connected by modern technology, such as computerized mailing lists or low-cost WATS phone lines.
3. They represent major resource investments of members—such as in the case of bicycle producers, whose entire livelihoods are tied up in the group involved, as against the consumers of bicycles, for whom investment in a bicycle is not anywhere near as important.
4. They involve those characteristics that give people status in society—such as race or ethnicity.
5. They involve feelings about a single issue that are so intense as to overpower concerns about other issues.
6. They are composed of people who are able to participate actively in politics; that is, people who have time and money to spare.

Interest groups may be more or less organized and more or less vigilant and alert on policy matters that concern, or ought to concern, them. They are not necessarily organized in ways that make them politically effective; very often the paid lobbyists of interest groups spend more time trying to alert their own members to the implications of government policies than they spend lobbying with politicians.[59]

In American politics, interest group activity is lively and ubiquitous, even when it is not particularly effective or meaningful in terms of policy outcomes. We shall be concerned with three characteristics of interest groups. First, membership in these groups may be quite important in giving voters a sense of affiliation and political location. In this respect, interest groups may act the way parties do, helping to fill in the voter's map of the world with preferences, priorities, and facts. Second, interest groups are important because of their partisan political activities; they may actively recruit supporters for candidates and aid materially in campaigns. Third, interest groups may influence party policy by making demands with respect to issues in return for their own mobilized support. The extent to which interest groups can "deliver" members' votes, however, is always problematic; to a great extent interest group leaders are the prisoners of past alliances their group has made. Even so, various ethnic votes, the farm vote, the labor vote, the youth vote, the consumer vote, and many other "votes" are bandied about as though they were political commodities that can be manipulated easily in behalf of one or another candidate. Yet, in the case of some of the most vocal groups, they have no membership at all and only exist as lobbying organizations.[60]

When the use of election statistics and opinion polls was in its infancy, claims to guarantee group support or threats to withdraw it could be analyzed only intuitively, and no one could tell with any certainty whether these claims had substance. The appearance of voting studies and the development of public opinion analysis have created new opportunities for the purveyors of bloc votes and new difficulties for the interested but necessarily amateur citizen and public official. How are they to evaluate these important political claims backed up by impressive and complicated arrays of data?

The usual argument is that if one or another candidate captures the allegiance of a particular bloc, that bloc's pivotal position or large population in a state will enable the fortunate aspirant to capture all of the state's electoral votes and thus win the election. But of course no one combination of states totaling more than a majority of electoral votes is more critical, valuable, or pivotal than any other such combination. In a fairly close election the defection of any number of combinations of states to the other side would spell the difference between victory and defeat.

Appeals to various groups are conditioned by time, place, and circumstance. There is little doubt that under some conditions during some elections some social characteristics of voters and candidates may have some relevance to the election results. Finding the conditions under which specified social characteristics become relevant to voter choice is difficult. We know that in a competitive political system various participants (parties, interest groups, leaders) put forward candidates and issues designed to capture the allegiance of various groups. Rarely is it possible to appeal to one group alone, not only because there are so many different groups, with all sorts of conceptions of policy, but also because each individual may have many social characteristics that are potentially relevant to his or her voting decision. While some people may be so single-minded that they have only one interest that is important in determining their vote—race, religion, ethnic background, income, feelings about abortion or the environment—most of us have multiple interests that sometimes conflict. Ecological interest groups, for example, may have less success in areas where environmental concerns conflict with employment opportunities than in areas where the two do not conflict. The worse the economic conditions, the stronger the difficulty. Concern about increasing unemployment may influence how some voters feel about the governmental support of people who are not working. Much depends on the tides of events, which may bring one or another issue to the forefront of the voter's consciousness and incline him toward the candidate he believes best represents his preferences on that matter.[61] Today, the enormous size of governmental transfer payments in money, such as Social Security, and in goods, such as food stamps, may lead recipients and providers alike to see a close cash connection between public policy and their individual welfare. Long-term social trends, as well as candidates' strategies, have much to do with the impact of appeals to bloc votes.

In each election members of the various groups that make up the American voting population turn out to vote, dividing their loyalties in varying ways between the major parties. To determine the contribution that a particular group makes to a party, it is necessary to know three things: how big the group is, how many of its members actually vote, and how devoted its members are to one party or another.

For example, let us look at the contribution of votes of poor people—defined as those whose incomes are below $3,000 through 1980 and $5,000 in 1984 and 1988. Basing his analysis on Michigan Center for Political Study polls, Robert Axelrod has shown that the contribution of the poor to the total Democratic vote has fallen from 28 percent in 1952 to only 5 percent in 1980, 10 percent in 1984, and 6 percent in 1988.[62] This trend can be accounted for in any—or all—of four ways: (1) more of the nonpoor voted Democratic in recent years, diluting the contribution of the poor; (2) fewer people voted Democratic in recent elections; (3) the poor declined as a percentage of the overall population; (4) raising the threshold of what it takes to be officially poor affected the result.

If one wishes to know a group's contribution to the Democratic vote, Axelrod's analysis is excellent. Since most people have overlapping characteristics—being, say, white, female, Catholic, and a union member—it would also be useful to try to identify the contribution of each attribute alone. Using multivariate methods, Stanley, Bianco, and Niemi show that, when controlling for other characteristics, being poor and urban did not, from 1952 to 1984, contribute to the Democratic vote. By separating subjective identification with the working class from being a union member, they are able to show that belonging to a union still creates a strong push toward Democratic allegiance. Being Jewish, being black, and being female propel people toward the Democrats. So too does being Catholic, working class, or native southern white. The pro-Democratic bias of these latter groups, however, has declined since the 1950s.[63]

While the poor have not been an important part of the Democratic coalition in recent years, African-Americans have established themselves

TABLE 1.3 *Percentage Contribution to Democratic Coalition of African-Americans and Other Nonwhites, 1952–1988*

Year	Percentage Contribution to Democratic Votes
1952	7
1956	5
1960	7
1964	12
1968	19
1972	22
1976	16
1980	22
1984	25
1988	19

Sources: Robert Axelrod, "Where the Votes Come From: An Analysis of Electoral Coalitions, 1952–1968," *American Political Science Reveiw* 66 (March 1972), pp. 11–20; Axelrod; Letter to the Editor, *American Political Science Review* 68 (June 1974), pp. 727–730; Axelrod, Letter to the Editor, *American Political Science Review* 72 (June 1978), pp. 622–624; Axelrod, Letter to the Editor, *American Political Science Review* 76 (June 1982), pp. 393–396; Axelrod, "Presidential Electoral Coalitions in 1984," *American Political Science Review* 80 (March 1986), pp. 281–284. For 1988, American National Election Studies, Center for Political Studies, University of Michigan; University of California, Berkeley, State Data Program.

as a substantial component: from 5 percent to 7 percent in 1952–1960 to 12 percent in 1964, and 19 percent in 1968. In 1972 the percentage rose again, to 22 percent. In 1976, their contribution fell for the first time, reaching 16 percent, largely as a result of the return of many Democratic voters who defected in 1972. In 1980 the African-American percentage of Democratic voters was again at 22 percent and in 1984 it went up to 25 percent, falling to 19 percent in 1988 as Michael Dukakis attracted more white voters than Carter in 1980 or Mondale in 1984. The African-American population has remained a relatively constant 11 percent of the total population. Their vastly increased contribution since the 1960s has been the result of a near doubling of their turnout throughout the nation, of their high loyalty to the Democratic party, and of fluctuations in the Democratic voting of white voters.

While union members and their families made up a third of all Democratic votes in the 1950s, their contribution fell slightly to 28 percent in 1968 and rose again to 32 percent in 1972, 1976, and 1980. They are important to the Democratic party because a quarter of all adults are in union families, their turnout is reasonably good, and they vote more Democratic than other people. Although only half of union members voted Democratic in 1980, the overall defection among other Democrats was so great that union members still voted 9 percent more Democratic than others. Whereas union families contributed four times as many votes as African-Americans to the Democratic party in 1960 (25 percent of the total), union families contributed only slightly more Democratic votes (30 percent) in 1984 and in 1988 (27 percent).

Catholics comprise roughly a third of the population and they provide a third of all Democratic votes. In 1952 and 1956, southerners voted about 10 percent more Democratic than the rest of the country. In more recent elections they have been slightly more Republican than other people, though they moved back to the Democrats in 1976 and 1980, when a southerner headed the Democratic ticket. They gave a quarter of their votes to the third-party movement of George Wallace in 1968. African-American southerners stayed with the Democrats in that year, but white southerners split their presidential vote among all three parties. In 1984 and 1988, the Republicans received very strong support from southern whites. Despite overwhelming opposition from southern blacks, the Reagan/Bush ticket exceeded their national share of the popular vote in every southern state.[64]

A major change has been the increase in the votes of young people, that is, those under thirty years of age. Until 1972, they were not part of any party coalition and their low turnout reduced any impact that their 18 percent of the population might have given them. Because the voting age has been lowered to eighteen, and because of the baby boom after the Second World War, their proportion of the population has increased to 28 percent, more than half again what it was a few years ago. Are they now making a big difference?

"Whatever else young voters are," Wolfinger tells us in a well-advised note of caution, "they are not harbingers of future outcomes."[65] The reason is that most of the time people under thirty do not divide their vote differently than the rest of the population. The belief that the youth vote was pro-Democratic began in 1972, when it was true, but such a result has not manifested itself since. A similar tale, only in the opposite, pro-Republican direction, has been told of the big youth vote for Ronald Reagan in 1984. Actually as Table 1.4 shows, the youth vote did not differ from other age groups in that year, while in 1988, Michael Dukakis received his strongest support from the oldest and the youngest voters.[66]

The Republican coalition appears to be constituted as follows: white people, who comprise approximately 90 percent of the U.S. population, vote anywhere from 3 to 5 percent more Republican than the general population. The comparatively small size of the black population means that even in 1960, when Richard Nixon got about a quarter of the black vote, 97 percent of his total came from whites; 99 percent of his vote came from whites in 1968, 98 percent in 1972. Ninety-nine percent of Ronald Reagan's votes in 1980 came from whites. If one can conceive of nonunion families and Protestants as "groups" in the usual sense, they

TABLE 1.4   *Vote for Democratic Presidential Candidate by Age Group, 1964–1984*

Age	1964	1968	1972	1976	1980	1984	1988
18–29	72%	38%	47%	51%	34%	40%	47%
30–44	69	47	34	48	37	42	45
45–59	70	37	31	52	37	39	31
60+	59	40	29	50	47	39	49

Sources: For 1964–1980, the National Election Studies of the University of Michigan Center for Political Studies; for 1984 and 1988, *The New York Times* (November 10, 1988), reprinted in Harold W. Stanley and Richard G. Niemi, *Vital Statistics on American Politics*, 2nd ed. (Washington, D.C., 1990), p. 100–101

make up about 75 percent of the population and vote 5 percent more Republican than the nation as a whole. The Republican party gets its vote, then, from white people, nonunion members, northerners, and Protestants outside the central cities. Although Republicans received 60 percent majorities or better from all these groups in 1972, they were able to attract at most 53 percent from any of them in 1976, and no more than 56 percent in 1980. In 1984, however, the Republicans again received over 60 percent of the vote from each of these groups.[67]

One of the largest groups of all, women, provides an example of a group membership whose meaning may be changing. At one time gender could not be shown to have a strong partisan effect; what weak tendency existed at the time of *The American Voter* (1960) showed women as slightly more Republican.[68] In 1980, however, women were substantially less pro-Reagan than were men,[69] and thus made up a much larger part of the Democratic than of the Republican coalition. We do not know, however, whether this division is permanent. Throughout 1981, differences between men and women appeared in public opinion polls that asked about party identification, and it became commonplace to refer to President Reagan's "gender gap."[70] Yet the *New York Times* 1982 election-day surveys showed only small differences between men and women voters.[71] In 1984, women voted 6 to 9 percent less for Reagan, depending on which exit poll you believe. Women cast a majority of their votes for Reagan, but Reagan's margin among women was smaller than it was among men, so women kept a distinctive orientation, which appears to favor liberal Democrats more than conservative Republicans. In 1988, the gender gap was only four points according to the Gallup poll, six or seven points according to the National Election Survey, CBS/*New York Times* and NBC/*Wall Street Journal*, polls or ten points according to CNN/*Los Angeles Times* figures.[72]

The case of the "women's vote" should alert us to some of the complexities of group interest. Not all women are the same; richer women are more Republican and poorer more Democratic, just like men. Thus group memberships are crosscutting. The "interests" of a given group may be of greatest interest to only a subset of members. Thus the Equal Rights Amendment, a "women's issue," was of greatest importance to highly educated women. A difference between men and women may also reflect not failure in appealing to one, but success at appealing to the other. Thus there can be "women's" issues like abortion and "men's" issues like gun control for hunters, and what can be read as a defection of women from the Republicans may equally mean a defection of men from the Democrats.[73] Moreover, a difference in one election may or may not prefigure a permanent difference in basic coalitions; as political consultant Celinda Lake argues, the political candidate choices in 1980 may have maximized the possibility of a gender gap.[74]

Democrats have a problem with white males and Republicans have a problem with women in general. There is no doubt about the numbers, only about the explanation. It is possible that the egalitarian bent of the Democratic party has attracted women and repelled men. The reason is that Democrats include women among the deprived minorities for whom affirmative discrimination is in order, leaving white males above the poverty line as the residual category who must help all the rest. The Republican party's emphasis on opportunity rather than on more equal outcomes, by contrast, leaves the existing status or privileges of white and more affluent males untouched. In a corresponding manner, white women of low income may still see the Democratic party as providing them with substantive benefits while middle and upper-middle income women, influenced by the feminist movement, may see Republicans as opposed to their views on social issues, such as affirmative action and abortion. As Ethel Klein tells us, "Surveys indicate that women tend to be more liberal than men on a variety of issues, including defense, environmental protection, social services, women's rights, and economic security."[75] Women are more concerned with egalitarian issues—fairness to the poor, unemployment—and less likely than men to support defense spending.[76] If defense spending is seen as taking away from social welfare, the contrast increases.

Turnout varies enormously among different groups in the population, as Appendix B shows, rising with income, occupational status, education, and age. Since Republicans are disproportionately located in the high-turnout groups and Democrats in the low, this tends to give Republicans electoral advantages that in some measure, varying from election to election, make up for the preponderance of Democrats in the potential electorate.

Both Democratic and Republican voters exist in virtually all groups, however. The experience of 1984 showed that increased voter registration alone would not necessarily automatically benefit the Democrats. There was talk on the Democratic side of forging a new party alignment along economic class lines through a massive registration campaign aimed at poor people, African-Americans, and youth. And 12 million new voters were registered. The Republican party and the conservative Moral Majority organized drives of their own. According to CBS and *New York Times* exit polls, nearly half of the poorest segment of the population (with incomes under $12,500 per year) voted for Reagan. And whereas there was a 31 percent increase in registration among southern blacks, three times as many new whites registered and they voted preponderantly for Reagan. Indeed, 72 percent of all southern whites voted for him. Although new female voters supported Reagan less than men, they still gave him a 57 to 42 percent margin.[77] This supports Raymond Wolfinger and Steven Rosenstone's conclusion that if voting turnout were increased so that everyone voted in national elections the results would be much the same.[78]

It is possible, then, to analyze party coalitions in terms of the group memberships of the people who vote regularly for one party or another. Likewise, it is possible to consider the differential impact of different candidates on these various groups.

The picture of voters and interest groups we have drawn thus far can be generalized. Presidential campaigns and elections are events that activate the personal loyalties of voters. The amount of new information about candidates or issues that citizens ordinarily need in order to vote or hold casual conversations about the election is slight, because the political component of their personal identities is reasonably stable and familiar to them. So long as their main reference groups do not change, party loyalty and membership in interest groups provide a shortcut to voter preferences and minimize the costs of getting information about the specifics of the issues and candidates in any particular election year.

Interest groups act as intermediary agencies that help voters to identify their political preferences quickly by actively soliciting their members' interest in behalf of specific candidates and parties and, more importantly, by providing still another anchor to voters' identities. This helps voters fix their own position quickly and economically in what otherwise would be a confusing and contradictory political environment.

Although interest groups in the past have differed over policy, they have not (at least since the acceptance of industrial unions in the 1930s and black organizations in the 1960s) denied the rights of opponents to advocate their policy preferences. But, in one significant respect, that is no longer true. "Public interest" lobbies have attacked the legitimacy of "private interest" groups. Political parties, labor unions, trade associations, and religious groups are examples of such private interest groups, intermediary organizations that link citizens and their government. Many are "special interest" groups—groups, that is, with special interests in public policy. Part of the program of public interest groups such as Common Cause or Ralph Nader's various organizations is to reduce the power of private, special interests and substitute their own services as intermediary organizations. Typically, public interest groups have fewer—sometimes vastly fewer—members than private interest groups.[79] They rely on the mass media to carry their messages to the population at large, and their success is an indication of the extent to which American voters now rely on mass media rather than group membership to get their political orientations and opinions.

Laws have been passed and constitutional amendments proposed by public interest groups that restrict the amounts of money unions and corporations can contribute to political campaigns and use in lobbying. On the whole, however, these laws have been unsuccessful in curbing interest group activity. What has happened is that interest groups have found new ways within the law to advance their interests. One such device is the political action committee. From 1974 to 1982 the number of political action committees (PACS) organized by business and unions more than tripled, increasing from 608 to 2,193 in 1982; in the next six years, PACs doubled again to a 1988 total of 4,268. The bulk of the original increase was accounted for by the rise in corporate PACs from 89 in 1974 to 1,763 in 1984, but these PACs grew slowly in the next four years, reaching a total of 1,954 in 1988.[80] PACS are created to collect and disburse political contributions. They must contribute to more than one candidate, and the amount they may give to any one candidate is limited. In 1976, amendments to the Federal Election Campaign Act enabled individual companies or labor unions to establish multiple PACS, thus multiplying the amount of money that they could funnel to any single candidate. Surprisingly, corporate PACS have not favored Republican campaigns as much as might be expected. Instead, the predominant trend in congressional elections has been to support incumbents over challengers, and since nationwide there are far more Democratic than Republican office holders, Democrats have managed partially to offset the Republican preferences of corporate donors.[81]

While an individual citizen is still prohibited from contributing more than $25,000 to federal candidates during any given year, the Supreme Court decision in *Buckley* v. *Valeo* (1976) removed any such restrictions from PACs. Thus, "a corporate or union political action committee can collect donations and contribute an unlimited sum of money to unspecified numbers of candidates or committees so long as no contribution exceeds $5,000.''[82] In addition, once a PAC ''contributes to five or more federal candidates, [it] can make unlimited independent expenditures . . . on behalf of candidates or parties. . . .'' (e.g., advertising on behalf of a candidate independent of that candidate's campaign in print or electronic media).[83] Not surprisingly, prospective presidential candidates themselves are organizing PACs as a way of developing political alliances.

The rise of PACs to prominence is an ironic result of misplaced idealism. In the 1950s, reformers thought that it would be a good idea if local parties, which were based on jobs and conviviality, were converted to more idealistic concerns. It was thought that the replacement of a politics of patronage with a politics of issues would lead to party government in which informed activists could hold public officials responsible for their policy positions. As government grew and parties weakened, however, two things happened: business corporations, concerned about what government was doing to them, founded and reinvigorated their own interest groups, and other citizens formed and joined new groups to press their particular concerns. Instead of integrative party government, therefore, the weakening of parties facilitated further fragmentation into what are called ''single-issue special interest groups,'' such as those concerned (for and against) with gun control or abortion. The emphasis on issues has led to fragmentation, manifested in the explosive growth of political action committees.

A second irony is that the PACs have been created in response to congressional efforts to restrict the role of money in elections. In 1943, Congress, following up an earlier law against corporate spending, forbade direct spending by labor unions. Soon thereafter, the more militant of the union federations, the Congress of Industrial Organizations (CIO), formed a political action committee financed by a separate fund collected from its membership, as well as a National Citizen's Action Committee to solicit contributions from the community at large. When the labor federations merged in 1955, the new AFL-CIO created its own Committee on Political Education (COPE) to collect and inject money into campaigns. COPE is commonly regarded as the model of the modern PAC.

But that was only the beginning. Government intervened again in 1971, 1974, and 1976 with the passage of the Federal Election Campaign Act (FECA) and subsequent amendments. By limiting the amount of money any individual or company could contribute, FECA reduced the role of large contributors while at the same time giving incentives for the formation of groups of small contributors. Once the courts decided that money raised and spent in politics was protected under the first Amendment as a necessary adjunct to political speech and expression, the way was open for committees to proliferate, each concentrating on the issues and candidates of their choice.[84] With no obligation to govern, no limit on new committees, and no necessary connection to any other issue, PACS became an electoral rival to political parties. Now governmental intervention is being proposed as a further remedy for the presumed ills caused by the last round of intervention. The question to be considered is whether to try once more to limit PACs or to reduce their influence.

Public interest lobbies which represent not direct material interests like corporations and unions but "issue" interests like tax reform and reform of voting laws have also sought to weaken the power of party leaders and strong party identifiers as compared with citizens who are weakly identified with parties and who emerge during a particular election campaign or in response to a current issue. The stress on ease of entry into internal party affairs—more primaries, more conferences, more frequent and more open elections to party bodies—leads, given the fact that party membership occurs in the first place by self-activation, to the domination of parties by activists who have time and education and are able to take the trouble to go to meetings. What kinds of people have these characteristics? Among others, they are the middle and upper-middle class professionals who predominate in supporting Common Cause, Nader's Raiders, and other public interest lobbies. Thus, among interest groups, if money matters less as a resource, business matters less; if time and talk and education matter more, ordinary workers matter less. As leaders of labor, business, and the parties lose power, organizers of public interest lobbies gain.

These public interest lobbies are not necessarily all on one side of the ideological spectrum. People who defend corporate capitalism as well as those who attack it can organize public interest law firms. And they do.

Two advantages have helped public interest groups flourish. One is a product of modern technology and the other has been generated by government. The use of computerized mailing lists has permitted these groups to tap contributions from large numbers of people who do not otherwise participate directly in group activities, but rather become privileged spectators to group leaders' battles over public policy. This opportunity for vicarious participation not only produces ready cash, but also simplifies somewhat the tasks of leadership. Instead of having to satisfy an active membership that might make diverse or contradictory demands, only the top leadership need be consulted. Leaders of public interest groups are frequently poorly paid, accepting low income as a sacrifice for their cause. Moving from one group to another, they reduce organization overhead by providing experienced lobbying at small cost.

The second advantage is that people who contribute to public interest groups are entitled to count these monies as tax deductible. When the group wishes to undertake activities incompatible with eligibility for deductibility, it often establishes a separate educational or litigious arm that can receive tax-deductible contributions. Without tax deductibility, the survival of some of these groups would be in doubt. The tradeoff is that they are required to engage in educational activities rather than overt lobbying, which may be a distinction without a difference. In addition, some of these groups achieve a status as legally authorized intervenors before regulatory commissions, a role that entitles them to payment for their activity. In this sense, such public interest groups are partially subsidized by government.

Parties

A third aspect of the social framework—along with voters and interest groups—that will help us to account for the strategies of participants in presidential elections is the nature of political parties in this country. Here we discuss parties as organizations rather than as symbols for voters. As organizations parties are devoted to maintaining or increasing their own opportunities to exercise political power primarily through sponsoring candidates for public office.

By "political power" we mean the ability to make decisions or to influence decision making by governments. Instrumental to this goal is access to those offices and officials legally entitled to make such decisions.[85] Access, in turn, depends in part upon participation in staffing the government, either by selecting officials to fill appointive offices (patronage) or by significantly influencing the nomination and election of elected officials. Since elected officials are usually empowered to select appointed officials, access to elected officials is often instrumental to the dispensation of patronage. There are, of course, numerous ways of gaining access to public officials, but participation in their original selection is the primary avenue of access used by political parties.[86]

An additional goal that political parties may from time to time seek is the expression of the political views of their most active and influential members. When party activists seek power primarily over the party, and only secondarily over the government, we refer to them as "purists." Purists wish their views to be put forth by the parties without much equivocation or compromise, and although they otherwise seek to win elections, they do not care to do this at the expense of self-expression.[87] In the purist conception of things, instead of a party convention being a place where a party meets to choose candidates who can win elections by pleasing voters, it becomes a site for passing resolutions and for finding a candidate who will embody the message delegates seek to express. In short, purists support parties of advocacy.

At each level of government, the elected chief executive (mayor, governer, president) generally has the most political power. As a result the party organizations depend more upon controlling these offices than on any other source for their political power. In addition, parties are accountable for the activities of chief executives elected with their endorsement. Accountability means that when the party endorses a candidate, it designates him or her as its agent before the electorate. The fortunes of the party depend on the success of party candidates. Candidates come and go, but parties and electorates remain. The party organizations, therefore, are quite concerned about selecting suitable officeholders, since it is assumed that the actions and identities of these men and women will in the long run determine the extent and location of the party's appeal within the electorate and its record of success at the polls.

The party is greatly dependent upon its officeholders for its political power; these officeholders in turn often have great discretion in the distribution of rewards to the party. Party members expect that officeholders will seek to strengthen themselves within the organization by the judicious dispensation of favors and patronage. As people who have won office at the head of party tickets, elected chief executives will probably come closer than other individuals to possessing the control over the party organization that will enable them to impose their own preferences on party organizations. Indeed, where parties are weak, they may become mere appendages of the major officeholders who use the label and manipulate the machinery until the next ad hoc collection of activists mobilizes around a new leader.

State party organizations are not simple in their internal workings. Sometimes elected chief executives run them; sometimes they are run by coalitions of party chieftains representing the local organizations of several large cities or counties. Sometimes party officials and elected officials work cooperatively; sometimes they work at cross-purposes. A strong national committeeman in a state party organization whose party occupies the presidency may find he is the main avenue of access in the distribution of federal patronage if there are few elected officeholders in the state with whom he might have to share power. On the other hand, there are instances of governors who have felt that their chances of continuing personal victory would improve if they thoroughly disassociated themselves from the party whose label they nominally bore, causing the party organization in the state to shrivel on the vine. A strong party organization, well led, can force on an executive choices suitable for the party's purposes even if they conflict with alternative choices more likely to enhance the executive's position. A weak party organization may have the actual conduct of election campaigns torn entirely from its grasp, as happens with increasing frequency at the national level, where presidential candidates, once nominated, have all the authority and most of the money. Leaders of party organizations frequently are at odds with the party's elected officeholders for a variety of reasons. Many elected officials see their party leaders as potential threats to their positions; many party leaders see the officeholders as ungrateful louts with whom the organization is unfortunately saddled.

Even so, what professional party leaders ordinarily care about most is getting their candidates into office and keeping them there. Other considerations are usually secondary. Party leaders are neither for nor against policies in the abstract; they are concerned with policies as means to the end of officeholding. If new policies help win elections, they are for them; if they help lose elections, they are against them. If officeholders are popular, party leaders have to accept them; if they are unpopular, threatening to bring the party into disrepute, party leaders will turn against them. Where parties are purist, activists control candidates. The purpose of such parties is to espouse policies of which party activists approve. If they can do that and win, so much the better for them; if the price of purism is defeat, so much the worse for the candidate. If a choice has to be made by purist activists, purism outside office is better than power in government.

It is not the case that professional party officials lack all interest in issues. As Herbert McClosky found as far back as the mid-1950s, party officials emphasize much more than they minimize policy differences as compared with their citizen supporters.[88] As Table 1.5 reveals, there is considerable issue distance between members of the Republican and Democratic national committees and party supporters. Democratic committee members are more liberal and Republican committee members more conservative than their respective party's rank and file.

As Table 1.6 shows, this is also true for delegates to national party conventions. CBS/*New York Times* surveys for 1988 delegates show Republican delegates more conservative and Democratic delegates more liberal than registered Republicans or Democrats. There are huge differences on the size of government or on the funding of abortions. On some issues, Democratic delegates are quite close to voters. These include taxing people with higher incomes and supporting the Equal Rights Amendment. There are other issues in which Republican delegates are closer to the populace than are Democrats. These include size of government, sympathy for Palestinians, school prayer, and the death pen-

TABLE 1.5 *Views of Members of the Democratic and Republican National Committees and Party Supporters, 1981*

	Democratic		Republican	
	Committee	*Rank & File*	*Committee*	*Rank & File*
Political Philosophy				
Liberal	36%	24%	1%	11%
Moderate	51	42	31	33
Conservative	4	29	63	51
Military/Defense Spending				
Increase	22	48	89	60
Decrease	18	13	1	5
Keep Same Level	51	36	7	31
Equal Rights Amendment				
Favor	92	62	29	46
Oppose	4	29	58	44
Too Much Government Regulation of Business				
Agree	35	59	98	72
Disagree	49	30	1	22

Source: Adapted from Martin Plissner and Warren Mitofsky, "Political Elites," *Public Opinion* (October/November 1981), pp. 47–49.

alty.[89] Whereas the general public, or at least those registered in one of the major parties, take liberal positions on some issues and conservative positions on others, the delegates are extraordinarily consistent. Presumably, this is what is meant by having an ideology.

Though political party leaders try to pursue policies which they believe will enhance their political power and to avoid unpopular points of view, it is clear that they are far from indifferent to the substance of policy. Because they are more interested and active than most citizens, party leaders also tend to care more about the policies with which they have to deal. In fact, some politicians who hold public office make a specialty of being policy oriented. At times they may deliberately incur some unpopularity in order to serve their policy preferences, although they are unlikely to go so far as to lose an election on purpose. The heavy losses of the Republicans in the 1964 election and the presidential landslide against the Democrats in 1972 are extreme cases of purist control of conventions, and they are unusual. Professional party leaders regard policy as a result of an interaction among legitimate political demands—as a bargainable product—and not, as purists regard it, as a set of logical or ideological imperatives.[90] For example, President Reagan favored tax cuts, but in 1982, when other aspects of his program were at stake, supported a tax increase. Similarly, Walter Mondale, the 1984 Democratic nominee, had

TABLE 1.6   *Views of the Delegates/Voters, 1988*

| | Delegate Survey | | CBS/NYT Poll, July 1988 | |
	Republican	Democrat	Regular Rep.	Regular Dem.
Ideology				
Liberal	0%	43%	11%	26%
Moderate	36	43	44	42
Conservative	59	5	40	28
Size of Government[1]				
Small	81	14	59	33
Big	4	56	30	56
Federal Funding Abortion				
Favor	16	57	28	32
Oppose	69	22	62	56
Gay Rights Law				
Favor	26	65	28	43
Oppose	58	18	57	40
Sympathy for Palestinians				
More sympathy	28	50	22	26
No more	46	22	53	49
Government Spending				
Defense	72	10	53	34
Social Programs	13	75	39	55
Death Penalty				
Favor	88	49	79	64
Oppose	6	38	15	27
School Prayer[2]				
Favor	51	22	72	67
Oppose	34	65	25	26
ERA[2]				
Favor	34	86	68	80
Oppose	51	4	25	11
Bal. Budget Amendment[2]				
Favor	77	38	80	77
Oppose	13	47	11	9
Top Tax Rate				
Increase	19	67	61	63
No change	64	14	32	27

[1] CBS/*New York Times* poll, May 1988.
[2] CBS/*New York Times* poll, August 1988.
Source: "The Making of the Delegates, 1968–1988," *Public Opinion* (September/October 1988), p. 46.

been for free trade, but in the course of seeking labor support, came out for protection in the automobile and steel industries.

How strong are the major political parties? The answer depends in part on which parties we have in mind at what time. Congressional parties are generally believed to have experienced a decline in partisanship since the turn of the century. But the Republican party in the House of Representatives showed a high level of cohesion in the 1970s and later gave President Reagan remarkably unified support. House Democrats did not vote together nearly so often but if one eliminated certain southern Democrats, the "Dixiecrats" of the 1940s and 1950s and the "boll weevils" of the late 1970s and early 1980s, the remaining mainstream and liberal Democrats looked a lot more cohesive. Party realignment in the South over the last twenty years, adding conservative Republicans to the House and subtracting Dixiecrats from the Democratic caucus, has increased Democratic party cohesion in Congress. The national committees of the two parties waxed and waned in strength—in the 1940s and 1950s a politically informed person might even have known the names of the national chairmen. The Republican National Committee, under Chairman William Brock, began in the late 1970s to raise large sums of money from a broad network of individual donors to provide aid to state parties, and to help candidates and state parties professionalize their operations.[91] The Democratic National Committee, more haltingly and less successfully, began to follow suit. In 1983 and 1984 the Republican party raised $297.9 million; the Democrats $98.5 million. In 1987 and 1988, the Republican party raised $263.3 million, while the Democratic party raised $127.9 million.[92]

In spite of considerable efforts by the national Democratic party to tighten up qualifications for voting in the presidential primaries, political parties in America as yet do not have elaborate procedures of membership, dues, and formal organizational structure. They are constituted differently in different localities and exist primarily to make nominations for and elect candidates to a variety of state and local offices. They are regulated primarily by state, not federal, law. Given the vast diversity among state and local parties and the periodic changes they undergo, it is not easy to characterize their effectiveness. At the turn of the century and through the 1940s, state party politics in most states was dominated by incumbent governors or national committeemen. There were virtually no permanent state party organizations. Central committees were, so far as it is known, largely dormant. By the early 1960s, a few state chairmen were paid full time, and most but not all states had a permanent party headquarters, as well as at least one paid professional.[93] By 1980 the long-standing practice of moving the state party headquarters to the home of the chairman had in most states been abandoned.[94] Nevertheless, modest increases in the organizational capacity of state parties are compatible with loss of control over nominations and campaigns to candidates and activists.

Owing to the lamentable lack of research on state parties, we cannot say how many states now have permanent headquarters with professional staff who recruit candidates, raise money, and help campaigns. But the best evidence suggests their number is growing.[95] State chairmen now have seats on the national committee. They mediate between national rules and state practices. They are conduits for the growing services—recruitment, polling, fund raising, issue development, vote mobilization—provided by the national parties.[96]

What used to be a loose federation of state parties at the national level is slowly being converted—by changes in party rules and by judicial decisions—into a more centralized structure. Thus our national parties combine elements of both decentralization and centralization. The most obvious indicator of continuing decentralization is that national parties are organized on a geographical basis with the state units as the constituent elements. The party organizations from different states meet formally by sending delegates to national committee meetings, and most importantly, by coming together at national conventions to nominate a president. The strongest indicator of nationalization is the guidelines that are set out at the national level which, especially for Democrats, are becoming increasingly important in determining who these delegates will be.[97] Still, it is the states who choose their representatives to national party bodies; the national committees and conventions do not choose officers of state parties. On the Democratic side, until recently, the permanent national party organization was not in a position to help the state parties, having neither the funds, nor the personnel, nor the contacts to contribute substantially to the nomination or election of candidates for Congress or local offices, who must run within state boundaries.[98] Now, following the lead of Republicans, the Democratic National Committee and the Democratic Congressional Campaign Committee provide a modicum of campaign services.[99] The Republican National Committee and the National Republican Campaign Committee have sizeable staffs who maintain lists of effective campaign managers, consultants, poll takers, and accountants, going so far as to buy blocks of services that then can be allocated to close races. The Republicans, Paul S. Herrnson finds, are "much more effective in targeting their campaign management services to competitive candidates than the Democratic Party organizations."[100]

The operation of the presidential coattail, whereby a popular president brings out supporters who also vote for other candidates of his party, has declined drastically over time. This decline matters for governance because a coattail effect, in a system of separated powers, would operate to connect presidents and members of Congress of their own party more closely. In addition to replacing congressmen from the other party with members of the president's party, the belief on the part of congressmen that the president has support in the members' own districts creates incentives for them to support the chief executive's policies.[101] Thus it has been found that the most faithful supporters of presidents are freshman legislators who came into office during a landslide victory.[102] Ferejohn and Calvert conclude that the disinclination to vote a straight party ticket, has worked so as to ". . . weaken the principal cohesive force in American politics." With that weakening, they speculate, "the capacity of the political system to supervise social and economic change has eroded."[103]

In any event, presidential coattails, even when operating at maximum effectiveness, only can exist when there is a presidential election. They do not help state parties and candidates who must try to win every year in numerous elections at the state and local level. And there is also the possibility (nowadays perhaps probability) that reverse coattail effects will operate as unpopular presidents do damage to other members of their party running for office.

Increasingly, members of Congress are self-starters who do not depend on state parties. Before the turn of the century, party caucuses nominated candidates, and voters supported party slates based on long ballots prepared by party organizations. The desirability of working through parties was evident. The advent of the direct primary and the printing of official rather than party-printed ballots meant that candidates could not rely on parties for nomination and did not need to rely on them to be part of a slate of party candidates. Voters could now easily vote for candidates of different parties for the various offices. As time went on, ticket-splitting became more common. Coming closer to the present day, the need for money to go on television, as constituencies expanded in size, and for dedicated workers, who tend to care more about issues than about party, in the absence of state party ability to provide these resources, gradually separated candidates from weakened party organizations. Unless and until state parties gain greater control over nominations and gather resources to help in campaigns, candidates are left to their own devices.[104]

When and where they are strong enough, state parties have substantial powers enabling them to share in making national policy and to be influential in the nomination and election of senators and representatives. The states have their own sources of patronage, as well as a share in federal patronage through their members of Congress and senators. The very circumstances that the states are separate constitutional entities engenders a drive for autonomy as those who hold places of prestige and profit in the state governments and parties seek to protect their jurisdictions, much as the framers of the Constitution hoped they would. Federalism, however, is much more than a legal fact. The states have great vitality because there are distinct, numerous, and vigorous ethnic, religious, racial, and economic groups that are disproportionately located in specific geographic areas and that demand separate recognition. State organizations, therefore, become infused with the purposes of groups who use their state parties for the recognition and enhancement of their separate identities and needs. Italians in Rhode Island, Jews and African-Americans in New York, dairy farmers in Wisconsin, wheat growers in Kansas, gay rights advocates in California, and many others make the idea of a noncentralized system a reality.[105]

Each of the state parties is composed of different people with somewhat different interests to protect and demands to make. Control over state parties must be exercised from within each state, since the various states do not control one another and the national party exercises only partial control. This is the essence of what is meant by a decentralized party system in which power is dispersed among many independent state bodies. Efforts, which in recent years have been quite successful, to centralize control of the criteria for delegate selection to national conventions may lead state parties to adopt two sets of rules—one for state and local nominations and another for federal—leading to even greater fragmentation of the party system.

Thus, despite rule changes which have tended to nationalize the parties, the national parties remain in many respects coalitions of state parties, meeting every four years for the purpose of finding a candidate and forging a coalition of interests sufficiently broad to win a majority of electoral votes. Increasingly, though, the national conventions exist mainly to ratify the results of the numerous primary elections that precede them. State parties are not generally as effective as candidates themselves in mobilizing support among primary electorates, and so it is less and less true that presidential nomination processes entail making a coalition of state parties and party factions—southern and northern Democrats, coastal and midwestern Republicans—who disagree on some major policy issues. Instead of compromise and coalition building, prospective candidates must build personal organizations state by state, mobilize their followers, and energize their individual factions in state primary elections. The cumulative effect of coming out ahead of other contenders—not necessarily winning a majority—is what makes for a successful presidential candidacy. By downgrading the necessity for compromise within the party and emphasizing the benefits of factional mobilization, the new rules of the presidential nomination process, which we discuss in the third chapter, expose the parties to certain risks. The most significant of these are the risks of spectacular failure in the general election, or, worse, an inability to govern in the event of a victory because of a failure to see the need for coalition building.[106]

The two major parties, as we have seen, gather their electoral support from somewhat different groups in the population, but no party has a monopoly of support from any of these groups; each party draws significant, and often indispensable, support from almost all categories.[107] In a close election the ability of a party to increase its support within one group, say, 20 to 30 percent may be crucial, even though that group still votes overwhelmingly for the opposition. The strategic implications of these remarks color all of national campaign politics: when they are trying to win, the parties try to do things that will please the groups consistently allied to them without unduly alienating other groups.

The temptation for political parties to avoid specific policy commitments in many areas, therefore, is very great. The American population is so extraordinarily varied—crisscrossed by numerous economic, religious, ethnic, racial, sectional, and occupational ties—that it is exceedingly difficult to guess the total distribution of policy preferences in the population at any one time. Even where issues like social security and unemployment compensation appear to be settled, many questions—should benefits be taxed or the rules of eligibility altered—remain. It is even more difficult to predict how these aggregations of actual and potential interest groups might react to shifts in party policy and positions, and still more hazardous to prophesy what different policy commitments might do to the margin of votes required for victory. This pervasive problem of uncertainty makes the calculations of gain from changes in policy positions both difficult and risky, and suggests that the interests of parties and candidates frequently are best served by vague, ambiguous, or contradictory policy statements that will be unlikely to offend anyone. The advantages of vagueness about policy are strengthened by the facts that most citizens are not interested in policy or are narrowly focused on a few issues, and that only a few groups demand many specific policy commitments from their parties and candidates.

Yet, despite all this, political leaders and parties do make policy commitments that are often suprisingly precise, specific, and logically consistent. Thus, we must consider not only why the parties sometimes blur and avoid commitments on issues, but also why they often commit themselves to policies more readily than their interest in acquiring or retaining office would appear to require.

Part of the answer may arise from the fact that the parties serve slightly different functions for their own activists than for people who vote but are otherwise largely disengaged from politics. Party activists are people who are much more interested in politics and attentive to political issues than the general population. The interest and attentiveness of political activists leads them to formulate and elaborate political opinions and preferences. Their desires to make these preferences internally consistent and consistent with the preferences of their party certainly lead to demands upon the party leadership for policy positions that are reasonably clear and forthright.[108] Activists also mutually reinforce their opinions when they interact with one another, which further leads them to press their opinions upon their party. When candidates with the same general political outlook compete for support of voters, as a large flock of Republican hopefuls did in 1988, the positions they take in the primary season may even exaggerate their policy differences.

The interest groups most closely allied with each party make policy demands that parties must meet to some extent. While it is true that voters are generally interested in only a few specific policies, interest group leaders and their full-time bureaucracies are manifestly concerned. If they feel that the interests they represent are being harmed, they may so inform their members or even attempt to withdraw support from the party at a particular election. Should voters find that groups with which they identify are opposed to the party with which they identify, they may temporarily support the opposition party, or they may withdraw from participation and not vote at all. Consequently, the party finds that it risks losing elections by ignoring the demands of interest groups. The demands of many of these groups conflict, however. If unions object to antipollution devices because they increase costs and decrease car sales, for example, labor and ecology groups cannot both be equally satisfied. If the costs of increasing worker safety compete with the costs of welfare payments, both cannot be obtained at the same level. Therefore, the parties may attempt to mediate among interest groups, hoping to strike compromises which, though they give no one group everything, give something to as many groups as they can. The increasing number of single-issue groups, of course, makes mediation difficult. Jimmy Carter, Walter Mondale, and Geraldine Ferraro discovered this when Catholic bishops, who wanted a strong antiabortion stand, rejected their efforts to remind them of a common interest in social welfare policies.

The contradictory pulls of vagueness and specificity are further exemplified in Jimmy Carter's 1976 campaign. He slid by such potentially divisive issues as amnesty for draft evaders or resisters—"a classic example of how to say something and not piss off people," as his press advisor Jody Powell put it—by saying he preferred pardons, which implied wrong had been done but had been forgiven. On the proposed B-1 bomber, Carter said the decision should be made by the next president, leaving listeners to guess what he might do. On abortion, he was personally opposed but fudged on the role of government. This led a Carter speechwriter to quit with a public blast, declaring, "I am not sure what you believe in other than yourself." Yet, time after time, as in his proposal for a more progressive income tax or for a ten-cent-a-gallon duty on imported oil, candidate Carter was attacked when he became specific. His poll taker, Pat Caddell, attempted to resolve the dilemma during the campaign:

> We have passed the point when we can simply avoid at least the semblance of substance. This does not mean the need to outline minute, exact details. We all agree that such a course could be disastrous. However, the appearance of substance does not require this. It requires a few broad, specific examples that support a point.[109]

Not being magicians, candidates have a hard time coming up with many "broad, specific" policies. Aside from his desires for tax cuts and higher defense spending, Ronald Reagan avoided specifics in 1980 and 1984. The utility of doing this was illustrated in his 1984 debates with Walter Mondale. Upon being challenged about social security, Reagan took the pledge not to reduce benefits, thereby greatly reducing his future flexibility. On the other hand, Reagan's vagueness made it more difficult to convert his landslide victory into a policy mandate. George Bush's extremely clear promise of "no new taxes" in 1988 may have been good presidential campaign politics, but it hurt him badly with congressional Republicans when he found he had to move away from that position a year or so later.

Throughout the years the opposing political parties have become identified with somewhat different policies. When new candidates arise they may bring with them somewhat new policy preferences. But there are bound to be many areas of policy on which they are not informed or do not have strong preferences. In such cases the existing set of policies traditionally associated with the parties provides the candidates with a useful economizing device. They can accept the going positions and concentrate on the policies that they may wish to revise, supplant, or present anew. This tack is bound to be popular with the party faithful, who have been brought up on the rallying cries of the past, who have learned to prefer what their party prefers, and who respond with vigor and enthusiasm to the cues provided by mention of their party's chief stocks-in-trade. Just as voters commonly use parties as a means of cutting their information costs on issues and candidates, and activists use them as reference groups, so may candidates use the parties' traditional policy positions to ease their burden of innovation.[110]

After a period of confusion in the 1960s and 1970s, the political parties are again becoming reasonably useful guideposts for the faithful. For forty years the New Deal structured the nature of political conflict in the United States. Those who were for or against a greater role for the federal government, for or against public or private electric power, for or against government-supported medical care for the aged and a host of other issues, knew immediately where their partisan loyalties stood. When the Republicans lost the 1964 election with Barry Goldwater, huge Democratic majorities were elected to both houses of Congress, and the Eighty-ninth Congress effectively enacted the agenda of the New Deal. This helped alter the content of partisan conflict at the national level. Since then new issues have arisen in bewildering profusion and new groups have come to public attention, clamoring to determine the shape of public policy. At first, these groups and issues were not closely linked to either party. Such issues as environmental pollution, law and order, prayer in schools, gun control, and abortion have now begun to take on firm identification with the major political parties. While no one is for pollution or against prayer, a certain sorting out of party positions has begun to occur. Most Democratic officeholders are for stronger—that is, more expensive—antipollution measures, more extensive gun control, no official prayer, and government support of freely chosen abortion, and most Republicans go the other way.

President Reagan contributed to the reinvigoration of party differences with his effort at across-the-board reduction of nondefense federal expenditures accompanied by significant tax cuts. During the 1980 campaign he argued for this in only the most general way, with many assurances that nobody would suffer untoward consequences, because of his belief—embodied in what is sometimes called "supply-side economics"—that the return of large sums of money to the private sector would spark a resurgence of the economy leading to increased government tax revenues. This did not happen. But by lowering income tax rates for everyone, the Reagan administration prevented Democrats from raising the "fairness" issue in the way that they did against President Bush's proposal to reduce taxes on the sale of business assets in the 1990s.

In the past, a relatively few party leaders controlled the decisions of a large proportion of the delegates to conventions. Delegates to national conventions were chosen as representatives of the several state party organizations, apportioned according to a formula laid down by action of previous national conventions. While it is true that official decisions are made at national conventions by a majority vote of delegates, American party organizations were often centralized at state and local levels and many delegates' votes were controlled by state party leaders. Such hierarchical controls as actually existed on the state and local levels asserted themselves in the national convention. Until recently the probabilities were fairly good that both major parties at any given time would have succeeded in electing a substantial number of governors and mayors of important cities; the chances were also fairly good, therefore, that a substantial number of delegates would be controlled hierarchically. Some states, of course, were badly split, with no one holding the lever to much more than his own vote.[111]

Normally, state party organizations were unified by incumbent governors. Without the centralizing forces of state patronage and coherent party leadership embodied by a leader in the governor's chair, state parties tend to fragment into territorial jurisdictions that can be played off one against another by astute aspirants for the presidential nomination. The lack of strong leadership at the state level also means that within the delegation a set of presidential preferences and strategies for pursuing them is less likely to be worked out in advance and agreed upon by all elements. Decentralized state parties thus become happy hunting grounds for early starters in the presidential sweepstakes. Early starters can— indeed increasingly they must—move into each state, make alliances and receive commitments from various state party activists, and build delegate strength from the ground up.

The importance of governors at national conventions (and along with them hierarchical control of state delegations) has diminished over the past quarter-century. There has been a little noticed but important long-term decline in the number of governorships that are up for election in years during which presidents are also running for office, as Table 1.7 indicates. From the thirty-three governorships that were open to election in 1944, the number declined to twelve in 1988. Many states are changing the two-year gubernatorial term to a four-year term and are providing for the gubernatorial election in the middle of the president's term of office. This is intended to isolate gubernatorial elections from national electoral currents, but it also means that the number of state delegations to national party conventions controlled by governors decreases as the motivation of governors to protect their own fortunes by finding popular presidential candidates also decreases. This trend thus far has had its most pronounced effect upon the Republican party, where the number of Republican governors up for election in presidential years has declined from twenty in 1944 to five in 1988. To the extent that delegates are pledged to candidates, of course, as almost all of them are, gubernatorial influence does not matter unless conventions go into multiple ballots.

This fact helps account for the willingness of Republican delegates to nominate Barry Goldwater even though he could reasonably have been expected to hurt the party's chances in many states. There were Republican state leaders in 1964 who winced at the thought of a disastrous defeat in November, but there were fewer such leaders than there might have been because there were fewer (that year, sixteen) Republican gov-

TABLE 1.7 *Number of Gubernatorial Elections in Presidential Election Years (Excluding Hawaii and Alaska)*

Year	Number of Elections
1944	33
1948	31
1952	31
1956	31
1960	27
1964	26
1968	25
1972	21
1976	24
1980	10
1984	13
1988	12

Source: World Almanac 1944, 1948, 1952, 1956, 1960, 1964, 1968, 1972, 1976, 1980, 1984, 1988.

Number of Republican Governors Up for Election in Presidential Election Years (Excluding Alaska and Hawaii)

Year	Number of Republican Governors Up for Election
1944	20
1948	19
1952	15
1956	16
1960	11
1964	7
1968	8
1972	11
1976	6
1980	3
1984	6
1988	5

Source: World Almanac 1944, 1948, 1952, 1956, 1960, 1964, 1968, 1972, 1976, 1980. For 1984: Austin Ranney, ed., The American Elections of 1984 (Durham N.C., 1985), p. 338. For 1988: Richard W. Scammon and Alice V. McGillivray, eds., America Votes 18 (Washington, D.C., 1989).

ernors at the Republican convention. The advantages accruing to Goldwater by declaring an early candidacy under these circumstances were obvious. Governors might have had sufficient hierarchical control over their delegations to keep them from precipitously joining the Goldwater bandwagon. The absence of central leadership on a state-by-state basis meant that delegates were freer to follow their personal preferences and also free to weigh ideological considerations more heavily than they could have done if they had been responsible to a leader who would suffer badly if Republicans were defeated for state offices. Similar considerations affected Democrats from 1972 to 1980, as a look at the decline in the attendance of senators and congressmen at national conventions reveals. From 1952 to 1968, senators and congressmen frequently played a role in the nomination process. But after the reforms of 1968 went into effect, as Table 1.8 reveals, they stopped even putting in an appearance in significant numbers as national convention delegates. This separation of the nomination process from subsequent processes of governing was as good an index as any of the precipitous decline of party power. Those who did the selecting were not the same as those who lived most intimately with the results. Recognition of this defect led the Democratic party to adopt the recommendations of its Hunt Commission to reserve about 15 percent of the delegate seats in 1984 for a large number of the party's office holders. Thus we see a sharp reversal of the downward trend with over 60 percent of senators and representatives in attendance at the 1984 convention. The superdelegates were overwhelmingly for Walter Mondale, and this fact helped stabilize Mondale's nomination campaign at points when it looked like he would be overrun by Gary Hart. Superdelegates are unlikely to vote against a candidate who emerges as the front runner in the primary elections and caucuses. They can, however, if they act together, hasten the nomination of a candidate who looks as though he is going to win anyway.

We have been saying that the distinctive functions of political parties—

TABLE 1.8   *Convention Attendance of Democratic Elected Officials*

	Percentage of Democratic U.S. Senators Who Were Voting Delegates or Alternates	*Percentage of Democratic U.S. Representatives Who Were Voting Delegates or Alternates*
1956	90%	33%
1960	68	45
1964	72	46
1968	68	39
1972	36	15
1976	18	15
1980	14	15
1984	62	68
1988	85	85

Data were drawn from official Convention Calls for each year.

Sources: Commission on Presidential Nomination and Party Structure (Morely A. Winograd, chairman), *Openness, Participation and Party Building: Reforms for a Stronger Democratic Party* (Washington, D.C., January 1978), p. 18; and Nelson W. Polsby, "The Democratic Nomination," in Austin Ranney, ed., *The American Elections of 1980* (Washington, D.C., 1981), p. 57; for 1984, Thomas E. Mann, "Elected Officials and the Politics of Presidential Selection," in Austin Ranney, ed., *The American Elections of 1984* (Durham, N.C., 1985), p. 124. For 1988, *Official Proceedings of the Democratic National Convention 1988* (Washington, D.C., 1988), pp. 29–173.

selecting candidates and campaigning for office—have atrophied as a result primarily of changes in the rules of delegate selection and have been replaced by entrepreneurship by candidates working through the mass media. Since candidates self-select and campaign for themselves through the media, it would not be surprising if the electorate, observing what has happened, pays more attention to the prime movers, the candidates, and less to their party labels. There is good evidence that this is exactly what has happened. As Martin Watternberg reads the data provided by the Inter-University Consortium for Political and Social Research,

> One possible explanation for why parties have declined in importance is that for various reasons candidates no longer need the parties in order to win elections. . . . In other words, the stands which candidates take on the issues may no longer be linked to voters' perceptions of the parties. The parties may still stand for certain broad principles and groups, but when it comes to specific policies, candidates now stand above parties rather than with them. . . .
>
> The reason for party decline has not been that people no longer see any important difference between the parties. . . . In the voters' minds, the parties are losing their association with the candidates and the issues which the candidates claim to stand for.[112]

The Electoral College

Another element of the strategic environment within which the drama of a presidential election is played is that peculiarly American institution, the Electoral College. American presidential elections are not decided directly by popular vote. Instead, popular votes are collected within each state, and each state casts all of its electoral votes for the candidate receiving the most popular votes within the state. This "winner take all, loser take nothing" approach is called a "unit rule."[113] We will explain some consequences of this rule presently.

Each state is allowed as many electoral votes as it has senators and representatives in Congress. Thus, all states, no matter how small, have at least three electoral votes. This means that sparsely populated states are overrepresented by the Electoral College. In 1988, 200,116 Alaskans influenced the disposition of three electoral votes, which gives a ratio of one electoral vote for every 66,705 voters. In New York, on the other hand, 6,429,753 voters went to the polls and voted for thirty-six electors, a ratio of one electoral vote for every 178,604 voters. In California, 9,757,150 voters for forty-seven electors produced a ratio of one electoral vote for every 207,599 voters.[114] One might conclude, therefore, that each Alaskan had about three times as much influence on the outcome as each Californian. But this is not entirely valid.

Why not? Because the unit rule of the Electoral College provides that the candidate having the most votes in a state receives the entire electoral vote of the state. This means that each Alaskan was influencing the disposition of all three of Alaska's electoral votes, and each Californian was helping to decide the fate of all forty-seven of California's votes. Ask any politician whether he would rather have three votes or forty-seven— the answer is immediately apparent. Thus the Californian gets more attention, which means the candidates may promise more to California voters even though each one of them does not matter so much. In fact, the present method of electing the president tends to give greater power to the large, populous states, not the small, empty states, because the large states can deliver to the winner large blocs of the votes he needs to win. Consequently, presidential nominees tend to come from big states and tend to run on platforms likely to appeal to interest groups that cluster there. They concentrate their campaigns in the big population centers, and, as politicians know, they stand or fall on the big state votes.[115] In 1976, for example, Jimmy Carter and Gerald Ford used strategies that emphasized the same seven states—New York, New Jersey, Pennsylvania, Ohio, Illinois, Michigan, and California—with Carter adding Indiana and Ford including Texas.[116]

Conclusion

As politicians develop their strategies for winning nomination and election to the presidency, they will have to keep in mind numerous facts about participants that exist in their political environment and probably are not subject to change by anything they may do. Among these are the following facts:

1. Most voters are usually not sufficiently concerned with specific policies to change their votes in response to policy appeals.
2. Voters usually vote the way they do out of party habit. Party allegiance is relatively stable. Major shifts in party identification are caused by cataclysmic events but smaller shifts, linked to issue positions, do occur.
3. Voters may not turn out in great numbers, and therefore it is necessary to use intermediary organizations and party activists to help turn out one's own voters.

4. Parties usually seek to win elections but may occasionally prefer to express the views of their activists as their major goal.

5. Either party has a reasonably good chance to win the election; the Democrats because they are in the majority, the Republicans because they are more likely to turn out.

6. Intermediary organizations such as interest groups and party organizations can be activated by policy commitments and reaffirmations and promises of access to governmental decision making.

7. Each party consists of a coalition of interest groups and state and local parties.

8. Increasingly, primary electorates determine presidential nominations.

9. The Electoral College puts a premium on votes from large two-party states.

Most or all of these basic facts about participants are well understood by presidential candidates and their managers. In addition, they must consider certain basic facts about the other resources available to them, to which we now turn.

2

The Strategic Environment: Resources

The Distribution of Resources

Certain resources that, at any given time, are disproportionately available to Democrats and Republicans play a significant part in the strategic environment of presidential elections. Possession of the presidential office, skill in organization, knowledge of substantive policies, a reputation for integrity, facility in speechmaking, ability to devise appealing campaign issues, personal wealth, stamina—all can be drawn upon to good advantage in a presidential campaign. There are more resources available to parties and candidates than any one book could deal with exhaustively. But some resources obviously are going to be more important than others, and the importance of different resources varies from occasion to occasion. It would be sensible to regard as especially important those resources that one side monopolizes—such as the presidential office—and those resources that can be easily converted into other resources, or directly into public office—such as money, which can be used to buy competent staff, newspaper space, television time, and so on.

Although political resources are distributed unequally between the parties, in a competitive two-party system such as ours the inequalities do not all run in the same direction. Sometimes Republican candidates reap the benefits; sometimes Democrats do. One result of these inequalities of access to different resources, however, is that different strategies are more advantageous to each of the two parties. Let us examine the effects on election strategies of three resources commonly held to be extremely important—money, control over information, and the presidential office.

Money

Presidential campaigns are terribly expensive. Radio and television appearances, newspaper advertising, travel for the candidate and his entourage, mailings of campaign material, buttons and placards, maintaining a network of campaign offices, taking polls, and raising money itself—all cost a great deal of money.[1] It is estimated that the various party committees (the Republican and Democratic national committees, the House and Senate campaign committees of both parties, and various ad hoc volunteer committees that spring up in each campaign) at the national level spent approximately $20 million in 1960, roughly $100 million in 1972, $143 million in 1980, $299 million in 1984, and $328 million in 1988.[2] Substantial sums were also spent by state and local organizations on behalf of the presidential candidates. Total political costs for all candidates at all levels of government amounted to something like $200 million in 1964, $425 million in 1972, $1.2 billion in 1980, $1.8 billion in 1984, and $2.7 billion in 1988.[3] The huge costs involved inevitably raise serious questions about the relationship between wealth and decisions in a democracy. Are presidential nominating and electoral contests determined by those who have the most money? Do those who make large contributions exercise substantial or undue influence as a result? Is the victorious candidate under obligation to "pay off" his major financial contributors? Do those who pay the piper call the tune?

This was certainly the reasoning that inspired the post-Watergate political reforms of the mid-1970s which attempted to take money as an influence out of presidential elections.[4] A taxpayer-supported federal election fund has been established, and the two major parties are entitled to draw upon it in equal amounts to finance the conduct of their general election presidential campaigns. The fund is available to the candidates of the two parties—once these candidates are picked—provided they do not collect or disburse money from any other source or coordinate their campaigns with citizens who are spending their own money in the candidates' behalf. Under this system each major party candidate spent $46.1 million in 1988, not an overwhelming sum, given the size of the electorate. The original 1974 law provided funding which was adequate at least to move the presidential candidates around the country and to get them on television. Missing were billboards, buttons and bumper stickers, and evidence of strong coordination between local and national presidential campaigns. The omission of these sorts of efforts may well have contributed to President Carter's impression, once he was elected in 1976, that he owed his election to nobody.[5]

In 1979 the Federal Election Campaign Act (FECA) was amended to allow local parties to make expenditures on billboards, buttons, and other forms of campaign advertising and on get-out-the-vote drives, without counting toward overall limits of the campaign. However, even with these changes there are strong incentives to centralize spending, and energizing grass-roots activity remains difficult. The major point is that materials put out by national committees, even if distributed by local committees, count toward the national committee limit. Naturally, the national committees prefer to spend their limited resources for their own needs. So the effect is either to force local committees to create original material or to abstain from visible support of their presidential candidate.[6]

Federal contributions also are available to contestants in primary elections, on a matching basis, insofar as they are able to raise money in small denominations from a variety of states. The best methods for qualifying for a federal subsidy of a primary campaign are (1) to make appeals through the mails, through telephone marketing and via personal appearances at events to known party contributors and (2) to hold fund-raising performances, since the donated services of celebrities have been held to be exempt from contribution limitations.[7] Thus, being able to raise money through mass means is a newly significant skill, conferring special power on professional practitioners of the arts of mail solicitation and celebrity hunting. These professionals are the new fat cats of campaign finance, along with the professional managers of PACs, the all-purpose campaign contribution clubs set up to comply with strict federal rules limiting campaign contributions by individuals and various sorts of corporate entities.[8]

Before these elaborate limitations were established in the mid-1970s, however, the evidence was slight that presidential elections were unduly influenced, never mind "bought" by monied interests. In the general election—that is, after the primaries—Republicans did spend more than Democrats in most places, but the difference was not as overwhelming as some would suppose. The Democratic percentage of major party post-nomination expenditures from 1932 to 1980 varied from a low of 33 percent in 1972 (when McGovern lost) to a high of 51 percent in 1960 (when Kennedy won); the average was about 41 percent.[9] Although the Johnson forces spent more money in 1964 than Kennedy's had in 1960 (the Democrats in 1964 managed to spend $12 million), Goldwater's forces spent $17.2 million, significantly more than Johnson's.[10] Total expenditures of both parties were high in absolute terms, but outlays per voter per party were quite modest, running in the 1972 election to about $1.31 for each of the 76.02 million voters.[11] One of the startling facts of the 1988 election was that, in contrast to all other presidential campaigns of this century except 1960, the Democratic candidate managed to outspend the Republican by a substantial (though not, evidently, electorally significant) margin.[12]

"Contrary to frequent assertion," said Alexander Heard, an expert on campaign finance, "American campaign monies are not supplied solely by a small handful of fat cats. Many millions of people now give to politics. Even those who give several hundred dollars each number in the tens of thousands."[13]

The most obvious and most important conclusion in our view is that even in the era when the parties were free to spend whatever they could raise and were not subjected to the limitations of the public finance law, money did not buy election victories. The candidates and party with the most money did not always win. Otherwise, Republicans would have won every election but two in the past fifty years, and we know, in fact, that Democrats won eight of the fifteen presidential contests from 1932 to 1988 and seven of the eleven from 1932 to 1972. Nor does there seem to be a correlation between the amount of money spent and the extent of electoral victory in national elections.[14] In 1968, for example, the Republican party outspent the Democrats by more than two to one, yet they won the election by a mere half-million out of the 72 million votes cast. One would expect that money would flow into the coffers of the party that is believed to have the best chance of victory. Yet with the possible exception of 1968, there does not seem to have been a single presidential election in this century that any competent observer believes would have turned out differently if the losing candidate had spent more money than the winner. We can at once eliminate all the Democratic victories but one (Kennedy in 1960) because the Democrats spent less than the Republican losers. Dwight Eisenhower was so popular that his two elections now seem to have been certain, whether or not he had a substantial campaign surplus. No doubt part of the reason he had so much money to run with was his personal appeal to the people who contribute to campaigns, and they might well have given to him even if he had run as a Democrat. Spending in 1960 was virtually even. It does not seem reasonable to blame Nixon's loss on a lack of money. However, given the closeness of the election, a large Republican financial advantage (as existed in 1972) might well have helped put Richard Nixon in the White House eight years earlier than he actually arrived, in January 1969.

Nixon in the election of 1968 had a great deal of money—indeed, probably a surplus—and Humphrey had less than he needed to make an effective race. Because the final outcome of the election was so close and the financial situations of the two major parties so disparate, 1968, it may be argued, is the single exception to the rule. Even so, it seems more plausible to argue that it was not lack of money but rather the deep divisions within the Democratic party (in part reflected in a diminution of contributions) that hurt even more. Had Vice-President Humphrey, the most creative liberal legislator of the quarter century after the Second World War, with impeccable credentials on civil rights and social welfare, received a rousing send-off instead of emerging bloody and half-beaten from the Democratic Convention, the election results might well have been different. But the party could not contain its differences on the Vietnam war.

In 1972, Richard Nixon's Committee to Reelect the President (CREEP) raised a colossal amount of money—and judging from the revelations of Watergate, spent much of it foolishly. Had they not possessed money to burn, it is doubtful whether a break-in at the Democratic party headquarters would have ranked high enough to consider funding. The Democrats, meanwhile, had to make do with much less (though more than in 1968), but nobody believes that more money would have helped Senator McGovern's hapless candidacy. Since the 1972 elections, both major party presidential candidates have drawn equally from the federal election fund. The Republicans who won the period from 1900 to 1928 did so with large majorities, as befits the party that then enjoyed the allegiance of most of the voters. The problem, then, is not to explain why money is crucial, but, on the contrary, to explain why it is not.

No one doubts that money is important; parties and candidates, not to speak of ordinary mortals, can hardly function without it. If a candidate could not raise any money, or only a pitifully small amount, he would be dreadfully handicapped and might not be able to run at all. But this situation has never arisen—although Humphrey in 1968 came close—after the national convention had made its choice. The first part of our explanation, therefore, is that the differences in spending ordinarily have not been so great as to give any candidate an overwhelming advantage. So long as the poorer candidate could raise the minimum amount necessary to mount a campaign—that is, to hire employees, distribute literature, go on radio and television a few times, get around the country, and so on—he could do most of what he had to do. In other words, spending more than the minimum amount necessary to run a campaign did not confer significant advantages. Like other goods, money is subject to diminishing returns. People may get tired of being bombarded with literature and harangued by speakers. The candidates sometimes worry about overexposure lest they go the way of certain television celebrities who were seen once too often. Accusations of "trying to buy the election" may arise if too much time is taken on television. Indeed, there may be resentment if favorite programs are taken off the air to accommodate candidates who seem to have had more that their say. We know that many voters are relatively impervious to bombardment by the opposition, and all the handouts in the world will not make them change. The actual result of an extensive assault by the richer party may be to give those who oppose that party additional reasons to intensify their opposition.

Given the necessary minimum amount of money, the less affluent candidate in the general election can count on a good deal of free publicity. Presidential campaigns are deemed newsworthy by the news media and are extensively reported. While Democrats may get somewhat less space than Republicans in the shrinking number of newspapers that openly display their partisanship in their news columns, they still get some, and they do better in the magazines and on the air. To some extent the candidates can make news. John Kennedy's grappling with the religious issue, Walter Mondale's choice of a woman as his running mate, Dwight Eisenhower's dramatic promise to go to Korea, Jimmy Carter's efforts to rescue the hostages in Iran or to negotiate them out, and George Bush's pledge: "Read my lips, no new taxes," all made headlines at little or no financial cost. The television debates in 1960, 1976, 1980, 1984, and 1988 attracted millions of viewers, numbers far in excess of the usual political broadcasts for which fees had to be paid.

The factor of skill must also be considered. Money can be spent for unrewarding purposes which actually rebound against the candidate. Democratic strategists during the 1930s were delighted at the expenditures made by the Liberty League on behalf of the Republican candidates. The strategists considered the expenditures to be an ideal target for their charges that the Republicans were the party of privilege. Much of the negative advertising during the presidential election of 1980 and the congressional elections of 1982 was regarded as more of a burden than a benefit to the candidates it was supposed to help. Money spent may unwittingly get the opposition to the polls. As Edward Kennedy showed in his disastrous interview with Roger Mudd in 1980, a poor performance on unpaid-for television may harm a candidate no matter how much is spent in other ways. The man who says the wrong thing may deeply regret the wealth that made it possible for him to disseminate his statement widely. The methods by which money is raised, as Nixon learned to his sorrow, may do more to hurt a president when he is in office than they ever did (or could have done) to help when he was campaigning. Or, consider Gary Hart, whose 1988 campaign suffered not only from scandal but also from financial disarray. Plagued throughout the campaign by the debts lingering on from his previous (1984) effort, Hart suffered the embarrassment of having a large fundraiser interrupted by federal marshals, called in by one of his creditors to seize any available receipts. Then it was revealed that some of the moneys he had still not repaid had been funneled into his 1984 campaign illegally by Stuart Karl, a Los Angeles videotape entrepreneur and Hart supporter.[15]

Other things being equal, of course, it would be nice to have more money to spend than the competition. But conditions are rarely, if ever, equal. The fundamental party allegiances of the population, the state of the economy, religious and ethnic affiliations, the personalities of the candidates, performance assessments of an incumbent president—all appear to be more significant in determining the outcomes of elections than the differences in total party spending. Despite the cries of harried party money raisers, the Democrats always seemed to come up with enough to get by. There is always the hope of victory. It remains true that the most expensive election is the one you lose.

Money probably makes a greater difference at the prenomination stage than later on. Having money early to aid in making a good showing helps raise money to sustain oneself throughout the primaries. Eisenhower and Taft each spent about $2.5 million on their nominating campaigns in 1952.[16] McGovern spent $12 million in 1972 on the way to his nomination.[17] Jimmy Carter spent $12.4 million in 1976 and—as an incumbent president—$19.6 million in 1980.[18] In 1984, Walter Mondale spent $26.2 million while Ronald Reagan—despite the lack of serious competition for the Republican nomination—spent $25.9 million.[19] In 1988, both the winning nominees had more money to work with than their rivals; Bush spent $27.7 million, and Dukakis spent $28 million.[20] By January 1, 1988, the Dukakis campaign had raised more than twice as much as any other Democratic candidate, a deficit difficult to overcome in the front-loaded primary system.[21] Of course inflation explains much of this growth in spending. The candidate who wishes to enter primaries and conduct a national drive to obtain delegates may be dissuaded through lack of the minimum amount necessary to get started. The press will not "take seriously" a candidate who cannot qualify for federal matching funds on January 1 of the election year by raising sufficient money in small amounts in 20 different states beforehand.

Money, however, is only one factor. Estes Kefauver in 1952 put on a vigorous campaign despite his relative lack of wealth. Had he not been bitterly opposed by party leaders, or had he won all the primaries he entered, as Kennedy did in 1960, he might have won the nomination. As it was Kefauver lost to Stevenson, whose command of wealth was the least of his political assets. In 1968, Nelson Rockefeller spent over $7 million—mostly his own money—in his effort to impress Republican delegates with his strength in the public opinion polls, but the effort was fruitless.[22] In 1976, Jimmy Carter won the nomination of his party through the primaries without a great campaign war chest, and incumbency, not money, was his great resource in 1980. It was not Ronald Reagan but John Connally who had the most Republican money in 1980, but Reagan won anyway.[23]

Having money manifestly does not guarantee victory in primaries. In 1984 there was a negative relation between Gary Hart's spending and his share of the vote. Hart was most successful in those states in which he was outspent by Walter Mondale. On the other hand, Hart lost four of the five major states in which he outspent Mondale by two to one or more.[24] Michael Robinson notes that "Hart had little money to spend when he was winning; he had plenty of money to spend as he lost. Spending and winning are unrelated; it is the 'drunken sailor' syndrome in presidential politics, spending what you have, regardless."[25] One can always argue that a small sum at a critical moment, if only one knew beforehand, might have been crucial. "If I'd only known then what I know today," Morris Udall lamented to an interviewer, referring to his decision (because of a money shortage) to stop advertising during the last week of the 1976 campaign in Wisconsin, where he lost by 5,000 out of 670,000 votes.[26] Since Udall came in second six times, losing three times to Carter by a tiny margin, any number of "it might have beens" (including an entry by Senator Henry Jackson into New Hampshire, which could have prevented Carter from getting started) might well have made the difference. Thus it cannot successfully be argued that a candidate who ran so long and so often in so many primaries lost only because he lacked money for a week.

Skill and strategy in using resources matters as much as having them. Witness a memorandum written to Morris Udall by his campaign manager: "We've got a reputation, frankly, as the sloppiest campaign in memory. No one knows who is in charge. . . ."[27] In 1976, Birch Bayh's indecision about entering primaries, Henry Jackson's taking Pennsylvania for granted, Hubert Humphrey's waiting until the California primary, when it was too late, Jimmy Carter's failing to see Maryland was not for him and getting involved in a pointless scrap with Governor Jerry Brown of California, all this and more mattered. It also mattered that Carter's strategy of running early and everywhere was a good strategy that paid off. Carter not only was able to run because he could raise money, he was able to raise money on the strength of his early victories.

Other candidates, however, may have been adversely affected by lack of funds. Nelson Rockefeller in 1960 is a curious example. Apparently he decided not to contest the Republican nomination that year in part because he could not raise the cash, or, one assumes, the enthusiasm that cash contributions symbolize among like-minded party financiers.

During the 1960 Kennedy-Humphrey primary campaigns in West Virginia, charges of vast Kennedy spending were made. Certainly Kennedy's ready cash did him no harm. In retrospect, however, it does appear that he was decidedly more popular with the voters than his rival, Hubert Humphrey.[28] Would more money have enabled Humphrey to turn the tide? Humphrey's campaign was badly managed and severely underfinanced, and in part this led the press to accord him less serious treatment than he might otherwise have merited. Had Humphrey had as much money to spend on campaigning as Kennedy, for as long a period of time, the tide might conceivably have turned in the other direction.[29] There were, nonetheless, other candidates—Johnson and Symington, for example—who had plenty of money but who chose not to contest the primaries. It is exceedingly difficult to get reliable information on an event that involves a decision not to act, such as a political candidate's decision not to run because he could not raise the money. There is no literature on this subject. But undoubtedly there have been some prospective candidates whose inability to raise cash has proved fatal to their chances of being considered for the nomination. Whether this failure represents inability to satisfy the monied classes or to convince enough people that the candidate is serious and worthy is difficult to say in the abstract. A more important question concerns whether there has been systematic bias in favor of or against certain kinds of candidates that consistently alter the outcomes of presidential nominations. We can immediately dismiss the notion that the richest person automatically comes out on top. If that were the case, Rockefeller would have triumphed over Goldwater in 1964 and Nixon in 1968, and Taft over Eisenhower in 1952. In 1976, Ronald Reagan's personal wealth eclipsed Gerald Ford's, as, in 1980, Edward Kennedy's did Jimmy Carter's. Nevertheless, in both instances, the incumbent president beat the challenger. Indeed, for candidates who accept public funds, the maximum personal contribution allowed is now $50,000. In 1988 only three candidates came close to this limit, and three others made loans of a similar size to their campaign organizations. Richard Gephardt's $50,000 must be compared with the $7 million or so that his campaign consumed. Of the $27.7 million spent by George Bush to win the Republican nomination, only $2,000 came out of his own bank account.[30]

The ability to raise money is not only a matter of personal wealth but also of being able to attract funds from others. Does this mean that only candidates attractive to the wealthy can run? The question is not so much whether it helps to be rich but whether candidates who favor the causes of the rich have the advantage over those who favor the poor. There is little evidence to support such a view. Given the nature of the American electorate, no candidate would openly admit to being the candidate only of the rich. Candidates holding a variety of views on economic issues—

most of which are highly technical—manage to run for the nominations of both parties. If candidates are generally chosen from among people who differ but little on most substantive issues, the reason is not because the rich are withholding their money from the more radical candidates. Rather it is because the distribution of opinions in the electorate renders the radicals' cause hopeless. Our conclusion is that it is nice to be rich; some candidates who lack funds may be disadvantaged. From the standpoint of the total political system, however, the nomination process does not appear to bar candidates who are otherwise acceptable to the electorate.

The Federal Election Campaign Act Amendments of 1974 were explicitly designed to reduce the influence of money in the electoral process. Whether they have accomplished this goal is difficult to calculate. The reform bill does establish a $1,000-per-person limit on contributions to any one candidate's primary, runoff, or general election campaigns, together with an overall limit of $25,000 on contributions by a single individual to all federal candidates in any one year. Organizations of all kinds are limited to $5,000 per candidate per contest. Since there is no limit on how large or small a donating group may be, or on how many donor organizations there are, it is possible that state and regional affiliates of businesses, unions, consumer groups, or what have you could each contribute the maximum amount up to a total of $250,000. This is the loophole through which political action committees (PACs) were formed, and, in recent years the number of such organizations is growing.

Political action committees have more impact on Congressional than presidential elections. They raise money from individuals to employ in campaigns either as direct contributions to a candidate or to fund separate but complementary campaigns. The latter was the technique of the National Conservative Political Action Committee (NCPAC), which in both 1980 and 1982 ran negative ad campaigns against liberal incumbents. A few PACs, like NCPAC, were created by direct mail entrepreneurs. Most PACs are products of established organizations—unions, corporations, trade associations, "public interest" lobbying groups—and thus are vehicles for those organizations' leaders to collect funds from members. The degree to which donors to PACs are in one way or another coerced into giving is yet to be discovered. Since what is required under the current rules is a large number of contributions of middling size, Herbert Alexander and Monica Bauer have argued that "the large contributor, in effect, has been replaced by the large solicitor."[31] These solicitors include PAC managers, corporation CEOs, direct mail consultants, and entertainment industry promoters—all of whom have access to those in position to give a thousand dollars to a political campaign.

The president of Common Cause, Fred Wertheimer, says "PAC money has a major and negative impact on the legislative process. Not only do PAC contributions provide access and influence for the donors, but special interest PACs have played a key role in the growing fragmentation of our political process."[32]

A PAC practitioner, Bernadette A. Budde, Political Education Director, Business-Industry Political Action Committee, argues the contrary viewpoint:

> PACs are a positive force in American politics for a number of reasons: First, and most important, participation in a PAC provides an opportunity for personal involvement in politics. What once might have seemed an obscure, remote activity engaged in by candidates and a few activists is now within the reach of all citizens. Second, PAC dollars offer opportunities for candidates without personal wealth to run for office. Third, PACs help to elect candidates who, while perhaps not supported by a major party, do represent the view of a large segment of the electorate. Fourth, PACs assist candidates in effectively managing their campaigns and budgets. Finally, PACs reinforce the basic concept of American politics—that all viewpoints an be heard and that public policy is best formed when created in a context of open competition between interests.[33]

PACs are controversial; in spite of the large membership of some, they symbolize "special interest" use of money in politics. In the 1984 and 1988 campaigns, a number of Democratic candidates appealed to this sentiment by forswearing use of PAC funds in seeking the nomination. Since presidential nomination campaigns operate with federal matching grants and with spending limits, such a "sacrifice" is easier in presidential campaigns than in congressional races. Indeed, much of the fear of PACs focuses on their use to influence Congress because members of Congress on committees with jurisdiction over a given matter frequently receive funding from the interested PACs. PACs matter less to presidential elections than to congressional, state, and local races, accounting for only 1.4 percent of total contributions during the 1988 presidential campaign. The moral high ground—at least in the eyes of many journalists and other observers—could be captured at relatively low cost for such candidates as Gary Hart, Pierre du Pont, and Michael Dukakis who forswore PAC contributions entirely. Pat Robertson was unable to claim total abstinence, having received, in the course of his campaign, a grand total of eight dollars from PAC sources. PAC funds figured more prominently in the campaigns of Bush, Dole, Gephardt, and Gore.[34]

One can argue both that PACs reduce citizen activity and that they increase it. The relation of PACs to parties is still developing. Their rise may be a symptom of party decline, for if parties controlled the resources for election, candidates would not need PACs. To the extent that PACs orient themselves to candidates rather than parties, they contribute to party decline by increasing the ability of candidates to build their own organizations. And to the extent that PACs favor incumbents, they decrease the need for incumbents to show party loyalty and they stifle rather than encourage competition. Yet PACs may in the long run be useful to parties. As PACs proliferate (there are now more than 4,000), they need to cooperate, and for PAC leaders as for voters parties can become organizing symbols. The ideological PACs—which probably should include not just conservative groups such as Jesse Helms's National Congressional Club, but the labor unions as well—line up virtually on party lines.

Richard Richards, former chairman of the Republican National Committee, expressed the tensions in the emerging relationship of PACs and parties. Ideological PACs that openly affiliate with a party, he believes, are useful in accumulating small contributions whose donors may "even sit on the Committee and watch how it is spent and allocate the money to people who have [their] interests at heart. . . ." The independent expenditure committees, which can spend as they please so long as they do not formally coordinate their activities with a party or candidate, make Richards unhappy. He feels that they can confuse the campaign and compete with the party for the loyalty of candidates. "The candidates say," he continues, "the party didn't do anything for me. I don't owe the party anything"[35]

Through trial and error candidates have discovered new ways of using PACs to their advantage. Befitting their proclivity toward technological innovation, Republicans went first. Well in advance of the 1980 presidential campaign, Republican candidates Ronald Reagan, George Bush, Robert Dole, and John Connally formed PACs of their own. The strategic advantage lay, first, in the ability of PACs to do more for candidates than the individuals who made them up. Whereas individuals are legally allowed to contribute a maximum of $1,000 per candidate for federal office per election, under the law PACs could contribute $5,000 per election to House and Senate candidates and individuals could give as much as $5,000 per presidential candidate to a PAC. More important, the money spent independently by PACs did not count toward the individual state or overall limits on spending that were applicable once a candidate sought matching funds. Thus personal PACs allowed candidates to travel, to help local candidates and gather their support, to build up lists of donors, and otherwise to prepare for the nominating campaign. By 1981, Walter Mondale and Edward Kennedy had established personal PACs. Indeed, Mondale did the Republicans one better by using large amounts of "soft money," that is, funds raised outside of federal law, say for state-level PACs, but that could be spent to help a presidential candidate.[36]

The most recent logistical breakthrough in presidential campaign finance was discovered in 1976, and is now known as the candidate sponsored, or "pre-candidacy" PAC. Since federal campaign finance restrictions apply to candidates only after they have registered themselves as such with the FEC, would-be Presidents of the United States have begun to delay their official announcements as long as possible. In the meantime, they can form political action committees devoted to the "National Interest" (Bruce Babbitt), "Prosperity" (Jack Kemp), "Freedom" (Pat Robertson), or (in Robert Dole's case) simply "America." The advantages of the personal PAC are several. First, donations of up to $5,000 per year (as opposed to $1,000 for the FEC-sanctioned campaign committee) may be accepted, and without any expenditure limitations attached. Secondly, neither fund raising nor spending by the PAC is counted toward legal limits once the candidate's official candidacy is declared. Contributors tapped at this initial stage can contribute again once the official campaign is launched.

Such early money is not superfluous. George Bush's Fund for America's Future was used to "hire a national staff of 50 persons . . . hire political organizers in Iowa, New Hampshire, and Michigan . . . develop direct mail fund-raising programs, prepare policy papers, and conduct polls" in the several years preceding the 1988 election.[37] In an era of the permanent campaign, these tasks must be started well in advance of the starting whistle.

What began in 1976 with Reagan's Citizens for the Republic (founded in part by contributions left over from his defeat in the Republican primaries that year), is now an established norm. Gearing up for the 1988 race, ten of the eventual fourteen candidates founded PACs. Spending on these enterprises was, according to Alexander and Bauer, "more than twice the combined amounts spent in advance of the 1980 and 1984 elections." Bush, Dole, and Kemp led the charge, and the Democrats followed at a more leisurely pace (Dukakis abstained altogether).[38]

Michael Malbin describes the developing interaction between the rise of PACs and the professionalization of campaigns:

> Paid professionals are less likely than individual corporate executives to give candidates early "seed money" for sentimental reasons: On the other hand, the professionals are more likely to share political information about competitive races, and move together to influence those races during a campaign's closing weeks. Professionals working for business groups also tend to be more "practical" and less ideological than individual corporate contributors. They are less likely to be satisfied with such honorific re-

wards as ambassadorships, and more interested in electing people who will at least listen to their technical legislative concerns.[39]

This suggests that professional lobbyists control the distribution of funds so as to maximize their group's influence over legislation. Sometimes this is the case. More often, however, the local people who raise the money also have the greatest say over how to spend it.[40]

More important than PACs for presidential elections are the 1974 act's provisions for public financing of presidential primaries, conventions, and campaigns. To be eligible for matching public funds, candidates in a presidential primary have to raise, on their own, at least $100,000, including $5,000 from each of twenty states or more. Only the first $250 of each individual contribution can be matched by the federal government. The total amount of matching funds available to each candidate contesting the primary elections is adjusted for inflation. In 1988, the limit was $11.6 million.[41] It is clear that early money, widely dispersed in modest amounts, is thrice blessed: once for helping a candidate get an early start, once for generating federal matching, and once for multiplying the disparity in private contributions by government aid. If two candidates raised $100,000 and $200,000 respectively, the difference between them would be half as much ($100,000) before matching as afterward ($200,000).

The two major parties get over $9 million apiece for their national conventions from the Presidential Election Campaign Fund. This fund comes from the money automatically assigned to it from the U.S. Treasury when citizens check the box on their tax forms permitting an allocation of one dollar per form to this purpose. Minor parties may receive lesser amounts based on the percentage of the total vote their candidates have received in a past or current election. Thus new parties have to compete at a disadvantage. To the extent that past presidential elections are used as a basis for calculating support, there is also a danger that a lapse of four years will distort a party's popularity, and the outpouring of third-party sentiment in one year will subsidize the perpetuation of the party four years later, when popular sentiments have shifted.

During the presidential election campaign, major party candidates can get more than $46 million each from the public fund.[42] They may forego this sum if they choose to do so and opt for private financing instead. It is likely, however, that they will settle for the public bird in the hand. If they go public, they cannot also raise money privately, and this release from private fund raising is a blessing few presidential nominees are likely to reject. They may also suspect that choosing private financing would alienate some voters. Each of the fifteen major party contenders in 1988 accepted matching funds, and therefore was subject to the FEC rules. Again, minor parties are eligible on a proportionate basis, depending on the votes they received at the last general election, so long as they obtained a minimum of 5 percent of the vote.

Each candidate, finally, is required to establish a single central campaign committee through which all campaign contributions are funneled and reported. Specific banks must be designated as depositories of campaign funds. Many committees may be called to contribute funds, but only one can be chosen to spend them. These stipulations add to the already strong disclosure provisions of the 1971 Federal Election Campaign Act, the attempted circumvention of which was exposed during the Watergate revelations and subsequent trials and convictions.

There were difficulties with the 1971 act and the 1974 amendments. The act was cumbersome, requiring reporting of small sums, and discouraged local campaign activity. It was also parsimonious, providing too little money to conduct adequate national campaigns. It caused political candidates and parties to become dependent on the timing of regulatory decisions. As these and other problems became apparent, the act was altered again in 1979 so as to allow state and local parties to do more and to lessen the reporting requirements for all concerned. Herbert Alexander and Brian Haggerty wrote an admirable summary of this detailed piece of legislation, which imposed new changes upon old ones.

Among its major provisions, the 1979 amendments:

- Exempted candidates who receive or spend $5,000 or less on a campaign from filing disclosure reports; the same applied to party committees under certain circumstances.
- Raised the level for itemized reporting of contributions and expenditures from over $100 to in excess of $200 and raised from $100 to $250 the threshold for reporting independent expenditures.
- Reduced the maximum number of reports a candidate is required to file during a two-year cycle.
- Permitted an individual to exclude from reportable contributions an amount up to $1,000 in behalf of a candidate or $2,000 in behalf of a political party, in volunteer expense connected with providing his home (as for a fund-raising event), food, or personal travel.
- Allowed state and local party groups to buy, without limits, buttons, bumper stickers, handbills, brochures, posters, and yard signs for voluntary activities, and to conduct voter registration and get-out-the-vote drives on behalf of presidential tickets without financial limit.
- Increased from $2 million to $3 million the allotment of federal funds for the Democrats and Republicans to finance their nominating conventions.[43]

Making the process even more Byzantine is the requirement that campaign organizations fill out forms not only for their overall fundraising and spending but also of their expenditures within each state. Each candidate is allowed a ceiling of $200,000 or 16 cents per eligible voter, whichever is greater, within each state.[44] If readers think it takes accountants and lawyers to keep up with all this, they are on their way to uncovering another reason for the increasing costs of campaigns.

Watergate was in part a scandal about campaign finance. It was revealed, for example, that the Justice Department negotiated a settlement of an antitrust suit with the ITT Corporation soon after an ITT subsidiary, the Sheraton Corporation, agreed to supply $400,000 worth of services to the Republican Party if the party would locate its 1972 national convention in San Diego. Sheraton's offer was only part of a package put together by San Diego civic leaders, in competition with other cities around the country whose visitors' bureaus also wanted to attract one or both national party conventions.[45]

Now that the law provides over $9 million in public financing to each national party for its national convention, it forbids parties to spend more than that on the conventions. It is unclear, however, whether this ban includes the various "in kind" services that traditionally have been provided: automobiles from the major manufacturers, free hotel rooms for the national committee roughly on a ratio of one free room for every ten paid for, special police protection and trash collection service, and so on. The Democrats' 1988 meeting in Atlanta managed to spend $22.5 million, more than twice the presumed legal limit.[46] This is one of the most difficult of the questions faced by the bipartisan Federal Elections Commission established for the purposes of monitoring compliance with campaign expenditures laws and distributing public money under provisions for public financing of elections.

There are four broad issues raised by these regulations on money. The least troublesome is the issue of public disclosure of campaign financing. In federal campaigns, all contributions in excess of $200 and expenditures by candidates and committees in excess of $200 must be publicly reported under the Federal Election Campaign Act of 1971. The availability of this information led Common Cause in 1972, and others since, to compile and publish lists of contributors to congressional campaigns. These compilations document the unsurprising news that some senators and representatives attracted donations from contributors having business before the committees on which they sat, and that some Senate and House races attracted money from sources far away from the state or district concerned. As well they might; a few hundred thousand dollars invested in Delaware or South Dakota could help to elect a sympathetic congressman or senator as readily as several million dollars invested in New York or California.[47]

When these contributions are matters of public record, voters can decide for themselves whether or not their representatives are still able to represent them adequately. Against this clear public gain must be weighed the possible chilling effects of publicity on the financial angels of small, unpopular parties. Safeguards against this difficulty are not at present in the law, and so far First Amendment protections of free speech have not been successfully invoked against disclosure on the grounds that disclosure inhibits political expression by chilling support for unpopular parties.[48]

A second feature of the new law is a provision for the public financing of presidential election campaigns, which, as we have said, currently offers over $46 million of public funds to each of the major party candidates, lesser amounts to minor parties, and matching sums to presidential candidates in primary elections. Among the policy issues raised by public financing are: How much should minor parties get? Should not some method be found so that people rather than legislatures allocate public funds to the parties of their choice? In light of the nearly $100 million spent by the major party candidates in 1972, the last presidential year before public finance went into effect, is not $90 million twenty years later too low to provide adequate political communication in a nation as large and diverse as ours? A comparative study by Howard Penniman suggests that, contrary to popular opinion, American elections actually cost less per voter than those of other democracies.[49] Although actual spending in 1988 showed a considerable 54 percent jump from the previous presidential election, the trend over time is less disturbing: real campaign spending in 1988 was four times the 1960 figures.

United to this last question is, of course, the question of whether

TABLE 2.1   *Presidential Spending: 1960–1984 (Adjusted for Inflation, 1960 = 100)*

Year	Actual Spending	CPI (1960 Base)	Adjusted Spending*
1960	30.0	100.0	30.0
1964	60.0	104.7	57.3
1968	100.0	117.5	85.1
1972	138.0	141.2	97.7
1976	160.0	192.2	83.2
1980	275.0	278.1	98.9
1984	325.0	346.8	93.7
1988	500.0	385.4	126.5

*All spending figures are in millions of dollars and include prenomination, convention, and general election costs.

Sources: Herbert E. Alexander and Monica Bauer, *Financing the 1988 Election*, p. 21; from Citizens Research Foundation.

private expenditures should be prohibited where public expenditures are used. Any limitation on campaign expenditure limits political communication, a class of speech that one would think would be especially protected by the First Amendment. In practical terms, limits on campaign spending constitute an incumbent's protective device, since challengers almost always have a greater burden of making their names known. When expenditures are limited, political competition is inhibited. At present, however, the courts have held that Congress can set expenditure limits as a condition of accepting public subsidy except when politicians are spending their own personal money, which it is their unlimited right to do.[50]

The final issue raised by recent legislation is the issue of limitations on contributions. Here, once again, a First Amendment problem is encountered, since voluntary political contributions of their own money by citizens as a means of political advocacy can readily be construed as exercise of free speech. Against this must be weighed a general public interest in seeing to it that politicians are not unduly influenced by people who have large financial interests. May it not be that those who contribute or raise money in large amounts thereby gain influence not available to others? Aware that the answer to this question is not a simple one and certainly does not dispose of the First Amendment problem, we would say, "Yes, but not overly much." As one fund raiser said of Washington: "This town works on personal relationships. Any time there's an opportunity to develop those relationships, it's a plus. The most anybody figures they can get in this business is access. You can't buy a vote. What you can do is say, 'Listen, I've helped you.' "[51]

What contributors or fund raisers (the financial middlemen) get to begin with is access to centers of decision making. That is why a lot of PAC money goes to incumbent legislators. Control over money certainly makes it easier to "get in the door" and present one's case. Persons of wealth, however, are likely to have substantial interests that would provide them with good access whether or not they made contributions. If no significant interest feels disadvantaged by what these contributors want, they may well be given the benefit of the doubt. But in matters of great moment, where the varied interests in our society are in contention, it is doubtful whether control over money goes very far with a president. There are many reasons for this.

In the first place, there are many issues on which a candidate is likely already to be publicly committed. Suggestions that he change his position during the campaign are likely to be met with little favor. If the matter is important enough to be mentioned, it has to be considered in relation to its vote-getting potential. Forced to make a choice, nominees are far more likely to prefer votes to dollars. And even if a miscalculation is made in public, candidates generally prefer not to reverse their field and appear vacillating and inconsistent. Money may be given in the expectation of future favors. To spell this out in detail would appear unseemly, however, and is likely to be rejected outright.[52] The moral sense of the candidates would most likely forbid such a thing. If not, the good political sense of their advisers (certainly after, if not before, the adventures of the Keating Five) would suggest that the consequences of discovery are much worse than any possible benefits. Thus, any strings attached to a gift are likely to be vague and cloudy, subject to all sorts of interpretations. When they are not, the risks of exposure are so great that the costs of corruption are as likely to be as high for the contributors as for the public.

Once a president assumes office, he is in a much stronger bargaining position. Contributors are likely to need him much more than he will need them: he can do more to affect their fortunes than they can to affect his. A president may at that point refuse to acknowledge any alleged agreement on policy concessions in return for contributions. Wealthy contributors frequently give to both parties and, in any case, are often found on opposite sides of public issues. For candidates to give in to one of them may simply incur the wrath of others.

A decline in contributions from one source may be made up by funds from another. The president's need to gain or maintain support from voters, the limits placed on his powers of decision by what congressmen, bureaucrats, and interest groups will accept, and his own preferences all place drastic constraints on benefits contributors get from campaign contributions. In brief, money becomes much less important to the things a president needs to do while he is in office. Contributors may be heard to complain in the hurt tones of Henry C. Frick, who, after visiting Theodore Roosevelt at the White House, said, "We bought the son of a bitch and then he did not stay bought."[53] The foregoing analysis should help to explain why presidential politicians do not "stay bought," whatever their debt to their financial supporters.

It would be amazing if the exponential growth in the regulation of private industry did not lead the business community to seek advantages and governmental officials to confer them. The fact is that what government does—an airline route or a television license here, a tax ruling or an import quota there—can have an enormous impact on the fortunes of private people. Businessmen, as we have learned from investigations of the fund-raising practices of the Nixon Committee to Reelect the President, feel they must act defensively. They may give to a campaign fund not so much to steal a march on their competitors as to make sure they are not left behind. Thus, for example, airlines may give to protect their routes.[54] Because government power is so pervasive, business people, not knowing when or where they might need a friend, frequently give to the campaigns of both parties. Deregulation makes this less necessary. So does public finance of elections.

Though the parties usually seem to raise enough money to get by, the activities that go into finding money are likely to give the candidate a few traumatic experiences. Each successive presidential campaign tends to be run by different people, who have to start from the beginning. When Adlai Stevenson was nominated in 1952, he downgraded large contributions and appointed Beardsley Ruml his chief fund raiser. Ruml tried to get most of what he needed from small contributions, and he got more than usual from small givers, but not nearly enough.[55] His predecessor was Edwin Pauley, who raised funds for Truman. Pauley was an oilman who had a wide acquaintanceship among the wealthy. He was adroit in having his claims recognized by such groups as road builders and construction firms, who could expect to benefit from Democratic policies. Until the Kennedy campaign, the Democrats continued to live, at best, from hand to mouth, day to day, crisis to crisis. In 1948 President Truman found himself stranded without funds on his campaign train in the middle of Oklahoma. Few people wished to contribute to what was thought to be a sure defeat. The governor and a few others on the train decided that something had to be done, and found the money. Humphrey was nearly out of money in the midst of his seemingly hopeless 1968 campaign when a plea for funds was inserted as an afterthought at the end of a nationwide television speech from Salt Lake City, in which he pledged a bombing halt in Vietnam. Enough money came in to pay for the program twice over. Again, the essential wherewithal was forthcoming, but the attendant tension is hardly the best atmosphere in which to conduct a political campaign.[56]

In 1964, "when Republican chances of victory over Johnson were never rated much brighter than those of a snowflake in Austin," the Republicans raised more money than they had in any previous campaign. And, in contrast with previous campaigns, the money came not from big business but primarily from "small donations sent in by hundreds of thousands of contributors, many of whom had never before contributed to a national campaign." The GOP collected 651,000 small, individual contributions in 1964. Candidates who generate intensely enthusiastic personal followings seem to be more capable of raising money from small contributors than less appealing representatives of the parties. For example, George Wallace always raised a great deal of money this way, and in 1976 he was the first Democrat to qualify for federal primary matching funds, some eighteen months before the election.[57] This appeal may explain why followers of Barry Goldwater, despite his huge loss in 1964, went on to take control of the national Republican party. Sharply defined views, whether on the right or the left of the political spectrum, are particularly an asset in direct-mail fundraising. The generally acknowledged Democratic pioneer of this technique was George McGovern in 1972, who succeeded in bringing in over 600,000 contributors and $15 million in contributions.[58] More recently, Jesse Jackson has gone to the bank with direct mail. "The major difference," between Jackson's dismal 1984 receipts and his 1988 successes, was "the explosion of direct mail."[59]

In order to pay off the sizeable debt left over from the 1968 presidential campaign, the Democrats took to the airwaves and put on a number of fund-raising telethons. These raised more than $2 million each, after costs. In recent years, the Democrats have also practiced other methods of debt reduction, including the painful business of negotiating with creditors to see if they would settle for less than 100 cents on the dollar.

Gary Hart had terrible difficulty paying off his 1984 campaign debt. Media attention to the complaints of his creditors led to much bad publicity as Hart opened his ill-fated campaign for the 1988 Democratic nomination. Political parties and candidates, in consequence of these sorts of maneuvers, have gotten a name for themselves as bad credit risks. As a result, television stations and newspapers usually require payment in advance. Airlines and the telephone companies—both regulated industries, after all, and hence vulnerable to the wrath of newly elected officials—have been edging gingerly toward similar requirements.

Campaign reform laws have encouraged candidates to switch to the attraction of small donations by mass appeals through the mails. The incentive to solicit small sums is created by limits on large contributions and by linking matching funds to receipts from individuals under $250. Mail solicitation has become a large and sophisticated business, and a whole new class of professional political managers who know about such things—which mailing lists yield the best results, how to write a mail solicitation, how to organize and account for returns—has grown up.[60] Indications are that raising money from the American public may be becoming more difficult. The percentage of Americans contributing to political causes or individuals running for office declined from 12.5% to 7.2% between the 1984 and 1988 election cycles. Part of this drop may have been due to the repeal in 1986 of federal income tax credit for political contributions.[61]

Money and the way it is raised are sensitive to changes in the rhythms of the election year. Gradually, since the beginning of this century, and recently at an increasing pace, key events in the nominating contest have occurred earlier and earlier in the presidential election cycle. And so early events—especially primaries—have an increasing influence on the strategies of potential and actual candidates. Under the party system that existed before the post-1968 reforms, most national convention delegates were selected in state caucuses and conventions over the two years before the election. After the establishment of primary elections in some states in the 1920s, a fifth to a quarter of delegates were selected in this fashion over a five-month period from February through June of the election year. As primaries became more important, even decisive, from the late 1960s on, there was still time between the earliest primaries and the latest ones for candidates to raise money to start and hope to raise more by doing better from one primary to another. "Super Tuesday" in 1984 and 1988, by bunching primaries in March, created an extremely narrow window for fund raising. The number of separate state primaries occurring on the same day in 1988 was raised to fifteen. This vastly increased the importance of raising sufficient funds ahead of time so that candidates could last through and beyond this date. Candidates who cannot do so lose before they have even started. Thus a long-distance race was converted into a middle-distance race, and now into a short series of frantic sprints.

"Presidential money," as Michael S. Berman, a long-time Democratic strategist put it, "is winner money. It's success money."[62] Success means doing well in the Iowa caucuses and then in the New Hampshire primary the week after. Then Super Tuesday occurs. If by then no one candidate has the nomination sewn up, all those who remain in the race need to have enough money left over to contest the coming primaries.

The importance of early money is enhanced by matching provisions that institutionalize the advantages of already having money. For candidates it is not merely having what they need but having it from the right sources (to get matching funds) and in the right places (to meet state limits) and at the right time (as early as possible).

Under the prevailing regulations, there is a new definition of nominating campaign efficiency, namely, the proportion of money raised to matchable money. In 1984, Mondale got about 55 percent of his contributions in primary matching money while Reagan got 65 percent. Legal and auditing advice is at a premium. A Republican attorney, in remarking on the complexity of the statutes and the Federal Election Commission interpretations, commented, "I'm terrified of the 1988 campaign; there probably isn't a candidate who'll obey the laws."[63]

Among the complexities is the possibility that candidates can lose and then regain matching funds. In 1984, winning just 5 percent of the vote in New Hampshire on February 28 and 8 percent in Vermont's March 6 nonbinding primary, Jesse Jackson ran afoul of the provision that if in two consecutive primaries a candidate receives less than 20 percent of the primary vote, and has not formally told the FEC that he or she was not a willing candidate at least twenty-five business days before the primary, then thirty days after the second primary, eligibility to receive matching funds is lost. It can be regained if, in a subsequent primary, the candidate receives at least 20 percent of the vote, as Jackson did on March 13th in Georgia.[64]

Another issue concerning the financial regulation of presidential elections is whether, as it is said in certain Latin American countries, a law should be passed to mandate that existing laws be observed. Campaign spending in excess of mandated limits, according to Herbert Alexander and Monica Bauer, "only brings an FEC fine in the amount of the overspending, months after the event, and is considered by pragmatic candidates as a cost of 'doing business.' "[65] Summing up the combined effects of legal and illegal circumventions of FEC regulations, they add:

> [T]he 1988 election period, in which candidate spending limits were set by law at $46.1 million, found more than twice as much spent, mainly by combinations of candidate and party committees at the state and local levels. The erosion of the effectiveness of the contribution and expenditure limits represents a return to big money—public and private, hard and soft, candidate and party. It threatens the general election public funding concept, that full public funding would be provided, with minimal national party participation, and effective expenditure limitations.[66]

This does not necessarily mean that too much money is being spent on presidential campaigns or that this money is skewing the democratic process (separate topics that have been discussed above), but only that the government's attempts to limit spending and efforts to supplant private money with public money have not been terribly effective.

A representative summary opinion on campaign fund raising comes from Peter B. Teeley who helped Vice President Bush: "A lot of people say two years is too long a time. But it's really a ten-year process."[67] Without quite going that far, it is apparent that nominations for the presidency have become an unintended combination of a maze and an obstacle course.

Today the financing of presidential elections is broken into two phases: before the nomination, when federal subsidies supplement the fundraising activities of candidates, and after the nomination, when federal subsidies provide all the money to the major parties to run their presidential campaigns. Expenditures independent of candidates by political action committees—buying ads on television or in the newspapers, or campaigning via direct mail, for example—are permitted by law, and play an increasing part in presidential elections. However, this sort of independent access to the voting public is by no means as pervasive as the ordinary access to voters provided to those nonpoliticians who own and operate the news media.

Control Over Information

Control over information is thus a major political resource. Information does many things other than help voters to change their minds—that rare phenomenon. It helps people keep in touch with the progress of the campaign, gives the party faithful indications of the effectiveness of their side, and acquaints voters with the candidates' major arguments. Information helps to guide and channel both the enthusiasm and content of participation, and therefore control over information and its dissemination is a significant political resource.

As we scan the major information media it appears that, generally speaking, newspapers are somewhat more partisan in their straight news coverage than are most radio and television stations. A political party that feels discriminated against over the air can complain to the Federal Communications Commission, which may take such complaints into account when the offending station's broadcast license is up for renewal. This makes station management jumpy and is a strong incentive for balanced coverage.[68] There is no such legal limitation on the freedom of newspapers and magazines to be one-sided in the presentation of the news, and indeed, it has again and again been discovered that the printed media avail themselves rather extensively of this freedom. Many newspapers enjoy monopoly positions in their communities, and much of the detailed political information available comes from the press. For these reasons the character of press coverage of presidential elections is a matter of strategic importance.

Historically, partisanship in news coverage has generally tended to favor the side that is most often endorsed editorially by the press, namely, the Republicans. Repeated studies have shown that the Republicans usually are the favorite party of the newspaper executives who determine editorial policy in most newspapers. They have also shown that whatever biases exist in news reporting, in placing stories in papers, in location and size of headlines, and so on, systematically have favored the Republicans.[69] The election of 1964, when newspapers gave a slight edge to President Johnson, provided the only exception; in 1968 and thereafter newspapers returned to form.

Yet, paradoxically, Democratic candidates for president do not seem to be harmed excessively by pro-Republican sentiments in the press, even among voters who rely heavily upon newspapers as sources of civic information. In recent decades Democrats like Franklin Roosevelt, Harry Truman, John F. Kennedy, and Jimmy Carter have gained office despite the fact that a vast majority of the press was editorially against them. If electoral votes had been apportioned within each state by the number of newspaper endorsements for each candidate, the 1976 count would have been Ford 538, Carter 0. If they had been apportioned on the basis of the circulation of these papers the count would have been Ford 489, Carter 49. The actual result, of course, was Ford 240, Carter 297. In 1980 and 1984, Republican years, endorsements more or less matched electoral results: 1980 numbers were Reagan 444, Carter 46 (with 48 electoral votes in states where newspaper endorsements were evenly balanced) on the basis of the number of endorsements. On the basis of newspaper circulation, the result would have been Reagan 385, Carter 139 (and 14 for ties). The electoral college result was Reagan 489, Carter 49. The 1984 count would have been 491 to 8 (39 tied) favoring Reagan on the basis of endorsements, and 429 to 99 (10 tied) on the basis of newspaper circulation. The actual result was Reagan 525, Mondale 13.[70] In 1988, the pattern of Republican-dominated endorsements was somewhat disrupted. Sixty-three percent of newspapers which responded to the quadrennial *Editor and Publisher* poll did not report an endorsement, although those which did support a candidate overwhelmingly chose Bush. In thirty-eight states a plurality of papers were reported as "uncommitted" or "do not endorse," including every large state; in seven states a plurality supported Bush, and only in Vermont did a majority of newspapers endorse Dukakis (five were tied).[71]

Despite the seeming Republican edge, the days of the crusading editor who owned his own paper and used it as a vehicle to propagate his own political doctrines are largely gone. In our time, newspapers with substantial circulations are much more likely to be part of corporate chains devoted primarily to making money for their stockholders.[72] The costs of publication are high. In order to show a profit, papers must have a high circulation and a good deal of advertising. This is difficult to achieve in the midst of competition among several papers and with television and accounts for the trend toward consolidation. Reader attention is gained by emphasizing human-interest stories—sports, crimes, local personalities, and the high jinks of movie stars. Especially outside the major metropolitan areas, political news, though it does have a place, is downplayed because most readers are not terribly interested in politics. An excessive emphasis upon public affairs, therefore, is unlikely so long as appeal to readers is a prime consideration.

This certainly has drawbacks for civic education. But for present purposes, it means that the possibilities for political propaganda are much less than they otherwise might be, because public affairs do not get much space.[73] Advertising is gained by convincing advertisers that it will pay them in terms of increased sales. The periodic appeals of conservatives requesting business people to place or withhold advertising as a form of political coercion usually fall on deaf ears, because the motives of those who pay are commercial rather than political. Both the paper and its advertisers are likely to shy away from political controversy; it tends to make enemies rather than friends and is commonly believed to be bad for business. The result is that much of the time newspapers are rather bland. Such political opinions as they do express are watered down so they will not give offense. These opinions, far from being their central concerns, tend to be sporadic and aimless, rather than representative of a coherent political ideology.[74]

These tendencies are strengthened by a prevailing belief that papers ought to be nonpartisan in their news stories and present both sides of the issues of the day. However much the norm of impartiality may be honored in the breach, it provides a standard that to some extent holds down partisanship. More than that, the belief that newspapers should report what happens rather than editorialize in their news columns has many other attractions for editors. It enables them to avoid the hostilities engendered by political controversy; it lessens problems of editorial judgment, thus decreasing their work load; it enables them to select items that they think will enhance their readership; it provides editors with a defense against the charge of giving too much prominence to causes and candidates that may be unpopular with advertisers or influential readers. The norm of impartiality, however, leaves the papers open to manipulation by political strategists who can create sensational news stories. During the heyday of Senator Joseph McCarthy, for example, journalists slowly became aware of the extent to which they aided him by publicizing his charges because they were "news" rather than ignoring or carefully evaluating them.[75] During presidential campaigns, application of the same standard gives candidates who are opposed by newspapers the opportunity to enter at least some of its news stories because whatever they say is "news." If they should be incumbents, their exposure will be greater because presidents of the United States get attention for the smallest things they and their families do.

The desire to cut costs has at least one favorable consequence for increased impartiality in news stories. There is today a growing reliance on material put out by the giant news services, the Associated Press, United Press International, and the *New York Times*, Knight-Ridder, *Los*

Angeles Times, and *Washington Post* services. These news-gathering agencies serve a wide clientele having a broad spectrum of opinions. They therefore endeavor to prepare stories that will prove acceptable to various shades of opinion.[76] Presenting what happened with a minimum of slanted commentary is a good way to do this, though the wire services are by no means perfect in this respect. The final product, however, is closer to the canons of impartiality than would be the case if each paper prepared stories in accordance with its editorial position.

In 1988, this trend continued with the introduction of the Presidential Campaign Hotline, a fancy electronic information service that keeps all subscribers abreast of the latest campaign developments. The eighteen-to-twenty-two-page daily printout consists of published campaign material from a wide range of newspapers and magazines, summarized highlights of television network news shows, commentary and analysis by the pundits, and current survey data. The Hotline also allows the candidates to contribute up to two hundred words each on any subject. Douglas Bailey, one of the creators of the service, describes it this way:

> This is not a newspaper. It's a news wire. It allows the political press corps to keep track of things they are not covering, lets the candidates send a daily message to editors and provides a means for media subscribers to make sure they don't let any news slip between the cracks.[77]

The Hotline swiftly became the bulletin board of campaign professionals from all the campaigns, where they could—and did—communicate with each other.

While it remains true that candidates favored by newspapers receive better treatment and somewhat greater coverage than others, there is one compensating factor in presidential campaigns that has not received the attention it deserves. Although the papers are generally conservative and Republican, political correspondents are comparatively more liberal and Democratic.[78] Most of the same standards of professional practice that constrain right-wing partisanship by publishers also damp down left-wing partisanship by journalists. As Michael Robinson has shown, while reporters may lean to the left, it's hard to find this bias in their copy.[79]

Hard, but not impossible. Overt expressions of partisan bias are regarded as unprofessional in news columns, and may even be veiled in articles labeled as "analysis." In at least two ways, however, news coverage that has a differential impact on the fortunes of candidates can be observed in contexts that are formally understood to be neutral territory.

In the first place, it is permissible under standard journalistic norms to entertain a general pro-underdog bias. Journalists pride themselves in their calling to "comfort the afflicted and afflict the comfortable." Comforting any sizeable body of afflicted persons may be well beyond the capacities of the news media.[80] It is far easier to afflict the comfortable, since this merely entails maintaining a pro-forma skepticism about the presumably self-interested pronouncements of incumbents of high office. Incumbents escape this presumption only rarely. In the early stages of a foreign crisis, when there is a rally round the flag effect, incumbents are permitted the luxury of being described as speaking in behalf of all the people. This frequently does wonders for their public opinion ratings. Ordinarily, however, Americans are instructed by the media to take their leaders' views with a grain of salt.[81]

Secondly, and more fundamentally, illustrating Bernard Cohen's observation that the news media tell their consumers what to think *about*, there is the issue of "framing." How issues are framed matters over the long run because frames determine the terms within which alternative solutions are debated, and, indeed they frequently serve to define the very nature of the problem.[82] Thus whether or not environmental degradation, global warming, carcinogenic cranberries, inadequate schooling, unemployment, inflation, and so on are seen as problems at any given time is not entirely controlled by scientific measurements of the underlying phenomenon in question.[83] In part their status as problems is determined by how people feel about them at any given moment, and these feelings are, in turn, partially determined by how the news media write about them. Thus the very problems our leaders are called upon to solve may differ from era to era according to ebbs and flows of public attention to them. Politicians work hard to seize control of this public agenda, and have a considerable impact on its contents. So, too, we would argue, do the autonomous decisions of journalists, who give and withhold credibility to leaders according to their own collective judgments about issues and the seriousness with which politicians are addressing them.

In 1960 John F. Kennedy, who was popular with reporters, got some favorable extra attention. Richard Nixon, who was not so popular with them, quite understandably complained.[84] By 1968, Nixon was a battle-scarred veteran who could watch with grim satisfaction as the press pursued the early Republican front runner, the relatively inexperienced George Romney. Jules Witcover comments:

> Romney, Nixon reasoned correctly, had not yet learned the lessons about the press that Nixon's experience had taught him, and even if he had, he could not go into hiding. A moratorium on politics by a former Vice-President, Presidential candidate and conspicuous globe-trotter would make little difference, since his face and his views already were widely known in the country; Romney, however, needed exposure in large doses

on the national scene if he hoped to graduate to the status of a national candidate. That exposure, Nixon was confident, would be Romney's downfall. . . . Meanwhile, Nixon himself could sit back, let Romney's destruction happen, and emerge all the stronger by virtue of the contrast between the way he and Romney conducted themselves in the pre-election year shakedown.[85]

In 1972, Nixon carried his strategy of avoidance even further, programming himself into local television spots in key places around the country and totally bypassing exposure to possible hostile questions from news correspondents.[86] He used the norm that the president's statements are news to get the coverage he wanted. Ronald Reagan, with his affable personality and long experience in show business, did exceedingly well with the men and women of the media in 1980. Jimmy Carter's efforts to portray him as an ogre, insensitive to poor people, or a warmonger were contradicted by Reagan's media coverage. By comparison, President Carter had far less favorable press notices. In 1984 underdog Walter Mondale got much better press coverage than incumbent Ronald Reagan but this apparently made little difference to the voters.[87]

Are ordinary citizens actually influenced in their opinions and voting choices by the newspapers they take? We used the word "take" advisedly, because the fact that a newspaper enters a home is no guarantee that its political news and editorials will be read. Most people pay little enough attention to politics; they often read nothing or just scan the headlines without carrying away much of an impression. Analyses of tons of newspaper clippings showing political propaganda by the press mean very little if these stories are never read.

When stories and editorials are perused with some care, the reader's perception of what has been written may differ markedly from the writer's intentions. An editorial may not be clear in intent, particularly if it is hedged by qualifications or watered down to minimize offense, as it often is. Frequently, the reader pays attention only to those parts of the piece that substantiate his own opinions. Opinion studies have demonstrated the remarkable capacity of people to filter out what they do not wish to hear and come away with quite a different impression than an objective analysis of an editorial or article would warrant. Indeed, the reader may interpret the story to mean precisely the opposite of what it intends. A criticism of Harry Truman for being vituperative, for example, could be taken as a commendation of his fighting spirit, just as a condemnation of Jimmy Carter for being obstinate could emerge as praise for his high principles.[88] Ronald Reagan's "detachment" could be seen by some observers as incompetence, by others as being above politics.

Stories and editorials may also be interpreted as they were meant to be and still be rejected as invalid. There is a great deal of suspicion of the press in the United States.[89] Party identification is so powerful that it is likely to overwhelm almost anything a paper says. Obviously millions of citizens have no difficulty remaining and voting Democratic while reading Republican newspapers. Group loyalties are another force that may lead to rejection of opinions in newspapers. Face-to-face groups in unions, on the job, in fraternal, religious, and ethnic organizations, may generate opinions of their own. If these differ from those in the newspaper, members of the group are provided with defense against the persuasion of the press. Group pressures of this kind are likely to be far more influential than what is written in a paper. The group may also reinforce what the paper says, but this represents an intensification rather than a change of opinion.[90]

Consider a puzzle concerning the political impact of the *New York Daily News*, a tabloid that in the 1930s and 1940s had a circulation in the millions. If those who read the *News* all through those years had voted against Franklin D. Roosevelt, as the paper repeatedly recommended in vitriolic terms, Roosevelt certainly would never have carried New York City by the huge margins he did. At the same time it seems strange that so many people who not only voted for but revered FDR in New York continued to read a newspaper whose editorials bitterly attacked their hero. The Democratic readers of the *News* apparently managed to get the best of both worlds. They read the paper they liked and voted for the man they favored without noticing the apparent contradiction. For them, perhaps, there was no contradiction. They either did not pay attention to the editorials, or they blocked out the unfavorable ones completely, or they interpreted them to mean something favorable to FDR. Voting studies document instances where people who wanted to vote for Harry Truman in 1948 convinced themselves that the incumbent president was against price controls; some people who preferred Dwight Eisenhower in 1956 apparently had no difficulty in believing that he surely favored medical care for the aged.[91]

Or, let us consider the case of the opposite of the *New York Daily News*, the gray, sober, responsible *New York Times*. After the *Times* came out for John F. Kennedy in the closing weeks of the 1960 presidential campaign, various political pundits speculated on the probable impact of this endorsement by so august and respectable a source. Our theory about voting behavior would lead us to be wary of claiming much influence for the *Times*, not because its readership is too indifferent to heed a call to reason, but because of the kind of people who read this paper. One has to be terribly interested in politics to read through the *Times* as far as the editorial page. Precisely because of this interest, *Times* readers are likely to identify with a major party and to resist changing their allegiance. An endorsement from the *Times*, therefore, however respectable, could hardly shake these devoted party people in their fundamental loyalty. The vacillating, the doubtful, and the uninformed who cannot make up their minds are far more likely to read comic books or *Modern Romance* than the *New York Times*, with its surfeit of "dull" news about political events.[92]

One paper which may have more of an impact is the *Manchester Union Leader*. This paper has neither the resources nor the circulation of the better known *Times*. However, its location—New Hampshire, site of the nation's first presidential primary—and its unabashed partisanship have made the *Union Leader* a force to be reckoned with. The paper's attacks on front-runner Muskie (and his wife) helped derail Muskie's 1972 campaign. In 1980, after an upset victory by George Bush in the Iowa caucuses, Ronald Reagan's candidacy appeared to be in serious trouble. David Moore argues convincingly that the *Union Leader* played a key role in Reagan's recovery and his victory in the New Hampshire primary. Moore finds that readers of the *Union Leader* were much more favorably disposed toward Reagan than nonreaders. This is not surprising given the stories the *Union Leader* was running. Representative headlines included—"George Bush Is a Liberal"; "Only a Bush Leaguer"; and "God Has Chosen Reagan to Lead This Country."[93]

This shows the great difference between primary and general elections. In primaries, when party loyalty is no help in sorting out the choices, cues from the news media may matter. In general elections, where choices are better structured, the news media are less influential.

No doubt the monopoly position of most newspapers in local communities makes the dissemination of opposing views more difficult than it might be in the presence of competition from a newspaper of a different outlook. But there are ways of getting around this. Other publications may enter the home—magazines and pamphlets that are religious, ethnic, union, fraternal, and even political in their focus—and these may contain contrary notions of public policy and candidate preference. True, only a relatively few persons read the political magazines, but these people are likely to be opinion leaders, people who take an active interest in public affairs and from whom others seek advice. The availability, therefore, of little magazines of many shades of opinion permits the opinion leaders to receive and then disseminate on a personal basis information that may counteract whatever is in a newspaper. And there is the pervasive influence of television, which has put so many afternoon newspapers out of business, and is now the favorite means by which citizens inform themselves of the rudiments of the daily news.[94]

What, then, is the significance of newspapers in presidential campaigns? We have suggested that the press is by no means immensely influential. Its major importance probably lies in two directions: presenting some kind of information about the candidates and the campaign to its readers and intensifying the predispositions held by people who tend to agree with the paper's preferences. Under some circumstances, also, a united press can force politicians to pay attention to a particular range of issues. Candidates would undoubtedly rather have the press on their side than against them. But they can and do win in the face of opposition from the press.

It may be that the newspapers people read subtly condition their attitudes in ways now unsuspected and that this has some effect on their opinions and voting choices.[95] One study, by Robert S. Ericson, suggests that when a newspaper in a monopoly position endorses a presidential candidate, that endorsement slightly influences the prevailing trend. Ericson found no influence for the press in 1968, a close election, but some in the polarized contest of 1964, when the usual Republican predominance lessened, and in 1972, when it intensified. The press matters more, it appears, as a conveyer of information during landslides, when its effect on the outcome matters less.[96]

Whatever impact the press has varies enormously with circumstances. Against a well-known and immensely popular president (such as Franklin Roosevelt in 1936 or Ronald Reagan in 1984) with publicity resources of his own, the impact of the press may be negligible. Against a little-known candidate, such as Adlai Stevenson in 1952, the attitudes communicated by the press—say, aloofness, overintellectuality, indecisiveness—may be more significant. Yet we know from voting studies that in 1952 Stevenson was favorably regarded by Democrats who identified him with his party.[97] The sheer number of different issues that may become relevant during a presidential campaign may either neutralize or intensify the influence of the press, depending on whether they are "pocketbook" issues that are grasped with relative ease by voters or "style" issues that owe their experience as issues to the attention paid them by the mass media.

The Role of Television

As a news medium, television reaches more voters than the newspapers. As an advertising medium, it soaks up enormous amounts of the money allocated to candidates under the law. As a medium of political influence, television makes a considerable difference.

Television news coverage plays a significant role in determining who wins the nomination in the first place. Early in the nomination process, when there are many prospective candidates, those candidates who are "taken seriously" by the news media, and especially by television, have a much better chance to survive the primaries and caucuses. Because the delegates to national party conventions are picked mostly by primary electorates, favorable exposure to mass electorates through the mass media—expensively by buying advertisements, or inexpensively by receiving news coverage—is absolutely necessary for hopeful candidates.

There is a tendency, brought on by the brisk competition among the three major television networks, for television news to deal rather ruthlessly with candidates, declaring them "winners" and "losers" with great rapidity on primary election nights, based on projections from early returns and exit polls. The competitive pressure to see a pattern even when the outcome is not terribly clear is overwhelming. Thus, on the night of the early-bird Iowa caucus in 1976 Jimmy Carter was proclaimed a big winner for bagging 29 percent of the vote. This was more than any of his rivals—the next in line was Birch Bayh with 11 percent—but far less than the 39 percent that went to uncommitted delegates. In 1988, Richard Gephardt, who led a large field of Democrats with 31 percent of the votes in Iowa, was much less lucky than Carter. The networks were more interested in Pat Robertson's unexpectedly strong showing on the Republican side.[98]

Television journalists, in common with their colleagues in print, make every effort to nail down "expectations" against which the performance in early primaries of candidates can be measured: Lyndon Johnson beat Eugene McCarthy as a write-in candidate in New Hampshire in 1968, but McCarthy did so much better than "expected" that the fact of his strong showing dominated the news and shortly drove Johnson out of the race altogether. Likewise, Gary Hart did unexpectedly well in 1984 in Iowa, and John Glenn did unexpectedly badly.

So television interacts powerfully with the delegate-selection process—especially early on, before popular images of the various candidates are fully established—and makes a difference to political outcomes. The media want excitement: That is what sells newspapers and captures viewers for the television news. From this need to compete follows a proclivity to adopt a horse-race metaphor and before election evening to overemphasize the closeness of races. Even when the results of surveys appear conclusive, the media suggest the race is still open. A close race keeps the adrenaline flowing. So, according to the study by C. Anthony Broh, reporters

(1) avoid predictions if they are definitive; (2) avoid reporting percentages if they are not close; (3) report the attitudes and preferences of subgroups that cast doubt on the outcome; (4) compare polls to a time period that can

demonstrate a narrowing or constantly close gap between the candidates;
(5) report voter reaction to spectacles of the campaign; (6) distort results
that do not generate excitement; and (7) question the validity of polls that
show a wide gap. Furthermore, they interpret methodological ambiguities
involving undecided voters and sampling error in ways that maximize
shifts in campaign support.[99]

Decisions favoring horse-race excitement and sensationalism eventually produce premature closure on apparent winners, not only on election
night, but also in the course of interpreting to viewers what has happened.
Consequently, the news media tend to start bandwagons early in the
election season and hasten the outcome of nomination processes.

Building bandwagons, however, conflicts with the recent tendency of
print and media journalists to give severe scrutiny to people in (or who
might get in) public office. So early front runners, like Republican George
Bush in 1980 or Democrat Gary Hart, before his flame-out in 1988, are
in some jeopardy.

The influence of media coverage of primaries could not be better illustrated than by the Mondale-Hart-Glenn rivalry of 1984. In the Iowa
caucuses on February 25th, attended by around 85,000 people, Mondale
got 45 percent to Hart's 16 percent, McGovern's 13 percent, and Glenn's
5 percent. Despite Mondale's huge victory and the relatively small number of people who voted—Hart got just 12,600 votes—the media made
the nominating contest into a two-man race. Glenn suffered a near knockout blow. Hart's media coverage, with hardly a negative voice, rose
dramatically, while Mondale's shrank. After Hart's victory in the New
Hampshire primary, where he got most of the votes of Democrats who
made up their minds after the Iowa caucuses, Hart briefly became the
front runner. At once, as Gary R. Orren reports, "In a daily series of
biting critiques . . . all three networks attacked Hart's credibility." On
March 13th, "Super Tuesday," with four state caucuses and five primaries, amidst generally mixed results, Hart received 35 percent and Mondale 31 percent of the popular vote. Yet "the media message was that this
was a Mondale victory, or at least a split decision." Apparently, Mondale
was helped by no longer being considered the front runner.[100] It cannot
be said that the voting results, rather than the media interpretation of these
results, carried the day.

After the nominations are made, if equal-time provisions of the Federal
Communications Act are waived by a special act of Congress, as they
sometimes are, the networks are able to give or withhold legitimacy to
third-party candidates more or less at will. This greatly affects the capacity of such candidates to mount a credible challenge to the candidates
of the two major parties. For example, in 1980 John Anderson lost

ground steadily after he was excluded from the televised debate between major candidates, more or less at Jimmy Carter's insistence.

Because they lend themselves easily to television coverage, primary elections and other "open" delegate selection mechanisms that lead to pledged delegates receive a lot of attention from television journalists.[101] This has made it hard for state party leaders to maintain control over party nominations. In effect the news media have been a major influence in transferring power over the nomination process from state party leaders to candidates and primary electorates.[102]

As an advertising medium television has gained greatly from the laws requiring a strict accounting of candidate expenditures. As compared with the numerous decentralized commitments of money that might occur in a grass-roots campaign, it is relatively easy to keep close watch over expenditures by buying television time for the presidential candidate's campaign. This has tended to centralize campaigns, and to make candidates increasingly dependent on television to carry their message. No wonder, then, that public relations specialists and experts in the use of television have increasingly turned up on presidential staffs since the days when actor-director Robert Montgomery coached candidate Eisenhower.[103]

We conclude that newspapers, magazines, and television stations do not conspire together (or within their own industries) to control the outcomes of nominations and elections. Because print and media journalists do share similar biases, being far more liberal and suspicious of authority than the general public,[104] and because they face similar institutional imperatives to converge on a coherent horse race, no conspiracy is required to create a correspondence of views. Similarly, although they try, as we have seen, candidates do not succeed in molding or manipulating the media to their liking. What we see most often is behavior that is not essentially manipulative or conspiratorial but mutual and interactive. The media and the candidates depend on each other for news to report and for favorable reporting to such a degree that each anticipates the actions and reactions of the other.

Observers are correct in noting the extent to which the media are not merely reporting the campaign, but centrally important to the campaign. No candidate has enough time or money or energy to reach all or most of the people necessary to get nominated and elected. There was a time, as far back as 1968 or 1972, when it was still possible for a candidate to go from small early primaries to larger later ones, gaining strength along the way. Nowadays there are too many primaries and too many groups and too many voters to manage without making use of the media. Most people get their news from the media, and early reports of progress are essential to a candidate's later success. Therefore, candidates must estimate how their actions are likely to appear in the news. Such questions as which primaries to enter or how much emphasis to put on them or how much attention to pay to which issues must be considered from the standpoint of the impression they will create on television.

Candidate choices continuously interact with media interpretations. R. W. Apple's *New York Times* story on the 1976 Iowa caucuses was widely credited with making Carter a front runner. Coverage of the 1984 Iowa caucuses, as we have seen, was equally important.[105] And, for all we know, had there not been numerous network and newspaper polls before the 1976 Republican convention showing Ford ahead, Reagan might have been able to maneuver better against a background of uncertainty. Knowing that dramaturgical stereotypes (who the good guys are, who the leaders are, who's out in left field, and so on) tend to persist, and that the front runner of today may be carried along only by early exposure, journalists may seek to resist perpetuating them.[106] This, however, is hard to do, because it must be done within certain rules of the news gathering business. Newspapers and television news programs require leads. Ignoring an act can be as dangerous as attending to it, since under- and overexposure may be evident only in retrospect. Since they need news, the media are swept along by the tide of events to which they contribute and in which they swim, very much like the rest of us.

Michael Robinson, a leading student of the media, observes that in 1984, "most of our basic notions and axioms of presidential politics in a network news era did not pan out."[107] The first axiom he challenges is that the incumbent, Ronald Reagan, had "an invisible shield: a teflon coating" so thick that the media never turned bad news into reporting critical of him, and that what bad press the president got did not reduce his popularity. William Adams has shown that Reagan's unpopularity increased with every rise in unemployment, that his popularity midway through his first term was lower than that of the six preceding presidents, and he began his second term with a lower rating than Richard Nixon did his.[108] For every evening news item that said or implied something favorable about Ronald Reagan during 1983, there were thirteen critical comments.[109] And they hurt his popularity. A glance at Table 2.2 shows that Reagan got over six times as many "bad press" items as Mondale.[110] Indeed, had it not been for later interpretations of the event, Reagan might even have been thought by citizens to have come out well from his first debate with Mondale.[111] Evidently, this negative treatment did not persuade most voters to turn against Reagan, since he won an overwhelming victory.

Perhaps other news stories, not so directly political, helped the incumbent. Michael Robinson notes:

TABLE 2.2   *Number of "Bad News" and "Bad Press" Pieces for Each of the "Final Four" National Candidates September 3 through November 5, 1984*

	Reagan	Mondale	Bush	Ferraro
"Bad news" pieces	34	8	4	19
"Bad press" pieces	81	13	15	6
Total	115	21	19	25

Source: Michael J. Robinson, "News Media. Myths and Realities," in Kay Lehman Schlozman, ed., *Elections in America* (Boston, 1987), p. 147.

In the fall the media elite broadcast—and rebroadcast—almost all of Reagan's best one-liners. In the summer they sounded like another George Bush as they did the cheerleading for the U. S. Olympic team. . . . After the Olympics, the big news story was the "new patriotism." All the free media did feature after feature about it. Would anybody expect that sort of thing to help the Democrats or Mondale? No, but the story was more or less true, more or less news, and tailor made for mass audiences in an Olympic victory year. So the story kept on coming.[112]

Past studies of media have focused on the written and spoken word. In an ingenious new analysis, Doris Graber managed to code the fa-

TABLE 2.3   *Positive Mentions of Candidate Traits: Poll versus Media Images*

	Reagan	Mondale
Competence		
Poll	76%	86%
Words	13	72
Pix	65	95
Leadership		
Poll	70	51
Words	41	46
Pix	87	98
Integrity		
Poll	78	80
Words	24	81
Pix	62	100
Empathy		
Poll	61	76
words	26	76
Pix	79	100

N = 2.2257 for the polling samples (though not all respondents answered all trait questions) and 750 trait mentions for Reagan and Mondale. Poll = NES sample; Words = verbal analysis only; Pix = audiovisual and visual analysis.

Source: Doris A. Graber, "Kind Pictures and Harsh Words: How Television Presents the Candidates," in Kay Lehman Schlozman, ed. *Elections in America* (Boston, 1987), p. 134.

vorable and unfavorable aspects of pictures in the 1984 campaign. As she says,

> On balance, in both words and pictures the nightly newscasts favored the Democrats. Pictures accented their virtues more and their flaws less. They made Democrats look closer to ordinary people than Republicans. Purely verbal trait descriptions also were far kinder to Democrats than to Republicans. Nevertheless, several countervailing factors tended to make coverage more balanced. These included the facts that Reagan's good pictures were generally better and more varied and interesting than Mondale's, that Reagan received the lion's share of coverage, and that a disproportionate share of this coverage emphasized traits favoring him. Moreover, Reagan and Bush were shown less frequently under attack by hecklers than was true of their Democratic rivals.
>
> A similar analysis for Mondale shows . . . the Democratic candidate received far higher positive scores on television than his Republican rival. Looking at purely verbal presentations, Mondale's television images showed comparatively small deficits for competence and leadership (14 and 5 percentage points) coupled with a tiny advantage (1 percentage point) for integrity and an even score for empathy. When it comes to the picture story, the trait images that emerge from television are so positive for Mondale that they exceed positive poll ratings in all categories. The differences are moderate for empathy, integrity and competence (24, 20 and 9 points). They are wide for leadership (47 points), for which the public gave Mondale exceptionally low scores.[113]

In short, the public rated Reagan more favorably and Mondale less favorably than their television coverage. Although pictures of Reagan may have helped counterbalance the extremely critical media coverage, the gap between public perceptions of his traits as reported in opinion polls and media reporting remained impressively large. Was this negative reporting offset by positive coverage of the Olympics and the "new patriotism"? Would less unfavorable treatment have led to an even larger victory for Reagan and other Republicans? Perhaps. Without the ability to rerun the election with different coverage, it is very difficult to tell. The influence of the media may be more in negative reporting on politics than in their favoritism toward any party.

Experimental studies, which tend to focus the attention of respondents far more than the real-world experience of television does during an election campaign, demonstrate that exposure to media stimuli do have effects on political attitudes.[114] Insofar as media stimuli reach ordinary voters, we would expect their effects to be negative toward incumbents, front runners, and positive toward those perceived to be underdogs.

Incumbency as a Resource: The Presidency

The presidency is one resource which, in any given election year, must of necessity be monopolized by one party or the other. When an incumbent president seeks reelection, he enjoys many special advantages by virtue of his position. He is, to begin with, much better known than any challenger can hope to be. Everything the president does is news and is widely reported in all the media. The issues to which the president devotes his attention are likely to become the national issues because of his unique visibility and capacity to center public attention on matters he deems important. To this extent, he is in a position to focus public debate on issues he thinks are most advantageous. The president can act and thereby gain credit. If he cannot act, he can accuse Congress of inaction, as Truman did in 1948 and Ford did in 1976. Since Truman won and Ford lost, this strategy, like all strategies in an uncertain world, evidently has mixed effects. Should he face a crisis in foreign affairs, and there are many, he can gain by doing well or by calling on the patriotism of the citizenry to support its chief executive when the nation is in danger. But if the problem lingers, as the Vietnam war did for Lyndon Johnson and the Korean war did for Truman, the continuing crisis soon becomes a lasting liability. A significant example of a foreign crisis took place during the 1980 campaign, when Iranian students seized the American embassy in Teheran on November 4, 1979, taking American diplomats hostage just as Edward Kennedy announced that he would run for the Democratic nomination against the incumbent president Jimmy Carter. Before the hostage crisis began, Kennedy was outdistancing Carter in the polls by 54 percent to 31 percent (with 15 percent undecided). Soon, however, Democrats rallied around the flag, and Carter's ratings shot up to 48 percent, with 40 percent for Kennedy and 12 percent undecided. Carter announced that he would suspend active campaigning, and he used his crisis responsibilities as a reason to refuse to meet his rivals in debate. He continued to campaign from the White House rose garden, however, and with great success.[115]

Unfortunately, the crisis dragged on too long, and President Carter's popularity ultimately suffered a serious decline, reverting to its precrisis level. Thus this episode also shows that the president cannot count on continued popularity if his policies do not appear successful to the electorate. President Nixon, to make a similar point in a different context, made repeated use of national television to mobilize support for his Vietnam policy. So long as his administration's actions were in accord with general public desires for withdrawal, even if gradual, the president did well in the polls. When he sent troops into Cambodia instead of withdrawing them from Vietnam, however, it was less clear that his fellow citizens approved of that course of action.[116]

As the symbol of the nation, the president can travel and make "nonpolitical" speeches to advance his candidacy subtly while his opponent is open to charges of "blind partisanship" in troubled times. Should his opponent claim that he can do a better job, the president need hardly make the obvious response that he is the only candidate who has had experience in a job for which there exists no completely appropriate prior training. Moreover, as Nixon did in 1972, presidents can campaign by doing their jobs, while challengers, as George McGovern discovered, have to manufacture positions that may dissolve upon close scrutiny or criticism.

The life of the incumbent is not necessarily one of undiluted joy. If the economic situation takes a turn for the worse, if terrorists strike, if a race riot erupts, if another nation is lost to hostile forces, whether Communist or fundamentalist, he is likely to be blamed. Whether he is really to blame or not, as president he is held responsible and has to take the consequences. Herbert Hoover felt deeply the sting of this phenomenon when the people punished the incumbent president for a depression that Hoover would have given much to avoid.[117]

The incumbent has a record; he has or has not done things, and he may be held accountable for his sins of omission or commission. Not so the candidate out of office, who can criticize freely without always presenting realistic alternatives or necessarily taking his own advice once he is elected. John Kennedy's "missile gap" of his 1960 campaign turned out to be something of a chimera after he got into the White House, and he never found it possible to act much differently toward the Matsu-Quemoy situation near mainland China than did Dwight Eisenhower, despite their overpublicized "differences" about this question during the campaign. Richard Nixon could complain about the problem of "law and order" in 1968 without promising anything more concrete than a new attorney general, which he would have appointed anyway. In 1980 candidate Reagan said "Ask yourself if you are as well off today as you were four years ago" and voters—for the most part erroneously—responded as Reagan hoped, in the negative.[118] Candidate Reagan was able to blame "stagflation," the unwelcome combination of high inflation and unemployment, on President Carter. The considerable Republican losses in the 1982 congressional elections, combined with the ability of Democrats to blame the Republican president for unemployment, placed Reagan in the same difficult defensive position his predecessor had been in a few years earlier. Reagan's popularity returned with economic recovery but, as the Iran-Contra affair showed, even a so-called "teflon" president has difficulty escaping blame when things go wrong on his watch. The incumbent is naturally cast as the defender of his administration and the challenger as the attacker who promises better things to come. We cannot expect to hear the person in office say that the opposition could probably do as well or to hear the challenger declare that he really could not do any better than the incumbent, although in a political system that encourages moderation and has enormous built-in inertia, like the American system, both statements may be close to the truth.

While his opponent can to some extent permit himself to be irresponsible or carried away by exuberance, the president cannot detach himself from office while campaigning, and he must recognize that other nations are listening when he makes statements. The president's very superiority of information may turn out to be a handicap, if he cannot make certain statements or reveal his sources for other statements without committing a breach of security. His opponent can attack his record, but the incumbent may have difficulty finding a comparable record to assail on the other side—unless, of course, the challenger succeeds at making his own proposals the issue. Both Goldwater and McGovern managed to do this. And Walter Mondale's promise of higher taxes provided ammunition for President Reagan's 1984 reelection campaign.

Barring catastrophic events—depression, war, scandal—the president's power is most certainly strong enough to assure him of renomination within the limits imposed by the anti-third-term (the Twenty-second) amendment to the Constitution. This is not merely because his is the greatest, most visible office in the land, with all sorts of patronage and other controls over the potential delegates. There is, in addition, the fact that his party can hardly hope to win by repudiating him. To refuse him the nomination would, most politicians feel, be tantamount to confessing political bankruptcy or ineptitude.

This rule was bent but not broken in 1980 by Kennedy's opposition to Carter and in 1976 by the Reagan challenge to Ford. Nor was it broken in 1968. The challenges of Eugene McCarthy and Robert Kennedy to Lyndon Johnson in that year demonstrated that the costs of party insurgency are high: not only do insurgents rarely win their party's nomination; their party also usually loses the election in years when party insurgency is strong. It was not only the fact that Senator Edward Kennedy sought to take the nomination away from Jimmy Carter in 1980, but also that he persisted right up through the convention, refusing to give Carter his wholehearted endorsement, that hurt the Democrats. Consequently candidate Carter was unable to focus on his Republican opponent as early as he would have liked.

The presidential power over national conventions has historically extended to (1) the right to renomination, or to designate the party nominee, effectively exercised in almost all of the conventions since the Civil War in which the president interested himself in the outcome; (2) the power to dictate the party platform; (3) the power to designate the officers of the convention; (4) the power to select many delegates. This privilege was especially potent historically in the case of Republican delegations during the days of the one-party Democratic South. In those days Republican presidents, until the passage of the Hatch Act taking federal employees out of partisan politics, drew upon southern federal patronage appointees to man this sizeable convention bloc.

The constitutional amendment limiting presidents to two terms did not change the power of a two-term incumbent radically. The party still must run on the presidential record, and the outgoing president still seems likely to control the management of the convention. Before President Roosevelt broke the two-term tradition, outgoing presidents controlled conventions even when no one expected them to run again. Presidents Truman and Johnson were also very influential in 1952 and 1968, when they were not candidates for reelection.[119]

The decline of the influence of state parties in national conventions and the rise of primary elections makes presidents less influential than they once were. Presidents have a harder time controlling primaries than controlling party leaders, and this affects presidential power over conventions. Overt attempts to designate a successor are riskier for an outgoing president in a system dominated by primaries, for the risks of failure are high.

There are those who believe that, like other democratic countries, the United States is going through a crisis of ungovernability.[120] In this view, any incumbent is vulnerable because he cannot satisfy the expectations of increasingly well-educated and articulate critics and their audiences in the electorate, who want results but are not willing to pay the costs. The presidency, therefore, becomes an albatross, and successive presidents are doomed to defeat. We do not fully accept this thesis, but note that it becomes far more plausible with the decline of parties that are capable of transmitting demands to leaders as well as moderating and channeling public opinion. It is one thing to demand that government take on new responsibilities; it is another to couple that demand with a refusal to give government the necessary resources, especially acceptance of its authority to carry out these tasks. Without parties to mediate between leaders and followers, government is indeed in a double bind: damned if it doesn't act and damned if it does.

Incumbency as a Liability: The Vice-Presidency

Yet the incumbent president does have some advantages; it is the incumbent vice-president who is seeking to succeed an incumbent president of his own party who suffers the most. His is the unhappy lot, as Nixon discovered in 1960, and Humphrey in 1968, of getting the worst of all possible worlds. He suffers from the disadvantages both of having to defend an existing record and of being a new face. He cannot attack the administration in office without alienating the president and selling his own party short, and he cannot claim he has experience in office. It may be difficult for him (think of Hubert Humphrey on Vietnam) to defend a record he did not make and may not wholly care for. His is the most difficult strategic problem of all the candidates.[121]

George Bush in 1988 was the first vice-president to succeed a retiring president of his own party since Martin Van Buren succeeded Andrew Jackson in 1837. Why, despite the historical rarity of the event, did Bush win? He obtained the nomination of his party largely, it appears, because primary voters in the Republican party considered him the logical successor to Ronald Reagan, and Reagan was extremely popular at the end of his second term. This may help also to explain why Bush won the election. At least three theories—all of them meritorious—have been invoked to explain his success.[122] They refer, respectively, to peace and prosperity, to the conduct of the campaign, and to structural properties of the parties and the nominating process. The first theory is refreshingly straightforward. It says, simply, that if nothing is badly disturbing the electorate, then incumbents will do well. George Bush was of course not an incumbent president, but as the sitting vice-president he was as close to an incumbent president as it is possible to be without actually being an incumbent president. In the election incumbents whether they were Democrats or Republicans did extraordinarily well for all offices, as they do in conditions of peace and prosperity. And most, of course, were Democrats. Those scholars who use fancy models to attempt to forecast elections have, on the whole, employed assumptions stressing such variables as the condition of the economy somewhat in advance of the election and they all produced numbers suggesting a Bush victory.[123] Indeed some of them did so even during the spring and summer months when Michael Dukakis was leading George Bush by a wide margin in the public opinion polls.

The second theory also seems to us entirely plausible. It points out that Vice-President Bush ran an effective campaign and Governor Dukakis did not. Jerry Roberts of the *San Francisco Chronicle* gave an excellent summary of professional opinion on this subject, noting the following features of the Dukakis campaign:

> A fatal reluctance to respond to Bush's bareknuckles attacks. The Republican hit Dukakis as weak on defense and soft on crime, attacking him over the Pledge of Allegiance, prison furloughs and the death penalty. By the time Dukakis fired back in late fall, it was too late. Many voters by then believed the attacks because they had gone unanswered.
>
> A failure to find a consistent campaign theme. Running against peace and prosperity, Dukakis tried campaigning on competence, the middle class squeeze and the unfairness of Bush's attacks before settling on traditional Democratic economic populism in the closing weeks of the race.
>
> A disastrous media campaign. Matched against Bush's state-of-the-art television commercials—which meshed precisely with the message he was delivering on the campaign trail—Dukakis' shifting set of ads had little impact. They were produced by a series of media specialists and drafted by committee, and were criticized as confusing, obscure and without much content.
>
> "We absolutely should have won this race," said California Democratic Party Chairman Peter Kelly. "What happened was George Bush defined Mike Dukakis before Dukakis defined himself."[124]

It is possible to dwell too long on particulars of the campaign. There is unusually strong agreement among campaign professionals that Dukakis campaigned badly in the general election. This overlooks the fact that he did well enough in the primary season and in dealing with Jesse Jackson thereafter and in his vice-presidential pick. There is, likewise, strong agreement that the Bush campaign was well tailored to make the best of his chances, conveniently overlooking the selection of Dan Quayle. So if we accept the professional assessment of the effects of the campaign—as on the whole we do—we must do so in the face of the fact that every winning campaign looks better in retrospect and every losing campaign looks worse that it probably was.

Of the third theory we are especially fond, because it helps understand not only the election of 1988 but the entire set of presidential elections over the last twenty years and not only presidential elections, where Republicans have been so successful, but also the great and persistent anomaly in the American political system in which there is Republican success in presidential elections while at the same time Democratic dominance overall, as measured by electoral success at all other levels, party identification, and party registrations. Essentially, the argument is that since the drastic reforms of the presidential nominating process that took place in the wake of the chaotic 1968 Democratic National Convention, the system has changed radically from a coalition-building regime to a factional-mobilization regime. Over the long run this harms Democrats and helps Republicans in the general election because the Democrats, although they are the larger of the two parties, are also far more factionally fragmented and therefore greatly disadvantaged in a long nomination process in which there are no incentives or occasions for coalition formation. Because the Republicans are much more easily mobilized and coordinated through their basic ideological similarities, the lack of coalition-building incentives harms them less.[125]

Bush nevertheless also had to contend with the disadvantages of the vice-presidency. Thomas Riley Marshall, the genial Hoosier who was Woodrow Wilson's vice-president, once observed that the office he had in the Capitol was so little protected from tourists that they used to come by and stare at him like a monkey in the zoo. "Only," he complained, "they never offer me any peanuts." This is the way vice-presidents have viewed their constitutional office, not just its physical setting, for a long time. "Not worth a pitcher of warm spit" was the bowdlerized version of John Nance Garner's rueful conclusion in the mid-1930s. "A mere mechanical tool to wind up the clock" was the way the first vice-president, John Adams, described himself. "My country has in its wisdom contrived for me the most insignificant office that was the invention of man."

The main constitutional function of the vice-president is to wait. As Mr. Dooley once said, "Every morning it is his business to call at the White House and inquire after the President's health. When told that the President was never better, he gives three cheers and departs with a heavy heart."[126] Clearly this is not much of a job for a major political leader who is used to active leadership. Yet suppose a sudden tragedy should befall the president. Can we afford in the inevitable days of uncertainty that follow such an event to replace him with anything less than a major political leader who can step into the breach immediately, do the president's job, and do it well? This is the first and fundamental dilemma of the vice-presidency and, as the quotation from John Adams amply testifies, it has been with us since the founding of the Republic. From this dilemma flow the problems characteristic of the modern vice-presidency.

We can date the modern vice-presidency from April 12, 1945, the day Franklin Roosevelt died. The next day his successor, Harry S. Truman, remarked to some newspapermen: "Boys, if you ever pray, pray for me now. I don't know whether you fellows ever had a load of hay fall on you, but when they told me yesterday what had happened, I felt like the moon, the stars, and all the planets had fallen on me." Truman had been a respected but not a leading senator before he assumed the vice-presidency. In his three months in that office, Vice-President Truman saw President Roosevelt only a few short times. As vice-president he had not been told of the Manhattan Project to build the atomic bomb. Sticking closely to the duties prescribed under the Constitution, Mr. Truman spent most of his time on Capitol Hill, presiding over the Senate. His knowledge of the affairs of the executive branch and of foreign and military operations was the knowledge of an experienced legislator and not the inside information routinely available to top policymakers in the Roosevelt administration: Mr. Truman wrote later, "It is a mighty leap from the vice-presidency to the presidency when one is forced to make it without warning."[127]

Since Harry Truman made the leap in the waning days of World War II the world has grown more complicated, and so has the presidency. Efforts have accordingly been made to update the vice-presidency to meet modern conditions. The vice-president now sits with the National Security Council as a matter of right; under President Eisenhower, the vice-president attended all meetings of the cabinet at the president's invitation and presided in the president's absence. In addition to his Capitol Hill quarters, Vice-President Johnson had a suite of offices in the Executive Office Building adjacent to the White House. For a while President Nixon moved Spiro Agnew to an office down the hall from his own. Nelson Rockefeller was not only made head of the Domestic Council by President Ford, but also was allowed to bring in his own men as top staff assistants in this presidential agency. Vice-President Mondale, with an office in the White House only a few doors away from the Oval Office, was given an unprecedented full, though junior, partnership by President Carter. Vice-President Bush's relations with President Reagan were complicated by worries among the Reagan staff about Mr. Bush's future ambitions, a common enough difficulty between presidents and vice-presidents, somewhat exacerbated in this case by their differences in age and in political outlook. But Bush kept the White House office. And he played a part in foreign policy.

Since 1945, presidents have made greater efforts to involve vice-presidents in various administration activities: goodwill tours abroad, occasional attempts to promote legislation on Capitol Hill, honorific jobs "coordinating" programs to which the president wants to give a little extra publicity, and, especially, political missionary work around the country—speeches and appearances on behalf of presidential programs. These are tasks of the modern vice-president. In return for continuous briefing on the entire range of problems confronting the government, vastly improved access to the president, and a closer view of the burdens of the presidency, the modern vice-president must carry some of these burdens himself. Which burdens he carries, how many, and how far are up to the president. Naturally a vice-president may withhold his cooperation, but if he does, he impairs his relationship with the president. This is bound to affect his capacity to fulfill the constitutional obligation of the vice-presidency, which is to be genuinely prepared in case of dire need.

No vice-president is in any sense the second in command in a president's administration. In truth, he is entirely removed from any chain of command in the government. This guaranteed the independence of the vice-president in the days of Aaron Burr, John C. Calhoun, Charles Dawes, and other free spirits who have occupied the office. Today, the situation is quite different: it is much easier for high members of a president's administration to maintain independence from the presidency. Top administrative officials can constitute a loyal opposition on government policy within the executive branch because their obligations run in at least three directions: upward to the president, downward to the agencies whose programs they supervise within the administration, and outward to the clientele their agencies serve. Political executives serve the president best who serve their clients with devotion and promote the interests of their agencies with vigor. Executives know, moreover, that if in the process they conflict too much with presidential plans or priorities, the president can always fire them. If the president fails them in some serious way, they can resign, as Attorney General Richardson did when President Nixon ordered him to remove Special Prosecutor Archibald Cox during the memorable "Saturday Night Massacre" of October 1973, or as Secretary of State Cyrus Vance did from the Carter administration in 1979 over the aborted rescue mission to Iran.

The vice-president can hardly fulfill his constitutional responsibilities by resigning, nor, in midterm, can he be dismissed. He has no anchor in the bureaucracy, not interest group constituency. Thus, uniquely in the executive branch, the modern vice-president must discipline himself to loyalty to the president.

This sometimes has painful consequences for vice-presidents, especially when they attempt to emerge from the shadow of the president and run for the presidency on their own. It is scarcely necessary to note Vice-President Humphrey's difficulty in persuading opponents of the Vietnam war that he and President Johnson were not Siamese twins. Even after four years out of office, Walter Mondale found himself criticized for President Carter's perceived failures. Vice-President George Bush was alternatively attacked as servile and insufficiently loyal.[128] Like Humphrey and Nixon before him, Bush found it difficult to run independently on his own record.

There seems to be no way for a vice-president to avoid the dilemmas built into the office. Unless he is scrupulously loyal to the president, he cannot get the access to the president that he needs to discharge his constitutional function; when he is loyal to the president, he is saddled, at least in the short run, with whatever characteristics of the president or his program the president's enemies or his own care to fasten on him. He sits there in the limelight, visible, vulnerable, and for the most part, powerless.

From 1836 until 1960, when Richard Nixon was nominated, no incumbent vice-president was put forward for the presidency. Since 1960, many vice-presidents—Humphrey, Ford, Johnson, Rockefeller, Mondale, Bush—have tried for the presidency. It may be that the name recognition of vice-presidents or, as Howard Reiter suggests, the decline of the ability of party leaders to select their own candidate, has made vice-presidents leading candidates for the presidency.[129] Some—Truman, Johnson, and Ford—became presidents before seeking election as their party's presidential nominee, but the others did it on their own. Now even defeated vice-presidential candidates, from Lodge to Muskie, to Shriver to Mondale and Dole launch their own presidential nominating efforts four years later.

As long as vice-presidents have some chance eventually to run for the presidency, as they do at present, and are not arbitrarily excluded from further consideration as independent political leaders in their own right, there will be plenty of takers for the vice-presidential nomination. This contributes to the strength of political parties. Vice-presidential nominees can balance tickets, help to unite a warring party, and campaign effectively with party workers and before the public—as, for example, Senator Lyndon Johnson did with conspicuous success in the election of 1960, and both George Bush and Walter Mondale did in 1980. Thus, vice-presidential nominees can help elect a president. It is after the campaign is over that the vice-president's problems begin.

Convertibility of Resources

Clearly, the social framework within which presidential election strategies must be pursued distributes advantages and disadvantages rather importantly between the parties. We have attempted to explain why the unequal distribution of key resources such as money and control over information do not necessarily lead to election victories for the parties and candidates who possess and use most of these resources. Might there not, however, be a cumulative effect that would greatly assist those who possessed both more money and more control over information? This effect may exist, but it could not be of overwhelming importance, since the Democrats, who are usually disadvantaged in both respects, have won more than half the elections since 1932. We can suggest a few reasons for Democratic strength despite these disadvantages. First, the Democrats are able to convert other resources into money and control over information, thereby narrowing the gap during campaigns. Second, the Democrats have superior access to other important resources which may counter the Republican superiority in money and control over the media of information.

Once the Democratic party assumed the presidency in 1933 and held it for twenty years, it was able to use the resource of official position to collect campaign funds because contributors wanted access to the winner. The Democratic candidate could also get greater news coverage because the incumbent president's activities are newsworthy no matter what his party. The alliance of the Democrats with the large industrial unions has, at times, meant that the party has received contributions in the form of personal electioneering, for which the Republicans had to lay out cash or do without. The superiority (perhaps the mere existence) of Democratic organizations in cities of large populations with strategic impact on the Electoral College has sometimes led to the availability of election workers who did not have to be paid in cash—at least not in cash the presidential candidate had to raise during the campaign. Public funding has brought expenditures in the general campaign to a fairly even level. The fact that Democrats still maintain a lead over Republicans in party identification is perhaps the most effective resource in the Democratic arsenal.

These Democratic assets are still important, but in each case the Democratic advantage has been declining. The Republicans have controlled the White House (and the benefits that entails) for twenty of the last twenty-four years. Unions and urban political organizations are less important and smaller than they once were and are facing difficult times. The assistance they can offer the Democrats is limited. Finally, the Democratic edge in party identification has shrunk in recent years. The Democrats' ability to counter Republican assets has eroded.

3

The Nomination Process

Obtaining the presidential nomination of a major political party in this country has never been easy. Today, however, this process has grown even more time consuming, expensive, and complicated. The "shadow phase" of the campaign, "the long organizational period before the television cameras turn the light of public attention on the race," is lengthening.[1] This is because of changes in the rules governing the conduct of candidates, activists, and party regulars in the preprimary period, during the actual delegate selection phase, and at the national party conventions themselves.[2]

Before the Primaries

Once upon a time, not so long ago, there was a gap between one presidential election campaign and the next one four years later. This gave a little breathing space during which, we assume, politically active citizens occupied themselves with such unexciting business as, for example, making a living (for those out of office) or governing (for those in office). What has caused this gap to shrink so drastically, in spite of the entreaties of reformers and the complaints of journalists?

As we see it, the spreading out of preconvention party skirmishing, extending first to the primary phase and now to a lengthy preprimary period, is, in part, a result of rules changes over the last two decades. These changes govern delegate selection to the national convention, and especially the national convention of a party that has no incumbent president eligible for reelection.

The rules changes have increased the number of people each candidate for the nomination must reach and, if possible, convince of his worthiness. The more people you have to reach, the more time and money it takes to do the job. We reserve for later a consideration of whether this can be called a democratization of the candidate selection process. There is something to be said on both sides of that proposition. For the moment, however, let us put ourselves in the shoes of the candidate for a presidential nomination who confronts the following rules of the game. As we will see, most of the rules, and most of the constraints, apply to Democrats.

1. For Democrats, all convention delegates must be selected according to rules requiring that state parties "assure that such delegates have been selected through a process in which all Democratic voters have had full and timely opportunity to participate. . . ."[3] This must be done by all states within a three-month period (which three months to be determined by the Democratic National Committee), and each individual state must set candidate filing deadlines thirty to ninety days before the election. This process must result in state delegations that are evenly divided between men and women.[4] In general, this means candidates must contest in primary elections. Whereas only sixteen states held primaries in 1968, thirty-three primaries were held in 1988. With the exception of Wisconsin and Montana, which historically have had "open primaries" in which any citizen can participate, the rules of the Democratic party do not permit Republicans to participate in selecting Democratic candidates. Since Democrats wish to expand rather than narrow the primary electorate, they do allow independents, whose support they seek at election time, to vote in their primaries.[5] Changes in state law—such as changes requiring primaries—generally apply to both parties; thus state responses to the post-1968 Democratic rules helped transform the Republican nominating process as well.[6]

2. Candidates of either party may be eligible for federal funding of their primary expenses of more than $10 million each if they can raise at least $5,000 cash in each of twenty or more states before the primary (only the first $250 of each contribution being eligible for matching).

3. In the Democratic party, any candidate in a statewide primary who receives more than 15 percent of the vote obtains a proportionate share of the delegates per congressional district. The Republican party has no such minimum threshold. Delegates are apportioned to each state by a formula that gives added weight to states that voted Republican in the last presidential, congressional, and gubernatorial elections. Thus, Republican candidates for the nomination have an incentive to win in states that go Republican in national and state

elections; but each state has its own rules apportioning delegates to candidates.

4. Democratic elected officials (members of Congress and governors) as well as officials of the Democratic National Committee have automatic seats as delegates and voting rights in the convention, and are not required to pledge their support to any candidate as a condition of delegate status. This will account for 15 percent of the Democratic delegates in 1992.

The first overall constraint on the system is that the more people you have to convince, the longer it takes. And so the nomination process has become very long. The second overall constraint is that the more restrictions that are placed upon the expenditure of money, the harder it is for newcomers to attract public notice to get into the race. And this too dictates an earlier start to the campaign. Anybody whose name is known ahead of time—movie stars, sports figures, incumbents of high office—gets a boost. Whereas by March 12, 1988 the major parties chose one-third of their delegates, by that date in 1984 only a quarter had been selected.[7] Moreover, proportionate rules for counting votes encourage Democrats to enter more primaries for the simple reason that there are delegates to be had even if one does not win a majority. And primaries generate attention, which means more people will be enticed out of the woodwork to make financial contributions that the government will then match.

In part, no doubt, candidates will be reading the lessons of the post-reform era since 1972 into future election years. For among the axioms of conventional wisdom to bite the dust in 1972 was the notion that an early announcement of candidacy was a sign of a weak candidate, and that it therefore behooved front runners to avoid an early disclosure of their plans, with all the inconvenience and running around that an active campaign entails. This coyness destroyed the chances of the 1972 early Democratic front runner, Senator Edmund S. Muskie. In 1976, this lesson was greatly reinforced as Jimmy Carter, an outsider, parlayed early, narrow wins in Iowa, New Hampshire, and Florida into the presidency itself. Thus the congressional elections of 1978 were barely over before a variety of Republicans announced their candidacies for the 1980 race and began to qualify for federal support. And two Democratic candidates qualified for the 1984 federal subsidy by the end of the first week of 1983.[8] By June 1987 seven candidates were campaigning for the Republican nomination and seven for the Democratic,[9] and the Democratic front runner, Gary Hart, had already been sidelined because of publicity surrounding charges of adultery.[10]

In some respects, the 1972 preconvention race in the Democratic party provided an interesting transition between old and new practices. The 1968 convention had been marked by rioting in the streets and charges that party leaders had "stolen" the nomination for their favorite, Hubert Humphrey. So between 1968 and 1972, delegate selection rules were substantially revised. The new rules were written in such a way as to placate the element of the party that was most disaffected in the debacle of 1968, namely, the left wing. This may have been done in part because party leaders who both acquiesced to and enforced these changes were reasonably confident that placating the left in this fashion would merely legitimize throughout the party the eventual selection of a broadly based, centrist candidate.[11]

Early in the 1972 election season, at least two such candidates were extremely visible to party leaders: Senator Edward Kennedy and, after the Chappaquiddick incident put Kennedy out of action, Senator Edmund Muskie of Maine. By early 1971, Muskie was leading President Nixon in Gallup trial heats. Consequently, giving in on party rules must have seemed to centrist party leaders a low-cost proposition. As the leading Democrat in all polls, Muskie concentrated his early efforts upon securing endorsements from party notables. But operating under obsolete strategic premises, Muskie failed to announce his candidacy until January 4, 1972. In April, 1971, Muskie's campaign director Berl Bernhard said:

> There's no real necessity to [announce early]. . . . When you do it, you should be ready to do a bit more than just announce. You do it to maximize your position; you don't do it just for the ritual. The announcement is the clarion call to people who want to work for you to get ready. The most important thing Ed Muskie can do right now, rather than announce, is to talk about substantive issues.[12]

As of that month, Richard H. Stewart, Muskie's press secretary said:

> I thought Muskie was in awfully good shape. The money was flowing in fairly well in keeping with Muskie's standing in the polls. I figured that all we had to do was sit and wait, and that it was only a matter of a few months before Muskie would win the nomination. . . .[13]

By the time the Muskie organization woke up to the fact that what was required was state by state campaigning to win the popular support of a loyal Muskie faction of voters, it was much too late. George McGovern, whose initial standing in the public opinion trial heats was negligible, out-organized Muskie in most early states, which is to say he put together an enthusiastic group of die-hard workers mobilized around anti-war sentiment. So by the time Muskie got around to announcing his candidacy formally, Senator George McGovern had already won the allegiance of and organized the most energetic segment of the party. McGovern's was the only organization that employed grass-roots activists in large numbers. Like Goldwater among Republicans in 1964, McGovern won not because he was the most popular candidate among his fellow partisans, but because he was best organized to move into state primaries and state party conventions and take them over from party regulars.

Since 1976, the position of state party leaders has been reduced to making deals to support one or another candidate in the state primary or caucuses. And the candidate's job is to attract support from state party leaders by looking like a probable winner in primaries.

So the lessons of the preprimary period have become clear: before the delegate selection season begins candidates must organize to achieve personal visibility. Visibility is important because in order to win it is necessary to appeal to voters in primary elections and caucuses. Organization is important because that is what it takes to turn out voters. Because many candidates begin the election season with presidential hopes, the course of selection is a winnowing process in which the successive hurdles of the weeks in which primaries and caucuses are held knock off more and more hopefuls until only one survivor is left. Before these events the candidate's tasks are to raise money and to give personal attention to states that will select delegates early in the process. Increasingly it is thought that this sort of work cannot be done by a public official who at the same time holds a responsible job. This is not a hard and fast rule, as Michael Dukakis's success in the nominating process shows, but politicians remember the Jimmy Carter did nothing but campaign for the presidential nomination for a full year before the first primary of 1976, and that Edmund Muskie chose to attend to his Senate responsibilities in 1971, when he should have been out campaigning. In the run-up to the 1984 election, Walter Mondale was far better off as an ex-senator and ex-vice-president than he would have been as an incumbent officeholder.

During the long preprimary phase the candidates also undergo ideological preparation. Knowing that most of the voters in Republican primaries are right of center, Vice-President Bush, Representative Kemp, and Senator Dole spent a lot of time in 1987 honing their remarks (and shading their voting records) toward this part of the spectrum. Similarly, the fact that the dominant faction of the Democratic party is left of center has not been lost among Democratic contenders. As an adviser to a rival candidate described Gary Hart's preprimary activities in 1987, "He saw how liberals and labor dominated things in 1984 and he's determined he'd not going to let anyone get to his left."[14]

Part of the preprimary task of the candidate is to achieve the status of being "taken seriously" by the news media. Part of being taken seriously requires that a candidate should have won some major election for public office. In addition, the news media pay attention to signs that candidates are hiring competent campaign staff—fund raisers, lawyers, accountants, poll takers, media buyers, advance men, speech writers, issue analysts, spotters of political talent in the early states—and are establishing a beachhead in these first battlegrounds. All this activity is highly visible to the increasingly watchful news media, who in turn pronounce candidates to be "serious" or "not serious," with attendant consequences for public visibility and credibility with donors of campaign funds.

Preprimary activities thus take up more and more time and absorb more and more resources in preparation for the primary elections, which in 1988 selected delegates in thirty-three states, and the state party caucuses.[15]

Iowa and New Hampshire

The party rules that provide for all delegate selection to take place in the year of the election also prescribe that the selection processes—state caucuses and primaries—take place within a limited period of time. Two exceptions, based on accidents of history, have thus far always been granted by the Democratic party, and the Republicans have always gone along. Iowa, which selects its delegates through a series of broadly participatory local, regional, and state conventions, has a license to be first in the nation. And New Hampshire, the nation's first primary, comes next—in recent years, within a week.[16]

In 1988, Iowa selected fifty-two Democratic delegates and thirty-seven Republican delegates to their respective national party conventions, 1.2 percent of all Democratic delegates and 1.4 percent of all Republican delegates. Iowa's small size notwithstanding, the initial stage of the selection process, the February 8 precinct caucuses, received highly attentive media coverage, very much in keeping with the extraordinary attention these caucuses have received in previous years. In 1984, according to an actual count of news coverage appearing on all three television networks plus in the New York Times, Iowa, with 2.5 percent of the U.S. population, received 12.8 percent of the total news coverage accorded the presidential race from January to June.[17]

Owing to the hospitality of the University of Iowa Political Science Department, in February, 1988 a few political scientists had the pleasure of actually going to Iowa and watching the caucus of the Democratic party of the 4th precinct of Johnson County, 289 or 287 strong, depending on the count you use, all gathered together in the auditorium of the

Lincoln School of Iowa City, Iowa. Before the Democrats got their act together on the evening of February 8, it was possible to observe the 4th precinct Republican meeting—in the Lincoln School's kindergarten room, as it happens. There they were, about sixty Republicans, sitting decorously on those tiny little kindergarten chairs, chatting quietly and behaving just as though they were waiting for a string quartet concert to begin. The Democrats, true to form, put on a noisier and more cheerfully disorderly show of selecting nine delegates to the Johnson County caucus of the Democratic party a month hence. The county caucus would send delegates to the congressional district convention a month after that, and they in turn elected delegates to the Iowa state convention who sent delegates to the national convention of the Democratic party in July.

At least on the Democratic side, the Iowa precinct caucuses had something directly to do with the actual selection of actual delegates to the national convention. On the Republican side, the numbers breathlessly reported on the networks were the outcome of a straw poll ballot, conducted at the precinct caucuses, and phoned into the networks just like the real delegate divisions on the Democratic side. After the straw poll was conducted, Republican delegates to the next level up were selected in each precinct, without any necessary connection to the straw poll.

As David Oman, co-chairman of the Iowa Republican party, described the process the week before to the *Presidential Campaign Hotline:*

> Essentially we have one very large straw poll taken in 2500 different locations simultaneously. . . . Those at the caucus will be given small cards and will mark on these cards their choice for president. The cards will be tallied. . . . Our straw poll is not tied to the process of choosing delegates. After the poll is taken and reported, the caucus will then pick its precinct committeeman and committeewoman, then pick the men and women who will got to the Republican county convention, and then discuss the platform.[18]

The county conventions met in March and picked delegates to district conventions, which met in June on the eve of the state convention. The district conventions selected three national convention delegates for each district and the the state convention selected the rest. Thus the straw poll might or might not predict the results of the delegate selection process accurately in any given year. In 1988, the preferences of the eventual delegates were sixteen for Dole, twelve for Bush, two each for Robertson and Kemp, and five uncommitted.[19]

On the Democratic side, the caucuses are more immediately consequential. As Phil Roeder, Communications Director of the Iowa State Democratic Party described it ahead of time to the *Hotline:*

. . . at 7:30 PM on caucus night in 2489 precincts people will start to break into candidate preference groups. . . . They will physically divide into different groups for each candidate and in most instances there is an uncommitted group as well.[20]

These groups elect delegates according to the number of delegates each precinct is entitled to by virtue of its population. Groups preferring various candidates are allocated delegates depending on what proportion of the people who show up to the caucus are in each group. Groups that are too small to receive delegates have the option of breaking up and their members can migrate to their second choices or to the uncommitted group, or they can seek as a group to combine with one or more other small groups so as to be eligible to receive a delegate. Each of the groups then selects their delegates to the county convention. Democratic delegates selected in this fashion are, unlike the Republican delegates, usually pledged to a presidential candidate as they move up through the county and district conventions to the state convention.

Given the complications in ascertaining what the actual outcomes of the precinct caucuses are, it is a wonder that there is so much media coverage of the Iowa caucuses. Nevertheless, the coverage is there, because the Iowa caucuses are, in effect, the gateway to a long and complex nomination process, and all players and all observers very much want whatever information they can glean from the Iowa precinct caucuses if only to position themselves for the next round. The media need to know to whom to give special attention. Financial supporters of various candidates want to know whether it is worthwhile to continue to give, or to steer, money to their first choices or whether it is time to jump to other alternatives. Voters want to know which candidacies are viable, which futile.[21]

Thus the grounds for paying special attention to the Iowa caucuses are that the system as a whole is conspicuously front-loaded, and Iowa is furthest to the front. What does it mean to have a front-loaded nomination process?

The temptation to ignore history is ever-present. Each quadrennial nomination sequence has plenty of elements of uniqueness, and our entire historical experience of presidential elections yields very few instances at best. Even further constraining a historical view is the fact that whatever happened before the drastic changes of the post-1968 reforms should probably be ignored on the grounds that the system overall was fundamentally altered by these reforms. It is the reforms that front-loaded the presidential nominating process.[22] Consequently, considering evidence from 1968 and before is bound to be drastically misleading as a guide to the structural constraints and strategic opportunities that shape the choices of contemporary actors. So we are left, in effect, with exactly ten historical data points, five Democratic, five Republican, representing the elections of 1972, 1976, 1980, 1984 and 1988. And these, owing to the effects of incumbency, can be reduced even further.

1972. In 1972 the Iowa caucuses were for the first time set early in the year, on January 24. This date was arrived at because the Democratic state convention was to be held on May 20 owing to the availability on that date of a suitable hall. Working backward from May 20, adequate time had to be provided to prepare for each of the earlier stages of the process, and the entire sequence had to be completed within the same calendar year as the national convention. Thus the January date.[23]

In 1972, the Republican incumbent, Richard Nixon, had only token opposition in Iowa from two Representatives in Congress, Paul (Pete) McCloskey of California on his left and John Ashbrook of Ohio on his right.

The Democratic caucuses, on the other hand, were quite important. As we have seen, the presumed front runner, Senator Edmund S. Muskie, of Maine, was operating under obsolete strategic premises, and had failed to announce his candidacy until January 4, 1972. Neither Muskie nor Senator George McGovern invested much effort in Iowa. The day after the first-round caucuses the newspaper reported unofficially, with incomplete returns, that Muskie beat McGovern in the precinct caucuses in Iowa 35.5 percent to 22.6 percent with 35.8 percent uncommitted. The unexpected closeness of this margin pushed Muskie into overwork and an unaccustomed public display of emotional behavior in front of the building housing the offices of the *Manchester Union Leader* in New Hampshire.[24] By the time the news media analysts were finished with the New Hampshire results, prior "expectations" that the U.S. Senator from a neighboring state should win an overwhelming victory—over 50 percent—completely dominated that fact that Muskie had in fact won once again (46 percent to 37 percent). Because his win was four or five points less impressive than "expected", Muskie support—especially financial support—began to dry up, and he withdrew from the race altogether by April 27.

The Muskie presidency was nibbled to death by ducks before it began. This extraordinary spectacle gave unmistakable evidence of the fact that changing the rules had changed the game. Preconvention skirmishes were no longer simply important evidence to be taken into account by party leaders in making nominations: they were the contest itself.

Iowa did not administer the coup de grace to Muskie: that happened in New Hampshire. At most what happened in Iowa energized the participants in the New Hampshire primary and structured the alternatives for New Hampshire voters.

1976. Once again an incumbent was running on the Republican side. This time, however, Gerald Ford was the incumbent. Ford had never been a Republican presidential nominee and he was not an eloquent defender of his presidency. He was faced by a serious challenge from Ronald Reagan. Iowa came out in a dead heat between the two; both ended up with eighteen delegates to the national convention. Ford won the official straw poll the night of the precinct caucuses, but only by a small margin. R. W. Apple of the *New York Times* characterized the Republican effort in Iowa by both candidates as "all but invisible, with only marginal organizational efforts by the supporters of Mr. Ford and Mr. Reagan."[25] Ford's victory in New Hampshire made him the front runner for renomination, although Reagan rallied later in the year.[26]

On the Democratic side, the candidate who focused hardest on Iowa was Jimmy Carter. Hamilton Jordan, Carter's campaign manager, put together a strategy that was exactly three events deep, requiring strong showings in Iowa and New Hampshire, and a careful positioning as the anti-Wallace southerner in the Florida primary.[27] The Carter strategy dovetailed nicely with those of his main competitors. Henry Jackson's campaign was designed to start late: a token effort in Iowa (January 19) and New Hampshire (February 24) followed by an unequivocal win in Massachusetts (March 2), only a week later. After all, Massachusetts's 104 delegates greatly exceeded the Iowa-New Hampshire combination of 64. Thus Jackson's decision to play from "strength."[28]

Morris Udall's campaign was strategically incoherent. First Udall made an effort in Iowa, then, in an attempt to stretch his resources to cover as many primaries as possible (there were thirty Democratic primaries in 1976) Udall's campaign slacked its Iowa effort. As news coverage focused even more strongly on Iowa, however, Udall at the last minute recommitted resources to the race.[29] He was too late. Although he finished as high as second in seven primaries in 1976, in Iowa Udall came in fifth with 5.9 percent of the vote behind uncommitted with 37 percent of the caucus vote, Jimmy Carter with 28 percent, Birch Bayh with 13 percent, and Fred Harris with 10 percent.

The next day, R. W. Apple minimized the strong uncommitted sentiment and created the first major instance in which the Iowa caucuses combined importantly with mass media spin to launch a presidential candidacy. His story on the front page of the *New York Times* read:

> Former Governor Jimmy Carter of Georgia scored an impressive victory in yesterday's Iowa Democratic precinct caucuses, demonstrating strength among rural, blue-collar, black, and suburban voters.
>
> Mr. Carter defeated his closest rival, Senator Birch Bayh of Indiana, by a margin of more than 2–1, and left his other four challengers far behind.

The uncommitted vote, which many Iowa politicians had forecast at more than 50 percent, amounted to only about a third of the total, slightly more than that of Mr. Carter.[30]

This article, with its strong and coherent story line, cast a long shadow. It contained many elements that in later years would worry journalists— notably the use of such a word as "impressive" (to whom?) in the lead of what ostensibly was a news story and the belittling of the uncommitted vote because of the disappointed "forecasts" or expectations of anonymous politicians.

Elizabeth Drew's diary for the day after the Iowa caucuses said:

This morning, Carter, who managed to get to New York on time, was interviewed on the CBS Morning News, the Today Show and ABC's Good Morning America also ran segments on Carter. On the CBS Evening News, Walter Cronkite said that the Iowa voters have spoken "and for the Democrats what they said was 'Jimmy Carter.' "[31]

This coverage set the stage for New Hampshire, where Carter alone ran as a centrist Democrat and received 28.4 percent of the vote. Although he filed a slate of delegates, Jackson sat the primary out, and no fewer than four candidates, Udall (at 22.7 percent), Sargent Shriver (at 8.2 percent), Fred Harris (at 10.8 percent), and Birch Bayh (at 15.2 percent) divided the liberal Democratic vote.

1980. By 1980, it was beginning to be understood that there was no such thing as a successful presidential strategy that ignored early delegate selection events. President Carter's managers worked hard to structure the order in which states selected delegates so as to maximize favorable publicity impact, seeking to move southern primaries up to the head of the line.[32] Carter, aided by a rally round the flag at the start of the Iranian hostage crisis, beat Edward Kennedy in Iowa 59.1 percent to 31.2 percent. Iowa momentum helped Carter amass a majority of delegates far more quickly in 1980 than he had done in 1976.[33]

On the Republican side, Iowa nearly did the frontrunner, Ronald Reagan, in. Saving his energy, Reagan campaigned only eight days in the state and passed up the major all-candidate Republican debate. Caucus turnout on the Republican side jumped to 110,000 participants from a mere 22,000 in 1976. Howard Baker, an interested party, remarked that the Iowa caucuses had become "the functional equivalent of a primary". George Bush edged Reagan 31.5 percent to 29.4 percent in the straw vote, and as Jack Germond and Jules Witcover observed, the Iowa caucuses served in 1980 to clear "the underbrush of candidates with little future . . . establishing a definite pecking order among those who remained."[34]

Only a drastic change of strategy (including the replacement of John Sears, the strategist) and some extraordinarily vigorous propagandizing by the *Manchester Union Leader* saved Ronald Reagan's bacon by aiding his comeback in New Hampshire. David W. Moore wrote:

> In the 1980 primary campaign, the *Union Leader* provided an immense amount of information about the candidates, especially a great deal of negative information about one candidate [Bush] and positive information about the other [Reagan]. If ever a news source can influence voters' opinions, the *Union Leader* should have influenced voters during that campaign. And it did. . . .
>
> On average, readers of the *Union Leader* were more likely than non-readers to support Ronald Reagan by a margin of 35 to 40 points, a pattern that held true whatever a voter's ideological predisposition (from strong conservative to liberal). Indeed, a simultaneous comparison of numerous factors demonstrates that the *Union Leader* was overwhelmingly the most important influence on the choice Republicans made in the primary election.[35]

Whatever the overall influence of the *Union Leader*, New Hampshire's major news outlet, that influence is at its maximum in addressing Republican primary voters. Reagan campaigned energetically, and ambushed Bush at a key New Hampshire debate by "spontaneously" agreeing to let also-rans onto the platform. It also helped Reagan enormously that the gap between Iowa and New Hampshire was a full month (January 21 to February 26), thus permitting *Union Leader* publicity to counteract Iowa momentum. In 1976, that gap had helped Carter, a "winner" in Iowa; in 1980, it helped Reagan, a "loser."

By the 1980 election the strong interdependence between early delegate selection and media publicity could easily be observed. The "pecking order" of which Germond and Witcover wrote was, after all, a fabrication chiefly valuable in the construction of coherent news stories. The success of Jimmy Carter in 1976, and even more striking, the failure of Henry Jackson, suggested that it would be hard, perhaps impossible, to ascertain the preferences of primary electorates unmediated by the news—and news media evaluations—of how the various candidates were doing. And these characterizations could easily take on the coloration of self-fulfilling prophecies.

1984. Nothing doing on the Republican side; Reagan's incumbency meant no contest in Iowa. Democratic rules were rewritten ostensibly to counteract media influence: states were required to select delegates within a three-month "window" so that many states would act on any given

Tuesday, thus (it was hoped) confounding media attempts to start a single unified bandwagon. The effort was a failure, in part because both Iowa and New Hampshire received exemptions from the window, and continued to act first. On the Democratic side, Walter Mondale overwhelmed everybody, collecting 44.5 percent of the vote in a large field of contenders. Gary Hart came in second with a dismal 14.8 percent of the vote.

This was enough to identify Hart, rather than John Glenn, who finished in sixth place with 5.3 percent of the vote, as the strongest non-Mondale candidate. The news media constructed a horse race out of the unpromising material of the Hart candidacy, gave him extraordinary news coverage for the ensuing week, and boosted him into a win in the New Hampshire primary.[36]

It seems clear enough why the news media need a horse race, given their extraordinary investment in delegate selection coverage and the logic of their competition for business. Iowa caucuses help the news media sort out the story: it was the Iowa caucuses in 1984 that decreed that Gary Hart and not John Glenn should be the ''unexpected'' horse to make the race against Mondale, and it was the media that made the horse race.

1988. In 1988, with only one week separating Iowa and New Hampshire, the two events might have been expected to interact strongly. Governor Michael Dukakis entered Iowa as the Democratic candidate with the most money and the best organization in the most states—but not in Iowa—and with extremely high and favorable name recognition in New Hampshire, whose Democratic voters are mostly located on the fringes of the Boston metropolitan area. This meant that the only chance the other candidates had to neutralize the favorable impact that the New Hampshire primary was bound to have on the fortunes of the Governor of Massachusetts was in Iowa.[37]

In the event, the Iowa Democratic result did not help the winner there in New Hampshire, mainly because what happened on the Republican side in Iowa had such a strong impact on the Democratic race. The big story of Iowa 1988—and there always has to be one big story—was that Pat Robertson came in second and George Bush came in third in the Republican straw poll. And that is how the story played in the news media for the week between Iowa and New Hampshire. Obviously, that was bound to have some impact on the Republican race—but not as much as on the race on the Democratic side. Because the Robertson blip absorbed so much attention it spoiled the chances of the Democratic winner, Richard Gephardt, to capitalize on his Iowa win to become the focal alternative to Michael Dukakis in New Hampshire.

In 1984 Gary Hart was able to parlay a 15 percent second place showing into a media spin that made him the winner in New Hampshire, as figures on late-deciding Democrats showed.[38] In 1976, Jimmy Carter was able to pull out in front of the pack with 29 percent of the vote in the Iowa caucuses. In 1988, a 31 percent win was not enough for Gephardt to turn the same trick. Indeed, the *Wall Street Journal* reported that in the week between the Iowa caucuses and the New Hampshire primary the coverage Gephardt got on the network evening news programs actually diminished from the week before—from 6:05 minutes to 4:55 minutes.[39] Thus it is not farfetched to argue that although the winner in Iowa did not win the nomination of either party, Iowa did in fact play an influential role in determining the 1988 outcome.

What do these historical vignettes teach?

1. Candidates ignore Iowa at their peril. This does not mean that doing badly in Iowa is sufficient to lose everything, or that doing well is sufficient to win everything. It does mean that Iowa can be a tremendous help or a tremendous hindrance to each and every candidacy.

2. This is so not because of Iowa's size but because of its temporal primacy: Iowa results, plus media spin, structure the alternatives for the New Hampshire primary. These two events together plus media spin structure alternatives for everything that follows.

Doing well *in* Iowa takes organization as well as good publicity, because organizations get people to caucuses and sustain their loyalty as the public shufflings and reshufflings take place, especially at the Democratic caucuses themselves. Doing well as the *result* of Iowa, however, chiefly requires good publicity: spin control so as to hold adverse expectations to a minimum, but also, if possible, the good luck to be the story that the national news media converge upon coming out of Iowa and as the first primary approaches. The closer the next event in time, the narrower the temporal gap between Iowa and New Hampshire, the greater the potential that both events can be interpreted together, and thus the more influential the news media response to Iowa and New Hampshire overall in the election year.

Primaries

Between 1968 and 1972 the Democratic Commission on Party Structure and Delegate Selection (the McGovern-Fraser Commission) developed a set of rules and guidelines subsequently adopted by the national party concerning the selection of delegates to national party conventions. They wanted to make delegate selection more open and representative. So they issued eighteen new regulations that opened up meetings to all comers, gave those who came the right to vote, scheduled their delegate choices closer to the fall general election, and included various demographic groups in proportion to their size in the population. This had the immediate effect of greatly increasing the number of primaries (see Figure 3.1). Seeing that their delegates could be challenged in eighteen new ways, state party leaders in numerous states decided to let all the candidates contend in what they assumed would be regarded as fair and open primaries. Thus, from 1968 to 1975, fourteen new states adopted primaries as their method for choosing delegates to the Democratic National Convention. More important, as James Lengle and Byron Shafer explain:

> The increase in the number of "effective" primaries was even greater . . . because (required) reforms upgraded previously less significant arenas into serious campaign sites. In fact, the biggest rise in the number of delegates along the primary route came not from new entries but from changes in old ones. In 1968, nearly half of all primaries had been "advisory," i.e., either voters would express a Presidential preference but delegates would be chosen independently in party conventions, or, more commonly, a Presidential preference could not be logically connected with the separate vote for delegates. By 1972, the linkage between candidate preference and delegate selection had been tightened so much that the free agents of past primaries—"favorite sons," "bosses," and "uncommitted" delegates—had almost disappeared.[40]

The "front-loading" of the presidential nomination process, which began in 1968, proceeded apace in 1988. Whereas in mid-March of the presidential election year of 1984 both parties had chosen around a quarter of their delegates, by 1988 this proportion had increased to one-third. In the recent past, candidates without substantial financial resources for their campaigns had counted on strong showings in early primaries to give them the momentum they needed to raise more money and then carry on into the rest of the primaries. With primaries coming earlier and earlier, and more of them bunched together, that will be far more difficult in the future.[41]

Primaries are important largely because most delegates are selected in them and because the results represent an ostensibly objective indication of whether a candidate can win the election. The contestants stand to gain or lose far more than the growing number of delegate votes that may be involved. Success in early primaries—even those, like New Hampshire, where there are only a handful of delegates at stake—takes on enormous importance because the mass media focus on front runners, giving them a great advantage in publicity. This makes front runners' appeals for money both directly to groups of fat cats and through the mails more

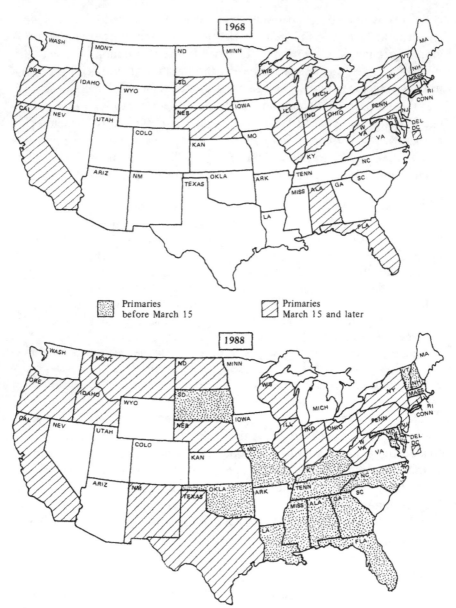

Primaries before March 15

Primaries March 15 and later

Neither Alaska nor Hawaii holds presidential primaries. 1988 dates based on tentative list by Congressional Research Service.

FIGURE 3.1   *Presidential Primaries More and Earlier*
Source: Rhodes Cook, "In 88 Contest, It's What's Up Front That Counts," *Congressional Quarterly Weekly Report* (August 23, 1986), p. 188.

successful, bringing advantages in the later primaries, where name recognition is a significant determinant of the vote. It also greatly reduces the capabilities of lagging candidates to catch up.

This means that early and vigorous participation in primaries is now the only strategy available to serious presidential aspirants. As his political advisor, Hamilton Jordan, told President Carter in 1979, "It is absolutely essential that we win the early contests and establish momentum. If we win the early contests, it is difficult to see how anyone could defeat us for the nomination. Conversely, if we lose the early contest(s), it is difficult to see how we could recoup and win the nomination." In order to improve the president's chances in 1980, his preconvention organization managed to advance the dates of several southern primaries, where he expected to do better, and to delay Connecticut's for a month. All this was done in 1979 before the rival organization of Senator Edward Kennedy had gotten started.[42]

It was not always thus. It made no sense for a man situated as Richard Nixon was in 1960—the heir apparent—to enter a primary unless he believed that he was quite certain to win. This stricture applied with special force to any candidate who was well ahead in delegate support. All he could gain was a few additional votes, while he could lose his existing support by a bad showing in the primary, since this might be interpreted as meaning that he could not win the election. The candidate who was far behind or who had to overcome severe handicaps, however, had little or nothing to lose by entering a risky primary. If he won, he demonstrated his popularity; if he lost, he was hardly worse off than if he had not entered the primary at all. Such was the case in 1960 when John F. Kennedy quieted the apprehensions of Democratic politicians about the religious issue by winning in Protestant West Virginia.[43] In 1964 Barry Goldwater needed a primary victory in California to show uncommitted delegates that he had voter appeal, even though at the start of the primary campaigns he had been a prominent candidate. He accepted the risk of losing the nomination if he lost the primary because he needed proof of popularity to get the votes necessary for nomination.[44] Nixon, who had lost the presidency in 1960 and the governorship of California in 1962, had a similar problem in 1968. He had to enter the primaries in order to dispel his "loser" image.[45]

Those who live by the primary may be done in by it as well. In 1980, after Governor Jerry Brown of California received only a tenth of the primary vote in New Hampshire, he staked everything on the Wisconsin primary, which, because he came in a distant third, terminated his candidacy. Similarly, when Senator Edward Kennedy lost the Illinois primary in 1980 to President Carter two to one in votes and 165 to 14 in delegates, it was widely believed that his inability to win in an industrial, ethnic, populous state where he had the support of the famous Chicago machine doomed his chances.[46] On the Republican side that year, John Anderson tried to distinguish himself as a Republican moderate by espousing conservative economic policies and liberal social policies. But he was unable to win a single primary; after a loss in Wisconsin, where he had placed his last hopes, he withdrew from the Republican nominating contest, emerging as an independent candidate for president. Anderson was too far out of line with the preferences of people who vote in Republican primaries.[47] Something similar happened in 1984. Senator John Glenn attempted to establish himself as the moderate alternative to front runner Walter Mondale. A sixth place finish in Iowa—behind "uncommitted"—dealt his candidacy a blow from which it never recovered.[48] Gary Hart, who came in second to Mondale in the Iowa caucuses, even though he had only 16 percent of the vote, nevertheless became the focus of news media attention in the following week and the overwhelming non-Mondale choice in the New Hampshire primary and thereafter.

A significant part of the nomination process includes trying to manipulate what the mass media say about primary elections both before and after they take place. In a primary with many contenders, a defeated candidate may attempt to gain advantage from what may be regarded as an ambiguous result by claiming that the person who actually won was allied to him ideologically. The results may then be viewed as a victory for the ideology rather than defeat for the candidate. After Robert LaFollette had won an overwhelming victory in the 1912 Republican primary in North Dakota, Theodore Roosevelt issued a statement "claiming an immense progressive victory." He even went beyond this to count the LaFollette delegation as part of the Roosevelt camp once it had cast "a complimentary vote for LaFollette."[49]

Rockefeller supporters in 1964 hailed the New Hampshire Republican primary, which Henry Cabot Lodge won, as a defeat for Goldwater and a victory for the moderate wing of the Republican party. Something similar went on in 1968; supporters of both Eugene McCarthy and Robert Kennedy claimed that all those who had voted for either man in the primaries had voted against Hubert Humphrey, who was nowhere on the ballot.[50]

Nowadays, the emphasis on mobilizing one's own faction, on momentum, on attaining visibility, financial support, and active followers by winning early, makes it necessary to attack rather than defend allied candidates. But it is still necessary to attempt to influence the interpretations news media put on events, to engage in "spin control." Senator Henry Jackson in 1972 expected to run well in certain districts in Florida, winning perhaps a plurality of delegates statewide, but not necessarily coming out in front when the entire statewide vote was tabulated. To make the most out of his expected heavy vote in and around Miami and to minimize his expected weaknesses elsewhere, his staff spoke of the state as containing some fifteen primaries—one for each of its congressional districts. When the expected happened, some of the story stuck, but the sheer complexity of reporting so many separate contests frustrated the strategy, and Jackson appeared the loser.[51]

Because so many candidates enter primaries, the results may be ambiguous, with a scattering of votes spread among many candidates. Nevertheless, the news media require interpretations that sort out winners and losers more decisively and so, as we have seen, how results are interpreted is often more important than the actual numbers. The contestant who loses but does better than expected may reap greater advantage from a primary than the one who wins but falls below expectations. It is, therefore, manifestly to the advantage of a candidate to hold his preelection claims down to minimum proportions. Kennedy tried in 1960 to follow this advice in Wisconsin but the press, radio, and television took note of his extensive organization and of favorable polls and in advance pinned the winner-by-a-landslide label on the senator from Massachusetts.[52] Early predictions in the 1968 New Hampshire primary were that Eugene McCarthy would receive somewhere around 10 percent of the vote. When he eventually polled 42 percent—against Lyndon Johnson's 48 percent write-in vote—it was widely interpreted as a victory, in part because it was so unexpected.[53] George McGovern benefited from a similar process in 1972.

Primaries thus have major effects on candidates and their strategies. They require candidates to raise money so that they become credible early. They require attention to the way in which results are perceived regardless of their direct impact on delegate selection. Primaries must therefore be analyzed in relation to the ways they affect public opinion, and this in turn is mediated by the news media.

The design of the nomination process itself has its own independent influence on outcomes. As we have seen, the early Iowa caucuses and the first-in-the-nation New Hampshire primary have exceptional impact. Several southern states banded together in an attempt to have a stronger influence in 1988 by scheduling their primary elections all on the same day, as early as possible. They were rapidly joined by a small flock of other states, turning March 8, 1988 into "Super-Tuesday" with primaries in Alabama, Florida, Georgia, Kentucky, Louisiana, Maryland, Massachusetts, Mississippi, Missouri, North Carolina, Oklahoma, Rhode Island, Tennessee, and Texas. Everyone can see that moving so may primaries up so early will accentuate the "front loading" of the campaign. A quick knockout will be every candidate's ambition. The "exhibition season," when candidates display their policies and capabilities to party activists, donors, and the media will be pushed back even earlier. The first delegate-selection round, which in 1988 was the Iowa and Michigan caucuses for Democrats and Republicans respectively, and the New Hampshire primary for candidates from both parties, may, in the words of Republican consultant John Sears be "more at the end of the process than at the beginning,"[54] and serve to eliminate many candidates.

Is this elimination round more or less important if a super-Tuesday continues to come hard on the heels of New Hampshire? A delegate-rich contest very early may provide a little life after New Hampshire. But because Iowa and New Hampshire are so close to super-Tuesday, whatever momentum candidates gain in those two states might provide the major influence on super-Tuesday voting.

In short, Iowa and New Hampshire might give some candidate "momentum" going into super-Tuesday. Momentum, apart from overwhelming victories and crushing defeats, depends in part on how well candidates have been able to influence expectations and how thoroughly the media converge on an interpretation of who is ahead and behind. Small, separate primaries maximize the ability of candidates to make their own statements to voters. The larger the number of primaries on any given day, the greater the number of voters, the larger the geographical spread, the less "impression management" candidates are able to do and the more the media take over this activity. In this respect, super-Tuesday increases media influence.

The varying rules of the major parties for counting primary votes make a difference to candidate strategies. Under Republican rules, state primaries and caucuses may (and most do) follow plurality "winner take all" procedures. This gives a strategic opportunity not available to Democrats. A Republican late bloomer, by winning later "mop-up" primaries, conceivably could hope to overcome a front runner's early lead. Ronald Reagan in 1976, for instance, though he won no primaries until late March, almost took the nomination from Gerald Ford by getting all the delegates from such large states as California and Texas. Democratic party rules requiring proportional representation, however, make it difficult for lagging Democratic candidates to catch up. Even if front runners falter, proportional representation slows their momentum only a little in the later primaries.

What helps a candidate overcome an early poor showing? "One of the problems of being a dark horse," notes Hart's 1984 poll taker, Dotty Lynch, "is that you need some true believers with you. Without an issue like George McGovern had in 1972 or a [devoted, ethnically based] constituency like Jesse Jackson has, a lot of people give up on you and you may give up on yourself."[55] Raising enough money up front to outlast disappointing showings obviously is also important. The two factors—a loyal activist following and the capacity to raise money early—may be but do not have to be connected.

The existence of candidates with narrow but intense follows leads us to ask how such candidates might be affected by a super-Tuesday or a similar regional primary. If moderate or more broadly based candidates are more numerous and divide the great middle among themselves, it is quite possible for such a candidate to do extremely well. Under Republican "winner take all" rules, candidates with small but intense followings are less likely to prevail, because a substantial majority of party identifiers oppose them. The Reverend Pat Robertson in 1988 was a good test of this proposition. Following proportional representation procedures, Democrats presumably would be more likely to reward with delegates candidates who have narrowly focused but intense followings. The Reverend Jesse Jackson was a good test of this deduction. And in 1988 Jackson lasted longer than Robertson did.

In addition, super-Tuesday may magnify differences in candidates' fund-raising capacities. Albert Gore and Michael Dukakis outspent Richard Gephardt, the winner of the Iowa caucuses, by a two-to-one margin in southern and border super-Tuesday states. No candidate had the resources—in time or money—to campaign seriously in each state. But those with the money to do so were able to offer competition in more areas, and may have reaped more delegates as a result.[56]

Finally, there is the question of how well the designers of super-Tuesday—predominantly southern Democratic party leaders—have managed to enhance the chances that a candidate they favor will succeed. It is required, of course, in the first place that such a candidate be lured into the race by the prospect of doing well on super-Tuesday. If nobody strongly favored by southern party leaders becomes a candidate, they will have lost their gamble. Likewise they lose if super-Tuesday simply becomes the day in which the winners of Iowa and New Hampshire sort out the nomination between themselves. In this eventuality, super-Tuesday will merely have enhanced the importance of the two earlier, more easily reported events. Finally, super-Tuesday may divide the resources of all candidates and cause all of them to do only moderately well or worse. This strengthens the hand of candidates with intensely loyal followings. Chief among these in the Democratic party of 1988 was Jesse Jackson, presumably not the person the designers of super-Tuesday had in mind when they sought to increase the influence of white southern moderates in the presidential selection process.

The idea behind the creation of the super-Tuesday primaries was two-fold: (1) to give the South a larger voice in presidential nominating politics, and (2) by switching from caucuses to primaries and holding those primaries relatively early in the campaign, that is, before it was all decided, they hoped some more moderate or conservative Democratic politicians would be in the race, thereby attracting voters into the primaries. But it was not to be. Turnout in super-Tuesday primaries in 1988 was only 25.5 percent as compared to 33.8 percent for the other primaries.[57]

Jesse Jackson did especially well on super-Tuesday because he kept his already high level of support of black voters and he extended that support to liberal and highly educated white voters. Though Jackson kept appealing to blue-collar workers, his actual strength was among the better educated because they and not poorer people were the mainstay of liberalism. In all the primaries, except for New Hampshire and Pennsylvania, Jesse Jackson was the first choice of the most liberal voters. The more liberal a white person was, the more that person was likely to vote for Jackson. As Cain, Lewis, and Rivers report, ". . . white-collar white Democrats were more likely than blue-collar white Democrat to favor aid for abortion, oppose mandatory AIDS testing, endorse additional domestic spending and support defense cuts. Indeed, on a number of issues, upper-class white voters were more liberal than Hispanic and black democrats—for instance, on banning abortions (compared to Hispanics), defense cuts, . . . and favoring a tax hike." What separated Jackson's white and black supporters was the considerably more conservative stance his black supporters took on social issues.[58]

In the event, super-Tuesday did help Jackson. It ended the candidacy of Richard Gephardt. It kept the southern moderate candidate, Senator Albert Gore, in the race. This harmed the front runner, Governor Dukakis, and thus helped Jackson who with his small but devoted following and his thirst for publicity was determined to persist until he could appear on television at the national convention.

Thus the design of the presidential primary process continues to be an ongoing saga of trial and error. A good summary of the way in which the various forces are aligned is Rhodes Cook's:

> Regardless of the different nominating rules, . . . there is a dynamic affecting both parties that makes early defeats devastating. No candidate in either party in recent years has mounted a successful comeback during the mop-up period.[59]

The rising importance of primaries, and of public opinion polling, has had a profound impact on the behavior of party leaders. The results of early polls and primaries are covered extensively by the news media. This creates pressure on party leaders to commit themselves quickly to the front runner. The political consequences are clear, as William H. Lucy says:

> If primary winners are nearly always nominated, then it behooves would-be leaders to bargain with candidates early in the primary process in order to be on board when their support is still valued. Or, if the preprimary poll leader is nearly always nominated, then this fact would be a cue for party leaders to start to choose sides even before the primaries began. In addition, if candidates leading the polls believed that success in the primaries depended but little on support by political leaders, then the assets with which they would be willing to negotiate with political leaders might be reduced in number and value. As compared with political leaders, those with plentiful campaign funds or media skills might increase their bargaining potential.[60]

Though the demand for more primaries originally came from politicians challenging their party establishments, the cause was quickly picked up by the networks. The role of television journalists, Richard Rubin contends, lay "in legitimating the process as the genuinely democratic way to choose convention delegates." Television, unlike print journalism, finds it easier to cover exciting primary races rather than processes of deliberation and negotiation among a few party leaders in caucuses and conventions. The special needs of television, Rubin writes, are

> reflected by the medium's broad use of sports analogies (such as the "horse race") to describe primary campaigns. Television needs a shorthand method to compress and dramatize events, and has settled comfortably on sporting phrases to describe and simplify a complex process. Candidates are "leading the pack," "closing fast," "sagging in the stretch," and "gaining ground," as the medium strives to treat their competition in language suggestive of movement and vitality. The "game analogy" is prominent in the treatment of all media, but its prominence, as Thomas Patterson has demonstrated, is greater on television (and in weekly news magazines) than in newspapers. The looser story line in newspaper versus television reporting and a larger "news hole" enables it to move beyond these analogies to cover intricate, complex, and talky political activities in more detail than television easily accommodates.[61]

Aside from "the vastly disproportionate time given primaries compared to other selection methods," Rubin found that the primaries were often called open and democratic and the winner labeled the popular choice of the voters even if the results were ambiguous.[62]

By reporting as they do, the electronic media alter the character of presidential nominations. Since primary voters lack the guidance that the endorsement of political parties provides during general elections, and since primary events are often full of uncertainty, media reporting of who is ahead or behind or how seriously candidates should be taken assumes considerable importance. Were officials of political parties able to select their own candidates, the media would matter much less. But with primaries replacing caucuses and conventions, it is fair to say that candidates have to care much more about how they do on television than on whether they please leaders of their party.

Is the selection of presidential candidates best carried out by party leaders bargaining in conventions or by the mass electorate voting in primaries? In order to prepare ourselves for discussing this question, we need to know something about the kinds of information possessed by those who do the selecting. Do primaries convey enough information to those who vote about a candidate's character, competence, issue positions, electability, and capacity to govern? What the media do best is to provide information on the viability of candidates, their standing in the nomination race. Primary voters soak this information up. Substantial evidence exists that voters read opinion poll results and gather other impressions of viability, and these exert considerable influence over voting decisions. But information on policies, character, and leadership ability is comparatively low and is absorbed slowly.[63] "It appears safe to conclude," John G. Geer writes, "that most primary voters do no compare the issue positions of candidates when voting."[64] One reason is that primary voters do not perceive much issue distance between the candidates, perhaps because, being members of the same party, there is in fact not that much difference of opinion among the candidates. Another reason may be that candidates are purposely unclear. Since it may well be advantageous for candidates to appeal differently to various audiences, they may, like Michael Dukakis or George Bush, appear moderate to some people, liberal to others, and conservative to still others.

There are bandwagon effects in primaries. Gary Hart rose from 2 percent of national support early in February 1984 to 33 percent in three weeks. Jimmy Carter went from near obscurity, 0.7 percent in January 1976, to 29.3 percent by mid-March. As Collat, Kelley, and Rogowski define the term, "a bandwagon effect may be said to exist if a given decision maker supports, from among some set of contenders, not the contender he most prefers, but the contender who seems most likely to win."[65]

Evidently the strength of their preferences on issues or on leadership ability must be very low if voters can be swept along with the sheer momentum of events. On what basis, then, do citizens choose? As the nominating campaign moves along, voters do develop feelings about the personality of the candidates. In a study of primary voters in Los Angeles, California, and Erie, Pennsylvania, Geer demonstrates that comments centered on the candidates' personalities dominate the reasons given for voting in primaries.[66] (See Table 3.1.)

Since much of the debate in the primary is about who among members of the same party can provide the best leadership, Geer thinks voter concentration on candidates is reasonable. Others will disagree. Brady and Hagen argue that "primaries seem to be seriously flawed by forcing voters to commit to candidates before they can learn about . . . policy positions, electability and leadership ability of those standing for the nomination. . . . American primaries force people to choose before they are ready. . . ."[67]

The political parties have written their rules in a way that makes if difficult to avoid primaries. It is no one thing but the whole confluence of events that has conspired to emphasize them. Now that the national party conventions ratify rather than choose candidates, the function of reducing uncertainty about which candidates are ahead and behind is transferred from successive convention ballots to the sequence of primaries.

It could be said that primaries are more important than general elections because primaries do more to limit the choices available to voters. Since the effects of primaries are cumulative, it is especially important to study how earlier events affect later ones. Larry Bartels argues that the nomination victories of Republican Gerald Ford and Democrat Jimmy Carter in 1976 were due to the accumulation of momentum, with over half of Carter's support in primaries coming from his early successes.[68] Perhaps the most interesting preliminary finding comes from a study by Richard Brody and Larry Rothenberg showing that voter turnout declines

TABLE 3.1 *Reasons for Supporting a Candidate for Nomination*
The Density of the Open Ended Comments (in Percent)

	N	"Person-ality"	Issues	Ideology	Group	Cam-paign	Other	Don't Know
Erie Democrats	264	70.1	10.2	.8	9.5	8.7	.4	.4
Erie Republicans	101	79.2	15.8	2.0	0	2.0	1.0	0
LA Democrats	270	68.9	15.9	5.2	1.9	7.8	.4	0
LA Republicans	161	73.9	19.9	3.1	0	1.2	1.9	0

Source: John G. Geer, *Nominating the President: An Assessment of Voters in Presidential Primaries* (New York, 1989), p. 77.

toward the end of the primary season.[69] This makes sense to us; if the early primaries dominate the process, then it would follow that people would see less purpose in turning out for later ones.

In 1968, only seventeen states selected delegates by primary. By 1980 thirty-two states used primaries, and in 1988, the number was thirty-three. In 1968 only 36.7 percent of delegates were selected by primary. In 1988 the percentage was approximately 65 percent.[70] So who runs in primaries now? In an increasing number of states all recognized candidates are placed on the ballot by a state official whether they wish to enter the fray or not. A convergence of opinion, whether justified or not, that no candidate is legitimate without exposure in primaries makes it difficult to stay out. The more primaries there are, the harder they are to miss. And there is an added inducement for candidates to enter. Delegates on a statewide basis often are allocated proportionally, which means that even losing candidates can frequently pick up a few delegates.

Since primaries have become so important—indeed, indispensable—for presidential nominations, it increases our interest in such questions as: Which candidates, and which interests they represent, are advantaged or disadvantaged by primaries? Will radicals, conservatives, or moderates do better or worse with more extensive use of primaries? Are citizens' preferences more or less likely to be reflected in the results? If not citizens', then whose preferences will be met? How do the rules for counting votes affect the results? We begin with this last important question because it turns out that the way votes are counted in large measure determines whose preferences count the most.

No one pretends that primaries are perfect representations of the electorate that either identifies with a particular political party or is likely to vote for the party's leading vote getter. For one thing, voters are not allowed to rank their preferences, so a candidate's popularity with voters who gave their first-choice votes to others is unknown. It is quite possible for a candidate to be the first choice of the largest clump of voters but to be only the fourth or fifth choice of all voters taken together. In 1972, for example, the candidates of the Democratic party's right and left—Wallace and McGovern, respectively—won pluralities in more states than any other candidates, yet they also attracted widespread opposition. This opposition was ineffectively expressed in the primary process. Voter turnout in primaries is usually much lower than in the general election and is likely to contain a larger proportion of dyed-in-the-wool party supporters than would be true in a general election. Austin Ranney has shown that average turnout in primaries is approximately 27 percent of all people voting age, compared with roughly double that in the presidential election.[71] It is not so much low turnout, however, as the combination of low turnout with plurality elections that biases the results. In 1972 Senator McGovern had a plurality in six states. In those states his total primary vote compared with the total vote cast in the general election ranged from 4 to 22 percent. Clearly, his primary voters could not have been a representative sample of those who actually voted in November.[72]

Nevertheless, it may appear that McGovern was entitled to most of the primary delegates because he won more often than any other candidate. This would depend, however, on how the votes were counted. There are three basic ways of counting votes. One if winner take all: whichever candidate gets a plurality of votes in the entire state gets all the delegates. Another is proportional: all candidates who pass a certain threshold, say, 15 percent, divide the delegates among them in accordance with their percentage of the vote. A third is congressionally districted: after delegates are allotted (by population or past party vote or both) to districts, the candidate who wins a plurality in each area gains all of its delegates. What would happen if all the votes in the 1972 Democratic primaries were recomputed by following any of the three rules consistently, rather than according to the actual melange of rules that determined the 1972 delegate allocation? Which candidates and, more importantly, which interests would have prevailed?

Consider the situation in Pennsylvania. Had the primary been run under a winner-take-all rule, Hubert Humphrey would have gained all 182 votes. Under the actual districted rule, however, Humphrey received only ninety-three votes, though that was substantially more than the sixty-six he would have gotten had proportional rules been in effect. James Lengle and Byron Shafer, close students of the situation, point out: "In fact, the difference [in delegates] between winning Pennsylvania Winner-Take-All and . . . proportionately is greater than the total number of delegates available in twelve out of the first fifteen primaries."[73] The point is not that Humphrey "wuz robbed," since McGovern might well have been nominated anyway, but that the rules matter a great deal. And they contributed to the interpretation of the results: McGovern's thirty-nine votes were considered excellent in a state where he was not expected to run well, and Humphrey's total of ninety-three was downgraded for the opposite reason, whereas the entire 182 would have been considered a real victory.

The crucial importance of looking good early in order to enhance future prospects means the determining whether certain rules help or hinder various candidates is in part a matter of timing. If one counts the late California primary of 1972, which George McGovern won under the winner-take-all system, for example, then winner-take-all was good for McGovern. In the early primaries, such as Pennsylvania, which kept

McGovern going, if winner-take-all had applied, he might not even have been in the race by the California primary. Once a candidate is ahead, proportional voting rules help put him over the top whether he wins or not. That is how Jimmy Carter won the nomination in 1980, although he lost five of his last eight primaries.

Rumination about the three rules reveals the kinds of constituencies (and hence interests) they are likely to favor. Winner-take-all gives more power to populous and competitive states, which have a large number of delegates. These are, Texas and Florida excepted, the states of the Northeast and California, known for their large concentration of urban voters, ethnic minorities, and union laborers. The proportional rule favors noncompetitive areas because in these places a high degree of support for a single candidate pays off. The congressional district rule would fractionate the large states, where many candidates could get some support, but not the smaller, less competitive states that have a few homogeneous districts. That is why Governor Wallace did so well wherever the proportional rule was in force. It should be evident, as Lengle and Shafer conclude, that:

> The widespread adoption of Districted primaries after 1968, or the prohibition of Winner-Take-All primaries after 1972, were not, then, just inconsequential decisions to hand out delegates via a certain mechanism. They were far-reaching, if almost accidental, choices about the type of candidates who would bear the party's standard, the type of voters who would have the power to choose those standardbearers, and the type of issues with which both groups would try to shape history. They were, in short, a decision on how to (re)construct the Democratic party.[74]

The Carter primary results in 1976 are not easy to assess. For one thing, he won most primaries by such tiny margins that almost any setback, however slight, might have sunk him without a trace. Two further things can be said: one is that most electoral devices overreward

TABLE 3.2 *How the Rules of the Game Affected Delegate Distributions, 1972 Democratic Primaries*

	Winner Take All	Proportional	Districted	Actual Results
Humphrey	446	314	324	284
Wallace	379	350	367	291
McGovern	249	319	343	401.5
Muskie	18	82	52	56.5
Others	0	27	6	59

Source: James Lengle and Byron Shafer, "Primary Rules, Politician Power, and Social Change," *American Political Science Review* 70 (March 1976), pp. 25–40.

winners, and 1976 was no exception; the other, which is more striking, is that Carter did much better in the states that had primaries for the first time in 1976. According to Gerald Pomper, "The Georgian won nearly two-thirds of the delegates from these thirteen new primary states. . . . Without the aid of these supporters, it is quite conceivable that Carter would have been denied the Democratic nomination."[75] Most of the delegates picked in the new primaries were in the border states, home territory for both Jimmy Carter and the resurgent Republican conservatism that favored Ronald Reagan.[76]

The purpose of the McGovern-Fraser Commission, which rewrote Democratic delegation selection rules prior to the 1972 elections, was to take control of the presidential nomination away from state and local party officials as well as from national officeholders, and give it over to party activists attached to candidates and elected through primaries with safeguards to assure representation of those deemed insufficiently represented: women, youth, racial minorities. Seeking to improve upon this version of representativeness, the Mikulski Commission of 1976 outlawed the plurality or winner-take-all primary and required some form of proportional representation from the states. Thinking this might be going too far, the Winograd Commission of 1980 allowed "loophole primaries," providing that if delegates were elected by congressional district, the plurality rule could operate. While the McGovern-Fraser Commission had ruled out ex officio delegates who were not pledged to a candidate and not elected in the regular way, the Winograd Commission, fearing that ties between parties and officeholders and thus between electioneering and governing were weakening, increased the size of state delegations by 10 percent in order to accommodate party and elected officials.[77] Nevertheless, these ex officio delegates had to declare a candidate preference and were subject to the same demographic rules of representativeness as all other delegates. Although the proportion of governors participating in the nominating convention shot way up, that of senators and representatives declined even further. It seemed that the need to declare one's preference very early and to compete with other legislators created disincentives to participate.[78]

After the crushing defeat of the Democrats in 1980, a presidential election year that ushered in a Republican Senate majority for the first time since 1954, and Jimmy Carter's seeming ineffectiveness in office, a lot of soul-searching went on among party leaders. Could representativeness and ineffectiveness go hand in hand? Had the new rules taken the party away from its electoral base? Was the absence of politicians, both party and public officials, a sign that insufficient attention was being paid both to getting elected and to governing?

The 1981–82 Commission on Presidential Nomination, chaired by Governor James B. Hunt, Jr. of North Carolina, was established to try to right the wrongs of the McGovern-Fraser reforms by encouraging stronger linkages between politicians and the presidency. Citing ample evidence that "delegates were ideologically unrepresentative of Democratic voters," the Hunt Commission thought that bringing politicians back into the nominating process might convince voters of the Democratic party's moderate character. They also believed that "elected officials might provide that missing element of peer review, whereby candidates for the presidency are screened by politicians who have dealt with them personally, instead of just observing them on television."[79] The hope, moreover, was that by giving politicians a greater voice in the presidential nomination there would also be greater cooperation in the business of government.

Contrary arguments were voiced within the Hunt Commission. Opponents said essentially that giving power to politicians would take power away from people. They feared that if these politicians, who could be uncommitted delegates, swung the convention decision in a close contest, the legitimacy of the outcome would be called into question. They feared that guidelines such as the equal division between men and women would be destroyed by creating a separate class of still largely male superdelegates.

Other members of the Hunt Commission thought these super-delegates too few and too weak. Coming in at the end of the process, all they would be able to do was affirm its outcome.[80] In the end, about 15 percent of the slots for delegates were reserved for uncommitted party and public officials. In each state, positions were reserved for the party chair and vice chair, and up to three-fifths of the members of Senate and House caucuses could serve as delegates. The remainder of the unpledged delegates were turned over to state parties with the suggestion they be given to governors and mayors of large cities. Finally, 305 delegates, corresponding to the additional number provided by the Winograd Commission, were allotted to pledged elected and party officials.[81]

So far we have only the results of the 1984 and 1988 Democratic nominating processes to gauge the effects of these rules changes. In 1984, the uncommitted delegates overwhelmingly supported Walter Mondale, and did so not late in the convention but relatively early in the primary season. Whether Mondale could have won without them, or, as is more likely, they helped sustain his strength during his bid, the unpledged delegates did matter.

How did the rules for counting votes toward delegates affect the outcome in 1984? Where Jesse Jackson's highly concentrated 18 percent of the vote got him just 10 percent of the delegates, and Hart came out even with 36 percent of the vote and the delegates, Mondale won 49 percent of the delegates with 39 percent of the vote. Jackson was hurt by the concentration of his support in largely black area. Hart's results were proportional because he happened to win mostly in states following proportionate rules. Mondale was helped because he won in big states with bonus "winner take more" systems, which the Democrats outlawed again after the 1988 contest.[82]

Do the Hunt Commission reforms enhance the prospects of moderates with close ties to party officials, as they were intended to do? Walter Mondale fit this description and, as we have seen, the rules in 1984 worked to his advantage. Still, reserving 15 percent of convention seats for party officials may not be enough to reverse the trends we have discussed earlier. The declining role of state parties, the greater emphasis on primaries, and the logic of primary election choice all favor candidates with intense factional followings over moderate insiders.

In any case, for party officials to play a moderating role, they must be moderate. Recent trends toward party polarization make this somewhat less likely. As conservatives—mostly Southerners—have left the Democratic and moved into the Republican party, conflict between the parties might substitute for conflict within them. Certainly, the prospects of a conservative Democratic or a liberal Republican presidential candidate have diminished. To the extent this is so, party officeholders may no longer be the bastions of moderation they once were. To test this hypothesis, we would like to know whether the views of politician delegates are closer to or further from those of Democratic voters than are delegates chosen through primaries or caucuses. We do know that politician delegates are more loyal to their party, 85 percent saying they support its candidates every year compared to two-thirds of the other delegates. Tom Mann argues that some politicians at the 1984 convention tried to push the Democratic party platform further to the left. Similarly, some Republican delegates from the House of Representatives pushed hard to the right.[83]

Where once it was useful to be the second choice of 90 percent of all delegates, today first choices—even of as few as 30 percent—are far preferable. This is a good measure of the change over the last two decades in the nomination process. Whether the country will do better with presidents who are the strong preference of party minorities rather than the weak preference of party majorities remains to be seen. One key test for presidents selected by modern processes will be what happens when they attempt to gather the support they need to govern—or, even more significantly, what happens to them and to their governments if they neglect to make the attempt. The warning words of a British observer, Anthony Teasdale, merit careful consideration:

> One irony of the primaries may thus be that in the name of greater democratic participation, nominations more often go to those less representative of party opinion. A second irony seems to be that in pursuit of more authoritative and legitimate government, primaries often favour candidates with less governmental experience, reduce the usefulness of party, increase popular expectations of politicians, and generally make America more difficult to govern. . . .
>
> Above all, by establishing direct personal contact between candidates and the mass electorate, primaries erode the importance of party as an intermediary between the elected and the elector in the United States. Candidates establish their own national organization, with their own mobile campaigners now imported into States as necessary. In government, this weakens the attachment of party loyalty which might give the President additional leverage to secure action on his proposals in Congress and the States.[84]

State and District Conventions

The 1988 results in Michigan, Virginia, Hawaii, and elsewhere show that as party activists become less moderate than party electorates their impact will be greater on caucuses than in primaries. The strong commitments of party activists to participate are amplified in those states where it is possible by showing up at a caucus or a convention to take over the nomination process even though their numbers are not great. These conditions were clearly best illustrated by the 1988 success of Reverend Pat Robertson on the Republican side and Reverend Jesse Jackson on the Democrat side.[85]

In 1988 approximately 64 percent of the delegates at the Democratic convention were chosen in primaries. Fifteen percent were unelected super-delegates. State and district conventions chose the other 20 percent. In the past this process has provided relatively few contests over the selection of delegates. But taking over the state and district conventions that chose the delegations to the party convention was the heart of Barry Goldwater's strategy in 1964 and an important aid for George McGovern in 1972. Jimmy Carter's 1976 showing in the early Iowa caucuses—where he beat all his competitors except "uncommitted"—was a central feature of his strategy.[86] The anti-Johnson forces' belated realization in 1968 that state conventions contained so much of the action prompted them to demand, and get, substantial changes in the rules governing the selection of delegates for the next convention. These included abolition of unit-rule voting in state and district conventions and a rule that delegates to the national convention had to be chosen in the year of the convention itself rather than at some earlier time, as had been the case in some states.[87]

In the past, attempts by candidates to influence delegates chosen outside of primaries were usually made after these delegates were selected by state parties. The first strategic requirement for the candidate seeking to influence these delegates was an intelligence service, a network of informants who could tell him which delegates were firmly committed, which were wavering, and which might be persuaded to provide second- or third-choice support. Advance reports on the opportunities offered by internal division in the state parties, the type of appeal likely to be effective in each state, and the kinds of bargains to which leaders were most susceptible were also helpful. The costs of this information were high in terms of time, money, and effort, but it was worthwhile to the serious candidate who needed to know where to move to increase his support and block his opponents.

These days no one wants to wait for delegates to be chosen before trying to influence them. The idea is for candidates to get their supporters selected as delegates. By the time they are selected, delegate are likely to be committed to a particular candidate or point of view. In any event, they cannot be selected before the year of the election. The same forces that persuade candidates to begin their drive for the nomination ever earlier impel them to begin the hunt for delegates ahead of time.[88] Since fund raising must go on in at least twenty states to attract federal matching money, it can be combined with the identification of local allies, who eventually will be designated delegates if the candidate does well in the state selection process.

The major change between past and present stems from weaknesses in the party system. When and where there were strong state party organizations in the past, aspiring candidates had to deal with them. Decisions on whether to enter a primary or influence delegate selection were mediated through party leaders. If party leaders thought a contest in a state would be divisive, candidates would have to worry about incurring their enmity. The decline of state parties in the nomination process has lowered these obstacles. Relatively small numbers of activists without a continuing connection to the party may mobilize around a candidate and, by appealing to caucus attenders and primary electorates, overwhelm the party regulars. If the test is numbers of followers who will come to a particular meeting, rather than present party position or past service, an activist surge can carry the day, as McGovern and Goldwater demonstrated so well.

Aspirants for nomination vary greatly in the degree to which they know other politicians throughout the country. Men like Richard Nixon, Hubert Humphrey, and Barry Goldwater, who traveled extensively and gave assistance to members of their party, simply needed to keep their files up to date in order to have a nationwide list of contacts. When the time came they knew from whom they could request assistance in gathering information, persuading delegates, and generally furthering their cause. Candidates who lacked this advantage had to take special steps in order to build up their political apparatus. In paving the way for Franklin D. Roosevelt's 1932 nomination, James A. Farley began early by sending invitations to Roosevelt's inauguration as governor of New York to party leaders throughout the country. Most invitations were refused, but a valuable correspondence grew out of this approach. Farley next sent a small manual containing a few facts about the New York Democratic party organization to people throughout the country. The response encouraged a follow-up pamphlet which presented, without comment, the New York gubernatorial vote in every county since 1916. It was intended to be impressive testimony of FDR's vote-getting ability. When many people wrote back expressing an interest in FDR's candidacy, offering suggestions, or just saying "thanks," Farley replied with a personal message and endeavored to keep up the contact through further letters, phone calls, and even a phonograph record. Later, in 1931, Farley took a trip through the West, ostensibly to visit the Elks Convention in Seattle, but actually to contact over 1,000 party leaders in all but three states west of the Mississippi. Upon Farley's return, every one of his contacts received a personal letter.[89]

This is more or less the method candidates must use in building their personal organizations in state after state, and especially those states who choose their delegates early in the election year. In addition, candidates have to be well known to get a start. Instead of heading toward the Elks, a candidate's manager now march toward the media.

Nowadays every candidate seeks to sway voters, not party leaders. Thus the sort of organization that candidates need includes poll takers, fund raisers, and media experts. Indeed, it may not be too much to say that a key question for candidates today is which poll taker or manager to attract to his campaign rather than which party leaders.[90] Now everybody believes, and with good reason, that the early aspirant gets the nomination. Candidates will need more publicity than they used to have and they will need it earlier than they used to have it to compete in the future.

The delegates to national party conventions are selected state by state, in conventions or primaries or by a combination of the two methods.[91] They are the outcomes of processes that are slightly different in their legal requirements and political overtones in each of the states, the District of

Columbia, and the territories—all of which send delegations to both party conventions. For the Democrats, however, these requirements are subject to supervision at the national level.

National parties, strengthened by the LaFollette decision of the Supreme Court,[92] have taken a strong hand in determining such matters as who may participate in the selection of state delegations, the demographic composition of delegations, and the timing of selection processes. This has led to various sorts of maneuvering by state parties. The abolition of winner-take-all elections and the Democrats' establishment of a relatively narrow band of time during which delegates must be selected have inspired many states to move the date of delegate selection as far forward as possible, so as to increase their influence on the overall outcome.[93] Things have moved so fast so far, however, that by 1988 a third of the delegates were chosen at the earliest possible moment, on super-Tuesday. When Senator Robert Dole referred to the "make-or-break" year, he was not pointing to 1988, the election year, but to 1987, when the preparation work was done.[94]

There are many different methods in use among the states for selecting delegates. The three main modes of selecting delegates are: (1) direct election, (2) the caucus or convention, (3) the binding preference primary. In addition the Democratic party has several special categories of delegates; each state is required to send its representatives to the Democratic National Committee, its governor if of the right party, and the party's state chair and its vice chair, it being understood they would go uninstructed. Other places for unpledged delegates are taken up by Democratic members of Congress selected by the Senate Democratic Conference and House Democratic Caucus. Although the Republican party has no such category as super-delegate, it does recommend that the state delegation be representative of the communities from which they came, a suggestion honored in the breach.[95] Thus, as convention time approaches, all states will have selected delegates who are already pledged to various candidates.

Prenomination Strategies

The first strategic decision facing an avowed candidate used to be whether to attempt to become a front runner by entering primaries, barnstorming the country, and publicly seeking support at state conventions. The advantage of this strategy was that a candidate might build up such a commanding lead (or appear to) that no one would be able to stop him at the national convention. Nowadays the possibility that some other candidate might become unstoppable early, reinforced by the larger number of primaries and a federal subsidy for primary contestants, obviously makes early entry necessary for all candidates.

The disadvantage used to be that an open campaign might reveal the inability of some candidates to acquire support or might lead other candidates to band together to stop the front runner. The front runner's success, then, depended on his ability to predict accurately both how he would fare compared with others in open competition and what others would do when they discovered his lead. He could, for example, try to anticipate whether this activity would stimulate a coalition of opponents who were otherwise unlikely to get together. Exactly this happened to Jimmy Carter in 1976 when, after an initial period of disbelief, everyone else in the race, without formal coordination, directed their fire at him. Richard Gephardt had the same problem in 1988. If such a coalition seemed likely, the candidate would issue communications playing down the extent of his support. But this tactic might discourage new supporters who would have been attracted by a display of strength. Since proportional allocation allows even primary losers to gain delegates, and since funds depend on visibility, running openly is much more attractive than it used to be. Indeed, it is mandatory. The rising total of pledged delegates from caucuses and primaries means that a candidate who avoids them, as Hubert Humphrey did in 1968, is certain to end up without delegates.

The dark horse used to be a candidate who avoided open campaigning. Like Stuart Symington in 1960, or Richard Nixon in 1964, the dark horse was content to be everyone's friend and no one's enemy.[96] As Abraham Lincoln wrote to a supporter in 1860 describing his dark-horse strategy: "My name is new in the field, and I suppose I am not the first choice of a very great many. Our policy, then, is to give no offense to others— leave them in a mood to come to us if they shall be compelled to give up their first love."[97] The strategy of the dark horse was to combine with others to oppose every front runner. His hope was that when no front runner was left he would appear as the man who could unify the party by being acceptable to all and obnoxious to none. The dangers the dark horse faced were that he would enter the convention with too little support to make a strong bid or that some other dark horse would prove preferable. How much support was enough to make a serious bid but not enough to be shot at as a front runner? How far behind the front runner could a candidate permit himself to get without becoming entirely lost from sight? Either an intuitive ability to guess or an exceedingly accurate apparatus for collecting information on the strength of candidates, as well as on the likely effect of different levels of strength on other delegates, had to be part of the serious dark horse's equipment.

With nominations decided before the convention meets, there is no longer room for outsiders of this sort. With so few uncommitted delegates, there is little point in wooing or stampeding the uncommitted as Wendell Willkie did successfully in 1940. Nor is there room for the strategy used by 1952 backers of Dwight Eisenhower, who some party leaders imposed on others in order to increase their party's election chances. Whether party leaders with this sort of commitment exist today is debatable; even if they did, however, they would be less likely than in the past to challenge the candidate who has done best in the primaries because bargaining among politicians increasingly has become suspect as a legitimate form of decision making. For politicians to substitute their judgment for those of party voters requires the belief that they have special qualifications that would justify others deferring to them. Whether or not politicians think they have such qualifications, they may well doubt that voters, or the news media, think so.

The best chance for a dark horse in the future is likely to be a deadlocked convention, something that has not happened for over thirty years. Well-known party leaders who have run before and have achieved great visibility, like Hubert Humphrey or Edmund Muskie in 1976, can afford the luxury of hoping lightning will strike without doing too much to stimulate it. But the fact that both these men lost out to a new and inexperienced face—Carter, who ran in the primaries—is a lesson that future dark horses are bound to heed. If the candidates who entered the primaries and arrived at the convention with pledged delegates are unacceptable to a majority, presumably the party will either have to go back to someone it passed over or break up. So what are the conditions in which a dark horse might emerge as the nominee? If no candidate arrives at the convention with either a majority or a strong plurality of delegates, the convention may have to decide. Or if one candidate gets more primary votes and another more delegates, neither may make it. In such circumstances, especially if opinion polls show the leading candidates losing to the opposition party in the general election to come, a highly visible governor or senator might conceivably be drafted. But it is unlikely. Efforts by candidates to bargain for a place on the ticket may also seem "too political" to be acceptable. Increasingly, by convention time there is a clear front runner. The vast majority of delegates are now pledged to those who actively compete in primaries and state conventions, leaving the dark horses with two few delegates to affect the outcome.

At the Convention: Housekeeping

While the selection of a site for the convention has often been inter-preted as one of the preballot indicators of various candidates' strength, in the past it usually was the rather routine outcome of the weighing of one major and several very minor factors. The major factor was the size of the convention city's proffered contribution to the national party com-mittee. This contribution—in cash or in services—came partly from the city government but mostly from various business groups—hotels, restaurants—which stood to profit from a week-long visit of 6,500 del-egates and alternates, their families and friends, and thousands of media representatives, dignitaries, and convention personnel. The cloud over the offer of several hundred thousand dollars by the Sheraton hotel chain as part of San Diego's bid to host the 1972 Republican convention, as well as the reaction to Watergate, has inspired some changes. The federal government now makes available a sum of over $8 million to each of the national parties to finance their nominating conventions, thereby lessen-ing the pressure to acquire cash contributions or contributions in kind.[98] A variety of other factors, however, may tip the balance between cities. San Francisco was chosen by Democrats in 1984 partly because the party was having trouble in the West and partly because the city had a popular female Democratic mayor.[99] Other factors include the quality of facili-ties, the suitability of the convention hall to the television networks, hotel and entertainment accommodations, and the caliber of the local police force. For example, Philadelphia's James Tate headed as large and as loyal a Democratic organization in 1968 as Chicago's Richard Daley, and his city was closer geographically to Lyndon Johnson in Washington, but Philadelphia simply could not provide 20,000 first-class hotel rooms.[100] All things being equal, an incumbent president is likely to prefer a city near enough to Washington to allow him to keep close tabs on convention business and travel easily back and forth to the convention while at the same time playing his role away from it as "president of all the people." And, naturally, the president's wishes will not be furthest from the minds of the members of the site-selection committee of the national committee, which does the choosing. In addition, they will have in mind some other political factors. The Republicans in 1968, by selecting Miami Beach for the first Republican convention ever held south of the Mason-Dixon line, may well have facilitated a "southern strategy" if they intended to pursue one. In 1988, both parties wanted to bolster their strength in the South, Republicans because they were gaining and Democrats because they were declining, and so the Democrats selected Atlanta and the Republicans New Orleans.[101]

For the 1992 Republican convention the issue came down to Houston or San Diego. In 1990, Texas elected a Democratic governor, Anne Richards, whose speech at the 1988 Democratic convention described George Bush as having been "born with a silver foot in his mouth." On these grounds, San Diego, where former mayor, now governor, Pete Wilson could greet them, looked like a better bet. But the convention's home community has to come up with around $15 million, and California, with its two senatorial elections, reapportionment fights, and seven new House seats, was going to need a lot of political money for its own purposes in 1992.[102] The Republicans might have chosen New Orleans, but for the unfortunate emergence in Louisiana of David Duke, formerly of the Klu Klux Klan, as the Republican candidate for Senate in 1990.

The parties prefer to bring their publicity and their business to cities and states where the mayor and the governor are friendly members of the party, since this may give added access to (and control of) public facilities. The aloof attitude of California's Governor Jerry Brown toward the site-selection committee of his party evidently tipped the decision of the Democrats toward New York City in 1976 and away from Los Angeles.[103] In 1984, the fact that the party chairman, Charles Manatt, was a Californian, may have tipped the balance back to San Francisco for the Democrats. The desire to maintain the autonomy of the convention from demonstrators, who were involved in the Democratic debacle in Chicago in 1968, led to a choice in 1972 of Miami Beach, where a causeway facilitated crowd control.

The time of a convention varies between mid-July and late August. There are two general statements to be made about it. One is that the "out" party will normally hold its convention before the "in" party, on the theory that its candidate will need more of a publicity boost earlier. In 1976, 1984, and 1988 this put Democrats before Republicans, and in 1964, 1968, and 1980 it was the other way around. Also, if there is an incumbent president, he will schedule the convention to fit his timetable. At its most momentous, the convention may coincide with an international peace offensive; in 1968, the date of the Democratic convention seems to have been set with nothing more in mind than President Johnson's birthday.

Once assembled, the national convention is a mass meeting in which the participants necessarily play widely varying and unequal roles. The candidates and their chief supporters are busily, perhaps frantically, perfecting their organizations and trying to maintain their communications with as many of their delegates as they can. In the old days, "pledged" delegations were actively supporting their candidate while "bossed" delegates negotiated for the disposal of their votes. The leaders of these delegations were the people who conducted negotiations among the delegations when an impasse developed. There were also factional leaders and independent delegates within state delegations who played an important part in determining what their delegation or a part of their delegation would do. They bargained within their delegation rather than among the various state delegations. Now, the roles of both of these relatively autonomous types of politicians have sharply diminished, since most delegates will come to the convention pledged to one or another presidential candidate. This will mean that candidate organizations, not state party leaders, will have to do the bargaining. But it will be hard for them to bargain if they cannot transfer the votes of their supporters; it will be even harder if the nomination has already been decided in caucuses and primaries. In setting the stage for their balloting, therefore, we will deal first with candidates and their organizations and then with the delegates.

Candidates and Their Organizations

At the national convention, before the balloting for the presidential nomination starts, one or more days are consumed in a variety of party rituals: making speeches, seating delegates, presenting the platform, and so on. During that time delegates and their leaders mill about, exchanging greetings and gossip. It is this set of circumstances that challenges even the most efficient candidate organization.

There is a wide divergence among candidate organizations. They range from the comprehensive, integrated, and superbly effective to the fragmented, uncoordinated, and virtually nonexistent. We can only suggest the range of organizational alternatives through some general comments and a few examples.

The first modern candidate organization at a national convention, tied together with sophisticated communications equipment, was the expensively mounted organization of Senator John F. Kennedy in 1960. His communications network provided him with a continuing and accurate stream of vital information.[104] He wanted detailed personal information about as many delegates as possible in order to know how they were likely to vote and how they might best be persuaded to stay in line or to change their minds. More than a year before the convention the Kennedy-for-President organization started a card file containing information on people throughout the nation who might be delegates and who might influence delegates. Included on each card was the prospective delegate's name, occupation, religion, party position, relation (if any) to the Kennedy family or its leading supporters, ambitions, policy preferences if strongly held, and likely vote. This was brought up to date before convention time and entries were made in a central register as new information developed. Thus when it appeared that a delegate needed to be reinforced or might not vote for Kennedy, his card was pulled and the information was used in order to determine the best way to convince him.

In order to keep an up-to-date and, when necessary, an hour-by-hour watch on developments within the state delegations, the Kennedy organization assigned an individual coordinator to each state. This person might have been a delegate or an observer, such as a senator or a member of the candidate's staff. When it was deemed inadvisable to choose a delegate for fear that any choice would alienate one faction or another, a person outside the state was chosen. These liaison men kept tabs on individual delegates and maintained a running record of the likely distribution of votes. When necessary, the liaison men sent messages to the candidate's headquarters and reinforcements were sent to bolster the situation. At the Kennedy headquarters the seriousness of the report would be judged and a decision made on how to deal with it. Senator Kennedy himself might call the wavering delegate, one of his brothers might be dispatched, a state party leader might intervene, or some other such remedy might be applied.

In the hurly-burly, crush, and confusion of convention activity, it cannot be assumed that messages sent are received or that decisions are communicated to those who must carry them out. The Kennedy organization took great care to establish a communications center that would receive messages and locate the intended recipients and that could send out instructions and receive feedback on the results. In this pre-beeper era, each key staff person was required to phone his whereabouts periodically to a central switchboard. This made it possible for the Kennedy forces at the convention to deploy and reassign their people on a minute-by-minute basis as developments required.

A system set up only to deal with emergencies would have limited usefulness to a candidate who wanted regular reports so that he could appraise them in a consistent way. Every morning every liaison man assigned to the Kennedy headquarters attended a staff meeting at which he deposited with the secretary a report on his activities for the previous day. These reports were sent to what was called the "secret room" and the information was transferred to state briefing files. From these files, a daily secret report on delegate strength was written and given to the candidate and his top advisers.

At the morning staff meetings, Robert Kennedy, who acted as campaign manager for his brother, would ask each liaison man for his estimate of the number of Kennedy votes. Keenly aware of the dangers of seeming to want high estimates, Robert Kennedy challenged the liaison men if he felt that their estimates were too high, but not if they appeared too low. On occasion he would reprimand a liaison man for including a delegate as a certain Kennedy supporter when other information indicated that this was not true. The success of this procedure was indicated by the fact that when the alphabetical balloting had reached Wyoming on the first (and last) ballot, the Kennedy organization's estimate of their delegate strength was proved correct within a one-vote margin.[105]

The danger of confusion and mishap is multiplied during the ballot because the convention floor is filled and it is difficult to move about freely. To deal with this, the Kennedy organization arranged for telephones on the convention floor. Six were set up beneath the seats of chairmen of friendly delegations who were seated around the gigantic convention hall. These phones were connected to the Kennedy headquarters outside the hall. Inside the headquarters, staff members sat near the telephone and simultaneously scanned several television sets to look for possible defections. Had the pretested telephone failed to work, walkie-talkie radios were available to take their place.[106]

By comparison with the Kennedy efforts, most of the organizations that have successfully nominated presidential candidates in American history have been uncoordinated, diffuse affairs. For example in 1952 none of the various factions in the Democratic party that favored the nomination of Adlai Stevenson had the wholehearted cooperation of their candidate; information gathering was casual and tactical maneuvers were in some cases hit upon accidentally or as afterthoughts. The factions working for the Stevenson nomination did not cooperate to a significant degree and squabbled on occasion. Yet Stevenson was nominated; his success came about because he was the second choice of an overwhelming number of delegates who could not agree on any of their first choices and the first choice of a significant number of leaders in spite of his disinclination to pursue the nomination in an organized fashion.[107]

We have devoted so much space to the Kennedy organization because, unlike the Stevenson example, it became a harbinger of the future. McGovern's organization in 1972 was like Kennedy's only more so—more telephones, more communications apparatus, more file cards. These extremely organized efforts created some tension within the McGovern camp because delegates who prided themselves on independent thinking did not always appreciate a series of communications on each issue coming before the 1972 convention telling them how to vote or—equally insulting—allowing them a free choice if a given matter was not considered important.

The McGovern organization worked wonderfully on the platform. A free vote was permitted on giving Indians first choice in the distribution of federal land. Proposals for a guaranteed national income of $6,500 and for minority rights for homosexuals were opposed and defeated. Last-minute additions to reassure supporters of Israel and a commitment to keep troops in Western Europe were supported and passed. Commands went down the line, obedience came up the line, since it was all for the cause.

At the 1976 convention, Jimmy Carter was superbly organized but did not need to be because his nomination was already in the bag. An interesting contrast emerged at the more closely contested Republican convention. Following recent practice, the President Ford Committee installed an effective communications apparatus. Rather than rely entirely on the geographic leaders of their earlier delegate monitoring operation, the President Ford Committee divided the convention floor into zones, whose floor leaders wore red hats, tied by telephone to the Ford trailer and to subleaders responsible for each state. By contrast, Ronald Reagan relied on style and ideology rather than hierarchy and division of labor. As a convention leader said, "Our conservatives don't like to be told what to do, and they don't need to be. The Ford people need all that hardware because they can't count on their delegates to vote with them consistently." F. Christopher Arterton, who observed the convention, believes that at crucial moments, as when the Mississippi delegation caucused on the floor before a crucial vote, Reagan "was handicapped by key coordinators having too fight their way through jammed aisles."[108]

At the 1984 Democratic convention, the Mondale nerve center was composed of fourteen delegate trackers in a trailer, thirty-five cluster organizers (clusters were groups of states) covering 300 to 350 delegates each, sixty state whips, and 390 lines whips responsible for seeing to it that delegates fulfilled their pledges. Thus by the 1980s, all serious candidates brought to the convention as part of their normal equipment a full complement of electronic communications gear. All had trailers parked near the convention hall in which they could monitor trends on the floor and entertain friends and allies. What was extraordinary about the Kennedy effort in 1960 has, with the passage of time and the progress of technology, become commonplace.

Delegates and Caucuses

While candidate organizations have clearly increased their control over delegates, it is still important to know something of the delegates themselves. Who are they? What do they believe? How loyal to their parties are they? Excellent studies of convention delegates allow us a perspective on the changing nature of party activists. In recent conventions, delegates, pledged in state primaries and caucuses, have had little flexibility in the choice of the party's nominee. Still they play a role in platform debates and establishing the image the party projects on television. If we should ever have a deadlocked convention, in which delegates are released from their pledges, delegate attitudes and behavior will be of the utmost importance.

Each of the major parties has its own distinctive style and norms. "Republicans," Jo Freeman observes, "perceive themselves as insiders even when they are out of power, and Democrats perceive themselves as outsiders even when they are in power."[109] This difference can be elaborated: Republicans in convention are relatively unified, while Democrats think of themselves as members of subgroups. As the more hierarchical party, Republicans stress loyalty to the chosen leader and the organization. The more varied and egalitarian Democratic party, in Freeman's words, "has multiple power centers that compete for membership support in order to make demands on, as well as determine, the leaders."[110] For Democratic delegates, therefore, subgroup caucuses are significant reference groups. The component parts of the Republican party, states and geographic regions and ideological factions, do not maintain robust lives outside the party structure, as do the Democratic caucuses of African Americans, gays, Asians, and so on, nor do they make decisions and proposals so much as serve as conduits of information to delegates. At national conventions Democrats go to caucuses, as Freeman says, while Republicans go to receptions. Republicans "network" with the candidate organizations while Democrats make demands. Democrats expect their nominee to pay attention to their problems while Republicans are more likely to think that the winner ought to get his way until the next time.[111]

There are four identifiable categories of convention activists: (1) a small number of managers of candidate organizations, (2) in the Democratic party a set of not necessarily committed elected officials (the superdelegates), (3) a shrinking proportion of state leaders who control votes other than their own and who in the past might have participated in high-level negotiations on the disposition of these votes, and (4) leaders of caucuses representing interest groups and demographic categories. The rise of these caucuses deserves special comment.

The demographic identities of the delegates to the Democratic National Convention since 1972 have been determined only in part by the kinds of people who supported candidates who won delegates in primaries and state conventions. Since 1972, the rules have modified the demographic makeup of the delegations. The Democratic Commission on Party Structure and Delegate Selection, headed by George McGovern, required state parties to take "affirmative steps to encourage representation . . . of young people [and] . . . minority groups in reasonable relationship to their presence in the population of the States."[112] The best study we have of the immediate effects of this requirement is William Cavala's aptly titled article "Changing the Rules Changes the Game," which deals with California. After observing what happened there, we shall note the effects on the composition, policy preferences, and behavior of delegates as a whole.

California had a winner-take-all primary in 1972, the last in the country. According to past practice, the candidate who won this primary election would choose his delegates on the basis of recommendations made by his leading supporters around the state. The major criterion for delegate selection was the degree to which a possible delegate's past record or present resources suggested he could help the party in the coming campaign. Thus high party officials, officeholders, and financial contributors, most of whom were white, male, and over thirty, fit the bill.

This traditional system had its drawbacks. It gave candidates a splendid opportunity to unmake friends by failing to appoint people to the delegation. And space was always limited. This meant a certain amount of bargaining; people who wanted to be selected could refuse to help with the campaign or delay their contributions until they had first been rewarded with a delegate's position. Thus California political leaders did not oppose changes in the rules that imposed de facto quote requirements and removed the choice of delegates to the congressional district level. At the time, this seemed to be an opportunity to connect convention rewards with party performance.

In each congressional district, delegate selection meetings were held on behalf of each candidate well in advance of the primary. Some of these meetings were dominated by traditional interest group forces. But these were mostly the meetings of the traditional centrist candidates— Hubert Humphrey, Henry Jackson, and the early front runner, Edmund Muskie. Not so the meetings of the eventual winner of the primary, George McGovern. At the McGovern district meetings there were large turnouts of white liberal activists who had not previously been involved in local and state politics. "In contrast to campaign professionals," Cavala writes, "who saw delegates as basically campaign personnel, the assembled activists viewed them as moral ambassadors. . . ."[113] Thus prior experience in campaigns was often viewed as a disqualification, presumably on the ground that the nominee had been tainted. Activists found the instructions on quotas congenial because they believed in both demographic (race, age, sex) and issue representation. They soon broke up into black, Hispanic-American, and women's caucuses, whose members bargained with one another for representation. The concern of these caucuses was with group interests rather than party or candidate interests. Hence women who had been active for

McGovern were slighted in these mini-caucuses in favor of those whose attention was focused on women's rights. Racial minorities received a double bonus. The McGovern campaign committee urged extra representation in districts where minorities predominated in order to enhance electoral prospects. This was done. But they did not anticipate that areas with few minority people would also feel it necessary to have minorities on their slate.

What about white males over thirty years of age? They, presumably, did not have a shared interest requiring separate representation. Only 8 percent of the McGovern delegates selected at district meetings met this description. Jewish men, who had in the past supplied a great deal of money for Democratic politics in the state of California, and many of whom backed McGovern, were evidently not considered a minority because they were nowhere to be found. To find Jews one had to look at the female side of the delegation. The final result was a delegation consisting of 41 percent of minority-group members, whose presence in the general California population hovered around 18 percent.

As an aid in obtaining party unity during the campaign for the general election, the primary winner traditionally chose a few delegates from the losing slates. A few members of the winning slate were asked to resign, and supporters of other presidential nominees were salted in. However, the new breed of delegates refused to give up a single place. Consequently, organized labor, which had supported Humphrey, had hardly any representation in the California delegation, and officeholders were noticeable by their absence. Hence the manpower and money these groups provided in the campaign came to McGovern late and in smaller amounts.[114]

Party rules regarding primaries now give delegates chosen as representatives of the various candidates little or no freedom of choice at the convention so long as their candidate is still in contention. Demographic caucuses have some impact on party platforms and convention resolutions, however, and so it is worthy knowing whether delegates who were chosen under quotas are as representative as delegates in previous years and whether their preferences were like the preferences of voters who identify with the Democratic party.

The new rules have succeeded in increasing the proportion of blacks, women, and youth at the past five Democratic conventions. But if delegates are stratified by income and education, it becomes clear that political activists are still a rather elite group. Table 3.3 gives income figures for 1972 for both parties, figures that over the years have not changed much.

Educational differences were even more striking in 1972. About three

TABLE 3.3   *Incomes of Delegates and Party Identifiers*

Democrats Income

Identifiers, 1971		Delegates, 1972	
Less than $9,000	48%	Less than $10,000	14%
$9,000 to $15,000	30%	$10,000 to $20,000	36%
Over $15,000	22%	Over $20,000	50%

Republicans Income

Identifiers, 1971		Delegates, 1972	
Less than $10,000	43%	Less than $20,000	23%
$10,000 to $15,000	42%	$20,000 to $50,000	54%
Over $15,000	15%	Over $50,000	23%

Source: Jeane J. Kirkpatrick, "Representation in the American National Conventions: the Case of 1972," *British Journal of Political Science* 5 (1975), pp. 265–322.

in five delegates from both parties had college degrees, compared to one in four among rank-and-file Democrats and one in three of rank-and-file Republican identifiers. Among the Democratic delegates, 65 percent of McGovern's people had college degrees, compared to 33 percent for Wallace, 40 percent for Humphrey, and 56 percent for Muskie. Professional people predominated among the delegates, with lawyers in the forefront, except among McGovern supporters, where teachers were predominant. As Jeane Kirkpatrick concludes, "The delegates to both conventions were an overwhelmingly middle to upper class group. . . ."[115]

The reformed Democratic party has run into ideological problems which previously were associated with the GOP. Herbert McClosky's classic study comparing delegates to the 1956 conventions with ordinary voters uncovered an important source of difficulty for the Republican party that has persisted through the years. Republican voters and Democratic voters tend to think more or less alike on most policy issues. Ordinary voters of both parties in turn had attitudes in McClosky's data close to those of Democratic leaders but relatively removed from the attitudes of Republican leaders.[116] This suggested that Republican activists, by satisfying themselves with a candidate and platform, would court unpopularity and defeat. The 1964 experience is frequently cited as evidence of this.

In 1972, quite similar risks passed to the Democratic camp. On a broad range of issues, Democratic delegates, especially McGovern delegates, were far from most citizens, including supporters of the Democratic party. In fact they differed from the preferences of Democratic voters on most issues even more than did Republican delegates. On welfare policy, most voters gave priority to work, while most Democratic delegates were more interested in eradicating poverty. On busing, only 3 percent of the McGovern delegates were strongly opposed, in contrast to 71 percent of voting Democrats. On law and order, over three-fourths of the delegates cared more about the rights of the accused, compared to one-third of the voters. On Vietnam, 7 percent of the voters but 57 percent of the McGovern delegates were opposed to giving an aid whatsoever after American withdrawal. Only on inflation did Democratic voters and delegates agree on the importance of governmental action.[117]

Politics involves feelings not only about issues but also about groups. Toward one group—politicians—delegates in both parties in 1972 were more favorable than voters. On unions, business, and liberals, Democratic voters and delegates were together. But on political demonstrators, civil rights leaders, black militants, the military, and people on welfare, Republican delegates were closer to Democratic voters, who were very far indeed from Democratic delegates. On all issues and group attitudes, McGovern delegates were found to differ more with Democratic voters than the supporters of any other candidate. There is certainly good reason to believe this, since although a majority of delegates voted for George McGovern at the 1972 convention, McGovern lost 40 percent of the vote of Democratic identifiers in the general election.

Were these differences caused by the new quota rules of the Democratic party or by divergences between voters and activists on other grounds? All McGovern supporters shared the same political attitudes whether they were male or female, white or black, young or old. Thus demographic quotas clearly cannot be blamed for the disparity in views between 1972 Democratic delegates and voters. Perhaps what happened is that activists in both parties, enjoying high social and economic status but without professional commitment to party unity or party organization, grew at once farther apart from one another and from the voters. The participant sectors of the parties were far more polarized in 1972 than they had been in the 1940s and 1950s in two directions—one party from the other at the elite level, and elites in both parties from their followers.[118]

Party Ideology and Political Polarization Since 1972

The major study of the 1976 and 1980 convention delegates, Warren E. Miller and M. Kent Jennings' *Parties in Transition*, reports that while Democratic delegates and activists continued to support McGovern's

1972 policy preferences, they became less purist and more committed to electing candidates and to supporting their party.[119] Miller and Jennings conclude that "the amateurs' enthusiasm for ideological purity at the expense of party was apparently short-lived."[120] We have come to a related conclusion: internal changes in the parties merged purism and professionalism because party loyalty and issue commitment became more nearly equivalent. Looking at the table Miller and Jennings use to support their argument (Table 3.4), we see that while purism declines and support of party rises, agreement on "selecting a nominee who is strongly committed on the issues" is nearly unanimous. From 1972 through 1980, Miller and Jennings found "large absolute differences in terms of what are widely recognized by elites as conservative and liberal positions."[121] Dramatic differences between the parties "provide striking evidence of party polarization at the elite levels." They report:

> . . . The basic data demonstrate more than simple differential affinity; they also demonstrate differential antipathy. . . . This element of differential rejection and antipathy, when coupled with the element of differential

TABLE 3.4   *Interparty Differences on Issue Positions and Group Evaluations Among Convention Delegates, 1972–1980*

Issues	
Abortion Permissiveness	16
Relations with Russia	25
Inflation/Unemployment	31
Defense Spending	31
Environmental Protection	33
Busing for Integration	35
Liberal-Conservative Self-Placement	38
Equal Rights Amendment	50
Groups	
Blacks	20
Pro-Life	21
Business Interest	26
Gay Rights	30
Environmentalists	32
Moral Majority	35
Union Leaders	38
Antinuclear	39
Women's Liberation Movement	40
Conservatives	47
Liberals	50
Democrats	55
Republicans	60

Entries represent the absolute value of Republican mean scores minus the Democratic mean scores.

Source: Warren E. Miller and M. Kent Jennings, with Barbara Farah, *Parties in Transition: A Longitudinal Study of Party Elites and Party Supporters* (New York, 1986), pp. 164–167.

TABLE 3.5   *Goals for Nominating Conventions*

	Democratic Delegates			Republican Delegates		
	1972	1976	1980	1972	1976	1980
Policy-Oriented						
Standing firm for position even if it means resigning from party	43	31	30	25	31	27
Playing down some issues if it will improve the chances of winning	58	66	62	70	73	71
Selecting a nominee who is strongly committed on the issues	95	94	95	93	95	96
Party-Oriented						
Counting service to the party heavily in nominating candidates	70	81	84	88	85	84
Working to minimize disagreement within the party	82	87	87	92	89	86
Minimizing the role of the party organization in nominating candidates for office	28	23	20	18	19	23
Encouraging widespread participation in making most party decisions	93	91	92	93	92	93

These seven responses were offered to the following questions: In thinking about decisions that are made at the conventions, which positions do you favor and which do you oppose?

Entries are the proportion who responded "strongly favor" or "favor."

Source: Warren E. Miller and M. Kent Jennings, with Barbara G. Farah, *Parties in Transition: A Longitudinal Study of Party Elites and Party Supporters* (New York, 1986), p. 97.

approval, not only produces the extreme differences between the parties in terms of group evaluations, but it also implies a marked polarization of attitudes toward groups going well beyond varying degrees of favorableness. In this sense the opinion cultures of the two elites are truly antagonistic.[123]

What explains this party polarization? The more continuously active the delegates over the years, Miller and Jennings show, the greater the polarization among Republicans and Democrats.[124] In fact, partisan conflict was considerably less among the 1972 delegates who later dropped out of presidential nominating politics than among those who stayed in. Both turnover and individual change resulted in greater party polarization by 1980.[125]

It appears that 1972 was a deviant year for Democrats. Prior to that time, Democratic delegates were closer in issue preferences to Democratic identifiers and voters than were Republican delegates to those who identified with and voted for Republicans. That older relationship, first measured and identified by Herbert McClosky in 1956, reasserted itself in 1976. Indeed, by 1980, Democratic delegates were about as close to Republican identifiers as Republican delegates were.[126]

What accounts for the greater distance between Republican activists and voters in 1980 compared to 1972? The least conservative activists and hence those closest to the rank and file tended to drop out. The activists who replaced them were more conservative. And those who remained active from 1972 onward themselves became progressively more conservative.[127] While there were few changes in delegate selection rules among Republicans, except, of course, those driven by state legislation forcing them to imitate Democrats, there were apparently profound internal changes among the population of delegates.

Had the 1980 delegates supporting George Bush constituted a majority at the Republican National Convention, the delegates as a whole would have been far more moderate and therefore closer to Republican voters. Since ordinary voters of both parties are centrist, the more conservative the Republican delegates and the more liberal the Democrats, the further each gets from the bulk of their voters. Among Democrats, 1980 delegates supporting Senator Edward Kennedy were furthest from the party's citizen supporters but not nearly so far as the Reaganites were from rank-and-file Republicans.[128]

Pundits and party ideologists like to talk about massive swings of public opinion to the right and left. Yet endless surveys suggest modest changes at most in mass opinion. Hidden within that mass, however, may be larger movements to the left or right among those who identify more strongly with the major parties. Elite opinion is evidently more volatile, exaggerating much smaller changes among the voting public.

Studies of delegate issue preferences and preferred spending allocations by the University of Michigan Center for Political Studies, from 1984 data, reveal that the parties remained polarized (Table 3.6, Table 3.7). The only issues on which there was consensus between the parties were spending less on foreign aid and more support for science and fighting crime. Every of the issue—domestic policy, defense policy, foreign policy, the environment, prayer, abortion, even social security, which for years was uncontested between the parties—reveals large differences.[129]

The Center analysts concluded, moreover, that there was "a deep schism among Republican delegates, much deeper than those which separated the policy preferences of supporters of the major Democratic candidates." On only one issue, busing, which was declining in saliency,

TABLE 3.6   *Policy Preferences Among National Convention Delegates, 1984*

	Democrats	Republicans
Environmental Regulation		
Relax	14%	65%
Middle	13	19
Tighten	73	16
Abortion		
Never forbidden	53	23
Permitted if woman would would have difficulty caring for the child	23	19
Permitted only if life and health in danger	21	51
Never permitted	3	8
Equal Rights Amendment		
Approve	90	28
Disapprove	10	72
Prayer in Schools		
Allowed	15	56
Allowed if silent	19	31
Not allowed	67	14
U.S. in Central America		
Less involved	74	12
Middle	14	17
More involved	13	71
Defense Spending		
Decrease spending	83	16
Middle	12	28
Increase spending	5	56
Detente with USSR		
Try to get along	76	31
Middle	14	20
Big mistake to try hard to get along	10	49
Busing		
Busing to achieve integration	42	4
Middle	17	6
Keep children in neighborhood schools	41	90

Source: Center for Political Studies, Institute for Social Research, "Convention Delegate Study Report to Respondents" (Ann Arbor, 1985), p. 4.

were Democratic delegates more disunited than Republicans. Everywhere else, even on defense spending, Star Wars, prayer in schools, and abortion, on which the Reagan administration had taken a definite stand, Republicans were far more divided than Democrats.[130]

Amidst overwhelming support for the renomination of President Reagan in 1984, Reagan administration policies were far less popular: three-fourths of the delegates preferred stronger environment protection and opposed cuts in social security benefits, and 60 percent opposed a constitutional amendment to ban abortion. Forty percent even opposed higher

TABLE 3.7   *Preferred Budgetary Allocations Among National Convention Delegates, 1984*

	Reduce	*Same*	*Increase*
Crime			
Republicans	8%	40%	52%
Democrats	5	49	46
Education			
Republicans	50	36	14
Democrats	4	19	77
Social Security			
Republicans	29	65	6
Democrats	6	56	37
MX			
Republicans	23	45	32
Democrats	88	11	2
Medicare			
Republicans	38	56	6
Democrats	6	50	44
Science			
Republicans	15	45	40
Democrats	8	41	52
Foreign			
Republicans	73	25	2
Democrats	50	41	9
Minorities			
Republicans	64	43	3
Democrats	14	46	40
Star Wars			
Republicans	14	29	57
Democrats	84	11	4

Source: Center for Political Studies, Institute for Social Research, "Convention Delegate Study: Report to Respondents" (Ann Arbor, 1985), p. 5.

defense spending. Democrats at the 1984 convention did not have anything like this degree or range of disagreement.[131]

A diagnostic issue, both because it raises questions of equality and reveals differences in cohesion within the parties, is the participation of women in politics. Kent Jennings' data testing "agreement that men are better suited emotionally for politics," reveals that in 1972 almost three-quarters of Republican and half of Democratic men delegates agreed (Table 3.8). By 1984, only a fifth of Democratic males thought that women were not as well suited as me compared to two-fifths of Republican males. While the parties had moved in the same egalitarian direction, by 1984 Democratic women were virtually unanimous while only a fifth of the men would subscribe to the old prejudice. Two-fifths of Republican men and one-fifth of the party's female delegates held on to

TABLE 3.8   *Agreement That Men Are Better Suited Emotionally for Politics Among Delegates to National Party Conventions*

	Men	Women
Democrats		
1972	47%[*]	19%
1984	19	4
Republicans		
1972	74	43
1984	42	21

[*]Tau-Correlations between sex and the full range of responses are, for the Democrats, .38 in 1972 and .29 in 1984; for the Republicans, .33 in 1972 and .32 in 1984.

Source: M. Kent Jennings, "Women in Party Politics" (report prepared for the Russell Sage Foundation, Women in the Twentieth Century American Politics Project, January, 1987), p. 57.

this traditional view. This constituted a significant minority of Republicans, while Democrats were far more united.[132]

Three-fourths of Democratic and two-fifths of Republican women delegates felt that they would not have been delegates at all except for affirmative action rules.[133] Among Democratic delegates, women were consistently the most liberal on most issues, especially in their positive appraisal of spending on health and welfare services and their negative view of defense. Though their differences with already liberal Democratic male delegates are not large, Jennings concludes, "they definitely bespeak an element of liberal ideology that serves to alter the ideological cast of the Democratic conventions and, at a further remove, the composition of the party cadres and leaders." Though Republican women are moderately more liberal than the party's male delegates, Democratic women, Jennings says, "are infinitely closer to Democratic men than to Republican women."[134]

Thus party still mattered more than gender in organizing the political preferences of party activists. As Jennings says, "The vast dissimilarities in ideological orientation according to party tend to swamp what modest differences are provided by gender."[135] But the influx of women has added to the Democratic party's liberal stance. Republican women are relatively conservative for women but are nevertheless liberal for Republicans, and so the net effect of their growing participation has somewhat diminished the ideological cohesion among Republican delegates.

A table prepared by Barbara G. Farah (Table 3.9) on the composition of delegates from 1944 to 1984 reveals that the big change over that time lies in a four-and-a-half-fold increase in the participation of women. Much smaller changes involve decreases in delegates with less formal

TABLE 3.9 *Delegate Surveys Forty Years Apart*

| | 1944 | | 1968 | | 1976 | | 1984** | |
	Dem.	Rep.	Dem.	Rep.	Dem.	Rep.	Dem.	Rep.
By sex								
Men	89%	91%	87%	83%	67%	69%	49%	54%
Women	11	9	13	17	33	31	51	46
By education								
High school or less	24	23	NA	NA	NA	NA	11	12
Some college	18	18	NA	NA	NA	NA	18	25
College grad	12	16	10	—	21	27	20	28
More than college degree	46	41	44	34	43	38	51	35
Average Age (in years)	52	54	49	49	43	48	44	51
By Occupation								
Lawyer	38	37	28	22	16	15	17	14
Union leader	2	—	4	—	6	—	6	—
Executive	9	10	27	40	17	30	14	26
Other profession/ teacher	24	35	8	2	26	12	36	27
Public official	11	6	13		12	9	9	6
Housewife	6	5	*	*	7	15	4	13
Never Attended Convention Before	63	63	67	66	80	78	74	69
By Ideology								
Liberal	*	*	*	*	40	3	50	1
Moderate	*	*	*	*	47	45	42	35
Conservative	*	*	*	*	8	48	5	60

*Questions not asked in these years. **1984 figures are a combination of the CBS News poll, the *New York Times* poll, and the *Los Angeles times* poll; the 1968 and 1976 figures come from the CBS News poll. The occupation categories are not exactly the same for the 1944 study and the later polls. That will explain the discrepancy between "executive" in the early year and the later ones.

Source: Barbara G. Farah, "Delegate Polls: 1944 to 1984," *Public Opinion* 7 (August/September, 1984), p. 44. Reprinted with permission of American Enterprise Institute for Public Policy Research.

education, lawyers, and public officials. The categories of executive and teacher, where there have been considerable changes, deserve further examination.[136]

From 1972 to 1976, a good half of female Democratic delegates were employed in the public sector, either in government itself or in public education. This was also true of a little over a third of Democratic male delegates. Among Republicans, somewhat more than a third of female and just under a fifth of male delegates were some sort of government employee. Over a quarter of all delegates were union members, most of them from teachers' and other public sector unions. For women in particular, then, Jennings concludes, "Public employment is a key route to the avenues of party power."[137]

As the traditional party of government, it is to be expected that Democratic delegates would come more heavily from the public sector. This may also explain why they seek higher spending on domestic programs. But there is nothing inherent in public sector employment that would necessarily lead to a preference for lower spending on defense, or against military intervention in Central America, or for liberal positions on social issues. For that we must look to an ideological explanation. Jo Freeman conjectures that

> [t]he 1984 conventions solidified the direction in which both parties had been moving for the previous ten years. The Democrats adopted the feminist perspective on all public issues directly affecting women and made it clear that women, under feminist leadership, were an important part of the Democratic coalition. The Republican party adopted antifeminist positions on almost every issue. Its public script was written by Phyllis Schlafly. But it didn't repudiate women; instead it affirmed their importance by showcasing them extensively and devoting more real resources to help women, as individuals, get elected, than the Democratic Party has done.[138]

What happens when party and ideology conflict? A "requirement of participating in the mainstream of the party," Freeman says, "is that one not become an electoral liability. NOW (National Organization of Women) demonstrated its awareness of this rule by endorsing Democratic men running against Republican feminist women, arguing that anyone who supports Reagan's economic program, and . . . doesn't support pro-choice [on the abortion issue], is not really a feminist."[139]

Evidence from representative governments throughout the world demonstrates that voters have more moderate views than elected officials who in turn are more moderate than party activists.[140] In 1984 there was poll evidence sustaining this view, showing Democratic voters to be slightly and delegates vastly more liberal than the average of the general population, except on national health care. Moreover, Democratic delegates grew more liberal from 1980 to 1984.[141] While the general public prefers smaller government and lower taxes far more than do Democratic elites, the public also likes welfare and health spending a lot more than Republican elites do. We conclude that when party elites talk about the great issues that separate them, they are not talking about the public, which is much more moderate, but about themselves.

With the increase of ideological consistency among activists in the major parties has come a decline in their party loyalty. While Republican delegates have consistently seen themselves as stronger party supporters than have Democrats, delegates from both parties (with the exception of

TABLE 3.10   *Delegates to the Left of Rank and File and Public, 1984*
Our polling of the Democratic delegates in San Francisco showed they were philosoph-
ically to the left of most Americans and most Democrats especially on some key issues
like the budget and military involvement abroad.

Here's how the delegates measured up against the Democratic rank and file and the public
at large on some of these issues.

	Public	Democrats	Delegates
Ratify ERA			
Blacks are long way from the same chance as whites	55	63	85
CIA should help friendly governments and undermine hostile governments	40	36	14
Reinstitute the draft	49	51	26
U.S. should take all steps including force to stop communism	63	59	22
Government should raise taxes to deal with deficit	23	22	53
U.S. can meet security obligations with smaller military budget	49	59	85

However, our polling showed some issues on which the delegates, their fellow Democrats
and the general public agree.

	Public	Democrats	Delegates
Government should stop building nuclear power plants for safety reasons	56	64	65
Government should institute national health care program	71	81	70

Numbers are percentage in agreement.

Source: Peter Begans, ''The ABC News/*Washington Post* Poll.'' survey #'s 0122–0125, p. 4.

TABLE 3.11   *Positions Taken by the 1984 Delegates Compared to Predecessors in 1980*

	1984	1980
Ratify ERA	91	86
Blacks are long way from having some chance as whites	85	79
CIA should help friendly governments and undermine hostile governments	14	30
Reinstitute draft	26	39
Government should stop building nuclear power plants for safety reasons	65	48
Governments should institute a national health care program	70	65

Numbers are percentage in agreement.

Source: Peter Begans, ''The ABC News/*Washington Post* Poll,'' survey #'s 0122–0125, p. 4.

the 1976 Democratic convention when there were moderate Carter delegates) show a steady decline in strong party support.[142]

Asked to say who they represented at the convention—the party organizations, a candidate support group, an interest group, or voters—Democrats from 1972 to 1984 overwhelmingly went with their favorite candidates. Their support for party never went above 25 percent. Their adherence to special groups has grown in recent years to 22 percent, double that of Republicans.[143]

The best 1984 data on the ideology of party activists compared to rank-and-file partisans, comparable to earlier (1972 to 1980) studies, shows that Democratic and Republican rank-and-file voters are identifiably apart on issues and reference groups, and that activists differ much more than nonactivists (see Table 3.12).[144] Where the rank and file are 32 points apart on the scoring system used by Warren Miller, whose findings these are, party activists are 108 points apart, over three times further away.

Between 1980 and 1984, whether one refers to ideological self-designation or issue position (busing and blacks remaining exceptions), both rank-and-file and activist Democrats became more liberal, the activists, as usual, in a more pronounced way. Particularly interesting is the very large movement toward opposition to defense spending.

Even more fascinating is the checkered position of Republicans. Overall, activists moved in a slightly more liberal direction, while the rank and

TABLE 3.12   *Ideology and Policy Preferences, 1984, for Partisan Activists and Rank-And-File Party Followers*

| | Democratic Party | | Republican Party | |
	Activists	Rank and File	Rank and File	Activists
Ideological Self Designation	64*	12[12]	−40*	−84*
Abortion	57	20	10	−28
Moral Majority**	94	15	−1	−2
Aid to Women	65	21	−11	−45
Women's Movement**	73	49	−26	−53
Blacks**	76	54	45	−1
Busing	4	−61	−80	−83
Defense	84	16	−27	−42
Detente	69	9	−26	−16
Central America	65	33	9	−66
Average	+65	+17	−15	−43

Minus means more conservative and plus more liberal.

Source: Warren E. Miller, Blazer Lecture on "Ideology and Polarity in American Politics," March 9, 1987, University of Kentucky, Lexington.

TABLE 3.13   *Changes in Ideology and Policy Preferences, 1980 to 1984, Party Activists and Rank-and-File Party Followers*

| | Democratic Party | | Republican Party | |
	Activists	Rank and File	Rank and File	Activists
Ideology	+11	+6	+2*	+1*
Abortion	+19	+11	−4	−8
Moral Majority	+7	+1	−1	+13
Women's Movement	+27	+16	−29	+13
Blacks	+1	−8	0	−19
Busing	+12	−3	+5	+3
Defense	+74	+58	+10	+32
Detente	+25	+2	−21	+22
Average	+22	+12	−5	+7

Entries reflect percentage point changes in group means between 1980 and 1984. A plus indicates a net shift in the liberal direction; a minus indicates a shift in the conservative direction.

Source: Warren E. Miller, *Without Consent: Mass-Elite Linkages in Presidential Politics* (Lexington, Ky., 1988), p. 17.

file became marginally more conservative. As the activists began the period far more conservative than the rank and file, these movements brought the two groups closer together.

In summary, trends in the ideological dispositions of party activists in the two parties seem to reflect changes in the composition of the two delegate populations. Notably, Republican delegates include more women and more ex-Dixiecrats; Democratic delegates also include more women and fewer conservative southerners. Thus Democratic delegates are becoming somewhat more liberal, and Republicans more mixed and less cohesive. Similar trends can be observed in the Democratic caucus of the House of Representatives, where the subtraction of a large number of Dixiecrat seats over the last twenty years has led to the emergence of liberal mainstream sentiment expressed through caucus action.

In her report on the 1988 Democratic convention, Jo Freeman observes that ''. . . to a greater extent than ever thought possible, when contemporary feminists first made demands at the 1972 convention, women [had become] insiders.''[145] Women held a large number of top positions, including Dukakis' campaign manager, Susan Estrich. Women had become so strong that in 1984 Walter Mondale sought an early endorsement from the National Organization for Women ''. . . and ceded 'sign-off' authority in all platform language concerning women to Mary Jean Collins, NOW's Action Vice President that year.''[146] In 1988 a number of different people performed the same function. A hitch developed because of the desire of Paul Kirk, Jr., and many others in the Democratic National Committee, to avoid the old style platforms with their endless lists of promises, which they believed would only spur charges of overspending and overpromising, in favor of a short and general statement. In the end, after many meetings, the women got what they wanted, though not all in the same section. So the platform speaks of ''the fundamental right of reproductive choice,'' ''equal access to governmental services. . . ,'' ''pay equity for working women'' and ''family leave policies that no longer force employees to choose between their jobs and their children or ailing parents.'' There are three mentions of child care.[147] When representatives of feminist groups met with the drafting committee to get their preferences into the document, Irene Natividad of the National Women's Political Caucus remarked that ''a lot of the major players were our folk.''[148]

Feminists had a lot less to do with the Republican platform. There was no chance of them getting abortion rights into the platform, but they were successful in getting the Republican party for the first time to adopt a plank endorsing support for child care. Republicans were interested in protecting women. Thus they cited statistics on the growth of mothers in the labor force. The most interesting exchange occurred when a Republican feminist proposed that "the Republican party strongly support the efforts of women to achieve parity in government, and is committed to the vigorous recruitment, training and funding of women candidates at all levels." This caught the Bush people by surprise. Who could be against having women as candidates? But funding was another matter. So "funding" was replaced with "campaign support."[149]

In the 1930s, Republican party values were highly individualistic, favoring both less domestic and less foreign involvement by the government. The struggle within the Republican party to nominate Dwight Eisenhower was an explicit attempt from within to change these values, a fight between the Main Street and the Wall Street factions of the party. During the Eisenhower presidency the Republican party came to a grudging acceptance of social security and related measures and a more active stance in the international arena. Making the Republican party safe for internationalism was Eisenhower's central goal in office. Thus Republican disputes with Democrats from the 1960s onward were largely confined to domestic issues (bigger versus smaller government). The Republican party today is a coalition of economic libertarians and social conservatives. The GOP has always had a traditional belief in the importance of social order. Integral to this view was a belief that there are inherent differences among people that justified their taking on different roles in society. Recently the Republicans have received an influx of fundamentalist Christians—mainly southern—who have a patriarchal conception of desirable social differences, with a corresponding belief that there are large moral differences between right and wrong. The politicization of these fundamentalists occurred, at least in part, because of court decisions prohibiting prayer and permitting government funding of abortions, conditions that had not existed prior to the 1960s and 1970s.[150]

On social issues, the Republican party's free enterprisers have not been happy with their party's opposition to abortion or its advocacy of prayer in schools. Economic conservatives frequently believe that defense spending is too high. The party's growing number of female activists, while generally opposed to abortion, have been less opposed than Republican men.

As for the party's social conservatives, their emphasis on family, order, and obedience to a strict moral code has led them to dislike government intervention in economic affairs that they believe individuals should handle for themselves or within their community. Believing in hierarchical principles, however, they are somewhat more disposed than free marketers to approve of social welfare, especially medical programs.

Thus although Republican activists remain far more socially homogenous than are their Democratic peers, ideological differences among active Republicans have increased. The great contemporary divide between the parties is over whether opportunity (Republicans) or more equal outcomes (Democrats) should be the guiding norm for American public policy.

Now we can guess why in the midst of a considerable change in policy preferences, wholesale party realignment fails to appear: the major parties have realigned themselves internally. This is most evident in the South as newcomers and young voters have become increasingly Republican.[151] There is also considerable movement in and out of each party, thus facilitating their greater homogeneity. Whether and to what degree the electorate supports the new directions of the parties remains to be seen; we will appraise the evidence in the next chapter. But the older view that the major parties were essentially alike, which was never true, is even less true today.

The consequences of ideological polarization, which is what we have been describing, are well-known: heightened conflict and perhaps political instability. According to the theory of crosscutting cleavages, when people agree on some issues and disagree on others the need to call upon each other for support moderates the severity of conflict. Polarization, by putting the same people in opposition on issue after issue, increases antagonism.

The Conventions

By the time of the nominating convention, most delegates are pledged and a probable winner has emerged. The convention merely ratifies the result. Sometimes there is a little suspense if the numbers are close, as the Republicans demonstrated in 1976 with Ronald Reagan's down-to-the-wire battle with President Ford. And so it is still worthwhile to explore what happens in the increasingly rare instances of contested conventions where decisions are actually made. Under these circumstances, there is uncertainty at the time of the convention about who will be the nominee. In an uncertain convention, delegates crave information on what is going to happen and when. For some of them, of course, the convention is a spectator sport, since they will be acting under instructions from the voters in their state primary or from their state party leaders. Even so, they will want to know who is ahead and who is behind and what the chances are of majority agreement on one of the leading candidates. Rumors are rife because no one has been able to establish an unshakable claim of victory, because it is to the advantage of more than one aspirant to be thought to be winning, and because people like to speculate. In the grip of uncertainty, the delegates grasp for any objective information that may be gleaned from the events of the convention itself.[152]

Before the balloting on the candidates begins at the convention, there often are votes on the seating of contested delegations, a plank in the platform, or some rule governing convention life (such as a loyalty pledge), or there is conflict over who is to be permanent chairman. If some of the candidates become identified with one or the other side on these preliminary votes, the results may be considered a test of who is likely to win the nomination. Thus, candidates who choose sides may prejudice their chances of nomination. They must calculate the effects of the loss of such a vote. In 1932, Franklin Roosevelt nearly lost his bid for the nomination by coming out against the two-thirds rule then required for nomination. Fortunately, FDR's supporters at the convention discovered that the opposition to the change in rules was greater than the opposition to FDR, and he beat a hasty retreat from his previous position.[153]

In the 1952 Democratic convention, the issue was the seating of the Virginia delegation. Adlai Stevenson's patron, Colonel Jack Arvey of Illinois, describes the strategic problem from his perspective:

Cook County Chairman Joe Gill and I were having dinner . . . when one of our ward committeemen came running over to tell us an important roll call vote was under way on the seating of Virginia. . . . Gill and I hurried back into the hall. Illinois had already been recorded 45–15 against seating Virginia. It suddenly dawned on us what was happening. The strategy of the Kefauver backers and the Northern liberal bloc was to try and make impossible demands on the Southern delegates so that they would walk out of the Convention. If the total convention vote was thus cut down by the walkout of delegates who would never vote for Kefauver, then the Tennessee Senator would have a better chance of winning the nomination. Our Illinois delegation quickly huddled and then changed our vote to 52–8 in favor of seating Virginia.

The eight opposed included Senator Douglas and other backers of Kefauver.[154]

In 1976, in a last-ditch effort to stave off a narrow defeat for the nomination, Ronald Reagan named a moderate Republican senator, Richard Schweiker of Pennsylvania, as the man he would pick as his running mate if he were to be nominated. Reagan forces attempted to change the rules so as to compel President Ford to disclose his vice-presidential choice in advance. They failed to do so, signaling to everyone that Ford had enough votes to win.[155]

A challenge to the seating of delegates (i.e., whether they were properly selected and might take their seats and vote at the convention) might also tell the story. Eisenhower's victory in 1952 was signaled by challenges to Taft delegates, and McGovern showed he would win in 1972 by beating Humphrey's forces on the seating of the winner-take-all California delegation. The decision of the credentials committee to allow contested delegates from California, who intended to support McGovern, to vote on the challenge was an early and significant sign. At the Democratic convention of 1980, the Carter forces beat back an attempt instigated chiefly by Kennedy supporters to change the rules so as not to require delegates to vote for the candidates to whom they had been pledged. Since a majority of the delegates were already pledged to Carter, Kennedy's only hope was to give them room to change their minds. As soon as this effort failed, Kennedy withdrew his candidacy altogether.

Many of the same strategic considerations hold in relation to conflicts that may develop over the permanent chairman. This struggle may be important because the chairman has significant procedural powers at the convention. He can speed up adjournment to give a particular candidate time to make bargains, or he can harm another's chances by refusing to recognize a state delegation about to go over to that candidate at a crucial moment. The importance of being chairman was demonstrated by the senior Senator Henry Cabot Lodge at the 1920 Republican convention, when he wanted to permit party leaders to find a way out of an impasse that had developed. Shortly after the fourth ballot, Senator Reed Smoot of Utah moved to adjourn the proceedings. A resounding "no" echoed throughout the auditorium as Lodge put the motion to a vote and immediately declared the convention adjourned.[156] Twenty years later, at another Republican convention, Senator John Bricker of Ohio asked Chairman Joseph Martin for a recess before the sixth ballot; this would have given the Taft and Dewey forces time to make a deal. Partial to the Willkie cause, however, Martin refused the request and the balloting continued, ending with victory for Willkie.[157] A similar situation developed at the 1976 Republican convention when the Ford forces gaveled through a voice vote on the foreign policy plank instead of risking a roll call that might have shown less strength than was desirable for their candidate.

Unless victory appears assured, it may be unwise for a candidate to challenge. An alternate strategy is to accept an unfavorable chairman but to put forth a stream of publicity stressing the chairman's partiality, so that he feels under continuous scrutiny and may bend over backward to avoid charges of favoritism. Nowadays, however, the usual practice is for representatives of the leading candidates to agree upon major personnel of the convention—keynote speaker, permanent chairman, platform committee chairman, credentials committee chairman—well ahead of the convention itself. If they do not, the outcome of the ensuing struggle over the chairmanship becomes a signal of the strength of the contenders, depending on whether the person they favor gets the position.

Virtually any action can take on added significance if it reveals information hitherto unavailable to all. In the 1932 Democratic convention a vote on seating a contested delegation was taken under conditions that freed many delegates from the unit rule which required state delegations to vote together as a block. This revealed which delegations were closely divided, information that imposition of the unit rule had helped to hide.[158]

While candidates are being nominated, and during the balloting, demonstrations—which are largely prearranged—take place on the floor. These raucous displays are meant to let everyone know that a candidate has many loyal supporters. A demonstration at a crucial moment, it is hoped, might ignite the spark of enthusiasm among the multitude of uncertain delegates. But, as supporters of Adlai Stevenson learned in 1960, this can work only when delegates are really uncertain and uncommitted. Nowadays, because delegates are completely committed, demonstrations serve to show enthusiasm for the benefit of the television audience.

Currently, the convention is more than anything else an opportunity for the nominee to garner a little favorable advertising, and events of the convention are now orchestrated for that purpose. First and foremost, therefore, the candidate wants a united party.[159] Party leaders who are in a position to disrupt unity may extort small advantages from the nominee, a significant strategic resource in recent years of Jesse Jackson's candidacy.

As Jackson approached the Democratic convention of 1988, he made speeches demanding a greater role in the party, threatening a floor fight over the party platform, "and renewed his threat to challenge Bentsen's [vice-presidential] nomination."[160] Dukakis's backers voted down Jackson's platform proposals. These would have raised taxes to much higher levels, frozen military spending, tilted more to the Palestinian side in their conflict with Israel, and pledged the United States not to be the first to use nuclear weapons. In return, Jackson temporarily won changes in Democratic party rules, cutting the number of super-delegates nearly in half and requiring that all delegates be awarded to candidates on a proportional rather than a winner-take-all basis. All along, Jackson's complaint had been that it was undemocratic for him to have fewer delegates than votes as a proportion of the whole convention.[161] In order to preserve the peace, Dukakis gave in on the procedural issues, just as Humphrey gave in to McCarthy delegates in 1968 and granted them the formation of what became the McGovern Commission.[162]

The Balloting

Politicians who wish power in government try to contribute to the majority essential for the nomination of the candidate they believe will be the winner. Given the front-loading of the nominating contest, this means guessing a year or more ahead of the conventions who will win in the caucuses and primaries or, if their candidate drops out during the prenomination phase, switching to the front runner. In the days when decisions were made at conventions or at any time when uncertainty exists about the outcome, there is a strategic rationale for the bandwagon behavior that has been seen in operation at many conventions. When delegates believe that one presidential aspirant is certain of nomination, they will attempt to go on record as voting for that aspirant as quickly as possible. Delegates committed to a favorite son candidate will trade their votes for access (or what they hope will be access) to the candidate they think most likely to win nomination. Note the differences in these two statements. In the first, delegates know which candidate will win and hope to earn his gratitude by voting for him. In the corollary, delegates are less certain of the outcome, hence their commitment to an aspirant is more costly for that aspirant in terms of future favors. The prospective candidate, in these circumstances, often makes promises to delegates of future access in return for their support.

At a contested convention, aspirants, who lead in votes for the nomination must actually win the nomination by a certain time or else their chances of eventually winning decline precipitously, even though they remain temporarily in the lead. This is true when delegate support is given to candidates in anticipation of victory. When this victory does not materialize quickly, delegates may question their initial judgment. Thus, the longer candidates remain in the lead without starting a bandwagon, the greater the possibility that their supporters will vote for someone else. In order to maximize future access, delegates prefer to support the eventual winner before he achieves a majority. They therefore are guided by what they expect other delegates to do and are constantly on the alert to change their expectations to conform to the latest information. This information may be nothing more substantial than a rumor, which quickly takes on the status of self-fulfilling prophecy as delegates stampede in response to expectations, quickly realized, about how other delegates will respond. The strategies that a candidate in a multiballot convention adopts depend, therefore, not only on showing that he or she can win, but also on the candidate's position in the convention. A candidate who can keep gaining support, no matter how slightly, is still in contention, because it is assumed that he may have more strength in reserve. But the front runner who begins to manifest any decline, or even in some cases a leveling off in votes, on successive ballots can expect uncommitted delegates to conclude that he has shot his bolt and begin to shift their support to more promising prospects.

Considered as a source of information, the balloting indicates whether a candidate is gaining or falling behind. One strategy sometimes used in this connection is to "hide" a few votes on early ballots by giving them to others and reclaiming them little by little to show a steady increase.[163] Or a candidate may decide to bide his time and delay making his bid. In that case a weak initial total of votes is not likely to be commented upon because the front runner occupies the center of attention. Later, a dark horse may occasion surprise by a rapid climb and may hope that most delegates will decide to hitch their wagons to a rising star.

The importance of indicators of uncertainty in contested conventions has been studied empirically. Eugene B. McGregor, Jr., shows that "the candidate making the largest gain from the first to the second ballot went on to win the nomination . . . in eight . . . out of the ten most recent multi-ballot conventions . . . held since 1892. . . ." The exceptions, such as the 103-ballot Democratic convention in 1924, are the result of "extreme ideological divisions" such as between urban, Catholic "wets" (who opposed a constitutional prohibition on alcoholic drinks) versus rural, Protestant "drys" (who favored Prohibition) at that time.[164]

Aspirants sometimes combine their voting strength in the convention in order to prevent a front-running candidate from gaining a majority. They will then try to negotiate the nomination among themselves. Should favorable circumstances for such bargaining arise, it will be interesting to see whether the media and the public find "behind the scenes" decision making acceptable to their modern sensibilities.

If the front runner's anticipated victory promises other aspirants insufficient access, they may defeat him by preventing a bandwagon in his favor. An apparently successful case of combining against the front runner occurred in 1920 when Harry Daugherty, Harding's manager, realizing that General Leonard Wood had to be defeated to give Harding a chance, offered to lend Illinois Governor Frank Lowden every vote he could spare until the governor passed Wood in the balloting. Then the alliance would be terminated. "Certainly you couldn't make a fairer proposition," Lowden responded, and the agreement was consummated.[165] The good old days of "lending" votes may be no more, however, because under the primary rules governing the obligations of delegates, candidates may be unable to exercise this kind of control over them. Even if delegates are able to switch after a first ballot, they may not be willing to take orders.

Rational aspirants who lead but lack a majority will bargain and promise access to leaders representing the requisite number of votes if they believe that no bandwagon will develop without stimulation. They may offer the vice-presidential nomination to one or more leaders of important states; they may hint at cabinet posts, patronage, or preferred treatment; they may explore concessions on policy. But before they can bargain, candidates must know with whom to bargain. And among those delegations or caucuses that might be swayed, they must find the ones amenable to what they can offer. This promises to be either very difficult or absurdly simple. If almost all delegates are pledged, the remaining few should be easy to find. If there is a multiballot convention, however, and if the delegates released do not give their allegiance to others who can dispose of their votes, many individual delegates will have to be reached. The importance of maintaining an apparatus for obtaining this information was evident in the past. If there is ever a multiballot convention in the future, such an information-gathering capability will become indispensable because there will be so many more "bits" of data to keep in mind, with the proliferations in the number of delegates and the lack of party leaders to organize them.

The bargaining process itself may be an excellent source of information on what delegates are likely to do under a variety of circumstances. Candidate organizations may carry out a series of probing actions to discover what delegates want, what they will take, what they will give in return. Out of the negotiations may emerge the beginnings of a commonly held picture of the shape of events to come.

Bargains may be tacit rather than explicit, made through intermediaries rather than by principals. Exactly what was promised may not be entirely clear or may be distorted later on. The delegate who wishes to collect what he believes to be his due may have trouble securing effective guarantees. Thomas Dewey never quite had the same understanding that Representative Charles Halleck of Indiana did about an offer of the vice-presidency in return for support of the Indiana delegation in the Republican convention of 1948.[166] One delegate to the 1960 Democratic convention told reporters that he was the nineteenth person to be offered the vice-presidency by the Kennedy forces. Under the circumstances, he allowed as how he would take cash.[167] Proffering positions in return for support has declined of late, possibly because contested conventions have also declined. Despite the distaste with which these deals are regarded, they may rise again; in case bargaining is necessary, what else will candidates have to bargain with?

It is possible that much less material reward for support comes out of the convention than is commonly supposed. An incoming president, for example, may well decide to handle patronage through the dominant party faction that helped him at a convention. Nevertheless, if delegates believe that rewards are likely to follow support, as many apparently do, their actions will conform to his belief. Since politics plays an important part in the lives of many delegates, ability to identify with the nominee may confer an important sense of political involvement (as a Reaganaut or a Kennedyite) that is valued in and of itself.

In the absence of quick agreement at the convention, the demonstrations and adjournments give party leaders, if there are any, time to meet to try to find a candidate who can receive a majority of votes. This is the "smoke-filled room" of convention lore. Its inhabitants try to work out an agreement that will meet their desires, but they are severely limited in their choice by their estimate of what the people will accept at the polls and what the other delegates will stand for. Delegates have independent influence and different interests and there may be only a limited range of agreement among them.

The essential trick is to convince others that one's preferred view of what will happen is the correct one. This is apparently what took place in the 1920 Republican convention, when Harry Daugherty succeeded in convincing party leaders that a deadlock was inevitable and that only Harding could break it. Much the same kind of thing occurred in 1844 when Gideon Pillow and George Bancroft spread the word that Lewis Cass, John C. Calhoun, or Martin Van Buren could not possibly win, but that James Polk would carry the day.[168]

In order to break a deadlock, it is necessary to convince some delegates that the candidate they prefer cannot win and that they would be well advised to switch to one who can. The leaders at the 1920 Republican convention decided to communicate this point convincingly by calling for several additional ballots during which nothing changed.[169] This also helped to assure losing party factions that their candidates had a fair chance. At the 1924 Democratic convention, however, which operated under a two-thirds rule and went to 103 ballots, the lengthy voting apparently did not communicate the hopelessness of their cause to the leading candidates. Not only did incompatibility and intransigence block bargaining, but short-lived booms kept arising, an indication that the delegates shared no common view of future events.[170] The shock to loyal party members was so great that eight years later John Nance Garner chose to submerge his own chances and throw the 1932 convention to Franklin Roosevelt rather than risk another agonizing stalemate.[171]

Most of this is now history; television and primary elections have shortened convention procedures, made demonstrations largely pointless, facilitated internal communications at conventions, and given delegates a lot less to communicate about. But the contrast between brokered conventions, in which candidates and party leaders bargain over the nomination, and ratifying conventions, merely registering a result decided in primaries and state caucuses, is worth keeping in mind, we think, for the purpose of reminding readers that conventions are capable of more than they currently do.

The Vice-Presidential Nominee

When the convention finally selects its presidential candidate, it turns to the anticlimactic task of finding a running mate. Vice-presidential nominees are chosen to help the party achieve the presidency. Party nominees for president and vice-president always appear on the ballot together and are elected together. Since 1804, a vote for one has always been a vote for the other.

The vice-president occupies a post in the legislative branch of the government that is mostly honorific, and his powers and activities in the executive branch are determined by the president.[172] The electoral interdependence of the two offices gives politicians an opportunity to gather votes for the presidency. Therefore, the prescription for "ideal" vice-presidential nominees is the same as for presidential nominees, with two additions: they must possess those desirable qualities the presidential nominee lacks, and they must be acceptable to the presidential nominee.

The vice-presidency is the most frequent position from which presidents of the United States are drawn. Just under a third of our forty-one presidents were at one time vice-presidents. Five were later elected to the presidency in their own right; eight first took office upon the death of a president; and of course Mr. Ford succeeded because of President Nixon's resignation. American history has given us fourteen good reasons— one for each man who succeeded to the presidency—for inquiring into the qualifications of vice-presidents and for examining the criteria by which they are chosen.

The presidential candidate who has firm control over his nomination is in a position to use the vice-presidential slot to help win the election. This is what Abraham Lincoln did in 1864 when he chose a "War Democrat," Andrew Johnson, whom he hoped would add strength to the ticket. In the same way, John F. Kennedy chose Lyndon Johnson to help gather southern votes, especially in Texas, and Richard Nixon chose Henry Cabot Lodge of Massachusetts in 1960 to help offset the Democratic party advantage in the Northeast. In 1964 President Johnson chose an outstanding liberal, Senator Hubert Humphrey, of Minnesota. Johnson's own credentials as a liberal Democrat down through the years were not strong; when Kennedy picked him as vice-president he was opposed on these grounds by many labor leaders and by leaders from several of the most important urban Democratic strongholds.

Recent vice-presidential candidates sometimes have been distinguished politicians who had a great deal to recommend them. But the help the could offer their parties was undoubtedly an important consideration. In choosing Senator Humphrey, President Johnson adhered to the familiar strategy of ticket balancing, as Kennedy had done in choosing him. President Ford, with his midwestern and congressional background, may have had the same thing in mind when he chose a more liberal eastern establishment figure, Nelson Rockefeller, to be his nominee for vice-president; threats from the right wing of the Republican party to his own nomination chances caused him to switch away from Rockefeller by the next convention when he picked Senator Bob Dole. Jimmy Carter, meanwhile, chose a popular senator, Walter Mondale, in part to make up for his own lack of "insider" qualifications. Michael Dukakis did the same thing when he picked Senator Lloyd Bentsen of Texas. And Reagan, more securely tied to the Republican right wing than Ford, leaned toward the moderate side of his own party in picking George Bush.

Spiro Agnew was chosen in 1968 because, with the Democrats badly divided and Nixon assured of the nomination, it was important to find a running mate who was not (at least not then) hated by anyone. Nixon had seen the results of a poll indicating that all of the leading candidates for the vice-presidency would hurt his chances of election more than they would help him. Agnew was little known outside his home state of Maryland, had been a Rockefeller supporter, had defeated a Democratic segregationist in his gubernatorial race, was a member of one of the "new" ethnic groups (Greek-American), and impressed Nixon with his person qualities. At the time of his selection, he was, as he himself said, not exactly a household word. No one suspected that he would later become one—as the first vice-president to resign in return for which he avoided a criminal indictment.[173] Walter Mondale's choice of Representative Geraldine Ferraro did not fit the pattern of ideological ticket balancing; her views were quite similar to his own. Instead it was hoped that the historic choice of a woman on a major party ticket could help exploit the "gender gap" that had emerged in 1980. Far behind in the polls, Mondale may also have been hoping that a bold move would invigorate his campaign. Richard Brookhiser argues that "The best justification for Mondale's audacity, though, was that it was audacious. . . . Prudent losers remain losers. The first woman on a major party ticket might shake things up."[174]

Sometimes a presidential candidate will try to help heal a breach in the party by offering the vice-presidential nomination to a leader of a defeated party faction. Or the presidential candidate may try to improve his relationships with Congress by finding a running mate who has friends there. Humphrey balanced his ticket in 1968 by choosing Senator Edmund Muskie, a quietly eloquent, moderate man, a member of an ethnic group (Polish-Americans) concentrated in the cities of the eastern seaboard, to balance his own midwest populist background and fast-talking style.

A Republican presidential candidate from the East will try to pick a vice-president from the Midwest or Far West. It has been thought desirable, as in the case of Reagan (California) and Bush (Texas) for both to reside in large, two-party "swing" states. With the mode of delegate selection among Democrats biased in favor of one-party states (owing to the abolition of the unit rule and the winner-take-all primary), however, this tendency may no longer prevail. None of the Democratic presidential nominees since the post-1968 rules changes has been from a large state. But a liberal Democrat running for president will frequently try to find a more conservative running mate. If it is impossible to find one person who combines within his or her heritage, personality, and experience all the virtues allegedly cherished by American voters, the parties console themselves by attempting to confect out of two running mates a composite image of forward-looking-conservative, rural-urban, energetic-wise leadership that evokes hometown, ethnic, and party loyalties among a maximum number of voters. That, at least, is the theory behind the balanced ticket.

There have been times when a president has insisted on having his personal choice selected as vice-president. Andrew Jackson was adamant about running with Martin Van Buren and Franklin Roosevelt went so far as to write out a refusal to accept the Democratic nomination in 1940 when party leaders balked at the thought of Henry Wallace. The presidential nominee clearly is expected to have a lot to say about his running mate. More and more in recent years the expectation has been that the presidential candidate personally makes the choice after due consultation with party leaders. Indeed, failure to act decisively may well be regarded now as a sign of weakness. Yet there have been times when presidential candidates have not wished to become involved in internal party battles and have let the convention decide. William Jennings Bryan would not even allow his own Nebraska delegation to signal his preferences by voting on the vice-presidential nomination at the 1896 Democratic convention, and Adlai Stevenson preferred to let Estes Kefauver and John F. Kennedy fight it out for the prize in 1956.

When especially able politicians have appeared in the vice-presidential office from time to time, this may have been more because of the blessings of Providence than because of wise actions on anyone's part. If good results require noble intentions, then the criteria for choosing vice-presidents may leave much to be desired. Why should the great parties, we might ask, not set out deliberately to choose the candidate best able to act as president in case of need? Should ticket balancing and similar considerations be condemned as political chicanery?

In a 1956 speech, former Vice-President Henry A. Wallace declared: "The greatest danger is that the man just nominated for President will try desperately to heal the wounds and placate the dissidents in his party. . . . My battle cry would be—no more deals—no more balancing of the ticket." In 1964, the Republican party evidently also endorsed this view. The selection of the 1964 Republican vice-presidential nominee, Representative William Miller of upstate New York, was intended to violate criteria used in the past for balancing the ticket. Although he came from a region different from Barry Goldwater and, unlike Goldwater, was a Catholic, Miller was chosen primarily because of his ideological affinity with the presidential candidate. The special style of Goldwater and his supporters required that consistency of views, opposition to the other party on as many issues as possible, and refusal to bargain prevail over the traditional political demands for compromise, flexibility, and popularity.[175] This was also apparently the sentiment of many Republicans in 1976. Yet the candidate of the conservatives that year, Ronald Reagan, said he would choose as his running mate a liberal Easterner, Senator Richard Schweiker of Pennsylvania. This was his last-ditch attempt to win the nomination, and it was a gamble he lost. But it was consistent with Mr. Reagan's view four years later, when he said:

> There are some people who think that you should, on principle, jump off the cliff with the flag flying if you can't have everything you want. . . . If I found when I was governor that I could not get 100 percent of what I asked for, I took 80 percent.[176]

From the standpoint of the electoral success of candidates, balancing the ticket seems only prudent. But there are other reasons for ordinary citizens to prefer that candidates make an effort in this direction. One of the chief assets of the American party system in the past has been its ability, with the exception of the Civil War period, to reduce conflict by enforcing compromise within the major factions of each party. A refusal to heal the wounds and placate dissidents is nothing less than a declaration of internal war. It can only lead to increased conflict within the party. Willingness to bargain and make concessions to opponents is part of the price for maintaining unity in a party sufficiently large and varied to be able to appeal successfully to a population divided on economic, sectional, racial, religious, ethnic, and perhaps also ideological grounds. To refuse entirely to balance the ticket would be to risk changing our large, heterogeneous parties into a multiplicity of small sects of "true believers" who care more about maintaining their internal purity than about winning public office by pleasing the people.

There is obvious good sense in providing for a basic continuity in policy in case a president should die or be disabled. But his need not mean that the president and vice-president should be identical in every respect, even if that were possible. Within the broad outlines of agreement on the basic principles of the nation's foreign policy and of the government's role in the economy, for example, a president would have no great difficulty in finding a variety of running mates who appealed to somewhat different groups, or who differed in other salient ways. To go this far to promote party unity, factional conciliation, and popular preference should not discomfort anyone who realizes the costs of failing to balance the ticket.

Actually there is little evidence to suggest that vice-presidents add greatly to or detract severely from the popularity of presidential candidates with the voters. By helping unite the party, however, and by giving diverse party leaders another focus of identification with the ticket, a vice-presidential nominee with the right characteristics can help assure greater effort by party workers, and this may bring results at election time. Even if balancing the ticket does not help the party at the polls, it may indirectly help the people. It may aid our political parties to maintain unity within diversity and thereby to perform their historic function of bringing our varied population closer together.

Why, then, did George Bush pick Senator Dan Quayle as his running-mate? We suggest that such a choice was well within the traditions of the American vice-presidential selection process, and that Quayle had some assets and lacked some liabilities that Bush may have been more aware of than others who observed the process closely.

For example, Vice-President Bush had reason to believe Quayle would not alienate Republican voters, or activists. His record as a regular Republican in the House and Senate was comforting. So were his views on abortion, which tracked with the dominant Republican pro-life position. He had recently won an election in Indiana by an impressive margin, and two leaders of the Bush entourage, Robert Teeter and Roger Ailes, reported favorably on his campaign. The Vice-President may also have been seeking a running mate who would not openly second-guess him, as Robert Dole and Jack Kemp almost certainly would have done.

Considerations such as these have frequently led to vice-presidents who were clearly not their party's second best choice for the presidency. Spiro Agnew, Henry Wallace, and the thirty-eight-year-old Richard Nixon were none of them weighty figures in their respective parties at the time they were picked to be vice-presidential candidates. The choice of Dan Quayle thus very much followed a well-worn American pattern.[177]

The Future of National Conventions

One of the lessons of recent presidential elections is that national conventions are declining in importance as decision-making bodies.[178] They are not now taken seriously as decision-making instruments of the party of an incumbent president. The turnover of delegates from convention to convention is very high, averaging about 80 percent.[179] This suggests that large numbers of delegates are recruited by national candidates rather than by local parties. The successes of out-party nominees from John Kennedy in 1960 through Ronald Reagan in 1980, as well as the post-1968 changes in the rules of the Democratic party, make it increasingly necessary for delegate commitments to be made earlier and earlier in the nomination process, even when the nomination of the party out of office is being contested among several factions.[180] State party leaders are no longer a significant part of the process except as delegates allied to candidates.

The large number of first-ballot nominations in recent years shows that important things are happening in the out-party before the convention meets. Nationwide television coverage of the primaries gives early candidates a head start on the free publicity of the election year. Private polls (as well as those published in the newspapers) put more information about the comparative popularity of candidates in the hands of party leaders earlier than before, and the fact that there are so many polls from so many sources gives these polls, if they agree, greater credence. The proliferation of primaries sends national candidates into more and more states in search of committed delegates. The pressure is great upon state party leaders to choose up sides early in the election year—before national publicity creates a rush of sentiment in one direction or another that takes matters wholly out of their hands. Those early decisions must, perforce, take place at widely separate places on the map. This enhances the bargaining power of candidates who can deal with party leaders piecemeal under these circumstances, rather than having to face them en

TABLE 3.14   *Number of Presidential Ballots in National Party Conventions,*
1928–1988

Year	Democrats	Republicans
1928	1	1
1932	4	(1)
1936	(1)	1
1940	(1)	8
1944	(1)	1
1948	(1)	3
1952	3	1
1956	1	(1)
1960	1	1
1964	(1)	1
1968	1	1
1972	1	(1)
1976	1	(1)
1980	(1)	1
1984	1	(1)
1988	1	1

First-ballot total   14/16   14/16
                          (6 incumbents)   (5 incumbents)
Combined (Democrats and Republicans) first-ballot nominations:
Nonincumbents   17/21
Incumbents   11/11

Nominations won by incumbents are in parentheses.

masse at a convention, where they once had an opportunity to wheel and deal with one another.

As mass media increase their saturation coverage of early events in the election year, and as early primary elections become more and more important, successful candidates (at least of the party out of office) increasingly must have access to large sums of money, a large personal organization, and an extra measure of skill and attractiveness on the hustings and over television. In these circumstances, other resources—such as the high regard of party leaders—are less important. Thus, early candidacy, opulent private financing (preferably gathered by a mail campaign that pulls in small contributions fully matchable by the federal subsidy), good, early personal publicity, and strong personal organizations, such as characterized the Kennedy, Goldwater, Nixon, McGovern, Carter, Reagan, and Dukakis preconvention campaigns, can overcome strong misgivings on the part of party leaders, who in any event control fewer and fewer votes at the convention.

There are a few countervailing tendencies. The existence of proportional and districting rules in Democratic party primaries plus the federal financial incentives that entice candidates of middling promise into the race were designed, in part, to decrease the probability that one candidate would have a clear majority before the convention. A bare victory in the last big primary that produced a bumper crop of delegates under a winner-take-all rule, like the one in California that carried McGovern in, became impossible after the winner-take-all rule was abolished. Jimmy Carter won his great victory at the 1976 convention with only a little more than one-third of the delegates pledged to him. It may be that, current history to the contrary notwithstanding, at some future time one-third or so will not be enough to stampede a convention.

The same trends that might at some time make it harder to win decisively before the convention also would make bargaining difficult once there. Proportional and district primaries give the advantage to the more extreme candidates because they place a premium on the intense commitments of candidate enthusiasts; so does the weakness of party organization and the proclivity of educated activists with time on their hands to be stylistically purist and ideologically distant from voters. In part this problem may have been mitigated by the 1982 decision of the Democrats to admit public officeholders to the convention as unpledged delegates. Over 15 percent of the 1992 convention will be constituted in this fashion.

A healthy political party requires activists as well as voters. So long as the policy preferences and group identifications of these two populations are reasonably compatible, their differing interests can be reconciled by bargaining. Once they grow far apart, however, the tension between them may become unbearable until one or another leaves their ancestral party. In Europe this tension frequently takes the form of a clash between the militant party activists and the more moderate parliamentarians interested in winning elections. Since it is the parliamentarians who elect the party leaders in parliament, including the prime minister, they have real resources with which to combat the militants. The separate elections of senators and congressmen and the federal system in the United States, however, take the presidential nomination outside of normal politics. Congressional and gubernatorial candidates rarely run on as radical or conservative a basis as the rhetoric of their activist supporters might suggest, and they participate less than they used to in picking the presidential nominee. Thus, these elected officials have much less of a stake in the presidency. On the Democratic side the party leaders who used to guard that stake were so weak or absent during the conventions after 1968 that the Democratic Hunt Commission of 1982 provided for a large number of members of Congress to be welcomed as unpledged delegates.

What is remarkable, when one thinks of it, is that special arrangements should have to be made to bring party officeholders back into the conventions or to allow the people who probably know most about the candidates to support whomever they think best. Leaving the politicians who have to appeal to the electorate out of the process, we think, is a poor way to choose candidates for the greatest national office.

Bringing into the convention a bloc of uncommitted ''super-delegates'' from officeholders and public officials might appear on the surface to reflect a desire to give the convention greater discretion in choosing a candidate. Not so: evidently the chairman of the Democratic National Committee and others wanted to assure a consensus behind a candidate well before the convention meets. The chairman's concern was that the nominating decision would not ''be taken away from the millions who do participate in our primaries and caucuses and be given to a few in the 'back rooms' of a brokered convention.''[181]

In 1984 the ''super-delegates'' went early and massively for Mondale. Jesse Jackson and Gary Hart supporters, as part of their price for uniting behind Mondale, got agreement that the Democratic National Committee would appoint these super-delegates later in the 1988 process, after the caucuses and primaries were over.[182] Would placing politicians at the national conventions in this fashion lead to different convention choices?

There would have to be differences in candidate preference between these politicians and the other delegates. And the other delegates, pledged to various aspiring candidates, would themselves have to be split, since if they were united, they would have more than enough for a majority.[183]

Just as the news media have interacted with political forces to produce the ratifying rather than the deciding convention, so the two have combined to give the conventions their electoral meaning. Deprived of their decision-making role, the conventions become the first opportunity for campaign publicity with the party united behind a single candidate. Not having to worry about winning the nomination at the convention itself, candidates can more carefully consider how they want to manage the presentation of their party for advertising purposes. Asked to appraise the importance of national conventions, we would have to say that they have changed from being the big guns of the nominating process to the first shots of the election campaign.

Now the candidates may want their delegates to look presentable to television viewers, but they are not in a position to do much about it. They can, as we have seen, assure the presence of delegates pledged to them, making sure the delegates do their duty by voting for them. So far, from the candidate's point of view, so good. While the delegates have mostly pledged their votes, however, they have not hocked their souls. As Jimmy Carter discovered in 1980, platform issues were all the more important to delegates by virtue of the fact that they had no other decisions to make. What is more, delegates who have come to a convention to express support for their varied lifestyles can do that simply by being who they are and showing up on television. Black or white, male or female, straight or gay, liberated or conventional, the delegates make a statement about what they stand for simply by being there.

To appear before the public, of course, delegates must get on television. What gets across to the voter is what television journalists choose to put on. Aside from the few obligatory famous names, the usual principles apply—controversy and deviance make better copy than uncomplicated gestures of support. Whatever the delegates appear to be, television accentuates that pattern at its leading edges, stressing differences rather than similarities with the past. Should voters look in and say to themselves and friends and neighbors that these delegates are not "my kind of people," candidates may find that their ability to project a certain image is overwhelmed by contrary notions that voters have gathered for themselves.

4

The Campaign

Once the conventions are over, the two presidential candidates traditionally "relax" for a few weeks until Labor Day, when they ordinarily begin their official campaigning. From that day onward they confront the voters directly, each carrying the banner of his political party. How do the candidates behave? Why do they act the way they do? And what kind of impact do their activities have on the electorate?

For the small minority of people who are party workers, campaigns serve as a signal to get to work. How hard they work depends in part on whether the candidates' political opinions, slogans, personalities, and visits spark their enthusiasm. The workers may "sit on their hands," or they may pursue their generally unrewarding jobs—checking voting lists, mailing campaign flyers, ringing doorbells—with something approaching fervor. They cannot be taken for granted; activating them and imbuing them with purpose and ardor is perhaps the first task of the candidate.

A second task, growing in importance, is generating favorable media coverage. The sheer size of the electorate and the fact that many if not most citizens get their knowledge of politics from television means that it has become the chief intermediary not only between candidates and voters, but also between candidates and party workers.

For the majority of the population, most of whom are normally uninterested in politics, campaigns call attention to the advent of an election. Some excitement may be generated and some diversion (as well as annoyance) provided for those who turn on the TV to find that their favorite program has been preempted by a political speech. The campaign is a great spectacle. Talk about politics increases, and a small percentage of citizens may even become intensely involved as they get caught up in campaign advertising.

For the vast majority of citizens in America, campaigns do not function so much to change minds as to reinforce previous convictions. As the campaign wears on, the underlying party identification of most people rises ever more powerfully to the surface. Republican and Democratic

identifiers are split further apart—polarized—as their increased awareness of party strife emphasizes the things that divide them.[1] (See Table
4.1.)

The Center for Political Studies at the University of Michigan has
found over the years that about three-quarters of those in its sample who
are eligible to vote claimed a party identification; of these, three-fifths
were Democrats. A sizeable shift in party identification occurred during
1984, narrowing considerably the Democratic lead. James Sundquist and
Thomas Cavanaugh describe what occurred:

> From 1950 until the summer of 1984, Gallup polls showed a consistent and
> substantial Democratic advantage over the Republicans in party identifi-
> cation. In the nation as a whole the Democrats always claimed more than
> 40 percent of the electorate, and usually 45 to 48 percent, while Repub-
> lican identification was always below 35 percent and, for the last quarter of
> a century, 29 percent or less. But this longstanding, one-and-one-half-
> party relationship gave way during the fall campaign when all the major
> polling organizations found the GOP nearing parity with the Democrats.
>
> Surprisingly, the movement toward Republicans as measured by suc-
> cessive Gallup polls was not gradual; it took place in a single ten-week
> period. Until then the election and inauguration of Ronald Reagan and the

TABLE 4.1 *Party Identification*

	1972	1974	1976	1978	1980	1982	1984	1986	1988
Strong Democrat	15%	18%	15%	15%	17%	20%	17%	18%	18%
Weak Democrat	26	21	25	24	23	24	20	23	18
Independent Dem-ocrat	11	13	12	14	11	11	11	11	12
Independent	13	15	15	14	13	11	11	12	11
Independent Re-publican	11	9	10	10	10	8	12	11	14
Weak Republican	13	14	14	13	14	14	15	15	14
Strong Republican	10	8	9	8	9	10	12	11	14
Other	1	3	1	3	3	2	2	NA	NA
Total	100	100	100	100	100	100	100	101	101

Question: "Generally speaking, do you usually think of yourself as a Republican, a Democrat, an
Independent or what? Would you call yourself a strong Republican or a not very strong Republican?
Would you call yourself a strong Democrat or a not very strong Democrat? Do you think of yourself
as closer to the Republican Party or to the Democrat party?"
NA: Not available

Sources: J. Merrill Shanks and Warren E. Miller, "Policy Direction and Performance Evaluation:
Complementary Explanations of the Reagan Elections" (paper prepared for delivery at the 1985
Annual Meeting of the American Political Science Association, New Orleans, August 29–September
1, 1985), p. 12; Paul R. Abramson, John H. Aldrich, and David W. Rhode, *Change and Continuity
in the 1988 Elections* (Washington, D.C., 1990), p. 204 based on NES post-1986 and pre-1988
elections surveys.

first three and one-half years of his administration had brought the GOP no accretion of strength above its historical base. . . . Through the first half of 1984, party identification figures still displayed the familiar three-to-two ratio—virtually identical with the pre-Watergate 1972 figures.

But a shift in strength from the Democrats to the Republicans began to appear in late June and continued through Labor Day—essentially the period spanning the two party conventions. . . . Whatever the causes, by early September the partisan balance had shifted to 39 percent Democratic, 35 percent Republican, and 26 percent independent, where it remained essentially unchanged for the rest of the campaign and through the first three months of 1985.[2]

At this point, it is difficult to determine whether this shift will prove long lasting. The Republican surge of 1984 receded in later surveys and the spread between the two parties stabilized at a Democratic advantage of about 10 points. This seemed to suggest the following dynamic: that at least some voters were making up their minds to vote for Ronald Reagan's reelection, and were bringing their party identification into harmony with their presidential choices. For many others, party identification guides presidential selection rather than the other way around. These voters are more Democratic than Republican.[3]

The outstanding strategic problem for Democratic politicians who wish to capitalize on long-standing party habits is to get their adherents to turn out to vote for Democratic candidates. Democrats therefore stress appeals to the faithful. They try to raise in their supporters the old party spirit. One of the major problems, as we reported in Chapter 1, is that most citizens who identify with them are found at the lower end of the socio-economic scale and on that account are less likely to turn out to vote than those with Republican leanings. So the Democrats put on mobilization drives and seek in every way to get as large a turnout as possible. If they are well organized, they scour the lower-income areas. They provide baby-sitters, cars to get the elderly and infirm to the polls, and, occasionally, inducements of a less savory kind to reinforce the party loyalty of the faithful. Whether the neutral campaigns put on by radio, television, and newspapers to stress the civic obligation to vote help the Democrats more than the Republicans depends on whether, in any given locality, there are more Democrats who are unregistered because they are poor and uneducated than Republicans who are unregistered because they have recently moved. Raymond Wolfinger and his colleagues, who have studied the matter closely, conclude that nationwide the partisan advantage is about a wash.[4]

For Republicans involved in presidential nominating politics, the most important fact of life is that their party is the minority party in the United

States. In presidential elections in which considerations of party are foremost, and allowing for the greater propensity of Republicans to turn out to vote, it was plausibly argued in 1960 that the Democrats could expect to win around 53 or 54 percent of the vote.[5] Nowadays it appears that the Republicans have better presidential prospects. The party's share of citizens who actually vote (40 percent in 1980) is considerably greater than the proportion of voters in the eligible general population (34 percent in 1980). The gap the Republicans have had to overcome has diminished since the 1960s, from 20 percent (54 percent Democratic versus 34 percent Republican) to 12 percent (52 percent Democratic to 40 percent Republican) in the 1980s. Additionally, Democratic voters have been much more likely to defect to a Republican candidate than Republicans to defect to Democrats.[6]

In part, this may be a result of the party reforms that have been somewhat more significant in changing the Democratic that the Republican party. From 1952 to 1968, the most recent prereform period, Democratic defections averaged 18 percent. Since the post-1968 reform, while Republican voting defections have remained stable at around 10 percent, Democratic defections have risen by half. (See Table 4.2.)

A further factor is the marginal Republican advantage in the Electoral College. Owing to the fact that Republicans frequently do better in sparsely populated states, it has been estimated that the Democrats need over 52 percent of the total vote to gain a majority in the Electoral

TABLE 4.2 *Party Loyalty in Presidential Elections, 1964–1988*

	Percent of Party Identifiers Voting for Their Party's Presidential Candidate	
	Democrats	*Republicans*
1964	89	73
1968	68	87
1972	58	91
1976	79	85
1980	67	85
1984	73	92
1988	82	91

Except in 1984 independents who say they lean toward a party are included in that party's identifiers. If these partisan independents were excluded, party loyalty would appear a bit lower in most of these presidential elections.

Sources: For 1964–1980, the National Election Studies of the University of Michigan Center for Political Studies, for 1984, the CBS News/*New York Times* poll, reported in the *New York Times* (November 8, 1984). For 1988, Gerald Pomper, "The Presidential Election," in Pomper, ed., *The Election of 1988: Reports and Interpretations* (Chatham, N.Y., 1989), p. 133. Table adapted from Wolfinger, "Dealignment, Realignment, and Mandates in the 1984 Election," in Austin Ranney, ed., *The American Elections of 1984* (Washington, D.C., 1985), p. 281.

College. We conclude that while Republicans have to come from behind, the predisposing factors are sufficiently close so that Republicans have a good chance of winning, and either major party can win a presidential election.

The decline in party identification from something over three-quarters to just above two-thirds of the adult population may lead to questions about its continuing importance. Yet it is doubtful that independent voters are or will soon become the decisive voters in presidential elections. For one thing, about two-thirds of all independents have leanings; scratch an independent and underneath you are likely to find an almost-Republican or a near-Democrat, and those who are left are least likely to turn out. Thus the actual proportion of the vote contributed by "pure" independents, who do not lean toward either party, is no greater now than thirty years ago. This is no mere artifact of the way a survey question is asked; the voting behavior in presidential elections of independents who lean one way or another much more closely resembles that of either Democrats or Republicans than it does other independents.[7] The likelihood of these different sorts of "independent" voters coalescing into a meaningful mass and becoming a cohesive force in national politics is thus remote.[8]

Explaining Party Appeals

Peace and Prosperity?   There are two straightforward ways of explaining victories and defeats in the presidential elections: one is that voters simply express their party preferences. Except for the election of 1984, when some polls reported near equality in the size of the two major parties, this explanation fails to account for Republican victories. The other is that voters are reacting to the condition of the nation. No incumbent since the Second World War has failed to win reelection when the nation was peaceful and prosperous. When there is no war, presidential popularity and per capita national income or unemployment track one another extraordinarily well.[9] (See Figure 4.1.)

The trouble with this current-condition type of explanation is that it usually comes after the fact of the election. But it can be made to sound plausible. In 1964 the nation was at peace, the economy was strong, and the Republicans nominated a candidate, Barry Goldwater, then considered far too conservative for most voters. Lyndon Johnson won by a landslide. By 1968 the war in Vietnam had led to severe protests, especially from within the Democratic party, and inflation was rising. Lyndon Johnson did not run and his successor as a candidate, Hubert Humphrey,

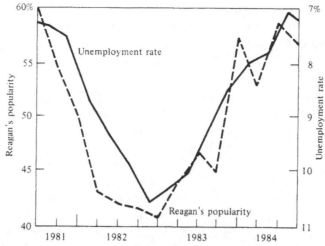

FIGURE 4.1   *Unemployment and Approval of Reagan*
Sources: Scott Keeter, "Public Opinion in 1984" in Gerald M. Pomper, ed., *The Election of 1984: Reports and Interpretations* (Chatham, N.J., 1985), p. 94; from the *New York Times* (October 26, 1984). Data from the Bureau of Labor Statistics do not include military.

refused to disavow the war. Republican Richard Nixon won. With the nation at peace and relatively prosperous, with Nixon continuing and expanding Democratic domestic programs, and facing a Democratic candidate, George McGovern, then regarded as too extreme, Nixon was reelected in 1972 by a large margin. After Nixon resigned as a result of Watergate, his successor, Gerald Ford, ran for reelection amidst the beginnings of "stagflation"—rising rates of unemployment and inflation. Yet the nation was at peace and the economy was not that bad. Jimmy Carter, a centrist Democrat whose views were close to most voters, and who ran as an outsider, barely beat Ford. By 1980, economic conditions had deteriorated and people were ready to try more conservative policies. Reagan beat Carter. In 1984 and 1988 there were peace and relative prosperity. Reagan and then Bush each won big. Except in 1976, when Watergate and Ford's pardon of Nixon were imponderables, public reactions to current conditions may have decided the election.

Shifting Party Identification?   This does not suggest that voting attitudes have undergone radical changes over a twenty-year period. But the absence of wholesale change does not signify no change, and apparently Reagan's large victory in 1984 was accompanied by some change of party identification toward the Republican party.

Over the decade from 1972 through 1982, as Warren Miller and Merrill Shanks show, the Democratic party retained its advantage in party identification.[10] Suddenly, in 1984, however, there was a decline in self-placed party identification among Democrats and an increase among Republicans, thus cutting the Democratic margin in half in two short years. Who changed and why? And how is this connected to the much-mentioned decline in overall party identification during the late 1960s and 1970s?

Miller and Shanks help answer these questions by dividing voters into fifteen age groups according to the time they were first eligible to vote. Over time their main finding is the continued attachment to party of all but one age group—those who began voting after the 1964 elections. The eighteen-year-olds who became eligible to vote in 1972 revealed much weaker attachment to party than older voters. As the oldest voters who began voting in 1932 or earlier grew smaller in proportion to the whole population of voters and the youngest age group grew larger, attachment to party proportionately declined. Actually, the party attachment of the oldest twelve of the fifteen age groups had increased by 1980. What happened, we now know, is that lowering the voting age to eighteen in 1972 "added a set of young adults who were anything but strong partisans at their point of entry."[11] Just as it is not rejection of the political system but rather registration procedures that make it difficult for mobile Americans to vote that significantly decrease voting rates, it is not dissatisfaction with party but the extension of the franchise to young people, who are not yet well connected to the political system, that resulted in the reported decline in party identification.

Age versus Youth?   Does the vote of young people in 1984, then, explain the strength of President Reagan's victory? Yes, in part, but in part, no. It does not because startling changes among older citizens have been left out. The oldest age groups evinced a remarkable 24 percent shift, becoming 12 percent less Democratic and 12 percent more Republican. Shanks and Miller write that "the pattern of shifts suggests an astounding rate of actual conversion as people who had been weak Democrats in 1980 became Republicans, and most often strong Republicans, in 1984." The youngest voters were mobilized in favor of Reagan but their shift of 9 percent was average for the nation.[12] By 1988 the Republican advantage among voters aged eighteen to twenty-nine had stalled. Once again young voters split 37 percent Republican to 37 percent Democrat in their party identifications, as they had in 1984, but Bush received only 52 percent of the vote of voters in that category, as compared with the 59 percent that Reagan received in 1984.[13]

Merging of Ideology with Party   If by ideology we mean consistency among views on public policy spanning a broad array of issues,[14] party elites, as exemplified by convention delegates, have become more ideological since 1972. What about party identifiers and voters?

When ordinary people place themselves on a scale of liberalism and conservatism from 1972 to 1984, the most impressive finding is how little change there has been. The plurality of self-designated conservatives remains constant. There has been a moderate decline in those who think of themselves as centrists. No evidence here of a tide toward conservatism or of a movement toward the Republican party. (See Table 4.3.)

What is the connection between ideology and party identification? In 1984 the growth in Republican identification came largely from self-designated conservatives rather than from moderates or liberals. In the youngest group with a college education, 28 percent of conservatives switched in identification to Republicans while only 1 percent of liberals and moderates followed this trend. The middle-aged college-educated cohort stuck to the Democrats. The oldest cohorts went Republican.[15] Higher levels of education tended to make older people Republican and to keep middle-aged citizens Democratic, with the youngest cohorts propelled most readily by their ideology. Shanks and Miller conclude:

> The consistent articulation of conservative ideas by a successful and remarkably popular president may have persuaded many lifelong Democrats, who have also been lifelong conservatives, that the time has come to reject their partisan roots and declare allegiance to the conservative Republican party of Ronald Reagan. As a consequence, their party identifications have changed with no change in their ideological orientations or their issue preferences.[16]

Can citizens continue to think of themselves both as Democratic and conservative? There was a time when the two designations went com-

TABLE 4.3 *Ideological Self-Designation of Voters in Presidential Elections, 1972–1988*

	1972	1976	1980	1984	1988
Liberal	20%	18%	19%	20%	17%
Moderate	26	26	19	24	23
Conservative	28	31	32	33	38
Not Placed	26	25	30	23	22
Total	100	100	100	100	100
N					
Plurality; conservatives / liberals	(1,662)	(1,720)	(886)	(1,290)	(1,225)
	+8	+13	+13	+13	+21

Source: J. Merrill Shanks and Warren E. Miller, "Partisanship, Policy, and Performance: The Reagan Legacy in the 1988 Election," *British Journal of Political Science* 21 (Spring 1991).

fortably together, especially in the South. But the growing liberalism of Democratic activists and the corresponding conservatism of Republican activists may make that self-designation seem increasingly out of place. The same problem exists for liberal Republicans. If there continue to be large issue differences between elite Democrats and Republicans, it then becomes harder to maintain discrepant party identifications and ideologies.

The Gender Gap and Party Support   Ideology and performance evaluations are not the only factors likely to affect party allegiance in the 1990s. The identification of a phenomenon known as the "gender gap" calls attention to the fact not only that women are voting more Democratic but also that men are voting more Republican. Observing Democratic party losses in party identification from 1980 to 1984, a period in which the gap between the parties narrowed significantly, we find them concentrated among white males as well as among young people, southerners, and those with less than high school education. Even when most women vote Republican, as they did in 1984 and 1988, they follow the national trend less than men.[17] Why? Is there anything about the changing role of women in American society that might make them more disposed to be liberals and hence Democrats?

Apparently, there is. Historically, women have been less inclined than men to favor the use of force to resolve conflicts. In 1952, for instance, as Everett C. Ladd and Karlyn H. Keene point out, 45 percent of the men questioned were willing to use whatever force was necessary in South Korea, compared to 33 percent of the women. Indeed, one of the earliest polls the Gallup organization carried out (in 1936) found that considerably more men than women (63 percent to 47 percent) favored the death penalty in cases where a life was taken. In regard to social issues, however, women remain a big more conservative than men.[18]

Even on what are usually referred to as women's issues, such as abortion or voting for female candidates, the differences between men and women are relatively small. By the late 1970s, however, new issues arose separating men and women more substantially than in the past. Women grew considerably more supportive of social measures, such as giving government responsibility for taking care of people who needed jobs or income, and they were also more risk-averse in regard to the consequences of technology, favoring stricter regulation than men. Consequently, a plurality of women favor a larger government that provides more services while a majority of men prefer smaller government.[19]

The differences in party identification among men and women are striking; though the figures vary a bit among surveys, men identify with the Republican party by a ratio of 39 to 26 but women identify with the Democratic party by 37 to 32 percent.[20] Is there a male or female gender gap? Both, we think, but for different parties. Confirmation of these general findings come from focus groups conducted by the *Wall Street Journal* in blue-collar suburbs surrounding Detroit. The Democratic pollster who conducted these groups, Peter Hart, concluded: "It's as though you are in two separate worlds." The women feel more vulnerable economically, he believes. They are therefore less willing to take risks in order to increase their opportunities. By contrast, the men interviewed think that the emphasis on competition, on staying the competitive course, as Ronald Reagan put it, will pay off. "The men tend to say, 'Look at where we've come from,' " Hart says, but "the women tend to say, 'Look how far we've got to go.' "[21] Asked whether they view themselves as risk takers, 42 percent of the men said they did compared to 27 percent of the women.

Women have distinctive, and more liberal, policy preferences and their vote is strongly connected to their place in the life cycle. Women are more concerned than men about unemployment and want government to do more about it. They are employed in public agencies in higher proportions than males. Women also favor lower expenditures on defense and higher on social services. Their foreign policy is against military intervention and in favor of arms control and other negotiated agreements. They favor gun control and oppose the death penalty. Women favor equal rights more than men, not only in regard to ERA but also for the poor and minorities. These issue preferences are robust; it is not so much the presence of a women on the ballot but a person favoring their preferred positions that captures their allegiance.[22] In 1988 this resulted in a one percent advantage for George Bush among women voters while he maintained a 16 percent edge among men. Women voted 52 percent for Democratic candidates for the House of Representatives and only 45 percent for Republicans, while men favored Democratic House candidates by a 51 percent to 45 percent margin.[23]

Of course gender does not exhaust life's possibilities, or the bases of political allegiance. Among other things, women may be young or old, married or single, working at home or in paid employment, and they may have many, few, or no children. If social situation affects political leanings, we would expect the most conservative women to be those involved most deeply in traditional family roles—wife, mother, homemaker. The most liberal (or feminist) women should be single, childless, professional. And women with conflicting characteristics, say a married mother of three who works full-time outside the home, should rank in between. Table 4.4, though not a perfect confirmation of this hypothesis, comes pretty close:

married women voted much more heavily for Bush in 1988 than single women, working women supported Dukakis a lot more than nonworking women, and working women who were married were more evenly split.[24]

It appears that when women's responsibilities are confined mostly to looking after themselves, that is, when they are single, working or not, they vote more Democratic; when their social concerns extend to husbands and families, they vote more Republican; and when they are cross-pressured, they come out in between.

While Republicans have a female problem, Democrats have a male problem. Women who vote are differently attracted to the different parties because of the preoccupations characteristic of their place in the social structure. It should not be surprising that men react to corresponding incentives. If they look at themselves as likely to marry and provide for children, paying taxes to support social services for nonworking individuals may not appeal to them. And white working males, so it seems, are the only major social grouping that the Democratic party does not regularly refer to as an oppressed minority deserving of special consideration. Since 1968, as Table 4.5 shows, white males over thirty have deserted the Democratic party to a degree far greater than most voters.

TABLE 4.4   *Women's Vote for President, 1984 and 1988*

	1984			1988		
	Reagan	*Mondale*	*Reagan minus Mondale*	*Bush*	*Dukakis*	*Bush minus Dukakis*
Younger, married, working women	61%	39%	+22%	58%	42%	+16%
Younger, not married, working	50	50	Even	48	52	− 4
Younger, married, not working	64	36	+28	52	48	+ 4
Younger, not married, not working	33	66	−33	36	64	−28
Older, married, working	55	45	+10	51	49	+ 2
Older, not married, working	41	59	−18	36	64	−28
Older, married, not working	62	38	+24	48	52	− 4
Older, not married, not working	56	44	+12	52	47	+ 5

Sources: Evans Witt, "What the Republicans Have Learned About Women," *Public Opinion* 8 (October/November, 1985), p. 49. Reprinted with permission of American Enterprise Institute for Public Policy Research. For 1988, American National Election Studies, Center for Political Studies, University of Michigan: University of California, Berkeley, State Data Program.

TABLE 4.5   *Party Votes of White Males over Age Thirty*

	1956	1960	1964	1968	1972	1976	1980	1984	1988
Republicans	57	47	36	47	71	51	55	62	62
Democrats	42	53	65	39	29	49	37	38	38
Third Party*	—	—	—	14	—	—	8	—	—
Democratic Margin for White Males Over 30	− 14	+ 6	+ 29	− 8	− 42	− 2	− 18	− 24	− 24
Democratic Margin for Nationwide Electorate	− 20	0	+ 35	− 7	− 28	+ 2	− 12	− 16	− 4
Difference	+ 6	+ 6	− 6	− 1	− 14	− 4	− 6	− 8	− 20

*Anderson in 1980, Wallace in 1968.

Sources: American National Election Time Series, 1952–1984 (machine readable data file); for 1988, American National Election Studies. Center for Political Studies, University of Michigan: University of California, Berkeley, State Data Program.

Underdog Strategies

If the Democrats have more party identifiers, the strategic alternatives available to Republicans can hardly be regarded as secret. They can be boiled down to a few possibilities. First, Republicans can attempt to deemphasize the impact of party habit as a component of electoral choice by capitalizing upon a more compelling cue to action. The nomination of General Eisenhower, the most popular hero of World War II, overrode party considerations and is a clear example of the efficacy of this strategy.[25] Efforts to play upon popular dissatisfaction in a variety of issue areas, such as "stagflation" in 1980, also exemplify this strategy, but these dissatisfactions must preexist in the population and must be widespread and intense before they will produce the desired effect. When issues do come to the fore in a compelling way, the payoff to the advantaged party is sometimes enormous, because these are the circumstances under which new party loyalties can be created. Or the Republican candidate can do as Ronald Reagan did in 1980 and emphasize popular themes of patriotism and national renewal, while hoping his opponent's personal unpopularity will keep enough Democratic voters at home to make a Republican victory possible. The Republican candidate also can stress the issue differences between his party and the other, as Goldwater did in 1964 and Bush, less stridently, in 1988. When Democratic policies are popular, as they were in 1964, this tactic is suicidal. But when they are unpopular, as was the case for "liberalism" and "crime" in 1988, stressing differences works very well.

Some imaginative writers have suspected that conservative elements of the population are in fact alienated from politics and sit in the wings, frustrated, immobilized, and without party loyalties, until someone pursuing a Goldwater-like strategy gives them the "choice" they are looking for. In 1964 they called this a "hidden vote" theory. But it was a canard. What evidence we have points to the probability that the dedicated conservatives who are sufficiently interested in politics to hold strong opinions about public policy do in fact belong to political parties and participate actively in them. These people are almost all Republicans. This is true even in the South, where many of these people used to vote Democratic.[26]

Another assumption underlying the hidden-vote theory is that in 1964 it would have been possible to attract this mythical vote in substantial numbers without losing the allegiance of large numbers of more moderate people. Not so. Goldwater aroused great antipathy among the general population. Louis Harris surveys found that sizeable majorities in the general population defined themselves as opposed to positions that they believed Senator Goldwater held.[27] And they let him know at the polls.

1980 and 1984: Realignment at Last?

The strategies discussed above are *underdog* strategies. Nixon won, in part, by downplaying his programmatic differences with the Democrats. In any case, his personal victories were not matched by gains lower down on the ticket. In the 1950s and 1960s, the Republicans seemed doomed to a permanent minority status. Then in 1980 something happened—or so it appeared. The Republicans did so well in electing Ronald Reagan over Jimmy Carter that it was widely assumed that at long last a party realignment was about to occur.[28]

This assessment proved to be quite wrong, as 1988 once again demonstrated, but it was understandable that such an idea should have arisen. After all, virtually every presidential election brings with it something anomalous, unusual, novel, and hence interesting in the way events sort themselves out. Afterward, pundits and political analysts set about patting and palpating the body politic, trying to discover what, if anything, has really changed. Usually, the correct answer is not much. The political habits of voting Americans, while subject to mood swings, are pretty stable on the whole. The same old parties—Democrats and Republicans since 1860—divide up most of the political offices. Every once in a great while, however—the 1860s, the 1890s, and the 1930s are examples—for one reason or another the very terrain shifts and recontours itself under the political parties, and we have a significant party realignment: new, more or less permanent, majorities and minorities, a new sort of ideological consensus, new participants in politics, or all three.

Partisan realignments are such intellectually stimulating events that it is no wonder that political observers are awaiting the next one with some impatience. And so, of course, are hopeful beneficiaries of the new dispensation. So it should come as no surprise even to the most casual follower of American politics that the 1980 election, like so many of its predecessors, would provoke at least a few political analysts to announce a party realignment, and that the definitive demise of the party system dominated by the New Deal coalition was finally at hand. All those doomsaying prophets who hoisted their umbrellas in vain way back during the Eisenhower years, waiting for the sky to fall on the Democrats, could at long last hear the pitter-patter of something or other just above their heads.

An elected incumbent president, for the first time since Herbert Hoover in 1932, had been defeated for a second term of office. And, even more surprisingly, the Senate, after twenty-six years, had a Republican majority. "For the first time in a generation," David Broder wrote in the *Washington Post*, "it is sensible to ask whether we might be entering a new political era—an era of Republican dominance."[29]

The sort of answer one might give to such a question is not wholly devoid of significance in the world of partisan politics. If it can plausibly be argued that a realignment has taken place, then presumably it can be claimed that the legislative program of the president is, as an attempt to fulfill an electoral mandate, the most accurate available translation into law and public policy of an authentic majority sentiment among the people at large. This programmatic mandate is something grander and more impressive than merely the entitlement to hold office: that sort of entitlement is something a president gets by winning the election, by whatever margin, in the Electoral College. The winner of a programmatic mandate, on the other hand, has a talking point of considerable weight in the continuing process of persuasion that goes on as the president interacts with the people whose cooperation he needs to accomplish his goals. Armed with a mandate, a president can speak with a stronger voice in setting the terms for the consideration of legislative alternatives. Without a secure mandate, presidents must give ground to other elected officials, to the claims of tradition, of expertise, of political expediency.

So the discussion of mandates in the 1980 election carried some political freight along with it. The beliefs of political actors about the proper interpretation of the electoral results color the ways in which they treat one another in Washington. The impressive legislative victories won by

President Reagan during his first year in office suggested that more than a few politicians were convinced that the 1980 elections had indeed produced what the president's poll taker, Richard Wirthlin, labeled "a political Mount Saint Helens."[30] Steven V. Roberts of the *New York Times* located the legislative successes of President Reagan's first year in his "overwhelming electoral victory, and the outpouring of public support for his policies generated by a politically savvy White House."[31]

The evidence for the emergence of a new majority backing the president's program was, however, extremely thin. It was based on three considerations: (1) the size of Mr. Reagan's victory, (2) the results in the Senate, and (3) the results in the House of Representatives. None of these could stand much scrutiny as a basis for believing that the 1980 election created a policy mandate.

While it is true that Governor Reagan defeated President Carter for the presidency by an overwhelming landslide in the Electoral College, 489 votes to 49, the actual numbers of voters for the two candidates—43.9 million to 35.5 million—were much closer, or, as percentages of the two-party vote, 55 percent to 45 percent. The electoral vote landslide was the third biggest in the twentieth century, but in percentage of the two-party vote ten other twentieth-century presidential elections gave their winners more impressive majorities.

In the end, 46 percent of the age-eligible population did not vote for president, a percentage of stay-at-homes larger than in any election since 1948. And there was a sizable third-party vote, constituting 4.4 percent of the age-eligible population, or 5.7 million votes. Thus, as a proportion of all age-eligible voters, 27 percent voted for Ronald Reagan for president, while 73 percent did not. This impaired President Reagan's right to govern not one whit, but it did, of course, bear significantly on the resources of popularity on which he might expect to draw.

The next ground for the belief that the 1980 election constituted a significant break with past policies was the fact that the United States Senate changed hands and brought in a Republican majority. Because Republican presidential landslides have generally failed to resonate farther down the ticket, as in 1972 and 1956, the fact that at the senatorial level the Republicans did well in 1980 takes on significance. Nine Democratic incumbents lost in the general election to Republicans, and no Republican incumbent lost to Democrats. Out of nine open seats, seven went Republican. There was a Republican gain in the Senate of twelve seats, for an overall majority of fifty-three to forty-seven seats.

Some of the defeated senators were well-known liberals: Frank Church of Idaho, Birch Bayh of Indiana, John Culver of Iowa, George McGovern of South Dakota, and Gaylord Nelson of Wisconsin were all beaten by conservative Republican members of the House running strongly conservative campaigns. This led David Broder to comment:

> The election was plainly more than a repudiation of Jimmy Carter. . . .
> [W]as there an ideological message in the 1980 vote? There sure was. . . .
> [Y]ou had to be dense to miss . . . a flat-out repudiation of basic economic,
> diplomatic, and social policies of the reigning Democratic liberalism.[32]

Yet the fact is that the change in the ideological and party balance of the Senate indicated no great surge at the level of voters. By aggregating the vote totals for thirty-three Senate seats, and excluding the vote for Democratic incumbent Russell Long of Louisiana, who ran unopposed, we discover that 3 million more votes were cast for Democratic than Republican candidates.

How can this have happened? Senatorial electorates, following state boundaries, are of greatly unequal size. On the whole, Republicans won the closely contested races, and won in some very small states—New Hampshire, Idaho, Utah, the Dakotas, Nevada—while Democrats won most of the senatorial landslides, notably in California, where Alan Cranston was reelected by a margin of 1.6 million votes. Of the fifteen races where the winner received 55 percent of the vote or more, eight were won by Democrats. In the eighteen close races where the winner got less than 55 percent of the vote, fifteen were won by Republicans.

The Reagan landslide failed to overturn the Democratic majority in the House of Representatives, but it did reduce that majority by thirty-three seats, from 276 Democrats to 243 out of 435 seats. The party balance in the House reverted to the identical number—243 Democrats to 192 Republicans—as occurred after the Nixon hairbreadth 1968 victory over Hubert Humphrey, which few mistook for a realignment. That was just one Democratic seat less than was produced by the 1972 Nixon landslide against McGovern, which was also not a realignment. In the midterm elections of 1970 and 1974, the Democrats picked up twelve and forty-seven seats, respectively. In the 1976 presidential election, the old New Deal coalition elected Jimmy Carter president and 292 Democrats to the House. As Robert Axelrod's research showed:

> For the Democrats, the New Deal Coalition made a comeback in 1976. For
> the first time since the Johnson landslide of 1964, the Democrats got a
> majority of the votes from each of the six diverse majorities which make
> up their traditional coalition: the poor, blacks, union families, Catholics,
> southerners, and city dwellers.[33]

In the context of the previous few elections, what the House electoral results of 1980 showed was a set of outcomes well within normal expectations, not anything remotely approaching a realignment.

We have so far considered evidence favoring the proposition that the 1980 election was the occasion of a fundamental party realignment in which President Reagan received a programmatic mandate. We must conclude that this evidence is weak if not contradictory to that argument.

If ever there were presidential election results that looked like they conferred a mandate, 1984 should have been the year. President Reagan's 525 electoral votes (lacking only those of Walter Mondale's home state of Minnesota and the District of Columbia) constitute a modern record. More votes were cast for him than for any other candidate in history. Outside of New England, the upper Midwest and the upper Far West, Reagan received more than 57 percent of the vote everywhere with large sections giving him over 62 percent. Why, then do we still doubt there was anything like a mandate?

To be effective, a presidential mandate must carry over to Congress. In 1984, the Democrats won the close Senate races. Consequently, Democrats gained two seats. Whatever claim the president might have laid to a new mandate was challenged by the power of incumbency—among the 15 senators running for reelection, eight received over 70 percent of the vote, four got over 60 percent and only three (two Republicans and one Democrat) were defeated by tiny margins.[34] Not only did they hold their own in the Senate in 1984, the Democrats gained control of the Senate in 1986. In 1984 the House results followed the usual pattern in connection with huge Republican presidential majorities: Republicans gained only fourteen seats, not nearly enough for a majority. They did best in the open (nonincumbent) races, taking five of fourteen seats previously occupied by Democrats and losing only one Republican seat. That gave Republicans a gain of four. Seven of the fourteen incumbent Democrats who lost were southerners. Four Republican incumbents also lost.[35] Not much to carry out a mandate here.

It is not change, in fact, but continuity that is the main story of the 1984 elections for the House of Representatives as it was for the Senate. Among the 254 Democrats running for reelection, 240 won, a 94.4 percent success rate. The Republican success rate was an astounding 98.1 percent (151 out of 154). Indeed, a good 80 percent of incumbent Republicans increased their winning margin, as did 47 percent of incumbent Democrats.[36]

It may be, as Normal Ornstein suggests, that when a presidential election is about ratifying past performance, as 1984 was, the voters may well decide (if things are so good) to keep the entire team, Congress as well as president.[37] This seems to have been the case also in 1988. It may also be that, as Kevin Phillips maintains, Republicans suffer an unusual disadvantage in House elections. Since they are (or have been) better educated, they turn out more. Consequently, in largely Republican districts, the margins of victory were more like 150,000 to 200,000 rather than the 50,000 margins that Democrats may achieve in their low turnout districts. In this sense, the Democratic vote is more efficient than the Republican per representative elected. Even if district boundaries were drawn to even out these differences, Phillips estimates that Republicans would have to get 52 to 53 percent of the national vote to capture the House.[38]

Despite his lower vote in 1980, there was more reason for Reagan to make a claim to a mandate in that year than in 1984. Although voters differed with Reagan on social issues, from ERA to abortion, they did want more spent on defense, less spent on welfare, and lower taxes. And that, in Reagan's first term, is more or less what they got. But by 1984, voters had turned moderate on these matters, wishing neither a return to the pre-1980 situation, nor to go as far as the president.[39] The lesson here is twofold: first, an American presidential election is ordinarily limited to a choice among candidates, and is not an issue referendum; second, in thinking about candidate and issue preferences, voters may decide they want a candidate even if they do not wish to endorse his policies.

Since 1937 or thereabouts, public opinion polls have been asking voters about their party affiliations. The long-term stability of the responses has been notable. There seems to be no room for doubt that over the four-and-a-half-decade period for which such figures exist, persons claiming identification with the Democrats have outnumbered Republicans in the general population, and, until recently, by large numbers. This would surprise nobody who has been attentive to election results over this same stretch of years. Only twice in the entire generation since Franklin Roosevelt's first election in 1932—after the elections of 1946 and 1952—have the Republicans controlled both houses of Congress. When landslides have favored Democrats—for example, in 1934, 1936, 1958, 1964, and 1974—massive Democratic majorities have resulted in Congress, and shock waves have been felt farther down on the ticket, for example, in state assemblies. After the 1980 elections, however, looking at the system from the bottom up, the Republicans got no such advantage. Although Republicans gained some seats, the Democrats were still comfortably ahead, with 4,497 state legislative seats, compared with 2,918 for the Republicans. And Democrats controlled sixty-three state chambers, compared with thirty-four controlled by Republicans.

At the beginning of 1984 there were 7,363 state legislators of whom 4,624, or 63 percent, were Democrats. Newspaper reports said that the Republicans gained around 300 legislative seats in the elections of 1984. So, 4,324 out of 7,363 means the Democrats held 59 percent of the seats after the Republican landslide. Or, to quote the outgoing Republican governor of Delaware, Pierre du Pont, "Of the 6,243 state legislative seats contested in 1984, Republicans lost 58 percent of them."[40] After the election the Republicans controlled thirty-two out of ninety-eight legislative chambers, or one-third. Before Reagan's 1984 landslide, there were thirty-five Democratic governors, fifteen Republican governors. After the landslide, there were thirty-four Democratic governors, sixteen Republican governors. Over the thirty-two years from Dwight D. Eisenhower's first election until 1984, 7,392 congressional elections were held, and the Democrats won 4,372 of them, or 59 percent. Over the same period, 587 senatorial elections took place. There have been 331 Democratic winners, or 56.4 percent.[41]

The election of 1984, far from constituting a sharp break with the past, actually followed a rather stable pattern that has been more or less well established over the last fifty years. During these last five decades we have had fourteen presidential elections. Ten of them—two-thirds—have been part of what we could call a "landslide sequence" (see Table 4.6).[42] In the first election in the sequence a candidate is elected president. The second time around he wins a resounding personal triumph, in an enormous landslide. This happened to Roosevelt in 1936, to Eisenhower in 1956, to Johnson, standing in for Kennedy, in 1964, to Nixon in 1972, and to Reagan in 1984. Seen in this context, 1984 does not seem so unusual.

TABLE 4.6 *Landslide Sequences: Presidential Landslides and Congressional Outcomes*

Year	Winner of the Presidency	Percentage Margin in Two-Party Vote	Electoral Vote Margin	Net Result in Congress compared with Last Midterm	
				House	Senate
Democratic					
1932	Roosevelt	+18	+413	+92D	+12D
1936	Roosevelt	+24	+515	+11D	+ 6D
1960	Kennedy	+ 0.7	+ 84	+37D	+ 2D
1964	Johnson	+23	+434	+37D	+ 2D
Republican					
1952	Eisenhower	+11	+353	+22R	+ 1R
1956	Eisenhower	+16	+384	+ 2D	0
1968	Nixon	+ 0.7	+110	+ 3R	+ 5R
1972	Nixon	23	503	+ 7R	+ 2D
1980	Reagan	+10	+440	+33R	+12R
1984	Reagan	+18	+512	+14D	+ 2D

Sources: Richard M. Scammon, ed., *America Votes* 15 (Washington, D.C., Congressional Quarterly, 1983). Nelson W. Polsby, "The Democratic Nomination and the Evolution of the Party System," in Austin Ranney, ed., *The American Elections of 1984* (Durham, N.C., 1985), p. 42.

The pattern of Democratic benefit further down the ticket from land-slides is also well established.[43] It is a little hard to see this in 1936, because Roosevelt came into the election with sixty-nine Democrats out of ninety-six Senators, and 333 Democrats out of 435 House members. This was the result of the 1934 election, the only midterm election in the twentieth century when the president's party gained seats. Even so, in 1936 the Democrats bumped up against the ceiling of possibility, winning eleven more House seats and six more Senate seats to go with Roosevelt's advantage of 515 electoral votes and 24 percent of the popular vote. In 1964, Johnson's margin over Barry Goldwater was 23 percent of the popular vote and 434 of the electoral votes. Democrats picked up two Senate and thirty-seven House seats. This is what Democratic landslide sequences look like: When the presidential candidate does well, the party does well.

Republican sequences follow a different pattern. Eisenhower's great popular victory in 1956 gave him a net advantage of 384 electoral votes and a 15 percent popular vote margin over Adlai Stevenson. There were no net gains for Republicans in the Senate and a net loss of two Republican seats in the House. In 1972 Nixon's margin was 503 electoral votes and 23 percent of the popular vote, yet Republicans picked up only seven seats in the House and Democrats gained two Senate seats.

Reagan's 1984 victory was like that: an 18 percent margin in the popular vote, and 512 in electoral votes, and yet the Democrats gained two Senate seats and suffered a net loss of only fourteen seats in the House. In 1980, when Reagan's personal margin was only 10 percent, the Republicans picked up twelve seats in the Senate (mostly by very small margins) and thirty-three House seats. But there was no realignment, nor even much of a mandate, as we all discovered at the 1982 midterm election when the Democrats bounced back with a net gain of twenty-six House seats.

Nobody viewed the 1988 election as a realigning election. Although it is extremely unusual for a vice president directly to succeed a president of his own party, the rest of the 1988 election results fell well within normal expectations. It is worth reciting the 1988 numbers: Bush led Dukakis by eight points in the popular vote, 53 percent to 46 percent. He had a winning margin of 315 electoral votes. Yet there was no change at all in the Senate and the Democrats actually picked up two House seats. In the wake of the highly successful Iraq war of 1991, when President Bush's approval ratings hit all-time highs, it is plausible to foresee a repetition of the landslide sequence in 1992. Indeed an anticipation of such a result undoubtably served to delay the entry of Democratic hopefuls into the race in 1991. Where in recent elections prospective candidates of both parties were busily courting voters and making party alliances in Iowa and New Hampshire well before the year of the election,

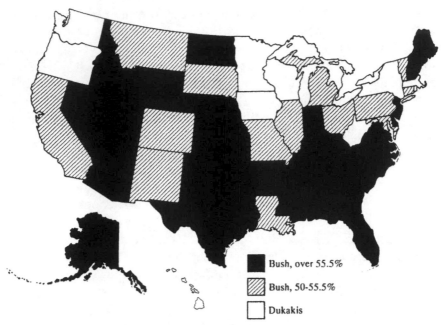

FIGURE 4.2   *The Presidential Vote in 1988*
Source: Gerald M. Pomper, ed., *The Election of 1988: Reports and Interpretations* (Chatham, N.J., 1989).

an eerie silence descended on the Democrats a year before the 1992 contest.[44] A look at history shows that a 1992 Bush landslide would not be unusual. What would be unusual would be the extension of President Bush's popularity to his party—and especially to nonincumbent candidates of his party—farther down the ticket.

How is it possible to maintain a political system in which Republicans do extremely well in presidential elections and Democrats do extremely well otherwise? Such a phenomenon is clearly impossible in a system lacking a separation of powers, giving voters no chance to make the disparate choices that add up to this peculiar pattern of results. But the separation of powers, long ballots, and a large array of electoral choices all exist in the American political system. And Americans take advantage of the opportunity to diversify their political portfolios. Rock-ribbed Republican states of the mountain region have in recent years overwhelmingly preferred Democrats for governor. A Republican governor of California faces a phalanx of Democratic state constitutional officers elected statewide: lieutenant governor, secretary of state, controller, treasurer. In 1990 Californians broke precedent to elect a Republican attorney general to keep Pete Wilson company. Nationally, Democrats run the House and, once again, since the 1986 elections, Democrats run the

Senate. And so on. But the fact that a formal opportunity exists for voters to split their tickets does not require them to do so. Presumably this is the fact—that they do so—that needs explaining.

There seem to be three types of explanations that might account for all this, and all have their advocates: (1) massive autonomous changes in the electorate itself, changes that are making people more Republican than they used to be; (2) Republican strength at the top of the ticket— the magical influence of Ronald Reagan and other attractive Republican presidential candidates; (3) Democratic weaknesses at the presidential level.

As to the first, there is a problem of simple logic: If people are becoming more Republican, why does this show up decisively only in the voting for president? Is there any reason why grass-roots realignments should start at the top of the ticket? Perhaps there is a reason: the great visibility of the presidential race as compared with other races on the ballot. But if this is how a modern realignment works, it works through a mechanism that focuses on candidates, not parties, and helps Republican presidential candidates, not Republicans generally. The weight of evidence seems to be against the proposition that realignment has gone further than the presidency, except in the South. There we can see ample evidence of realignment as northern migrants have combined with native converts to greatly strengthen the Republican party. As Table 4.7 suggests, in a thirty-year period, the number of Republicans representing the old Confederacy in Congress has risen steeply. All this has been at the expense of conservative Democrats; the prospects of liberals in the Democratic parties of the South are at worst unchanged.[45]

In the aftermath of the 1984 landslide, the newspapers were full of copy extolling Ronald Reagan and his magic bullet. And yet the president's popularity did not seem to extend to any of the baggage that a

TABLE 4.7 *Republicans in the House of Representatives*

Election Year	National Number of Republicans	Percentage of Seats	Non-South Number of Republicans	Percentage of Seats	South* Number of Republicans	Percentage of Seats
1960	176	40	170	52	6	6
1970	180	41	154	47	26	25
1980	192	44	153	47	39	36
1990	167	38	128	40	39	34

*The states of the old Confederacy: Ala., Ark., Fla., Ga., La., Miss., N.C., S.C., Tenn., Tex., Va.

Sources: Guide to U.S. Elections (Washington, D.C., 1975), pp. 841–844, 866–870; Richard M. Scammon and Alice V. McGillivray, ed., *America Votes 18* (Washington, D.C., 1989); *Congressional Quarterly Weekly Report* (November 10, 1990), p. 3802.

president normally carries with him—for example, approval of the way he was doing his job. Roughly on the occasion of his second inaugural, an ABC News/*Washington Post* poll gave a national sample of Americans an opportunity to grade President Reagan's handling of eleven national problems. His overall score was mediocre, and, significantly, many of those giving him mediocre scores were people who had voted for him. In the words of the *Post*'s Barry Sussman, "People who gave Reagan only a C grade overall tended to vote for him last November . . . by a ratio of better than 2 to 1."[46]

The third explanation makes more sense to us: that the Democrats have hurt themselves in the course of their internecine warfare since the 1968 election and that the reforms of the delegate selection process that they instituted have made it harder for them to mobilize their broad coalition in behalf of their presidential candidates. Harder, that is, than for Republicans, who have a narrower coalition and more internal ideological agreement. Because delegates are now selected mostly in primary elections, the task of a presidential candidate is to proceed, state after state, to mobilize voters who will give him their exclusive loyalty and their first-choice vote. The idea is not to win a majority but to come out ahead of the other candidates. Whoever comes out ahead in enough early contests wins the nomination.

So the basic technique for winning requires the mobilization of a faction, not coalition-building. Nowadays, there is no institutionalized occasion for factions to be reconciled and for coalitions to be built. National conventions, with their pledged delegates and their role reduced to ratifiers of primary election results, cannot do the job. So in recent elections the Democrats, with all their factional rivalries and stylistic differences and ideological disparities, have had to face the Republicans, a party which for all its internal differences is far more homogenous and ideologically united than the Democrats.[47]

Partisan Advantage in the Electoral College?

One approach to the analysis of party competition in presidential elections is to go methodically state by state assigning probable electoral votes to one party or another. From the time of Reconstruction forward into the 1960s—nearly a century—it was understood that the states of the former Confederacy—the "Solid South"—would always go Democratic in presidential elections. This meant that the Democrats always started with all the southern electoral votes in their column, and they needed to carry correspondingly fewer states than the Republicans to add up to a win.

Today some analysts propose that the Republicans have a similar advantage in the Electoral College—a group of states that they are virtually assured of winning, states like the Mountain States which in recent elections have faithfully gone Republican for president. Democrats, conversely, do not seem to be able to count on any electoral votes beyond the three assigned to the District of Columbia and they must fight for the rest. Thus, goes the argument, the Republicans have a natural advantage in presidential elections owing to their superiority in being able to count on safe electoral votes.[48]

We offer a note of caution. The Solid South of old was profoundly Democratic territory in ways unmatched by Republicans anywhere in the contemporary era. In most parts of the South the Republican party did not exist and elected no sheriffs, no county officers, no state legislators, no governors, senators, or members of Congress. Indeed, Republicans not infrequently made no nominations for these offices. This is not remotely the way it is in any of the allegedly safe Republican states today. Consider the Mountain States. One, Montana, is predominantly Democratic. All the others have recently elected and reelected Democrats to high public office: governor, senator, member of Congress, and so on. Democrats as varied as Cecil Andrus, Dennis DeConcini, Morris Udall, Roy Romer, Timothy Wirth, Jeff Bingaman, Bruce King, Wayne Owens, and Scott Matheson have prospered politically in the allegedly inhospitable soil of the Mountain Sales.

An even stronger case can be made that states other than the Mountain States that may have rewarded Republican presidential nominees with their electoral votes in recent years cannot be taken for granted. There is scant basis for the belief that Republicans have solid turf they can count on no matter what may happen any more than the Democrats do. Both will have to work for their electoral votes. As for enough electoral votes to win, any winning combination will accomplish this job. Of course we expect Utah and Idaho to be in the Republican column and the District of Columbia and Hawaii to go Democratic. But not automatically.

Recent Trends in Party Realignment

The term "party realignment" is usually taken to mean a massive change in voter loyalties from one of the major parties to another. Realignment could also refer, of course, to the appearance of one or more third parties with significant portions of the vote, thus creating a multiparty system. It could also signify the replacement of one or both of the major parties by new parties while maintaining a two-party system. Although this realignment by replacement is not on the current political agenda, we will ask later why there has been no sizable third party and whether one might be in the offing.

Is it *voters* who are changing position or the more restricted group of *party identifiers?* Is it *party activists* and/or *party officials* that are realigning themselves? The reason for making such distinctions is that one or more of these realignments can happen independent of the others. Activists but not identifiers or voters can be switching sides. Alternatively, voters can change sentiments while party activists do not. When all elements that make up a party are changing in the same direction at the same time, interpretation is relatively straightforward, and it can be assumed the same forces are causing everyone to shift. But if some elements are going one way and others are staying put or going a different way, a more variegated explanation must be sought. Either elites and rank-and-file members have become estranged, suggesting room for the rise of a new party, or a time lag exists after which elites and voters should show greater issue agreement.

In addition, the discussion of realignment suffers from confusion of two related but different questions. One of these—Who is ahead?—refers to the relative power of the parties in the electorate, either in garnering votes or in regard to party identification. Since the Republican party's presidential candidate has won all but one election since 1968 and the Democratic party has (except for a brief period around the 1984 election) maintained its lead in identification and in electoral results at levels lower than the presidential, answers to this question depend on specifying exactly whose power is being compared. Another question—Who has changed from party A to party B?—focuses attention on the demographic or geographical sources of change, whether by new mobilization or conversion.

Theory about party realignment is sufficiently well developed in political science to have produced at least two contending schools of thought about the dynamics of change in the general population when realignments occur. One school says that party realignments are caused by voters changing their minds, and, over time, their party affiliations come into conformity with their commitments on issues.[49] According to this school, a 1980 realignment ought to have been visible in the defections of conservative Democrats who made a down payment on what in due course would have been a conversion to regular Republican loyalty. In order for this argument to work with 1980 data, it ought to be possible to show a fair amount of ideologically motivated voting. The Michigan survey suggests that self-identified conservative Democrats were more likely to vote for Reagan than those who said they were liberals.[50] This makes sense: Reagan was, after all, the more conservative candidate. But it remained to be seen whether Reagan could make permanent converts of them. Among many he did, especially the oldest Democrats.

Another theory of party realignment emphasizes not conversion of voters from one party to another but mobilization of previously quiescent nonvoters.[51] On the face of it, any election in which there is low turnout, as was the case in 1980, 1984, and 1988 is an unlikely realigning election through the workings of this theory, simply because it is large numbers of new voters who are supposed to do the realigning of the parties. Turnout in 1988 amounted to about 50 percent; around 91 million citizens stayed home while only 49 million voted for Bush. The Bush voters added up to only a little over a quarter (26.9 percent) of those who could have registered and voted.[52] Nevertheless, it is worth a look at new voters. In 1980 and 1988 new voters were not Reagan or Bush voters overwhelmingly, but in 1984 they did strongly support Reagan. Will 1992 be a Bush landslide that repeats Reagan's 1984 success with new voters?

The different positions of African-American and Hispanic voters pose interesting dilemmas for these groups and for the major political parties. African-Americans (see Table 4.8) are largely Democratic in their vote. Historically their turnout has been low, but in 1988 the proportion of black people who voted (51.1 percent) was not much lower than that of whites (59.1 percent).[53] This makes them vitally important to the Democratic party. However, if black voters, as the political phrase has it, "have nowhere to go," their bargaining power is reduced. That is why talk is heard about running an African-American candidate for president, not in the expectation of victory, but as a means of putting pressure on Democrats in Congress and on Democratic candidates for the presidential nomination to undertake appropriate actions and make pledges so that the "black vote" will no longer be taken for granted. This strategy may backfire; African-American voters might actually face a choice between one of their own, whom some would want to support lest their threat be perceived as hollow, and taking responsibility for the defeat of a Democratic candidate. Such a defeat would indeed make the threat good, but it would also perpetuate Republican rule.

Republican party leaders would very much like greater African-American support. A party that wants to win and to govern must draw support from all sectors of the population. Yet the policy preferences of African-American leaders for higher federal spending on social welfare conflict with the minimal government stance of the Republican party.

TABLE 4.8 *Party Identification of Racial Groups*

	1952	1956	1960	1964	1968	1970	1972	1974	1976	1978	1980	1982	1984	1986	1988
Whites															
Strong Democrat	21%	20%	23%	24%	12%	16%	12%	16%	13%	12%	14%	16%	15%	14%	14%
Weak Democrat	26	23	25	25	25	23	25	20	23	24	22	23	20	21	16
Independent Democrat	10	6	9	9	10	11	12	12	11	14	12	11	9	10	10
Independent	6	9	9	8	11	13	13	13	14	15	14	11	6	12	12
Independent Republican	7	9	7	6	9	9	11	10	11	10	11	9	14	13	15
Weak Republican	14	14	14	15	16	16	14	15	16	14	16	16	18	17	15
Strong Republican	14	16	16	12	11	10	11	10	10	9	9	11	16	12	16
Apolitical	2	3	1	1	1	1	1	2	1	2	2	2	1	2	2
Blacks															
Strong Democrat	31	27	27	52	56	43	37	43	35	37	46	53	42	42	39
Weak Democrat	22	23	21	22	29	34	31	25	36	30	27	26	26	60	24
Independent Democrat	10	6	5	8	7	8	8	15	14	15	9	12	16	12	18
Independent	4	7	12	6	3	10	12	10	8	9	6	5	5	8	6
Independent Republican	4	1	4	1	1	0	3	1	1	2	3	1	5	2	5
Weak Republican	8	12	10	5	1	4	4	1	3	3	2	2	1	3	5
Strong Republican	5	7	7	2	1	0	4	3	2	3	3	0	3	2	1
Apolitical	17	18	14	5	3	1	2	3	1	2	4	1	2	2	3
Hispanics															
Strong Democrat											25	13	16	25	24
Weak Democrat											28	40	26	27	19
Independent Democrat											2	15	13	10	16
Independent Independent											18	13	18	16	13
Independent Republican											10	2	9	2	8
Weak Republican											7	6	8	12	10
Strong Republican											7	4	6	6	8
Apolitical											5	6	3	2	1

Sources: For 1952–1978, Warren E. Miller, Arthur H. Miller, and Edward J. Schneider, *American National Election Studies Data Sourcebook, 1952–1978* (Cambridge, 1980), p. 89; for 1980–1986, American National Election Time Series, 1952–86, Center for Political Studies, University of Michigan: University of California, Berkeley, State Data Program. For 1988, American National Election Studies. Center for Political Studies, University of Michigan: University of California, Berkeley, State Data Program. Data rounded to nearest percent.

There are two possible routes to accommodation: one is that Republicans convince some African-American voters that they will be better off with policies that emphasize growth of the private sector; the other is that the Republican party moderate its position at the cost of alienating some of its present supporters. It cannot be desirable for the nation to have party differences reinforce racial cleavages.

The position of Hispanics is difficult to analyze. They are, in the first place, not one, but several ethnic groups, depending on place of origin (Cuba, Puerto Rico, Mexico, Central America). They vary also in the length of their residence in the United States, all the way from new arrivals to leading citizens of the state of New Mexico who trace their family trees back hundreds of years in the same territory. Hispanics are the fastest growing ethnic group, adding to their population by high birth rates and a considerable "undocumented" immigration from Mexico in particular and Latin America in general. They could become 20 percent of the potential electorate, and their various choices of political affiliation may well be fateful ones. Cuban-Americans in south Florida have recently elected their first member of congress, a Republican, as many Miami Cubans are. This contrasts with the older settlement of Cuban-Americans around Tampa, who are predominantly Democratic. Most of the other Hispanic-Americans are Democrats in their presidential voting.

Realignment Reconsidered

It is not only the evidence of the 1980s, but the far stronger evidence of trends since 1972, that enables us to conclude that there has been a considerable internal reshuffling of activists within the Democratic and Republican parties. This process has unfolded slowly. It constitutes a meaningful change, even though it is not the classic realignment of voters that definitively changes the parties so that the majority becomes the minority and vice versa. Instead we observe a deepening and intensification of preexisting positions—Democrats becoming more liberal and Republicans more conservative, and an increase in the coverage of these positions over a much wider range of issues, from defense spending to foreign policy to ecology to various matters concerning social behavior. Thus there has been a polarization of the major party activists consisting in party of the conversion of southern conservative Democrats to the Republican party and of some liberal Republicans to the Democratic party.[54]

Party identifiers in the general public have either become a little more

Republican or not changed very much, leaving the Democratic party with a clear but diminished advantage. Among party identifiers there is evidence of ideological consistency. Thus the opinions of identifiers cohere in the same directions as their respective party activists, though not as strongly. Identifiers are of course more interested in politics and public policy than the general public. Being loyal as well, identifiers are more likely to learn what stands they ought to take from their respective party activists and leaders. As party elites become more consistent in their views, therefore, party identifiers follow suit. And those who are at odds with their party—say, Democrats who favored war against Iraq or prayer in schools or Republicans who opposed the Strategic Defense Initiative or are permissive with respect to abortion—can expect to suffer more discomfort than in the past when party positions were fuzzier. As liberal comes more unequivocally to mean Democratic and conservative to mean Republican, people who identify with a given party for historical or habitual or traditional or other reasons unrelated to ideology will become more uncomfortable.

Yet the views of the public at large appear largely unchanged over the last decade or two. There is little evidence of anything except small movements in issue positions. Self-identifications as liberal or conservative have remained stable with conservatives consistently outnumbering liberals and a large number identifying as centrist or moderate. Nevertheless, when votes in the 1980s are related to voters' self-identifications and issue positions, the more conservative supported Republican candidates for president and the more liberal went for Democrats.[55] Whether these particular candidates generated an ideological response among voters or whether voters already felt that way is an open question.

If there has been a growth of both liberal and conservative ideology, then we can expect increased polarization among the major parties and heightened levels of conflict over public policy. If party activists and, to a much lesser extent, identifiers are becoming more polarized, but voters are not, the question must arise of whether there is room for a third party whose issue positions would be closer to those of the citizenry.

James Q. Wilson says: "The central change that has occurred in American party politics in the last twenty years has been the realignment of party elites."[56] Wilson notes that a sitting Democratic president, Jimmy Carter, was challenged for renomination in 1980 by a more liberal challenger, Senator Edward M. Kennedy, and an incumbent Republican president, Gerald Ford, was challenged in 1976 by a more conservative rival, Ronald Reagan. In 1956 Democratic delegates were close in issue positions to Democratic voters, while from 1972 on delegates of both major parties were fairly far from their party's voters. Twice as many Democratic delegates as rank-and-file Democrats called themselves liberal in 1980 according to a CBS News/*New York Times* poll, whereas in 1984 according to a *Los Angeles Times* survey that number had increased to four times. And where a third more Republican delegates than rank-and-file Republicans called themselves conservative in 1980, half did the same in 1984. These sharp liberal-conservative differences, Wilson maintains, citing the accompanying table by William Schneider (see Table 4.9), show up in congressional votes, House and Senate, across a spectrum of issues. Democratic and Republican politicians are internally cohesive and differ substantially from each other.[57]

Wilson thinks that elite realignment may have made mass realignment—"a sharp enduring change in the coalitions supporting each party"—less likely. As party elites grow further from party voters, and from the general public, he reasons, they are less likely to select generally appealing candidates. Candidates who appeal to party leaders are less likely to appeal to voters.

Party polarization is not just a statistical artifact; it is observed by voters. Whereas from 1952 to 1976, 46 to 52 percent of the electorate saw important differences between the major parties, 58 percent did so in 1980 and 63 percent in 1984. "This greater public perception of philosophical differences between the parties," Martin Wattenberg suggests, "may well be one of the most long-lasting changes in the political system from the Reagan era."[58] We think that the Reagan era saw the continuing liberalization of the Democratic party as well as the growing conservatism of Republicans.

On the other hand, Wattenberg argues that candidate-centered nomination processes mean that party identification will come to mean less to most voters. He shows that while voters perceive more differences be-

TABLE 4.9   *Members of Congress Voting on Liberal Side of Issues, by Party, 1983*

Kind of Issue	House Democratic	House Republican	Senate Democratic	Senate Republican
Economic	85%	8%	93%	7%
Social	75	27	91	18
Foreign and Military	82	9	85	7

Source: The Baron Report (May 7, 1984). Percentages computed by William Schneider.

tween the parties than formerly, they are also less likely to believe that one or the other party would do a better job on specific issues they find important. Thus party polarization may be less important than the declining relevance of party to voters.

Theory and Action

The issues of realignment discussed above are of great interest to students of American politics. Realignments help shape the "playing field" upon which electoral competition takes place. As presidential candidates enter the fall of an election year, however, they have more immediate concerns on their minds. Specifically, they want to know what sort of campaign will maximize their chances for victory in November. Can any theory tell them what to do?

The contents of election campaigns appear to be largely opportunistic. The swiftly changing nature of events makes it unwise for candidates to lay down all-embracing rules for campaigning that cannot meet special situations as they arise. Candidates may prepare for battle on one front and discover that the movement of events forces them to fight on another. Yet on closer examination, it is evident that the political strategist has to rely on some sort of theory about the probable behavior of large groups of voters under a few likely conditions. For there are too many millions of voters and too many thousands of possible events to deal with each as a separate category. John Maynard Keynes pointed out years ago, quite rightly, that politicians who most loudly proclaim their avoidance of theory are generally the victims of some long-dead economist or philosopher whose assumptions they have unknowingly assimilated. The candidates must simplify their picture of the political world or its full complexity will paralyze them; the only question is whether or not their theories, both explicit and implicit, will prove helpful to them.

What kind of organization shall they use or construct? Where shall they campaign? How much time shall they allocate to the various regions and states? What kinds of appeals shall they make to what voting groups? How specific shall they be in their policy proposals? What kind of personal impression shall they seek to create or reinforce? How far should they go in castigating the opposition? These are the kinds of strategic questions for which presidential candidates need answers—answers that necessarily vary depending on their party affiliations, their personal attributes, whether they are in or out of office, and on targets of opportunity that come up in the course of current events. Let us take up each of these questions in turn, taking care to specify the different problems faced by "ins" and "outs" and by Democrats and Republicans.

"Ins" and "Outs"

While incumbents may have disadvantages to offset some of their advantages, as we saw in Chapter 2, challengers face their own set of problems. They may not be well known and may find that much of their effort must be devoted to publicizing themselves. All the while, the president is getting reams of free publicity and is in a position to create major news by the things he does—a tariff on imported oil, proposals for balancing the budget, announcing major new programs for highways and public works.[59] Or the incumbent may play president for the press without risking exposure on issues. Gerald Ford's chief of staff in 1976 admitted this made things easy for his candidate. "Let's face it," he said, "we played to television's problems. We knew that their measure of fair treatment was equal time. So we would go out in the Rose Garden and say nothing—just sign a bill—and we'd get the coverage."[60]

As the symbolic leader of the nation, the incumbent is well placed to utilize patriotic themes. Reporter Sam Donaldson described the 1984 Reagan campaign in these terms: "The essence of the Ronald Reagan campaign is a never-ending string of spectacular picture stories created for television and designed to place the president in the midst of wildly cheering, patriotic Americans. . . . God, patriotism, and Ronald Reagan, that's the essence this campaign is trying hard to project."[61] That this did not seem altogether to please Mr. Donaldson probably suggested to Mr. Reagan that he had good reason to use this strategy.

The candidate aspiring to office may find that he lacks information, which puts him at a disadvantage in discussing foreign policy and defense issues. Frequently, the president offers as a matter of courtesy, or strategy, to supply both party nominees, or his opponent, with regular briefings. The out-party candidate may deliberately keep from finding out too much, however, for fear that he be held back in his criticism by an implied pledge not to use information the president has furnished to him. Perhaps the major advantage the challenger possesses is his ability to criticize policies freely and sometimes in exaggerated terms, whereas the incumbent is often restrained by his current official responsibilities from talking too much about them. Obligations to other nations, for example, may restrain a president from talking about changes in foreign policy or from tipping his hand in situations like Vietnam or the Middle East. Knowing too much is not necessarily helpful if inside information leads one to ignore the forest for the trees. Ordinary citizens would have had no difficulty telling a national television audience that the Soviet Union had armed forces in and exerted considerable control over Poland in 1976. President Ford, with other relevant but confidential things on his mind when he debated Jimmy Carter, answered differently and caused a furor.[62]

While the incumbent has a going organization, molded and tested through his years in office, the challenger has to build one, usually from scratch. The mechanics of electioneering are no simple matter; they cannot be entrusted wholly to amateurs. Not only must candidates get to their various speaking engagements on time, but they also need to have some good idea of the audience they are addressing and what kind of approach to take. In the hurly-burly of the campaign, where issues and plans may change from day to day, where yesterday's ideas may have to make room for today's problems, where changes of schedule are made in response to the opportunities and dangers suggested by private and public polls, a poor organization can be severely damaging. The troubles of Adlai Stevenson present a case in point. His apparent distaste for the niceties of organization in 1956 hurt him badly. He was excessively rushed going from one place to another and thus lost the composure and thoughtfulness which should have been his most valuable assets. If he continually made speeches that were inappropriate for his audiences, it may have been because he was badly informed about who his audience would be, not because he was talking "over people's heads." For instance, once during the 1956 campaign he made a speech in New Haven redolent with allusions to Yale and Princeton, with punch lines depending on knowledge of what the "subjunctive" was, to an audience that happened to be composed largely of old-time Democratic party workers from around Connecticut.[63] In 1976, Republican vice-presidential candidate Bob Dole did especially badly in his debate with Walter Mondale because he was too aware of his immediate audience—a mixed group of savvy partisans who enjoyed his inside jokes and partisan jibes—and forgot that his main impression, the one that counted, would be made to the relatively unsophisticated television audience.

In 1972, because George McGovern and his staff were tired, and busy preparing for the challenge to their California delegates, they did not check as carefully as they might have into their vice-presidential nominee's background. What was to be the rousing opening of Walter Mondale's 1984 campaign sputtered when his advance men failed to produce a crowd.[64] Geraldine Ferraro's hesitation about making her husband's tax returns public hurt her and her running mate badly both because it appeared she was hiding something and because the press would not allow them to speak about anything else. To be sure, some mix-ups, if not outright fiascoes, are inevitable given the frantic pace and the pressure of time. Resilience is not the least qualification of a presidential candidate.

The risks and rewards of a special campaign organization are illustrated by President Nixon's decision in 1972 to bypass entirely the Republican party in setting up his Committee to Reelect the President (CREEP). This comported with Nixon's desire to insulate himself as much as possible from the fortunes of the Republican party. On behalf of the incumbent president, Maurice Stans, Herbert Kalmbach, and others had no difficulty raising enormous amounts of money. Some estimates of the total take range up to $60 million.[65] At CREEP, meanwhile, persons of low character and no common sense devised plans to spend the money. One such plan has become famous, since it entailed bugging the headquarters of the Democratic National Committee, the botching of which led to the president's near-impeachment and to the unraveling of the Nixon presidency.

Two little-noticed facts about the CREEP operation deserve mention here. The first is that by raising money in this fashion, President Nixon starved other Republican candidates who had to rely on many of the same sources for cash. The second is that apparently the president and his employees had no intention of sharing the proceeds with other Republicans. Yet when Nixon's downfall came, he dragged numerous Republicans down with him, at a minimum by spoiling the party's chances at the next election. This illustrates the profound stake political parties have in the caliber of their presidential candidates.

The Professionalization of the Campaign

Presidential candidates have never lacked for willing accomplices in their quest for office. In the first generally acknowledged partisan election battle of 1800 the crucial New York campaign was led by Alexander Hamilton (for the Federalists) and Aaron Burr (for the Democratic-Republicans). With the resumption of party competition in the 1830s, campaign managers assumed primary responsibility for the conduct of the battle, a pattern that has continued to the present.

Contemporary campaigns have evolved into something qualitatively different from the pattern of the previous century. The "professionalization'' of the campaign is not new—old-time party managers were extremely interested in monetary rewards for their services—but what is new is that modern consultants are business professionals, not party professionals. The individuals who directed the first century-and-a-half of presidential elections were closely tied to one or another of the political parties. Secondly, the technologies and strategies at the disposal of modern consultants to "sell" their candidates have transformed the entire process of running for the nation's highest office.

What is the nature of this new campaign animal, the "consultant"? The business of consulting, though still relatively new, has already reached a considerable degree of specialization and diversity.[66] There are still old-style generalists who coordinate campaigns from top to bottom, but increasingly the business of the campaign is subcontracted to firms who specialize in a particular aspect of the process. *Campaigns and Elections,* the trade magazine of political consultancy, lists the following major categories of consultants (along with sixty-seven further subcategories) in their "Complete Guide to Political Products and Services": advertising agencies, attorneys, campaign promotional materials, campaign training, computers, general consulting, field operations, opposition research, press relations, scheduling and advance, speech coaching, speech writing, targeting, voter contact, direct mail, fund raising, grass roots, media, political publications, printing, research and polling, and telephone/voter contact.[67]

Polls The first significant use of polls within a campaign or organization occurred in 1960, when surveys taken by Louis Harris helped guide John Kennedy's campaign in key primary states.[68] Polling of various kinds is now a major industry, but only a small number of the hundreds of polling firms handle political races. Just a few names— Republican pollsters such as Robert Teeter of Detroit's Market Opinion Research, Inc., and Richard Wirthlin of Decision Making Information, and Democrats such as Peter D. Hart and Irwin "Tubby" Harrison— tend to dominate at the national level. Teeter began polling in Richard Nixon's 1968 campaign. He was the lead pollster in Gerald Ford's nearly successful underdog campaign in 1976 (Ford faced an initial deficit of 62–29 in the polls). And he was the polling chief for George Bush in both 1980 and 1988. For about fifteen years, from the McGovern campaign in 1972 to Gary Hart's 1984 effort, Patrick Caddell was the Democrats' dominant figure. He began developing sophisticated polling techniques as a precocious seventeen-year-old high school senior in Jacksonville, Florida and took his first presidential poll for

George McGovern in 1972 while still a senior at Harvard. He polled for the Carter campaign in 1976 and 1980. According to journalist Michael Barone, Caddell's great contribution was to exploit the theme of alienation: "[I]t was he who counseled McGovern to appeal to supporters of George Wallace on the grounds that they all wanted a change and a removal of the people in power in Washington." But, says Barone, Caddell became something of a "Johnny-one-note." He again pushed the alienation theme in Carter's 1976 campaign, this time with success, and in 1979, when he urged Carter to make his famous "national malaise" speech.[69]

The modern pollster's role goes far beyond gathering data. "There's no question that our role has changed from collector of facts to interpreter and strategist," Wirthlin has said.[70] What should be the major campaign themes—or, at least, which would be most attractive to the electorate? Should the candidate attack his opponent's record? If so, how? Which regions and states should be emphasized? What is the proper role of the vice-presidential candidate? The campaign pollster helps make these and a variety of other crucial campaign decisions, like which states to visit and which groups within the electorate to court.

The first nationwide polls in behalf of candidates typically begin many months before the first caucuses or primaries. These initial polls, called "benchmark polls," are based on twenty- to thirty-minute interviews with large samples (up to 4,000 nationwide) of potential voters. The object is to determine everything from current candidate preferences to issue positions. Of course, at this stage, most voters will not have even heard of, say, Jimmy Carter in 1975 or Michael Dukakis in 1987, but nevertheless pollsters begin to form campaign strategies based on the "mood" of the electorate. Later, there are shorter polls to update the horse race in key states or to test newly developed issues and themes; a second of benchmark-length survey is often conducted at the start of the fall campaign.

Kathleen Hall Jamieson explains how these polls can determine campaign themes, drawing an example from Ronald Reagan's successful 1980 campaign:

> In June 1979, [Reagan pollster] Richard Wirthlin conducted a national study of "six scenarios for the future." Given a choice from among options ranging from "less is better" to "America can do," the majority preferred the "America can do" theme.
>
> The "can do" theme pervaded Reagan's advertising. "Don't let anyone tell you that inflation can't be controlled. It can be, by making some tough decisions to cut federal spending."[71]

In primaries, candidates can use polls to detect opportunities to surpass the media's expectations. Louis Harris analyzed 1960 polls in West Virginia and discovered that although conventional wisdom considered the primary a sure loss for Kennedy, JFK in fact had considerable support. Thus, the Kennedy campaign targeted the state for a critical "upset" victory.[72] In 1988, the Dukakis campaign used the same strategy in the Wisconsin primary against Jesse Jackson. In its preprimary polls, the press showed a tight race, but Tubby Harrison's numbers revealed a double-digit lead for Dukakis. According to Christine Black and Thomas Oliphant, "Dukakis' aides . . . privately reasoned that the bigger Jackson became in the press, the harder he would fall, and Dukakis would rise if Harrison's data were accurate."[73] As it turned out, the Wisconsin results were as Harrison had foreseen: 48 percent for Dukakis, 28 percent for Jackson, and 17 percent for Gore. The surprisingly large margin— actually not a surprise for Dukakis—deflated Jackson's support, and Dukakis went on to win all subsequent primaries.

Campaigns monitor any number of "target voters"—blocs of the electorate who are considered key swing votes—to determine which themes should be stressed. The Dukakis campaign targeted two major groups: white Reagan Democrats (about 10 percent of the voters) and white independents (about 20 percent of the voters). In a September 19 memo, Dukakis's pollsters—Tubby Harrison, Clifford Brown, and Lynda Powell—had grim news about the first target group: "After the Democratic convention, we led by 69% to 25% among white Reagan Democrats; in the most recent survey . . . Bush led 54% to 41%." They suggested that to recapture this group, Dukakis should emphasize his commitment to "building a strong economic future," argue that the current state of the economy was one of "false prosperity," and talk about how overseas economic competition was threatening U.S. economic stability.[74]

For the second group—white independents—the pollsters noted that prior to the Republican convention, Bush and Dukakis split evenly, but by mid-September, Bush led 62 percent to 31 percent. These voters were disproportionately concerned about Dukakis's lack of "presidential" qualities. "In sum," concluded the polling team, "the most important move we can make to regain our position among white independents is for [Dukakis] to appear strong and presidential. Given our acute liberal-conservative outlook problem among this group, emphasizing patriotism and toughness are equally important."[75] The pollsters also paid close attention to white men, who were disproportionately pro-Bush. Said an earlier memo: "Among white men, Bush leads by 61% to 34%; among white women, he leads by 55% to 39%.[76]

The Dukakis campaign attempted to determine which of Bush's weaknesses would win over the target groups. According to one memorandum:

Voters were read a series of factual negative statements about George Bush's record, and then were asked for each statement whether or not the information contained in that particular statement made them less or more inclined to support Bush. Set forth below are the percentages of . . . white Reagan Democrats (WRD) and white independents (WI) who, for each statement, say the information makes them "much less" inclined to vote for Bush:

	WRD	WI
Opposed 60-day plant closing notice	26	16
Cutting capital gains tax for rich	37	23
Opposed medicare, tried to raise premiums	41	25
Chaired terrorism task force/Ayatollah	38	31
Supposed to stop flow of drugs into South Florida	43	31
Changes his stand: abortion/gun control	29	26
Supported cutbacks in education loans	34	30
Japan task force/trade deficit	22	20

Overall, the item that seemed most effective was the one alleging that Bush had been put in charge of reducing the drug flow into South Florida, but while he was in charge, drug imports tripled.[77] The Dukakis team decided not to stress this particular issue. "We weren't going to win on crime or defense," said Harrison. "We didn't want the campaign waged on those issues. They're not our strengths. That's the Republicans' turf."[78]

Polling within particular states allows campaigns to decide which states to contest fiercely and which to downplay. By the final weeks of the 1988 campaign, pollsters realized that with a few possible exceptions, the Republicans were solidly ahead in the entire South and Mountain West regions. As Republican pollster Vincent Breglio noted, "Approximately 125 to 135 electoral votes in eighteen or nineteen states were going to end up in the Republican column unless a major mistake was made."[79] With approximately 130 electoral votes out of reach, Dukakis had to win his 270 votes from the remaining 408. But Bush needed only 140 of those 408 to win entrance to the White House. That is why talk among Democrats of a "fifty-state strategy," a strategy emphasized at their convention in Atlanta, quickly subsided. For Dukakis to win, he virtually would have had to sweep the Northeast, the industrial belt, and the Pacific. Both candidates spent little time in states where Dukakis was far behind—there was no point since the outcome was not likely to change—and therefore a small group of large, close states received the bulk of candidate visits in the final weeks.[80]

In addition, polling results help the campaign decide how to utilize the vice-presidential candidate. In an October 10, 1988 post-debate memo, Dukakis's pollsters noted that Lloyd Bentsen had won the vice-presidential debate against Dan Quayle "hands down." They said:

> Opinion of Senator Bentsen, now for the first time, has an impact on the trial heat. Even though its impact is small, opinion of Senator Bentsen now has as much of an impact on voter choice as opinion of Reagan. . . . These findings argue strongly for using Senator Bentsen's growing stature among the voters for something more important than Quayle-bashing while memories of the debate are fresh—thereby turning Senator Bentsen's favorability into a permanent asset.[81]

Focus Groups   Focus groups have been a tool of communication and advertising researching for forty years. But it was not until the 1980s that they became an integral part of campaign strategy. The ideal group is about a dozen to fifteen people. A much smaller number is likely to place too much of a burden on each individual, while more tends to reduce each member's participation. A moderator guides the discussion, focusing on matters of interest to the campaign. Discussions are lengthy—anywhere from one and a half to three hours—so that respondents have a chance to express their feelings.

Unlike opinion polls, which depend for their validity on randomly selecting a cross section of voters, focus groups are usually structured to be socially and intellectually homogenous, "so that the numerous inter-acting demographic variables do not confuse the issues; to be most productive, all the participants must be on the same wavelength."[82] The composition of the various groups depends on the needs of the campaign. In 1988, the Bush team interviewed white, Catholic Reagan Democrats, because they were considered a critical swing group. The idea was for Bush to pursue those groups that voted for Reagan but were in danger of drifting back toward the Democrats.

Focus group interviewing violates most of the accepted canons of survey research. As William D. Wells of the University of Chicago Graduate School of Business said:

> Samples are invariably small and never selected by probability methods. Questions are not asked the same way each time. Responses are not independent. Some respondents inflict their opinions on others; some contribute little or nothing at all. Results are difficult or impossible to quantify and are not grist for the statistical mill. Conclusions depend on the analyst's interpretive skill. The investigator can easily influence the results.[83]

With so many defects, why have focus groups become so widely used in political campaigns? Part of the reason is that they are fast and relatively cheap—a few thousand dollars as opposed to $20,000 to $25,000 or more for quantitative studies. But the more important reason is that pollsters believe that focus groups allow an opportunity for greater depth than regular polls. The subject's deeper feelings and half-formed thoughts emerge, and in his or her own words. "Focus groups allow you to put flesh on the bones," Democratic pollster Mark Mellman says; they provide "a sense of texture you can't get from a poll."[84] While focus groups do not produce the raw numbers of traditional polls, in both cases the art of the pollster requires a sensitive reading of the implications of the data, whether that data consists of nervous laughs at the mention of Willie Horton's rampage or 36.75 percent of respondents favoring some policy issue.

Using focus groups in 1988, Bob Teeter discovered that none of Bush's positive campaign issues impressed voters. The issues that tested strongest were the attacks on Dukakis which became the Bush campaign themes: "liberals," death penalty, taxes, furloughs, and the flag.[85] The Dukakis campaign also used focus groups extensively and, interestingly, found many of the same sentiments in the population that the Reagan people were discovering. "We polled. We had extensive focus groups," said Susan Estrich, Dukakis' campaign manager. "You know, you can go wrong, but you don't go wrong for lack of trying—at least in the general election we were polling constantly. We were focus grouping their ads probably as much as they were."[86] The polls and focus groups enabled the Democrats to identify their weaknesses. "They told us that we were vulnerable on the liberal-conservative issues and on crime," said Irwin "Tubby" Harrison. "We looked at Dukakis's involvement in the prison furlough program in Massachusetts early and knew we had a problem. There was a possible vulnerability on defense, on taxes, and on capital punishment, too."[87]

But recognizing a problem and remedying it are two different things. The pollster reigns supreme at the former task but there may be little he can do about the latter. Dukakis's closest aide, Nicholas Mitropoulos, suggested that the Governor was uncomfortable responding to Bush's attacks. "Dukakis deep down inside is just a good guy and felt that . . . the American people were going to see that these issues were not real issues," Mitropoulos said. "He wanted to take the campaign on the high road . . . he wanted to stay positive."[88] A Bush pollster, Vincent Breglio, took a different view. "Dukakis tried to explain away the furlough program, Boston harbor, his Pledge position," Breglio said. "It just didn't work."[89]

Another wrinkle, overnight tracking, has become critical in the last weeks of an election. Rare until recently, tracking polls have "become de riguer in the business," says Democratic pollster Paul Maslin.[90] Shifts in sentiment among voters are "tracked" by calling approximately one hundred voters each night, asking a half dozen very specific questions, usually about perceptions of the latest ads, issues, or the candidates. With each increment of new respondents, the responses from six-day-old interviews are dropped. Thus, rolling averages can be calculated. The overnight figures facilitate fine-tuning of a campaign in the crucial last days.

In late October of 1988, Dukakis made a last-minute surge, narrowing the gap with Bush, who was so distressed by Dukakis's improvement that aides tried to keep the tracking numbers from him. "Bush would start each morning agreeing that they [the numbers] were bad for him," Peter Goldman and Tom Mathews report, "but his resolve not to ask would typically break down by, say, 8 A.M. 'What did Teeter tell you?' he would ask urgently. 'Have you heard from Teeter?' " As a result of Teeter's disconcerting tracking results, the entire Bush team worked feverishly right up to election day.[91]

While plenty of attention has been focused on the mistaken or misleading results of polling, the real story of polling is perhaps contained in the fact that, taken together, polls are reasonably accurate indicators of public sentiment. Thus they are a better tool for shaping campaign strategy and content than anything else presently available, and this, in the uncertain universe of the presidential campaign, is all that is really necessary to make polls indispensable to the candidate.

One need only consider the information sources that used to govern campaign strategy to appreciate the significance of the advent of modern polling techniques. Nineteenth- and early twentieth-century campaign indicators consisted of reports from precinct captains and state party leaders, crowd size and response, newspaper editorials and letters to the editor, the candidate's mail, man-in-the-street interviews, and pure hunches. Most of these indicators were unreliable. Editorials may signify the views of only a few newspaper owners; letters to the editor represent a lot of writing by a rather small number of activists; crowd responses can be manipulated, or variously "interpreted"; party leaders may let candidates know only what they wish them to hear. Polls, on the whole, are better data.

Television in the Campaign

Television Advertising   Campaigns spend a lot of money on political television commercials. Though they are not normally the main cause of defeat or victory, it is generally acknowledged among media consultants that advertisements can make some difference. Commercials serve a variety of purposes. They can be used to establish name identification, or to improve a candidate's personal image. They can focus on campaign issues, targeting key subgroups in the population. Or they can be used to attack the candidate's opponent. This practice has come to be called negative advertising.

There is no standard formula for a political ad, but there are standard time-slots. When introduced in the 1950s TV advertising was generally produced to fill five-minute slots. One-minute spots predominated in the 1960s and 1970s, to be eclipsed in the late seventies by the thirty-second ad. Finally, around 1982, the now-popular ten-second spot was introduced.[92]

After the advertisement is filmed, edited, and approved by the candidate, a schedule of airing is prepared that is supposed to reach the right people. Every ad campaign is somewhat different, and must be crafted to attend to the unique assets and deficits of the candidate. But amidst the varying styles of each campaign, a relatively small number of tried-and-true themes have established themselves over the last several decades; they are the advertising consultants' tool-kit, from which virtually every television campaign is built. There is the "man-in-the-street" ad, sometimes scripted and sometimes culled from actual interview footage, showing the average voter (or the average member of a targeted constituency group) endorsing the candidate's accomplishments or general integrity. The "sainthood spot" might include features from the candidate's life story mixed with political accomplishments. The "news-look" ad combines the legitimacy of experts and legitimacy of television newscasters who relate facts about the candidate's record. The "apology" ad is used, usually out of desperation, when a liability develops that is considered so serious to the candidate's chances of election that he must personally apologize to the electorate. "Cinema-verite" spots offer the audience a view into the life of the candidate as he is working, walking, or addressing another audience, while the older "talking head" approach (still a staple of spot ads) places the candidate directly in front of the camera so that he can talk personally and directly with the audience. The "issue-position" spot defines the candidate's record on an issue of high salience to the electorate or to a swing group of voters.[93]

One measure of the centrality of television advertising in the current campaign process can be found in the recently developed "back-'n-forth" ad. This innovative format begins with an excerpt from an opponent's spot ad which is then "answered" in the second sequence, an ad-within-an-ad. This is possible because technological developments have enabled campaigns to produce television ads faster, cheaper, and more easily. Campaigns can respond to the opposition's latest round of advertising in a matter of days.

Of course, media consultants work closely with pollsters as they develop ads. In the 1988 campaign, the results of focus groups and polls were instrumental in devising the ad campaign. When pollster Robert Teeter discovered that Michael Dukakis was vulnerable on the prison furlough issue, Roger Ailes ran what professionals considered the single most potent ad of the campaign: "Revolving Door." The ad showed a prison guard and a long line of convicts walking through a revolving gate while the announcer explained that Dukakis' "revolving-door prison policy gave weekend furloughs to first-degree murderers not eligible for parole." It grimly concluded: "Now Michael Dukakis says he wants to do for America what he has done for Massachusetts. America can't afford that risk."[94] The ad hit Dukakis where it hurt, implying that he was soft on law and order issues.

In the background was the story of Willie Horton, a murderer who while on furlough raped a woman and beat her husband. Democrats complained that exploitation of the Willie Horton case was racist. The Bush campaign responded that they have never used Horton in an ad. But state Republican parties did. Commentators are still debating whether the Bush campaign (and, in particular, Ailes) instructed, consented, or knew about the independent Republican state committees' decision to run ads featuring Horton's face.

It is important to note that ad-makers are not always guided by the pollster's revelations. In the 1980 general election, ads showed Carter working long hours at the White House. "The responsibility never ends," said the voice-over. "Even at the end of a long working day, there is usually another cable addressed to the Chief of State from the other side of the world where the sun is shining and something is happening." But polls said that voters never doubted that Carter worked hard. They doubted whether all the hard work was paying off; this crucial point—Carter's effectiveness—was not addressed in the ad.[95]

Targeting   Media masters attempt to place political commercials so as to reach the right viewing audience. "Dissimilar kinds of people," Larry Sabato notes, "watch and listen to different sorts of programs at various times of the day. The better educated, information-oriented, undecided voters have been found to cluster around late news shows." A media manager might go after such a group with information-packed ads, or spots discussing issues. Middle-aged housewives, Sabato believes, are partial to family-oriented or charismatic image spots during afternoon soap operas.[96]

The latest frontier in targeting promises to extend this strategy by exploiting the rapidly expanding media-market of cable television. Well over half the households in the country now subscribe to one or more cable systems.[97] The audiences watching cable channels are often more socially and culturally homogenous than audiences tuned to even the smallest local television station. Also, according to one researcher, cable audiences tend to be more politically active than regular television viewers, raising the prospect of media advertising aimed at recruiting not just voters, but also volunteer campaign workers.[98] Richard N. Neustadt, a communications law attorney, predicts:

> When we watch the narrowcasting [approach of cable] networks, we may see campaign ads and news programs showing candidates advocating bilingual education on Spanish channels, defending Social Security on channels aimed at the elderly, or playing football on sports channels.[99]

Cable television, in the words of Richard Viguerie, "could be to the politics of the 1990s what direct mail was to the 1970s."[100]

The Sound Bite   Television advertising is not necessarily the most important source of political information for the electorate. In fact, when compared with state- or district-wide campaigns, the presidential campaign relies much more heavily on free media than paid media. "In a sense," media consultant Robert Squier says, "presidential candidates are their own spot-makers as they get their messages across on the stump before the TV cameras."[101]

The press, not the public, is the audience for much of what candidates do while running for the presidency. John Buckley, press secretary to Jack Kemp, estimated that, "If you discount travel time, I'd say that the media take a third of a candidate's entire day. It's not just the news conferences, but one-on-one interviews, hotel room press briefings, radio and TV shows, editorial board discussions, back-of-the-car interviews and conversations."[102]

In the 1988 campaign, the contrast between the two campaigns' abilities to control the news agenda was widely regarded as significant. Bush's media advisors planned the vice-president's appearances in camera-ready settings that provided excellent videotape for the newscasts. In front of a defense plant in St. Louis, he talked up America's need to remain strong. Dukakis made speech after speech in front of the backdrop of a drab blue curtain, behind a wooden podium.

Another Bush success was the ability to manufacture "sound bites"—one-liners that he knew would be broadcast on television. "Dukakis gives me the impression that he is opposed to every new weapon since the slingshot," said Bush. NBC used the line immediately, and the other networks followed suit when he repeated the line a few days later. "I wouldn't be surprised," Bush said in another sound bite, "if [Dukakis] thought that a naval exercise was something you find in Jane Fonda's workout book."[103]

The Other Media

Thus far, we have spoken of the news media as if they were a monolithic entity. But there are all sorts of news outlets with differing biases, needs, and audiences. A great deal of a candidate's attention is devoted to stories destined for the racial, religious, and ethnic interest-group press. The circulations of these publications may not be huge, but it is assumed that they have readers who are concerned with topics of special interest to smaller and more attentive constituencies. A story on religion in politics in a religious journal may do more to convince people than much greater coverage in the daily press.

Radio   Though generally ignored by political and academic commentators, radio remains a staple in the advertising diet of presidential campaigns. The main advantage over television, of course, is cost. With an audience that is more demographically focused than even cable television, radio also offers a campaign the opportunity to pitch a narrow slice of the electorate. The McGovern campaign, for example, was the first to take aim at the rock 'n' roll audience, which at the time consisted largely of eighteen- to twenty-one-year-olds just enfranchised by the Twenty-sixth Amendment.[104]

Newspapers   The grandfather of all political advertising, newspapers have clearly lost out in the bid for campaign advertising dollars in the contemporary period. Consultants, according to one survey, consider the effect of a print ad to be "almost negligible."[105]

Several factors account for this revolutionary change in campaign strategy. First, people tend to view newspapers as less credible than other media as sources of information. Secondly a newspaper ad can be more easily ignored than a television or radio spot. Thirdly, the portion of the electorate that reads newspapers is more highly educated and more politically committed than that portion that attends to electronic media, and therefore less likely to be swayed by advertising of any sort. "If you want to communicate to the politicians, take out a newspaper ad. If you want to communicate with the voters, use radio and television." Such is the orthodoxy among the consultants.[106]

One continuing attraction of newspapers for the presidential campaign has nothing to do with advertising. "Some candidates," according to Democratic pollster Bill Hamilton, "particularly on the Democratic side, are forced to buy newspaper ads if they want to get the paper's endorsement."[107]

Video Cassettes Two-thirds of the electorate now own videocassette recorders, and the fact has not been lost on political consultants. Walter Mondale become the first presidential candidate to produce a video cassette for mass circulation during the 1984 campaign. The purpose in this case was fundraising, but the trend is clearly to use the new medium to replace personal campaigning. Eleven of the thirteen major party candidates in 1988 distributed videos of themselves. "Video parties" were held by the thousands in New Hampshire before the state's primary elections.

Why the sudden popularity? Luntz explains:

At a cost of from $10,000 to $40,000 . . . , home videos are relatively inexpensive to prepare, and can also save the campaign money by using video footage for their television advertising, or vice versa. These cassettes allow the candidate to appear "in person" at five or even fifty places at once, and are designed to give voters a personal sense of the candidate, not just a recitation of proposals or issues.

As John Buckley, Jack Kemp's press secretary, put it, "It's the political equivalent of cloning."[108]

Computer Telemarketing Automated dialing devices were once thought to be the technological successor to direct mail. These "tape recorded messages and interactive response systems" were designed to conduct automatic polling and fundraising drives. The usual advantages of time and money can be found over human phone banks, and the machines are capable of some pretty impressive maneuvers. They pause when the respondent answers, register the response, and choose an appropriate sermonette with a personalized message from the candidate.

The trouble is, no one appears to be listening. Voters, surprisingly enough, "want human contact. Even if they like the person on the tape, they won't pay much attention to the message if it isn't live," reported one frustrated pollster.[109]

Satellites The first use of satellite broadcasting in a presidential campaign is described by Richard Armstrong:

> During one . . . impossible week in 1984, when both Florida and Georgia
> were preparing for their primaries, Walter Mondale took an hour out of his
> campaign schedule in Georgia to go to an Atlanta television studio. [Frank]
> Greet [the first consultant to capitalize on the new satellite technology] had
> arranged for an "uplink" to a satellite and had made appointments with the
> news anchormen of Miami's three biggest television stations. As Mondale
> stared into the camera, each Florida newsman took turns asking him ques-
> tions over long-distance phone lines. Mondale's replies were shot in At-
> lanta, relayed by microwave to an uplink dish outside the city, beamed
> 22,300 miles in space to a satellite over the equator, reflected back to the
> downlink dishes in three Miami television stations, and recorded for use on
> the evening news later that day.[110]

The result? Mondale captured the lead spot on all three network-
affiliated stations in Miami. As his face appeared on the screen behind the
anchormen, each repeated the questions asked earlier in the taped satellite
interview. "To the viewers it appeared to be a live interview in the
studio, a real coup for the local news team. But as virtually everyone in
southern Florida watched Mondale "live" on local TV, Mondale himself
was busy meeting his commitments in Georgia.[111] Mondale, one technological step ahead of his opponent John Glenn, managed to appear in
three places while actually campaigning in none, and scooped up the
nightly news programs in the process.

In addition to conducting press conferences in situations where the
candidate and the press audience he is trying to reach are on different
parts of the earth, satellite communications can be used to disseminate
stories to local media across the country, to bring the candidate into direct
contact with potential donors at several locations, and to bring the many
local chapters of the campaign together for one, big television conference.

Braintrusters: Advising the Candidate

Everyone has advice for the would-be president. In the old days most
of the policy advice came after the general election as the victor prepared
to assume office. Nowadays the advising process has been incorporated
into the process of campaigning. The function of the policy advisor, in
other words, is no longer simply to help the future president govern, but
to help the candidate define and publicize the campaign's position on the

"issues." Every campaign has extensive contacts with academics and policy analysts who draw up position papers on specialized issues of foreign and domestic policy and help set the general ideological tone of the campaign. The experts do this to position themselves to have influence if their candidate wins, and the candidate takes the advice because no single politician can be an expert on every issue.

The increasing duration of presidential campaigns means that candidates sometimes decide what issues to emphasize as many as two or three years in advance of the election. It is at this initial period, long before a candidacy is officially announced, that decisions on national policy issues will be made. "If you're . . . in the policy-advising business," explains Pat Choate, an issues specialist, "you must move on that time schedule." Introducing a novel idea later on, during the heat of the campaign, is risky: first because the candidate may gain the reputation of an opportunist or a waffler, and second, because there will be no opportunity to test the new idea for technical or political feasibility, to get its "rough edges smoothed out."[112]

Since in the course of the campaign the candidate is expected to offer judgments on events occurring in the world as they break into the news, every campaign has to keep handy access to advisors in different policy areas who can be contacted during emergencies. News of a crisis in international finance surfaced as the Reagan campaign was in flight, remembers Martin Anderson, Reagan's policy research coordinator in 1980. By the time the plane had touched down at the next location the campaign had contacted Milton Friedman and Arthur Burns, formulated a response, and issued a press release.[113]

Campaign policy experts come in three flavors, according to Janne E. Nolan, Gary Hart's foreign policy and defense advisor in the 1984 campaign: those who believe in the issues they are pushing, those adrenaline junkies attracted by the chance to participate in the events of a presidential campaign, and those who have attached their ambitions to a particular candidate in the hope of achieving a position in a new administration.[114]

Policy advisors, even of the third type, are a very different breed from poll takers and media consultants. With the exception of the candidate's most senior policy coordinator(s), they are usually not paid. Their ties to the campaign may be tenuous, and they all have nonpolitical careers. Well-known academics may offer advice in an informal capacity to several campaigns in the same election.

Not surprisingly, there is a certain degree of tension between the "flack masters and [the] idea mongers," as Richard Allen (of the latter camp) puts it. "[P]eople in flackery don't know ideas and wouldn't know if one hit them at a great rate of speed," continues Allen, who headed the foreign policy issues team on the Republican side for the Reagan elections.[115]

There may, however, be some justification for this, in light of the demands of the presidential campaign. "There's a big difference," explains William A. Galston, Mondale's issues director in 1984, "between having a position paper and having a politically salable commodity."[116] "If an idea can't be communicated to the public, then it won't be part of the campaign," concludes John Holum, Hart's issues man in 1984 and 1988. Someone, in other words, must administer the "test of political marketability."[117]

Professionalization Reconsidered

Professionalization of the political campaign has advanced, by all accounts, considerably further in the United States than anywhere else among the world's democracies. What is the cumulative effect of the introduction of modern polls, media campaigns, fundraising efforts, and the consultants who run these operations on the conduct of the presidential campaign? Does the new agenda-setting mechanism of the opinion poll change the character and conduct of presidential campaigns? Have the political consultants altered the substantive content of politics? Are they in it for the money, or do they have their own ideological axes to grind?

Some of the murkiness in the consultant-client relationship clears away if one looks closely at the initial phases of the relationship. Although candidates are more typically to be found in the role of the suitor it is not at all unusual for consultants to go candidate-shopping if they are short on contracts in a particular election cycle. Once the initial contact has been made the two sides begin a bargaining process over a contract that, if signed, will formalize responsibility, set payment agreements, and establish general ground rules that will guide their interactions over the course of the campaign. Whether this courtship process is consummated or not depends on the resources each side brings to the bargaining table. The key resources, for both parties, are money and a winning reputation. Candidates are looking for the hottest consultant their money can buy—which generally means the firm with the best recent win-loss record on their side of the ideological spectrum. Consultants likewise prefer winners over probable losers (so they can protect their record) and fat cats over lean. Neither side wants to end up with a partner who is ideologically or personally incompatible.[118]

Not surprisingly, topflight consulting firms are besieged with offers from candidates and would-be candidates. Direct-mail champion Richard Viguerie has claimed (with possible exaggeration) to have turned down 98 percent of the campaigns that requested his help.[119] Big-name presidential hopefuls are similarly able to pick and choose, while no-name candidates must often wait patiently until relatively late in the game and settle for whomever is left. Sometimes a prominent consultant will take on a long-shot candidate to advance a political agenda, or because of a personal friendship. Even if the campaign is not generously bankrolled the publicity attached to running a presidential campaign may lead to future business opportunities for the firm.

How powerful are the consultants within the campaign organization? The candidate-client relationship varies considerably from case to case, depending on the experience and stature of each party and the terms of the original contract. It is the candidate, all agree, who draws the "bottom line," who approves the general strategy of the campaign. However, having done this many candidates apparently prefer to absent themselves from the nitty-gritty choices of the campaign. One survey found that 44 percent of a population of consultants agreed that candidates generally backed off from making decisions on the priority of different issues on the campaign. Most "were neither very involved nor influential in the day-to-day tactical operation of the campaign."[120]

Consultants (not a shy and self-deprecating group of people) will gladly tell you all about the power they enjoy—and should enjoy— as campaign managers. Robert Squier, for instance, a media advisor who works for Democrats, says:

> It is very possible to go through an entire campaign with a candidate, and when it is all over, they have no idea what went on. It is not to our advantage to explain to them. It is to our advantage to get them to do what we want—what's best for them—with the least amount of fuss.[121]

Explanations for consultant imperialism can be found in several related developments. The increasingly advanced technology involved in the campaign process means a candidate must hire technocrats to do most of the work. Volunteers, family and friends, and party leaders will tend to be sidelined to one degree or another because they lack technical experience in law, accounting, media productions, advertising, and the like.

Moreover, the brief and tenuous life of the average campaign organization (which, even in the age of the "permanent campaign" lasts only a year or so as an active entity) means that the candidate needs in addition to expertise a base of organizational capacity and institutional experience to draw upon. Instead of having to build a national organization from scratch it is now possible—and often necessary—to buy one ready-made.

"All-service" consultants will cover all contingencies, from general strategy to licking stamps.[122]

Have consultants made presidential campaigns more ideological? Probably not. With the exception of a few ideologically motivated firms consultants tend to be game-players, not advocates. Fund raising and direct-mail firms (an overlapping set of categories) can afford to be more pure than other sorts of consultants since they are holding the purse-strings and since they generally target a narrow range of politically motivated donors.[123]

However, Larry Sabato notes, "For most consultants ideology is a surprisingly minor criterion in the selection of clients."[124] The business logic of consultancy militates against an approach that would limit a firm's clientele, and the game-playing logic of the campaign itself demands the use of any strategy that will win, regardless of its ideological consequences.

Do consultants help candidates obfuscate and blur the issues? With candidates from both parties being coached to court the swing vote in the middle, perhaps consultants contribute to a "Tweedledum-Tweedledee" effect in presidential elections. Mitchell E. Daniels, Jr., from the Republican side says, "You tend not to make major gaffes, because somebody will spot them. On the other hand, you may not take very many bold actions, because someone will be very nervous."[125]

Have the consultant corps lowered standards of conduct in presidential elections? Even though the candidate is ultimately responsible for all campaign decisions, the use of paid political consultants may change the range of campaign options available and the type of strategies ultimately chosen. Consider the case of negative campaigning. "I love to do negatives," declares Bob Squier. "It is one of those opportunities in a campaign where you can take the truth and use it just like a knife to slice right through the opponent. I hate the kind of commercials that are just music and pretty pictures."[126] This bit of refreshing candor raises the possibility that the average consultant may in fact be different from the average politician. One study found that, "most media consultants admitted often having considerable difficulty in convincing their clients to go negative."[127]

Candidates are aware, of course, of most of what goes on in their name, but it is in any case easier to sign on the dotted line and have someone else take care of your dirty business for you than to have to haul the bodies away yourself.[128] Other commentators point out that there are limits to what campaigns can say on television, limits that did not apply to old-fashioned campaigns run by thousands of semi-independent and localized party bosses, newspapers, and partisans.

Do consultants undermine partisanship? There is no doubt that consultants have replaced party leaders as major actors in the campaign process. But the decline of party leaders was not caused by consultants; it was caused by changes in the party nomination and election system. Consultants' ideological slates are not completely blank. They retain, as a group, strong partisan affiliations and do not work both sides of the street. "[P]arty affiliation," according to one study, "is by far the most important factor considered by consultants in selecting their clients, outweighing a candidate's electability, ideology, or financial standing."[129] "I only do Republican races," said one media advisor, "because when I did Democrats we were given a lot of hell."[130]

Where to Campaign

In deciding where the campaign, the candidates are aided by distinctive features of the national political structure that go a long way toward giving them guidance. They know that it is not votes as such that matter but rather electoral votes, which are counted on a state-by-state basis. The candidate who wins by a small plurality in a state gains all of that state's electoral votes. The candidates realize that a huge margin of victory in a state with a handful of electoral votes will not do them nearly as much good as a bare plurality in states like New York and California, with large numbers of electoral votes. So their first guideline is evident: campaign in states with large numbers of electoral votes. There is not much point, however, in campaigning in states where they know they are bound to win or to lose. Thus, states that almost always go for a particular party receive less attention. The original guideline may be modified to read: campaign in states with large numbers of electoral votes that are doubtful. In practice, a "doubtful" state is one where there is a good chance for either party to capture the state. Politicians usually gauge this chance by the extent to which the state has delivered victories to both parties within recent memory. Candidates of both parties thus spend more time in New York, Ohio, Illinois, Pennsylvania, Texas, Florida and California than they do elsewhere. The closer the election contest overall, of course, the greater the likelihood that there may be more close races. As the campaign wears on, the candidates take soundings from the opinion polls and are likely to redouble their efforts in states where they believe a personal visit might turn the tide. In 1976 Hamilton Jordan had these matters worked out to mathematical extremes—awarding points to states based on these sorts of considerations, and then allocating campaign days to each of them for his candidate, Jimmy Carter, the vice-presidential candidate, and members of the Carter family.[131]

Here we once again come across the pervasive problem of uncertainty. No one really knows how much value in changed votes or turnout is gained by personal visits to a particular state. By the time the campaign is under way, most voters have made up their minds.[132] Opponents of the candidate are unlikely to go to see him anyway and one wonders what a glimpse of a motorcade will do to influence a potential voter. Yet no one is absolutely certain that whistle-stop methods produce no useful result. Visiting various localities may serve to increase publicity because many of the media of communication are geared to "local" events. It also provides an opportunity to stress issues such as farm policy or unemployment that may be of special significance to citizens in a given region. Party activists may be energized by a look at or a handshake with the candidate. New alliances, such as the one that emerged in 1964 between Goldwater and many long-time Democratic sectors of the Deep South, can be solidified. So rather than let the opportunity pass, the candidates usually decide to take no chances and get out on the hustings. They hedge against uncertainty by doing all they can.

Consider the case of John Kennedy in Ohio. He traversed that pivotal state several times in the 1960 campaign and exerted great physical effort in getting himself seen traveling there. But when the votes were counted, he found himself on the short end. The future president professed to be annoyed and stumped at why this happened. An analysis of the voting returns showed that Kennedy's vote was correlated with the percentage of Catholic population in the various counties.[133] Kennedy made a considerable improvement over the Democratic showing in 1956, but that was not enough to win. Seeing that he was far ahead in every poll, Ronald Reagan in 1984 geared his appearances to helping out congressmen in close races. As we know, this did not work well enough to alter many outcomes. Despite evidence of this kind, which suggests that personal appearances may be overwhelmed by other factors, visits to localities will undoubtedly continue. Who can say, to take a contrary instance, that Kennedy's visit to Illinois in 1960 did not provide the bare margin of a few thousand votes necessary for victory?

There was a time when presidential nominees faced the serious choice of whether to conduct a "front porch" campaign or to get out and meet the people. The first president to make a campaign speech, William Henry Harrison at Columbus, Ohio, in June 1840, was scolded for his pains: "When," the Cleveland Adviser asked, "was there ever before such a spectacle as a candidate for the Presidency, traversing the country advocating his own claims for that high and responsible station? . . . Never! . . . the precedent thus set by Harrison appears to us a bad one."[134] Advice to speak more while saying less was not long in coming.

The aristocratic Nicholas Biddle, whose "monster bank" had been abolished by President Andrew Jackson, suggested that Harrison

> . . . say not one single word about his principles, or his creed—let him say nothing—promise nothing. Let no committee, no convention, no town meeting ever extract from him a single word about what he thinks now, or what he will do hereafter. Let the use of pen and ink be wholly forbidden as if he were a mad poet in Bedlam.[135]

A candidate like Warren Harding, who his sponsors felt would put his foot in his mouth every time he spoke, was well advised to stay home. "Keep Warren at home," Boise Penrose, Republican boss of Philadelphia, was reputed to have said about Harding. "If he goes on tour, somebody's sure to ask him questions, and Warren's just the sort of damn fool that'll try and answer them."[136] More hardy souls, like William Jennings Bryan, took off in all directions only to discover that to be seen was not necessarily to be loved. An underdog, like Harry Truman in 1948, goes out to meet the people because he is so far behind. A favored candidate, like Thomas Dewey in 1948, goes out to meet the people to avoid being accused of complacency. Everybody does it because it is the fashion, and the spectacle of seeing one's opponent run around the country at a furious pace without following suit is too nerve-wracking to contemplate. It is beside the point that no one knows whether all this does any good. Richard Nixon seems to have learned from his enervating experience in 1960, when he pledged to visit each and every state and the had to follow through despite a severe illness. In 1968 he ran a different kind of campaign, taking account of the fact that radio and television made it possible to reach millions without leaving the big metropolitan areas. Nixon did a small amount of traditional campaigning, which was faithfully chronicled by the press corps that followed him around the country. But more basic to his strategy was the technique of fixing upon regional centers and making major appearances and speeches in these places, followed by elaborate, regionally oriented television commercials that reached the voters directly—"over the heads," so to speak, of the news media that were covering and interpreting only the part of the campaign they could see, which did not include Nixon's television programs.[137] Nowadays most candidates follow a regional strategy geared to television markets. But as the candidate heats up, if they look like losers, as Walter Mondale discovered, they feel obliged to heed the advice that more activity might turn the tide.

In Jimmy Carter's famous 1976 *Playboy* interview, in which he spoke of having lusted in his heart, he also said that "the national news media have absolutely no interest in issues at all. . . . The travelling press have zero interest in any issues unless it's a matter of making a mistake. . . . There's nobody in the back of this plane who would ask an issue question unless he thought he could trick me into some crazy statement."[138] Whether or not the specific charge was true, the general idea has some cogency. The campaign is about choosing a president. Since most issues are complex, and most voters aren't interested, the media seek issues that do double duty, illuminating an area of interest and displaying a candidate's fitness to govern.

Unfortunately, a candidate's mistakes can fall in this category, though what counts as a mistake depends on what doubts about the candidate exist in voter's minds. President Ford's advisors told him, based on considerable interviewing, that many voters who otherwise liked him thought he was "not smart enough" or sufficiently competent or commanding. His remark in the well-publicized 1976 San Francisco debate with Jimmy Carter about Poland not being under Soviet domination, which he kept repeating because he did not want to seem to be acquiescing to the fact on behalf of the United States, was a serious mistake and hurt him so much because it hit him where he was vulnerable. Carter was vulnerable to charges of being arrogant and devious. This is why his *Playboy* interview hurt him. "It demonstrated," Carter told in interviewer, "a confirmation of Ford's proposal to the American people that I was not quite to be trusted. . . ."[139] and that was not all. At the end of the *Playboy* piece, Carter, thinking the tape was off, appeared to disparage Lyndon Johnson. Asked about this in Texas, Jimmy Carter seemed to say not that he had been mistaken but that someone else had misrepresented what he said. This put a further strain on his credibility.

In order to avoid making mistakes, Carter tended to repeat the same prepared speeches. His chief policy planner, Stuart Eizenstadt, repeatedly urged him to vary the menu. After he delivered speeches, however, the future president answered questions from the audience, saying what he believed, because that, he thought, was the way to be open and honest. This practice would invite reporters to attend to Carter's extemporaneous comments rather than to the particular points a speech was supposed to make. Thus Carter got into trouble on such "issues" as his criticisms of the head of the Federal Bureau of Investigation, seeming to say he would increase taxes of middle-income people, and appearing to approve of "ethnic purity." In this context, it is not surprising that dealing with issues fell from favor in the Carter camp. Hamilton Jordan, Carter's chief of staff, confessed, "I don't care if we ever have another issues speech."[140] This is a great pity. The interested public would benefit by hearing the candidates give spontaneous answers to questions. The "genuine Carter," like the more relaxed Mondale outside the television studio, might have imparted to their candidacies a more human quality. By contrast, Ronald Reagan, who did so much better with set speeches than with press conferences, was wise to stage-manage events.

Issues

"Never in recent memory," Martin Wattenberg writes about 1988, "has a campaign been so widely criticized for being both overly bitter and devoid of substantive issues."[141] There is no doubt that Wattenberg has accurately captured prevailing opinion in large parts of the media and the general public. Only 5 percent of voters polled after the election felt that the 1988 campaign had been positive while 68 percent believed it had been negative. But was this perception accurate? The rise of mudslinging, in Wattenberg's view, is due to the decline of party identification in the electorate. "When party identification predetermined most voters' choices, candidates had little incentive to get down in the mud in an attempt to rip their opponent to shreds. Strong partisans would see their party's candidates in a favorable light no matter what the charges. Campaigns therefore centered on rallying loyal troops." Whatever the ostensible decline of parties, however, Wattenberg continues, "the proportion of swing voters has risen dramatically. Thus, a strategy of sharp personal attacks has more potential payoff in today's era of candidate-centered rather than partisan politics."[142]

Is there some litmus test that can be applied to determine whether a matter of concern to some people is or is not a genuine issue? Aaron Wildavsky's parents, for instance, were strong Democrats because they believed that President Franklin Delano Roosevelt, together with his wife Eleanor, who made a point of attending numerous Jewish weddings and bar mitzvahs, would protect them against abuse. Wildavsky's father had been beaten in a pogrom in the Ukraine when he was nine years old and had stayed in a hospital for eight months. Should his son have told his father that the point of getting a Ph.D. is that the old man didn't know what a true issue—say the tariff or asbestos in schoolrooms—was? If the people affected are themselves to determine what matters to them, as we think appropriate, then their concerns, whatever they are, deserve consideration.

The complaints about negative campaigning in 1988 came from such incidents as the Bush campaign harping on the importance of reciting the pledge of allegiance in schools and complaining about the Willie Horton case. To those discomforted by discussion of such matters, these are false issues because they appeal to unworthy sentiments. The pledge of allegiance issue suggests that the Democratic party and its candidates are less than patriotic, and the Horton furlough was a not-so-subtle invocation of racist sentiment.

Differences about what counts as an issue depend in part on what matters to people. And different people may have different concerns. Whereas increasing availability of childcare and creating a national health plan mattered to almost twice as many Dukakis as Bush voters in 1988, for instance, Bush voters cared more by similar large margins about strengthening national defense and the death penalty. Defense mattered more to Bush voters 72 to 37 percent whereas the health plan mattered more to Dukakis voters 62 to 32 percent and the death penalty 57 to 38 percent.[143] What was widely perceived as negative campaigning also reflected some real differences in the sorts of public policies preferred by activists in the two parties.

Domestic Issues, Foreign Issues   On the broad range of domestic affairs and "pocketbook" issues, the Democrats, since the New Deal, have been highly favored as the party most voters believe will best meet their needs. Statements like "The Democrats are best for the working man" and "We have better times under the Democrats" abounded when people were asked to state their feelings about the Democratic party. The Republicans, on the other hand, were viewed as the party of depression under whose administration jobs were scarce and times were bad.

These attitudes have had considerable staying power through the years. In 1987 and again in 1990 *Times Mirror* asked samples of American adults "What does it mean to be a Democrat? What does it mean to be a Republican?" and got the spontaneous replies listed in Table 4.10.

A campaign in which the salient issues are economic, therefore, is more likely to aid the Democrats than the Republicans[144] Of course, if the incumbent president is Democratic and the economy is faltering, emphasizing economic issues may not do him much good. Since the advent of "stagflation" under the Democrats in the late 1970s, the Republican party has more often been deemed the party of prosperity. (See Table 4.11.) The party that is in office when people are suffering does badly.

The Democratic party's modern task has been to be liberal in several senses of that word. It promises something for everyone. There are extensions of social welfare programs financed by the federal government, increased minimum wages for the underpaid, medical insurance for new groups of people, better prices for the farmer, irrigation for arid areas, flood protection for river basins, and so on. No one is left out, not even businessmen, who are promised prosperity and given tax benefits. Although voters say they are in favor of these programs, they do not like the

TABLE 4.10   *What Does It Mean To Be a Republican?*
(Unprompted Replies)

Top Mentions	1987	1990
Conservative	21%	22%
Rich, powerful, monied interest	18	21
Business-oriented	13	10
Not for the people	5	4
Against government spending	5	6

What Does It Mean To Be a Democrat?
(Unprompted Replies)

Top Mentions	1987	1990
For working people	21	18
Liberal	18	18
Too much government spending	7	3
Cares for poor, disadvantaged	7	7
For social programs	7	9

Source: See *The Polling Report* (October 1, 1990), and Times Mirror Center for the People and The Press press release (undated).

TABLE 4.11   *Which Party Is Better for National Prosperity?*

	Rep.	Dem.
November 1951	29%	37%
January 1952	31%	35%
October 1956	39	39
October 1960	31	46
October 1964	21	53
October 1968	34	37
September 1972	38	35
August 1976	23	47
September 1980	35	36
September 1984	50	33
September 1988	52	34

"No difference"/"No opinion" (categories not separated by Gallup) not shown. This category ranges from 16 to 34%.

Source: Surveys by the Gallup Organization. Table adapted from *Public Opinion* 7 (December/January, 1985), p. 38; 1988 data from George Gallup, Jr., *The Gallup Poll: Public Opinion 1988* (Wilmington, 1989), p. 165.

spending totals that emerge from them. Hence the tag of being run by the "special interests," especially labor unions, which hurt Mondale in 1984. Should the issue become "excessive spending" as leading to inflation or huge deficits or decreasing investment, Democrats would be at a disadvantage.

Republicans were once clearly on the defensive in the realm of domestic policy, a situation stemming from the fact that they were in office when the Great Depression of 1929 started, and during two sizable but shorter depressions more recently (1970–71, 1982–83). They try to play down economic issues when their president is in office during a depression, and play them up when the Democrats are in office or their party is in power during good times. Republicans attack the Democrats as the party that likes to tax and spend, tax and spend. The Republican candidate is thus well placed to benefit if the issue becomes one of excessive spending. As most spending programs are quite popular, however, the candidate is well advised to be vague concerning the exact aspects of excessive spending he or she opposes. Ronald Reagan in 1980, for example, directed his attacks mainly against "inefficiency" and "waste," and ran on a platform which promised tax cuts that would actually raise tax revenues.[145] On the other hand, the Republican candidate is understandably upset at Democratic insinuations that he and his party have not become fully reconciled to Social Security. Indeed, when Walter Mondale challenged him during a 1984 debate, President Reagan promised not to cut Social Security then or the next year or ever.

In the realm of foreign affairs and defense policy, the Republicans may be regaining the traditional advantage they were losing. The fact that the Democrats occupied the presidency during the First and Second World Wars, the Korean War, and the initial stages of heavy American involvement in Vietnam once convinced most voters that Democrats tend to lead the country to war. Republicans were then known as the party of peace, a position underscored by Senator Dole in the 1976 vice-presidential debate when he said: "I figured up the other day, if we added up the killed and wounded in Democrat wars in this century, it would be about 1.6 million Americans, enough to fill the city of Detroit."[146] Senator Goldwater in 1964 had people believing he would intervene in a great many places, and so the Democrats became the party of peace, a feeling reinforced during Jimmy Carter's presidency and—early in his presidency—by President Reagan's belligerent rhetoric (see Table 4.12). Thus for most of the past decade the Democrats have enjoyed the advantage of being considered the peaceful party. At the same time however desiring peace also led Republicans to be identified as the party that, especially following President Reagan's sponsorship of a big defense buildup, cared most about defense.

The distinction between domestic and foreign policy has always been a bit artificial. It has been maintained because of the ability of the United States to insulate its domestic economy from international forces. Today that ability is diminishing. The decline of the dollar in foreign exchange compelled the Carter administration to pursue a deflationary policy cutting spending, advocating less monetary expansion, selling bonds tied to foreign currencies. In 1987, the Reagan administration came under similar pressure. Energy prices, which obviously affect everyone, are set by the international market or by OPEC, not by the United States government. The Reagan administration wanted to reduce trade barriers to serve its foreign policy, but had a hard time beating back protectionist forces worried about domestic unemployment.

Whereas the major parties once enjoyed long-term advantages in foreign or domestic policy, these have lately become more sensitive to evaluations of performance. For example, the fact that Jimmy Carter was the only president in office when national income declined during an election year has given the Democrats a turn at being blamed for a depression and lately Republicans have gotten higher marks than Democrats, once again, as the party of peace. Moreover foreign and domestic economic policy may not be the only issue areas that over the long run will matter to voters. Environment and social issues might become more salient.

TABLE 4.12   *Which Party Is Better for Peace?*

	Rep.	*Dem.*
September 1951	28%	21%
January 1952	36	15
October 1956	46	16
October 1960	40	25
October 1964	22	45
October 1968	37	24
September 1972	32	28
August 1976	29	32
September 1980	25	42
September 1984	39	38
September 1988	43	33

"No difference"/"No opinion" (categories not separated by Gallup) not shown. This category ranges from 26 to 51%.

Sources: Surveys by the Gallup Organization. Table adapted from *Public Opinion* 7 (December/January, 1985), p. 38; 1988 data from George Gallup, Jr., *The Gallup Poll: Public Opinion 1988* (Wilmington, 1989), p. 167.

Social Issues   What about the third great cluster of problems, the "social issues"—variously labeled (and understood) as law and order, domestic violence, race relations, abortion, ecology, school prayer, and gun control—that involve lifestyles as well as distributions of benefits?[147] As Richard Scammon and Ben Wattenberg point out, the first three have grown enormously in prominence to voters over the past two decades: "Suddenly, some time in the 1960's, 'crime' and 'race' and 'lawlessness' and 'civil rights' became the most important domestic issues in America."[148] Ecology has been politicized mostly in a Democratic direction while being against abortion has become a Republican issue. It is difficult to tell whether this entire cluster of issues works consistently for or against a particular political party. Presumably, everyone is against crime.

Social issues are affecting the parties in different ways. The Republican party may be thought of as a coalition of social conservatives and free market libertarians. So long as it concentrates on economic issues, both factions can usually agree on limited government. But on social issues the libertarians favor individual choice, and are against government intervention even to protect traditional values.

Democratic activists, as we have seen, despite their social heterogeneity, are more united than previously on some issues. A growing belief in equality, in the advisability of diminishing differences among people (women and men, black and white, straight and gay, rich and poor) has led them to measure social, economic, ecological, and defense issues by a similar standard. Defense is antiegalitarian when it is perceived as taking funds from domestic welfare programs; the protection of defenseless creatures and saving workers from chemicals made by rich corporations are seen as a distributive issue; social issues involve the protection of weak groups (women, minorities) from strong groups (men, whites).

Whether agreement on this complex of positions surrounding greater equality of condition unites rank-and-file Democrats is another matter. As the larger of the two major parties, spanning the entire country, the Democrats have in the past experienced difficulty in uniting on any programmatic principles. One consequence of the migration of conservative southerners into the Republican party has been to facilitate the emergence of a more ideologically coherent Democratic mainstream, but as recently as the *Times-Mirror* survey of political attitudes in 1987 (reported in *The People, Press and Politics*), the Democrats at the grass-roots level divided into *four* separate and distinct blocs of voters whereas the Republicans were split into two groups on issues.

One measure of the ideological heterogeneity of the Democratic and

Republican parties is provided in Table 4.13. In the University of Michigan's American National Election Studies, respondents have been asked to indicate their positions on policy issues by placing themselves on a series of seven-point scales; and to indicate how favorably they view a variety of politically active groups by rating each group on a 100-point "feeling thermometer." In Table 4.13, we have tried to assess how united or divided each party is by calculating the standard deviation of party identifiers' responses to these questions. As the table clearly shows, the Democratic rank and file are more divided on the vast majority of issues and in their feelings toward important political groups. Similar results are found for all the years in which results are reported. On some issues, the differences between the two parties is not large; in other cases, however, the Democrats' standard deviation is more than 50 percent larger than the Republicans'.

Presentation of Self

Another set of strategic problems concerns the personal impression made by the candidates. A candidate is helped by being thought of as trustworthy, reliable, mature, kind but firm, devoted to family, and in every way normal and presentable. No amount of expostulation about the irrelevance of all this ordinariness as qualification for an extraordinary office wipes out the fact that candidates must try to conform to the public stereotype of goodness, a standard that is typically far more demanding of politicians than of ordinary mortals. Gary Hart's precipitous withdrawal from the 1988 race for the Democratic nomination following charges of adultery tells a part of the story. Because the media now feel obliged to report on such matters, their importance is bound to grow. Back in John F. Kennedy's time, reporters knew of his philandering but would have thought it wrong to say so in public.

It would be an excruciating process for a candidate to remodel his entire personality along the indicated lines. What the candidates actually try to do is to smooth off the rough edges, to counter what they believe are the most unfavorable impressions of specific aspects of their public image. Kennedy, who was accused of being young and immature, hardly cracked a smile in his debates with Nixon, while the latter, who was said to be stiff and frightening, beamed with friendliness. Michael Dukakis, suspected of excessively pacific leanings, allowed himself to be driven around in an army tank.[149] George Bush was told to lower his voice so as to subdue the impression that he was a "wimp."[150] Kennedy restyled his youthful shock of hair, and Nixon thinned his eyebrows to look less

TABLE 4.13   *Internal Agreement on the Issues of, by Party*

	Republican Stnd. Dev.	Democratic Stnd. Dev.	Difference (Dems. − Reps)
1972 Seven-Point Scales			
Busing	1.200	1.925	0.725
Student unrest	0.520	1.976	0.456
Aid to minorities	1.792	2.117	0.325
Guaranteed job	1.815	2.082	0.267
Health insurance	2.293	2.496	0.203
Rights of accused	1.986	2.174	0.188
Marijuana	1.930	2.114	0.184
Tax rate	2.227	2.405	0.178
Urban unrest	2.013	2.168	0.155
Vietnam	1.816	1.948	0.132
Ideology	1.144	1.266	0.122
Inflation	1.472	1.550	0.078
Role of women	2.263	2.312	0.049
Pollution	2.024	1.976	−0.048
1972 Feeling Thermometers			
Ministers who protest	25.152	31.057	5.905
Black militants	17.848	23.559	5.711
Civil rights leaders	26.284	31.280	4.996
Urban rioters	15.073	19.477	4.404
The military	18.611	22.803	4.192
Marijuana users	21.629	25.510	3.881
Radical students	20.122	23.913	3.791
Policemen	15.410	18.690	3.280
Big business	18.537	21.163	2.626
Women's liberation movement	26.350	28.135	1.785
Labor unions	22.667	21.456	−1.211
1976 Seven-Point Scales			
Busing	1.306	1.979	0.693
Guaranteed job (post-election)	1.479	1.818	0.339
Aid to minorities	1.815	2.133	0.318
Guaranteed job	1.784	2.079	0.295
Rights of accused	1.955	2.209	0.254
Marijuana	2.006	2.247	0.241
Ideology	1.117	1.355	0.238
Tax rate	2.157	2.334	0.177
Health insurance	2.232	2.392	0.160
Role of women	2.074	2.123	0.049
Urban unrest	1.874	1.911	0.037
1976 Feeling Thermometers			
Black militants	20.236	23.767	3.531
Policemen	15.389	18.221	2.832
Civil rights leaders	1.274	23.879	2.605
The military	18.370	20.645	2.275
Radical students	19.643	21.710	2.067
Marijuana users	23.703	25.514	1.811
Big Business	20.000	20.550	0.550

TABLE 4.13   *Internal Agreement on the Issues of, by Party (continued)*

	Republican Stnd. Dev.	Democratic Stnd. Dev.	Difference (Dems. − Reps)
People on welfare	20.605	20.878	0.273
Labor unions	21.383	20.983	−0.400
Women's liberation movement	21.998	21.490	−0.508
1980 Seven-Point Scales			
Preferential hiring	0.873	1.409	0.536
Aid to minorities	1.330	1.735	0.405
Defense spending	1.218	1.564	0.346
Guaranteed job	1.610	1.919	0.309
Ideology	1.102	1.399	0.297
Ideology (post-election)	1.026	1.228	0.202
Women's equality	1.911	1.855	0.044
Inflation v. unemployment	1.442	1.456	0.014
Policy towards Russia	1.809	1.815	0.006
Services v. spending	1.790	1.766	−0.024
1980 Feeling Thermometers			
Black militants	21.887	26.137	4.250
The military	20.448	22.850	2.402
Radical students	20.690	22.710	2.020
Civil rights leaders	22.343	23.337	1.034
Big business	21.840	22.784	0.944
Labor unions	21.588	22.302	0.744
Evangelicals	25.460	26.008	0.548
Women's liberation movement	25.851	26.103	0.252
People on welfare	22.297	22.489	0.192
Environmentalists	22.701	20.392	−2.309
1984 Seven-Point Scales			
Busing	1.169	1.699	0.530
Defense spending	1.348	1.694	0.346
Russia	1.634	1.974	0.340
Aid to minorities	1.439	1.681	0.242
Government help for women	1.508	1.732	0.224
Guaranteed job	1.637	1.784	0.147
Ideology	1.178	1.308	0.130
Central American involvement	1.655	1.769	0.114
Services v. spending	1.483	1.509	0.026
Women's role	1.855	1.783	−0.072
1984 Feeling Thermometers			
Black militants	21.272	24.702	3.430
The military	18.408	21.810	3.402
Big business	18.819	22.050	3.231
Gays and lesbians	24.414	27.098	2.684
Evangelicals	24.223	26.522	2.299

TABLE 4.13   *Internal Agreement on the Issues of, by Party (continued)*

	Republican Stnd. Dev.	Democratic Stnd. Dev.	Difference (Dems. − Reps)
Civil rights leaders	23.003	24.428	1.425
Anti-abortionists	27.272	27.474	0.202
Labor unions	23.674	23.806	0.132
People on welfare	21.385	21.473	0.088
Women's liberation movement	23.831	22.131	− 1.700
1988 Seven-Point Scales			
Ideology	1.184	1.360	0.176
Government services	1.493	1.528	0.035
Defense spending	1.413	1.625	0.212
Health insurance	1.957	1.918	− 0.039
Guaranteed jobs	1.611	1.884	0.273
Aid to blacks	1.542	1.992	0.450
Aid to minorities	1.638	1.942	0.304
Russia	1.700	1.862	0.162
Women's role	1.838	.853	0.015
1988 Feeling Thermometers			
The military	18.254	21.735	3.481
Big business	19.632	22.165	2.533
Gays and lesbians	24.554	27.337	2.783
Evangelicals	24.121	25.095	0.974
Civil rights leaders	20.702	23.387	2.685
Anti-abortionists	29.144	29.777	0.633
Labor unions	22.958	23.759	0.801
People on welfare	20.150	21.797	1.647

Respondents are party identifiers.
Feeling thermometer standard deviations do not include respondents who did not know where to rate group or could not judge group.

Source: American National Election Time Series, Center for Political Studies, University of Michigan, Ann Arbor.

threatening. Jimmy Carter made intimate revelations to show he was not cold and calculating but serious and sincere. Gerald Ford was photographed a lot around the White House to show he was in command. Ronald Reagan smiled and ducked when Jimmy Carter tried to portray him as dangerous. And just as Kennedy made it possible for Roman Catholics to be considered for the presidency, Reagan broke the taboo on divorce. The little things that some people don't like may be interpreted favorably by other people. Hubert Humphrey was alleged to be a man who could not stop talking. His garrulousness, however, was just another side of his encyclopedic and detailed knowledge of the widest variety of public policies. He might have talked too much to suit some, but the fact that he knew a lot pleased others. Was George McGovern kindly and compassionate? Or just wishy-washy? Was Ronald Reagan amiable and charming or was that a vacuous expression on his face?

The political folklore of previous campaigns provides candidates with helpful homilies about how to conduct themselves. Typical bits of advice include the following: always carry the attack to your opponent; the best defense is offense; separate the other candidate from his party; when in doubt as to the course that will produce the most votes, do what you believe is right; guard against acts that can hurt you because they are more significant than acts that can help you; avoid making personal attacks that may gain sympathy for the opposition. Unfortunately for the politicians in search of a guide, these bits of folk wisdom do not contain detailed instructions about the conditions under which they should and should not be applied.

The experience of Adlai Stevenson suggests a familiar dilemma for candidates. Shall they write (or cause to have written for them) new speeches for most occasions, or shall they rest content to hammer home a few themes, embroidering just a little here and there? No one really knows which is better. Stevenson is famous for the care he took with his speeches and the originality he sought to impart to his efforts. Had he won office he might have established a trend. As it is, most candidates are likely to follow Kennedy and Nixon, Johnson and Goldwater, and Carter and Ford in using just a few set speeches. Ronald Reagan's virtuoso shuffling of his well-worn index cards, with their anecdotes of questionable accuracy, seems to have served him well enough. In view of the pervasive inattention to public affairs and political talk in our society, this approach may have the advantage of driving points home (as well as driving mad the news correspondents who must listen to the same thing all the time).[151] Newspaper people and television journalists who cover the campaigns complain quite a lot about the repetitiousness of presidential candidates, as though the campaign should be designed mostly to amuse them. This ranks high on the list of unsolved (and no doubt unsolvable) problems of American democracy: how to appeal to the relatively inattentive American people without totally alienating the superattentive mandarins of the news media through whom a candidate must reach the rank-and-file voter.

More important, perhaps, is the desirability of appearing comfortable in delivery. Televised speeches are the major opportunities for a candidate to be seen and evaluated by large numbers of people. Eisenhower's ability to project a radiant appearance helped him; Stevenson's obvious discomfort before the camera hurt him. On this point we have evidence that those who listened to Stevenson's delivery over radio were more favorably impressed with him than those who watched him on TV.[152]

Jimmy Carter's "paste-on" smile and rigid bearing contrasted poorly with Ronald Reagan's easy grin and relaxed manner, though these surface indicators, like Gerald Ford's alleged clumsiness, may have nothing to do with performance in office. Both George Bush and Michael Dukakis were regularly said to be either awkward or excellent before the camera, the "unbiased" critique from the pundits generally varying with the candidates' standing in the polls.

The major difficulty with the strategic principles we have been discussing is not that they are too theoretical, but that they do not really tell the candidates what to do when they are mutually incompatible. Like proverbs, one can often find principles to justify opposing courses of action: "Look before you leap," but "He who hesitates is lost." Nixon in 1960 could not take full advantage of international affairs without hitting so hard as to reinforce the unfavorable impression of himself as being harsh and unprincipled. Kennedy could hardly capitalize on the Rooseveltian image of the vigorous leader without attacking the foreign policy of a popular president. The result is that the candidates must take calculated risks when existing knowledge about the consequences of alternative courses of action is inadequate. Hunch, intuition, and temperament necessarily play important roles in choosing among competing alternatives.

Television Debates

The famous television debates of 1960 between Nixon and Kennedy provide an excellent illustration of the difficulty of choosing between competing considerations in the absence of knowledge of the most likely results. With the benefit of hindsight, many observers now suggest that Nixon was obviously foolish to engage in the debates. Let us try to look at the situation from the perspective of each of the presidential aspirants at the time.

Kennedy issued a challenge to debate on television. The possible advantages from his point of view were many. He could use a refusal to debate to accuse Nixon of running away and depriving the people of a unique opportunity to judge the candidates. Among Kennedy's greatest handicaps in the campaign were his youth and the inevitable charges of inexperience. Television debates could and did help to overcome these difficulties by showing the audience not so much that Kennedy was superior in knowledge but that there was not that much difference in the information, age, and general stature of the two men. Whatever administration skills or inside information Nixon might have had would not show up on the screen as the candidates necessarily confined themselves to broad discussions of issues known to all politically literate people.

Kennedy could only guess but he could not know that Nixon would not stump him in an embarrassing way in front of millions of viewers. But Kennedy understood that despite the reams of publicity he had received, he was unknown to many voters, much less known than the vice-president. Here was a golden opportunity to increase his visibility in a sudden and dramatic way. And his good looks would not hurt him with those who like to judge the appearance of a man.[153] Nixon was in a more difficult position. To say no would not have been a neutral decision; it would have subjected him to being called a man who was afraid to face his opposition. Saying yes had a number of possible advantages. One stemmed from the numerical disadvantage of the Republican party. Normally, most people do not pay very much attention to the opposition candidate, making it difficult to win them over. Televised debates would provide a unique instance in which huge numbers of people attracted to both parties could be expected to tune in attentively. Nixon had good reason for believing that if he made a favorable impression he would be in a position to convince more of the people he needed to convince (Democratic identifiers) than would Kennedy. The risk that Kennedy might use the opportunity to solidify the support of those attracted to a Democrat simply had to be taken. Another potential advantage that might have accrued to Nixon arose from his previous political life. He had been labeled by some people as "tricky Dick," an untruthful and vindictive man. This picture might have been supplanted on television by the new Nixon of smiling visage and magnanimous gesture who had it all over his opponent in knowledge of public affairs. Nixon had to judge whether his handicap was serious or whether it was confined to confirmed liberals whose numbers were insignificant and who would never have voted for him in any event. He also had to guess whether it would be worthwhile to overcome his own disabilities.[154] Perhaps a record of success in debate situations going back to high school was not irrelevant in guiding Nixon to his eventual decision to go on television with his opponent.[155]

Surveys taken after the event suggest that Nixon miscalculated.[156] But if he had won the election instead of losing it by a wafer-thin margin, he would hardly have been reminded of any error on his part, and there would probably have been discussions of what a brilliant move it was for him to go on TV.

The election of 1964 presented an entirely different set of circumstances. President Johnson, an incumbent enjoying enormous personal popularity at the head of the majority party, had nothing to gain and everything to lose by debating his rival. And so, despite strenuous efforts by Senator Goldwater and his allies to involve the president in debates, none were held.

By 1968, observers were beginning to question whether candidates would ever again seek an epic confrontation with one another on the 1960 model. What seems to be required before the occurrence of such a debate is two major candidates equally eager for such a battle. If one is an incumbent, or feels himself securely in the lead, there is little incentive to debate. Hubert Humphrey pursued Richard Nixon fiercely on this point in 1968, but Nixon prudently refrained from a debate that would needlessly have risked his chances of victory. His excuse in 1972 was that a president in office could not tell all he knew.

Because inertia had begun to work against the idea of debates, the fact that they occurred again in 1976 was somewhat surprising. Neither candidate had been elected to the presidency, but Gerald Ford, the less articulate of the two, was the incumbent president. Although the Democrats did not do especially well in the debates, Ford's side, the Republicans, which had the most to lose by debating, undoubtedly lost ground twice. One time was when Ford left the impression that in his opinion Eastern Europe was not under Soviet domination, an occasion for a week's worth of "clarifications." The other was when Senator Robert Dole, his vice-presidential running mate, misjudged the audience entirely and bounced partisan one-liners ineffectually off the beatific brow of Senator Walter Mondale, thus spoiling one of the few chances the Republicans had to woo Democratic voters.[157]

The strategy of participation in presidential debates was well illustrated in the 1980 Democratic party primaries. In the fall of 1979 President Carter's public popularity was exceedingly low, Senator Kennedy's was exceedingly high, and Governor Brown of California was struggling for recognition as a serious candidate. Thus, every candidate had an interest in participation: the president needed it because he was way behind; Senator Kennedy needed it because he was still a challenger; and Governor Brown needed it most of all because he considered himself a good debater and hoped to show that he could hold his own with the front runners. Then the Iranian seizure of American hostages served almost instantly to raise the president's popularity. Senator Kennedy's popularity plummeted after he gave an embarrassingly bad television interview to Roger Mudd and had difficulty explaining the Chappaquiddick incident. Thus, the situation changed. President Carter no longer stood to gain a lead but to lose one, so he bowed out of the debates on the grounds that it would be inappropriate to campaign while the hostages were being held, a circumstance that might continue almost indefinitely. The senator and the governor protested in vain. Hurt worst of all, Brown lost the chance to share the limelight with the president, which, at that stage, might have given him the public prominence he needed.

In 1980 there were problems in deciding what to do about including the major independent candidate, John Anderson, in debates. President Carter refused to publicize Anderson, and so in the end only one debate took place instead of a series, and it was held very late in the campaign only between Carter and his Republican challenger, Ronald Reagan. On balance it seems to have helped Reagan, who may have lost on high-school debate rules but projected a benignity that was helpfully at odds with the picture of a dangerously radical opponent that Jimmy Carter was trying to paint.[158] So Carter became another incumbent who lost ground by submitting to a staged debate.

There were two presidential debates in 1984; after the first it looked as if the incumbent had lost ground. A series of negative news and television stories told the public the president had performed badly. A *Wall Street Journal* article suggested that perhaps Reagan's age was catching up with him.[159] Challenger Walter Mondale moved up slightly in the polls. Perhaps Mondale could come from behind to win. In the second debate, President Reagan put in a stronger showing and the age issue was put to rest. "I will not make age an issue of this campaign," the president joked. "I am not going to exploit, for political purposes, my opponent's youth and inexperience."[160] Reagan regained the large lead he had held throughout the campaign and went on to a landslide victory.[161]

The strategic imperatives surrounding debates seem to be emerging with some clarity. Debates can hurt incumbents. Challengers have far less to lose, and may gain simply by keeping their countenance and appearing on the same stage with the holder of high public office. Opinion makers and the custodians of the flame of disinterested public spiritedness seem agreed that debates are wonderful exercises in public enlightenment. This scarcely seems credible to minimally intelligent viewers of the actual debates we have had, but this sentiment nevertheless exists, and may tempt candidates to engage in public debates against their better strategic judgment.[162]

Indeed, there is growing sentiment to institutionalize debates so that whether or not to participate in them will no longer be a matter for the candidates to decide for themselves. From the beginning, presidential debates have been run as a public service by the League of Women Voters who represented a nonpartisan perspective in working out the arrangements. This meant that the candidates could protect their own interests in deciding whether to debate and under what conditions. Much haggling took place over ground rules, as anxieties in the camps of candidates ran high over such matters as use of the presidential seal on the podium, or bad camera angles, or which journalists would moderate or ask questions. In 1987 the Democratic and Republican national committees formed a bipartisan commission to determine the format (number, location, ground rules) and run the debates. This was designed to reduce the power of candidates to influence the conditions under which they would appear. In a joint statement explaining why they thought they should control the debates, Paul G. Kirk, Jr., chairman of the Democratic National Committee, and Frank J. Fahrenkopf, Jr., chairman of the Republican National Committee, stated that

> we will better fulfill our party responsibilities; to inform and educate the electorate, strengthen the role of political parties in the electoral process and most important of all, we can institutionalize the debates, making them an integral and permanent part of the presidential process.[163]

Once a candidate is nominated, however, the leverage of the national committee to compel his participation largely disappears. Candidates find most of the alternative formats that have been suggested to them too risky. And so it is doubtful that the Presidential Debate Commission will have any more power over these events than the League of Women Voters used to have.

The Commission certainly had no such power in 1988 when debates were held under its auspices. By far the most memorable event of the debates was a question that Bernard Shaw of CNN put to Michael Dukakis early in the second debate asking whether Dukakis's views of capital punishment would change in a particular case, if his wife had been raped by a criminal. Dukakis treated this hypothetical question in a manner that commentators later said was too cool and impersonal to garner widespread admiration.

This confirms the conventional wisdom that debates are more about accidents and mistakes than about enlightenment on the capacities of candidates to govern. And it seems likely to reinforce the cautiousness of candidates with respect to these events.

Getting a Good Press

Although we have seen that newspapers—whether in editorials or news stories—do not markedly influence reader opinion when the strong cue of party is present, it is still important for a candidate to get the most favorable coverage possible. It usually does not pay to try to line up support from publishers who have already made up their minds before the campaign has officially started. But the candidates can and do assiduously court the newspaper, periodical, and television journalists assigned to them.[164] Not only do candidates throw parties for press and staff, but they follow their coverage and complain about it. Strong feelings within the Carter camp in 1976 that Ford was being let off too easily on issues but that Carter was being pressed, for example, led Carter to call a meeting at which he discussed his grievances with the press.[165] Ford's poll takers felt that media coverage of the debates reinforced the image of him as a bumbler from which they had been trying to escape. And in 1980 Carter complained about but could not counter the journalistic view of Reagan as a good guy.

In 1984, Mondale's backers felt President Reagan was avoiding the issues in a campaign that stuck to broad, patriotic themes. The "great communicator," they argued, was exploiting the media with his carefully staged events. Many in the media agreed and did negative stories about the Reagan campaign's manipulative tactics. Negative coverage of this sort gave the Reagan camp grounds for complaints of their own concerning an anti-Republican "spin" to nightly newscasts.[166]

The space a candidate gets in the paper, his time on television, and the slant of the story may depend to some extent on how the reporters regard him. If they find it difficult to get material, if they find the candidate suspicious and uncommunicative, this, too, may affect how much and what gets on the air or published. Little things, such as phasing news to meet the requirements of both morning newspapers and the evening network news shows, or supplying reporters with human-interest material, are helpful to the candidate. The personality of the candidate, his ability to command the respect of the rather cynical men and women assigned to cover him, may count heavily. Democratic candidates probably have to work a little harder at cultivating good relations in order to help counteract the editorial slant of most papers. But Republicans have to work harder to win the sympathies of reporters of liberal tendency who dominate the national press corps.[167] Both also must make the most of their opportunities in public appearances or radio and TV speeches. If what they say and do "makes news," and their press secretaries help promote the stories, they may get space through the desire of the newspapers to sell copies.

Finally, there is the overwhelming importance of staging the daily bit of news for the nightly television programs of the networks. Candidates know they will be on these programs every night; but doing and saying what? In order to seize control of the situation they stage little dramas: an announcement in front of the Statue of Liberty or in the midst of a picturesque slum; visits to a series of ethnic shops, delicatessens, farms, factories, and shopping centers. If the backdrop is right, the candidate thinks, the coverage may be too. And sometimes it is.

Negative Campaigning

In the closing days of what appears to be a close race, there may be a temptation for the parties, now thoroughly engrossed in the heat of battle, to loose a stream of negative advertising at the other side. How much of this they do and how often they do it is partially determined by the kind of people they are. In the long run, however, the standards of the voting population determine the standards of the candidates. Should it happen that vituperation is rewarded, we can expect to see it occur again. Should it prove to be the case, however, as in the Scandinavian countries, that departures from proper deportment are severely punished at the polls, candidates can be expected to take the hint. Alas, such elevated levels of morality have not yet been reached in the United States. In what appear to be modern lows for vulgarity and inanity, the 1986 congressional elections abounded with malicious and foolish negative advertising.[168] Why did this happen? *The New Republic* explains that

> The proliferation of negative ads is simply a result of the consultants' discovery that attacks make a more lasting impression on voters than positive commercials. More candidates are making the attacks personally, rather than working through stand-ins, because research shows that the ads work better that way. The surge in negative advertising has even given rise to the countertactic known as "inoculation": ads designed to answer potential negative ads even before the attacks air.[169]

The trend to "negative" ads reached the presidential campaign level in 1988, as George Bush's campaign sought to capitalize on the fact that Michael Dukakis was known to very few voters at the beginning of the campaign. As Bush's political advisor Roger Ailes said,

> We always knew we would have to define Dukakis . . . and whichever of us defined the other and ourselves most effectively would win. . . .
>
> You've got to understand that the media has no interest in substance. Print has a little more interest because they have to fill a lot of lines. But electronic media has no interest in substance.
>
> There are three ways to get on the air: pictures, attacks, and mistakes, so what you do is spend your time avoiding mistakes, staying on the attack and giving them pictures.[170]

One of the results of the Watergate scandals of the early 1970s is said to be the advent in the populace at large of a "post-Watergate morality" in which failure to abide by rules of common decency can be expected to be strongly disfavored. This does not necessarily provide much in the way of guidance to candidates, however. It may, in fact, be a gross violation of common decency, as elites understand such matters, to hurl an accusation at an opponent that forces him into a complex explanation that few people will understand. Yet it may be winning politics to indulge in such tactics under the incentives set up by post-Watergate morality. For example, there are frequently adequate and legitimate reasons of public policy for congressmen to travel abroad on public funds, even if they have a good time doing it. But woe betide the member of Congress who for one reason or another is forced to defend this case before an aroused electorate.

Many observers claim that Senator Edmund Muskie fatally injured his campaign for the 1972 Democratic nomination by showing too much emotion in response to a Republican smear that branded him a racist. Muskie, it is true, had in many prior campaigns managed with enormous success to show indignation at the moral lapses of opponents who attacked him,[171] but this time something went wrong, and he was widely criticized for showing the wrong demeanor.

Perhaps on this one occasion he should have taken a leaf from the book of Franklin Delano Roosevelt, who paid no attention to most accusations about him but seized on an attack involving his dog, Fala, to rib his opponents unmercifully for impugning an animal that could not reply.[172] If all else fails, it is always possible to take the advice attributed to a Chicago politician who said that in politics, as in poker, the way to meet scandalous charges is to "call 'em and raise 'em. If you are denounced as a fool, call your opponent a damned fool; if he says you are a crook, call him a robber; if he intimidates that you are careless with the truth tell your audience that he is a pathological liar."[173]

Why, we may wonder, are candidates supposed to behave in a more exalted fashion in politics and in the midst of a passionately fought contest than we would expect of them in other areas of life? Successful public officials, like successful business executives, union leaders, and people in other walks of life, deal with people as they are, not as they would wish them to be. Campaigning is concerned primarily with winning support; any secondary effects in may have, such as educating the public, are (unfortunately) incidental. If we wonder at the level of appeals made to us in elections, we need look only as far as our own qualities to get the answer. There are occasions when we might be thankful that our politicians do not fully reflect the ethical standards actually practiced in society. Knowledge of our own character may explain the wish and expose the fallacy of expecting politicians to be better than we are.

However, the standards of the voting population do not necessarily determine the actions of organized hecklers and mischief makers. Heckling has probably always been a part of any politics in which votes are publicly solicited, though Americans have never indulged in the practice to the degree that it exists in Great Britain.

The heckling in the 1968 campaign was different in scope from that of any other year in modern American politics. Both Hubert Humphrey and George Wallace had to face frequent, deliberate, disruptive activities by groups of young people whose aim was to prohibit them from speaking at all, rather than to "score points" on them through clever interruptions. To the degree that such heckling had any impact, in the end it probably gained a little sympathy for the candidate under fire. The hecklers had no candidate who might have lost votes by being identified with them and, in any event, their purpose was to show contempt for the electoral process rather than for any single candidate. In 1984, the heckling was less pervasive but did exist. Most notable were the opponents of abortion who harassed pro-choice Catholic Geraldine Ferraro. Their cries of "What about abortion?" were an aggravation to the vice-presidential candidate but had little impact on the vote.[174]

Both Carter and Ford in 1976 eschewed opportunities for mudslinging. When it looked like his fortunes were in decline, Carter was urged to link Ford explicitly to Watergate through his pardon of Nixon. Carter refused, saying, "It will rip our country apart."[175] Presented with an opportunity to accuse Carter of corruption in regard to the family peanut business, Ford squelched the matter.[176]

It is ironic that President Nixon and his campaign managers should have sought, in 1972, to adapt the tactics they attributed to the far-out left to their own uses. The contempt of insiders for a political system that nurtures them is a far more serious phenomenon than the antics of dissidents. Yet it appears that the Nixon campaign hired people to fake evidence tending to discredit former Democratic presidents and to harass Democratic presidential candidates by playing "dirty tricks" on them (such as ordering huge numbers of pizzas in their name). Presumably the passage of laws prohibiting such behavior in the future will be of some help, but the fact that the reelection campaign of a president of the United States sheltered such disgusting behavior is a shameful blot upon our history.[177]

In the United States we seem to be in a middle position in regard to mudslinging. It is not everyday practice, but neither is it a rarity. A glance at the history of presidential campaigns suggests that vituperation is largely irrelevant to the outcomes of campaigns and that its benefits are problematical.

Blunders

One hears much about campaign blunders, as if there really were objective assurance that another course of action would have turned out better for the unfortunate candidate. An example was Thomas E. Dewey's decision in 1948 to mute the issues, which was said to have snatched defeat from the jaws of victory.[178] A vigorous campaign on his part, it was said, would have taken steam out of Harry Truman's charges and would thus have brought victory to Dewey. Perhaps. What we know of the 1948 election suggests that it provoked a higher degree of voting on the basis of economic class than any of the elections that have succeeded it.[179] A slashing attack by Dewey, therefore, might have polarized the voters even further. This would have increased Truman's margin, since there are many more people with low than with high incomes. Had the election gone the other way—and a handful of votes in a few states would have done it—we would have heard much less about Dewey's blunder and much more about how unpopular Truman was supposed to have been in 1948.

A whole series of "mistakes" have been attributed to Richard Nixon in 1960, the year he lost the election by such a small margin. Here are two, culled from Theodore H. White's best-selling book on the 1960 campaign. On the civil rights plank of the Republican platform:

> The original draft plank prepared by the Platform Committee was a moderate one. . . . This plank, as written, would almost certainly have carried the Southern states for Nixon and, it seems in retrospect, might have given him victory. . . . On Monday, July 25th, it is almost certain, it lay in Nixon's power to reorient the Republican Party toward an axis of Northern-Southern conservatives. His alone was the choice. . . . Nixon insisted that the Platform Committee substitute for the moderate position in civil rights (which probably would have won him the election) the advanced Rockefeller position on civil rights. . . .[180]

On Nixon's failure to protest the imprisonment of Martin Luther King during the campaign:

> He had made the political decision at Chicago to court the Negro vote in the North, only now, apparently, he felt it quite possible that Texas, South Carolina, and Louisiana might all be won by him by the white vote and he did not wish to offend that vote. So he did not act—there was no whole philosophy of politics to instruct him.[181]

Hindsight is capable of converting every act of a losing candidate into a blunder. Victory can have the same effect in reverse. Consider the situation of Richard Nixon, 1968 version, as he dealt with the same southern-white/northern-black dilemma—in the same way. Theodore White reports:

> Nixon had laid it down, at the Mission Bay gathering, that none of his people, North or South, were to out-Wallace Wallace. He insisted, as he was to insist to the end of the campaign, that he would not divide the country; he wanted a campaign that would unify a nation so he could govern it. To compete with Wallace in the South on any civilized level was impossible. . . . Instead, Nixon would challenge Wallace in the peripheral states—Florida, North Carolina, Virginia, Tennessee, South Carolina. . . . It was only later that the trap within this strategy became evident—for, to enlarge his base in the Northern industrial states, Nixon would have to reach across the rock-solid Republican base there, across center, to the independents, the disenchanted Democrats, to the ghettos. But to do that would be to shake the peripheral strategy in the new South. And to hold to the course he had set for the peripheral strategy limited his call in the North.[182]

Nixon's strategy was aimed, in both years, at chipping off the "peripheral" southern states while not taking such a strong anti-civil rights position as to bring northern black voters to the polls in great numbers and to turn northern suburban whites against him.

In 1968, of course, he won; his margin over 1960 consisted of North Carolina, South Carolina, Illinois, and New Jersey. Would it have been a gain for him to "out-Wallace Wallace"? Not likely, in view of the heavy margins Wallace piled up in the states he did carry and his inability to do very well elsewhere. Would it have been a gain for Nixon to repudiate all possible anti-civil rights votes? Not likely, in view of the near unanimity against him of the black vote and probably of most strongly pro-civil rights white liberals. In short, did his strategy of equivocation almost win or almost lose the presidency for Richard M. Nixon in 1960 and/or 1968? Absent the opportunity to rerun these elections with different strategies, no one can say.

We have previously dealt with Nixon's decision to engage in television debates with Kennedy. Let us take a look at his decision on timing the 1960 campaign. Nixon calculated that the election was going to be very close because the Democrats were the majority party in the country and the Republicans lacked Eisenhower. Nixon reasoned, therefore, that the candidate who closed his campaign with the strongest spurt would be the winner.[183] Consequently he held his fire somewhat until the latter part of October, hoping thereby to peak his campaign while Kennedy's was falling off. This is precisely what he did, and Kennedy's supporters were worried that Kennedy had lost and Nixon had gained impetus in the last two weeks. Nevertheless, Kennedy won. What lesson might a future candidate derive from this experience? Nixon's strategy of timing has a common-sense ring to it. Yet it is really difficult to say whether it had meaning. Would he have done better to come to a peak earlier? Might the general public not have gotten tired of a full-blast effort straight through? There is no way of knowing. It is possible that Nixon lost because of his strategy, that he gained, though not enough, or that the strategy had no effect whatsoever. It would have been possible to use a successive survey of the same voters to check on whether votes were changed in his favor during the period he put on the steam, but other factors, such as the effects that the attention of researchers have on ordinary respondents, could also affect the outcome of such a study. Furthermore, there is no way of measuring how well he might have done had he pursued a different strategy.

How should George McGovern have treated the Eagleton affair of 1972? Had he failed to remove Senator Thomas Eagleton as vice-presidential nominee, the campaign might have revolved around charges, ill-founded or not, that Eagleton was psychologically unfit to succeed to the presidency if and when that became necessary. McGovern, moreover, felt that he had been taken in by Eagleton's failure to mention his past psychiatric treatment. Had McGovern kept Eagleton on the Democratic ticket, however, on the grounds that past illness should not disqualify for future activity, positive use might have been made of the events. If the Democrats were indeed the party of the people who needed help, this was certainly a good time to demonstrate it. Punitive Republicans might have been compared with compassionate Democrats. But there is reason to believe that McGovern activists threatened to abandon his campaign if he did not dump his running mate. These activists were apparently outraged at the thought that their issue preferences would be subordinated to discussion of mental illness. They were, of course, beaten before the race began, so they had nothing to lose by sticking to principle; but they did not know that then.

Gerald Ford's biggest mistake, if it was one, occurred long before his campaign began when at the end of his first month in office he pardoned Richard Nixon. Without the pardon, however, Nixon might have been on trial during or before the campaign, with even worse electoral consequences for Republicans. Moreover, the election of 1976 was sufficiently close that any number of changes might have altered the outcome.

Some perceptions of political reality are so overwhelming that everyone accepts them as true. According to Reagan strategist Richard Wirthlin, commenting on the 1980 campaign, ''there was no question, in our own minds . . . that if we could make this campaign a referendum on the performance of Jimmy Carter, we would win the election."[184] Patrick Caddell, who performed a similar role in the Carter campaign, agreed that "Looking at the perceptions that people had about the President, there was no way that we could survive either a primary or general election . . . if we allowed it to become a referendum on the first three years of the Carter administration. . . . We had to keep the campaign on the candidates and we had to try to keep it on the future—a movie about the future, as one of our analysts said, as opposed to a movie about the past. We would lose the latter flat out; we knew that."[185] Once the Carter campaign failed to convict Ronald Reagan of being too dangerous to elect, the contest was over. Still, it could have ended differently. As Everett Ladd concludes,

In the end the 1980 election became what the Republicans had hoped and the Democrats had feared—a referendum on the Carter administration. Some observers think it could not have been otherwise, in view of the depths of the public rejection of the Carter administration's performance. I do not accept this view. In my judgment it unfairly minimizes the impact of Reagan's campaign and insufficiently appreciates the importance of both the Republican candidate's performance and the strategic choices he made—including Reagan's impressive handling of his October 28 debate with Carter. In any case, what had been a close contest through September and October became an electoral landslide for the GOP, as the electorate resolved its indecision and voted no on the Carter administration.[186]

In 1984, the poll takers again agreed that the Democrats had to keep the campaign focused on the future.[187] How was this to be done? Mondale's strategy was a bold one. In an attempt to address the federal budget deficit, Mondale declared that he would raise taxes if elected. Was this a disastrous miscalculation as many later claimed? After all, who is in favor of higher taxes? The strategy seemed to emphasize one of Mondale's main weaknesses—an image as a liberal who liked to tax and spend, tax and spend. Yet there was a logic to it. By presenting a comprehensive budget plan, it was hoped, Mondale could overcome his party's reputation for fiscal irresponsibility. Moreover, the strategy would force President Reagan to deal with one of the failures of his first term—the budget deficit. Mondale lost the election by a landslide, so this maneuver is now seen as a blunder. It should be remembered, however, that it was well received by the press at the time and that Mondale was far behind well before he adopted this strategy. Besides, if Mondale kept hearing he was weak and indecisive, hitting everyone's pocketbook would show them another side to his character.

In 1988 Michael Dukakis declared that the campaign would be about "competence, not ideology." But he did not campaign competently, which would have required that he answer the barrage of charges the Bush campaign made in their attempt to introduce Dukakis—unfavorably—to the mass of American voters who had never heard of him.

The list of Dukakis's campaign errors, real and alleged, is a long one. The should-haves and should-not-haves are legion. When asked what he would do if his wife were raped—a question, one must admit, candidates have not usually been asked—he took it not as a request to pour out his emotions, an act he viewed with distaste as a put-on, but as a request for the kind of governmental policies that might cut down on rapes and murders. This presumably showed he lacked emotion and was heartless.

The candidate's critics speak of a "candidate possessed of little understanding of the voters or the election and, more important, of a candidate offering no compelling message or rationale for his campaign."[188] The first part of the criticism is merely a restatement of the fact that he lost, for had he won he would obviously have possessed the correct understanding. As for the second, he did offer a message, which was that he was the more competent of the two and that his party had better answers to questions of modern life. This was not, to be sure, the answer his critics wanted to hear but it was his genuine answer and it might have served him well if the electorate had felt they were in bad straits and needed a competent president.

As the *Times Mirror* National Survey reported in late September 1988, more voters were satisfied with the way things were than were dissatisfied, and this represented a change in the last few months.[189] Dukakis's detractors wanted him to portray himself as a populist, i.e., a harder liberal, claiming this would have rescued his campaign from the beginning. Not according to anything we know. The *Times Mirror* poll, in its own words, "Shows that Bush has succeeded in portraying the Massachusetts governor as a liberal by focusing on such issues as Dukakis's prison furlough program, his veto of 'pledge of allegiance' legislation, and his opposition to major weapons systems." Whereas 31 percent thought of Dukakis as a liberal in June, when he had a huge lead over Bush, while 46 percent considered him a liberal in September, when his support had dropped precipitously, we may well suspect that being perceived as liberal was not the best thing that could happen to a candidate.

Indeed, the proportion of people in the electorate who considered themselves to be more conservative than Dukakis increased from 22 percent in June to 35 percent three months later.[190]

Over and over again Dukakis told his campaign managers that he would not engage in mudslinging no matter what the provocation. Presumably this eminently desirable position was seen as a source of weakness. "How many times do I have to tell you?" an aide heard him say, "That's not me." What else is there to say to this but "Hooray!" The evidence from polls is that voters do not care for negative campaigning.[191]

Candidate Dukakis was also governor of Massachusetts and felt he should abide by a pledge to the citizens of that state to spend several days a week doing the job. He might have done better had he put full time into the campaign.[192] Dukakis failed to answer questions about national defense, which is, after all, a major presidential responsibility. He did not intervene to decide how to halt damaging internal squabbles in his campaign team. Almost from the beginning the organization of the campaign was poor in that phones weren't answered, supplies weren't provided, activities weren't coordinated.[193]

By September 1989 Dukakis had learned how to blame himself. "I have reluctantly come to the conclusion," he told students at the University of California, "that if they throw mud at you, you've got to throw it back."[194]

The problem, in our opinion, was not the candidate but the party. By the beginning of October, according to the Gallup Poll, Republicans led the Democrats by wide margins in regard to the two big issues of peace and prosperity. Another large-scale national poll, taken early on in May when Dukakis was supposed to have lost his edge, shows that except for items where Bush's long experience in national government gave him an edge, Dukakis came out very well.[195] What happened as a result of cumulative developments, including the fading of the Iran-Contra incident and the warming of relations between the United States and the Soviet Union, was that voter optimism began to rise. President Reagan's popularity went way up; confidence in the economy was rising. "Simply put," John Dillon wrote for the *Christian Science Monitor*, "Americans are feeling better about things."[196] The highest level of support for Dukakis naturally came from those citizens who felt that times were getting worse. Sixty-two percent of them voted for him. "Unfortunately for Dukakis," as Dillon commented, "there just aren't enough of those people."[197]

No election campaign is without its faults. What are we to make of

Vice-President Bush's explanation—his supporters were at country clubs helping their daughters come out—for his relatively poor showing in Iowa? His mispronouncements and Freudian slips might have become legendary. But he won.

Should the candidate arrive at a coherent strategy that fits reasonably well with what is known of the political world, he still will find that the party organization has an inertia in favor of its accustomed ways of doing things. The party workers, upon whom he is dependent to some extent, have their own ways of interpreting the world, and he disregards this point of view at some risk. Should the candidate fail to appear in a particular locality as others have done, the party workers may feel slighted. More important, they may interpret this as a sign that the candidate has written off that area and they may slacken their own efforts.

Suppose the candidate decides (as now, with expenditure limitations under the federal subsidy, all candidates must) to divert funds from campaign buttons and stickers to polls and television or transportation. He may be right in his belief that the campaign methods he prefers may bring more return from the funds that are spent. But let the party faithful interpret this as a sign that he is losing—where, oh where, are those familiar indications of his popularity?—and their low morale may encourage a result that bears out this dire prophecy. An innovation in policy may shock the loyal followers of the party. It may seem to go against time-honored precepts that are not easily unlearned. Could a Republican convince his party that a balanced budget is not sacred? Or a Democrat that it is? Both parties adopted these views, innovative for them, in 1984. But it left each of them unhappy. The Democrats were left without the rationale for deficit spending in behalf of good causes that had kept them going since the 1930s. The Republicans, who were in office when Reagan built up deficits of unprecedented size in peacetime, had more to worry about. Any adverse economic results—a too high or too low dollar on world markets, inflation, lack of industrial competitiveness, unemployment, a cloud of dust keeping food from growing—would surely be attributed to the deficit. Everyone knows what happens when a taboo is violated: bad things happen. If Republicans are not more frugal than Democrats, moreover, what are they good for? A selling job may have to be done on the rank and file; otherwise they may sit on their hands during the campaign. It may make better political sense (if less intellectual sense) to phrase the new in old terms and make the departure seem less extreme than it might actually be. The value of the issue in the campaign may thus be blunted. The forces of inertia and tradition may be overcome by strong and persuasive candidates; the parties are greatly dependent on their candidates and have little choice but to follow them, even if haltingly. But in the absence of a special effort, in the presence of enormous uncertainties and the inevitable insecurities, the forces of tradition may do more to shape a campaign than the overt decisions of the candidates possibly can.

Appendix

Forecasting the Outcome

As the time for voting draws closer, more and more interest focuses on attempts to forecast the outcome. This process of forecasting elections is not at all mysterious; it depends on well-settled findings about the behavior of American electorates, many of which have already been discussed. But it may be useful for citizens to understand how the "experts" go about picking the winner.

There are several ways to do it. One way, popularized by journalists Joseph Alsop and Samuel Lubell, is to interview the residents of neighborhoods where there are people who in the past have voted with great stability in one pattern or another. There are neighborhoods, for example, that always vote for the Republicans by a margin of 90 percent or better. Let us say that the interviewer finds that only 50 percent of the people he talks to tell him they are going to vote for the Republicans this time, but when he visits areas voting heavily Democratic, respondents continue to support the Democratic nominee heavily. A finding such as this permits the reporter to make a forecast, even though it is based on only a very small number of interviews that may represent not at all the opinions of most voters.

Reporters who use this technique very rarely make firm predictions about election outcomes. Instead, they concentrate on telling about the clues they have picked up: what they learned in heavily black areas, what the people in Catholic areas said, what midwestern farmers say, what people from localities that always vote with the winner report, and so on.[1] This technique is impressive because it digs into some of the dynamic properties of what goes into voting decisions. It reports which issues seem to be on people's minds. It examines the different ways in which members of different subgroups see the candidates and the campaign. It is also a technique that can be executed at relatively low cost. But it is unsystematic, in that people are not polled in proportions reflecting the

259

distributions of their characteristics in the population (so many men, so many women, so many white, so many black, and so forth). Thus the results of this technique would be regarded as unreliable in a scientific sense, even though they may enhance people's intuitive grasp of what is going on. The results are also unreliable in the sense that two different journalists using this method may come to drastically different conclusions, and there is no certain way of resolving the disagreement; nor is there any prescribed method for choosing between their conflicting interpretations.

The strength of forecasting from historical voting statistics has arisen out of the marvelous stability of American voting habits. But the weakness of such a technique is also manifest. Sometimes gross changes in population through immigration, or changes in the appeals of the parties to different voting groups will throw the historical two-party vote ratios in the sample area out of joint. Since the 1940s, voting habits, particularly at the presidential level, have become much less stable. When a forecast made with this technique is wrong, it is usually quite difficult to tell whether transitory or lasting causes are at the root of it. This limits the usefulness of the forecast greatly, since, in the end, it rests on assumptions that have only partial validity in any one election, and nobody can say precisely how or where or to what extent they may be valid.

A second technique is a variety of the foregoing type of analysis and is used by electronic computers at the radio and television networks on election night. The basic principle of these machines, for our purposes, can be described simply. They are given information about the past voting history of various locales. As these locales report their returns on election night, the machine compares this year's results with the information about previous years and arrives at a prediction of how this year's election will turn out when all the votes are counted. The system is exactly the same as we have already described for Alsop and Lubell, only the machine can be loaded with historical information about many localities—precincts, wards, and so on—and then the machine compares this historical information, not with voting intentions as expressed by a few interviewees, but with voting results as expressed by the whole voting population of the area. Networks now supplement this information with the results of exit polls, statements about voting behavior collected as voters leave the polling place. These findings can be fed into the computer very rapidly—well before votes are officially counted—and give the networks an early feel for what is going on. They do not tell us why nonvoters failed to vote, of course, and this may be important in the end in understanding a given election.

Television network projections have proven controversial in recent years. As the networks' techniques have improved, their predictions have been coming in earlier. In 1980, NBC proclaimed a landslide Reagan victory nearly three hours before West Coast polls closed. Many believed that this depressed turnout and affected the outcome of state and local races. This led to calls for legal prohibition of early projections. Thus far, legislation of this type has not been successful. The controversy, however, has led the networks to be more cautious.[2]

The final method for predicting elections is the most controversial and by all odds the most famous: polls. These are based on a few simple assumptions that have been found to be quite correct over the years. One is that people generally will tell you the truth if you ask them how they are going to vote. Another is that it is not necessary to ask everyone what he is going to do in order to get as accurate a forecast as if you had asked nearly everyone.

The polls are commercial operations and, these days, they are big businesses. In addition to the publicly available polls, such as the Gallup and Harris newspaper reports, politicians commission private polls. These are expensive. They entail writing up a list of questions and asking them all, and all in the same way, to several thousand people spread all over the country; collecting the answers; and figuring out what it all means. Each of these phases of the operation—writing questions, selecting the sample of the total population to be interviewed, interviewing, organizing the answers, and interpreting the results—requires skill and training. This expertise is what commercial polling organizations provide.

In the past, regrettably, some of these organizations have treated the technical aspects of their operation as trade secrets (which they are not) and have left the impression that their forecasts are the result of a particularly efficacious kind of magic. Since the fiasco of 1948, when pollsters were so sure of the result that they became professionally careless, there has been less ballyhoo and polling methods have become much more sophisticated. For example, instead of the quota-control method, most major polling firms use computer-generated random digit dialing telephone surveys. Because they are cheaper than door-to-door sampling, larger numbers of respondents can be contacted.

While far more Americans own phones today than in 1936, there are still, of course, many households that have no phone, and this may bias phone surveys. Telephone polling is often conducted in one night, a process that can introduce still more biases into the sample. "If you call Friday night in Texas, you never reach the parents of teen-age children because they're always at high school football games," says one polling consultant.[3]

Fearful of biasing their sample, Roper and Gallup use personal interviews instead of telephone surveys, and do not conduct one-night polls. They replaced the quota-control method of sampling with "stratified random sampling," in which neighborhoods and houses within neighborhoods are selected randomly to ensure the inclusion of areas representing a variety of economic levels. The new method is not perfectly random—if no one is home at a specified address, the interviewer is permitted to go next door—but it is far superior to the old technique and may be better than telephone interviewing.

In the days of Landon and Dewey victory predictions, pollsters did not account for differential turnout rates among those interviewed. Modern pollsters give substantial attention to identification of likely voters. It is not enough to merely ask the respondent if he intends to vote. According to one expert: "The general experience is that a simple question asking whether one plans to vote produces a gross overestimate of the size of the likely voter population."[4] Hence, many experienced polling organizations build corrections into their results based on assumptions about how many people in their sample will actually vote. Six of the factors used to differentiate likely voters from unlikely voters are:

1. *Eligibility:* now registered or plans to register.
2. *Behavior:* reported frequency of voting; voted in last election; ever voted in precinct where one lives.
3. *Intention:* plan to and certainty of voting.
4. *Affect:* how much thought given to the election.
5. *Values:* general interest in politics.
6. *Cognition:* knowledge of where to vote.[5]

Interpreters of polls should keep in mind the nature of pollster's assumptions and the resulting corrections.

Another polling improvement involves question wording and definition of poll results. In 1936, pollsters asked respondents how they would vote on election day, not their current preference. The results were interpreted as a prediction of how the election would turn out. For example, Roper asked: "For whom do you expect to vote next month?" The drawback of this approach was that many respondents who had a preference said they were undecided because they were reluctant to preclude the possibility that they might change their mind in response to new information or events. After 1948, when pollsters became sensitive to the sizeable shifts in voter sentiment that can occur, they decided to redefine their results not as predictions of how the election will turn out, but as measures of a candidate's standing at a particular time. Thus, they came to rely exclusively on wordings that asked about current preference rather than future intention, such as: "If the election were held today, would you vote for George Bush or Michael Dukakis?"[6]

As polling improved, it became more dependable. For example, the average deviation from election results of the Gallup Poll has been reduced from 3.6 percentage points in eight national elections from 1936 to 1950 to 1.2 percentage points in seven national elections from 1972 to 1984.[7] Today, many people accept polls' predictions as accurate and are surprised when polls prove incorrect.

The general reader will do well to keep a sharp eye on the following points as the polls begin reporting early in the campaign.[8]

1. How big is the population that is reported to be "undecided"? In some elections, members of this group cast the crucial ballots. In reporting their results poll takers have a rule that says: "If the undecided people were to cast their ballots in the same proportion as those who have made up their minds . . ." But wait. If those people were like the decided, they too would have made up their minds. Sometimes they do vote like early deciders, but sometimes they don't. Unfortunately, not enough is known about when they do and when they don't; the best advice we can give is to pay close attention to what the poll taker says he is doing about them, and if they are more than 10 to 15 percent of the population sampled, then place little confidence in the reliability of the reported outcome. Until these people make up their minds, it is too early to tell about the outcome.

2. Certain types of people are hard to get a hold of. People working in the evening, for example, may be difficult to contact because most polls are conducted then. And some voters do not want to be interviewed at all. Pollsters usually build in a correction to account for "unavailables" and "refused responses." That correction is often based—sometimes incorrectly—on the assumption that the opinions of those that were not contacted are the same as those who were. It is important to know how pollsters adjust their results to account for such measurement difficulties.

3. How stable is general sentiment in the population? Very often the polls will report wide swings from week to week. In 1960, the Gallup organization began averaging one week's totals with the previous week's part way through the campaign—without telling its readers.[9] This tended to depress the extent of an apparent shift of sympathy from Nixon to Kennedy, and it also tended to make the figures appear a great deal more stable and settled than they actually

were. In general, wide swings of sentiment from week to week mean that opinions have not crystallized sufficiently for a reliable prediction to be made. Hence the rush to Reagan in the last week of the 1980 election led to a much stronger showing for him than any of the major polling organizations predicted.

4. Some races are harder to forecast than others. Primaries, for example, are notoriously unpredictable. They involve fewer voters, more candidates, the absence of the stabilizing influence of party identification, a less-knowledgeable and committed public, and less-understood campaign and election rules than the general election.[10] Thus in primaries voter preference may form very late. In the absence of knowledge, voter's opinions are tenuous and subject to change.[11]

The major polling disaster of the 1988 primary season came in New Hampshire. Bush had led Dole by margins approaching two to one in the month before the primary. But his lead evaporated after Dole's victory in Iowa. Most late polls in New Hampshire showed Dole even, or slightly ahead of Bush.[12] But Bush won clearly, by more than nine points.

Over the course of the 1988 primary season, Gallup systematically overestimated support for Robert Dole (by averages of anywhere from 2.0 to 3.4 percent, depending on which type of poll is evaluated) while underestimating support for Pat Robertson (by from 4.5 to 5.6 percentage points) and Jesse Jackson (by from 4.3 to 6.4 percentage points). Both Robertson and Jackson drew much of their support from poor, rural areas, constituencies in which survey sampling is especially difficult.

Caucuses are even harder to forecast than primaries. The turnout is extremely small—often less than 200,000. Very small turnout makes forecasts difficult because if members of any particular group, such as blacks or Christian fundamentalists, turn out in larger numbers than expected, then the overall composition of the electorate changes dramatically. As Gallup president Andrew Kohut notes, it is hard to know which candidate's troops will mobilize their voters most effectively.[13]

Pollsters predicting the results of 1988 caucuses were mistaken in several key contests. The final *Des Moines Register* poll for the Republican Iowa caucus showed Robert Dole leading with 37 percent, followed by George Bush at 28 percent, Pat Robertson 13 percent, and Jack Kemp 11 percent. On election day, Robertson's "Invisible Army" materialized, and he ended up running second to

Dole, with 25 percent of the vote. In Michigan, pollsters predicted a big Dukakis victory. "Dukakis Ready to Bury Gephardt in Michigan," read a *Washington Times* headline based on a poll. Turnout among blacks in Detroit and all across the state was enormous. Jackson defeated Dukakis, 54 percent to 29 percent: 113,832, 61,750.[14]

5. Remember that the polls are based on a gross, overall, nationwide sample, but that presidential elections are decided by the distribution of votes in the Electoral College. Thus a really reliable prediction would have to include a state-by-state breakdown. This is prohibitively expensive, and so it is not done. If it were done, it would be possible to detect situations like the following: Candidate A has 49 percent of the popular vote in polls taken in all the populous states and 75 percent of the popular vote in sparsely settled states. He loses badly to Candidate B in the Electoral College, although it looked like it was going the other way. Poll takers generally caution that they are trying only to forecast the percentage distributions in the popular vote. Here again, if the result is closely divided at around 50 percent, then the poll may be quite close to being perfectly accurate but it would still forecast the wrong winner.

6. Some people never show up to vote on election day; these tend to be undecideds and Democrats (in that order) more often than Republicans, but in any event some sort of grain of salt has to be taken with results in order to account for the phenomenon of differential turnout. Most experienced polling organizations do build some sort of correction into their results based on assumptions about how many people in their sample will actually vote. (It is important to know precisely what this assumption is and what the resulting corrections are.

7. Many people feel that the samples used by poll takers—of 1,200 to 5,000 people—are inadequate to represent the feelings of the millions of Americans whose voting they are supposed to represent. This, by and large, is a false issue. Experience has shown that very few of the errors one makes with a sample of 3,000 are correctable with a sample of 15,000 or 20,000, although the expense of polling such a population rises steeply.[15]

Generally it is not a sampling error that is at fault nowadays when poll takers' predictions go awry, but illicit "cooking" of the data or incompetent interpretations of findings. One famous instance of a sampling error occurred when polling was in its most rudimentary stages. In 1936 the *Literary Digest* predicted a landslide for the Republican Alfred Landon.[16] When Franklin D. Roosevelt won overwhelmingly, the *Digest* became a laughingstock and soon thereafter went out of business. What had happened was simple enough. The magazine had sent out millions of postcards to telephone subscribers asking them how they intended to vote. The returns showed a huge Republican triumph. Surely, the *Digest* must have thought, we cannot possibly be wrong when our total response is so large and so one-sided. But, of course, something was terribly wrong. And that stemmed from the fact that only 2.3 million people responded out of 10 million recipients of the cards, and these were all voluntary respondents. So the *Digest* got its returns from a group in the population more likely to vote Republican and completely ignored the larger number of poorer people who were going to vote Democratic. There is a much greater tendency for people of wealth and education to return mail questionnaires so that there was a bias in favor of people likely to vote Republican.[17] As Peverill Squire says: "The 1936 *Literary Digest* poll failed not because of its initial sample, but because of the non-random response rate. Those who received straw vote ballots were strongly supportive of the president. But a slight majority of those who returned their ballot favored Landon."[18]

In 1948, a whole series of errors were made, but none of them seem to have been connected with the size of the sample. In that year, the Gallup, Roper, and Crossley polls all predicted that Governor Dewey would unseat President Truman. Among the problems with the polls that year, the following were uncovered by a committee of social scientists after the event.[19]

1. The poll takers were so sure of the outcome that they stopped taking polls early in the campaign, assuming that the large population of undecideds would vote, if they voted, in the same way as those who had made up their minds early in the campaign.

2. The undecideds voted in just the reverse proportions.

3. Many instances were revealed where polling organization analysts, disbelieving pro-Truman results, arbitrarily "corrected" them in favor of Dewey. The methods of analysis employed were not traced in any systematic way, however, because they could not systematically be reconstructed from records of the polling organizations.

4. Sampling error occurred not because of the size of the samples, but because respondents were selected by methods using the quota-control method instead of stratified random samples. Today, when virtually all American households have telephones (far more than in

1936) telephone surveys using sophisticated methods of random-ization have been developed, as we discussed earlier. Because tele-phone polls are cheaper than door-to-door sampling, larger numbers of respondents can be contacted.

Predicting presidential elections is largely a matter of satisfying curi-osity. It is a great game to guess who will win, and we look to the polls for indications of the signs of the times. But the importance of this kind of prediction is not great. After all, we get to know who has won very soon after election day with much greater detail and accuracy than the polls can supply. The bare prediction of the outcome, even if it is rea-sonably correct, tells us little about how the result came to occur. More may be learned if it is possible to break down the figures to see what kinds of groups—ethnic, racial, economic, regional—voted to what degree for which candidates. Yet our enlightenment at this point is still not great. Suppose we know that in one election 60 percent of Catholics voted Democratic and in another election this percentage was reduced to 53. Surely this is interesting; but unless we have some good idea about why Catholics have switched their allegiance, our knowledge has hardly ad-vanced. The polls often tell us "what" but seldom "why." There is, however, no reason why polling techniques in the future cannot be used to answer "why" questions.[20]

The usual polling technique consists of talking to samples of the pop-ulation at various points in time. The samples may be perfectly adequate, but different people constitute each successive sample as the interviewers seek out people who meet their specifications. It is difficult to discover with any reliability why particular individuals or classes of people are changing their minds because interviewers ordinarily do not go back to the same people who gave their original preferences. A panel survey is used to overcome this difficulty.[21] In a panel survey, a sample of the voting population is obtained and the very same people are interviewed at various intervals before election day and perhaps afterward. This tech-nique makes it possible to isolate the people who make up their minds early and those who decide late. These groups can be reinterviewed and examined for other distinguishing characteristics. More importantly, per-haps, those voters who change their minds during the campaign can be identified and studied. If a panel of respondents can be reinterviewed over a number of years and a series of elections, it may become possible to discover directly why some people change their voting habits from elec-tion to election. Another technique, more practical and cheaper than the panel survey, is the focus group.

The attentive reader may have observed that reports of party identification vary somewhat according to the observer. Poll data during the 1984 election campaign suggested that the gap had narrowed to zero or that it was as large a 19 percentage points. Why don't all reports agree?

One reason for discrepancies involves the time the poll was taken; the nearer to election day, the more likely that voters will bring their party preferences into line with their chosen candidates. A second reason is that different polls often sample somewhat different populations. Exit polls, for instance, sample only those who actually vote. Other polls report results only for registered voters or those who say they are likely to vote, which is different from sampling a cross-section of the population. The closer the population polled is to the actual electorate (which is, remember, far smaller than the total population eligible to vote), the more likely it is to reflect electoral influences. Thus exit polls, in view of Reagan's popularity, showed a greater gain in identification with the Republican party than polls of all those of voting age.

A third reason concerns wording. A question that includes a phrase such as "as of today" is more likely to tap current feelings than one that specifically asks the respondent to answer "usually" or "generally" or "regardless of how you may vote."

A test of these factors by Borrelli, Lockerbie, and Niemi reveals that they explain most of the discrepancies among polls reporting different figures in partisan allegiance. As they say,

> . . . all else equal, 1980 and 1984 polls that worded the partisanship question in a general way reported a Democratic-Republican gap roughly five percentage points larger than reported by polls that asked "as of today"; nonexit polls in those years reported gaps, on average, five points larger than did exit polls, polls taken more than 10 days before or after the election in 1984 reported gaps three points larger than did polls taken within 10 days of the election.[22]

There are a number of concerns about networks' practice of making early projections on election night. One concern is that voters who hear the early call will switch their vote. A "bandwagon effect" could come about if the projections inspired otherwise reluctant supporters of the announced victor to vote, or move the undecided to the winner's circle, or convert some of his opponent's supporters into vote switchers. There is also the possibility of an "underdog effect," where voters move toward the projected loser. A number of studies have been conducted on the matter, and the evidence suggests neither of the two effects exists in actual practice.

Another concern regards turnout. Critics of early calls maintain that voters in the West might be dissuaded from voting due to the projections. California Secretary of State March Fong Eu said that in 1980:

> [V]oter lines dissolved as people waiting to vote decided to go home instead when they heard the presidential race was over. . . . [V]oter-information telephones stopped ringing during the time when traditionally voters have had a hard time getting through because of heavy phone traffic. Would-be voters tell me how they decided to stay at home rather than vote when they had the network news.[23]

Researchers on the subject have started from different assumptions and have used varied data and methods, so it is little surprise that they arrive at divergent conclusions. While Laurily Epstein and Gerald Strom found no effect,[24] John Jackson concluded a potential decline in turnout of 6 to 12 percent.[25] A consensus of the data suggests the possibility of a small decline in affected areas, ranging from 1 to 5 percent.[26]

But, as many experts on the topic have noted, early calls must introduce new information to voters if they are to reduce turnout. The results of exit polls will not have any effect unless they change voter's perceptions about the closeness of the race.[27] This was the case in 1980, when prior to election day pollsters predicted a tight race, but election day exit polls indicated a Reagan sweep. This was not the case in 1984 and 1988, when exit polls simply confirmed what the preelection polls had already forecasted: a wide Republican win. Nor was it the case in the 1976 election, which had been predicted as close before election day and was also predicted as close by the exit polls.[28]

The potential for a decline in turnout is worrisome not only because turnout in American presidential elections has persistently declined since the early 1950s, but also because it may affect the outcome of both the presidential and local elections. In 1980, incumbent Democratic congressman James Corman lost his seat in California's twenty-first congressional district by about .5 percent—752 votes in a race where 153,770 were cast. Oregon Representative Al Ullman, the Chairman of the House Ways and Means Committee, lost his seat by a margin of approximately 1 percent. Would these candidates have won if not for networks' projections? Once again, the evidence is mixed. Jackson argues that Republicans are most likely to be affected by hearing the early results.[29] Michael X. Delli Carpini, on the other hand, concludes that the decline in affected districts was disproportionately Democratic.[30] The jury is still out on the matter.

Congressman Al Swift, a leading critic of early projection, argues that although the effect on turnout may be small, the effect on voter morale is not. This, he says, is the most pernicious effect of early calls by networks. Swift told an American Bar Association panel:

> Since John Kennedy was assassinated, this country has gone through a series of extraordinarily traumatic experiences. One of the results appears to be a growing public cynicism toward almost all our institutions. If, under these circumstances, you also begin to erode their confidence in the fundamental building block of a democratic society—the individual citizen's right to select, unimpeded, the people who will form the government—it seems to me that you have attacked something very precious to this country.[31]

In response to these concerns (and perhaps, out of a fear of restrictive legislation), all three major networks and Cable News Network pledged not to make projections for a given area until the polls close in that area. There is still, however, the possibility that reports from areas in which the polls have already closed (eastern areas of the United States) will affect turnout in areas where the polls are still open (the West). Some legislators have proposed to solve this problem by closing all polls in the continental United States at the same time. Federal legislation which would require uniform poll closing has passed the House twice, but has never succeeded in the Senate.[32]

5

Issues and Appraisals

In 1968 the Democratic party endured a season of turmoil: its incumbent president, Lyndon Johnson, withdrew his candidacy to succeed himself; a leading candidate to succeed him, Robert Kennedy, was assassinated; and its national convention was conducted amidst extraordinary uproar. In that convention, party leaders chose Hubert Humphrey, who had not entered a single primary, to be the party's candidate for the presidency. In the aftermath of that convention, a party commission on reform of the nomination process—the McGovern-Fraser Commission as it was called—was constituted and a year later brought in some proposals for changing presidential nominations. These were adopted by the Democratic party.

After every national nominating convention from 1968 through 1984, the Democrats have had such a commission; after the 1988 election, the Democrats convened a "committee" which, despite claims that it was not a successor to the five previous commissions, essentially performed the same function of reexamining and altering the rules governing nominating procedures. Table 5.1 gives pertinent facts about their leadership and their main effects. It is fair to say that for much of the last twenty-five years reform has been in the air. Even Republicans have been affected, since in some cases new state laws have had to be enacted to comply with changes in Democratic party regulations.

Previous chapters have incorporated the results of these reforms into the description we have given so far, concentrating on features of the presidential nomination process as it presently exists and on the political consequences that flow from our system as it is now organized. Some of these features have been part of the landscape of American politics for a generation or more; others are new, and the changes they may bring about lie mostly in the future. Nevertheless, if there is one certainty about presidential elections, it is that this process is subject to continuous pressure for change.

In this chapter we appraise some of these changes and proposals for

TABLE 5.1   *Reform Commissions of the Democratic Party, 1969–1990*

Name	Duration	Leadership	Main Effects
McGovern-Fraser	1969–72	Senator George McGovern, (S.D.); Representative Donald M. Fraser (Minn.)	Established guidelines for the selection of delegates; outlawed two systems of delegate selection.
Mikulski	1972–73	Barbara A. Mikulski, Baltimore City Councilwoman	Banned open cross-over primaries; replaced stringent quotas on blacks, women, and youths with nonmandatory affirmative action programs.
Winograd	1975–80	Morley Winograd, former chairman of Michigan Democratic Party	Eliminated loophole primary; shortened delegate selection season; increased size of delegations to accommodate state party and elected officials; required states to set filing deadlines for candidates 30 to 90 days before the voting.
Hunt	1980–82	Governor James B. Hunt, Jr. (N.C.)	Provided uncommitted delegate spots for major party and elected officials; relaxed proportional representation; ended ban on loophole primary; shortened primary and caucus season to a 3-month window; weakened delegate binding rule.
Fowler, or "Fairness"	1985	Donald L. Fowler, former chairman of So. Carolina Dem. Party	Slightly expanded superdelegate spots; allowed certain states to return to open cross-over primaries; lowered from 20 percent to 15 percent the threshold of primary voters candidates must surpass to receive delegates.
DNC Rules and Bylaws Committee	1989–90	Fowler and Anne D. Campbell (N.J.)	Slightly expanded superdelegate spots; re-banned loophole primaries.

Sources: Adapted from William Crotty, *Party Reform* (New York, 1983), pp. 40–43. Additional sources: Adam Clymer, "Democrats Adopt Nominating Rules for '80 Campaign," *New York Times* (June 10, 1978); Clymer, "Democrats Alter Delegate Rules, Giving Top Officials More Power," *New York Times* (March 27, 1982); Rhodes Cook, "Democrats' Rules Weaken Representation," *Congressional Quarterly Weekly Report* (April 3, 1982), p. 750; Austin Ranney, "Farewell to Reform—Almost," in Kay Schlozman, ed., *Elections in America* (Boston, 1987), p. 106; Rhodes Cook, "Democratic Party Rules Changes Readied for '92 Campaign," *CQ Weekly Report*, March 17, 1990; "Democrats Alter Nominating Rules," *CQ Weekly Report*, April 14, 1990.

future change of the American party system and its nomination and election processes. Because of the rapid reforms of the past few years, some of the impetus behind certain suggestions for further reform has slackened while other ideas seem likely to be pursued with renewed vigor. Few observers are satisfied with the nomination process as it now is. As past solutions lead to future problems, new proposals enter the agenda and old ones depart.

As times change, moreover, old concerns become outdated and new ones take their place. Under the party system of the 1950s and 1960s, for instance, with conservative Democrats and liberal Republicans reducing the agreement within their parties, the cry went out for greater party cohesion. Too little ideology was widely blamed for the lack of consistent party policy positions across a wide range of issues. How, it was then argued, could voters make a sensible choice if the parties did not offer internally consistent and externally clashing policy views? As evidence of ideological consistency within each party grows, however, the demand for internal cohesion may decline. In its place, one can confidently expect concern about the negative consequences of party polarization. In the same way, reforms stressing participation have been in due course modified by measures emphasizing experience, such as the creation of superdelegates. Thus the preoccupations of one era give way to those of its successors.

New proposals for change stem on the whole from two camps, which for purposes of discussion we wish to treat as distinct entities. One camp urges strengthened parties, not as the focus of organizational loyalties so much as the vehicles for the promulgation of policy. The other group urges "openness" and "participation" in the political process and has advocated weakening party organizations and strengthening candidates, factions, and their ideological concerns. Thus while both sets of reformers ostensibly disagree about whether they want parties to be strong or weak, this comes down to a difference in predictions about the outcome of the application of the same remedy, for both in the end prescribe the same thing: more ideology as the tie that binds voters to elected officials, and less organizational loyalty.

The Political Theory of Policy Government

The first branch of the party reform movement has its antecedents at the turn of the century in the writings of Woodrow Wilson, James Bryce, and other passionate constitutional tinkerers who founded and breathed life into the academic study of political science. The descendants of these thinkers have through the years elaborated a series of proposals that are embodied in a coherent general political theory. This theory contains a conception of the proper function of the political party, evaluates the legitimacy and the roles of Congress and the president, and enshrines a particular definition of the public interest. Different advocates of reform have stated this theory with greater or less elaboration; some reformers leave out certain features of it, and some are disinclined to face squarely the implications of the measures they espouse. We shall try here to reproduce correctly a style of argument that, though it ignores the slight differences separating these party reformers one from another, gives a coherent statement of their party reform theory and contrasts it with the political theory that critics of their position advance.[1] Since in time we may achieve much the kind of party cohesion that these reformers of yesteryear wanted, it is worthwhile to attend to the pros and cons of the debate their proposals brought about.

This group of party reformers suggested that democratic government requires political parties that (1) make policy commitments to the electorate, (2) are willing and able to carry them out when in office, (3) develop alternatives to government policies when out of office, and (4) differ sufficiently to "provide the electorate with a proper range of choice between alternatives of action."[2] They thus come to define a political party as "an association of broadly like-minded voters seeking to carry out common objectives through their elected representatives."[3] In a word, party should be based on policy.

Virtually all significant party relationships are, for these reformers, mediated by policy considerations. The electorate is assumed to be policy motivated and officeholders mandate conscious. Policy discussion among party members is expected to create widespread agreements upon which party discipline will then be based. Pressure groups are to be resisted and accommodated only as the overall policy commitments of party permit. The weaknesses of parties and the disabilities of governments are seen as stemming from failure to develop and support satisfactory policy programs. Hence it seems sensible to refer to this theory of party reform as a theory of "policy government." This theory suggests "that the choices provided by the two-party system are valuable to the American people in proportion to their definition in terms of public policy."[4] It differs from the participatory brand of party reform in that policy reformers believe they are revitalizing party organizations, whereas participatory democrats are likely to be indifferent to party organization.

Opponents of party reform believe that democratic government in the United States requires the minimization of conflict between contending interests and social forces.[5] Their ideal political party is a mechanism for accomplishing and reinforcing adjustment and compromise among the various interests in society to prevent severe social conflict. Where reformers desire parties that operate "not as mere brokers between different groups and interests but as agencies of the electorate," their critics see the party as an "agency for compromise." Opponents of party reform and policy government hold that "the general welfare is achieved by harmonizing and adjusting group interest."[6] In fact, they sometimes go so far as to suggest that "the contribution that parties make to policy is inconsequential so long as they maintain conditions for adjustment."[7] Thus, the theory of the political party upheld by critics of the party reform position is rooted in a notion of "consensus government." Advocates of policy government behave as if problems of consensus, of gaining sufficient agreement to govern, have already been solved. Believing that there is no problem of stability, therefore, they concentrate on change. Their critics downplay policy not because they think it unimportant but rather because they think the capacity to govern is more important than any particular policy. Fearing instability, they are less concerned with enhancing the system's capacity to change.

A basic cleavage between advocates of policy government and consensus government may be observed in their radically opposed conceptions of the public interest. For advocates of consensus government, the public interest is defined as whatever emerges from the negotiations, adjustments, and compromises made in fair fights or bargains among conflicting interest groups. They suggest no external criteria by which policies can be measured in order to determine whether or not they are in the public interest. So long as the process by which decisions are made consists of intergroup bargaining, within certain specified democratic "rules of the game," they regard the outcomes as being in the public interest.

For advocates of policy government, the public interest is a discoverable set of policies that represents "something more than the mathematical result of the claims of all the pressure groups."[8] A concept of the public interest, they argue, is necessary if we are to resist the unwarranted claims of "special interest" groups. While they suggest that there are ways of judging whether a policy is in the public interest, apart from the procedural test applied by supporters of consensus government, these methods are never identified. This lack of concrete criteria spelling out the public interest would not present great difficulties if policy government advocates did not demand that an authoritative determination of party policy be made and that party members be held to it. Information about the policy preferences of members is supposed to flow upward, and orders establishing and enforcing final policy decisions are supposed to flow downward in a greatly strengthened pyramid of party authority. Without criteria of the public interest clearly in mind, however, party leaders can define the public interest in any terms they find convenient.

If we were to have parties that resembled the ideal of this first set of party reformers, what would they be like? They would be coherent in their policies, reliable in carrying them out, accountable to the people, sharply differentiated and in conflict with each other, disciplined and hierarchical internally. Let us see, then, what it would take to create a party system of this kind.

For the parties to carry out the promises they make, the people responsible for making promises would have to be the same as (or in control of) the people responsible for carrying them out. This means, logically, one of two alternatives. Either the people who controlled party performance all year round would have to write the party platforms every four years at the national conventions, or the people who wrote the platforms would have to be put in charge of party performance. In the first case, the party platforms would have to be written by leaders such as the members of Congress who at present refrain from enacting laws favored by both national conventions. State and local political leaders would write their respective platforms. Under such an arrangement, very little formal, over-all coordination or party coherence seems likely to emerge. Since the main point of policy government is to create logically coherent, unified policy that makes possible rational choices by voters, we must reject this first alternative as a way to fulfill the demands of party reformers.

In fact, it is the second alternative that is most often recommended by advocates of policy government. National conventions must make policy that will be enforced on national, state, and local levels by means of party discipline, and the people who write the convention platforms must be put in charge. This arrangement also has a fatal defect: It ignores the power of the people who do not write the platforms. How are independently elected members of Congress to be bypassed? Will present-day local and state party leaders acquiesce in this rearrangement of power and subject themselves to discipline from a newly constituted outside source? Party reform has already gone some distance toward reducing the influence of these people in the presidential nomination process. Will they give up their independent capacity as public officials to make policy as well? Generally, we assume they will not.

One reformer says: "As for the clash of personal political ambitions in the United States, they are being completely submerged by the international and domestic concerns of the American public. War and peace, inflation and depression are both personal and universal issues; tariff, taxes, foreign aid, military spending, federal reserve policies, and hosts of other national policies affect local economic activities across the land. Politicians who wish to become statesmen must be able to talk intelligently about issues that concern people in all constituencies."[9]

But is it necessarily the case, as party reformers suggest, that the increasing importance of national issues will inevitably lead to placing greater power in the hands of party leaders with national (that is to say, presidential) constituencies? There is no necessary connection between political power in the national arena and the national scope of issues. National political power may rest upon local control of nomination, alliances with local interest groups, and many other bases. Even if national issues become more important, as they well may, this may only enhance the powers of the local interests best able to influence national policy— such as, for example, the people in the congressional districts that elect influential members of the House of Representatives. So far, the nationalization of policy has been accompanied by strengthened single-issue groups.

The people who have the most to lose from policy government are the leaders of Congress. As of now, the major electoral risks facing national legislators are local. This does not mean that legislators will necessarily be parochial in their attitudes and policy commitments. But it does mean that they are not necessarily bound to support the president or national party leader on issues of high local saliency. In order to impose discipline successfully, the national party must be able either to control sanctions presently important to legislators, such as nomination to office, or to impose still more severe ones upon them. At the moment our system provides for control of congressional, state, and local nominations and elections by geographically localized candidates, electorates, and (to a lesser extent) party leaders. Presidents are not totally helpless in affecting the outcomes of these local decisions, but their influence, especially considering the power of incumbent members of Congress to maintain themselves in office, is in most cases quite marginal.[10]

In the light of this, one obvious electoral prerequisite of disciplined parties is that local voters must be so strongly tied to national party issues that they will reward their local representatives for supporting national policy pronouncements, even at the expense of local advantage. To a certain extent, by virtue of the influence of national news media and the rising educational level of the electorate, as well as some increase in the general propensity of the most active citizens to think ideologically, this condition is being met. The issues on which the national party makes its appeal must either unify a large number of constituencies in favor of the party or appeal at least to some substantial segment of opinion everywhere. But even if this could be accomplished, it would be strategically unwise for parties to attempt to discipline members who lived in areas that are strongly against national party policy. This would mean reading the offending area out of the party. Therefore, reformers must show how they intend to contribute to the national character of political parties by enforcing national policies upon members of Congress whose local constituencies are drastically opposed to national party policy, or whose constituents do not pay attention to issues but care more for the personality or the constituent services of their congressman.[11] Insofar as leeway exists, let us say, for liberal northeastern Republicans—a diminishing breed—to support liberal programs and for conservative southern Democrats—who are also more scarce than they once were—to oppose them, the parties shall, in fact, have retained their old, "undisciplined," "irresponsible" shapes. Insofar as this leeway does not exist, splinter groups of various kinds are encouraged to split off from the established parties. This is a consequence regarded as undesirable by most party reformers.

There is another way of achieving disciplined parties that may be more promising. We have seen that party activists and, to a lesser but meaningful extent, legislators have become ideologically more coherent and distinct. This has not occurred by command but by evolution: northern liberal Republicans have moved into the Democratic party and conservative southern Democrats into the Republican party. As the parties have become more ideologically distinctive across a wider range of issues—social, environmental, and defense, as well as economic—those who feel most uncomfortable have been changing allegiances. For proponents of party cohesion, this is the good news. The bad news is that a strong party line breeds splits. Among Republicans this means the prospect of future conflict between free market libertarians and social conservatives. Among Democrats, factionalism has become so severe that it may be preventing them from mobilizing their historic edge in party identification for presidential elections.

A second method for reducing the independent power over policy of independently elected congressional leaders has begun to have an effect in national politics. This method addresses not the prospects for nomination and election of congressional leaders but rather their capacity to lead in Congress. Adherence to the conservatism of the majority of Republicans in Congress has in general been a prerequisite of leadership within the Republican party. Among congressional Democrats, however, more leeway has existed for congressional leaders—at any rate for committee chairmen, who in the past have been selected by seniority—to take whatever policy positions they pleased.

Since the mid-1950s, sentiment has grown in Congress that conservative Democratic committee chairmen should be more responsive to the policy preferences of the majority of the majority party, and in recent years the Democratic caucus of the House of Representatives has acted to remove committee chairmen they have regarded as unresponsive. This has not, however, proceeded strictly along ideological lines. One of the first chairmen to be removed, Wright Patman of Texas, was as liberal as any Democrat in the House, including his replacement, Henry Reuss of Wisconsin. Another chairman, Edward Hebert of the Armed Services Committee, was replaced by a leader ideologically indistinguishable from him on matters coming before the committee.[12] So, despite the unlimbering of a new weapon that has the potential of encouraging party responsibility in Congress, it has not been used consistently quite in this way, and concerns related to the management of Congress itself have thus far been more significant than the shaping or enforcement of party policy in the activities of the reactivated Democratic caucus.

The Evolution of a Second Branch of Party Reform

It should be obvious that party reforms are generally not politically neutral. From the 1940s to the 1960s they were designed almost entirely to strengthen the president and to weaken Congress, especially as Congress was then constituted. Advocates of policy government wanted more disciplined, pragmatic parties. Only the president, they believed, could provide the necessary leadership. Proposed reforms of the party system were in general also designed to help Democrats and weaken Republicans. The reasoning is this: Republican presidents represented a party generally unsympathetic to increased activity by the federal government. Hence they would be inclined to ask less of Congress, and thus they ran less risk of being stymied on matters of policy by a recalcitrant Congress. Democratic presidents, on the other hand, on behalf of the more liberal, more activist, and more innovative party, ask much more of Congress and customarily have to settle for much less of what they ask for.

It seems to us quite understandable that agitation for party reform, which during the late 1940s so excited the liberal academicians who were its chief proponents, died away to a whisper during the Eisenhower decade. In the early 1960s frustrated liberals took up their cudgels in the cause of party ''responsibility'' and presidential prerogative. The underlying aim, it appears, was to speed up the social changes that they desired by trying to rig the rules of the game more in favor of that political institution, the presidency, which then shared their policy preferences. In the 1970s and 80s, with Democrats firmly entrenched in Congress and

Republicans far more successful in electing presidents, the successors of these frustrated liberals are not as united in favor of a strong presidency as they once were.

The close connection between the desire for party reform and the policy preferences of reformers was illustrated in the late 1960s. Reformers could no longer complain about the failure of a conservative Congress to enact New Deal-type welfare measures; the Eighty-ninth Congress had taken care of that. Their attention became focused on foreign policy because they were outraged by America's continued involvement in the war in Vietnam. It turned out that presidents had become "imperial," and they were, if anything, more in favor of military involvement in Vietnam than were many members of Congress. The frustrations of reformers were centered on the inability of senators who favored an antiwar policy to persuade the president to withdraw American troops and commitments as fast as they would have liked. Hence, it was no longer feasible to advocate reforms that would enable presidents to pursue presidential foreign policies despite the reluctance of congressmen. Instead, reformers began to entertain notions of limitations on presidential prerogatives. It is, unfortunately, exceedingly difficult to stop presidents from doing things one doesn't like (such as, for example, fighting a war in Indochina) without also preventing them from taking actions of which one approves (such as, for instance, fighting inflation or unemployment). Since liberals want a strong presidency in domestic affairs and conservatives want a strong presidency in foreign affairs, the result is a phenomenon we all observe, namely, ambivalence about the power of the presidency.

Because it is not feasible to limit the damage presidents can do without also limiting the good they can do, the attention of many party reformers in the late 1960s focused on making the presidential nomination procedure more responsive to their preferences without regard to the strengthening of parties. They believed that if the nomination procedure were opened up to more party voters in primaries and to party activists in district and state conventions, they would have a better chance of nominating a candidate they preferred. Their immediate cause for complaint was the 1968 Democratic convention, in which they believed the fortunes of nominees like Eugene McCarthy and George McGovern were damaged by undemocratic modes of delegate selection. In view of the commanding margin of victory at the convention for Hubert Humphrey, it seems doubtful that different procedures, even if they had been enforced at the time, would have changed enough delegate votes to make a difference in the 1968 outcome. But it was strongly thought so at the time, and at that convention rules changes were begun that changed the face of politics in the Democratic party.[13] The assumption behind the views of the reformers who represented generally left-wing policy positions within the Democratic party was that if the people were given a choice they would support candidates with policy preferences more like their own. Their success in this regard has been mixed. In 1972 the reformed nominating system did help nominate the liberal George McGovern. In 1976, and again in 1980, however, the system produced a moderate, Jimmy Carter. Walter Mondale, the 1984 nominee, was a mainstream liberal Democrat strongly supported by party regulars. And Michael Dukakis, though clearly a liberal, was not the most left-wing Democratic hopeful of 1988; that honor probably belongs to Jesse Jackson.

Reform by Means of Participatory Democracy: An Appraisal

The efforts of those who advocate participatory democracy and who have attempted to make the Democratic party the vehicle of this approach to government have met with considerable success over the past twenty years. Here we wish to contemplate the theory of politics that underlies this position. Ordinarily, participatory democrats criticize the American political system in two respects. First, they argue that elections have insufficient impact on policy outcomes of the government. These critics see too weak a link between public policy and the desires of electoral majorities. Second, there is the critique of the electoral process itself, which argues that policy does not represent what majorities want because undemocratic influences determine election results. These criticisms are simpleminded in one sense and cogent in another. They are simpleminded in that they ignore the immense problems that would have to be overcome if we were truly serious about transforming America or any large diverse population into a participatory democracy. They are cogent in that responsiveness to majorities on questions of policy is a fundamental value that gives legitimacy to democratic government. The connection between such criticism and the legitimacy of government makes it important to deal at least briefly with some of the issues and problems that should be raised (and usually are not) by judgments of this fundamental nature.

The first and obvious question to ask is whether the criticisms are based on fact. Is the American system unresponsive to the policy desires of a majority of its citizens? Unfortunately, there is no unambiguous way to answer this question. If we focus our attention, for example, on the mechanics of the policy process, we find what appears to be government by minorities. In some policy areas a great number of people and interests, organized and unorganized, may have both a say in open hearings and some influence on the final product. But fewer individuals may be involved in areas dealing with other problems and policies, some of which will be of a specialized nature, of limited interest, and so on. Certainly it is true that even members of Congress do not have equally great influence over every decision: committee jurisdictions, seniority, special knowledge, party, individual reputation—all combine to weigh the influence of each member on a different scale for each issue.

So we must conclude that if we adopt direct participation in and equal influence over the policy decisions of our government (the decisions that "affect our lives") as the single criterion of democracy, then our system surely fails the test. So, we might note, does every contemporary government of any size known to us—possibly excepting two or three rural Swiss cantons.

Another approach might focus on public opinion as an index of majority desires. Using this standard a quite different picture emerges. The vast majority of policy decisions made by the government have the support of popular majorities. In cases where this is not true, the lack of "responsiveness" may have several causes, not all of them curable: (1) conflicts between majority desires and intractable situations in the world (for example, the desire to peaceably transform Iraq into a liberal democratic ally), or (2) public attitudes favoring certain sets of policies that may be mutually incompatible (such as the desire for low taxes, high expenditures, and balanced budgets); or (3) clear, consistent, and feasible majority desires that are ignored by the government because the desires are unconstitutional or antithetical to enduring values of the political system, to which leaders are more sensitive than popular majorities. Surveys, for example, have from time to time revealed majorities in favor of constitutionally questionable repressive measures against dissenters and the press. Criticisms of presidential elections are more difficult to assess. American politics does respond to the application of resources that are arguably nondemocratic and that cause the influence of different actors to be weighed unequally. In a truly democratic system, it could be argued, the system would respond to numbers and only numbers. All other methods of achieving political outcomes beyond the registering of preference by voting would be deemed illegitimate. As we have indicated, however, money, incumbency, energy and enthusiasm, popularity, name recognition, ability, and experience are all valuable assets within the structure of American politics. Should be system be condemned for this? Should we attempt to eradicate the influence of these resources? Before joining a campaign in behalf of this cause, it may be wise to consider for a moment why these unequally distributed resources are useful.

Possession of the relevant political resources could increase an individual's influence because candidates seek the support of such people. They do so because contenders need money to publicize themselves and their causes and because they need experienced and able allies to help them convey their image effectively to the voters. Political resources and the people who possess them are important, it turns out, because campaigns are important. And campaigns are important because the general public needs to be alerted to the fact that an election is near. Partisans must be mobilized, the uncommitted convinced, perhaps even a few minds changed. Resources other than votes are important because—and only because—numerical majorities must be mobilized.

American politics responds to diverse resources because many citizens are politically apathetic. Why is political apathy widespread? There are several alternative explanations. Perhaps it is because the system presents the citizenry with no real alternatives from which to choose. However, in the election of 1964 there was at least a partial test of this "hidden vote" theory, and the evidence is negative. And in 1972, another year when there was an unambiguous choice, nonvoting hit a high for elections up to then. Perhaps it is because the public has been imbued with a "false consciousness" that blinds them to their "real" desires and interests. This explanation is traditionally seized upon by the enlightened few to deny value to the preferences of the ignorant many. The people, we are told, are easily fooled; this testifies to their credulity. They do not know what is good for them; this makes them childlike. But when the people cannot trust their own feelings, when their desires are alleged to be unworthy, when their policy preferences should be ignored because they are not "genuine" or "authentic," they are being deprived of their humanity as well. What is left for the people if they are held to have no judgment, wisdom, feeling, desire, and preference? Such an argument would offer little hope for democracy of any sort, for it introduces the most blatant form of inequality as a political "given": a structured, ascribed difference between those who know what is "good" for themselves and those who must be "told." No doubt it is true that much of the time we do not know (without the advantage of perfect foresight) what is best for us. But that is not to say that others know better, that our consciousness is false but theirs is true. Persons who make the "false consciousness" argument do not believe in democracy.

A more hopeful and less self-contradictory explanation of political apathy might note that throughout American history a substantial number of citizens have not wished to concern themselves continually with the problems and actions of government. Many citizens prefer to participate on their own terms, involving themselves with a particular issue area or problem. These citizens' participation is necessarily sporadic and narrower than that of the voter interested in all public problems and actively involved in general political life. Many other citizens (surely a majority) are more interested in their own personal problems than in any issue of public policy.[14] These citizens meet their public obligations by going to the polls at fairly regular intervals, making their selections on the basis of their own criteria, and then supporting the actions and policies of the winner—whether they were their first choices or not. In the intervals, unless they themselves are personally affected by some policy proposal, most of these citizens may wish to be left alone. Given the complexity of issues and the uncertainty surrounding the claims of candidates, citizens may arrive at their voting decisions by asking themselves a simple, summary question: Are things (the domestic economy, world affairs) better or worse than they were? This is a reasonable way to decide but it does not offer much future policy guidance to political leaders.

The literature on apathy may say more about the values of the students of the subject than about the ostensible objects of their studies. Those observers who approve of existing institutions are likely to view apathy as relatively benign; people do not participate because they are satisfied and they trust institutions to do well by them. Those who disapprove of existing institutions naturally find the defect in the institutions themselves; people do not participate because they are denied the opportunity or because they rightly feel ineffectual. Observers who view individuals as capable of regulating their own affairs, by contrast, see them as deciding case-by-case whether it is worth the time and effort to participate. Projecting the investigator's preferences onto citizens does not seem to us a useful way of learning why this or that person chooses to participate in political life. As political scientists and citizens, we think self-government an ideal so valuable that we would not impose our own views on those who decide they have better things to do.

Studies have from time to time shown unfavorable citizen attitudes toward the political system, a phenomenon sometimes called "alienation." These attitudes do not explain low rates of voting participation, however; persons who score high in these unfavorable attitudes evidently participate at about the same rate as the nonalienated.[15] So we surmise that most citizens who do not vote fail to do so because they are concerned with other things important to them, like earning a living or painting a picture or cultivating a garden, and not because they feel it is so difficult to influence outcomes. In short, for them, politics is peripheral. Given the peripheral importance of politics in many peoples' lives, even a little bit of extra effort at making it easier to vote does make a difference in turnout. Were this not so, laws making it easier to register and to vote would not be as successful as they are in increasing voter participation.

Consider a society in which all citizens were as concerned about public matters as the most active. Such a society would not require mobilization: all who were able to would vote. The hoopla and gimmickry associated with political campaigns would have little effect: this citizenry would know the record of the parties and the candidates and, presumably, would make their reasoned choices on this basis. Should such an active society be the goal of those whose political philosophy is democratic? This question should not and cannot be answered without first addressing the problem of how such a society could be achieved.

Without attempting to be comprehensive, a few difficulties do merit some specific comment. First and foremost, political participation—as Aristotle made clear more than two thousand years ago—takes a great deal of time. For this reason (among others) a large population of slaves was felt to be a necessary concomitant of participatory government: it freed Athenian citizens from the cares of maintaining life and thus provided them the leisure time that made their political activity possible. But having rejected some hundred years ago this ingenious solution to the problems related to relatively large-scale participation, we must deal with the fact that the vast majority of our citizens must work for a living. Most Americans lack the disposable time that permits professionals and college students and other privileged people to choose their working hours. Most citizens lack the time, even if they had the temperament and training, to engage continually in politics. To the degree that representative institutions—political parties, legislatures, elected executives—are denigrated in favor of more direct modes of activity, the majority of the people will be without the means of participation through which they can most effectively make their will felt. In short, to impose requirements of direct participation on those desiring a voice in decisions would be to insure that the incessant few rather than the sporadic many would rule: thus the 1960s' slogan ''power to the people'' really proposed to replace a representative few, who are elected, with an unrepresentative few, who are self-appointed.

In a well-known work, the philosopher Jurgen Habermas has argued that the only way to legitimate a democracy, that is, for it to be considered a true democracy worthy of support, is for it to approximate the conditions of what he calls ''an ideal speech situation.'' Every person would be equally interested and active. Each would have equal rights, money, information, and all other resources necessary for effective participation.[16] What could be wrong with such an ideal? Nothing at all, we think. If it were to be realized in practice in a very diverse society, however, it might lead to surprising results. For in a diverse society there are bound to be people who may wish to express diverse values. Individualists, for example, adhere to the ideal of equality of opportunity so that people can be different, and some may consequently end up with more resources than others. This expresses a different equality than that postulated by Habermas. Other people, for example, Christian fundamentalists, may prefer a more patriarchal or hierarchical set of values in which different people occupy different statuses. Thus it is helpful to consider whether democracy is only about equality or whether it may be about enabling people who hold different values to live together peaceably.

There is a further explanation for the decline in participation that deserves consideration. If government is perceived to be the source of difficulty rather than the solution to problems, it would not be surprising if fewer people thought it worthwhile to contribute to the selection of those who would invariably do more harm than good. Whoever wins, the slogan would be, the people lose. Surprising as it may seem, both major parties have contributed to disparagement of government. In olden times, way back in the mid-1960s, the overarching issues were all too obvious: Conservatives (including most Republicans) who had to pay taxes for other people's programs were generally against expansion of the public sector, and liberals (including most Democrats) who spent other people's money on behalf of their constituencies were mostly in favor of expansion. Then simplicity began to give way to complexity. As the legitimacy of the political process was questioned by opponents of the Vietnam war, a disposition strengthened by the civil rights movement and the Watergate affair, spokesmen for beneficiaries began to attack social welfare policies as grossly inadequate and unfair, too little and too late, and tainted by the corruption of the system from which they stemmed. At the same time, as the system's capacity to detect failure by making sophisticated policy evaluations leaped ahead of its ability to deliver policy success, some former liberals became "neo-conservatives" who doubted the worth of many governmental policies and called attention to the disrepute the failures of policy brought upon government.

If it were true that welfare programs were a form of domination over poor people, harming instead of helping them, then Ronald Reagan should have been regarded as the savior of the poor, for he certainly promised and provided less of this domination. If it were the avowed aim of conservatives to rebuild respect for authority, denigration of the federal government as "the problem" is a poor way to prove their point. Why should President Reagan have been trusted to spend an increased defense budget wisely when he and his colleagues doubted the ability of the rest of the government to achieve effective results? And since effective government depends on a high-caliber civil service, why should all concerned think to gain by castigating public servants? This was no method for recruiting talented young people to serve in government, or for retaining the services of talented older people. When liberals think of themselves as outsiders to a government they deem insufficiently responsive, and conservatives consider existing governmental institutions inadequate to enforce traditional social norms, like deference to authority, governmental institutions decline in their capacity to attract the involvement of citizens. Neither Michael Dukakis nor George Bush campaigned by maligning the government in 1988. It may unfortunately be the case, however, that one campaign that is relatively free of bureaucrat-bashing is not enough to turn public attitudes around that have been ingrained over a longer period.

Thus there are practical difficulties with a theory that requires high levels of political participation. We raise this issue not because we are opposed in principle to the idea of an active, participatory, democratic society. By persuasion and political education the majority of our citizens might indeed be convinced that the quality of our shared existence could and should be improved through more continuous devotion to public activity. This is quite different from arguing that the rules of the game should be changed to disenfranchise those who presently lack the opportunity or desire to be active in this sense. We do not favor efforts to implement ideal goals when the preconditions and the means of achieving these goals do not exist. We do not favor actions that in the name of democracy (or under any other guise) restrict the ability of most of the people to have their political say.

Three Specific Reforms

Comprehensive reform of the party system rides in on tides of strong feeling. Until such feelings exist among party activists, rational advocacy looking toward reform is wasted; once such feeling exists, rational advocacy is superfluous. So the type of analysis we undertake here is bound to be uninfluential. We attempt it only because thoughtful citizens may find it instructive to consider the consequences of the best-laid plans. Once these consequences have had an opportunity to manifest themselves, however, a new generation of reform may be in order. After all, practically everything that reformers object to now was once somebody's favorite reform.

We suspect that the achievement of many—not all—of the specific objectives of party reformers would be detrimental to their aims and to those of most thoughtful citizens. Let us consider, for example, three specific reforms of governmental machinery that are commonly advocated to make the parties more responsive to popular will and more democratic. Party reformers often advocate a variety of changes in the nomination process, simplification of the process of registering voters, and modification or abolition of the Electoral College. Two of these reforms might well have exactly the opposite effects from those intended.

An Appraisal of the Nomination Process   In order to evaluate the nominating process, it would be helpful to suggest a set of goals that most Americans would accept as desirable and important.[17] The following seven standards appear to meet this test: any method for nominating presidents should (1) aid in preserving the two-party system, (2) help secure vigorous competition between the parties, (3) maintain some degree of cohesion and agreement within the parties, (4) produce candidates who have a likelihood of winning voter support, (5) lead to the choice of candidates who are reasonably well qualified, (6) lead to the acceptance of candidates as legitimate, and (7) result in officeholders who are capable of generating support for public policies they intend to pursue. We first look at some suggested alternatives to the current nominating system.

A national direct primary to select party candidates for the presidency has often been suggested. Many people took heart in 1968 from the way in which the piecemeal primaries around the country facilitated the expression of antiwar sentiment, and they noted that nonprimary states were on the whole less responsive to persons whose participation in party activities was largely precipitated by strong feelings about the war. Their conclusion was that primaries were rather a good thing and that, therefore, a national primary was in order.

We believe this would have serious disadvantages. First of all, it would have been self-defeating as far as the professed goals of many antiwar people who advocated it were concerned. By entering primaries one at a time in 1968, Senator Eugene McCarthy, and later Senator Robert Kennedy, were able to construct "test cases." We doubt that McCarthy, given the limitations of his resources before New Hampshire, could have even entered a national primary.

Charles O. Jones has said that in some respects we already do have a national primary, and that it is held in New Hampshire. He is entirely correct to call attention to the enormous influence that early delegate selection processes have on the fortunes of candidates later on. But the Iowa caucuses and New Hampshire primary do differ from a national primary in one major respect: they are small, and as Everett Carl Ladd says,

By leading off, manageable little Iowa and New Hampshire enable less well-known and well-heeled candidates to gain attention through presenting their wares to real people in real election settings. If a candidate with moderate resources, and previously lacking a national reputation, manages to impress a fair number of voters in these small states, isn't this laboratory experience of some considerable interest to the country?[18]

This merely points to a more general problem of financing national primary elections. It is quite probable that many candidates—perhaps as many as ten of them—might obtain enough signatures on nominating petitions or qualify by some other device to get on the ballot for a true, fifty-state national primary. In a year when there is no incumbent president in the race, it is not hard to imagine a crowd of challengers in both parties hustling all over the United States campaigning in such a primary. It would take, of course, enormous amounts of money. The parties could hardly be expected to show favoritism and so could not finance these candidates. Although government financing would no doubt be made available, this would have to depend upon demonstrated ability to raise money previously in order to discourage frivolous candidates. The pre-primary campaign, therefore, would assume enormous importance and would be exceedingly expensive. Nationwide challengers would have to have access to very large amounts of money. It would help if they were already well known. They would also have to be quite sturdy physically. Ordinarily, nobody would win a clear majority in a primary with a large number of contenders. Since all contenders would be wearing the same party label, it is hard to see how voters could differentiate among candidates except by already knowing one or two of their names in favorable or unfavorable contexts, by liking or not liking their looks, by identifying or not identifying with their ethnic or racial characteristics, by attending to their treatment in the press and in television news reports, or by some other means of differentiation having nothing whatever to do with ability or inclination to do the job, or even with their policy positions. Since patents on policy positions are not available, it is reasonable to suppose that more than one candidate would adopt roughly the same set of positions. Or they might, for the purpose of the primary, falsely portray themselves as disagreeing. Thus, voters would be fortunate if the intellectual content of the campaign consisted of quibbling about who proposed what first and, more relevantly, who could deliver better.

Suppose, then, that the primary vote was divided among several candidates. Suppose, as is the case for gubernatorial elections in some southern states, that ten or twelve aspirants divided the votes. One possibility is that the party nominee would be the candidate with the highest number of votes, say, 19 percent of those cast, a much less democratic choice than we now have, since who knows how the other 81 percent might have distributed themselves if they had known what the rank order of the candidates was going to be. Another possibility would be for the two highest candidates to contest a fifty-state runoff after the first primary and before the general election in a campaign that would begin to remind observers who can remember that far back of a marathon jitterbug contest. The party might end up with a good candidate, of course, if there was anything left of that candidate to give to the party in the real election campaign, which would follow. Then the poor candidate, if elected, would have to find the energy to govern. By following this procedure, the United States might have to restrict its presidential candidates to wealthy athletes.

We are not ready to give up at least some of the state primaries we now have, although it is now widely believed—and we agree—that we have too many. It is eminently desirable that it be possible in a number of states, separated geographically and in time, for test cases to be put to voters and for trial heats to be run among aspirants for high office. But a national primary would be like a steady diet consisting exclusively of dessert.

National primaries would also lead to the weakening of the party system. It is not unusual for a party to remain in office for a long period of time. If state experience with primaries is any guide, a prolonged period of victory for one party would result in a movement of interested voters into the primary of the winning party, where their votes would count for more.[19] As voters deserted the losing party, it would be largely the die-hards who were left. They would nominate candidates who pleased them but who could not win the election because they were unappealing to a majority in the nation. Eventually, the losing party would atrophy, seriously weakening the two-party system and the prospects of competition among the parties. The winning party would soon show signs of internal weakness as a consequence of the lack of opposition necessary to keep it unified.

A national primary might also lead to the appearance of extremist candidates and demagogues who, unrestrained by allegiance to any permanent party organization, would have little to lose by stirring up mass hatreds or making absurd promises. On the whole, the convention system of the past discouraged these extremists by placing responsibility in the hands of party leaders who had a permanent stake in maintaining the good name and integrity of their organization. Some insight into this problem may be had by looking at the historic situation in state elections in several southern states, where most voters voted only in the Democratic primary and where victory in that primary was tantamount to election. The result was a chaotic factional politics in which there were few or no permanent party leaders; the distinctions between the "ins" and "outs" became blurred; it was difficult to hold anyone responsible; and demagogues sometimes arose who made use of this situation by strident appeals.[20] The fact that under some primary systems an extreme personality can take the place of party in giving a kind of minimal structure to state politics should give pause to the advocates of a national primary.

We believe that very widespread use of direct primaries weakens the party system. It encourages prospective candidates to bypass regular party organizations in favor of campaigns stressing personal publicity, and it provides for no peer review, that is, consideration of the criteria of fitness to hold office, which can best be applied by those who actually know the candidates, who have themselves a heavy investment of time and energy in making the government work, and who know that they may have to live at close quarters with the results of their deliberations.

It is difficult to persuade those who participate only casually in politics, and those who tend to do so only when moved by a great issue of the day, that the intensity of their feelings does not confer a sweeping mandate. These feelings, no matter how worthy, do not make occasional participants more worthy than steady participants. They do not confer a special moral status upon latecomers to politics as compared with people who are already active. Party regulars or even party leaders cannot always be excluded on grounds of moral inferiority from decision making in the presidential nomination process.

The great virtue of state-by-state piecemeal primaries is, of course, that they provide a means—increasingly supplemented by polls—of gauging the popularity of various candidates and their effectiveness in public speaking under adverse circumstances. The virtue of conventions has been that by living at closer quarters than ordinary citizens with the results of the collective choice, party leaders can bring to the choosing greater knowledge and even, sometimes, a higher sense of responsibility.

It is generally conceded that Adlai Stevenson would have made a better president than Estes Kefauver, who ran and won in most of the primaries in 1952. Stevenson, for his entire career in elective office, was the product of selection by party leaders—in some cases even by "bosses"—who were knowledgeable and continuously involved in the political process, acquainted with what governing demanded and with the personal capabilities of the politicians among whom they chose. Walter Mondale, who withdrew from the 1976 preprimary sweepstakes because of a reluctance to spend a year in various motels around the country, was not a conspicuously worse—indeed by some standards he was a better—public servant than some of those who leaped joyfully into the fray. Mondale first served in the Senate by appointment and was picked by Jimmy Carter to be his running mate without the sanctification of an election. Yet nobody supposes Mondale was picked without regard for democratic constraints. When in 1984 Mondale decided either that motels had improved or he had become more ambitious, he certainly represented the views of the mainstream of his party. While it is doubtful that any Democrat could have beaten Ronald Reagan that year, few doubted that Mondale was well qualified to be president.

Giving politicians some rights to influence political choices is not per se an evil system. Unchecked by the ultimate necessity to appeal for votes it would no doubt degenerate. Political leaders certainly would not run a system that responded easily to short-run opinions of high intensity in the electorate, but sometimes this sort of system will pick a popular candidate over a candidate in whose personal capacities the delegates have more faith. This, we think, is what delegates to the Republican convention of 1952 did when they nominated Dwight Eisenhower over Robert A. Taft. Even when they decide to make a popular choice rather than go with their personal favorite, party leaders can invoke criteria of judgment unavailable to mass electorates.

In short, we believe that as long as there are many things we demand of a president—intelligence as well as popularity, integrity as well as speaking ability, private virtue as well as public presentability—we ought to foster a selection process that provides a mixture of devices for screening according to different criteria. The mixed system we advocate is not perfect, of course, but it is greatly superior to the unmixed nonblessing of the national primary.

The use of primaries at the state level has produced a variety of anomalous experiences: totally unqualified candidates whose names have resembled those of famous politicians have been nominated by innocent voters; ethnic minorities concentrated in one party have defeated attempts by party leaders to offer "balanced tickets," thus dooming to defeat their entire ticket in the general election; and palpable demagogues have defeated responsible candidates. All of these consequences may not persuade reformers that the increased use of direct primaries is not a good idea, but they must be faced. If we value political parties, which reformers often profess to do, then we must hesitate to cut them off from the process of selecting candidates for public office, to deprive them of incentives to organize, and to set them prematurely at the mercy of masses of people whose information at the primary stage is especially poor.

This is not, we suggest, an elitist doctrine. Responsible political analysts and advocates must face the fact that party identification for most people provides the safe cognitive anchorage around which political preferences are organized. Set adrift from this anchorage, as they are when faced with an intraparty primary election, most voters have little or nothing to guide their choices. Chance familiarity with a famous name or stray feelings of ethnic kinship under these circumstances seem to provide many voters with the only clues to choice.[21] Given the conditions of popular interest and participation that prevail, we question throwing the future of the party system entirely and precipitously into the hands of primary electorates.

What is more, a nomination process dominated by primaries gives the media great influence. This was illustrated in a dramatic way in the spring of 1987, when the front-running candidate for the Democratic nomination, Gary Hart, suddenly fell afoul of publicity calling attention to a close personal relationship that he evidently had with a young woman who was not his wife. This episode caused many thoughtful journalists to express concern about the extraordinary influence of the news media in the nomination process. Some journalists felt that they and their colleagues were unable to do justice to the special circumstances of the private lives of public figures, and that even public figures have rights to privacy in those areas of life that have little to do with the performance of public duties. Others argued that the way people behave in private is bound to affect the way they do their public chores.

Not long ago, when there was something like peer review in the nomination process, other politicians who were influential in the process and who knew the candidates could make assessments about the suitability of presidential hopefuls for office. Perhaps they would be forgiving in cases of alcoholism, chronic pettiness, bad temper, manic-depressive behavior, marital infidelity, laziness, bigotry, slowness of wit, vindictiveness, duplicity, stubbornness, or any of the other infirmities and imperfections that afflict human beings. Or perhaps not. At least, it was possible for reasonably well informed judgments to be made about the qualities of candidates by people who knew something about what these qualities were.

Today, presidential nominations are made almost entirely by primary electorates. What do these electorates know of the human qualities of the candidates? Typically, very little. But virtually all of what they do know comes via the news media. And so journalists, through no fault of their own, have had thrust upon them far greater responsibilities to tell what they know, and to find out whether what they suspect is true or not.

Not all candidates receive the same treatment, however. In 1972 the history of emotional depression of Thomas F. Eagleton, briefly the Democrats' vice-presidential candidate, weighed more heavily in the scale than did the history of receiving bribes of Spiro T. Agnew, his Republican opponent. Journalists found out about one but not the other in time to influence an election.

So we must wonder whether attention to any candidate's possible flaws of character ought not to be compared more conscientiously against flaws that some of the others may have. Surely, if these are qualities of candidates they will also be qualities of the presidents these candidates might become. But it is hard to predict just how these qualities will work in any given presidency. There is no foolproof method for making sensible inferences from private behavior about the conduct of public office. Can we suppose that a lazy candidate will be a lazy president? Possibly. Still, some candidates hate campaigning but love governing and may be mediocre in a stump speech but superb negotiating a legislative compromise.

What is worse, the opposite may be true, and a great campaigner may turn out to be an incompetent president. Equally serious difficulties may be in store for those who attempt to make inferences about the conduct of the presidency from knowledge of candidates' sexual irregularities (or regularities), drinking habits, relations with their children and grandchildren, and so on.

So what are ordinary citizens to do? Ignore information that might be relevant to our primary vote if we knew about it? Attend to information about candidates even though it may be irrelevant to their conduct of the presidency? If we could tell in advance the difference between relevant and irrelevant information, it would help. But mostly we cannot, nor can the journalists who must decide what to report and what not to report. So long as primary elections and, therefore, the votes of citizens matter as much as they presently do, the only hope of achieving informed choices is by means of publicly available information. Thus, it may be regrettable but it is understandable that journalists are leaning toward disclosure and away from the protection of candidates' private lives.[22]

Regional primaries, of which 1988's Super-Tuesday may be a harbinger, have apparent appeal as a halfway house between a single national primary and a multitude of state primaries. There are basically three "degrees" of regional primary that have been proposed thus far. The mildest form merely requires that all states holding presidential primaries schedule them for one of four sanctioned dates, spaced a month apart, and that all candidates on a list prepared by the Federal Election Commission appear on the ballot. A second type of proposal would group states into geographic regions. All states within a given region that choose to have a primary would be required to hold it on the same day, on the second Tuesday of a month between March and July. Further down the slippery slope is a plan to make primaries mandatory for all states.[23]

Under the regional primary system candidates would not have to campaign in as many distant places at nearly the same time; this would save them money and effort. Since each election would encompass a larger geographic area, however, the need to campaign earlier, to be better known at the start, and to have more money with which to begin would be even greater than it is now. It also seems likely that regional primaries would, in effect, push all states to hold primaries, thereby increasing the total territory a candidate must cover and the consequent cost of campaigning. The major advantage of regional primaries, assuming they were spaced about one month apart as in one plan, would be that both politicians and people could reconsider their earlier choices in the light of the latest information. Yet if delegates were pledged to candidates, the flexibility of bargainers in the event they were needed at the national conventions would still be diminished. In addition, the predilection of the media to simplify complex phenomena would mean that voters in states given later dates would have their choices severely constrained because of the results of earlier primaries. It is possible that conflicts among states may doom the entire enterprise. If not, we suspect that regional primaries, which create an opportunity to reconsider the rules of voting, will become stalking horses for a national primary. Thus all the difficulties of a national primary should be weighed as these partial alternatives are proposed. So long as the relevant choice is between a mixed system and a national primary, our choice lies with diversity.

The Decline of the National Convention   High on the list of practices that in the past were regarded as objectionable was the secret gathering of party leaders in the smoke-filled room. Some likened this to a political opium den where a few irresponsible men, hidden from public view, stealthily determined the destiny of the nation.[24] Yet it is difficult to see who, other than the party's leaders, should have been entrusted with the delicate task of finding a candidate to meet the majority preference. If head-on clashes of strength on the convention floor could not resolve the question, the only alternatives were continued deadlock, anarchy among scores of leaderless delegates splitting the party into rival factions, or some process of accommodation.

Let us suppose that some national convention in the future has real work to do, and because no single candidate has the nomination sewed up it must pick a nominee. Would we require that the smoke-filled room be abolished and with it all behind-the-scenes negotiations? All parleys would then be held in public, before the delegates and millions of television viewers. As a result, the participants would spend their time scoring points against each other in order to impress the folks back home.

Bargaining would not be taking place since the participants would not really be communicating with one another. No compromises would be possible; leaders would be accused by their followers of selling out to the other side. Once a stalemate existed, breaking it would be practically impossible, and the party would probably disintegrate into warring factions.

An extensive system of state primaries in which delegates are more or less compelled to vote for the candidate who wins in the state has led to the eclipse of negotiation processes without any formal action of a convention. Since delegates cannot change their positions except by direction of the candidate to whom they are pledged, there is little point in bring party leaders together for private conferences. Sharply increasing the number of pledged delegates introduces great rigidity into the convention because under conditions of stalemate no one is in a position to switch his support.

This more or less resembles the situation of the two parties today. Recent rule changes have led to the following contradiction: by fragmenting delegations, they have increased the chances of a contested convention, and by giving preference to pledged delegates they have decreased the likelihood that delegates will be able to bargain with one another. These conditions have been masked by the overriding influence of primaries and television which, by forcing earlier and earlier decisions, have spared the parties so far the consequences of a meaningful convention under conditions of extreme fragmentation. Failure to arrive at a decision to nominate a candidate acceptable to all could conceivably lead to withdrawal of the defeated factions from the party. Since the national party is unified, if at all, only by the choice of a presidential candidate, inability to bargain out an agreement invites serious party fragmentation. Therefore, if primaries do not produce a nominee who is certain to be ratified, what happens at a national convention will matter.

Even when the nominee has already been chosen, each party has a stake in the presentation it makes of itself to the public. Much criticism over the years has been leveled at the raucousness of demonstrations that take place on the convention floor while candidates are being nominated.[25] Criticism of demonstrations on the grounds that they are unseemly and vulgar seems to us to be trivial. There is no evidence to substantiate a claim that the final decision would be better in some way if demonstrations were banned. Undoubtedly, the demonstrations have in the past been overdone, but not in recent years owing to the requirements of television. Briefer demonstrations retain the attention of the vast television audience that both parties would like very much to influence in their favor. The dominance of primaries has actually made demonstrations into what their critics always said they were—purely stage-managed affairs with no relation to the final outcome.

The television coverage of the 1968 national conventions raised a number of questions concerning their management. We wonder if all the things that went wrong at the Democratic convention of that year were the result of willful mismanagement by Lyndon Johnson and Richard J. Daley or whether at least some of the difficulty can be attributed to the increasing unwieldiness of the convention. Delegates complained of an inability to attract the attention of the chair. The microphones allocated to each delegation on the floor were turned on and off at the rostrum, so it was impossible to use them to get the chair's attention. Attempts to telephone the chair from the floor were often ignored. Attempts to approach the rostrum were repulsed by security guards. Attempts to signal the chair were defeated by the noise and movement in the hall.

It is hard to see how such a huge and chaotic organization can conduct itself as a parliamentary body. In fact, plenary sessions of the convention have two functions—ceremonial and business. We think it is time to consider a separation of these functions. Ceremonial activities can take place in an amphitheater or a stadium. The general public can be invited. On such occasions there are two classes of people: performers and spectators.

When the convention is conducting its business, however, a different division of labor is involved, and a different decorum should prevail. If it is not possible for a convention to conduct itself as a parliamentary body when all 2,000 or 4,000 members are present, perhaps some democratic and equitable means could be found to restrict the number of official delegates so as to make communication among them feasible. In fact, one effect of reforms designed to increase the representativeness of delegations has been to increase the size of each state delegation. Quotas, whether implicit or explicit, have, according to this perspective, not only increased the numbers of delegates, but also decreased the probability that they could deliberate as a body. If, let us say, 1,000 delegates met at business meetings, much of the paraphernalia associated with meetings of 10,000 could be dispensed with. The number of guards and security officers could be cut. The business of keeping order could be placed where it belongs—in the hands of the chair, who directs sergeants-at-arms publicly, rather than in the hands of an anonymous functionary, who in 1968 at Chicago apparently felt free to dispatch security officers to harass delegates on the floor.

A smaller number of people on the floor, the possibility of spontaneous communication with the chair and with other members, and parliamentary decorum would unquestionably facilitate and properly dignify the business of the convention. It would also provide a warrant for the re-examination of the role of television cameras at national conventions.

We believe television and other news media should continue to cover national party conventions with all the care and energy they have always used. Though the networks have lost their enthusiasm for it, we would like to see full gavel-to-gavel coverage by all the major networks. But we question the propriety of wandering television and newspaper reporters on the floor of a convention. To be sure, so long as conventions continue in their present overblown form, reporters may as well be on the floor, since everyone else is. But if conventions were reduced in size and, for business purposes, maintained parliamentary decorum, perhaps it would be possible to deal with the problems created by news media representatives at national conventions. Neither Democrats nor Republicans alone will take the lead in grappling with this problem, because both fear the wrath of the media. Thus, academic observers are ideally situated to open this discussion.

We want to increase respect for presidential nominations by having them conducted in a serious atmosphere conducive to mature deliberation. The presence of hordes of correspondents on the convention floor introduces a discordant note somewhere between individual breast-beating and mass hysteria. The very presence of numerous reporters, with their microphones and television cameras, creates a carnival atmosphere. No one would ordinarily make an important decision surrounded by people hurriedly throwing questions. No one would take seriously a decision made by people constantly distracted from the main proceedings by side conversations.

A superabundance of TV cameras on the convention floor plays up to the worst instincts of the delegates, alternates, and hangers-on gathered there. It is hard for ordinary mortals to resist publicity; it is asking too much of convention attendees to forego an opportunity for national exposure. Yet the purpose of the convention (if it were again to become a decision-making body) is not only to make the delegates look good at home, but for them to make a wise choice where they are.

The mass media not only reports events; they create news. They are always after bizarre and unusual sights and sensational stories. If conflict and controversy is not inherent in a situation, they will seek to create it. A momentary misunderstanding on the floor might be cleared up later on, but reporters will jump in immediately to widen the breach. In 1980, for example, we could see television reporters leaving the floor of Madison Square Garden in hot pursuit of a small rump group of Alaskans; these few delegates wanted to distract television coverage with their boycott of the Democratic keynote address of Morris Udall, who as chairman of a

House of Representatives Interior Committee subcommittee had in some way offended them.

Imagine what football games would be like if they were reported as national conventions presently are. A quarterback is getting clobbered in the Super Bowl. His line is weak and defenders are pouring all over him. After the fifth interception, he receives a fearful blow. Before he can pick up his shattered bones a dozen TV reporters stick their microphones and cameras in his face, shouting questions at him. "Did you get good protection today?" "Anybody let you down, hey?" A few answers on the spot and the team might never be able to work together again.

Is it asking too much for nominations of future presidents to be conducted with at least the same dignity as presently obtains at football games? The press, radio, and television can broadcast the proceedings and report events from booths above the convention floor. No one but delegates and frail, elderly, unthreatening sergeants-at-arms should be allowed on the floor while the convention is at work. Ample interview facilities should be provided just off the floor. When delegates are wanted for an interview, a page should be sent to fetch them just as is done in Congress. "Ms. Smith," the page might say, "a network wants to harass you in room nine," and if Ms. Smith wants to be harassed she can walk off the floor to accomplish that mission.[26] The American people deserve full reporting of the national conventions; no one wants to limit the media in any legitimate coverage. But improving the conduct of national conventions and increasing public respect for their decisions are reasons enough to ask the media to pay a small cost for a large public benefit.

These proposals assume, of course, that the conventions have a good deal "maturely" to deliberate about. If the nominee is a foregone conclusion, as is now normally the case, then it may make sense to organize the convention as a ceremonial exercise. Even then, the parties might still want to regulate coverage to maximize the effectiveness of the ceremony.

The convention, as we have said, normally aids party unity in a variety of ways. It provides a forum in which initially disunited fragments of the national party can come together and find common ground as well as a common nominee. The platform aids in performing this function. In order to gain a majority of electoral votes, a party must appeal in some way to most major population groups. Since these interests do not always want the same thing, it is necessary to compromise and, sometimes, to evade issues that would lead to drastic losses of support.

Reformers' concerns with party platforms stem primarily from two assumptions: first, that there is a significant demand in the electorate for more clear-cut differences on policy; second, that elections are likely to be a significant source of guidance on individual issues to policy makers.

Yet both these assumptions are either false or highly dubious. As we have seen, on a wide range of issues leaders in both parties are much further apart than are ordinary citizens who have been separated by rather small differences.[27] To the often considerable degree that party platforms spell out clear and important differences on policy, this results far more from a desire of party leaders to please themselves than from any supposed demand from the electorate.

Some critics objected to the traditional convention's stress on picking a winner rather than the "best candidate," regardless of popularity. This objection is not compatible with the democratic notion that voters should decide who is best for them and communicate this decision in an election. Only in dictatorial countries does a set of leaders arrogate unto themselves the right to determine who is best regardless of popular preferences. An unpopular candidate can hardly win a free election. An unpopular president can hardly secure the support he needs to accomplish his goals. Popularity can be regarded as a necessary element for obtaining consent in demhocratic politics.

Although popularity is normally a necessary condition for nomination, it should not be the only condition. The guideline for purposes of nomination should be to nominate the best of the popular candidates. But "best" is a slippery word. A great deal of what we mean by "best" in politics is "best for us" or "best represents our policy preferences," and this can hardly be held up as an objective criterion. What is meant by "best" in this context are such personal qualities as experience, intelligence, and decisiveness. Nevertheless, it is not at all clear that an extreme conservative would prefer a highly intelligent liberal to a moderately intelligent candidate who shared his conservative policy preferences. Personal qualities clearly are subject to discount based on the compatibility of interests between voter and candidate.

For some critics the defect of conventions lies not only in their poor performance in nominating candidates, but also in their failure to become a sort of "superlegislature," enforcing the policy views of the platform upon party members in the executive branch and Congress. We have previously indicated that such enforcement is most unlikely to be achieved. Let us suppose for the purposes of argument that the conventions could somehow become much more influential on matters of national policy. How could either party retain a semblance of unity if the stakes of convention deliberations were vastly increased by converting the platform into an unbreakable promise of national policy? If one believes that an increase in heated discussion necessarily increases agreement, then the problem solves itself. Experience warns us, however, that airing sharp differences, particularly when the stakes are high, is likely to decrease agreement. At the 1964 Republican convention, for example, black delegates, bitter about the defeat of Governor Scranton's proposed amendment on civil rights to the GOP education plank, held a protest march around the Cow Palace and, when Barry Goldwater was nominated, announced that they would sit out the campaign.[28] This could not have helped Goldwater's chances of election. The fact that platforms are not binding permits a degree of unity necessary for the delegates to stay put long enough to agree on a nominee. By vastly increasing the number of delegates who would bitterly oppose platform decisions and possibly leave the convention, the binding platform would jeopardize the legitimacy of the convention's nominating function. Paradoxically, in such circumstances it would be difficult to resist the temptation to make the platform utterly innocuous in order to give offense to no one.

Even so, platforms do have a far from negligible impact on public opinion. Platform planks are enacted as governmental policy slightly more than half the time.[29] And programs favored by the public, according to opinion polls, are twice as likely to be enacted if they also appear in party platforms.[30] When large majorities favor programs, both parties are likely to put them in their platforms; when the public is somewhat more divided and important constituencies object, however, the parties are capable of going against popular majorities. Thus Republican platform planks on welfare and economic issues and Democratic provisions on labor unions and affirmative action tend to run counter to majority opinion.[31] The question of whom the parties are for, special or general constituencies, is resolved by going for the majority when it is substantial, and modifying that position when it conflicts with special party concerns.

There are good reasons for opposing the desires of those who love the conventions so much that they like to see them convene every year or two. For without a presidential candidate to nominate, conventions have little to do. If the purpose of these meetings is to give free advice to elected officials, there would seem to be little point to them. Congressmen are likely to pay as little attention to convention talk as they would to the pronouncements of any advisory committee that does not appreciate the context within which they operate. After all, members of Congress are subject to different risks and sanctions than are most delegates, and have no reason to be attentive to a party conclave for suggesting policies that may get them into trouble. The notion of getting delegates together under circumstances where their disagreements are certain to come out merely for the purpose of making recommendations does not seem promising.

The 1974 midterm conference in Kansas City of the Democratic party was notable not for its accomplishments, because there weren't any, but because it barely avoided a damaging party split over demographic quotas. Party activists returned from Kansas City bathed in good feeling—or was it sweat?—because they managed to avert outright catastrophe there. The Memphis Democratic conclave of 1978 provided only one high spot—an opportunity for Senator Edward Kennedy to upstage President Carter by advocating a popular but costly medical insurance scheme that the administration had put on the back burner. In 1982 nothing happened at the Philadelphia Democratic midterm convention. This was hailed as a great work of political engineering by Chairman Charles Manatt. The accomplishment of Democratic Party Chairman Paul Kirk in 1986 was even more astounding: He caused the midterm meeting to be abolished. So far as we can tell about a nonevent, it was not missed.

Especially now that they are an endangered species, the superiority of the traditional national conventions to the available alternatives is clear. Only the convention permits us to realize in large measure all of the seven goals—maintenance of the two-party system, party competition, some degree of internal cohesion, candidates attractive to voters, qualified candidates, acceptance of nominees as legitimate, and a connection between winning the nomination and governing later on—that we postulated earlier would commonly be accepted as desirable.

An Appraisal of Permanent Voting Enrollment   One reform that has received increasing attention and that presumably would have at least marginal effects on all stages of presidential elections without directly altering either the means of nominating candidates or the ways in which they campaign is universal automatic voter enrollment. A distinguishing feature of American national elections is the low share of the potential electorate that actually votes. As Table 5.2 shows, this is a consistent feature of modern presidential elections. One study suggests that the American system of voter registration may be responsible. It shows that the level of voter registration is easily the greatest influence (accounting for 80 percent of the variance) on the percentage of the population that actually votes, far greater than any other single factor usually cited in studies of voting by those registered and, in fact, greater than all such factors put together.[32]

Unlike the citizens of foreign democracies in which the government takes responsibility for registration, the American must prepare for the eventual vote by taking the initiative to register before the election, at a time in the political cycle when political information and interest are at a low point.[33] Since interest and information are important factors, the level of registration can be advanced or retarded by altering the time of year when voter registration rolls are closed or by changing the physical

TABLE 5.2   *Age-Eligible Voters Actually Voting*

Year	Democrat Voting	Republican Voting	Not Voting
1972	29,170,000	47,170,000	61,924,000
1976	40,831,000	39,148,000	68,485,000
1980	35,484,000	43,904,000	77,866,000
1984	37,577,000	54,457,000	81,180,000
1988	41,809,000	48,886,000	91,033,000

Source: Bureau of the Census, *Statistical Abstract of the United States 1990* (Washington, 1990) p. 262.

ease of reaching a registration point, and practicing political leaders are well aware of this.[34] As Stanley Kelley and his collaborators observe, "Local differences in the turnout for elections are to a large extent related to local differences in rates of registration, and these in turn reflect to a considerable degree local differences in the rules governing, and the arrangements for handling, the registration of voters."[35]

Proposals for universal automatic voter enrollment differ according to administrative arrangements for enrollment, the time when it would oc-cur, the duration of enrollment, and the level of government to which it would apply. The basic idea, however, is that the United States would be divided into election districts, and deputy registrars within them would go door to door, enrolling every citizen who did not refuse to be registered.[36]

When the United States is compared to other democratic countries, its voting rate is quite low. This may not necessarily imply greater apathy or alienation. Much of the problem lies in American impediments to regis-tration. When one looks at the percentage of *registered* voters who turn out, the United States compares more favorably. (See Tables 5.3 and 5.4.) Some areas of the United States make it far easier to register by allowing election-day registration. Table 5.5 shows that the consequences for voting turnout are impressive. In 1980 Minnesota voters turned out at a rate of nearly 20 percentage points above the national average. When citizens are registered, they turn out to vote.[37]

While the rest of the United States now lags behind the Minnesota performance, there was once a time—in an era when the impact of the president was remote, mass communication absent, and electronic voting equipment unheard of—when more than 70 percent of potential (not just registered) voters turned out in presidential elections. In the election of 1876, 82 percent of the possible voters turned out for the nation as a whole. Soon thereafter, however, harsh registration restrictions were in-troduced, cloaked in rhetoric about stopping corruption but aimed at keeping down the vote of "undesirable elements" (immigrants and black voters)—which they did. As Kelley et al. observe,

TABLE 5.3   *Ranking of Countries by Turnout in Their Most Recent National Election as of 1981*

Traditional Measure of Turnout[1]		Vote as a Percentage of Voting-Age Population[2]	
1. Belgium	94.6	1. Italy	94.0
2. Australia	94.5	2. Austria	89.3
3. Austria	91.6	3. Belgium	88.7
4. Sweden	90.7	4. Sweden	86.8
5. Italy	90.4	5. Portugal	85.9
6. Iceland	89.3	6. Greece	84.9
7. New Zealand	89.0	7. Netherlands	84.7
8. Luxembourg	88.9	8. Australia	83.1
9. W. Germany	88.6	9. Denmark	82.1
10. Netherlands	87.0	10. Norway	81.8
11. France	85.9	11. W. Germany	81.1
12. Portugal	84.2	12. New Zealand	78.5
13. Denmark	83.2	13. France	78.0
14. Norway	82.0	14. United Kingdom	76.0
15. Greece	78.6	15. Japan	74.4
16. Israel	78.5	16. Spain	73.0
17. United Kingdom	76.3	17. Canada	67.4
18. Japan	74.5	18. Finland	63.0
19. Canada	69.3	19. Ireland	62.3
20. Spain	68.1	20. United States	52.6
21. Finland	64.3	21. Switzerland	39.4
22. Ireland	62.2		
23. United States	52.6		
24. Switzerland	48.3		

[1] In the "Traditional Measure of Turnout," U.S. turnout is calculated as the percentage of the voting-age population, while turnout elsewhere is calculated as the percentage of registered voters.
[2] An anomaly exists between the right and left columns of this table (as well as between this table and Table 5.4) for five countries: Greece, Ireland, Italy, Portugal, and Spain. In each of these cases the vote as a percentage of voting-age population is higher than the vote as a percentage of registered voters. This is because there is a separate source for calculating the voting-age population. The less trustworthy number is the voting-age population figure. This often had to be estimated from old census data for present-day populations. For example, the Italian and Spanish numbers had to be projected from 1971 and 1970 census figures on the percentage of the population over 18.

Sources: The figures for the United States are from the *Statistical Abstract of the United States 1982–83*. The data for all other countries for the number of voters and the number of persons registered are from *The International Almanac of Electoral History*, 2nd ed., by Thomas T. Mackie and Richard Rose. The voting-age population was derived from the countries' Year Books. It was occasionally necessary to extrapolate the present age breakdown on the basis of the last census. Reprinted from David Glass, Peverill Squire, and Raymond E. Wolfinger, "Voter Turnout: An International Comparison," *Public Opinion* 6 (December/January, 1984), pp. 50–52.

turnout in presidential elections in the U.S. may have declined and then risen again, not because of changes in the interest of voters in elections, but because of changes in the interest demanded of them. . . . [Not only are] electorates . . . much more the product of political forces than many have appreciated. But also . . . to a considerable extent, they can be political artifacts. Within limits, they can be constructed to a size and composition deemed desirable by those in power.[38]

TABLE 5.4   *Turnout of Those Who Are Registered*

Vote as a Percentage of Registered Voters		Compulsion Penalties	Automatic Registration
1. Belgium	94.6	Yes	Yes
2. Australia	94.5	Yes	No
3. Austria	91.6	No (some)[1]	Yes
4. Sweden	90.7	No	Yes
5. Italy	90.4	Yes	Yes
6. Iceland	89.3	NA	NA
7. New Zealand	89.0	No (some)[1]	No
8. Luxembourg	88.9	NA	NA
9. W. Germany	88.6	No	Yes
10. Netherlands	87.0	No	Yes
11. United States	86.8	No	No
12. France	85.9	No (some)[1]	No
13. Portugal	84.2	NA	NA
14. Denmark	83.2	No	Yes
15. Norway	82.0	No	Yes
16. Greece	78.6	Yes	Yes
17. Israel	78.5	No	Yes
18. United Kingdom	76.3	No	Yes
19. Japan	74.5	No	Yes
20. Canada	69.3	No	Yes
21. Spain	68.1	Yes	Yes
22. Finland	64.3	No	Yes
23. Ireland	62.2	No	Yes
24. Switzerland	48.3	No (some)[1]	Yes

[1] Penalties apply only to small portions of the country or certain types of elections.
NA: Not available

Source: See Table 5.3. Compulsion penalty and automatic registration information are from G. Bingham Powell, "Voting Turnout in Thirty Democracies: Partisan, Legal, and Socio-Economic Influences," except for Canada and Spain. The information on these two countries is in Inter-Parliamentary Union, ed., *Parliaments of the World* (New York, 1976). Reprinted from David Glass, Peverill Squire, and Raymond E. Wolfinger, "Voter Turnout: An International Comparison," *Public Opinion* 6 (December/January, 1984), pp. 50–52.

Whether an expanded electorate would have any direct effect on primaries and delegate selection would depend on the particular enrollment plan adopted. At one extreme, if enrollment were held every four years in October and provided for continuation on the rolls only if the registrant voted in each election held in the district—state and municipal elections, as well as federal—reform would have little direct effect. If the canvass occurred in the spring, however, and registrants had to vote only once every four years to stay on the rolls, there would be a significant addition to the presidential electorate. Some have argued that this portends new strength for activists unconnected with parties, since this new group of voters would be far less tied to any political organizations than the already enfranchised groups. In general, however, nonvoters have preferences for candidates much like those who vote.[39]

TABLE 5.5   *Turnout in States with Election-Day Registrations (1980)*

State	Percent of the Voting-age Population Who Voted	Where to Register
Minnesota	70.1%	At polls on election day, City Hall, City Clerk, County Auditor
Wisconsin	67.2	Election day at polls with identification, Municipal Clerk or Board of Election Commissioners in counties where registration is required
North Dakota	64.8	No registration
Maine	64.6	Registrar of Voters, Board of Registration, Justice of Peace, Notary Public
Oregon	61.5	County Clerk
All U.S.	52.6	

Source: David Glass, Peverill Squire, and Raymond E. Wolfinger, "Voter Turnout: An International Comparison," *Public Opinion* 6 (December/January, 1984), p. 53.

While universal automatic voter enrollment deals with the means by which the share of the potential electorate that gets to the polls can be changed, there are a whole series of lesser reforms that deal with changes in the size of the potential electorate itself. The major limiting factors of this potential electorate are legal requirements concerning residence, age, literacy, criminal conviction, mental incompetence, and U. S. citizenship.

The most notorious of these restrictions has been the residence requirement. In a nation noted for the geographic mobility of its population, a majority of states required, as recently as 1972, one year within the state, three months within the county, and thirty days within the precinct to vote in any election, including presidential. In 1972 the Supreme Court ruled that thirty days was an ample period of time for the State of Tennessee to register its voters and declared its existing six-month state residency requirement an unconstitutional denial of equal protection. In two subsequent per curiam decisions, the court held that an extension to fifty days was permissible under certain conditions, but that this time period represented the absolute limit.[40]

In an important study, Squire, Wolfinger, and Glass show, first, that the extraordinary mobility of Americans leads to low voting turnout, and, second, that countering this effect would dramatically increase turnout. In order to vote in the United States, a citizen must register. But to stay registered, the citizen must live in the same place. Yet something like one-third of all adults change their home address every two years. If all movers were registered in their new residences, perhaps by using the post office change-of-address form for that purpose as Wolfinger suggests, these scholars estimate that national turnout, the proportion of eligibles who vote, would increase by 9 percent. They also conclude that "expanding the voting population in this way would produce no consequential advantage for either party."[41]

A number of other major groups are now kept out of the potential presidential electorate. While travelers and the ill are allowed to use absentee ballots, many depart or become ill too late to take advantage of this opportunity.[42] Aliens, legal and illegal, are not allowed to vote. Finally, in most states, convicted felons are permanently stripped of their voting rights. These three groups are not insignificant in size. William Andrews, in 1960, calculated that they contained nearly eight million potential voters.[43] As the number of aliens and of ex-felons has increased markedly since 1960 the figures today would surely be even larger.[44] The analysis of whether or not such groups should be allowed to become part of the electorate must be much the same as that for other nonregistrants. To the degree that voting is a means to distribute the political goods of a society, they presumably have as much (perhaps more) of a stake in its outcome as do other groups, and while some of them may be low in general political information, this would not be an adequate reason, in our view, to deprive them of the right to vote.

An Appraisal of the Electoral College   Close presidential elections, those in which the new president has only a narrow margin in the total popular vote, always lead to renewed public discussion of the merits of the Electoral College, since close elections remind people of the mathematical possibility that the candidate with a plurality of all the votes will not necessarily become president. Reform interest surges even higher when a regionally based third party, such as the party George Wallace led in 1968, becomes strong enough conceivably to prevent any candidate from having an electoral vote majority. This would drive the decision into the U.S. House of Representatives, which under the Constitution decides such matters when the Electoral College cannot.

The number of reform plans generated in the aftermath of the 1968 elections was legion. There were, however, only three basic alternatives to the present system proposed, and the rest were variations. One would abolish the Electoral College outright and weigh votes equally everywhere. The net effect of such a proposal would be to undermine slightly the current strategic advantage enjoyed by populous, two-party, urbanized states. It might also have some long-run effects on the two-party system itself, but these would depend on other changes in the social situation within the country. The second proposal would retain the apportionment of the Electoral College (which gives numerical advantage to the smaller, rural states) but abolish the unit-rule electoral vote (which operates strongly in favor of populous states). This proposal is quite extreme in its import, which would be to confer an additional political bonus upon states traditionally overrepresented in positions of congressional power. A third, quite similar, proposal also retains the apportionment of the Electoral College but distributes an Electoral College vote for the plurality vote winner in each congressional district and two additional electoral votes for the winner in each state. Since this system maximizes the strength of one-party states it could work to realign the presidential coalition in fundamental ways.[45]

The Constitution provides that each state, regardless of its population, shall be represented in the Senate by an equal number of senators. This means that the eight largest states, with just under 50 percent of the voters in 1988, have 16 percent of the senators. In the course of legislative proceedings, these sixteen senators' votes can be canceled by the sixteen votes of the senators from the eight least populous states, with 2.5 percent of the voters in the 1988 presidential election. At one point in the early 1960s an average vote in Nevada was worth eighty-five times as much as an average vote in New York in elections for the Senate. The imbalance roughly corresponds to the advantage that more populous, urbanized, two-party states enjoy in the Electoral College, and thus in access to the presidency.

The present Electoral College system, with its votes apportioned according to the total of Senate and House seats a state has, awarded on a "winner-take-all" basis state by state, does provide a clear advantage to two groups of states. It yields a secondary advantage to the smallest states, since their overrepresentation in the Senate guarantees them overrepresentation in the Electoral College; after the 1990 census, the seven states with three electoral votes each had a ratio of 268,000 or fewer citizens per electoral vote, while every state with thirteen or more electoral votes had a ratio of 475,000 or more citizens per electoral vote. But it is primarily the larger states, through the unit-rule principle, which benefit from the Electoral College. A candidate who can get a narrow majority in California alone can get almost as many electoral votes (fifty-four) as he could by carrying all of the sixteen smallest states (sixty); he can, mathematically, carry California by one vote and not receive any votes in those sixteen states and do just as well. This fact suggests that a presidential candidate should spend his energy in the larger states and tailor his programs to appeal to voters there, provided that energy expended there is likely to yield results.[46] In fact, the larger states are usually quite close in their division of the major party vote, while a fair number of the smaller states are more nearly "sure" for one party or the other. In 1988 the average share of the vote for the winner in the sixteen smallest states gave the winner an 18.7 percentage point margin of victory; in the eight largest states, on the other hand, the average margin of victory was 8.8 percent points. The large states are the home of many organized minorities, especially racial and ethnic minorities, and this has traditionally meant that both presidential candidates have had to pitch their appeals to attract these groups, or at least not to drive them off. Some of the critics of the current system have pointed to this advantage for the larger states, and especially their urban minorities, as a drawback of that system, to be reformed out of existence,[47] but most have concentrated their fire on the possibility of the "wrong winner," and the "undemocratic" nature of the unit rule.

Allowing a majority (or plurality) of voters to choose a president has a great deal to commend it. This is the simplest method of all; it would be most easily understood by the greatest number of people; it is the plan favored by the majority of Americans; and it comes closest to reflecting intuitive notions of direct popular sovereignty through majority rule.

Moreover, the outright abolition of the Electoral College, and the substitution of the direct election of the president, would reduce the importance of the larger states. It would mean that the popular vote margin that a state could provide, not the number of electoral votes, would determine its importance.[48] For example, under the present system a candidate who carries California by 144,100 votes (as Reagan did in 1980) has garnered one-sixth of the support he needs to win, while under the direct-vote system states like Massachusetts or Alabama can sometimes generate three and four times that much margin. In the two-party states, in which category most of the larger states fall, voters are cross-pressured in many ways, and a candidate can seldom count on defeating his opponent by a very large margin. The reason, then, that the large states lose influence is that this system switches influence from the close states to one-party states; in some states where one party's organization is weak, it is easier for the other party to achieve a large turnout at election time, and special rewards might be forthcoming for interest groups particularly strong within states that could provide a large margin of victory for their candidate. As candidates currently look with favor on those who can bring them support in the large states, because this spells victory, so might they be expected to look with favor on those who can bring them large popular margins in the one-party states, should that become the preferred strategy for winning. The emphasis would not be on which candidate was going to win the state, already a foregone conclusion, but by how many votes he was going to win. The small states do not gain, however, because even when they are one-party, they are not large enough to generate substantial voting margins. Direct election thus changes the advantage from the biggest and the smallest two-party states to the medium-sized one-party states, and these, in recent elections, happen most commonly to be located in the South.[49]

Table 5.6 lists all states having more than fourteen electoral votes and all states having more than a margin of 100,000 votes for the winner in 1988. It shows that the major gainers under a direct-election system would be southern states, for all eleven southern states would be "big states" because of their vote margin. Nine of the ten "big states" by the Electoral College method remain "big" by the popular vote criterion— but only Ohio and California exceeded Virginia in their importance to the presidential candidates. In 1976, the last close election, Ohio, Illinois, and New Jersey would have been "small states" under a direct election system, while seven southern states were among the twenty-one states with large popular vote margins. In that year, Jimmy Carter's margin of almost half a million Georgians would have made his home state the single most important.

This does not, of course, settle the matter, for one of the reasons that direct election is touted is that third parties cannot deadlock the process. In fact, those southern states with the largest 1968 margins were not powerful but weak, for they did not contribute to a winner but to a third-place loser.

How one feels about direct elections depends on (1) how one feels about the diminution of large-state influence and the gain by sundry other smaller states, (2) how much of a plurality one feels a newly elected president should have, and (3) how this plurality limit will affect others in the system.

Clearly, third-party votes under a direct-election system are wasted if the candidate with a plurality wins, no matter how small that plurality. If this is how the system is made to work, it is quite possible that future third parties will not benefit. At best, voters could express only their anger by voting for third-party candidates and this would be at the cost of fore-going the chance to decide an election. We suspect, however, that most Americans would feel uncomfortable with a president who, even though he won a plurality, was elected by, say, only 35 percent of the voters. One of the virtues of the present electoral vote system is that it magnifies the margin of a presidential victory (as, for instance, in 1988, Bush's 7.8 percent victory margin gave him 79 percent of the electoral vote), pre-sumably conferring added legitimacy and with it acceptance of the new president's responsibility to govern in fact as well as in title. Any system

TABLE 5.6 *Comparison of Popular Vote Margin with Electoral Vote Margin, 1988*

Electoral Vote Margin	Popular Vote Margin, 1988				
	Small (*less than 100,000*)		Large (*more than 100,000*)		
Small (13 or fewer)	Md.	Vt.	12-Va. (449)	10-La. (167)	
	Ct.	N.D.	12-Ind. (437)	9-Kt. (154)	
	Mo.	Del.	12-Ga. (366)	10-Minn. (147)	
	Wash.	N.M.	13-N.C. (347)	5-Neb. (139)	
	R.I.	Ha.	11-Tenn. (267)	7-Kan. (131)	
	Wis.	S.D.	9-Ala. (266)	3-D.C. (131)	
	Wyom.	Me.	7-Ariz. (249)	8-Iowa (126)	
	Alaska	Ore.	8-S.C. (235)	4-N.H. (118)	
	Mont.	W.Va.	5-Utah (221)	6-Ark. (118)	
	Nev.		13-Mass. (206)	8-Colo. (107)	
			8-Okla. (195)	4-Id. (107)	
			7-Miss. (194)		
Large (14 or more)	24-Ill. (95)		21-Fla. (962)		
			29-Tex. (684)		
			23-Ohio (477)		
			16-N.J. (423)		
			47-Cal. (353)		
			20-Mich. (289)		
			36-N.Y. (266)		
			25-Penn. (105)		

The number preceding the state is its number of electoral votes and the number following the state is its popular vote margin (in thousands). No popular vote margins or electoral vote margins are given for states in the upper left quadrant (states with fewer than 13 electoral votes and popular vote margins of less than 100,000).

of direct election would almost have to eliminate the majority principle in favor of some plurality, or it would clearly lead to much more, not less, deadlock; in three out of our last ten presidential elections, the winning candidate was without an absolute majority.

Reformers have generally agreed, though, that the winner must win by at least a substantial plurality; consequently the Electoral College reform amendment that passed the House in late 1969 provided for a runoff between the top two candidates if no one secured as much as 40 percent of the popular vote in the initial election.[50] The first effect of this provision would be to hand back influence to third parties; if one's candidate is going to have a second chance to win the office anyway, there is an incentive for any sizeable organized minority to contest the first election on its own. That the runoff would likely be used if it were provided for is suggested by the 1968 figures, when there was a fairly strong third-party candidate in the race. A fourth candidate would have needed to pull only 6 or 7 percent of the national total to keep either major party candidate from having the required 40 percent (Nixon won with only 43.4 percent, although he had 56.2 percent of the electoral vote).[51] Once this becomes even a plausible expectation, there is no reason for various intense minorities not to put up their own candidates, and visions of a white supremacist party, an African-American party, a labor party, a peace party, an environmentalist party, a right-to-life party, a farmers' party, and so on, appear. Whereas one of the strong points of the present system is that it enforces a compromise by penalizing all minorities that will not come to terms, the direct-election system could well encourage a continental European model, in which numerous groups contest the first election and then recombine for the second; at the very least, severe changes would be worked on the present convention system.[52] Should such a result occur in the future, the simplicity, ease of comprehension, and inherent majoritarian rightness of the direct-election solution would quickly disappear. One of the hidden effects of the Electoral College is to restrict the number of parties contesting for the presidency, which helps to focus the electorate on a limited menu of choices. In turn, this increases the chance that winners will have the backing of a sizeable number of voters and the legitimacy to lead Congress and the nation.

The direct-election plan passed by the House in 1969 received a warmer reception in the Senate than the previous time it appeared there—in 1956 it was voted down 66 to 17—but there were, not surprisingly, two major opposition groups. The first was the bloc of liberal senators from the biggest states, which had most to lose. The second was composed of some of the conservative senators from the smallest states, whom we have named as the group deriving second-greatest benefits from the current system. They argued that direct election would be a complete break with the federalism underlying our Constitution, since it would de facto abolish state boundaries for presidential elections.[53]

Another proposal, embodied in the 1950s in the unsuccessful Lodge-Gossett Resolution, is seen by some reformers as an acceptable "compromise" between outright abolition of the Electoral College and its retention.[54] In this scheme, the electoral vote in each state is split between the candidates according to their proportion of the state's popular vote. This may seem to be a procedural compromise, but it is a rather extreme reform in political terms. As Table 5.7 shows, the large, urban, two-party states would have been nearly eclipsed in the close election of 1976, in a way that direct election could not accomplish. Seven out of the ten largest states would not in 1976 have been able to provide their winner with a margin of even one full electoral vote, while thirteen other states would have been able to do so. Using 1980, 1984, and 1988 figures, large

TABLE 5.7 *Comparisons of Actual Electoral Vote Margins with Proportional Electoral Vote Margin, 1976*

Electoral Vote Margin	Proportional Electoral Vote Margin, 1976			
	Small (*1.00 or less*)		Large (1.00 or more)	
(13 or fewer)	All other states		9-Ala.	(1.2)
			6-Ariz.	(1.0)
			6-Ark.	(1.8)
			12-Ga.	(4.0)
			13-Ind.	(1.0)
			10-Minn.	(1.3)
			5-Neb.	(1.1)
			13-N.C.	(1.5)
			8-S.C.	(1.1)
			10-Tenn.	(1.3)
			4-Utah	(1.2)
			6-W.Va.	(1.0)
			3-D.C.	(1.9)
(14 or more)	45-Cal.	(0.8)		
	17-Fla.	(0.9)		
	26-Ill.	(0.5)		
	15-Mass.	(2.2)		
	21-Mich.	(1.2)		
	17-N.J.	(.4)		
	41-N.Y.	(1.8)		
	24-Ohio	(0.0)		
	27-Penn.	(0.7)		
	26-Tex.	(0.8)		

The number preceding the state is its actual number of electoral votes; the number following the state is its electoral vote margin under the reformed, proportional system.

states under Lodge-Gossett are congruent with large states in reality, but in close elections Lodge-Gossett does not preserve the advantage of large states.

Under proportional allocation of electoral votes, campaigning presidential nominees would have to give special attention to those states in which they felt a large difference in electoral votes could be attained. Once again, the proposed reform emphasizes the amount of difference within the state between the winner and the loser. In this case, however, the electoral votes of the states are divided rather than the popular votes. This effectively cancels out the advantage of the large states entirely. The fact that the Electoral College underrepresents the large states in the first place even further reduces their influence. The beneficiaries are again the one-party states, as well as the smaller states, since in any particular election West Virginia and Arizona, for example, may have more to contribute to the difference in electoral votes than Illinois, New Jersey, Ohio, or Texas.

There are two versions of this plan, one that divides electoral votes to the nearest vote and one that divides them to the nearest tenth of a vote. Most proponents favor the plan to divide them to the nearest tenth, since the nearest whole vote in many cases still would understate the closeness of the vote in a large number of states, especially those with few electoral votes to divide, and "representativeness" is the primary theoretical advantage of the plan. Since preventing deadlock is supposed to be one of the goals of the Electoral College reform, it is interesting to note that with the majority vote victory required by proponents of both plans, either the whole or the tenth-vote system would have thrown the 1968 election into the House of Representatives (Nixon, 235, Humphrey 221, Wallace 74; or Nixon 233.8, Humphrey 223.2, Wallace 78.8, others 2.2); and the system allotting electoral votes to the nearest tenth would have deadlocked the election of 1960 (Kennedy 264.8, Nixon 263.5, others 7.7).

The reduction in influence suffered by the large states under proportional proposals might mean, in effect, that the sparsely populated and one-party states would entirely dominate the national lawmaking process, unchecked by a president obliged to cultivate urban and two-party constituencies. The same problem is present if deadlock is dealt with by letting the plurality candidate win. Even with a plurality provision, splintering is facilitated under this plan because a party need only pull a fraction of a percentage point of a major state's total vote in order to get some electoral votes. The present system at least cuts off splinter groups without a strong regional base.

A third plan, the district plan, has been proposed as still another "political compromise" between the other two major reform proposals, on the grounds that since thirty-eight states must ratify a Constitutional amendment on electoral reform, the thirteen states with three or four electoral votes are not likely to support either of the first two proposals because each dilutes their current strength. The district plan would give a presidential candidate one electoral vote for every congressional district he carried, plus two more for every state. This is how electoral votes are now distributed in the state of Maine. It has been pushed largely by conservative senators; it is clearly the most radical of all the reform proposals in its effect on the U.S. political system, and it least advantageous to the big states. This system would have given Nixon victory in 1968 (289–192–57), but if it had already been in effect he probably would not have been running, since he would have won the election of 1960 (Nixon 278, Kennedy 245). Since the goals of electoral reform are supposedly to prevent the wrong man from winning, to avoid deadlock, and to do away with winner-take-all arrangements, it is hard to see what is offered by a system that (1) would have given the less popular candidate victory, (2) provides no more guarantee against deadlock than the present system (Wallace in 1968 got forty-five electoral votes under the actual system, but would have received fifty-seven under this one), (3) uses a winner-take-all principle, and (4) has the incidental feature of ending the activist character of the American presidency and giving policy control to one-party areas for the foreseeable future.[55] The election of 1988 would have come out the same way under all the plans for counting votes we have been considering. But it may be that plans to abolish the Electoral College, by damping down even large landslides, would bring stronger and more splinter parties into the electoral competition, thus changing the climate of electoral competition altogether.

Under the present Electoral College system, there has been no time since 1876 when any splinter group has been able to make good its threat to throw the election into the House. Even in 1948 Harry Truman won an Electoral College majority despite threats from both a third and a fourth party. In spite of the mathematical possibilities, not once in this century has the loser of the popular vote become president. On the other hand a direct-election plan that required a 40 percent plurality might well have forced a runoff in 1968. The proportional plan would have created deadlocks in two recent elections; and the district plan would have thrown the election to the popular vote loser in at least one recent case. In view of this analysis of the effect of electoral reforms, it is curious that many reformers have supported these changes in the Electoral College.

Underlying all of these arguments, of course, is the premise that most structural reforms "tend" to shift influences in certain ways. There may well be situations of social polarization that electoral system alternatives by themselves cannot paper over. But while we have argued that there is no better system than the current one, from the standpoint of the professed goals of most reformers, there is one minor change that would aid them. Under the present plan the electors who make up the Electoral College are in fact free to vote for whomever they wish. As an almost invariable rule, they vote for the winner in their state, but abuses are possible, and two within recent memory come to mind:

1. The unpledged electors chosen by citizens in Mississippi and Alabama in 1960 decided for whom they would vote only well after the election, treating the preferences of citizens as advisory, not mandatory. This clearly thwarts popular control.

2. This liberty allowed George Wallace to hope that he could run for president, create an electoral deadlock, and then bargain with one of the other candidates for policy concessions in exchange for his electors.

TABLE 5.8   *Electoral Outcomes under Various Plans*

	Present Plan	Direct Plan	Proportional Plan	District Plan
1988	Bush Wins	Bush Wins	Bush Wins	Bush Wins
	Bush 426	Bush 53.4	Bush 288.1	Bush 377
	Dukakis	Dukakis	Dukakis	Dukakis
	111	45.6	245.1	159
	Others 1	Others 1.0	Others 4.5	
1976	Carter Wins	Carter Wins	Carter Wins	Winner Unclear
	Carter 297	Carter 50.1	Carter	Carter 259
	Ford 240	Ford 48.0	269.5	Ford 257
	Others 1	Others 1.9	Ford 258.0	Unknown
			Others 10.5	27*
1968	Nixon Wins	Nixon Wins	Nobody Wins	Nixon Wins
	Nixon 301	Nixon 43.4	Nixon	Nixon 289
	Humphrey	Humphrey	233.8	Humphrey
	191	42.7	Humphrey	192
	Wallace 46	Wallace	223.2	Wallace 57
		13.5	Wallace	
			78.8	
1960	Kennedy Wins	Kennedy Wins	Nobody Wins	Nixon Wins
	Kennedy	Kennedy	Kennedy	Kennedy
	303	49.7	264.8	245
	Nixon 219	Nixon 49.6	Nixon	Nixon 278
	Others 15	Others 0.7	263.5	Others 15
			Others 7.7	

*Because several states did not have complete figures for presidential vote compiled by congressional district, we could not determine which candidate would have received those electoral votes.

An amendment making the casting of electoral votes automatic would dispel both of these possibilities.

A final gimmick deserves consideration, the creation of a private commission set up by the 20th Century Fund some years ago. They came up with a proposal for a National Bonus Plan, which would award 102 electoral votes en bloc (two for each state plus the District of Columbia) to the plurality winner of the nationwide popular vote. This plan would make it highly probable that no president could be elected who did not get more votes than the nearest rival. An additional feature is that candidates would be encouraged to get as many votes as they could even in states where they were pretty sure to lose because these would add on to the candidate's national popular total.[56] The Bonus Plan would guard against a minority president, preserve the form and the spirit of the constitutional structure and all this without encouraging splinter parties.

We have argued that there is no serious reason to quarrel with the major features of the present system, since in our form of government "majority rule" does not operate in a vacuum but within a system of "checks and balances.'' The president, for example, holds a veto power over Congress, which, if exercised, requires a two-thirds vote of each house to be overridden. Treaties must be ratified by two-thirds of the Senate, and amendments to the Constitution must be proposed by two-thirds of Congress or of the state legislatures and ratified by three-fourths of the states. Presidential appointments, in most important cases, must receive senatorial approval. The Supreme Court passes upon the constitutionality of legislative and executive actions. Involved in these political arrangements is the hope that the power of one branch of government will be counterbalanced by certain ''checks'' from another, the result being an approximate ''balance'' of forces. In our view, it is not necessarily a loss to have slightly different majorities preponderant in different institutions, but it is definitely a loss to have the same majority preponderant in both political branches while other majorities are frozen out. In the past the Electoral College had its place within this system. Originally designed to check popular majorities from choosing presidents unwisely, the Electoral College later on provided a ''check'' on the overrepresentation of rural states in the legislative branch by giving extra weight to the big state constituencies of the president.

Party Platforms and Party Differences

Having reviewed some of the major changes proposed by the party reformers, let us return to consider their key argument. Parties, reformers claim, are insufficiently ideological. The voters are not being offered clear choices and the parties, once in office, are not responsibly carrying out the promises made in their platforms. We argue that American parties do indeed differ—more so now than in the recent past—and that, much of the time, they respond to changes in voter sentiment. We feel that the ''solutions'' offered by reformers are unnecessary and would lead to consequences that even they might not desire.

Party platforms written by the presidential parties should be understood not only as ends in themselves but as means to obtaining and holding public office. It would be strange indeed if a party found policies like Social Security and unemployment compensation to be enormously popular and yet refused to incorporate them into its platform.[57] This would have to be a party of ideologues who cared everything about their own ideas and nothing about winning elections. Nor would it profit them much since they would not get elected and would never be in a position to do something about their ideas. Eventually, ideologues have to make the choice between pleasing themselves and winning elections.

Even when the major political parties are in the hands of moderate leaders, there are clear differences between the doctrines espoused by the two parties, and these are reflected in party platforms. Moreover, party platforms change over a period of time in a cyclical movement. The differences between the parties may be great for one or two elections, until innovations made by one party are picked up by the other. The net change from one decade to the next, however, is substantial. Let us begin when platforms are more or less alike. Their similarity begins to give way as it appears that certain demands in society are not being met. The minority party of the period senses an opportunity to gain votes by articulating and promising to meet these demands. The majority party, reluctant to let go of a winning combination, resists. In one or two elections the minority party makes its bid and makes the appropriate changes in its platforms. Then, in the ensuing elections, if the party that has changed its platform loses, it drops the innovation. If it wins, however, and wins big, the other party then seeks to take over what seem to be its most popular planks, and the platforms become more and more alike again.

We can see this cycle clearly in the New Deal period. The 1932 Democratic platform, though hinting at change, was much like the Republican one, especially in its emphasis on balancing the budget. A great difference in platforms could be noted in 1936 as the Democrats attempted to consolidate the New Deal and the Republicans stood pat. The spectacular Democratic triumph signaled the end of widely divergent platforms. By 1940 the Republicans had concluded that they could not continue to oppose the welfare state wholesale if they ever wished to win again. By 1952 the parties had come much closer to each other as the Republicans adopted most of the New Deal. Though the platforms of the major parties were similar to each other in both 1932 and 1952, the differences between 1932 and 1952 for either party were enormous.[58] In keeping with our finding that party leaders are, by historic standards, currently more polarized than usual, it is not surprising to find sharp differences in the party platforms for 1988.[59]

Sometimes reformers deplore what they regard as an excessive amount of mudslinging in campaigns, but they also ask that differences among the major parties be sharply increased in order to give the voters a clear choice. The two ideas are incompatible. It would be surprising if the parties disagreed more sharply about more and more subjects in an increasingly gentlemanly way. A far more likely outcome would be an increase in vituperation as the stakes of campaigns increased, passions rose, tempers flared, and the consequences of victory for the other side appeared much more threatening than had earlier been the case.

The case for the desirability of party reform used to rest on the assumption that American political parties were identical, that this was confusing and frustrating to American voters, and that it was undesirable to have a political system where parties do not disagree sharply. Now we have a chance to find out what happens during a period of relative party polarization.

Imagine for a moment that the two parties were in total and extreme disagreement on every major point of public policy, more so than they are in the United States. One would limit American military power to our borders, the other would intervene in every tense situation across the globe. One group would go all out to improve productivity; the other would put environmental values first. One group would stop Social Security; the other would expand it drastically. One group would raise tariffs; the other would abolish them. Obviously one consequence of having clear-cut parties with strong policy positions would be that the costs of losing an election would skyrocket. If parties were forced to formulate coherent, full-dress programs and were forced to carry them out "responsibly," and in full, then people who did not favor these programs would have little recourse. Clearly their confidence in a government whose policies were so little to their liking would suffer, and, indeed, they might feel strongly enough about preventing these policies from being enacted to do something drastic, like leaving the country, or not complying with governmental regulations, or, in an extreme case, seeking to change the political system by force.

The presidency of Republican Ronald Reagan may give pause to liberal reformers. Though Reagan's campaign rhetoric was too general to alarm voters, in many respects he played the part of the responsible-party president who proposed and attempted to carry out a wide-ranging program designed to modify if not to undo completely the efforts of his Democratic predecessors. There was no mistaking his thrust—less domestic government and more for defense. Indeed, if any president has performed according to the "responsible government" model, it is Ronald Reagan, who tried and to some extent succeeded, at least early in his administration, to carry out his campaign promises. If the results have not met with universal approval, citizens cannot say they were not forewarned as to the direction the candidate would take in the event he was elected. And if some citizens prefer more moderation and compromise, they should then consider whether they really want parties and candidates to carry out their pledges. Is the argument for party reform that the nation needs more Reagans, whether of the right or left? Evidently, given favorable political conditions such as existed in Lyndon Johnson's first term and Ronald Reagan's first year, or the extraordinary skill exercised by the promoters of the 1986 tax reform, coherent presidential programs enacted en masse by Congress are possible without constitutional reform or further changes, such as we have been discussing, in electoral machinery. It is necessary to have convinced party activists, determined and skillful leaders, and public consent. These are not always available, but they sometimes are. When they are not perhaps it is wise not to make the achievement of large changes too easy.

6

American Parties and Democracy

Over a relatively short period of time, a new sort of American political system has come into being. Among its features are high degrees of mass participation in hitherto elite processes, the replacement of political parties with the news and publicity media as primary organizers of citizen action and legitimizers of public decisions, the rise in the influence of media-approved and media-sustained interest groups, and the decline of interest groups linked to party organizations. Certain sorts of decision making are easy in a system structured in this way: simple voting, for example, in which alternatives are few and clear-cut. Complex decision making, in which various alternatives are compared one after the other, contingencies are weighed and tested tentatively, second and third choices are probed for hidden consensuses, or special weight is given to intensity of likes and dislikes, is extremely difficult in such a system. Therefore, much influence flows into the hands of those who structure alternatives in the first place—candidates and media stars.

But the job of the parties continues even as the party organizations decline in influence. For presidential elections, we have observed the replacement of the convention with primary elections as the most significant part of the process, and the rise of party activists who are more ideological and extreme than the rest of the population.

Because the American political system is moving toward a role for political parties that stresses their activities as policy advocates, it seems to us important to discuss at length the implications of this trend for democratic government. Our argument makes two main points. The first is that it is necessary for parties of advocacy in a democracy to receive mandates on public policy from popular majorities of convinced believers in their programs, but that this condition is not met in America because of the ways in which electorates actually participate in elections and conceive of public policy.

Our second point is that in view of the actual disposition of attitudes toward public policy in the electorate as compared with party elites, the fact that we are moving toward, or have actually entered into, an era of parties of advocacy poses some significant and largely unmet problems for American democracy. This is because it is not the policy preferences of the bulk of the electorate that are being advocated. Moreover, the implementation of policy requires the sort of institutional support that parties can orchestrate only if they have some permanency and are not required to give birth to themselves anew every four years, nominate a candidate, and then wither away.

Elections and Public Policy

No doubt uncoerced and competitive elections aid in making the political system open and responsive to a great variety of people and groups in the population. But it would not be correct to say that our elections transmit unerringly the policy preferences of electorates to leaders or confer mandates upon leaders with regard to specific policies. Consider the presidential landslide of 1972, which resulted in a Republican president but also in a Democratic Congress that was bound to disagree with him. Or the Democratic landslide of 1964 when the two major presidential candidates also had sharply divergent, consistent policy differences. Two years later, in the election of 1966, the Republicans regained much of the ground in Congress that they had lost. In 1980, Ronald Reagan won comfortably; by 1982, the Democrats had recouped. President Reagan won even more decisively in 1984; two years later the Democrats made a strong comeback and regained control of the Senate. In 1988, George Bush won a solid victory while his party lost two House seats and failed to gain in the Senate. Even in a landslide the mandate is at best a temporary, equivocal matter. And in any case elections that are even as clear-cut as these are rare.

It is easy to be cynical and expect too little from elections or to be euphoric and expect too much from them. A cynical view would hold that the United States was ruled by a power elite—a small group outside the democratic process. Under these circumstances the ballot would be a sham and a delusion. What difference can it make how voting is carried on or who wins if the nation is actually governed by other means? On the other hand, a euphoric view, holding that the United States is ruled as a mass democracy with equal control over decisions by all or most citizens, would enormously magnify the importance of the ballot. Through the act of casting a ballot, it could be arued, a majority of citizens would determine major national policies. What happens at the polls would not only decide who occupies public office; it also would determine the content of specific policy decisions. In a way, it is public office that would then be a sham because the power of decision in important matters would be removed from the hands of public officials. A third type of political system, in which numerous minorities compete for shares in policy making within broad limits provided by free elections, has more complex implications. It suggests that balloting is important but that it often does not and sometimes should not determine individual policy decisions. The ballot guides and constrains public officials, who are free to act within fairly broad limits subject to their anticipations of the responses of the voters and to the desires of other active participants.

It is evident that the American political system is of this third type. Public officials do make major policy decisions, but elections matter in that they determine which of two competing parties holds public office. In a competitive two-party situation such as exists in American presidential politics, the lively possibility of change provides an effective incentive for political leaders to remain in touch with followers.

But voters in presidential elections do not transmit their policy preferences to elected officials with a high degree of reliability. There are few clear mandates in our political system because elections are fought on so many issues and in so many incompletely overlapping constituencies. Often the same voters elect candidates to Congress and to the presidency who disagree on public policies. Thus, even if mandates could be identified they might well be impossible to enact because of inconsistency in the instructions issued to officials who must agree on legislation.[1]

Presidential elections are not referendums. The relationship between presidential elections and policies is a great deal subtler than the relations between the outcomes of referendums and the policies to which they pertain. In principle, the American political system is designed to work like this: Two teams of politicians, one in office, the other seeking office, both attempt to get enough votes to win elections. In order to win, they go to various groups of voters and, by offering to pursue policies favored by these groups, or by suggesting policies they might come to favor, hope to attract their votes. If there were only one office-seeking team, its incentive to respond to the policy preferences of groups in the population would diminish; if there were many such teams, the chances that any one of them could achieve a sufficient number of backers to govern would diminish. Hence the two-party system is regarded as a kind of compromise between the goals of responsiveness and effectiveness.

The proponents of a different theory would say that elections give the winning party a mandate to carry out the policies proposed during the campaign. Only in this way, they maintain, is popular rule through the ballot meaningful. A basic assumption in this argument is that the voters (or at least a majority of them) approve of all or most of the policies presented by the victorious candidate. No doubt this is plausible, but not in the sense intended because, as we have seen, a vote for a presidential candidate is often an expression of a party habit: particular policy directions are not necessarily implied in the vote. In addition, citizens may be voting not for but against a candidate or a past president, saying, in effect, no more of this but not necessarily more of the other party's policies. Most voters in the United States are not ideologically oriented. They do not seek to create or to adopt systems of thought in which issues are related to one another in some highly consistent manner. Caring about more than one value, they prefer a strong government here or a weak one there, or just not to decide at the present time. If this is the case, then voters can hardly be said to transmit preferences for a uniform stream of particular policies by electing candidates to public office.

Other basic objections to the idea that our elections are designed to confer mandates on specific public policies may also be raised. First, the issues debated in the campaign may not be the ones in which most voters are interested. These issues may be ones that interest the candidates, that they want to stress, or that interest segments of the press; but there is no clear reason to believe that any particular issue is of great concern to voters just because it gets publicity. Time and again, voting studies have demonstrated that what appear to be the major issues of a campaign turn out not to be significant for most of the electorate. In 1952, for example, three great Republican themes were communism, Korea, and corruption. It turned out that the communism issue, given perhaps the most publicity, had virtually no impact. Democrats simply would not believe that their party was the party of treason, and Republicans did not need that issue to make them vote the way they usually did. Korea and corruption were noticeable issues.[2] Yet how could anyone know, in the absence of a public opinion poll (and perhaps not even then), which of the three issues was important to the voters and which therefore conferred a mandate? There were, in any event, no significant policy differences between the parties on these issues—Democrats were also against communism and corruption and also wanted an end to the war in Korea. A broadly similar story can be told, as we have shown, for more recent elections, in which nobody was for welfare fraud or the waste of money by the Defense Department, everybody was for the flag, and nobody favored crime.[3]

A second reason why voting for a candidate does not necessarily signify approval of that candidate's policies is that candidates pursue many policy interests at any one time with widely varying intensity, so that they may collect support from some voters on one issue and from other voters on another. It is possible for candidates to get 100 percent of the votes and still have every voter opposed to most of their policies, as well as having every one of their policies opposed by most of the voters.

Assume that there are four major issues in a campaign. Make the further, quite reasonable, assumption that the voting population is distributed in such a way that those people who care intensely about one major issue support the victorious candidate for that reason alone, although they differ with her mildly on the other three issues. Thus, voters who are deeply concerned about the problem of defense against nuclear weapons may vote for candidate Jones, who prefers a minimum deterrence position, rather than Smith, who espouses a doctrine that requires huge retaliatory forces. This particular group of voters disagrees with Jones on farm price supports, on the overall size of government, and on national health insurance, but they do not feel strongly about any of these matters. Another group meanwhile believes that farmers, the noble yeomanry, are the backbone of the nation, and that if they are prosperous and strong, everything else will turn out all right. So they vote for Jones, too, although they prefer a large defense budget and disagree with Jones's other policies. And so on for other groups of voters. Jones ends up with all the votes, yet each of her policies is preferred by less than a majority of the electorate. Since this is possible in any political system where many issues are debated at election time, it is hard to argue that our presidential elections give unequivocal mandates on specific policies to the candidates who win.[4]

People vote for many reasons not directly connected with issues. They may vote on the basis of party identification alone. Party habits may be joined with a general feeling that Democrats are better for the common man or that Republicans will keep us safe, or vice versa—feelings too diffuse to tell us much about specific issues. Some people vote on the basis of a candidate's personality, or his "image." Others follow a friend's recommendation. Still others may be thinking about policy issues but may be all wrong in their perception of where the candidates stand. It would be difficult to distinguish the votes of these people from those who know, care, and differentiate accurately among the candidates on the basis of issues. We do know, however, that issue-oriented persons are usually in a minority, while those who cast their ballots with other things in mind are generally in the majority. Voters may want to move government in a more liberal or conservative direction, but desires of this sort are general and not specific in character.

Even if there is good reason to believe that a majority of voters do approve of specific policies supported by the victorious candidate, the mandate may be difficult or impossible to carry out. A candidate may get elected for a policy he pursued or preferred in the past that has no relevance to present circumstances. Some may have voted Republican in 1956 because Dwight Eisenhower got rid of the rascals in the Truman administration, or Democratic in 1976 in response to Watergate; but this did not point to any future policy that was currently in the realm of presidential discretion. John F. Kennedy promised in 1960 to get the nation moving. This was broad enough to cover a multitude of vague hopes and aspirations. More specifically, as president, Kennedy may dearly have wished to make good this promise by increasing the rate of growth in the national economy, but no one was quite sure how to do this. Lyndon Johnson was able to make good on many of his 1964 campaign promises on domestic policy, but observers after the election were hard put to distinguish his subsequent Vietnam policies from those promised by Barry Goldwater. The 1980 and 1984 elections can be seen as referendums on the economic performance of the incumbent administrations. Clearly voters thought the economy was doing poorly under Carter and better under Reagan. More than likely, however, it was the monetary policies of the Federal Reserve under the leadership of Paul Volcker, a Carter appointee, that produced the pro-Reagan electoral results. In 1988 George Bush campaigned vaguely and negatively, as well as successfully. Did he receive a mandate to reverse the condition complained of in one of his most successful TV commercials, to clean up Boston harbor?

Leaving aside all the difficulties about the content of a mandate, there is no accepted definition of what size electoral victory gives a president special popular sanction to pursue any particular policy. Would a 60 percent victory be sufficient? What about 51 percent or 52 percent, however, or the cases in which the winner receives less than half of the votes cast? And is it right to ignore the multitudes who do not vote and whose preferences are not directly registered? We might ignore the nonvoters for the purpose of this analysis if we were sure they were divided in their preferences between candidates in nearly the same proportions as those who do vote. But we cannot be sure this is the case. In practice, this problem is easily solved. Whoever wins the election is allowed to pursue whatever policies he pleases, within the very important constraints imposed by the checks and balances of the rest of the political system. This, in the end, is all that a "mandate" is in American politics.

Opinion polls may help the politician gauge policy preferences, but there are always lingering doubts as to the polls' reliability. It is not certain in any event that they tell the political leader what that leader needs to know. People who really have no opinion but who care little may be counted equally with those who are intensely concerned. Many people giving opinions may have no intention of voting for some politicians who heed them, no matter what. The result may be that a politician will get no visible support from a majority that agrees with him, but instead he will get complaints from an intense minority that disagrees. The people who agree with him may not vote, while those who differ may—as single-issue interest groups are reported to do—attempt retribution at the ballot box. Those who are pleased may be the ones who would have voted for the public official in any case. And unless the poll is carefully done, it may leave out important groups of voters, overrepresent some, underrepresent others, and otherwise give a misleading impression. The correlations that are made—say, showing that support comes disproportionately from certain economic or social groups—do not explain why some people, often a substantial minority, possessing these self-same characteristics act in the opposite way.

Let us turn the question around for a moment. Suppose a candidate loses office. What does this tell him about the policies he should have preferred? If there were one or two key issues widely debated and universally understood, the election may tell him a great deal. But this is seldom the case. More likely there were many issues and it was difficult to separate out those that did from those that did not garner support for his opponent. Perhaps the election was decided on the basis of personal images or some events in the economic cycle or a military engagement—points that were not debated in the campaign and that may not have been within anyone's control. The losing candidate may always feel that if he continues to educate the public to favor the policies he prefers, he will eventually win. Should he lose a series of elections, however, his party would undoubtedly try to change something—policies, candidates, organization, maybe all three—in an effort to improve its fortunes.

How do winning candidates appraise an election? What does this event tell officeholders and their parties about the policies they should prefer when in office? Some policies undoubtedly were rather vague, and specific applications of them may turn out quite differently from what the campaign suggested. Others may founder on the rock of practicality; they sounded fine but they simply cannot be carried out. Conditions change and policies that seemed appropriate a few months before turn out to be irrelevant. Democrats may prefer to spend more on welfare and Republicans to cut taxes, but huge deficits preclude both these aspirations. As the time for putting policies into practice draws near, the new officeholders may discover that they generate a lot more opposition than when they were merely campaign oratory. And those policies they pursue to the end may have to be compromised considerably in order to get the support of other participants in the policy-making process. Nevertheless, if they have even a minimal policy orientation, the newly elected candidates can try to carry out a few of their campaign proposals, seeking to maintain a general direction consonant with the approach that may—they cannot be entirely certain—have contributed to their election.

The practical impossibility in our political system of ascertaining mandates is one important reason why it is so difficult for parties to emphasize their function as policy advocates. It is, however, entirely possible for parties to adopt mandates that have little or no support in the general population. It is to the exploration of this possibility that we now turn.

Parties of Advocacy versus Parties of Intermediation

The presidential election process in the United States has undergone a major transformation. As late as 1952, a president of the United States could, and with good reason, dismiss a prospective Estes Kefauver victory in the New Hampshire primary as "eye-wash." Now primaries select most convention delegates, and combined with the effects of the media, have an overwhelming impact on the outcome of the nominating process.[5]

Behind the shift in the role of primary elections lie shifts in the roles of political activists, both candidate enthusiasts and party regulars, and changes in the powers and the significance of the news media. We believe that these changes and other changes that we have discussed—the shift to public financing not only of the general election, but also of primary elections, the vast increase in the number of primaries, and the new rules for converting votes into delegates—add up to a fundamental redefinition of the place of the national political parties in our public life. One way to characterize this redefinition is to say that the conception of parties as agents of consensus government has begun to fade. If we are right, then more and more we can expect candidates and party leaders to raise divisive issues and to emphasize party differences rather than papering them over.

Activists are now favored by the rules of the game, and officeholders and party officials comparatively disfavored. In the early days of preprimary activity, the people who become most active are apt to be those who have the most spare time, the most ideological commitment, and the most enthusiasm for one candidate above all others. Since the rules are now written to encourage activity at an earlier and earlier date, as a basis for federal subsidies during the primaries and as a prerequisite of being taken seriously by the news media, it follows that activists will have more to say about the eventual outcome of the nomination process. Party officials in the various states, on the other hand, who once preferred to wait until they could see a majority forming, under the new rules of the game must ally themselves with one or another active candidate early in the process, or forfeit their influence. This applies to everyone with the exception of the Democratic high officeholders who get a free ride to the convention and make up around 15 percent of the total number of delegates. By the time their peculiar skills and interests in majority building might be needed—for instance at a convention—it is too late for them to get into the process: most of the seats will have been taken by the enthusiasts for particular candidates who won in the various primaries and state conventions.

We can therefore ask how the emerging structure of presidential election politics helps and hinders political parties in performing the tasks customarily allotted to them in the complex scheme of American democracy. In essence, we would argue that the parties have been greatly strengthened in their capacities to provide advocacy and weakened in their abilities to provide intermediation or facilitate implementation in the political system. Ever widening consensus among party activists has been achieved at the expense of increasing dissensus within government. Thus party platforms become ever more consistent while government finds it increasingly difficult to relate revenues to expenditures.

Advocacy is strengthened because the rules of the game offer incentives to party leaders and candidates who are able to attract personal followings on an ideological basis. What is lost, in our view, is a capacity to deliberate, weigh competing demands, and compromise so that a variety of differing interests each gain a little. This loss would not be so great if the promise of policy government—to select efficacious programs and implement them successfully—were likely to be fulfilled in performance. But, on the record so far, this is doubly doubtful.

It is doubtful because for many of the problems that form the basis of political campaign discussion—crime, racism, hostility abroad—there are no known, surefire solutions. And second, even if we knew what to do about more of our problems, it is unclear that, given the ways in which various forces in our society are arrranged, presidents alone could deliver on their promises.

This last dilemma is especially poignant in the case of candidates who speak to a very wide spectrum of issues. Were they elected, then program implementation would depend on support in Congress, the bureaucracies, state and city governments, and elsewhere. The ability of such policy-oriented candidates to gain the agreement of others depends on many factors which typically are neither discussed nor understood in elections. Yet gaining the agreement of others is part of making policies work.

Policy government might enhance the legitimacy of government if it increased the effectiveness of programs, but the insensitivity of its advocates to the needs for consensus makes that unlikely. Under these circumstances, neither policy nor consensus, advocacy nor intermediation, is likely to be served.

Two factors account for the decline in the vital function of intermediation by parties. First, candidates have far fewer incentives than heretofore to deal with interest groups organized on traditional geographic or occupational lines, or with state and local party leaders. These leaders and groups have in the past provided links between national politicians and the people and have focused the hopes and energies of countless citizens upon the party organizations as meaningful entities in the nomination process. Nowadays, as we have been told by politicians as varied as Richard Nixon and Jimmy Carter, a candidate for the presidency need no longer build up a mosaic of alliances with interest groups and party leaders. Candidates such as Walter Mondale who do work to make these alliances are attacked for being beholden to "special interests." Now, through the miracle of the mass media (especially television), through mass mailings to appeal for money, and through federal subsidy if these mass mailings are successful, presidential candidates can reach every home and touch every heart and claim the allegiance of followers based on ideological appeals rather than concrete bargains.

This is the first sense in which parties have been diminished in their capacity to mediate between the desires of ordinary citizens and the policies of government: candidates no longer need parties to reach voters. In a second sense parties are losing the capacity to mediate between leaders and followers because the formal properties of plebiscitary decision making, such as occurs in primary elections, leave little room for a bargaining process to occur. Contingent choices are impossible to express straightforwardly through the ballot box. Thus a candidate who is acceptable to a sizeable majority but is the first choice of only a few would systematically lose out under the new rules to candidates who might be unacceptable to most voters but secure in their control over a middle-sized fraction (20 to 30 percent, depending on how many play the game) of first-choice votes.

It is in this powerful sense that we can say that "participatory" democracy, as the American party system has begun to practice it, is inimical to "deliberative" democracy. As more and different people have won the right to participate in the nomination process, the kinds of communication they have been able to send to one another have become improverished. They can vote, but they cannot bargain. They can make speeches, but they cannot deliberate.

Let us see what happens when a free spirit like George McGovern breaks through the network of old politicians and gets nominated for president. A piece of bad luck afflicts his campaign: his vice-presidential candidate, Thomas Eagleton, has concealed a medical history that may weaken the ticket. The *New York Times* writes, "Dump Eagleton." The *Washington Post* writes, "Dump Eagleton."

What does an "old" politics candidate do? Presumably he gets on the telephone and asks around among interest-group leaders and state and local party bosses, "Can we stand the flak?" "What do the partyworkers think?" "What do you think?"

What do "new" politics candidates do? Well, what choice have they? To whom can they place a telephone call other than the far-flung members of their immediate families? There is no negotiating with the editorial board of the *New York Times* in or out of a smoke-filled room. There is no give-and-take with the moderator of "Meet the Press." The moderator gives. Politicians take. So also in the preprimary process, where bad news can drive candidates out of contention before their candidacies are even tested by primaries or caucus activity, as happened to Gary Hart in 1987, even though he was far and away the Democratic front runner at the time.

We have no way of knowing whether the paradox of participation swallowing up deliberation has had the net effect of turning citizens away from political parties. It is in any event the case that by a variety of measures—nonvoting, propensity of voters to decline to identify with a political party, direct expressions of disapproval of parties—political parties have, like so many other institutions of American society, suffered substantial losses in public confidence. In our view, the most promising way for them to regain public confidence is to avoid factional candidates and to not only nominate and elect, but also to help good candidates govern.

What is objectionable about policy government? What could be wrong with so intuitively attractive an idea? Governments must make policies. Candidates must be judged, in part at least, on their policy preferences as well as on indications of their ability to perform when in office. Has there not been, in the recent past, too much obfuscation of issues and too little candor in speaking one's mind? Obviously our society needs more rather than less discussion of issues, greater rather than less clarification of alternatives. The problem is that the premises upon which policy government is based are false. Most people do not want parties that make extreme appeals by taking issue positions far from the desires of the bulk of the citizenry.[6] Perhaps people feel safer if their parties give them a choice, but they do not want losing to be a catastrophe. This may be why they see no great difficulty in voting for a president of one party and a Congress of another.[7]

Adherents of issue expression have so far managed to control only one presidential nominating convention at a time; but suppose they manage in the future to face off a right-wing Republican against a left-wing Democrat? The trends now misperceived as products of consensus government—alienation, nonvoting—as likely as not would show an alarming increase if the vast majority of citizens discovered that their preference had been disregarded and that they had nowhere to turn. Indeed, it may well be that the vastly increased participation of activists has, by making campaigns distasteful to the majority, led to the very decline in participation that they deplore.

It is one thing to say that policy options have been insufficiently articulated and quite another to create conflict and develop disagreements where these did not exist before. Political activists in the United States are more ideological and polarized than at any time since studies were first conducted in the 1930s, and possibly since the 1890s or even the Civil War. Should ordinary citizens be compelled to choose from policy alternatives that appeal to these activists, or are they entitled to select from a menu closer to their tastes? The question is not whether there will be issues, for inevitably there must be, but who will set the agenda for discussion and whether this agenda will primarily reflect differences in the population or among elites.

The objection to a party of advocacy is that it falsely justifies the rule by elites who impose on the great majority of people preferences to which the majority is largely indifferent or opposed. Policy government does not lead to participatory democracy, because participation does not in fact increase uniformly or democratically among the people. It decreases in the population as a whole and increases among certain selected elites, drawn from the upper-middle and upper classes, who have the time and inclination to engage in bouts of intense political activity.

Thus, the rationale behind parties of advocacy leads to plebiscitary democracy. If it is not only desirable for all citizens to vote in general elections but also for them to choose candidates through preelection primaries, it must be even more desirable for them to select governmental policies directly through referendums. Instead of rule by special interests or cliques of congressmen, the public's interest would supposedly be expressed by the public. Experience with referendums in California, however, suggests that this is not quite how things work in practice. Without measures for limiting the number of referendums voters may face at a given election, citizens are swamped by the necessity of voting on dozens of items. Elites, not the people, determine the selection and wording of referendums. And how they are worded is of course extremely important. Money—to arrange for signing petitions to get referendums on the ballot—becomes more meaningful than ever. The public is faced with a bewildering array of proposals, all sponsored by special interests that want a way around the legislature. To learn what is involved in a single seemingly innocuous proposal to raise somebody's salary or issue bonds takes hours of study. To understand twenty or more per election is unduly onerous. Are citizens better off guessing or following the advice of the local newspaper rather than trying to choose a legislator or a party to represent their interests? To take a famous case, were citizens or legislators better qualified to understand that Proposition 13 in California would not only keep property taxes down, which it was supposed to do, but would also, by depriving localities of resources, centralize control at the state level over many areas of public policy, which no one wanted? Were citizens of California, where referendums abound, wise to vote at widely separated intervals for so many mandatory expenditures as to make it difficult for the state legislature to mobilize resources to meet new needs?

A plebiscitary democracy, stressing the direct connection between candidates and voters, could not abide the Electoral College. Only direct democracy, mass voting for candidates, would do. Abolishing the Electoral College, however, as we have seen, would further decrease the need for forming diverse coalitions. Both the agents of consensus—mediating parties—and the fact of consensus—political leaders who nurture it—would decline.

After two decades of severe internal difficulty, when confidence in virtually all national institutions suffered repeated blows, the need for consensus-building parties seems clear. Ideological parties might be desirable for a people homogeneous in all ways except the economic; but can a multiracial, multiethnic, multireligious, multiregional, multiclass nation like the United States sustain itself when its main agents of political action—the parties—strive to exclude rather than include, to sharpen rather than dull the edge of controversy?

It is even doubtful that the rise of parties of advocacy leads to a more principled politics. If principles are precepts that must not be violated, when contrary principles are firmly embedded in the programs of opposing parties, one man's principles necessarily become another's fighting words. A few principles, such as those enshrined in the Bill of Rights, may be helpful in establishing boundaries beyond which governmental action may not go. A plethora of principles inevitably establishes competing sovereignties whose jurisdiction can be violated only at great peril. As being a Democrat increasingly requires adherence to liberal positions and a Republican to conservative positions, cross-cutting cleavages—people who support one another on some issues while opposing on others—will diminish. With officeholders opposing each other on more issues, and with more issues defined as moral issues, political passions are sure to rise. And so, we conjecture, will negative campaigning.

Compromise, of course, can also be a curse. If everything were bargainable, including basic liberties, no one would feel safe and, indeed, no one would be. Similarly, if candidates cared everything about winning and nothing about how they win, if they were not restrained by internal norms or enforceable external expectations, elections would become outrages.

Parties without policies would be empty; parties with only a narrow band of policies are dangerous. Without the desire to win elections, not at any cost but as a leading motive, there is no reason for politicians to pay attention to the people who vote. Winning requires a widespread appeal. Thus the desire to win leads to moderation, to appeals to diverse groups in the electorate, and to efforts to bring many varied interests together. This is why we prefer parties of intermediation to parties of advocacy. Parties of advocacy do not sustain themselves well in government. Thus they fail to assist political leaders in mobilizing consent for the policies they adopt, and this widens the gap between campaign promises and the performance of government.

Because so many of the rules of presidential election politics are changing, we cannot say with a high degree of assurance how parties, candidates, and voters will adapt to the new incentives and disabilities that are continuously enacted into law. We are confident only in asserting that the adaptations they make will be of enormous consequence in determining the ultimate capacity of the American political system to sustain the fascinating and noble experiment in self-government begun on this continent over two hundred years ago.

APPENDIX A   *Vote by Groups in Presidential Elections Since 1952*

	1952		1956		1960	
	Stev.	*Ike*	*Stev.*	*Ike*	*JFK*	*Nixon*
NATIONAL	44.6%	55.4%	42.2%	57.8%	50.1%	49.9%
SEX						
Men	47	53	45	55	52	48
Women	42	58	39	61	49	51
RACE						
White	43	57	41	59	49	51
Nonwhite	79	21	61	39	68	32
EDUCATION						
College	34	66	31	69	39	61
High School	45	55	42	58	52	48
Grade School	52	48	50	50	55	45
OCCUPATION						
Professional						
and Business	36	64	32	68	42	58
White Collar	40	60	37	63	48	52
Manual	55	45	50	50	60	40
Members of						
Labor Union						
Families	61	39	57	43	65	35
AGE						
Under 30 years	51	49	43	57	54	46
30–49 years	47	53	45	55	54	46
50 years and older	39	61	39	61	46	54
RELIGION						
Protestants	37	63	37	63	38	62
Catholics	56	44	51	49	78	22
POLITICS						
Republicans	8	92	4	96	5	95
Democrats	77	23	85	15	84	16
Independents	35	65	30	70	43	57
REGION						
East	45	55	40	60	53	47
Midwest	42	58	41	59	48	52
South	51	49	49	51	51	49
West	42	58	43	57	49	51

APPENDIX A   (*Continued*)

	1964		1968			1972	
	LBJ	Gold.	HHH	Nixon	Wallc	McG.	Nixon
NATIONAL	61.3%	38.7%	43.0%	43.4%	13.6%	38%	62%
SEX							
Men	60	40	41	43	16	37	63
Women	62	38	45	43	12	38	62
RACE							
White	59	41	38	47	15	32	68
Nonwhite	94	6	85	12	3	87	13
EDUCATION							
College	52	48	37	54	9	37	63
High School	62	38	42	43	15	34	66
Grade School	66	34	52	33	15	49	51
OCCUPATION							
Professional							
and Business	54	46	34	56	10	31	69
White Collar	57	43	41	47	12	36	64
Manual	71	29	50	35	15	43	57
Members of							
Labor Union							
Families	73	27	56	29	15	46	54
AGE							
Under 30 years	64	36	47	38	15	48	52
30–49 years	63	37	44	41	15	33	67
50 years and older	59	41	41	47	12	36	64
RELIGION							
Protestants	55	45	35	49	16	30	70
Catholics	76	24	59	33	8	48	52
POLITICS							
Republicans	20	80	9	86	5	5	95
Democrats	87	13	74	12	14	67	33
Independents	56	44	31	44	25	31	69
REGION							
East	68	32	50	43	7	42	58
Midwest	61	39	44	47	9	40	60
South	52	48	31	36	33	29	71
West	60	40	44	49	7	41	59

	1976 Carter	1976 Ford	1976 McC.	1980 Carter	1980 Reagan	1980 Andrsn	1984 Mondale	1984 Reagan	1988 Duk.	1988 Bush
NATIONAL	50%	48%	1%	41%	51%	7%	41%	59%	46%	54%
SEX										
Men	53	45	1	38	53	7	36	64	44	56
Women	48	51	*	44	49	6	45	55	48	52
RACE										
White	46	52	1	36	56	7	34	66	41	59
Nonwhite	85	15	1	86	10	2	87	13	82	18
EDUCATION										
College	42	55	2	35	53	10	39	61	42	58
High School	54	46	*	43	51	5	43	57	46	54
Grade School	58	41	1	54	42	3	51	49	55	45
OCCUPATION										
Professional and Business	42	56	1	33	55	10	34	66	NA	NA
White Collar	50	48	2	40	51	9	47	53	NA	NA
Manual	58	41	1	48	46	5	46	54	NA	NA
Members of Labor Union Families	63	36	1	50	43	5	52	48	63	37
AGE										
Under 30 yrs.	53	45	1	47	41	11	40	60	37	63
30–49 years	48	49	2	38	52	8	40	60	45	55
50 years and older	52	48	*	41	54	4	41	59	49	51
RELIGION										
Protestants	46	53	*	39	54	6	39	61	42	58
Catholics	57	42	1	46	47	6	39	61	51	49

	1976			1980			1984		1988	
	Carter	Ford	McC.	Carter	Reagan	Andrsn	Mondale	Reagan	Duk.	Bush
POLITICS										
Republicans	9	91	*	8	86	5	4	96	7	93
Democrats	82	18	*	69	26	4	79	21	85	15
Independents	38	57	4	29	55	14	33	67	43	57
REGION										
East	51	47	1	43	47	9	46	54	51	49
Midwest	48	50	1	41	51	7	42	58	47	53
South	54	45	*	44	52	3	37	63	40	60
West	46	51	1	35	54	9	40	60	46	54

*Less than one percent.
NA = Not Available
aNonunion.

Source: Gallup Monthly Opinion Index, December 1976, December 1980; The Gallup Poll, November 7, 1984, November 1988, Report No. 278.

APPENDIX B *Participation in National Elections, by Population Characteristics: 1968–1988*

Persons in thousands, as of November. Covers civilian noninstitutional population. For 1968, persons 18 years and over in Georgia and Kentucky, 19 and over in Alaska, 20 and over in Hawaii, and 21 and over elsewhere.

| | | 1968 | | |
| | | Persons Reporting They Voted | | Percent Reporting They Did |
Characteristic	Persons of Voting Age	Total	Percent	Not Vote
TOTAL	116,535	78,964	67.8	30.0
Male	54,464	38,014	69.8	27.6
Female	62,071	40,951	66.0	32.1
White	104,521	72,213	69.1	28.9
Black	10,935	6,300	57.6	38.5
18–20 years old	432	144	33.3	64.1
21–24 years old	11,170	5,707	51.1	45.6
25–34 years old	23,198	14,501	62.5	35.8
35–44 years old	22,905	16,223	70.8	27.1
45–64 years old	40,362	30,238	74.9	22.8
65 years old and over	18,468	12,150	65.8	31.9
Median age (years)	45.2	46.7	(x)	(x)
Metropolitan residence	40,778	27,461	67.3	32.7
Nonmetropolitan residence	40,778	27,461	67.3	32.7
North and West residence	81,594	57,970	71.0	29.0
South residence	34,941	20,994	60.1	39.9
Years of school completed:				
8 years or less	30,430	16,592	54.4	45.5
9–11 years	20,429	12,519	61.3	38.7
12 years	39,704	28,768	72.5	27.5
More than 12 years	25,971	21,086	81.2	18.8
Employed	70,002	49,772	71.1	28.9
Unemployed	1,875	977	52.1	47.9
Not in labor force	44,657	28,215	63.2	36.8

APPENDIX B   (*Continued*)

For 1972–1984, persons 18 years old and over in all states. Includes aliens. Figures are based on a population sample. Differences in percentages may also be due to overreporting of voting persons in the sample. Excludes persons who did not report whether or not they had voted.

		1972		
		Persons Reporting They Voted		Percent Reporting They Did Not Vote
Characteristic	Persons of Voting Age	Total	Percent	
TOTAL	136,203	85,766	63.0	37.0
Male	63,833	40,908	64.1	35.9
Female	72,370	44,858	62.0	38.0
White	121,243	78,166	64.5	35.5
Black	13,493	7,032	52.1	47.9
18–20 years old	11,022	5,318	48.3	51.7
21–24 years old	13,590	6,896	50.7	49.3
25–34 years old	26,933	16,072	59.7	40.3
35–44 years old	22,240	14,747	66.3	33.7
45–64 years old	42,344	29,991	70.8	29.2
65 years old and over	20,074	12,741	63.5	36.5
Median age (years)	42.4	44.9	(x)	(x)
Metropolitan residence	99,248	63,799	64.3	35.7
Nonmetropolitan residence	36,855	21,976	59.4	49.6
North and West residence	93,653	62,193	66.4	33.6
South residence	42,550	23,573	55.4	44.6
Years of school completed:				
8 years or less	28,065	13,311	47.4	52.6
9–11 years	22,277	11,587	52.0	48.0
12 years	50,749	33,193	65.4	34.6
More than 12 years	35,113	27,675	78.8	21.2
Employed	80,164	52,899	66.0	34.0
Unemployed	3,735	1,863	49.9	50.1
Not in labor force	52,305	31,001	59.3	40.7

APPENDIX B   (*Continued*)

		1976		
		Persons Reporting They Voted		Percent Reporting They Did Not Vote
Characteristic	*Persons of Voting Age*	*Total*	*Percent*	
TOTAL	146,500	86,700	59.2	40.8
Male	69,000	41,100	59.6	40.4
Female	77,600	45,600	58.8	41.2
White	129,300	78,800	60.9	39.1
Black	14,900	7,300	48.7	51.3
18–20 years old	12,100	4,600	38.0	62.0
21–24 years old	14,800	6,800	45.6	54.4
25–34 years old	31,500	17,500	55.4	44.6
35–44 years old	22,800	14,400	63.3	36.7
45–64 years old	43,300	29,800	68.7	31.3
65 years old and over	22,000	13,700	62.2	37.8
Median age (years)	41.5	45.1	(x)	(x)
Metropolitan residence	99,600	58,900	59.2	40.8
Nonmetropolitan residence	47,000	27,800	59.1	40.9
North and West residence	99,400	60,800	61.2	38.8
South residence	47,100	25,900	54.9	45.1
Years of school completed:				
8 years or less	24,900	11,000	44.1	55.9
9–11 years	22,200	10,500	47.2	52.8
12 years	55,700	33,100	59.4	40.6
More than 12 years	43,700	32,200	73.5	26.5
Employed	86,000	53,300	62.0	38.0
Unemployed	6,400	2,800	43.7	56.3
Not in labor force	54,100	30,600	56.5	43.5

APPENDIX B   (*Continued*)

Characteristic	Persons of Voting Age	1980		Percent Reporting They Did Not Vote
		Persons Reporting They Voted		
		Total	Percent	
TOTAL	157,100	93,100	59.2	40.8
Male	74,100	43,800	59.1	40.9
Female	83,000	49,300	59.4	40.6
White	137,700	83,900	60.9	39.1
Black	16,400	8,300	50.5	49.5
18–20 years old	12,300	4,400	35.7	64.3
21–24 years old	15,900	6,800	43.1	56.9
25–34 years old	35,700	19,500	54.6	45.4
35–44 years old	25,600	16,500	64.4	35.6
45–64 years old	43,600	30,200	69.3	30.7
65 years old and over	24,100	15,700	65.1	34.9
Median age (years)	40.7	44.6	(x)	(x)
Metropolitan residence	106,700	62,700	58.8	41.2
Nonmetropolitan residence	50,500	30,400	60.2	39.8
North and West residence	106,500	65,000	61.0	39.0
South residence	50,600	28,100	55.6	44.4
Years of school completed:				
8 years or less	22,700	9,600	42.6	57.4
9–11 years	22,500	10,200	45.6	54.4
12 years	61,200	36,000	58.9	41.1
More than 12 years	50,800	37,200	73.2	26.8
Employed	95,000	58,800	61.8	38.2
Unemployed	55,200	31,400	57.0	43.0

APPENDIX B   (*Continued*)

Characteristic	Persons of Voting Age	1984 Persons Reporting They Voted Total	1984 Persons Reporting They Voted Percent	Percent Reporting They Did Not Vote
TOTAL	170,000	101,800	59.9	41.1
Male	80,300	44,400	59.0	41.0
Female	89,600	54,500	60.8	39.2
White	146,800	90,100	61.4	38.6
Black	18,400	10,300	55.8	44.2
18–20 years old	11,200	4,100	36.7	63.3
21–24 years old	16,700	7,300	43.5	56.5
25–34 years old	40,300	22,000	54.5	45.5
35–44 years old	30,700	19,500	63.5	36.5
45–64 years old	44,300	30,900	69.8	30.2
65 years old and over	26,700	18,000	67.7	32.3
Metropolitan* residence				
Nonmetropolitan* residence				
North and West residence	112,400	69,200	61.6	38.4
South residence	57,600	32,700	56.8	43.2
Years of school completed:				
8 years or less	20,600	8,800	42.9	57.1
9–11 years	22,100	9,800	44.4	55.6
12 years	67,800	39,800	58.7	41.3
More than 12 years	59,500	40,200	67.5**	32.5
			79.1***	20.9
Employed	104,200	64,200	61.6	38.4
Unemployed	7,400	3,300	44.0	56.0
Not in labor force	58,400	34,400	58.9	41.1

APPENDIX B   (Continued)

| Characteristic | Persons of Voting Age | 1988 | | Percent Reporting They Did Not Vote |
| | | Persons Reporting They Voted | | |
		Total	Percent	
TOTAL	178,100	48,500	57.4	42.6
Male	84,500	47,700	56.4	43.6
Female	93,600	54,600	58.3	41.7
White	152,000	90,400	59.1	40.9
Black	19,700	10,100	51.5	48.5
18–20 years old	10,700	3,600	33.2	66.8
21–24 years old	14,800	5,700	38.3	61.7
25–34 years old	42,700	20,500	48.0	52.0
35–44 years old	35,200	21,600	61.3	38.7
45–64 years old	45,900	31,200	67.9	32.1
65 years old and over	28,800	19,800	68.8	31.2
Metropolitan* residence				
Nonmetropolitan* residence				
North and West residence	117,400	69,100	58.9	41.1
South residence	60,700	33,000	54.5	45.5
Years of school completed:				
8 years or less	19,100	7,000	36.7	63.3
9–11 years	21,100	8,700	41.3	58.7
12 years	70,000	38,300	54.7	45.3
More than 12 years	67,900	43,800	64.5[**]	35.5
			77.6[***]	22.4
Employed	113,800	66,500	58.4	41.6
Unemployed	5,800	2,200	38.6	61.4
Not in labor force	58,500	33,500	57.3	42.7

x—Not applicable

*Census Bureau has changed its definitions and this data is not now available. In past years there was little difference in turnout between these two categories.

**One to three years of college.

***Four years or more of college.

Source: U.S. Bureau of the Census, *Current Population Reports,* Series p-20. Nos. 192, 253, 359, and 405. From *Statistical Abstract,* 1974, p. 437; 1977, p. 491; 1981, p. 499; 1986, p. 256; 1990, p. 262.

Notes

Preface

1. "Seeking Legal Relief from Excessive Regulation of California's Parties" (mimeo, July 1982). The committee describes itself as "an organization of scholars, political practitioners and other citizens interested in strengthening our political parties. . . ."

Introduction

1. See Paul T. David, Ralph M. Goldman, and Richard C. Bain, *The Politics of National Party Conventions* (New York, 1964) for a lengthy treatment of the history of the national party conventions.

2. An excellent statement discussing signs of party strength may be found in Gerald M. Pomper, ed., *Party Renewal in America: Theory and Practice* (New York, 1980).

Chapter 1.   The Strategic Environment: Participants

1. In his major work on public opinion, V. O. Key, Jr., states, "for most Americans issues of politics are not of central concern. . . ." At another point Key summarizes the literature as follows: "In analysis after analysis of opinions on specific issues, sizable proportions of persons have been shown to lack an opinion" (*Public Opinion and American Democracy* [New York, 1961], pp. 47, 185). When asked, "What things are you most concerned with these days?" two out of three people in a representative sample of registered voters in New Haven, Connecticut, spoke of such personal matters as jobs, health, and children. Only one out of five cited local, state, national, or international affairs (Robert A. Dahl, *Who Governs?* [New Haven, 1961], p. 279). Further supporting evidence may be found in Julian L. Woodward and Elmo Roper, "Political Activity of American Citizens," *American Political Science Review* 44 (December 1950), pp. 872–875; and Samuel Stouffer, *Communism, Conformity and Civil Liberties* (Garden City, N.Y., 1955), Chapter 3. Stouffer, in his 1954 survey, found that "the number of people who said they were worried either about the threat of Communists in the United States or about civil liberties was,

even by the most generous interpretation of occasionally ambiguous responses, less than one percent. Even world problems, including the shadow of war, did not evoke a spontaneous answer from more than eight percent'' (p. 59). Using data from the University of Michigan's Center for Political Studies, Philip E. Converse estimates that those who have consistent and elaborately worked out political views on a variety of topics number about 3.5 percent of the voting population, and those who have some of these attributes number no more than 12 percent. He found that 17.5 percent of the population have attitudes with no issue content whatsoever. See his article ''The Nature of Belief Systems in Mass Politics,'' in David E. Apter, ed., *Ideology and Discontent* (New York, 1964), pp. 206–261, especially the table and commentary on p. 218. The elections of the 1960s and 1970s caused many political scientists to reexamine theories regarding the level of ideology among voters. Norman H. Nie and Kristi Andersen, in their article ''Mass Belief Systems Revisited: Political Change and Attitude Structure,'' *Journal of Politics* 36, 3 (August 1974), pp. 540–591, argue that later data contradict Converse's conclusions. Norman H. Nie, Sidney Verba, and John R. Petrocik take the argument one step further in *The Changing American Voter* (Cambridge, Mass., 1976), especially Chapter 10. There they argue that voters in the 1970s not only developed more consistent attitude structures but were able to assess the proximity of their attitudes to those of one candidate as compared with another, thereby enabling issue voting on a large scale.

These arguments have been attacked on methodological grounds. See John L. Sullivan, James E. Pierson, and George E. Marcus, ''Ideological Constraints in the Mass Public: A Methodological Critique and Some New Findings,'' *American Journal of Political Science* 22 (May 1976), pp. 250–269; and Eric R. A. N. Smith, ''The Levels of Conceptualization: False Measures of Ideological Sophistication,'' *American Political Science Review* 74 (September 1980), pp. 685–696; with comments by Paul R. Abramson, Nie, Verba, and Petrocik, and Smith himself in *American Political Science Review* 75 (March 1981), pp. 146–155. Additional criticisms have been made by David Repass, who suggests that voters' issue positions may be rationalizations after the fact (''Issue Salience and Party Choice,'' *American Political Science Review* 65 [June 1971], pp. 389–400). Philip E. Converse and Gregory B. Markus argue that issue voting has not increased in ''Plus Ca Change . . . The New CPS Election Study Panel,'' *American Political Science Review* 73 (March 1979), pp. 32–49. Finally, John L. Pierce and Paul R. Haynes have repeated Converse's original analysis for all presidential elections from 1956 through 1976. In ''Conceptualization and Party Identification: 1956–1976,'' *American Journal of Political Science* 26 (May 1982), pp. 277–387, they conclude that the amount of issue voting done by citizens has not changed much over a period of twenty years.

2. See Angus Campbell, Philip E. Converse, Warren E. Miller, and Donald E. Stokes, *The American Voter* (New York, 1960), pp. 89–115. Writing of the 1956 presidential election, for example, the authors say that the ''rate of turnout among persons of high interest exceeded that among persons of low interest by nearly 30 percent'' (p. 102). See also Gordon M. Connelly and Harry M. Field, ''The Non-Voter—Who He Is, What He Thinks,'' *Public Opinion Quarterly* 8 (Summer 1944), pp. 175–187. The work of the late Angus Campbell and his associates at the University of Michigan's Survey Research Center (later known as the Center for Political Studies), to which we will refer frequently, is based on

numerous sample surveys of the entire American voting population. These studies, which have been going on since 1948, have through the years increased in breadth and sophistication and at the moment represent the largest pool of data we have on the political attitudes of Americans. The work of the late Paul Lazarsfeld, Bernard Berelson, and their associates and successors at the Columbia Bureau of Applied Social Research has been going on since 1940. Rather than national sample surveys, the BASR group has collected data of a more focused kind, often limited to a single community. The BASR group pioneered the use of panel surveys, which consist of series of re-interviews with the same respondents. For a description and critique of these and other materials we shall be using, see Peter H. Rossi, "Four Landmarks in Voting Research," in Eugene Burdick and Arthur J. Brodbeck, eds., *American Voting Behavior* (Glencoe, Ill., 1959), Chapter 1; and Peter B. Natchez, "Images of Voting: The Social Psychologists," *Public Policy* 17 (Summer 1970), pp. 553–588.

3. The most comprehensive current study of voting participation—based on very large U.S. census surveys—is Raymond E. Wolfinger and Steven J. Rosenstone, *Who Votes?* (New Haven, 1980). See also Bernard Berelson, Paul F. Lazarsfeld, and William N. McPhee, *Voting* (Chicago, 1954), p. 25; Campbell et al., *The American Voter*, pp. 475–483; and Key, *Public Opinion and American Democracy*, pp. 195–199. For a detailed discussion of socioeconomic status and political participation, see Sidney Verba and Norman H. Nie, *Participation in America: Political Democracy and Social Equality* (New York, 1972), especially Chapter 8. For a sensitive but inconclusive discussion of the different forces influencing various types of participation, see Richard A. Brody, "The Puzzle of Political Participation in America," in Anthony King, ed., *The New American Political System* (Washington, D.C., 1987), pp. 287–324.

4. Campbell et al., *The American Voter*, pp. 120–134. Robert E. Lane concludes, "Over the long run party identification has more influence over a person's vote decision than any other single factor. . . ." (*Political Life* [Glencoe, Ill., 1959], p. 300).

5. In general, as the table below shows, voters are more likely to make up their minds early in landslide years.

Timing of Voters' Decisions in Presidential elections, 1948–1984

	1948	1952	1956	1960	1964	1968	1972	1976	1980	1984
Before the nominating conventions	37%	34%	57%	30%	40%	33%	43%	33%	42%	52%
During the conventions	28	31	18	30	25	22	17	20	17	17
During the campaign	25	31	21	36	33	38	35	45	40	30
Don't remember, not ascertained	10	4	4	4	3	7	4	2	1	1
Total	100%	100%	100%	100%	100%	100%	100%	100%	100%	100%
n =	424	1251	1285	1445	1126	1039	1119	1667	958	1402

Sources: For 1948–1980, William H. Flanigan and Nancy H. Zingale, *Political Behavior of the American Electorate,* 5th ed. (Boston, 1983), p. 159, from the Survey Research Center/

Center for Political Studies National Election Studies. For 1984, Warren E. Miller, *American National Election Study 1984: Pre and Post Election Survey File* (Second ICPSR Edition), (Center for Political Studies, University of Michigan: Inter-University Consortium for Political and Social Research), Codebook p. 417. Data rounded to the nearest percent. The authors are solely responsible for the analyses and interpretations of these studies.

Keith et al. show in the following table that "strong identifiers" are quite different from either "weak identifiers" or people who do not claim a party loyalty but will admit "leaning" to one or the other.

Mean Democratic Vote, 1952–1984

Strong Democrats	*84%*	*Strong Republicans*	*3%*
Weak Democrats	63%	Weak Republicans	13%
Independent Democrats	67%	Independent Republicans	11%
	Pure Independents 32%		

These are for white respondents only.

Source: Bruce E. Keith, David B. Magleby, Candice J. Nelson, Elizabeth Orr, Mark C. Westlye, and Raymond E. Wolfinger, *The Myth of the Independent Voter* (forthcoming).

Earlier research did not differentiate among the various sorts of independents and characterized the entire population of independents as comparatively uninvolved in politics, less interested, less concerned, and less knowledgeable than are party identifiers. These generalizations hold better for the truly nonpartisan subset of "pure independents." See Campbell et al., p. 143, and Berelson, Lazarsfeld, and McPhee, pp. 25–27. For a somewhat different treatment, see Robert Agger, "Independents and Party Identifiers," in Burdick and Brodbeck, eds., *American Voting Behavior,* Chapter 17. William H. Flanigan and Nancy H. Zingale use Michigan Center for Political Studies data to conclude, "In all recent elections the independents and weak partisans were more likely to make up their minds during the campaign, while the strong partisans characteristically make their decisions by the end of the conventions" (*Political Behavior of the American Electorate,* 3rd ed. [Boston, 1979], p. 174).

6. Berelson, Lazarsfeld, and McPhee, *Voting,* pp. 215–233. George Belknap and Angus Campbell state that "for many people Democratic or Republican attitudes regarding foreign policy result from conscious or unconscious adherence to a perceived party line rather than from influences independent of party identification" ("Political Party Identification and Attitudes Toward Foreign Policy," *Public Opinion Quarterly* 15 [Winter 1951–1952], p. 623).

7. Various voting studies previously cited contain substantial discussions of this subject. See Robert E. Lane, "Fathers and Sons: Foundations of Political Belief," *American Sociological Review* 24 (August 1959), pp. 502–511; Campbell et al., *The American Voter,* pp. 146–147; H. H. Remmers, "Early Socialization of Attitudes," in Burdick and Brodbeck, eds., *American Voting Behavior,* pp. 55–67. Key, *Public Opinion and American Democracy,* pp. 293–314, sums up in these words: "Children acquire early in life a feeling of party identification; they have sensitive antennae and since they are imitative animals, soon take on the political color of their family. . . ." (p. 294). See, especially, Fred I. Greenstein, *Children and Politics* (New Haven, 1965), Chapter 4. In a more recent work, Paul R. Abramson presents an interesting discussion of this familial link and the forces that later play against it. See *Generational Change in American Politics* (Lexington, Ky., 1975), especially Chapter 3 and 4.

8. ". . . People are more likely to associate with people like themselves—alike in political complexion as well as social position" (Berelson, Lazarsfeld, and McPhee, *Voting*, p. 83). See also Robert D. Putnam, "Political Attitudes and the Local Community," *American Political Science Review* 60 (September, 1966), pp. 640–654, and Ada W. Finifter, "The Friendship Group as a Protective Environment for Political Deviants," *American Political Science Review* 68 (June 1974), pp. 607–626.

9. Paul Lazarsfeld, Bernard Berelson, and Hazel Gaudet, *The People's Choice* (New York, 1944), pp. 16–28.

10. Lazarsfeld, Berelson, and Gaudet, *The People's Choice;* Angus Campbell and Homer C. Cooper, *Group Differences in Attitudes and Votes* (Ann Arbor, 1956); Woodward and Roper, "Political Activity of American Citizens," pp. 872–875; Key, *Public Opinion and American Democracy*, pp. 99–120, 121–181; Berelson, Lazarsfeld, and McPhee, *Voting*, pp. 54–76; Robert Axelrod, "Where the Votes Come from: An Analysis of Electoral Coalitions, 1952–1968," *American Political Science Review* 66 (March 1972); "Communication," *American Political Science Review* 68 (June 1974), pp. 717–720; "Communication," *American Political Science Review* 72 (June 1974), pp. 622–624; and "Communication," *American Political Science Review* 76 (June 1982), pp. 393–396. The following table is a summary of November and December, 1982, and January, 1983, Gallup polls, in which respondents were asked, "In politics, as of today, do you consider yourself a Republican, a Democrat or an Independent?" In recent elections, the Democratic advantage among Catholics has declined but among blacks it has grown. Robert Axelrod, "Presidential Election Coalitions in 1984," *American Political Science Review* 80 (March 1986), pp. 281–284.

11. V. O. Key, Jr., *Southern Politics* (New York, 1950), pp. 75–81, 223–228, 280–285. The formerly solidly Democratic South is becoming more evenly divided in its political loyalties because two trends have outweighed the effects of a third: the migration of Republicans into the South and the conversion of conservative southerners to Republicanism have not been made up for by the increasing turnout of black people who vote overwhelmingly Democratic in presidential elections.

Political Affiliation

	Republican	Democrat	Independent
National	32	39	29
Male	33	36	31
Female	31	42	37
White	35	35	30
Black	9	73	18
Hispanic	24	49	27
College Graduate	39	31	30
College Incomplete	40	31	29
High-School Graduate	30	39	31
Less than High-School Graduate	23	53	24
East	32	39	29
Midwest	31	35	34
South	31	43	26
West	37	38	25
18–29 Years	35	33	32

Political Affiliation (continued)

	Republican	Democrat	Independent
30–49 Years	30	38	32
50–65 Years	31	44	25
65 Years and Over	35	45	20
Income $35,000 and Over	39	32	29
Income $15,000–34,999	32	37	31
Income Under $15,000	27	47	26
Professional and Business	39	31	30
Other White Collar	35	36	29
Blue-Collar Workers	27	42	31
Skilled Workers	29	38	33
Unskilled Workers	26	45	29
Labor Union Members	26	44	30
Nonlabor Union Members	34	38	28

Source: The Gallup Poll: Public Opinion 1986 (Wilmington, Del., 1987), pp. 145–147.

12. Raymond Wolfinger and Michael Hagen, "Republican Prospects: Southern Comfort," *Public Opinion* (October/November 1985), pp. 8–13.

13. V. O. Key, Jr., "A Theory of Critical Elections," *Journal of Politics* 17 (February 1955), pp. 2–13; Campbell et al., *The American Voter,* p. 160. See, more generally, James Q. Wilson, *Negro Politics* (Glencoe, Ill., 1960). Barry Goldwater's 1964 candidacy intensified the Democratic loyalties of black voters. For more recent data on the black vote see Axelrod, "Presidential Election Coalitions in 1984," pp. 281–284.

14. See Duane Lockard, *New England State Politics* (Princeton, 1959); Dahl, *Who Governs?,* pp. 33–51, 216–217; Elmer E. Cornwell, "Party Absorption of Ethnic Groups: The Case of Providence, R. I.," *Social Forces* 38 (March 1960), pp. 205–210; J. Joseph Huthmacher, *Massachusetts People and Politics* (Cambridge, Mass., 1959), pp. 118–126.

15. Samuel Lubell, *The Future of American Politics* (New York, 1951), pp. 129–157.

16. This notion is developed by Anthony Downs, *An Economic Theory of Democracy* (New York, 1957).

17. William Lyons and John M. Scheb, II, "Ideology and Issue Space in the 1988 Election" (paper prepared for the 1989 Annual Meeting of the American Political Science Association, Atlanta, Georgia, August 30–September 1, 1989).

18. See Aaron Wildavsky, "Choosing Preferences by Constructing Institutions: A Cultural Theory of Preference Formation," *American Political Science Review* 81 (March 1987), pp. 3–21; and Michael Thompson, Richard Ellis, and Aaron Wildavsky, *Cultural Theory* (Boulder, Colo., 1990).

19. On Eisenhower see Campbell et al., *The American Voter,* pp. 55–57, 525–528, 537; and Herbert H. Hyman and Paul B. Sheatsley, "The Political Appeal of President Eisenhower," *Public Opinion Quarterly* 19 (Winter 1955–56), pp. 26–39. On McGovern, see Samuel L. Popkin, John W. Gorman, Charles Phillips, and Jeffrey A. Smith, "Comment: What Have You Done for Me Lately? Toward an Investment Theory of Voting," *American Political Science Review* 70 (June 1976), pp. 779–805. On Carter, see Merrill Shanks and Warren Miller, "Policy Directions and Presidential Leadership: Alternative Inter-

pretations of the 1980 Presidential Election," *British Journal of Political Science* 12 (July 1982), pp. 299–356.

20. The portions of this analysis that deal with voters and issues are taken from Chapter 8, "Public Policy and Political Preference," in Campbell et al., *The American Voter,* pp. 168–187.

21. See Hazel Gaudet Erskine, "The Polls: The Informed Public," *Public Opinion Quarterly* 26 (Winter 1962), pp. 669–677. This article summarizes questions asked from 1947 to 1960 of national samples of Americans designed to ascertain their information on current news topics. Similar data for 1935–1946 are contained in Hadley Cantril and Mildred Strunk, *Public Opinion, 1935–1946* (Princeton, 1951). In light of later work, Philip E. Converse was able to conclude: "Surely the most familiar fact to arise from sample surveys in all countries is that popular levels of information about public affairs are, from the point of the informed observer, astonishingly low" ("Public Opinion and Voting Behavior," F. I. Greenstein and N. W. Polsby, eds., *Handbook of Political Science,* Vol. 4 [Reading, Mass., 1975], p. 79).

22. The data on which this conclusion is based refer to issues in rather general categories such as "economic aid to foreign countries," "influence of big business in government," and "aid to education" (Campbell et al., *The American Voter,* p. 182). It is highly probable that the proportion of people meeting the requirements of having an opinion and differentiating among the parties would be substantially reduced if precise and specific policies within these general issue categories formed the basis of questions in a survey. See also Converse, "Public Opinion and Voting Behavior."

23. Campbell et al., in *The American Voter,* tentatively conclude that in the Eisenhower years, covered by their study, "people who paid little attention to politics were contributing very disproportionately to partisan change" (p. 264). Nie, Verba, and Petrocik argue that the American electorate has become more discerning in their electoral choices and that there has been an "increase in consistency among attitudes themselves, . . . increased relationship between attitudes and the vote, and [a] decreased relationship between party identification and the vote. The data suggest that the American public has been entering the electoral arena since 1964 with quite a different mental set than was the case in the late 1950s and early 1960s. They have become more concerned with issues and less tied to their parties" (*The Changing American Voter,* p. 166). Unresolved methodological problems cause us to regard these conclusions with some caution.

24. In the 1980 University of Michigan Center for Political Studies postelection survey, 35 percent of the respondents classified themselves as independents; of these respondents, only one-third did not further specify that they leaned either toward the Democratic or Republican party.

25. Arthur H. Miller, Warren E. Miller, Alden S. Raine, and Thad A. Brown, "A Majority Party in Disarray: Policy Polarization in the 1972 Election," *American Political Science Review* 70 (September, 1976), p. 760. The issues studied include: Vietnam withdrawal, amnesty for draft dodgers, reducing military spending, government health insurance, guaranteed standard of living, urban unrest, campus unrest, protecting the rights of those accused of crime, government aid to minorities, equal rights for women, abortion, legalization of marijuana, busing,

and a "liberal-conservative philosophic position." For similar findings, see Jeane J. Kirkpatrick, "Representation in the American National Conventions: The Case of 1972," *British Journal of Political Science* 5 (July 1975), pp. 265–322, and Kirkpatrick, *The New Presidential Elite* (New York, 1976).

26. Philip E. Converse, "Information Flow and the Stability of Partisan Attitudes," *Public Opinion Quarterly* 26 (Winter 1962), pp. 578–599. John R. Zaller describes some probable exceptions to Converse's model, which we generally follow: "Diffusion of Political Attitudes," *Journal of Personality and Social Psychology* 53 (November 1987), pp. 821–833.

27. Richard A. Brody, Benjamin I. Page, Sidney Verba, and Jerome Laulicht, "Vietnam, the Urban Crisis and the 1968 Presidential Election: A Preliminary Analysis" (paper delivered at the 1969 meeting of the American Sociological Association, San Francisco, California, September 1969). The authors polled four national samples of the electorate during the campaign and asked numerous questions about each issue. For a detailed interpretation of their Vietnam findings, see Benjamin I. Page and Richard A. Brody, "Policy Voting and the Electoral Process: The Vietnam War Issue," *American Political Science Review* 66 (September 1972), p. 979.

28. Page and Brody, "Policy Voting and the Electoral Process: The Vietnam War Issue," pp. 981–986.

29. Miller et al., "A Majority Party in Disarray," pp. 761–772.

30. J. Merrill Shanks and Warren E. Miller, "Policy Direction and Performance Evaluation: Complementary Explanations," *British Journal of Political Science* 20 (April 1990), pp. 143–235.

31. The major revisionist works are John E. Jackson, "Issues, Party Choices, and Presidential Voting," *American Journal of Political Science* 19 (May 1975), pp. 161–186; Jackson, "Issues and Party Alignment," in Louis Maisel and Paul M. Sachs, eds., *The Future of Political Parties* (Beverly Hills, 1975), pp. 101–125; Gregory B. Markus, "The Political Environment and the Dynamics of Public Attitudes: A Panel Study," *American Journal of Political Science* 23 (May 1979), pp. 338–359; Morris P. Fiorina, *Retrospective Voting in American National Elections* (New Haven, 1981); Charles H. Franklin and John E. Jackson, "The Dynamics of Party Identification," *American Political Science Review* 7 (December 1983), pp. 957–1973; and Charles H. Franklin, "Issue Preferences, Socialization and the Evaluation of Party Identification," *American Journal of Political Science* 28 (August 1984), pp. 459–475.

32. Campbell et al., *The American Voter*, p. 148.

33. V. O. Key, Jr., with the assistance of Milton C. Cummings, Jr., *The Responsible Electorate: Rationality in Presidential Voting, 1936–1960* (Cambridge, Mass., 1966).

34. Franklin, "Issues Preferences," p. 460.

35. Ibid., p. 474.

36. Fiorina, *Retrospective Voting in American National Elections* (New Haven, 1981), p. 84.

37. Donald R. Kinder and D. Roderick Kiewiet, "Sociotropic Politics: The American Case," *British Journal of Political Science* 11 (April 1981), pp. 129–161; and Douglas Rivers, "The Dynamics of Party Support in the American Electorate,

1952–1976'' (paper delivered at the 1980 Annual Meeting of the American Political Science Association, Washington, D.C.,August 28–31, 1980).

38. Converse, "The Nature of Belief Systems in Mass Publics"; and Converse and Markus, *"Plus Ça Change . . .* The New CPS Election Study Panel." We think it likely that what we perceive as aggregate party change in the electorate is actually a replacement of old voters by new. This process is strongly suggested for Canada by Richard Johnston in "Party Alignment and Realignment in Canada, 1911–1965," unpublished Ph.D. dissertation, Stanford University, 1976. V. O. Key also supported a mobilization-of-new-voters interpretation in "A Theory of Critical Elections," *Journal of Politics* 17 (February 1955), pp. 3–18. Arthur S. Goldberg's study of American data finds that children tend to defect from the party identification of their parents when the parents' party identification is atypical for their status and the children are relatively well educated ("Social Determinism and Rationality as Bases of Party Identification," *American Political Science Review* 63 [March 1969], pp. 5–25). And Kristi Andersen, in *The Creation of a Democratic Majority 1928–1936* (Chicago, 1979), p. 69, argues that "the surge in the Democratic vote in 1932 and 1936 came primarily from . . . newly mobilized groups": those who came of political age in the 1920s but did not vote until 1928, 1932, or 1936, and those who came of age between 1928 and 1936. On the other side, see the intriguing arguments for opinion change by individual voters in Robert S. Erikson and Kent L. Tedin, "The 1928–1936 Partisan Realignment: The Case for the Conversion Hypothesis," *American Political Science Review* 75 (December 1981), pp. 951–962.

39. Donald R. Kinder, "Enough Already About Ideology: The Many Bases of American Public Opinion" (paper delivered at the 1982 Annual Meeting of the American Political Science Association, Denver, Colorado, September, 1982) pp. 31–32.

40. Bruce E. Keith, David B. Magleby, Candice J. Nelson, Elizabeth Orr, Mark C. Westlye, and Raymond E. Wolfinger, "The Partisan Affinities of Independent Leaners," *British Journal of Political Science* 16 (April 1986), pp. 155–185.

41. Kinder, "Enough Already About Ideology," pp. 23–27. Kinder reports that "between 1956 and 1976, Democratically-inclined Independents voted 70 percent, on the average, for the Democratic candidate (compared to 64 percent for Weak Democrats), while Independent Republicans gave an average of 88 percent of their votes to the Republican nominee (compared to 85 percent for Weak Republicans)" (p. 27). See also Keith et al., "Partisan Affinities of Independent Leaners."

42. Kinder, "Enough Already About Ideology," pp. 27–29.

43. Ibid., pp. 29–31.

44. Nelson W. Polsby, *Consequences of Party Reform* (New York, 1983), p. 87; Raymond E. Wolfinger, "Dealignment, Realignment, and Mandates in the 1984 Election," in Austin Ranney, ed., *The American Elections of 1984* (Durham, N.C., 1985), p. 281; and Paul R. Abramson, John H. Aldrich, and David W. Rohde, *Change and Continuity in the 1988 Elections,* (Washington, 1990), p. 220.

45. See, for example, William J. Crotty and Gary C. Jacobson, *American Parties in Decline* (Boston, 1980) and Martin P. Wattenberg, *The Decline of American Political Parties: 1952–1980* (Cambridge, Mass., 1984).

46. Herbert F. Weisberg, "A Multidimensional Conceptualization of Party Identification," *Political Behavior* 2 (1980), pp. 33–60. See also Keith et al., "Partisan Affinities of Independent Leaners."

47. See Arthur H. Miller and Martin P. Wattenberg, "Measuring Party Identification: Independent or No Partisan Preference," *American Journal of Political Science* 27 (February 1983), pp. 106–121.

48. U.S. Bureau of the Census, *Statistical Abstract of the United States* (Washington, D.C., 1986), p. 255.

49. E. J. Dionne, Jr., "If Nonvoters Had Voted: Same Winner, But Bigger," *New York Times* National Edition (November 21, 1988), p. 10.

50. See Raymond E. Wolfinger, "How to Raise Voter Turnout," *New York Times* (June 6, 1990).

51. G. Bingham Powell, Jr., "American Voter Turnout in Comparative Perspective," *American Political Science Review* 80 (March 1986), pp. 18–43.

52. Greg W. Smith, "Party Organizations and Voter Turnout: The 1988 Elections" (paper prepared for delivery at the 1990 Annual Meeting of the American Political Science Association, San Francisco, August 30–September 2, 1990).

53. Carole Jean Uhlaner, "Turnout in the 1988 American Election" (paper prepared for delivery at the 1989 Annual Meeting of the American Political Science Association, Atlanta, Georgia, August 31–September 3, 1989).

54. U.S. General Accounting Office Report to the Chairman, Subcommittee on Elections, Committee on House Administration, House of Representatives, *Voting: Some Procedural Changes and Informational Activities Could Increase Turnout,* (Washington, D.C., November 1990), pp. 24–28.

55. Paul E. Meehl, "The Selfish Voter Paradox and the Thrown-Away Vote Argument," *American Political Science Review* 71 (March 1977), pp. 11–30.

56. For the early voting literature, see Campbell et al., *The American Voter*. Paul R. Abramson and John H. Aldrich, in "The Decline of Electoral Participation in America," *American Political Science Review* 76 (September 1982), pp. 502–521, state that "the erosion of partisanship in the electorate can explain between 25 and 30 percent of the decline in participation in presidential elections and even more of the decline in off-year congressional elections."

57. For the first half of the argument, see Abramson and Aldrich, "The Decline of Electoral Participation in America"; for the second, see Polsby, *Consequences of Party Reform.*

58. The theory of political behavior that takes as a major explanatory variable the social connectedness of actors is especially well explored in the work of Herbert McClosky and his students. See Jack Citrin, Herbert McClosky, J. Merrill Shanks, and Paul M. Sniderman, "Personal and Political Sources of Alienation," *British Journal of Political Science* 5 (January 1975), pp. 1–31. See also Wolfinger and Rosenstone, *Who Votes?* and Peverill Squire, Raymond Wolfinger, and David Glass, "Presidential Mobility and Voter Turnout," *American Political Science Review* 81 (March 1987), pp. 45–65.

59. See Raymond A. Bauer, Ithiel de Sola Pool, and Lewis Anthony Dexter, *American Business and Public Policy* (New York, 1963), pp. 323–399, especially p. 373. More recently, a similar argument is made in John R. Wright, "PACs,

Contributions, and Roll Calls: An Organizational Perspective,'' *American Political Science Review* 79 (June 1985), pp. 400–414.

60. Jeffrey M. Berry, *Lobbying for the People: The Political Behavior of Public Interest Groups* (Princeton, 1977).

61. See Seymour M. Lipset, Paul F. Lazarsfeld, Allen H. Barton, and Juan Linz, ''The Psychology of Voting: An Analysis of Political Behavior,'' in Gardner Lindzey, ed., *Handbook of Social Psychology* (Cambridge, Mass., 1954).

62. Axelrod, ''Where the Votes Come From: An Analysis of Electoral Coalitions, 1952–1968''; Axelrod, ''Communication,'' *American Political Science Review* 76 (June 1982), p. 394; and Axelrod, ''Presidential Election Coalitions.'' We wish to thank Ben Highton for updating the study for the 1988 election working from American National Elections Studies, Center for Political Studies, University of Michigan; University of California, Berkeley, State Data Program.

63. Harold W. Stanley, William J. Bianco, and Richard G. Niemi, ''Partisanship and Group Support Over Time: A Multivariate Analysis,'' *American Political Science Review* 80 (September 1986), pp. 969–976.

64. Wolfinger and Hagen, ''Republican Prospects.''

65. Wolfinger, ''Dealignment, Realignment, and Mandates,'' p. 290.

66. Ibid., p. 291.

67. Robert Axelrod, ''Communication,'' *American Political Science Review* 76 (June 1982), p. 395, and Axelrod, ''Presidential Election Coalitions.''

68. Campbell et al., *The American Voter*, pp. 483–494.

69. CBS News/*New York Times* 1980 exit polls showed men voting 54 percent Reagan to 37 percent Carter and women 46 percent Reagan to 45 percent Carter (Everett Carll Ladd, ''The Brittle Mandate: Electoral Dealignment and the 1980 Presidential Election,'' *Political Science Quarterly* 96 [April 1981], p. 16).

70. See Kathleen Frankovic, ''Sex and Politics—New Alignments, Old Issues,'' *PS* 15 (Summer 1982), pp. 439–448; and *Public Opinion* 5 (April–May 1982), pp. 21–32.

71. Adam Clymer, ''Polls Show a Married-Single Gap in Last Election,'' *New York Times* (January 6, 1983).

72. Paul Abramson, John Aldrich, and David Rohde, *Change and Continuity in the 1988 Elections*, pp. 123–125.

73. See the data in Frankovic, ''Sex and Politics.''

74. Celinda C. Lake, ''Guns, Butter and Equality, the Women's Vote in 1980'' (paper presented at the 1982 Annual Meeting of the Midwest Political Science Association, April 28–May 1, 1982).

75. Ethel Klein, ''The Gender Gap: Different Issues, Different Answers,'' *The Brookings Review* 3 (Winter 1985), p. 34.

76. Ibid., p. 37.

77. David Osborne, ''Registration Boomerang: The Democrats Delivered the Republican Vote,'' *The New Republic* (February 25, 1985), pp. 14–16.

78. Wolfinger and Rosenstone, *Who Votes?*

79. Berry, *Lobbying for the People*, p. 186.

80. Joseph E. Cantor, "PACs: Political Financers of the '80s," *Congressional Research Service Review* (February 1982), pp. 14–16; Xandra Kayden and Eddie Mahe, Jr., *The Party Goes On* (New York, 1985); and Harold W. Stanley and Richard G. Niemi, *Vital Statistics on American Politics*, 2nd ed. (Washington, D.C., 1990), pp. 100–101.

81. "Corporate Political Action Committees Are Less Oriented to Republicans Than Expected," *Congressional Quarterly* (April 8, 1978), pp. 849–854; and Theodore J. Eismeier and Phillip H. Pollock III, "A Tale of Two Elections: PAC Money in 1980 and 1984" (paper delivered at the 1986 Annual Meeting of the Midwest Political Science Association, Chicago, April 10–12, 1986).

82. Edwin M. Epstein, "Corporations and Labor Unions in Electoral Politics," *Annals of the American Academy of Political and Social Science* 425 (May 1976), p. 49.

83. Ibid., p. 50. For more on PACs, see Crotty and Jacobson, *American Parties in Decline*, pp. 100–155. An especially complete account is Edwin M. Epstein, "PACs and the Modern Political Process" (paper delivered at the conference on "The Impact of the Modern Corporation," Columbia University, New York, 1982). See also Michael J. Malbin, ed., *Parties, Interest Groups and Campaign Finance Laws* (Washington, D.C., 1980); Elizabeth Drew, *Politics and Money* (New York, 1983); and Eismeier and Pollack, "A Tale of Two Elections."

84. Frank J. Sorauf, "Parties and Political Action Committees in American Politics," in Kay Lawson and Peter Merkl, eds., *When Parties Fail* (Princeton, 1988), p. 16.

85. "Access" is the opportunity to press claims upon decision makers. This does not imply that those who have more access are more successful in pressing their claims, but it is generally supposed that claims have a better chance of realization when they are presented repeatedly and auspiciously to decision makers, and by "known" rather than "unknown" claimants. See David B. Truman, *The Governmental Process* (New York, 1951), pp. 264–270.

86. Our interpretation of parties is based largely on E. Pendleton Herring, *The Politics of Democracy* (New York, 1940); V. O. Key, Jr., *Politics, Parties and Pressure Groups*, 4th ed. (New York, 1958); David B.Truman, "Federalism and the Party System," in Arthur Macmahon, ed., *Federalism: Mature and Emergent* (New York, 1955), Chapter 8; Anthony Downs, *An Economic Theory of Democracy* (New York, 1957); and a burgeoning literature on state and local political party organizations. See especially Truman, *The Governmental Process*, pp. 262–287; Sarah McCally Morehouse, *State Politics, Parties and Policy* (New York, 1981); and David Mayhew, *Placing Parties in American Politics* (Princeton, N.J., 1986).

87. An acutely self-satiric evaluation of the purist mentality is contained in the following excerpt from Richard M. Koster's "Surprise Party," *Harper's* (March, 1975), p. 31: "Alan Baron, the sharpest of the young pros, who had coached the liberals brilliantly on the Mikulski and charter commissions, declared that, whatever happened, the conference was a success: we might lose organized labor, but we'd brought in God."

88. Herbert McClosky, Paul J. Hoffman, and Rosemary O'Hara, "Issue Conflict and Consensus Among Party Leaders and Followers," *American Political Science Review* 54 (June 1960), pp. 406–427.

89. Martin Plissner and Warren J. Mitofsky, "The Making of the Delegates, 1968–1988," *Public Opinion* 2 (September/October 1988), p. 46.

90. Herring, *The Politics of Democracy,* especially pp. 272–287. Recent research suggests that political activists who are at one stage recruited to politics by their strong views on one or another set of policy issues or their attachment to a candidate may in time become party regulars with a well developed taste for winning elections. See Robert T. Nakamura and Denis G. Sullivan, "Neo-Conservatism and Presidential Nomination Reforms: A Critique," *Congress and the Presidency* 9 (Autumn 1982), pp. 79–97.

91. See John F. Bibby, "Party Renewal in the National Republican Party," in Gerald M. Pomper, ed., *Party Renewal in America* (New York, 1980), pp. 102–115; and Cornelius P. Cotter and John F. Bibby, "Institutional Development of Parties and the Thesis of Party Decline," *Political Science Quarterly* 95 (Spring 1980), pp. 1–27.

92. Stanley and Niemi, *Vital Statistics on American Politics,* 2nd ed., p. 137.

93. William Prendergast, "Aspects of the Development of Republican State Organization" (paper delivered at the 1961 Annual Meeting of the American Political Science Association, St. Louis, 1961); Daniel M. Ogden, Jr., "Trends in Democratic State Party Organization" (paper delivered at the 1961 Annual Meeting of the American Political Science Association, St. Louis, 1961); Robert J. Huckshorn, *Party Leadership in the States* (Amherst, Mass., 1976), pp. 254–256; and Malcolm E. Jewell and David M. Olson, *American State Political Parties and Elections* (Homewood, Ill., 1978).

94. John F. Bibby, Robert J. Huckshorn, James I. Gibson, and Cornelius P. Cotter, *Party Organization in American Politics* (New York, 1984).

95. Ibid.

96. Ibid.

97. The structure of American political parties is treated, among other places, in Key, *Politics, Parties and Pressure Groups.* The Supreme Court now gives the national convention the right to regulate standards for admission to it, even overriding enactments of state legislatures on the subject of primary elections, and in this important respect national standards can be imposed on state party organizations. See *Cousins* v. *Wigoda,* 419 U.S. 477 (1975) and *Democratic Party of the U.S. et al.* v. *LaFollette et al.,* 450 U.S. 107 (1981). See also Everett Carll Ladd, Jr., with Charles D. Hadley, *Transformations of the American Party System* (New York, 1975); Austin Ranney, *Curing the Mischiefs of Faction: Party Reform in America* (Berkeley, 1975); William Crotty, *Party Reform* (New York, 1983); James Ceaser, *Reforming the Reforms* (Cambridge, Mass., 1982); Gary D. Wekkin, *Democrat versus Democrat* (Columbia, Mo., 1984); and Polsby, *Consequences of Party Reform.*

98. If the federal government ends up subsidizing the national committees instead of individual candidates, the next phase of party reform could give the national parties much greater leverage.

99. For a good brief account, see Richard Cohen, "'Party Help," *National Journal* (August 16, 1986), pp. 1998–2004.

100. Paul S. Herrnson, "Do Parties Make a Difference? The Role of Party Organizations in Congressional Elections," *Journal of Politics* 48 (August 1986), pp. 589–615; quote on p. 598.

101. John A. Ferejohn and Randall L. Calvert, "Presidential Coattails in Historical

Perspective," *American Journal of Political Science* 28 (February 1984), pp. 127–146.

102. David W. Brady and Naomi W. Lynn, "Switched Seat Congressional Districts: Their Effect on Party Voting and Public Policy," *Midwest Journal of Political Science* 17 (August 1973), pp. 528–543.

103. Ferejohn and Calvert, "Presidential Coattails," p. 142.

104. See Joseph A. Schlesinger, "The New American Political Party," *American Political Science Review* 79 (December 1985), pp. 1152–1169, for an interesting argument along these lines.

105. See William S. Livingston, "A Note on the Nature of Federalism," *Political Science Quarterly* 67 (March 1952), pp. 81–95.

106. Polsby, *Consequences of Party Reform,* passim.

107. See Robert R. Alford, *Party and Society* (Chicago, 1963), Chapter 6, "The Politics of Diversity." This reanalysis of a variety of surveys suggests that class-oriented voting in the United States, while it exists, does not polarize voters to the extent that can be found in Great Britain or Australia. See also Axelrod, "Where the Votes Come From," and "Communication."

108. Herbert McClosky et al., "Issue Conflict and Consensus Among Party Leaders and Followers." The authors, who compared large samples of Democratic and Republican leaders on twenty-four major public issues, conclude that "the belief that the two American parties are identical in principle and doctrine has little foundation in fact. Examination of the opinions of Democratic and Republican leaders shows them to be distinct communities of co-believers who diverge sharply on many important issues." They add, "little support was found for the belief that deep cleavages exist among the electorate but are ignored by the leaders. One might, indeed, more accurately assert the contrary, to wit: that the natural cleavages between the leaders are largely ignored by the voters" (pp. 425–426). McClosky et al. found in 1956 that on most issues, the Democratic party elite held positions not only closer to the Democratic rank and file, but also closer to the Republican rank and file than those of the Republican elite. While the party elites still differed significantly from each other in 1972, the tables had turned and the "Republican elite held views that were more representative of the views and values of rank-and-file Democrats than were the views of Democratic delegates." Jeane Kirkpatrick, "Representation in the American National Conventions," p. 287. Differences between the party elites have increased substantially since 1972; see Kent Jennings and Warren Miller, *Parties in Transition* (New York, 1986).

109. Martin Schram, *Running for President: A Journal of the Carter Campaign* (New York, 1977), pp. 92, 93, 114, 150.

110. That such burdens exist as a routine demand on presidential candidates is argued in Nelson W. Polsby, *Political Innovation in America* (New Haven, 1984).

111. In 1960, for example, Minnesota Democrats split among delegates friendly to Senator Hubert Humphrey, to Governor Orville Freeman, and to both. Freeman nominated John F. Kennedy for president. Senator Eugene McCarthy nominated Adlai Stevenson. And most of the delegation ended up voting for Humphrey.

112. Martin P. Wattenberg, "The Decline of Political Partisanship in the United

States: Negativity or Neutrality?'' *American Political Science Review* 75 (December 1981), pp. 941–950.

113. The unit rule is not prescribed in the Constitution or by federal law. Rather, it is the result of individual state action that provides, in all states except Maine, that electors for party nominees are grouped together and elected en bloc on a "general ticket" such that a vote for one elector is a vote for all the electors on that ticket, with the majority vote electing all electors for the state. Senator Thomas Hart Benton said in 1824, "The general ticket system . . . was the offspring of policy. . . . It was adopted by the leading men of [ten states] to enable them to consolidate the vote of the state. . . ." Thomas Jefferson had earlier pointed out that ". . . while ten states choose either by legislatures or by a general ticket it is folly and worse than folly for the other states not to do it." In short, once a few states maximized their impact by using the unit rule, the others followed suit. See *Motion for Leave to File Complaint, Complaint and Brief, Delaware* v. *New York*, No. 28 Original, U.S. Supreme Court, October term, 1966; and Neal R. Peirce, "The Electoral College Goes to Court," *The Reporter* (October 6, 1966). In Maine the electoral votes of each congressional district—of which there are two—are determined by the vote within the district, and the states' two electoral votes that it has by virtue of its senators are cast according to the overall vote in the state as a whole. Here is a summary of the law, taken from *Nomination and Election of the President and Vice President of the United States Including the Manner of Selecting Delegates to National Political Conventions* (Washington, D.C., 1980), p. 356:

Electors shall vote by separate ballot for one person for President and one person for Vice President. A presidential elector is elected from each congressional district and two at large. They shall convene in the Senate chamber in Augusta on the first Monday after the second Wednesday of December at 2:00 P.M. following their election. The presidential electors at large shall cast their ballots for President and Vice President of the political party which received the largest number of votes in the State. The presidential electors of each congressional district shall cast their ballots for the candidates for President and Vice President of the political party which received the largest number of votes in each congressional district.

114. Michael Barone and Grant Ujifusa, *The Almanac of American Politics 1990* (Washington, D.C., 1989), pp. 30, 81, 807.

115. Further confirmation of this view is provided by Steven J. Brams and Morton D. Davis, "The 3/2's Rule in Presidential Campaigning," *American Political Science Review* 68 (March 1974), pp. 113–134; Claude S. Colatoni, Terrence J. Levesque, and Peter D. Ordeshook, "Campaign Resource Allocations Under the Electoral College," *American Political Science Review* 69 (March 1975), pp. 141–152; and John A. Yunker and Lawrence D. Longley, "The Biases of the Electoral College; Who Is Really Advantaged?" in Donald R. Matthews, ed., *Perspectives on Presidential Selection* (Washington, D.C., 1972), pp. 172–203.

116. Schram, *Running for President*, p. 298.

Chapter 2: The Strategic Environment: Resources

1. Our discussion of money in elections owes a great deal to the work of Herbert Alexander who, over the years, has built up an unequaled store of knowledge on

this subject. Recent legislation affecting money in politics includes the Federal Election Campaign Act of 1971, and the Federal Election Campaign Act Amendments of 1974 2 USC 431. For a wide-ranging set of materials on election reform up to and including the 1971 act, see U.S.Senate Select Committee on Presidential Campaign Activities, *Election Reform: Basic References* (Washington, D.C., 1973). A compact summary of the state of the law as of 1975 is contained in U.S. Senate Subcommittee on Privileges and Elections of the Committee on Rules and Administration, *Federal Election Campaign Laws* (Washington, D.C., 1975). For a useful discussion of the law's political implications, see the American Bar Association, *Symposium on Campaign Financing Regulation* (Chicago, 1975) and Jo Freeman, "Political Party Contributions and Expenditures Under the Federal Election Campaign Act: Anomalies and Unfinished Business," *Pace Law Review* 4 (Winter 1984), pp. 267–296. Data about the 1980 election were supplied by Herbert Alexander from his *Financing the 1980 Election* (Lexington, Mass., 1983); 1984 data is from Herbert Alexander, *Financing the 1984 Election* (Lexington, Mass., 1987); and information for 1988 is from Herbert Alexander and Monica Bauer, *Financing the 1988 Election* (Boulder, Colo., 1991).

2. For 1960 figures, see Herbert Alexander, *Financing the 1960 Election* (Princeton, 1962), p. 10. Figures for 1964 are contained in Herbert E. Alexander and Harold B. Meyers, "The Switch in Campaign Giving," *Fortune* (November 1965), pp. 103–108. Figures for 1968 are contained in Herbert Alexander, "Financing Parties and Campaigns in 1968: A Preliminary Report" (mimeo, Citizens Research Foundation, Princeton,1969). Figures for 1972, 1976, and 1980 are contained in Alexander, *Financing the 1980 Election*, p. 110, Table 4–6; 1984 figures are from Alexander, *Financing the 1984 Election*, p. 81. 1988 figures are from Alexander and Bauer, *Financing the 1988 Election*, Table 1-1, p. 1–13.

3. Alexander Heard, *The Costs of Democracy* (Chapel Hill, 1960), pp. 7–8; Herbert E. Alexander, "Financing the Parties and Campaigns," in Paul T. David, ed., *The Presidential Election and Transition, 1960–61* (Washington, D.C., 1961), pp. 116–118; Alexander and Meyers, "The Switch in Campaign Giving," Alexander, "Financing Parties and Campaigns in 1968," p. 2; Herbert Alexander, *Financing the1972 Election* (Lexington, Mass., 1976), pp. 77–78; Herbert Alexander, *Financing the 1976 Election* (Washington, D.C., 1979), p. 166; Alexander, *Financing the 1980 Election*, p. 103; Alexander, *Financing the 1984 Election*, p. 82; and Alexander and Bauer, *Financing the 1988 Election*, p. 4.

4. See Edwin M. Epstein, "Corporations and Labor Unions in Electoral Politics," *Annals of the American Academy of Political and Social Science* 425 (May 1976), pp. 33–58.

5. Elizabeth Drew, conducting interviews during the Carter administration's first weeks in office, had this to report: "A man here said, '[Carter] spent so much time in the campaign saying that he didn't owe anybody anything that nobody thinks they owe him anything.' " "Our Far-Flung Correspondents: Settling In," *The New Yorker* (February 28, 1977), p. 87.

6. Freeman,"Political Party Contributions and Expenditures Under the Federal Election Campaign Act," pp. 280–287.

7. See Brooks Jackson, "Democrats, Outflanked in Previous Elections, Rival GOP in Financing of Presidential Race," *Wall Street Journal* (October 3, 1988), p. A22.

8. See Charles W. Hucker "Political Party Finances: It's David vs. Goliath," *Congressional Quarterly* (June 24, 1978), pp. 1607–1613; Charles W. Hucker,

"Campaign Consultants Portray Candidates as Fiscal Watchdogs," Congres-*sional Quarterly* (July 22, 1978), pp. 1857–1860; William J. Lanouette, "The Selling of the Candidates, 1978," *National Journal* (November 4, 1978), pp. 1772–1777; Edwin M. Epstein, "The PAC Phenomenon: An Overview," *Arizona Law Review* 22 (1980), pp. 355–372; Elizabeth Drew, *Politics and Money: The New Road to Corruption* (New York, 1983); Institute of Politics, John F. Kennedy School of Government, Harvard University, *An Analysis of the Impact of the Federal Election Compaign Act, 1972–1978,* prepared for the Committee on House Administration, U.S. House of Representatives (Washington, D.C., October 1979); and Larry J. Sabato, *The Rise of Political Consultants: New Ways of Winning Elections* (New York, 1981). For the interaction of celebrities and politics, see Ronald Brownstein, *The Power and the Glitter* (New York, 1990).

9. Heard, *The Costs of Democracy,* pp. 18–22, 39; Alexander, "Financing the Parties and Campaigns," p. 118; Alexander and Meyers, "The Switch in Campaign Giving"; Alexander, *Financing the 1972 Elections.*

10. Alexander and Meyers, "The Switch in Campaign Giving."

11. Alexander, *Financing the 1972 Election.*

12. Alexander and Bauer, *Financing the 1988 Election,* p. 42; see table accompanying note 14, below.

13. Heard, *The Costs of Democracy,* p. 6.

14. For expenditure figures, see ibid., pp. 17–24, and for 1956 on, see Alexander, *Financing the 1976 Election.* The table below is adapted from figures in both these books. On the state level, however, the story may be different. See Murray Levin and George Blackwood, *The Compleat Politician* (Indianapolis, 1962), pp. 227–243. In congressional elections the relationship is more complex; money helps to determine the chances and reflects perceptions of the chances of a challenger, as funding is needed to overcome incumbents' advantages, while contributors do not want to fund likely losers. See Gary C. Jacobson, *Money in Congressional Elections* (New Haven and London, 1980).

	Democratic Percentage of Two-Party Vote	Democratic Percentage of Two-Party Expenditures
1932	59	49
1935	652	41
1940	55	35
1944	52	42
1948	52	39
1952	44	45
1956	42	41
1960	50	51
1964	61	37
1968	49	35
1972	37	33
1976	50	47
1980	45	38

Sources: U.S. Bureau of the Census, *Statistical Abstract of the United States 1981* (Washington, D.C., 1981), p. 478; and Herbert E. Alexander, *Financing the 1980 Election* (Lexington, Mass., 1983), p. 109.

Comparable figures for years following 1980 are not available. Note that the table includes prenomination and general election expenditures. In 1984, when the Republicans had a strong, unopposed incumbent, they spent less than half of what Democratic candidates did prior to the convention. In the general election, however, Republicans spent more than Democrats by a large margin—$78.4 to $53.9 million—when "soft" money (money controlled by state and local parties, governed by state and local law, but spent in coordination with the candidate) and independent expenditures are taken into account.

In 1988, when both parties had competitive nomination battles, Republicans outspent Democrats in prenomination spending by a margin of $109.9 million to $83.5 million. In the general election campaign, the Democrats slightly outspent the GOP when all sources are considered:

Funding for the General Election, 1988 (in millions)

	Bush	Dukakis
Limited Funds		
Federal funding	$ 46.1	$ 46.1
National party	8.3	8.3
Unlimited Funds		
Coordinated expenditures[a]	32.5	51.5
Independent expenditures[b]	6.8	.6
Total	$ 93.7	$106.5

[a]Includes money spent by state and local parties, and money spent internally by labor unions, corporations, and associations.
[b]Does not include amounts to oppose candidates: $2.7 million against Dukakis, $140,428 against Bush/Quayle.

Source: Herbert E. Alexander and Monica Bauer, *Financing the 1988 Election*, Table 3.4, p. 41.

15. Alexander and Bauer, *Financing the 1988 Election*, pp. 27–28.
16. Alexander, "Financing the Parties and Campaigns," p. 119.
17. Alexander, *Financing the 1972 Election*, p. 98; and Alexander, *Financing the 1976 Election*, p. 169.
18. Alexander, *Financing the 1976 Election*, p. 246; Alexander, *Financing the 1980 Election; FEC Reports on Financial Activities 1979–1980, Final Report, Presidential Pre-nomination Campaign* (Washington, D.C., October 1981).
19. Alexander, *Financing the 1984 Election*, Table 4–2, p. 149.
20. Alexander and Bauer, *Financing the 1988 Election*, pp. 22–23.
21. Ibid., p. 34; Bruce Babbitt's 1988 attempts to cope with the high-tech requirements of a modern campaign without front-runner money are described in Maxwell Glen, "Running on a Shoestring," *National Journal* (April 25, 1988), pp. 998–1002.
22. Alexander, "Financing Parties and Campaigns in 1968," p. 9.
23. Connally had so much private funding that he chose to refuse federal matching funds so as not to be bound by spending limits. He won one delegate.
24. Michael J. Robinson, "Where's the Beef? Media and Media Elites in 1984," in Ranney, ed., *The American Elections of 1984*, pp. 173–177.

25. Ibid., p. 175.

26. Martin Schram, *Running for President: A Journal of the Carter Campaign* (New York, 1977), p. 55.

27. Ibid., p. 16.

28. See Theodore H. White, *The Making of the President, 1960* (New York, 1961), pp. 71–74.

29. See ibid., pp. 92–110, and Harry W. Ernst, *The Primary That Made a President: West Virginia* (New York, 1962), especially pp. 16–17, 29–31. Several factors appear to have contributed to Humphrey's difficulty in raising money. First and probably foremost, he had very little of his own to draw upon. Second Adlai Stevenson was being indecisive and refused to withdraw from contention. Thus, Stevenson's backers were encouraged to wait and see rather than switch monetary support to Humphrey. Had Stevenson not been in contention, Humphrey might have gotten more money. And third, Humphrey apparently was unwilling to do things that would severely alienate the other candidates or otherwise jeopardize his future associations in the party. He may, therefore, have been restrained from actions that would have aided him. A revealing passage in White, *The Making of the President, 1960* (pp. 109–110) indicates what may have been involved: "In New York, from which so much Stevenson money had originally come to Humphrey's coffers, [Connecticut] Governor Abraham Ribicoff, acting on Kennedy's instructions, warned all Stevensonians that if they continued to finance the hopeless campaign of Hubert Humphrey, Adlai Stevenson would not even be considered for Secretary of State. Where necessary, Kennedy lieutenants were even rougher; in Connecticut, Boss John Bailey informed former Connecticut Senator William Benton . . . that if he continued to finance Humphrey (Benton had already given Humphrey $5,000 earlier in the spring), he would never hold another elective or appointive job for Connecticut. . . ." Benton disputes this story. "It was wholly out of character for John Bailey to say anything like the words Teddy White ascribed to him . . . John Bailey did get in touch with me, but what he said was this: 'Since you gave $5,000 to Hubert's campaign, I want you to even the account by giving $5,000 to Jack Kennedy's campaign.' I told John that if Jack was nominated for the presidency, I would give him $10,000, which I later did." Sidney Hyman, *The Lives of William Benton* (Chicago, 1969), p. 529.

30. Alexander and Bauer, *Financing the 1988 Election*, pp. 22–25.

31. Alexander and Bauer, *Financing the 1988 Election*, p. 46.

32. Quoted in Edwin M. Epstein, "PACs and the Modern Political Process" (paper delivered at a conference on The Impact of the Modern Corporation, Columbia University, November 1982), p. 16. For similar arguments see Elizabeth Drew, *Politics and Money*, and William J. Crotty and Gary C. Jacobson, *American Parties in Decline* (Boston, 1980), pp. 100–105.

33. Quoted in Epstein, "PACs and the Modern Political Process," p. 17.

34. Alexander and Bauer, *Financing the 1988 Election*, p. 25.

35. Quoted in Kay Lawson, "Building Stronger Political Parties in the Eighties: Accountability vs. Power" (typescript, 1982).

36. Alexander, *Financing the 1984 Election*, pp. 173–174.

37. Anthony Corrado, "The Pre-Candidacy PAC Loophole," *The Boston Globe* (May 6, 1990), cited in Alexander and Bauer, *Financing the 1988 Election,* p. 28.

38. Alexander and Bauer, *Financing the 1988 Election,* pp. 14, 17; quote on p. 15; Brooks Jackson, "Politicians Turn to Special Groups to Raise Funds While Avoiding Presidential Campaigning Laws," *Wall Street Journal* (March 7, 1986), p. 46.

39. Michael J. Malbin, "The Problem of PAC Journalism," *Public Opinion* 5 (December/January 1983), p. 16.

40. See the excellent study by John R. Wright, "PACs, Contributions, and Roll Calls: An Organizational Perspective," *American Political Science Review* 79 (June 1985), pp. 400–414.

41. Alexander and Bauer, *Financing the 1988 Election,* p. 10.

42. The sum was set at $20 million in the Federal Election Campaign Act Amendments of 1974. Using 1974 as the base year, this number is increased annually by a cost-of-living adjustment, calculated by the Department of Labor. In1988 the sum was $46.1 million; U.S. Bureau of the Census, *Statistical Abstract of the United States 1990,* p. 55.

43. Herbert E. Alexander and Brian A. Haggerty, *The Federal Election Campaign Act: After a Decade of Political Reform,* Report of a Conference Sponsored by Citizens' Research Foundation, Washington, D.C., April 1981 (Los Angeles, 1981), pp. 28–29.

44. Alexander and Bauer, *Financing the 1988 Election,* p. 10.

45. Fund-raising scandals of the Nixon era are discussed in Mark V. Nadel, *Corporations and Political Accountability* (Lexington, Mass., 1976), pp. 27–28, 30–37.

46. Alexander and Bauer, *Financing the 1988 Election,* p. 28.

47. *1972 Congressional Campaign Finances,* 10 volumes (Washington, D.C., 1973).

48. *Buckley et al.* v. *Valeo et al.,* 424 U.S. 1 (1976). See also Daniel D. Polsby, "Buckley V. Valeo.: The Special Nature of Political Speech," *Supreme Court Review* (1976), pp. 1–43.

49. Howard R. Penniman, "U.S. Elections: Really a Bargain?" *Public Opinion* 7 (June/July 1984), pp. 51–53; see also Herbert Alexander, "Do the Presidential Candidates Need Even More Funds?" *San Diego Union* (October 9, 1988). For an analysis of media biases in reporting on PACs and campaign spending, see Frank J. Sorauf, "Campaign Money and the Press: Three Soundings," *Political Science Quarterly* 102 (Spring 1987), pp. 25–42.

50. In a per curiam opinion, the Court wrote:

The ceiling on personal expenditures, like the limitations on independent expenditures. . . , imposes a substantial restraint on the ability of persons to engage in protected First Amendment expression. The candidate, no less than any other person, has a First Amendment right to engage in the discussion of public issues and vigorously and tirelessly to advocate his own election and the election of other candidates. Indeed, it is of particular importance that candidates have unfettered opportunity to make their views known so that the electorate may intelligently evaluate the candidates' personal qualities and their positions on vital public issues before choosing among them on election day. . . . Section

608 (a)'s ceiling on personal expenditures by a candidate in furtherance of his own candidacy thus clearly and directly interferes with constitutionally protected freedoms.

Buckley v. *Valeo* 424 U.S. 1 (1976).

51. Bill Keller and Irwin B. Arieff, "Special Report: Washington Fund Raisers," *Congressional Quarterly* (May 17, 1980), p. 1335.

52. In October 1968, for example, multimillionaire Steward Mott offered to raise a million dollars for Hubert Humphrey, then in desperate need of cash. Mott "made it clear that the Presidential candidate would have to modify his views on Vietnam." Humphrey refused Mott's offer (Herbert Alexander and H. B. Meyers, "A Financial Landslide for the GOP," *Fortune* [March 1970], p. 187).

53. Quoted in Jasper B. Shannon, *Money and Politics* (New York, 1959), p. 35.

54. See Nadel, *Corporations and Political Accountability*, pp. 27–28, 32, on American Airlines' sense of being a victim of virtual extortion by the Nixon campaign.

55. Heard, *The Costs of Democracy*, pp. 249–258.

56. See ibid., and Shannon, *Money and Politics*, p. 59. On pp. 13–65, Shannon presents a colorful history of American experience in raising money for presidential campaigns.

57. Alexander and Meyers, "The Switch in Campaign Giving," pp. 103–108. In 1968, the Republican pattern of small giving continued, as it has since, augmented by the return to the fold of many large contributors who had defected to President Johnson in 1964. See Alexander, "Financing Parties and Campaigns in 1968."

58. Frank I. Luntz, *Candidates, Consultants, and Campaigns*, (Oxford, 1988), p. 147.

59. Duane Garrett, a San Francisco fund raiser, quoted in "In 1988, Jackson Money Trees Paid Off," *National Journal Convention Special* (July 23, 1988).

60. See Malbin, "The Problem of PAC Journalism." See also Tina Rosenberg, "Diminishing Returns: The False Promise of Direct Mail," *Washington Monthly* (June 1983), pp. 32–38.

61. Alexander and Bauer, *Financing the 1988 Election*, pp. 5–6.

62. Maxwell Glen, "Front-Loading the Race," *National Journal* (November 29, 1986), p. 2883. See also William Crotty and John S. Jackson, III, *Presidential Primaries and Nominations* (Washington, D.C., 1985), pp. 62–68.

63. Glen, "Front-Loading the Race," p. 2883; see also Carol Matlack, "Frayed Finance Law," *National Journal* (March 5, 1988), pp. 591–594.

64. Alexander, *Financing the 1984 Election*, p. 151.

65. Alexander and Bauer, *Financing the 1988 Election*, p. 18.

66. Ibid., p. 39; see Matlack, "Frayed Finance Law," and Alexander, "Do the Presidential Candidates Need Even More Funds?"

67. Glen, "Front-Loading the Race," p. 2883.

68. The provision of the Communications Act that focuses the attention of broadcasters so efficiently is section 315 which says, in part: "If any license shall permit any person who is a legally qualified candidate for any public office to

use a broadcasting station, he shall afford equal opportunities to all other such candidates for that office in the use of such broadcasting station" (*U.S. Code Annotated*, Title 47, section 315). Television stations have few programs of news commentary and these are not usually overtly partisan. (To be sure, the wealthier party may buy more TV time for its candidate, but we have already discussed the limitations of this resource.) Radio news commentary is more ubiquitous, but only those who initially agree with the more highly opinionated commentators are likely to tune in regularly. Consider, however, the impact of television coverage of the 1968 convention in Chicago. Two incidents will suffice to give a sense of the options open to television news directors under special circumstances:

[San Francisco Mayor Joseph] Alioto rose on screen to nominate [Humphrey]; back and forth the cameras swung from Alioto to pudgy, cigar-smoking politicians, to Daley, with his undershot, angry jaw, painting visually without words the nomination of the Warrior of Joy as a puppet of the old machines. Carl Stokes, the black mayor of Cleveland, was next—to second Humphrey's nomination—and then, at 9:55, NBC's film of the bloodshed had finally been edited, and Stokes was wiped from the nation's vision to show the violence in living color.

The Humphrey staff was furious—Stokes is their signature on the Humphrey civil-rights commitment; and Stokes' dark face is being wiped from the nations' view to show blood—Hubert Humphrey being nominated in a sea of blood.

Theodore H. White, *The Making of the President, 1968* (New York, 1969), pp. 300–302.

On the evening of August 28, 1968, according to Richard Pride and Barbara Richards, "NBC showed the same violent event, which lasted less than five minutes, from three different camera angles with three separate reporters and led viewers to believe it was one continuous battle lasting several hours" ("Denigration of Authority? Television News Coverage of the Student Movement," *Journal of Politics* 36 [August 1974], p. 640).

69. See Nathan B. Blumberg, *One-Party Press? Coverage of the 1952 Presidential Campaign in 35 Daily Newspapers* (Lincoln, Neb., 1954); Edwin Emery and Henry L. Smith, *The Press in America* (Englewood Cliffs, N.J., 1954), pp. 714 ff.; and Arthur Edward Rowse, *Slanted News: A Case Study of the Nixon and Stevenson Fund Stories* (Boston, 1975).

70. "11 Dailies Support Ford; 80 for Carter," *Editor and Publisher* (October 30, 1976), pp. 5, 12–13; and John Consoli, "Reagan Backed by 443 Dailies; Carter Trails with 126; Anderson with 30 and 439 Undecided," *Editor and Publisher* (November 1, 1980), pp. 9–13; "A Newspaper Majority for Reagan," *Editor and Publisher* (November 3, 1984), pp. 9–12.

71. Andrew Radolf, "Majority of Newspapers Don't Endorse," *Editor and Publisher* (October 29, 1988), pp. 9–10.

72. The classic formulation by A. J. Liebling is: "With the years, the quantity of news in newspaper is bound to diminish from its present low. The proprietor, as Chairman of the Board, will increasingly often say that he would like to spend 75 cents now and then on news coverage, but that he must be fair to his sharehold-

ers'' (*The Press* [New York, 1961], p. 5). Occasionally, there is evidence of an improvement in the news coverage in some communities when the papers have been taken over by the more responsible chains. Cases in point would include Philadelphia and San Jose, where the Knight-Ridder chain upgraded newspapers they purchased there.

73. Bernard C. Cohen, in *The Press and Foreign Policy* (Princeton, 1963), presents figures from a variety of sources on foreign affairs news (Chapter 4). His conclusion: ''The volume of coverage is low.'' See also Elie Abel, ed., *What's News, the Media in American Society* (San Francisco, 1981).

74. Here is an example, atypical but illuminating, of this aimlessness at work. Former House Speaker Joseph Martin in his memoirs describes the appearance of an editorial mildly critical of presidential candidate Thomas E. Dewey in Martin's own newspaper (Martin was nominally editor and publisher) on the day of Dewey's arrival in Martin's hometown during the 1948 campaign. ''Behind all this fuss was a very simple explanation. Having a small staff, the *Evening Chronicle* bought 'boilerplate' editorials prepared by a syndicate. The day of Dewey's visit, the editorial in question happened to be on the top of the pile, and a man in the composing room slapped it into the paper. Ironically, I never read the editorial until it was well on its way to fame'' (Joseph W. Martin, Jr., *My First Fifty Years in Politics,* as told to Robert J. Donovan [New York, 1960], pp. 196–197).

75. This issue is carefully studied and evaluated by Edwin Bayley, *Joe McCarthy and the Press* (Madison, Wis., 1981). See also Richard Rovere, *Senator Joe McCarthy* (New York, 1959), pp. 137, 162–69.

76. See Frank Luther Mott, *The News in America* (Cambridge, Mass., 1952), p. 110; and Emery and Smith, *The Press in America,* pp. 541 ff.

77. ''Electronic Update 1988,'' *National Journal* (November 21, 1987), p. 2967.

78. See William L. Rivers, ''The Correspondents after 25 Years,'' *Columbia Journalism Review* 1 (Spring 1962). On p. 5 he says, ''In 1960, 57 percent of the daily newspapers reporting to the *Editor and Publisher* poll supported Nixon, and 16 percent supported Kennedy. In contrast, there are more than three times as many Democrats as there are Republicans among the Washington newspaper correspondents; slightly more than 32 percent are Democrats, and fewer than 10 percent are Republicans. . . . More than 55 percent of the correspondents for newspapers consider themselves liberals; 26.9 percent consider themselves conservatives.'' More recently, see Stephen Hess, *The Washington Reporters* (Washington, D.C., 1981), pp. 87 ff.; S. Robert Lichter and Stanley Rothman, ''Media and Business Elites,'' *Public Opinion* (October/November 1981), pp. 42–46, 59–60; and William Schneider and I. A. Lewis, ''Views on the News,'' *Public Opinion* (August/September 1985), pp. 6–11, 58.

79. Michael J. Robinson, ''Just How Liberal is the News? 1980 Revisited,'' *Public Opinion* (February/March 1983), pp. 55–60.

80. For a definitive, thorough pictorial commentary, see Nathanael West, *Miss Lonely Hearts* (New York, 1933).

81. See Richard Brody and Catherine R. Shapiro, ''A Reconsideration of the Rally Phenomenon in Public Opinion,'' in Samuel Long, ed., *Political Behavior An-*

nual, Vol. 2 (Boulder, Colo., 1989); John E. Mueller, "Presidential Popularity from Truman to Johnson," *American Political Science Review* 64 (March 1970), pp. 18–34; and Kenneth N. Waltz, "Electoral Punishment and Foreign Policy Crises," in James N. Rosenau, ed., *Domestic Sources of Foreign Policy* (New York, 1967), pp. 263–293.

82. Amos Tversky and Daniel Kahneman, "Rational Choice and the Framing of Decisions," *Journal of Business* 59 (1986), pp. S251–78.

83. Aaron Wildavsky and Karl Dake, "Theories of Risk Perception: Who Fears What and Why," *Daedalus* 119 (Fall 1990), pp. 41–60.

84. See White, *The Making of the President, 1960*, pp. 333–338. Corroborative testimony is given by Benjamin C. Bradlee, *Conversations with Kennedy* (New York, 1975). On Barry Goldwater's press relations, see Charles Mohr, "Requiem for a Lightweight," *Esquire* (August 1968), pp. 67–71, 121–122.

85. Witcover, *The Resurrection of Richard Nixon*, p. 173. See also pp. 188–192.

86. Timothy Crouse, *The Boys on the Bus* (New York, 1972, 1973), pp. 189–190; Theodore H. White, *The Making of the President, 1972* (New York, 1973), pp. 251–268; Witcover, *The Resurrection of Richard Nixon;* and Joe McGinniss, *The Selling of the President, 1968* (New York, 1969).

87. Robinson, "Where's the Beef?" However, if the influence of television commentary is a guide, unfavorable reporting may well diminish a candidate's support from the higher levels it otherwise would have achieved. See Michael J. Robinson, "News Media Myths and Realities: What the Network News Didn't Do in the 1984 General Election," in Kay Lehman Schlozman, ed., *Elections in America* (Boston, 1987), pp. 143–177.

88. Elmo Roper observed that "on the civil rights issue [in 1948], Mr. Dewey draws the support of voters favoring exactly opposite things, and more than that, each side thinks Dewey agrees with them" (Hugh A. Bone, *American Politics and the Party System* [New York, 1955], p. 477). In 1968, the bulk of those voting for Eugene McCarthy in the New Hampshire primary were not Vietnam "doves," as McCarthy was, but were even more belligerent about the war than Lyndon Johnson. See Converse, "Public Opinion and Voting Behavior," p. 81.

89. When asked by the Gallup Poll in 1979 to gauge how much confidence they had in newspapers, among other institutions, 51 percent or the respondents said "a great deal or quite a lot," 47 percent said "some or very little" 1 percent said "none," and 1 percent had no opinion. The Gallup Poll, *Public Opinion 1979* (Wilmington, Del., 1980), p. 159. In 1980 only 42 percent said "a great deal or quite a lot." *Public Opinion 1980* (Wilmington, Del., 1981), p. 247. By 1986 the number of respondents saying "a great deal or quite a lot" had shrunk to 37 percent. *The Gallup Poll 1986* (Wilmington, Del., 1987), p. 275.

90. This paragraph summarizes the major findings of researchers on what has come to be called the "two-step flow" of information. See Elihu Katz and Paul F. Lazarsfeld, *Personal Influence* (Glencoe, Ill., 1955).

91. V. O. Key, Jr., *Public Opinion and American Democracy* (New York, 1961), p. 453.

92. Preponderant academic opinion argues that the media have little effect on candidate and issue preferences. See Benjamin I. Page, Robert Y. Shapiro, and Glenn

R. Dempsey, "What Moves Public Opinion?" *American Political Science Review* 81 (March 1987), pp. 23–44.

93. David W. Moore, "The Manchester Union Leader in the New Hampshire Primary," pp. 104–126 in Gary R. Orren and Nelson W. Polsby, ed., *Media and Momentum* (Chatham, N.J., 1987).

94. The table below shows the growing perference for television over newspapers as a primary source of news.

Source of most news:	1959	1961	1963	1964	1967	1968	1971	1972	1974	1976	1978
Television	51%	52%	55%	58%	64%	59%	60%	64%	65%	64%	67%
Newspapers	57	57	53	56	55	49	48	50	47	49	49
Radio	34	34	29	26	28	25	23	21	21	19	20
Magazines	8	9	6	8	7	7	5	6	4	7	5
People	4	5	4	5	5	4	5	4	4	5	5
Don't know/ no answer	1	3	3	3	2	3	1	1	—	—	—

Question: "First, I'd like to ask you where you usually get most of your news about what's going on in the world today—from the newspapers or radio or television or magazines or talking to people or where?"

Source: *Public Opinion* 2 (August/September, 1979), p. 30.

95. Examples would be instances where candidates were not known to voters before the campaign or where they ran without benefit of party labels, as in local nonpartisan elections. See Charles R. Adrian, "Some General Characteristics of Nonpartisan Elections," *American Political Science Review* 46 (September 1952), pp. 766–776; Charles E. Gilbert and Christopher Clague, "Electoral Competition and Electoral Systems in Large Cities," *Journal of Politics* 24 (May 1962), pp. 323–349, especially p. 344; and Raymond E. Wolfinger and Fred I. Greenstein, "The Repeal of Fair Housing in California: An Analysis of Referendum Voting," *American Political Science Review* 62 (September 1968), pp. 753–769.

96. Robert S. Ericson, "The Impact of Newspaper Endorsements on Presidential Elections" (paper delivered at the annual meeting of the American Political Science Association, 1974).

97. Angus Campbell, Philip E. Converse, Warren E. Miller, and Donald E. Stokes, *The American Voter* (New York, 1960), pp. 58, 530.

98. See Nelson W. Polsby, "The Iowa Caucuses in a Front-Loaded System: A Few Historical Lessons" in Peverill Squire, *The Iowa Caucuses and the Presidential Nominating Process* (San Francisco, 1989), pp. 149–162.

99. C. Anthony Broh, "Public Opinion, Polling and the Press: The Race for the Presidency" (working paper, Institute of Policy Sciences and Public Affairs, Duke University, 1979), p. 26.

100. Gary R. Orren, "The Nominating Process," in Austin Ranney, ed., *The American Elections of 1984*, pp. 53–54; for an analysis of network news and the 1984 campaign, see Allan R. Gutkin, "Network Coverage of the 1984 Campaign: From Iowa to New Hampshire," unpublished paper, Stanford University, 1984.

101. See Richard L. Rubin, *Press, Party and Presidency* (New York, 1981), pp. 191–

196. "Not only was [television journalists'] affirmation of primaries clear from the vastly disproportionate air time given primaries compared to other selection methods, but also numerous phrases attributing inherent democratic values to primaries appeared, sprinkled liberally throughout network news" (p. 193).

102. Nelson W. Polsby, *Consequences of Party Reform* (New York, 1983), passim.

103. For an early discussion of this phenomenon, see Stanley Kelley, *Professional Public Relations and Political Power* (Baltimore, 1956). See also Larry J. Sabato, *The Rise of Political Consultants: New Ways of Winning Elections* (New York, 1981).

104. S. Robert Lichter and Stanley Rothman, "The Media Elite and American Values," *Public Opinion* (October/November 1981), pp. 42–46, 59–60.

105. Gary R. Orren, "The Nominating Process," pp. 53–54.

106. See, for example, Jules Witcover's comments about reporters' attempts to deny Gerald Ford the advantage of the White House. Jules Witcover, *Marathon* (New York, 1977), pp. 528–556.

107. Robinson, "News Media Myths and Realities," p. 144.

108. William C. Adams, "Recent Fables About Ronald Reagan," *Public Opinion* (October/November, 1984), pp. 6–9.

109. Michael C. Robinson, Maura Clancy, and Lisa Grand, "With Friends Like These . . ." *Public Opinion* (June/July 1983), pp. 2–3. The possibility that the media may play a larger part than heretofore suspected in presidential elections is reinforced by a study of how opinion on public policy is affected by media coverage. Studying television reporting on various issues, and using before and after opinion polls on the same subject, Page et al. concluded that a "single, 'probably pro' commentary ["from the anchor person, reporters in the field, or special commentators"] is associated with more than four percentage points of opinion change. This is a startling finding . . ."; it has appeared in three separate studies by the authors. See Benjamin I. Page, Robert Y. Shapiro, and Glenn R. Dempsey, "What Moves Public Opinion?" *American Political Science Review* 81 (March 1987), p. 31.

110. Robinson, "News Media Myths and Realities," pp. 146–147; for an analysis of the effects of media coverage on the 1988 race, see David P. Fan and Albert R. Tims, "The Impact of the News Media on Public Opinion: American Presidential Election 1987–1988," *International Journal of Public Opinion* 1 (Summer 1989), pp. 151–163.

111. Ibid., p. 149.

112. Robinson, "Where's the Beef?" p. 202.

113. Doris A. Graber, "Kind Pictures and Harsh Words: How Television Presents the Candidates," in Schlozman, ed., *Elections in America*, pp. 127, 135. However, in 1988, media portrayals of Bush and Dukakis may have been closer to public perceptions; see Thomas E. Patterson, "The Press and Candidate Images," *International Journal of Public Opinion Research* 1 (Summer 1989), pp. 123–135.

114. Shanto Iyengar and Donald R. Kinder, *News That Matters*, (Chicago, 1986).

115. Nelson W. Polsby, "The Democratic Nomination," in Austin Ranney, ed., *The American Elections of 1980* (Washington, D.C., 1981), pp. 37–60; and *The Gallup Opinion Index*, Report #183 (December 1980), p. 51. Another example

occurred during the 1964 campaign, when United States vessels in the Gulf of Tonkin were fired upon and President Johnson took to the airwaves to promise vigorous defensive measures. In late July, just before the incident, he received favorable ratings from 59 percent of the voters, to 31 percent for Goldwater; in early August, just after the incident, the president's score went up to 65 percent, and Goldwater's declined to 29 percent (American Institute of Public Opinion Survey, released October 18, 1964). For other examples, see Nelson W. Polsby, *Congress and the Presidency* (Englewood Cliffs, N.J., 1986), p. 73.

116. Witcover, *The Resurrection of Richard Nixon,* pp. 462–463.

117. Howard S. Bloom and H. Douglas Price, "Voter Response to Short-Run Economic Conditions: The Asymmetric Effect of Prosperity and Recession," *American Political Science Review* 69 (December 1975), pp. 1240–1254.

118. A good indicator of whether or not people were better off in 1980 is real disposable income per capita, which according to the following figures taken from Survey of Current Business increased by about 10 percent in constant dollars between 1976 and 1980:

Disposable Personal Income Per Capita

	1976	1980
Current Dollars	$5,477	$8,176
1972 Dollars	4,158	4,571

Sources: U.S. Department of Commerce, Bureau of Economic Analysis, *Survey of Current Business* 61 (March 1981), p. 10; *Survey of Current Business* 62 (July 1982), p. 37.

119. For Truman, see Harry S. Truman, *Years of Trial and Hope* (Garden City, N.Y., 1956), pp. 499–503, and Alben Barkley, *That Reminds Me* (Garden City, N.Y., 1954), pp. 225–232. For Johnson, see White, *The Making of the President, 1968,* passim.

120. See Samuel P. Huntington, *American Politics: The Promise of Disharmony* (Cambridge, Mass., 1981); Huntington, "The Democratic Distemper," *The Public Interest* 41 (Fall 1975), pp. 9–38; Aaron Wildavsky, "The Past and Future Presidency," *The Public Interest* 41 (Fall 1975), pp. 56–76; and Wildavsky, "Government and the People," *Commentary* 56 (August 1973), pp. 25–32.

121. Much of the material in this section is adapted from Nelson W. Polsby, *Political Promises: Essays and Commentary on American Politics* (New York, 1974), Chapter 5.

122. The following discussion draws from Nelson W. Polsby, "The American Election of 1988: Outcome, Process, and Aftermath," Ernest Fraenkel Lectures (Berlin, 1989), pp. 1–23.

123. Ray C. Fair, "The Effect of Economic Events on Votes for President: 1984 Update," *Political Behavior* 10, No. 2 (1988), pp. 168–179; Larry Bartels, "Economic Consequences of Retrospective Voting" (July 1988), unpublished manuscript; Alan Abramowitz, "An Improved Model for Predicting Presidential Election Outcomes," *PS* 21 (Fall 1988), pp. 843–847.

124. Jerry Roberts, "What Dukakis Did Wrong," *San Francisco Chronicle* (November 10, 1988), p. A3.

125. Polsby, *Consequences of Party Reform.*

126. Finley Peter Dunne, *Dissertations by Mr. Dooley* (New York, 1906), p. 118.

127. Harry S Truman, *Memoirs: Year of Decisions* (Garden City, N.Y., 1955), pp. 19, 53.

128. Ross Baker, "The Second Reagan Term," in Gerald Pomper, ed., *The Elections of 1984: Reports and Interpretations* (Chatham, N.J., 1985), p. 150.

129. Howard Reiter, *Selecting the President* (Philadelphia, 1985), p. 119–120.

Chapter 3:   The Nomination Process

1. Ronald Brownstein, "Getting an Early Start," *National Journal* (November 29, 1986), pp. 2876–2881. The 1992 race started unusually slowly; in February 1991, not a single Democratic presidential hopeful was willing to travel to New Hampsire for that states's annual party fund-raising dinner."Have Mouth, Will Travel," *National Journal* (January 5, 1991), p. 3.; see also James A. Barnes, "Why Me?" *National Journal* (December 22, 1990), pp. 3070–3074.

2. Much of the discussion in this chapter is drawn from our own observations via the mass media of the nomination process, the personal observations of one of us who attended the Democratic National Conventions of 1960, 1968, 1972, and 1980 and the Republican National Conventions of 1964 and1980, and from a classic set of basic texts on American parties and elections, including Moisei Ostrogorski, *Democracy and the Party System in the United States* (New York, 1910); C. E. Merriman and H. Gosnell, *The American Party System* (New York, 1929); Peter H. Odegard and E. A. Helms, *American Politics* (New York, 1938); Pendleton Herring, *The Politics of Democracy* (New York, 1940); E. E. Schattschneider, *Party Government* (New York, 1942); D. D. McKean, *Party and Pressure Politics* (Boston, 1949); V. O. Key, Jr., *Politics, Parties and Pressure Groups*, 4th ed. (New York, 1958); H. R. Penniman, *Sait's Parties and Elections* (New York, 1952); Austin Ranney and Willmoore Kendall, *Democracy and the American Party System* (New York, 1956); William Goodman, *The Two-Party System in the United States* (Princeton, 1960); and Gerald M. Pomper, *Nominating the President: The Politics of Convention Choice,* 2nd ed.(New York, 1966).

   We also found quite useful a more specialized literatue on nominations, including Paul T. David, Malcolm C. Moos, and Ralph M. Goldman, *Presidential Nominating Politics in 1952,* Vols. 1–5 (Baltimore, 1954); Paul T. David, Ralph M. Goldman, and Richard C. Bain, *The Politics of National Party Conventions* (Washington, D.C., 1960); and Richard C. Bain *Convention Decisions and Voting Records* (Washington, D.C., 1960). More recent texts on party organization and presidential nominations that a student might find useful include Samuel J. Eldersveld, *Political Parties in American Society* (New York, 1982); Joel L. Fleishman, ed., *The Future of American Political Parties* (Englewood Cliffs, N.J., 1982); Howard Reiter, *Selecting the President* (Philadelphia, 1985); William J. Crotty and Gary C. Jacobson, *American Parties in Decline* (Boston, 1980); Gerald M. Pomper, *Elections in America: Control and Influence in Democratic Politics*, revised ed. (New York, 1980); Nelson W. Polsby, *Consequences of Party Reform,* (New York, 1983); and Everett Carll Ladd, Jr. with Charles D. Hadley, *Transformations of the American Party System,* 2nd ed. (New York, 1978).

3. Commission on Party Structure and Delegate Selection, *Mandate for Reform* (Washington, D.C., 1970), pp. 14–15.

4. See Democratic National Committee (Charles T. Manatt, Chairman), *Delegate*

Selection Rules for the 1984 Democratic National Convention (Washington, D.C., March 26, 1982). For a discussion of some of the consequences of the rules in the case of the 1980 convention, see Rhodes Cook, "Democrats Adopt New Rules for Picking Nominee in 1980," *Congressional Quarterly Weekly Report* (June 17, 1978), pp. 1571–1572.

5. On December 10, 1986, the Supreme Court ruled five to four that states could not compel parties to hold primaries closed to members of other political parties. The Court reaffirmed the right of the Connecticut Republican party to allow independents to vote in its primary. The majority (led by Justice Thurgood Marshall and joined by Justices William Brennan, Byron White, Harry Blackmun, and Lewis Powell) argued that the state government could not limit the associational rights of political parties in violation of the First Amendment to the Constitution. Their opinion did not reach the question of whether or not only independents but also members of other parties could be prevented by state laws from voting in any primary to which parties chose to admit them. In dissent Justice Antonin Scalia, joined by Chief Justice William Rehnquist and Justice Sandra Day O'Connor contended that "The Connecticut voter who, while steadfastly refusing to register as a Republican, casts a vote in the Repulican primary, forms no more meaningful an 'association' with the party than does the independent or the registered Democrat who responds to questions by a Republican Party pollster. If the concept of freedom of association is extended to such casual contacts, it ceases to be of any analytic use." In a separate dissent, Scalia joined Justice John Paul Stevens in arguing that since the Connecticut law did not apply to state offices it violated the constitutional provision that qualifications for voting for members of Congress be the same as those for the most numerous branch of the state legislature. 107 S. Ct. 557. See *Tashjian* vs. *Republican Party of Connecticut* 107 S. Ct. 544 (1986).

6. Rhodes Cook, "In '88 Contest, It's What's Up Front That Counts," *Congressional Quarterly Weekly Report* (August 23, 1986), pp. 1997–2002.

7. Maxwell Glenn, "Front-Loading the Race: Because of the Accelerated Timetable for the 1988 Presidential Nominating Contests, Ample Financial Resources Will Be More Important than Ever to Candidates," *National Journal* (November 29, 1986), p. 2882.

8. As the *New York Times* mused: "Now, a full year before the first 1984 delegate selection, the competition for attention among hopefuls is so intense that a new device has been introduced into national politics: the announcement of the announcement.

In mid-January, campaign planners for Senator Alan Cranston let it be known that the California Democrat would announce his candidacy February 2. The result: a small story, followed by a bigger one—more prominence than would have resulted otherwise. Planners for Senator Gary Hart observed this gambit and promptly let it be known that he would announce February 17. Planners for Walter F. Mondale said, not for attribution, that their man would do his thing on February 21; off the record, they said, the event would be in St. Paul. Later they distributed a schedule confirming these rumors.

Representative Morris K. Udall handled his different problem differently. His staff let it be known that he would announce his Presidential decision in a speech at the National Press Club last Wednesday. The day before, too late to affect attendance materially, a few reporters were told the Arizonan had reluctantly decided not to run after all.

Planners for Senator John Glenn, who is generally regarded as a little slower off the mark than the other Democratic competitors, have been willing to say only that they will not have an announcement about his announcement until March or April. Come to think of it, maybe that's a story."

Phil Gailey and Warren Weaver, Jr., "The New Announcement," *New York Times* (February 14, 1983).

9. The Republican candidates in June 1987 were Vice-President George Bush, Senator Robert Dole of Kansas, Delaware ex-Governor Pierre du Pont IV, the Reverend Pat Robertson, Representative Jack Kemp of New York, ex-Senator Paul Laxalt of Nevada, and former Secretary of State Alexander Haig. The Democrats were Massachusetts Governor Michael Dukakis, Senator Joseph Biden of Delaware, Reverend Jesse Jackson, former Arizona Governor Bruce Babbitt, Representative Richard Gephardt of Missouri, Senator Paul Simon of Illinois, and Tennessee Senator Albert Gore, Jr.

10. Tom Fiedler, "Sex Lives Become an Issue for Presidential Hopefuls," *Miami Herald* (April 27, 1987).

11. See William Cavala, "Changing the Rules Changes the Game: Party Reform and the 1972 California Delegation to the Democratic National Convention," *American Political Science Review* 68 (March 1974), p. 31, n. 20.

12. "Muskie Campaign: Cautious Pace by the Man in Front," *Congressional Quarterly* (April 16, 1971), p. 857.

13. Quoted in Ernest R. May and Janet Fraser (eds.) *Campaign '72: The Managers Speak* (Cambridge, Mass., 1973), p. 35.

14. *National Journal* (November 19, 1986), p. 2880.

15. Rhodes Cook, "In '88 Contest, It's What's Up Front That Counts," pp. 1997–2002.

16. Our discussion of Iowa and New Hampshire borrows freely from Nelson W. Polsby, "The Iowa Caucuses in a Front-Loaded System: A Few Historical Lessons," in Peverill Squire, ed., *The Iowa Caucuses and the Presidential Nominating Process* (San Francisco, 1989). See also Squire, ed., *The Iowa Caucuses;* Gary R. Orren and Nelson W. Polsby, eds., *Media and Momentum* (Chatham, N.J., 1987); "Special Report: Political Odd Couple"; W. John Moore, "Rural Prospecting"; and Burt Solomon, "Where America Is At," all *National Journal* (September 26, 1987), pp. 2394–2409; "When Iowa becomes Brigadoon," *The Economist* (January 9, 1988), pp. 21–22; "Iowa," *Congressional Quarterly Weekly Report* (August 29, 1987), pp. 1994–1997; and "The Iowa Democratic Caucuses: How They Work," *New York Times* (February 7, 1988).

17. William C. Adams, "As New Hampshire Goes" in Orren and Polsby, eds., *Media and Momentum*, pp. 42–59, esp. p. 43.

18. *Presidential Campaign Hotline* (January 4, 1988), pp. 15–16.

19. *Congressional Quarterly* (August 6, 1988), p. 2161.

20. *Presidential Campaign Hotline* (January 5, 1988), pp. 16–17.

21. Indeed, Henry Brady and Richard Johnston argue that the main educational effect of the entire primary process for voters is to inform them about candidate viability. See "What's the Primary Message: Horse Race or Issue Journalism" in Orren and Polsby, eds., *Media and Momentum*, pp. 127–186.

22. See Nelson W. Polsby, *Consequences of Party Reform* (New York, 1983) for the full argument to this effect, and, for copious evidence, Byron Shafer, *Quiet Revolution: The Struggle for the Democratic Party and the Shaping of Post-Reform Politics* (New York, 1983).

23. See R. W. Apple, Jr. "Iowa's Weighty Caucuses: Significance By Accident," *New York Times* (January 25, 1988). In 1976 the Iowa caucuses were held on January 19; in 1980 on January 21; in 1984 on February 20.

24. As Muskie told Theodore White:

   That previous week . . . I'd been down to Florida, then I flew to Idaho, then I flew to California, then I flew back to Washington to vote in the Senate, and I flew back to California, and then I flew into Manchester and I was hit with this "Canuck" story. I'm tough physically, but no one could do that. . . .

   Theodore H. White *The Making of the President 1972* (New York, 1973), pp. 81–82.

25. R. W. Apple, Jr.,"Carter Defeats Bayh by 2–1 in Iowa Vote" *New York Times* (January 20, 1976).

26. "Ford's 1976 Campaign for the GOP Nomination," *1976 Congressional Quarterly Almanac* (Washington, 1976), p. 900.

27. Elizabaeth Drew writes of Carter:

   Early successes and surprises were big elements in Carter's plan. . . . The basic idea was to show early that the southerner could do well in the North and could best Wallace in the South. . . . He visited a hundred and fourteen towns in Iowa, beginning in 1975 (and his family made countless other visits). . . .

   American Journal: The Events of 1976 (New York, 1977), pp. 143–144, 466–467. See also Jules Witcover, *Marathon: The Pursuit of the Presidency 1972–1976* (New York, 1977), p. 14.

28. See Drew, *American Journal,* Witcover, *Marathon,* passim.

29. See Witcover, *Marathon,* pp. 202–205; Drew, *American Journal,* passim; Martin Schram, *Running for President 1976* (New York, 1977), pp. 13–15.

30. Apple, "Carter Defeats Bayh." This was not the first time in 1976 that Apple had puffed Carter. Elizabeth Drew's diary of January 27, 1976 reported:

   A story by R. W. Apple, Jr. in the *Times* last October saying that Carter was doing well in Iowa was itself a political event, prompting other newspaper stories that Carter was doing well in Iowa, and then more new magazine and television coverage for Carter than might otherwise have been his share. *American Journal,* p. 6.

31. Drew, *American Journal,* p. 16.

32. Nelson W. Polsby, "The Democratic Nomination," in Austin Ranney (ed.), *The American Election of 1980* (Washington, 1981), pp. 47–48.

33. Ibid., p. 49.

34. Jack Germond and Jules Witcover, *Blue Smoke and Mirrors* (New York, 1981), p. 96.

35. David W. Moore, "The Manchester Union Leader in the New Hampshire Primary," in Orren and Polsby, eds., *Media and Momentum,* pp. 104–126, esp. pp. 116, 123.

36. Nelson W. Polsby, "The Democratic Nomination and the Evolution of the Party

System," in Austin Ranney, ed., *The American Elections of 1984* (Durham, N. C., 1985), pp. 36–65. In the eight day gap between Iowa and New Hampshire Gary Hart went from 10 percent in the public opinion polls to a 41 percent vote in the New Hampshire primary itself. See Peter Hart's comments in the *Presidential Campaign Hotline* (January 25, 1988), p. 19.

37. Mickey Kaus, et al., "Yes We Have a Front-Runner," *Newsweek* (July 20, 1987); Richard Berke, "Iowa Eclipsing New Hampshire Among Hopefuls," *New York Times* (September 6, 1987); Thomas B. Edsall and David S. Broder, "Dukakis's New Hampshire Campaign Not Unraveled by Biden Videotape," *Washington Post* (October 3, 1987); Mickey Kaus, et al., "Now, a Dukakis Fiasco," *Newsweek* (October 12, 1987); Maralee Schwartz, "Dukakis Still a Top Fund-Raiser," *Washington Post* (November 11, 1987); Gwen Ifill, "Bush and Dukakis Far Ahead in Poll," *Washington Post* (November 20, 1987).

38. See Polsby, "The Democratic Nomination and the Evolution of the Party System."

39. Monica Langley, "In Pre-New Hampshire Flurry, Images Prevail, and TV Coverage May be Pivotal to Candidates," *Wall Street Journal* (February 16, 1988), p. 64.

40. James Lengle and Byron Shafer, "Primary Rules, Political Power and Social Change," *American Political Science Review* 70 (March 1976), pp. 25–40; quote on p. 26.

41. Maxwell Glenn, "Front-Loading the Race: Because of the Accelerated Timetable for the 1988 Presidential Nominating Contest, Ample Financial Resources Will Be More Important Than Ever to Candidates," *National Journal* (November 29, 1986), p. 2882.

42. Stephen J. Wayne, *The Road to the White House: The Politics of Presidential Elections*, 2nd ed. (New York, 1984), p. 114.

43. See Harry W. Ernst, *The Primary That Made a President: West Virginia, 1960* (New York, 1962); Theodore H. White, *The Making of the President, 1960* (New York, 1961).

44. James Reston, "The Organized Disorder in California," *New York Times* (June 3, 1964).

45. See Jules Witcover, *The Resurrection of Richard Nixon* (New York, 1970), Chapter 10.

46. Wayne, *The Road to the White House*, pp. 23, 265.

47. Charles O. Jones, "Nominating 'Carter's Favorite Opponent': The Republicans in 1980," in Austin Ranney, ed., *The American Elections of 1980* (Washington, D.C., 1981), pp. 61–98.

48. Polsby, "The Democratic Nomination and the Evolution of the Party System."

49. Elting E. Morison, *The Letters of Theodore Roosevelt* (Cambridge, Mass., 1954), p. 525. See also George E. Mowry, *Theodore Roosevelt and the Progressive Movement* (Madison, Wis., 1946).

50. See, for example, Jack Newfield, *Robert Kennedy: A Memoir* (New York, 1969), p. 293. For a different view, see Richard Scammon and Ben Wattenberg, *The Real Majority* (New York, 1970), Chapters 7–8.

51. Further discussion can be found in F. Christopher Arterton, *Media Politics: The News Strategies of Presidential Campaigns* (Lexington, Mass., 1984).

52. See Ernst, *The Primary That Made a President;* White, *The Making of the President, 1960.*

53. See Theodore H. White, *The Making of the President, 1968* (New York, 1969), p. 89; Lewis Chester, Godfrey Hodgson, and Bruce Page, *An American Melodrama* (New York, 1969), pp. 79–99; Arthur Herzog, *McCarthy for President* (New York, 1969), p. 97; Newfield, *Robert Kennedy,* p. 218.

54. Cook, "In '88 Contest, It's What's Up Front That Counts," p. 1997.

55. Ibid., p. 1999.

56. Charles D. Hadley and Harold W. Stanley, "Super Tuesday 1988: Regional Results and National Implications," *Publius* 19 (Summer 1989), pp. 19–37; Linda Wertheimer, "The Stubborn Triumph of Michael Dukakis," *Washington Post* (June 12, 1988).

57. Barbara Norrander, "Turnout in Super Tuesday Primaries: The Composition of the Electorate" (paper prepared for delivery at the 1989 Annual Meeting of the American Political Science Assocation, Atlanta, August 31–September 3, 1989).

58. Bruce E. Cain, I. A. Lewis, and Douglas Rivers, "Strategy and Choice in the 1988 Presidential Primaries," *Electoral Studies* 8 (1988), pp. 23–48.

59. Cook, "In '88 Contest, It's What's Up Front That Counts," p. 2002.

60. William H. Lucy, "Polls, Primaries and Presidential Nominations," *Journal of Politics* 35 (November 1973), p. 833.

61. Richard L. Rubin, *Press, Party and Presidency* (New York, 1981), p. 194. The study cited is Thomas E. Patterson and Robert D. McClure, *The Unseeing Eye* (New York, 1976). See also Robert G. Kaiser, "T. V. on the Trail: A Three-Course Menu for Fluff," *Washington Post* (October 10, 1980).

62. Rubin, *Press, Party and Presidency,* pp. 191–193.

63. Henry E. Brady and Michael C. Hagen, "The 'Horse-Race' or the Issues: What Do Voters Learn from Presidential Primaries?" (unpublished manuscript, Harvard University, Center for American Political Studies, 1986). See also Henry E. Brady and Richard Johnston, "What's the Primary Message: Horse Race or Issue Journalism?" in Orren and Polsby, eds., *Media and Momentum,* pp. 127–186.

64. John G. Geer, "Voting in Presidential Primaries" (paper delivered at the 1984 Annual Meeting of the American Political Science Association, Washington, D.C., August 30–September 2, 1984), p. 6.

65. Ibid., p. 15.

66. Ibid., pp. 15–21.

67. Brady and Hagen, "The 'Horse-Race' or the Issues," pp. 38–39.

68. Larry M. Bartels, "Ideology and Momentum in Presidential Primaries" (paper delivered at the 1982 Annual Meeting of the American Political Science Association, Denver, Colorado, September, 1982). See also Larry Bartels, *Presidential Parties and the Dynamics of Public Choice* (Princeton, 1988).

69. Lawrence S. Rothenberg and Richard Brody, "Participation in Presidential Primaries" *Western Political Quarterly* 41 (June 1988), pp. 253–271.

70. See Glenn, "Front-Loading the Race," and Ranney, ed., *The American Elections of 1984,* p. 333. According to the Democratic National Committee each state was entitled to a given proportion of the total delegates to the 1988 Democratic National Convention. The entitlements of the thirty-three primary states were as follows:

New Hampshire	0.51%	Ohio	4.52%
Alabama	1.59	Connecticut	1.48
Arkansas	1.08	Wisconsin	2.30
Florida	3.87	New York	7.25
Georgia	2.18	Pennsylvania	5.06
Kentucky	1.56	Washington, D.C.	0.45
Louisiana	1.79	Indiana	2.24
Maryland	1.91	Nebraska	0.71
Massachusetts	2.79	West Virginia	1.05
Mississippi	1.14	Oregon	1.28
Missouri	2.19	California	8.93
North Carolina	2.33	Montana	0.54
Oklahoma	1.31	New Jersey	3.09
Rhode Island	0.63	New Mexico	0.68
Tennessee	1.99	South Dakota	0.43
Texas	5.20	Democrats abroad	0.19
Illinois	4.92	Total	77.17%

Since 15 percent of the delegates from each state were uncommitted "super-delegates," the proportion of delegates to the national convention by primary elections came to approximately 65 percent.

71. See Austin Ranney, "Turnout and Representation in Presidential Primary Elections," *American Political Science Review* 66 (March 1972), pp. 21–37 for the period 1948 to 1968. The same held true in 1976 when turnout averaged 28 percent in the primaries versus 54 percent in the general election. See Austin Ranney, *Participation in American Presidential Nominations 1976* (Washington, D.C., 1977), p. 20, and James Lengle, *Representation in Presidential Primaries: The Democratic Party in the Post Reform Era* (Westport, Conn., 1981), p. 10. In 1980 the figures were 25 percent in primaries and 54 percent in the general election (Ranney, ed., *The American Elections of 1980*, pp. 353, 364).

72. For an interesting argument along these lines, see Malcolm E. Jewell, "A Caveat on the Expanding Use of Presidential Primaries," *Policy Studies Journal* 2 (Summer 1974), pp. 279–284.

73. Lengle and Shafer, "Primary Rules, Political Power and Social Change," p. 28.

74. Ibid., p. 35.

75. Gerald Pomper, "New Rules and New Games in Presidential Nominations," *Journal of Politics* 41 (August 1979), pp. 784–805, quotation on p. 789.

76. Of the eight new primary states, the southern ones, Texas, Arkansas, Kentucky, and Georgia had 250 delegates, while Idaho, Montana, Nevada, and Connecticut combined had 95.

77. Dennis W. Gleiber and James D. King, "Party Rules and Equitable Representation: The 1984 Democratic National Convention," *American Politics Quarterly* 15 (January 1987), pp. 107–121.

78. Thomas E. Mann, "Elected Officials and the Politics of Presidential Selection," in Ranney, ed., *American Elections of 1984*, pp. 102–103.

79. Ibid., p. 103. See also David E. Price, *Bringing Back the Parties* (Washington, D.C., 1984).

80. Ibid., pp. 102–104.

81. Ibid., p. 105. See Glenn, "Front-Loading the Race," and Ranney, ed., *American Elections of 1984*, p. 333.

82. Mann, "Elected Officials and the Politics of Presidential Selection," pp. 105–106. For evidence that caucuses, and not primaries, have yielded the "best" proportional representation results, see Stephen Ansolabehere and Gary King, "Measuring the Consequences of Delegate Selection Rules in Presidential Nominations," *Journal of Politics* 52 (May 1990), pp. 609–621.

83. Mann, "Elected Officials," pp. 119ff.

84. Anthony L. Teasdale, "The Paradox of the Primaries" *Electoral Studies* 1 (April 1982), pp. 43–63; quotes from pp. 43–44, 49.

85. See Duane M. Oldfield, "Pat Crashes the Party: Reform, Republicans, and Robertson," Institute of Governmental Studies Working Paper 90–11 (Berkeley, 1990). Indeed, the Democratic National Committee was alarmed by a 1991 proposal in California to choose some of the state's Democratic delegates through caucuses, fearing that this would help candidates unlikely to draw general election support; see Katherine Bishop, "California Democrats Adopt Early Caucus System," *New York Times* (March 10, 1991).

86. Richard Reeves, *Convention* (New York, 1977), p. 180. Uncommitted delegates won 39 percent of the vote; Carter won 29 percent.

87. The Report of the McGovern Commission of the Democratic National Committee said,

    A minority of the Rules Committee of the 1968 Democratic National Convention brought to the floor a proposal to further 'democratize' the selection of delegates to future conventions. They proposed that the 1972 Convention shall require in order to give all democratic voters . . . full and timely opportunity to participate in nominating candidates, that (1) the unit rule be eliminated in all stages of the delegate selection process and (2) all feasible efforts [be] made to assure that delegates are selected through party primary, convention or committee procedures open to public participation within the calendar year of the national convention. This minority report of the Rules Committee, subsequently passed by the delegates assembled in Chicago, carried an unquestionably stern mandate for procedural reform.

    Mandate for Reform, a report of the Commission on Selection to the Democratic National Committee (Washington, D.C., April 1970), p. 15.

88. Indeed, one possible candidate, Morris Udall, bowed out of the 1984 race in early February 1983, saying that it was already too late to mount a serious campaign. See "Mondale, Askew Join Oval Office Aspirants," *Congressional Quarterly Weekly Report* (February 26, 1983), p. 434; and Martin Schram, "Udall Won't Seek Presidency in '84," *Washington Post* (February 10, 1983).

89. James A. Farley, *Jim Farley's Story* (New York, 1948), pp. 11–13; and Farley's *Behind the Ballots* (New York, 1938), p. 70; see also John F. Carter, *The New Dealers* (New York, 1934), p. 34.

90. See Brownstein, "Getting an Early Start," pp. 2876 ff.

91. See Thomas M. Durbin and Michael V. Seitzinger, Congressional Research Service, under the direction of J. S. Kimmitt, Secretary of the Senate, *Nomination*

and Election of the President and Vice-President of the United States Including the Manner of Selecting Delegates to National Political Conventions (Washington, D.C., 1980).

92. *Democratic Party of the U.S. et al.* v. *LaFollette et al.* 450 U.S. 107 (1981). In *LaFollette*, the national Democratic party sued the state of Wisconsin in order to defend the party's right to exclude from its national convention delegates selected in an open cross-over primary. The Court held that Wisconsin could not "constitutionally compel the National Party to seat a delegation chosen in a way that violates the Party's rules" (p. 107). For a full account, see Gary. D. Wekkin, *Democrat versus Democrat* (Columbia, Mo., 1984).

93. See Nelson W. Polsby, "The Democratic Nomination," in Ranney, ed., *The American Elections of 1980*, pp. 37–60.

In 1980, the manager of President Carter's renomination was especially active in attempting to manipulate the sequence in which delegates were to be chosen, so as to maximize favorable news coverage for the president. "The Jordan Memo," Martin Schram reports,

outlined plans for using White House pressure and influence to encourage state officials to shift the dates of various primary elections and caucuses—to create a "preferred version" of the 1980 calendar that would benefit Carter's campaign.

". . . The easiest way to establish early momentum . . . is to win southern delegates by encouraging southern states to hold early caucuses and primaries. . . . It is in our interest to have states that we are likely to win scheduled on the same day with states that we might do poorly in."

Martin Schram, "Carter," in Richard Harwood, ed., *The Pursuit of the Presidency 1980* (New York, 1980), p. 84.

94. David Shribman, "Presidential Hopefuls Start 'Make or Break' Year Gathering Funds, Endorsements and Good Ideas," *Wall Street Journal* (January 2, 1987), p. 30.

95. Darrell H. Rice, "The Mechanics of Delegate Selection: A Typology," *Political Science Teacher* 2 (Fall 1989), pp. 3–5.

96. See the articles on Symington in Eric Sevareid, ed., *Candidates, 1960* (New York, 1959); and Ralph G. Martin and Edward Plaut, *Front Runner, Dark Horse* (Garden City, N.Y., 1960). See also Nixon, *Six Crises* (New York, 1962).

97. Carl Sandburg, *Abraham Lincoln: The Prairie Years*, Vol. 2 (New York, 1926), p. 330. To an Indiana leader, Lincoln wrote that Republicans should "look beyond our noses and say nothing on points where we should disagree."

98. Alexander, *Financing the 1984 Election* (Lexington, Mass., 1987), p. 88.

99. *National Journal Convention Special* (July 21, 1983), p. 38. Dianne Feinstein, a Democrat, was elected on a nonpartisan ballot, as California law requires for local elections.

100. This is the number that White (*The Making of the President, 1968*, p. 259) estimates the Democrats needed for their convention. For a more recent example, see Eric Pianin, "Democrats Pick San Francisco as Site of '84 National Convention," *Washington Post* (April 22, 1983).

101. William Schneider, "Both Parties Embark on a Southern Strategy," *National Journal* (February 21, 1987), p. 436.

102. "Why Houston? Here's One Theory," *National Journal*, March 30, 1991, p. 719.

103. Reeves, *Convention*, p. 32.

104. Material on the Kennedy organization in 1960 is drawn from Fred G. Burke, "Senator Kennedy's Convention Organization," in Paul Tillett, ed., *Inside Politics: The National Conventions, 1960* (Dobbs Ferry, N.Y., 1962), pp. 25–39.

105. Ibid., p. 39.

106. Recognizing the importance of communication at the Republican convention of 1860, a supporter of Abraham Lincoln carefully seated all the solid Seward states close together and as far as possible from the states whose delegates were in some doubt about whom to support (Glyndon G. Van Deusen, *Thurlow Weed: Wizard of the Lobby* [Boston, 1947], p. 253). Mayor Daley arranged for something similar at the Democratic National Convention in 1968, but the level of protest about excessive security procedures and the lack of communications facilities reached such a pitch that whatever strategic advantages Daley might have hoped for evaporated.

107. See David, Moos, and Goldman, *Presidential Nominating Politics in 1952*, Vol. 1; Robert Elson, "A Question for Democrats: If Not Truman, Who?" *Life* (March 24, 1952), pp. 118–133; Albert Votaw, "The Pros Put Adlai Over," *New Leader* (August 4, 1952), pp. 3–5; Douglass Cater, "How the Democrats Got Together," *The Reporter* (August 19, 1952), pp. 6–8; Jack Arvey, as told to John Madigan, "The Reluctant Candidate: An Inside Story," *The Reporter* (November 24, 1953), pp. 19–26; and Walter Johnson, *How We Drafted Adlai Stevenson* (New York, 1955).

108. F. Christopher Arterton, "Exploring the 1976 Republican Convention: Strategies and Tactics of Candidate Organizations," *Political Science Quarterly* 92 (Winter 1977–78), p. 664.

109. Jo Freeman, "The Political Culture of the Democratic and Republican Parties," *Political Science Quarterly* 101 (Fall 1986), pp. 327–356; quote on p. 328. See also Byron Shafer, "Republicans and Democrats as Social Types: Or, Notes toward an Ethnography of the Political Parties," *Journal of American Studies* 20 (December 1986), pp. 341–354.

110. Freeman, "The Political Culture," p. 329.

111. Ibid.

112. Democratic National Committee, *Mandate for Reform*, p. 40. The Republican party adopted language encouraging the participation of women, young people, and black people in their conventions, but it has stopped short of requiring quotas.

113. Cavala, "Changing the Rules Changes the Game," p. 37.

114. Ibid.

115. Kirkpatrick, "Representation in the American National Conventions," p. 285.

116. Herbert McClosky, Paul J. Hoffman, and Rosemary O'Hara, "Issue Conflict and Consensus Among Party Leaders and Followers," *American Political Science Review* 54 (June 1960), pp. 406–427.

117. Jeane J. Kirkpatrick, "Representation in the American National Conventions," p. 304.

118. For extensive documentation, see Everett Carll Ladd, Jr. (with Charles D. Hadley), *Transformation of the Party System: Political Coalitions from the New Deal to the 1970's* (New York, 1975). See also their "Political Parties and Political Issues: Patterns in Differentiation since the New Deal," a Sage Professional Paper, *American Politics Series* (Beverly Hills, 1973), pp. 4–11.

119. In this, as in other matters concerning the 1976 and 1980 convention delegates, we rely upon Warren E. Miller and M. Kent Jennings, with Barbara G. Farah, *Parties in Transition: A Longitudinal Study of Party Elites and Party Supporters* (New York, 1986).

120. Miller and Jennings, *Parties in Transition,* p. 96.

121. Ibid., pp. 163–64.

122. Ibid., p. 166.

123. Ibid., pp. 166–167.

124. Ibid., pp. 175–177.

125. Ibid., pp. 187–188.

126. Ibid., pp. 203–205.

127. Ibid., pp. 218–219.

128. Ibid., pp. 221–223.

129. Center for Political Studies, Institute for Social Research, "Convention Delegate Study: Report to Respondents" (University of Michigan, Ann Arbor, 1985).

130. Ibid., pp. 3–5.

131. *National Journal Convention Daily* (August 2, 1984), p. 1 ff.

132. M. Kent Jennings, "Women in Party Politics," prepared for the Russell Sage Foundation Women in Twentieth-Century American Politics Project (Beverly Hills, January 1987).

133. Ibid., pp. 6–9.

134. Ibid., pp. 28, 32.

135. Ibid., p. 30.

136. Barbara G. Farah, "Delegate Polls: 1944 to 1984," *Public Opinion* (August/September 1984), pp. 43–45.

137. Jennings, "Women in Politics," pp. 11–12.

138. Jo Freeman, "Who You Know Versus Who You Represent," in Mary Fainsod Katzenstein and Carol McClurg Mueller, eds., *The Women's Movements of the United States and Western Europe: Consciousness, Political Opportunity and Public Policy* (Philadelphia, 1987), pp. 231–232.

139. Ibid., p. 242.

140. An important early work is Maurice Duverger, *Political Parties: Their Organization and Activity in The Modern State* (London, 1954).

141. Begans, "The ABC News/Washington Post Poll," pp. 4–5.

142. Center for Political Studies, "Convention Delegate Study," p. 2.

143. Warren Miller, *Without Consent: Mass-Elite Linkages in Presidential Politics* (Lexington, Ky., 1988), Chapter Two.

144. Center for Political Studies, Institute for Social Research, "Convention Delegate Study: Report to Respondents" (Ann Arbor, 1985), p. 1.

145. Jo Freeman, "Women at the 1988 Democratic Convention," *PS* (Fall 1988), p. 875.

146. Ibid., p. 876.

147. Ibid., p. 877.

148. Ibid.

149. Ibid.

150. See Daniel Walker Howe, *The Political Culture of the American Whigs* (Chicago, 1979). The very large *Times-Mirror* survey of September 1987, with 4,244 respondents, displayed as one of its principal findings: "The Republican party has two distinct groups: The Enterprisers . . . driven by free enterprise economic concerns, and the moralists, an equally large, less affluent and more populist group driven by moral issues and militant anti-communism." *The People, Press and Politics* (Los Angeles, 1987), p. 1.

151. See Nelson W. Polsby, "The Democratic Nomination and the Evolution of the Party System," and Raymond E. Wolfinger, "Dealignment, Realignment, and Mandates in the 1984 Election," both in Austin Ranney, ed., *The American Elections of 1984*, p. 289, p. 38.

152. See Ostrogorski, *Democracy and the Party System in the United States*, pp. 145–60, for excellent descriptions of convention confusion. Tillett, ed., *Inside Politics*, contains more up-to-date material in the same vein. Theodore H. White, *Making of the President, 1964* (New York, 1965), in contrast, describes the order and efficiency of conventions, like those in 1964, when there was no real contest for the nomination; see especially pp. 201–202. See also Ralph G. Martin, *Ballots and Bandwagons* (Chicago, 1964).

153. See Roy V. Peel and Thomas C. Donnelly, *The 1932 Campaign: An Analysis* (New York, 1935), pp. 92–93. Arthur Schlesinger, Jr., writes that strategist James Farley opposed the attempt to attack the two-thirds rule, "knowing well that not all delegates who were for Roosevelt were against the rule, and fearing that a defeat on this issue might set back the whole Roosevelt drive." Roosevelt backed down just in time (*The Crisis of the Old Order, 1919–1930* [Boston, 1957], pp. 299–300). See also Robert Morss Lovett, "Big Wind at Chicago," *The New Republic* (July 13, 1932), p. 228.

154. Arvey and Madigan, "The Reluctant Candidate," pp. 19–26.

155. See Jules Witcover, *Marathon* (New York, 1977), Chapters 31–33.

156. Wesley Bagby, "The 'Smoke-Filled Room' and the Nomination of Warren G. Harding," *Mississippi Valley Historical Review* 41 (March 1955), pp. 657–674.

157. Caroline T. Harnsberger, *A Man of Courage—Robert A. Taft* (Chicago, 1952), p. 146. See also Joseph Martin's memoirs, *My First 50 Years in Politics*.

158. Peel and Donnelly, *The 1932 Campaign: An Analysis*, pp. 95–96.

159. See Andrew Mollison, "Maestro of the Democrats," *The New Leader* (June 27, 1988), pp. 3–4. On the other hand, the leader of a united party may try to create excitement, as George Bush apparently intended to do in 1988 by refusing to reveal his choice for vice-president until the eve of the convention. James M. Perry and Ellen Hume, "Bush Aiming for Suspense as GOP Starts Convention," *Wall Street Journal* (August 15, 1988), p. 40.

160. Robert S. Boyd and Tom Fiedler, "Dukakis Hopes for Party Unity at Convention," *The Philadelphia Inquirer* (July 18, 1988).

161. "Dukakis-Jackson Accord May Avert Floor Fight," *Los Angeles Times* (June 26, 1988). See also E. J. Dionne, Jr., "Harmonious Convention Closes With Jackson Hugging Nominee," *New York Times* (July 22, 1988).

162. For the complete story, see Shafer, *Quiet Revolution.*

163. For instance, for the Roosevelt nomination in 1932: "Farley had held a few votes in reserve for the second ballot, knowing the importance of showing an increase each time round" (Schlesinger, *The Crisis of the Old Order, 1919–1933,* p. 306).

164. Eugene B. McGregor, Jr., "Rationality and Uncertainty at National Nominating Conventions," *Journal of Politics* 35 (May 1973), pp. 472–477.

165. Harry Daugherty, *The Inside Story of the Harding Tragedy* (New York, 1932), pp. 36, 46; and Mark Sullivan, *Our Times* (New York, 1926–1935), Vol. 2, p. 54. See also Bagby, "The 'Smoke-Filled Room' and the Nomination of Warren G. Harding," pp. 657–674.

166. See Jules Ables, *Out of the Jaws of Victory* (New York, 1959), pp. 65–68.

167. See Aaron Wildavsky, "What Can I Do? Ohio Delegates View the Democratic Convention," in Tillett, ed., *Inside Politics,* pp. 112–130.

168. See Edward Stanwood, *A History of the Presidency from 1788 to 1897* (Boston, 1898), pp. 206–225.

169. Sullivan, *Our Times,* Vol. 6, pp. 35–67. See also Daugherty, *The Inside Story of the Harding Tragedy,* pp. 41–55.

170. See Kent, *The Democratic Party,* pp. 483–505.

171. Ferdinand Lundberg, *Imperial Hearst* (New York, 1936), pp. 273–275; and Schlesinger, *The Crisis of the Old Order, 1919–1933,* pp. 304–308.

172. See Irving G. Williams, *The American Vice-Presidency: New Look* (New York, 1954); and Joel K. Goldstein, *The Modern American Vice Presidency* (Princeton, 1982).

173. The best accounts of the selection of Spiro Agnew are in White, *Making of the President, 1968,* pp. 244–253, and Witcover, *The Resurrection of Richard Nixon,* pp. 349–355. See also Richard Cohen and Jules Witcover, *A Heartbeat Away* (New York, 1974).

174. Richard Brookhiser, *The Outside Story* (Garden City, 1986), p. 155. In the event, Representative Ferraro's candidacy was mildly detrimental to the ticket. See Polsby, "The Democratic Nomination and the Evolution of the Party System," in Ranney, ed., *The American Elections of 1984,* pp. 36–65.

175. Most of the 130-odd Goldwater delegates we interviewed at the 1964 Republican convention were prepared to sacrifice victory if victory meant becoming a "me-too" party or "going against principles" by adopting what they termed the "devious and corrupt" balanced tickets of the past.

176. Quoted in Ross K. Baker, "Outlook for the Reagan Administration," in Gerald Pomper, ed., *The Election of 1980* (Chatham, N.J., 1981), p. 167.

177. See Peter Goldman, Tom Mathews, et al., *The Quest for the Presidency* (New York, 1989), pp. 314–320; Elizabeth Drew, *Election Journal: Political Events of 1987–1988* (New York, 1989), pp. 243–249; and Jack W. Germond and Jules Witcover, *Whose Broad Stripes and Bright Stars?—The Trivial Pursuit of the Presidency 1988* (New York, 1989), pp. 373–385.

178. This was noticeable even before the reforms of the 1968–1972 period. See

William Carleton, "The Revolution in the Presidential Nominating Convention," *Political Science Quarterly* 72 (June 1957), pp. 224–240.

179. Calculated for 1972–1984 from Reiter, *Selecting the President*, p. 64.

180. Obviously this entails risks as well as opportunities. George Romney was the first serious Republican candidate in the field in 1968, and the early exposure before he could put together a fully coherent position on the Vietnam issue almost certainly caused his downfall. See White, *Making of the President, 1968*, pp. 54–61, and Witcover, *The Resurrection of Richard Nixon*, pp. 171–191.

181. Rhodes Cook, "Dispute Over Convention's Role: Brushing Aside Complaints, DNC Approves Rules for 1988," *Congressional Quarterly Weekly Report* (March 15, 1986), p. 627.

182. Mann, "Elected Officials," in Ranney, ed., *American Elections of 1984*.

183. Reiter, *Selecting the President*, pp. 148–149.

Chapter 4: The Campaign

1. See Seymour M. Lipset, Paul F. Lazarsfeld, Allen H. Barton, and Juan Linz, "The Psychology of Voting: An Analysis of Political Behavior," in Gardner Lindzey, ed., *Handbook of Social Psychology* (Cambridge, Mass., 1954), pp. 1124–1175; Lazarsfeld, Bernard Berelson, and Hazel Gaudet, *The People's Choice* (Chicago, 1954), pp. 87–93; Berelson, Lazarsfeld, and William N. McPhee, *Voting* (Chicago, 1954), pp. 16–17; and Richard A. Brody, "Change and Stability in Partisan Identification: A Note of Caution" (paper delivered at the 1974 annual meeting of the American Political Science Association).

2. Thomas E. Cavanaugh and James L. Sundquist, "The New Two-Party System," in John E. Chubb and Paul E. Peterson, eds., *The New Direction in American Politics* (Washington, D.C., 1985), pp. 43–44.

3. By January 1985 the Republican surge had ended and the Democrats were once again the majority party in the polls. See accompanying table. Nelson W. Polsby, "The Democratic Nomination and the Evolution of the Party System," in Austin Ranney, ed., *The American Elections of 1984* (Washington, D.C., 1985), pp. 37–38.

Party Identification

A Republican Blip, 1984

	Democratic (%)	Independent (%)	Republican (%)	R/D Difference
All respondents	32	36	32	—
When "leaners" are distributed	44	8	47	3R

Source: CBS News/*New York Times* Poll conducted November 8–14, 1984.

A Democratic Restoration, 1985

	Democratic (%)	Republican (%)	R/D Difference
Among all adults	47	44	3D
Among registered voters	49	45	4D

Source: CBS News/*New York Times* Poll conducted January 14–17, 1985.

Continuity: September 1987

	Democratic (%)	Independent (%)	Republican (%)	R/D Difference
Among adults excluding those who said they belonged to other parties or had no party allegiance	42	28	30	12D

Source: Gallup poll conducted September 18–21, 1987.

4. There is another possibility: that voters who turn out only by being dinned at by the media are likely to be less stable in their political orientations and will therefore vote less for the party and more for the candidate whose name or personality seems more familiar to them. This, in a year when an Eisenhower is on the ticket, might well mean Republican votes. The most thoroughly documented research on the question suggests that increasing turnout by relaxing registration rules would have little or no effect on the partisan distribution of the vote. See Steven J. Rosenstone and Raymond E. Wolfinger, "The Effect of Registration Laws on Voter Turnout," *American Political Science Review* 72 (March 1978), pp. 22–48; and John R. Petrocik, "Voter Turnout and Electoral Preference: The Anomalous Reagan Elections," in Kay L. Schlozman, ed., *Elections in America* (Boston, 1987), pp. 239–259. Petrocik argues that the 1980 election did not fit the general pattern. Low turnout, he claims, seriously hurt Jimmy Carter.

5. Philip E. Converse, Angus Campbell, Warren E. Miller, and Donald E. Stokes, "Stability and Change in 1960: A Reinstating Election," *American Political Science Review* 55 (June 1961), pp. 269–280, especially p. 274.

6. Raymond E. Wolfinger, "Dealignment, Realignment, and Mandates," in Ranney, ed., *The American Elections of 1984*, pp. 277–296.

7. Ibid., pp. 278–282; and Bruce E. Keith, David B. Magleby, Candice F. Nelson, Elizabeth Orr, Mark Westlye, and Raymond E. Wolfinger, "The Partisan Affinities of Independent Leaners," *British Journal of Political Science* 16 (April 1986), pp. 155–185.

8. Wolfinger and his associates broke all independents into three categories, independent Democrats, independent Republicans and true independents (leaning toward neither party). They found that the partisan independents generally vote like normal Democrats or Republicans. True independents, however, act as swing voters, generally always voting for the winner. True independents have not increased in importance despite their growth in numbers, because that growth has been offset by a decline in their turnout rate. The turnout rate for true independents averaged nearly 10 percentage points lower than for either partisan independents or true partisans over the period from 1952 to 1974, and in the elections of 1972 and 1974 the difference was 20 percentage points. See Bruce E. Keith et al., "The Myth of the Independent Voter" (paper delivered at the 1977 Annual Meeting of the American Political Science Association, Washington, D.C.).

9. Scott Keeter, "Public Opinion in 1984," in Gerald Pomper, ed., *The Election of 1984: Reports and Interpretations* (Chatham, N.J., 1985), pp. 91–111.

10. J. Merrill Shanks and Warren E. Miller, "Policy Direction and Performance Evaluation: Complementary Explanations of the Reagan Elections" (paper deliv-

ered at the Annual Meeting of the American Political Science Association, New Orleans, August 29–September 1, 1985).

11. Ibid., p. 13.

12. Ibid., pp. 16–17. See also Wolfinger, "Dealignment, Realignment, and Mandates," pp. 290–292.

13. Adam Clymer, "Some Subtle Problems Undermine GOP Victory," *New York Times* (November 14, 1988). This article reports the results of a *Times*/CBS election-day exit poll of 11,645 voters.

14. See Phillip E. Converse, "The Nature of Belief Systems in Mass Publics," in David E. Apter, ed., *Ideology and Discontent* (New York, 1964), pp. 206–261.

15. Shanks and Miller, pp. 18–19.

16. Ibid., p. 20.

17. Clymer, "Some Subtle Problems."

18. Robert Y. Shapiro and Harpreet Mahajan, "Gender Differences in Policy Preferences: The Summary of Trends From the 1960s to the 1980s," *Public Opinion Quarterly* (Spring 1986), pp. 42–61.

19. Everett Carll Ladd and Karlyn H. Keene, "Gender in the 1988 Election," *The Ladd 1988 Election Update* II (September 1988).

20. Ibid., p. 335; see also Ladd and Keene, "Don't Overestimate the 'Gender Gap,' " *Wall Street Journal* (June 22, 1988), p. 22.

21. Michael McQueen, "The Gender Gap: Economic Issues Split Sexes in Their Choice of Bush or Dukakis," *Wall Street Journal*, (September 23, 1988) p. 1.

22. See Ethel Klein, "The Gender Gap: Different Issues, Different Answers," *The Brookings Review* (Winter 1985), pp. 33–37. See also her *Gender Politics: from Consciousness to Mass Politics* (Cambridge, Mass., 1984), especially Chapter 9, "The Women's Vote," pp. 140–164.

23. Clymer, "Some Subtle Problems."

24. Evans Witt, "What the Republicans Have Learned About Women," *Public Opinion* 8 (October/November 1985), pp. 49–52.

25. See Campbell et al., *The American Voter*, pp. 537–538; and Herbert H. Hyman and Paul B. Sheatsley, "The Political Appeal of President Eisenhower," *Public Opinion Quarterly* 19 (Winter 1955–56), pp. 26–39.

26. The study of right-wing ideologues and their supporters is more speculative than empirical. Nevertheless, there are a few straws in the wind, and all blow in the same direction. In 1962, Raymond E. Wolfinger and his associates administered a questionnaire to 308 "students" at an anticommunism school conducted by Dr. Fred Schwarz's Christian Anti-Communism Crusade in Oakland, California. Among the findings of this study were that 278 of the 302 persons in this sample who voted in 1960 (or 92 percent of those who voted) had voted for Nixon, and that 58 percent of those who answered the question chose Goldwater over Nixon for 1964. At about the same time, a nationwide Gallup poll showed Goldwater the choice of only 13 percent of Republicans. Raymond E. Wolfinger, Barbara Kaye Wolfinger, Kenneth Prewitt, and Sheilah Rosenhack, "America's Radical Right: Politics and Ideology," in David E. Apter, ed., *Ideology and Discontent* (New York, 1964), pp. 267–269. Analysis of various election returns and of a 1954 Gallup poll suggests that support for the late Senator Joseph McCarthy was importantly determined by party affiliation, with Republicans far exceeding Dem-

ocrats or independents in the ranks of his supporters. See Nelson W. Polsby, "Towards an Explanation of McCarthyism," *Political Studies* 8 (October 1960), pp. 250–271.

27. Louis Harris Survey News Releases (New York), July 13, 1964, and September 14, 1964. Some of the Harris survey findings on foreign affairs are shown in the table below:

Issue Differences Between Voters and Goldwater, 1964

Issue		Voters Describe Goldwater Position		Describe Own Position	
		July (*percent*)	Sept. (*percent*)	July (*percent*)	Sept. (*percent*)
Go to war over	For	78	71	29	29
Cuba	Against	22	29	71	71
Use atomic bombs	For	72	58	18	18
in Asia	Against	28	42	82	82
United Nations	For	42	50	82	83
	Against	58	50	18	17

Source: Louis Harris Survey News Releases (New York), July 13, 1964 and September 14, 1964.

28. This analysis of the 1980 election draws extensively on Nelson W. Polsby, "Party Realignment in the 1980 Election," *The Yale Review* 72 (Autumn 1982), pp. 43–54.

29. David S. Broder, "Is It a New Era?" *Washington Post* (November 19, 1980).

30. David S. Broder, "Election '80 Called 'Blip,' " *Washington Post* (September 5, 1981).

31. Polsby, "Party Realignment in the 1980 Election," p. 42.

32. Broder, "Is It a New Era?"

33. Robert Axelrod, "Communication," *American Political Science Review* 72 (June 1978), p. 622.

34. Norman Ornstein, "The Election for Congress," in Ranney, ed., *The American Elections of 1984*, p. 268.

35. Ibid., pp. 269–270.

36. Ibid., pp. 270–271.

37. Ibid., pp. 271–272.

38. Kevin Phillips, *American Political Report* 14 (January 11, 1985), p. 3; reported in William Schneider, "The November 6 Vote: What Did It Mean?" in Ranney, ed., *The American Elections of 1984*, p. 214.

39. Shanks and Miller, "Policy Direction and Performance Evaluation."

40. Pierre S. du Pont IV, "The GOP Isn't Doing Well Enough," *The Washington Post National Weekly Edition* (November 26, 1984), p. 24. See Iver Peterson, "Republicans Gain in State Legislatures," *New York Times* (November 11, 1984).

41. Commentators observe that in recent years Democratic state legislatures have rigged the boundaries of congressional districts so that small Democratic electoral majorities produce bumper crops of Democratic congressional seats. Democrats have enjoyed an advantage in recent years in the conversion of votes to seats. In the Senate an opposite result, greatly favoring Republicans, prevails. Even so,

over the thirty-year period, Democrats have dominated elections for both houses by almost exactly the same margin. See John T. Pothier, "The Partisan Bias in the Senate Elections," *American Politics Quarterly* 12 (January 1984), pp. 89–100. Norman J. Ornstein, in "Genesis of a Gerrymander," *Wall Street Journal* (May 7, 1985), argues that turnout is characteristically lower in Democratic-held districts; consequently the charge that the Democratic majority in Congress is the result of a gerrymander is, in all probability, spurious.

42. This discussion of landslide sequences is taken from Polsby, "The Democratic Nomination and the Evolution of the Party System," pp. 38–44.

43. This point is also made by Stanley Kelley, Jr., in *Interpreting Elections* (Princeton, 1983).

44. Rhodes Cook, "History a Tough Opponent for Democrats in 1992," *Congressional Quarterly Weekly Report* (April 14, 1990), pp. 1146–1151.

45. For evidence, see Nelson W. Polsby, *Consequences of Party Reform* (New York, 1983), pp. 110–113.

46. Barry Sussman, "Behind Reagan's Popularity: A Little Help from His Foes," *The Washington Post National Weekly Edition* (February 4, 1985), p. 37. See also David Rosenbaum, "Poll Shows Many Choose Reagan Even If They Disagree with Him," *New York Times* (September 19, 1984).

47. For a fuller discussion, see Nelson W. Polsby, *Consequences of Party Reform*. On the factional make-up of the parties, see the *Times-Mirror* poll, *The People, Press and Politics* (Los Angeles, September 1987), which shows the Republicans divided into two, the Democrats into four, factions.

48. See Steven J. Rosenstone, "Explaining the 1984 Presidential Election," *The Brookings Review* 3 (Winter 1985), pp. 25–32; and James Q. Wilson, "Realignment at the Top, Dealignment at the Bottom," in Ranney, ed., *The American Elections of 1984*, pp. 297–310.

49. See Robert S. Erikson and Kent L. Tedin, "The 1928–1936 Partisan Realignment—The Case for the Conversion Hypothesis," *American Political Science Review* 75 (December 1981), pp. 951–962.

50. See Warren E. Miller and J. Merrill Shanks, "Policy Directions and Presidential Leadership: Alternative Interpretations of the 1980 Presidential Election," *British Journal of Political Science* 12 (July 1982), pp. 299–356.

51. See, for example, Kristi Anderson, *The Creation of a Democratic Majority, 1928–1936* (Chicago, 1979).

52. See Thomas Ferguson and Joel Rogers, "The Myth of America's Turn to the Right," *The Atlantic Monthly* (May 1986), p. 51.

53. Bureau of the Census, *Current Population Reports: Voting and Registration in the Election of 1988*, Series P-20, no. 440 (October 1989), p. 4. Proportions in 1984 were even closer, and African-Americans may have registered and voted in higher proportions than whites; see Polsby, "Democratic Nomination and the Evolution of the Party System," p. 64.

54. The most complete set of published data bearing out these observations is "Is It Realignment? Surveying the Evidence," *Public Opinion* 8 (October/November 1985), pp. 21–31.

55. Shanks and Miller, "Policy Direction and Performance Evaluation: Complementary Explanations of the Reagan Elections." See also Miller and Shanks, "Policy

Directions and Presidential Leadership: Alternative Interpretations of the 1980 Election," *British Journal of Political Science* 12 (July 1982), pp. 299–356.

56. Wilson, "Realignment at the Top, Dealignment at the Bottom." "By an elite realignment, I mean a change in the identity and views of those persons who play important roles in the selection of the candidates, the writing of the platforms, the definition of the rules, and in conducting the affairs of each party." p. 300. See also John S. Jackson, III, David Bositis, and Denise Baer, "Political Party Leaders and the Mass Public: 1980–1984" (paper presented at the Annual Meeting of the Midwest Political Science Association, Chicago, April 19, 1987), who also argue that Democratic and Republican elites have become more polarized.

57. Wilson, "Realignment at the Top, Dealignment at the Bottom," pp. 301–302.

58. Martin P. Wattenberg, "The Hollow Realignment: Partisan Change in a Candidate-Centered Era," *Public Opinion Quarterly* 51 (1987), p. 61.

59. See Edward Tufte, *Political Control of the Economy* (Princeton, 1978), for a discussion of political effects of these sorts of activities.

60. Martin Schram, *Running for President* (New York, 1977), p. 342.

61. Michael J. Robinson, "Where's the Beef? Media and Media Elites in 1984," in Ranney, ed., *The American Elections of 1984*, p. 182.

62. Schram, *Running for President*, pp. 352–358.

63. The report of the speech in the *New York Times* (October 6, 1956) gives no indication of how it was received. The authors heard it delivered.

64. Richard Brookhiser, *The Outside Story* (Garden City, N.Y., 1986), pp. 231–232.

65. "The records . . . revealed that the 1972 Nixon campaign effort raised a record total of $60.2 million, $8 million more than the previously acknowledged total. The committee said that $56.1 million of this amount had been spent" (*Congressional Quarterly* [October 6, 1973], p. 2659).

66. See, for an early survey, Stanley Kelley Jr. *Professional Public Relations and Political Power* (Baltimore, 1956).

67. Special Issue: The Political Pages: C&E's Complete 1990 Guide to Political Products and Services, *Campaigns and Elections* 10 (February 1990), p. 4.

68. For a detailed account of the polling industry, see Larry Sabato, *The Rise of Political Consultants* (New York, 1981); see also Scott C. Ratzan, "The Real Agenda Setters: Pollsters in the 1988 Presidential Campaign," *American Behavioral Scientist* 32 (March/April 1989) p. 451; Mark Levy, "Polling and the Presidential Election," in *The Annals of the American Academy of Political and Social Science: Polling and the Democratic Consensus* (Beverly Hills, 1984); and Jerry Hagstrom and Robert Guskind, "Calling the Races," *National Journal* (July 30, 1988), pp. 1972–1976.

69. Michael Barone, "The Power of the President's Pollsters," *Public Opinion* 52 (September/October 1988), p. 4; for the circumstances of Carter's "malaise" speech, see Elizabeth Drew, "Phase: In Search of a Definition," *The New Yorker*, (August 27, 1979), pp. 45–73.

70. Gerald M. Goldhaber, "A Pollster's Sampler," *Public Opinion* 7 (June/July 1984), p. 50.

71. Kathleen Hall Jamieson, *Packaging the Presidency: A History and Criticism of Presidential Campaign Advertising* (New York, 1984), p. 429.

72. Sabato, *Rise of Political Consultants*, pp. 69–70.

73. Christine M. Black and Thomas Oliphant, *All by Myself: The Unmaking of a Presidential Campaign* (Chester, Conn., 1989) p. 128.

74. Memorandum from Tubby Harrison, Clifford Brown, and Lynda Powell, "Re: Target Voters and the Debate," September 19, 1988. This is one of a set of unpublished internal campaign memos and other reports from Dukakis's pollsters to the candidate.

75. Ibid.

76. Memorandum from Dukakis's pollsters (title and author unavailable), September 4, 1988.

77. Memorandum from Dukakis's pollsters, "Bush Negatives and Switching," September 9, 1988.

78. "Pollsters on the Polls: An Interview with Irwin 'Tubby' Harrison," *Public Opinion* 11 (January/February 1989), p. 5.

79. "Pollsters on the Polls: An Interview with Vincent Breglio," *Public Opinion* 11 (January/February 1989), p. 4.

80. Jack W. Germond and Jules Witcover, *Whose Broad Stripes and Bright Stars?* (New York, 1989), p. 416.

81. Memo from Dukakis's pollsters, "Why We Are Still Behind," October 10, 1988.

82. Danny N. Bellenger, Kenneth L. Bernhardt, and Jac. L. Goldstucker, *Qualitative Research in Marketing* (Chicago, 1976), p. 8.

83. William D. Wells, "Group Interviewing," in *Focus Group Interviews* (Chicago, 1979), p. 2.

84. Jerry Hagstrom and Robert Guskind, "Calling the Races," *National Journal* (July 30, 1988), p. 1974.

85. Peter Goldman and Tom Mathews, *Quest for the Presidency, 1988*, (New York, 1988) p. 358.

86. In David R. Runkel, ed., *Campaign for the President: The Managers Look at '88* (Dover, Mass., 1989), p. 157.

87. "Pollsters on the Polls: An Interview with Irwin 'Tubby' Harrison," p. 5.

88. Audio-tape of "Retrospective Analysis of Campaign '88: Process and Politics," an interview with Nicholas Mitropoulos at the University of California, Berkeley, February 22, 1989.

89. "Pollsters on the Polls: An Interview with Vincent Breglio," p. 51.

90. Hagstrom and Guskind, "Calling the Races," p. 1974.

91. Goldman and Mathews, *Quest for the Presidency, 1988*, p. 400.

92. Longer ads are occasionally produced, especially for small, low-cost media markets, but prime-time is dominated by ten- and thirty-second spots. Frank I. Luntz, *Candidates, Consultants, and Campaigns* (New York, 1988), p. 83.

93. Ibid., pp. 85–91.

94. Ibid.

95. David Chagall, *The New Kingmakers* (New York, 1981), p. 218.

96. Sabato, *Rise of the Political Consultants*, p. 182.

97. Luntz, *Candidates, Consultants, and Campaigns*, p. 210.

98. John Power, "Plug In To Cable TV," *Campaigns and Elections* 8 (September–October 1987), p. 54–57.

99. Luntz, *Candidates, Consultants and Campaigns*, p. 210.

100. Ibid.

101. Dom Bonafede, "Hey, Look Me Over," *National Journal* (November 21, 1987), p. 2967.

102. Ibid., p. 2965.

103. Germond and Witcover, *Whose Broad Stripes and Bright Stars?*, p. 403.

104. Luntz, *Candidates, Consultants, and Campaigns*, p. 107.

105. Ibid., p. 109.

106. Ibid., p. 110.

107. Ibid., p. 110.

108. Ibid., pp. 211–212.

109. Ibid., p. 214.

110. Richard Armstrong, *The Next Hurrah: The Communications Revolution in American Politics* (New York, 1988), p. 197.

111. Ibid., p. 198.

112. Ibid., p. 397.

113. Ibid., p. 397.

114. Ibid., p. 397.

115. Ibid., p. 393.

116. Ibid., p. 392.

117. Ibid., pp. 392–93.

118. Luntz, *Candidates, Consultants and Campaigns*, p. 52.

119. Ibid., p. 49.

120. Mark P. Petracca, "Political Consultants and Democratic Governance," *PS: Political Science and Politics* 22,1 (March 1989), p. 13.

121. Luntz, *Candidates, Consultants, and Campaigns*, p. 57.

122. Sabato, *Rise of Political Consultants*, p. 13.

123. Luntz, *Candidates, Consultants, and Campaigns*, p. 51.

124. Sabato, *Rise of Political Consultants*, p. 26.

125. Dick Kirschten and James A. Barnes, "Itching for Actions," *National Journal* (June 4, 1988), p. 1478.

126. Luntz, *Candidates, Consultants, and Campaigns*, p. 72.

127. Ibid., p. 112.

128. Occasionally the roles are reversed and consultants find themselves more "dovish" then their employers. In the 1972 general campaign, George McGovern ditched Charles Guggenheim, his media advisor, because the latter refused (on pragmatic grounds) to produce negatives. See Sabato, *Rise of Political Consultants*, p. 121.

129. Luntz, *Candidates, Consultants, and Campaigns*, p. 50.

130. Ibid., p. 50.

131. Jules Witcover, *Marathon* (New York, 1977), pp. 132–137.

132. See table accompanying note 5 to Chapter I.

133. Thomas Flinn, "How Nixon Took Ohio," *Western Political Quarterly* 15 (June 1962), pp. 276–279.

134. Nicholas von Hoffman, "Campaign Craziness," *The New Republic* (November 5, 1984), pp. 17–19; quote on p. 17.

135. Ibid., p. 17.

136. Ibid., p. 19.

137. Jules Witcover, *The Resurrection of Richard Nixon* (New York, 1970), pp. 237–239.

138. Schram, *Running for President*, p. 341.

139. Ibid., p. 292.

140. Ibid., pp. 341–342.

141. Martin P. Wattenberg, "The Hollow Realignment: Partisan Change in a Candidate-Centered Era," *Public Opinion Quarterly* 51 (1987), p. 61.

142. Ibid.

143. Times Mirror, "The People, the Press and Politics: Post-Election Typology Survey," Poll conduced for Times Mirror by the Gallup Organization (November 1988).

144. See, for example, the Gallup poll for June 25–28, 1982, in which 43 percent of a national sample said that the Democrats were the party best able to keep the country prosperous. Only 34 percent picked the Republicans (*The Gallup Report*, No. 204 [September 1982], p. 45). See also Campbell et al., *The American Voter*, pp. 44–59.

145. *Congressional Quarterly 1980 Almanac* (Washington, 1981). p. 59-B.

146. Transcript of presidential debates, *New York Times* (October 16, 1976). See also Campbell et al., *The American Voter*, pp. 44–59; and Angus Campbell, Gerald Gurin, and Warren E. Miller, *The Voter Decides* (Evanston, Ill., 1954), pp. 44–45, especially Table 4–3, p. 45.

147. See Henry A. Plotkin, "Issues in the Campaign," in Pomper, ed., *The Election of 1984*, pp. 48–52; Albert R. Hunt, "The Campaign and the Issues," in Ranney, ed., *The American Elections of 1984*, pp. 142–144; Schneider, "The November 6 Vote for President, pp. 239–242; Benjamin Ginsberg and Martin Shefter, "A Critical Realignment? The New Politics, the Reconstituted Right, and the Election of 1984," in Michael Nelson, ed., *The Elections of 1984*, (Washington, D.C., 1985), pp. 5–24.

148. Richard Scammon and Ben Wattenberg, *The Real Majority* (New York, 1970), p. 39; see also pp. 37–43.

149. Lloyd Grove, "When They Ask If Dukakis Has a Heart, They Mean It," *Washington Post Weekly Edition* (October 17–23, 1988), pp. 24–25.

150. Curt Suplee, "Bush's Candidacy Is Being Cooled Off by His Warmth Index," *Washington Post National Weekly Edition* (July 25–31, 1988), pp. 23–24.

151. See Theodore H. White, *The Making of the President, 1960* (New York, 1961), pp. 269–275; White, *The Making of the President, 1964* (New York, 1965), passim; and Timothy Crouse, *The Boys on the Bus* (New York, 1973).

152. Department of Marketing, Miami University, Oxford Research Associates, *The Influence of Television on the Election of 1952* (Oxford, Ohio, 1954), pp. 151–160.

153. See White, *The Making of the President, 1960*, pp. 282–283; and Herbert A. Selz and Richard D. Yoakum, "Production Diary of the Debates," in Sidney Kraus, ed., *The Great Debates: Kennedy versus Nixon, 1960* (Bloomington, 1977), pp. 73–126.

154. Ibid.; see also Richard M. Nixon, *Six Crises* (New York, 1962), pp. 346–386.

155. Earl Mazo, *Richard Nixon* (New York, 1959), pp. 21–22, 362–369.

156. See Katz and Feldman, "The Debates in the Light of Research: A Survey of Surveys," in Kraus, ed., *The Great Debates*, pp. 173–223.

157. See Charles Mohr, "President Tells Polish-Americans He Regrets Remark on East Europe," *New York Times* (October 9, 1976); and R. W. Apple, Jr., "Economy is Stressed by Dole and Mondale During Sharp Debate," *New York Times* (October 16, 1976).

158. See Hedrick Smith, "No Clear Winner Apparent: Scene is Simple and Stark," *New York Times* (October 29, 1980). After the election, Terence Smith of the Times wrote:

   The continual emphasis on Mr. Reagan's image as a hair-triggered proponent of American military intervention—the "war and peace issue" as it came to be called—may have been overdone, in the opinion of some Carter aides.

   In June, Mr. Powell was telling reporters that Mr. Reagan was "too benign" a figure to be painted as a warmonger, a la Barry Goldwater in 1964. "It wouldn't be believable," he said then.

   But beginning with his Middle Western swing the day after Labor Day, Mr. Carter stressed this point above all others, warning that the election was a choice between "war and peace." He did so because of private polls taken by Mr. Caddell that showed this to be the public's greatest hidden fear about the Republican candidate. The President was hoist by his own hyperbole, in the view of some Carter aides, who feel the President grossly overstated Mr. Reagan's record and aroused the public's skepticism about his argument. In the end, they feel, Mr. Reagan's cool, collected, nonthreatening performance in the debate defused the issue.

   "Carter Post-Mortem: Debate Hurt But Wasn't Only Cause for Defeat," *New York Times* (November 9, 1980).

159. Gerald M. Pomper, "The Presidential Election," in Pomper, ed., *The Election of 1984*, p. 76.

160. Brookhiser, *The Outside Story*, p. 272.

161. Hunt, "The Campaign and the Issues," pp. 149–158.

162. See Austin Ranney, ed., *The Past and Future of Presidential Debates*, (Washington, D.C., 1977).

163. *Oakland Tribune* (February 19, 1987). See also James A. Barnes, "Debating the Debates," *National Journal*, (February 28, 1987), p. 527; and Newton Minow and Clifford M. Sloan, *For Great Debates: A New Plan for Future Presidential TV Debates* (New York, 1987).

164. See Nixon, *Six Crises*, and especially White, *The Making of the President, 1960*, for a discussion of two candidates' contrasting attitudes toward their "camp" of reporters. For the 1964 election, see White, *The Making of the President, 1964*. For 1968, see Theodore H. White, *The Making of the President, 1968* (New York, 1969), pp. 327 ff. For 1972, see Crouse, *The Boys on the Bus*. For 1976,

see Jules Witcover, *Marathon* (New York, 1977). For 1980, see Jack W. Germond and Jules Witcover, *Blue Smoke and Mirrors* (New York, 1981), pp. 213–215, 260–264. On 1984, see Martin Schram, *The Great American Video Game: Presidential Politics in the Television Age* (New York, 1987).

165. Schram, *Running for President,* passim.

166. Michael J. Robinson, "Where's the Beef? Media and Media Elites in 1984," in Ranney, ed., *The American Elections of 1984,* pp. 173–177.

167. See Stephen Hess, *The Washington Reporters* (Washington, D.C., 1981); S. Robert Lichter and Stanley Rothman, "Media and Business Elites," *Public Opinion* 4 (October/November 1981), pp. 42–46, 59–60; and William Schneider and I. A. Lewis, "Views on the News," *Public Opinion* 8 (August/September 1985) pp. 6–11, 58.

168. For more on negative campaigning, see Sabato, *The Rise of Political Consultants*; and Luntz, *Candidates, Consultants, and Campaigns*; for an argument that 1964 featured the most negative ads, see Armstrong, *The Next Hurrah;* and for advice on how to run a negative campaign, see Rich Galen, "Nail the Opposition," *Campaigns and Elections* 9 (May–June 1988), pp. 45–49, and Galen, "The Best Defense Is a Good Offense," *Campaigns and Elections* 9 (October–November 1988), pp. 29–34.

169. "Our Cheesy Democracy," *The New Republic* (November 3, 1986), pp. 8–9.

170. Steven W. Colford, "Ailes: What He Wants Next: Bush Adman Aims Attack at Madison Ave.", *Advertising Age* (November 14, 1988), pp. 1, 67.

171. "In elections at home, which Muskie contests vigorously and wins by handsome margins despite the state's strong Republican orientation, he rarely mentioned his opponent's name, let alone attack him. He dwells instead on his own positive (and pragmatic) approach to problems. . . . Throughout the campaign he waits hopefully for his opponent to strike, in desperation, some more or less low blow in response to which Muskie can become magnificently outraged. Then, voice trembling with indignation but still without mentioning the opponent's name, he chastises the opposition for stooping to such levels, and thus manages to introduce a little color into the campaign. Usually the opposition obliges him: 'I can always count on the Republicans doing something stupid,' he once said with satisfaction" (David Nevin, *Muskie of Maine* [New York, 1972], p. 27).

172. Robert E. Sherwood, *Roosevelt and Hopkins* (New York, 1948), p. 821.

173. The effectiveness of underhanded tactics remains unknown. Dan Nimmo (*The Political Persuaders* [Englewood Cliffs, N.J., 1970], p. 50), argues that deviating from a vague sense of "fairness" that exists in the electorate may backfire. There is plenty of evidence on the other side as well. For a treasure trove of such material, see Stanley Kelley, *Professional Public Relations and Political Power* (Baltimore, 1956).

174. Brookhiser, *The Outside Story,* pp. 261–265.

175. Schram, *Running for President,* p. 369.

176. Ibid., pp. 362–363.

177. See Carl Bernstein and Bob Woodward, *All the President's Men* (New York, 1974), pp. 112–162, 197, 199, 251–253, 285–286, 328; and Senate Select Committee on Presidential Campaign Activities, *The Senate Watergate Report* (Washington, D.C., 1974).

178. See Jules Abels, *Out of the Jaws of Victory* (New York, 1959).

179. Robert Alford, "The Role of Social Class in American Voting Behavior," *Western Political Quarterly* 16 (March 1963), pp. 180–194; and Campbell et al., *The American Voter*, Chapter 13.

180. White, *The Making of the President, 1960*, pp. 203–204.

181. Ibid., p. 315.

182. White, *The Making of the President, 1968*, p. 331.

183. See Nixon, *Six Crises*, pp. 315–461.

184. "Face Off: A Conversation with the Presidents' Pollsters Patrick Caddell and Richard Wirthlin," *Public Opinion* 3 (December/January 1981), p. 5.

185. Ibid., pp. 2, 6.

186. Everett Carll Ladd, "The 1980 Presidential Election: In Search of its Meaning," typescript (February 3, 1981); see also "Face Off: A Conversation with the Presidents' Pollster Patrick Caddell and Richard Wirthlin," *Public Opinion* 3 (December/January 1981), p. 5.

187. "Moving Right Along?" Interview with Peter Hart and Richard Wirthlin, *Public Opinion* 7 (December/January 1985), p. 11.

188. David Shribman and James M. Perry, "Self-Inflicted Injury: Dukakis's Campaign Was Marred by a Series of Lost Opportunities," *Wall Street Journal* (November 8, 1988), p. 1.

189. " 'Liberal' Tag Hurts Dukakis, Times Mirror Survey finds," *Times Mirror News* (September 22, 1988).

190. Ibid.

191. For extensive recital of these critiques see Black and Oliphant, *All By Myself: The Unmaking of a Presidential Campaign*.

192. Shribman and Perry, "Self-Inflicted Injury," p. 1.

193. Karen M. Paget, "Afterthoughts on the Dukakis/Bentsen Campaign, *Public Affairs Report* 30 (January 1989), pp. 1–4.

194. *Daily Californian* (September 28, 1989), p. 5.; and John Jacobs, "Dukakis Admits Campaign 'Mistakes,' " *San Francisco Examiner* (October 14, 1989).

195. Michael J. Robinson, "Can Values Save George Bush?" *Public Opinion* (July/August 1988), p. 11. This is a *Times Mirror* poll conducted by the Gallup organization.

196. John Dillon, "Mood of America: Shifting to Bush?" *Christian Science Monitor* (September 29, 1988), p. 1, reporting on a *Times Mirror* survey.

197. Ibid., p. 28.

Appendix: Forecasting the Outcome

1. See, for example, Samuel Lubell, *The Future of American Politics* (New York, 1951); his "Personalities and Issues,' in Sidney Kraus, ed., *The Great Debates* pp. 151–162; and Joseph Alsop, "The Negro Vote and New York," *New York Herald-Tribune* (and elsewhere) (August 8, 1960). Reporting of this sort has become a feature of the election year coverage of the *Washington Post*. See, for example, Rowland Evans and Robert Novak, "Stronghold Lost," *Washington Post* (August 4, 1980).

2. On the import of early projections, see Philip L. Dubois, "Election Night Projection and Voter Turnout in the West," *American Politics Quarterly* 11 (July 1983), pp. 349–364. Dubois argues (against a number of other studies) that the early projections did have a significant impact on turnout. For a sophisticated analysis of the policy problems involved, see Percy Tannenbaum and Leslie J. Kostrich, *Turned-On TV/Turned-Off Voters: Policy Options for Election Projections* (Beverly Hills, 1983).

3. Rhodes Cook, "Topsy-Turvy Polls: Medium is the Message," *Congressional Quarterly* 46 (September 17, 1988), p. 2562.

4. Irving Crespi, *Pre-Election Polling: Sources of Accuracy and Error* (New York, 1988), p. 83.

5. Ibid., p. 91.

6. Ibid., pp. 96–97.

7. *Gallup Report 1986*, No. 254 (November), inside back cover.

8. These suggestions are drawn in part from a reading of the Report of a Committee of the Social Science Research Council, Frederick Mosteller et. al., *The Pre-Election Polls of 1948*, Social Science Research Council Bulletin 60 (New York, 1949).

9. Joseph Alsop, "The Wayward Press: Dissection of a Poll," *The New Yorker* (September 24, 1960), pp. 170–184.

10. Larry M. Bartels and C. Anthony Broh, "The Polls—A Review: The 1988 Presidential Primaries," *Public Opinion Quarterly* 53 (Winter 1989), p. 563.

11. Crespi, *Pre-Election Polling*, pp. 130–131.

12. Bartels and Broh, "The Polls—A Review," pp. 575–576.

13. Ronald Elving, "Rough '88 Raises Pollsters' Concerns," *Congressional Quarterly* 47 (August 19, 1989), p. 2191.

14. Christine M. Black and Thomas Oliphant, *All By Myself: The Unmaking of a Presidential Campaign* (Chester, Conn., 1989).

15. There are several sources about the technology and tactics of polling. George Gallup has published *A Guide to Public Opinion Polls* (Princeton, 1948). See also *Opinion Polls, Interviews by Donald McDonald with Elmo Roper and George Gallup* (Santa Barbara, 1962); Charles W. Roll, Jr., and Albert H. Cantril, *Polls: Their Use and Misuse in Politics* (New York, 1972); and Albert H. Cantril, ed., *Polling on the Issues: A Report from the Kettering Foundation*, (Cabin John, M.D., 1980). In 1972, Representative Lucien Nedzi held congressional hearings on the possible effects of information about polls on subsequent voting. See "Public Opinion Polls," Hearings before the Subcommittee on Library and Memorial, Committee on House Administration, House of Representatives, Ninety-Third Congress, First Session, on H.R. 5503, September 19, 20, 21, October 5, 1972. A further flap occurred in 1980, as the result of Jimmy Carter's concession of defeat and the television network predictions of a Reagan victory before voting was completed on the West Coast. See Raymond Wolfinger and Peter Linquiti, "Tuning In and Turning Out," *Public Opinion* 4 (February/March 1981), pp. 56–60; John E. Jackson, "Election Night Reporting and Voter Turnout," *American Journal of Political Science* 27 (November 1983); "Election Day Practices and Election Projections," Hearing before the Task Force on Elections of the

Committee on House Administration and the Subcommittee on Telecommunications, Consumer Protection, and Finance of the Committee on Energy and Commerce, U.S. House of Representatives, Ninety-Seventh Congress, First and Second Sessions December 15, 1981 and September 21, 1982; and Tannenbaum and Kostrich, *Turned-On TV/Turned-Off Voters*.

16. Robert E. Sherwood, *Roosevelt and Hopkins, an Intimate History* (New York, 1948), p. 86. See also Archibald M. Crossley, "Straw Polls in 1936," *Public Opinion Quarterly* 1 (January 1937), pp. 24–36; and a survey of the literature existing at that time, Hadley Cantril, "Technical Research," *Public Opinion Quarterly* 1 (January 1937), pp. 97–110.

17. Maurice C. Bryson, "The Literary Digest Poll: Making of a Statistical Myth," *The American Statistician* 30 (November 1976), pp. 184–185. As a matter of fact, this method produced a correct prediction in 1932, when the *Literary Digest* said that Roosevelt would win. Sampling error is tricky; an atypical sample may still give the correct prediction—by luck; but sooner or later, the law of averages is bound to catch up with it.

18. Peverill Squire, "Why the 1936 *Literary Digest* Poll Failed," *Public Opinion Quarterly* 52 (Spring 1988), p. 125.

19. Mosteller et al., *The Pre-Election Polls of 1948*.

20. Election day exit polls often come close to offering answers to the "why" questions. For an analysis of four different 1980 exit polls, see Mark R. Levy, "The Methodology and Performance of Election Day Polls," *Public Opinion Quarterly* 47 (Spring 1983), pp. 54–57.

21. See Paul F. Lazarsfeld, "The Use of Panels in Social Research," *Proceedings of the American Philosophical Society* 92 (November 1948), pp. 405–410.

22. Stephen Borrelli, Brad Lockerbie, and Richard G. Niemi, "Why the Democrat-Republican Partisanship Gap Varies from Poll to Poll," *Public Opinion Quarterly* 51 (Spring 1987), pp. 115–119; quote on pp. 117–118.

23. Elissa C. Lichenstein, ed., *Exit Polls and Early Election Projections* (American Bar Association, Washington, D.C., 1984), p. viii.

24. They argue, "the decision to vote—on the West Coast or anywhere else—is the result of a complicated combination of factors, none of which is related to information received on election day." Laurily Epstein and Gerald Strom, "Election Night Projections and West Coast Turnout," *American Politics Quarterly* 9 (October 1981), p. 486.

25. Jackson writes, "Overall turnout will be substantially reduced in an election in which new and unexpected information that one candidate has an early and decisive lead in the electoral college is reported to the public before the polls close." John Jackson, "Election Reporting and Voter Turnout," *American Journal of Political Science* 27 (November 1983), p. 633.

26. Seymour Sudman, "Do Exit Polls Influence Voting Behavior?" *Public Opinion Quarterly* 50 (Fall 1986), p. 338.

27. Ibid., p. 332.

28. Ibid., pp. 332–333.

29. Jackson, "Election Reporting and Voter Turnout," pp. 630–631.

30. Michael X. Delli Carpini, "Scooping the Voters? The Consequences of the Net-

works' Early Call of the 1980 Presidential Race,'' *Journal of Politics* 46 (August 1984), p. 890.

31. Lichenstein, ed., *Exit Polls and Early Election Projections*, p. 2.

32. Opponents complain about the complexity of a provision which would extend Daylight Savings Time in the West in order to achieve uniformity. Further, they say they fear that early poll closing times in the West would depress turnout there.

Chapter 5: Issues and Appraisals

1. There are many examples of the party reform school of thought. See, for example, Woodrow Wilson, *Congressional Government* (Boston, 1889); Henry Jones Ford, *The Rise and Growth of American Politics* (New York, 1898); A. Lawrence Lowell, *Public Opinion and Popular Government* (New York, 1913); William MacDonald, *A New Constitution for a New America* (New York, 1921); William Y. Elliott, *The Need for Constitutional Reform* (New York, 1935); E. E. Schattschneider, *Party Government* (New York, 1940); Henry Hazlitt, *A New Constitution Now* (New York, 1942); Thomas K. Finletter, *Can Representative Government Do the Job?* (New York, 1945); James M. Burns, *Congress on Trial* (New York, 1949); Committee on Political Parties, American Political Science Association, *Toward A More Responsible Two-Party System* (New York, 1950); Stephen K. Bailey, *The Condition of Our National Political Parties* (New York, 1959); James M. Burns, *The Deadlock of Democracy* (Englewood Cliffs, N.J., 1963); Lloyd N. Cutler and C. Douglas Dillon, "Can We Improve on Our Constitutional System?," *Wall Street Journal* (February 15, 1983); and Cutler, "To Form a Government," *Foreign Affairs* 59 (Fall 1980), pp. 126–143. The work of the Committee on Political Parties, representing the collective judgment of a panel of distinguished political scientists in 1950, is the statement we shall refer to most often. In 1971 a member of the committee published a thoughtful reconsideration of its main ideas. See Evron M. Kirkpatrick, "Towards a More Responsible Two-Party System: Political Science, Policy Science, or Pseudo Science?" *American Political Science Review* 65 (December 1971), pp. 965–990.

2. Committee on Political Parties, *Toward a More Responsible Two-Party System*, p. 1.

3. Ibid., p. 66.

4. Ibid., p. 15.

5. A sample of this literature might include E. Pendleton Herring, *The Politics of Democracy* (New York, 1940); Herbert Agar, *The Price of Union* (Boston, 1950); Malcolm C. Moos, *Politics, Presidents and Coattails* (Baltimore, 1952); Austin Ranney and Willmore Kendall, *Democracy and the American Party System* (New York, 1956); David B. Truman, *The Governmental Process* (New York, 1953); John Fischer, "Unwritten Rules of American Politics," *Harper's* (November 1948), pp. 27–36; Peter Drucker, "A Key to American Politics: Calhoun's Pluralism," *Review of Politics* 10 (October 1948), pp. 412–426; Ernest F. Griffith, *Congress: Its Contemporary Role* (New York, 1951); Murray Stedman and Herbert Sonthoff, "Party Responsibility: A Critical Inquiry," *Western Political Quarterly* 4 (September 1951), pp. 454–486; Julius Turner, "Responsible Parties: A Dissent from the Floor," *American Political Science Review* 45 (March 1951), pp. 143–152; William Goodman, "How Much Political Party Centraliza-

tion Do We Want?'' *The Journal of Politics* 13 (November 1961), pp. 536–561; and Austin Ranney, *The Doctrine of Responsible Party Government* (Urbana, Ill., 1954).

6. Herring, *The Politics of Democracy*, p. 327.

7. Ibid., p. 420.

8. Committee on Political Parties, *Toward a More Responsible Two-Party System*, p. 19.

9. Bailey, *The Condition of Our National Political Parties*, p. 20.

10. See David B. Truman, ''Federalism and the Party System,'' in Arthur W. Mac-Mahon (ed.), *Federalism: Mature and Emergent* (New York, 1962) p. 115–136. This situation is deplored in Cutler and Dillon, ''Can We Improve on Our Constitutional System?'' One remedy, changing the terms of office of congressmen and senators to coincide exactly with presidential elections, is analyzed in Nelson W. Polsby, ''A Note on the President's Modest Proposal,'' in Polsby, *Political Promises* (New York, 1974), pp. 101–107.

11. This is not at all uncommon. See, for instance, examples in Raymond A. Bauer, Ithiel de Sola Pool, and Lewis Anthony Dexter, *American Business and Public Policy* (New York, 1963), Chapters 16, 18 and 19; Richard F. Fenno, *Home Style* (Boston, 1978); and Bruce Cain, John Ferejohn, and Morris Fiorina, *The Personal Vote* (Cambridge, Mass., 1987).

12. The near removal in 1987 of Les Aspin as chairman of the House Armed Services Committee, however, was clearly based on policy differences, and so were several other threats to Democratic committee chairmen over the last decade.

13. A careful history of this process is Byron E. Shafer's *Quiet Revolution: Reform Politics in the Democratic Party, 1968–1972* (New York, 1983). For an analysis of consequences, see Nelson W. Polsby, *Consequences of Party Reform* (New York, 1983).

14. For strong evidence on this point, see Samuel Stouffer, *Communism, Conformity and Civil Liberties* (Garden City, N.Y., 1955), passim; and Julian L. Woodward and Elmo Roper, ''Political Activity of American Citizens,'' *American Political Science Review* 44 (December 1950), pp. 872–875. Two recent studies have examined the voters' desire not to be interfered with by the government as well as the importance of their private lives to them as compared with national issues. See Paul M. Sniderman and Richard A. Brody, ''Coping: The Ethic of Self-reliance,'' *American Journal of Political Science* 21 (August 1977) pp. 501–521; and Richard A. Brody and Paul M. Sniderman, ''From Life Space to Polling Place: The Relevance of Personal Concerns for Voting Behavior,'' *British Journal of Political Science* 7 (July 1977), pp. 337–360.

15. See, for example, Jack Citrin, Herbert McClosky, J. Merrill Shanks, and Paul M. Sniderman, ''Personal and Political Sources of Alienation,'' *British Journal of Political Science* 5 (January 1975), pp. 1–31; and Arthur H. Miller ''Political Issues and Trust in Government: 1964–70,'' along with the ''Comment'' by Jack Citrin, both in *American Political Science Review* 68 (September 1974), pp. 951–1001.

16. Jurgen Habermas, *Legitimation Crisis* (Boston, 1975).

17. An earlier statement of main themes in this section is Aaron B. Wildavsky's ''On the Superiority of National Conventions,'' *Review of Politics* 24 (July 1962), pp. 307–319.

18. Everett Carll Ladd, "Party Reform and the Public Interest" (paper prepared for delivery at the Brookings Conference on Party and Electorate Renewal, Washington, D.C., April 6–7, 1987). See, more generally, Gary R. Orren and Nelson W. Polsby, eds., *Media and Momentum: The New Hampshire Primary and Nomination Politics* (Chatham, N.J., 1987).

19. See V. O. Key, Jr., *American State Politics* (New York, 1956), Chapter 6.

20. V. O. Key, Jr., *Southern Politics* (New York, 1950), e.g., Chapter 3 (Alabama) and Chapter 9 (Arkansas).

21. Key, *American State Politics*, p. 216.

22. Nelson W. Polsby, "Was Hart's Life Unfairly Probed?" *New York Times* (May 6, 1987).

23. See Austin Ranney, *The Federalization of Presidential Primaries* (Washington, D.C., 1978), pp. 507; see also Commission on Presidential Nomination and Party Structure (Morley Winograd, Chairman), *Openness, Participation and Party Building: Reforms for a Stronger Democratic Party* (Washington, D.C., 1979), pp. 32–37.

24. A classical statement is Moisei Ostrogorski, *Democracy and the Party System in the United States* (New York, 1910), pp. 158–160. See also Elmo Roper, "What Price Conventions?" *Saturday Review* (September 3, 1960), p. 26.

25. The most famous account is still Ostrogorski, *Democracy and the Party System in the United States*, pp. 141–142.

26. At least one famous name from the world of television news apparently feels as we do about this problem. Walter Cronkite argues that "It is not necessary that we be admitted to the actual floor of the convention. There is a better way (such as the use of immediate off-floor interview booths) to cover the non-podium action in order to permit a more orderly convention procedure" (*The Challenges of Change* [Washington, D.C., 1971], p. 75).

27. See Herbert McClosky, Paul J. Hoffman, and Rosemary O'Hara, "Issue Conflict and Consensus among Party Leaders and Followers," *American Political Science Review* 54 (June 1960), pp. 406–427; Jeane Kirkpatrick, *The New Presidential Elite: Men and Women in National Politics* (New York, 1976); and John S. Jackson, III, et al., "Political Party Leaders and the Mass Public: 1980–1984" (paper presented at the Annual Meeting of the Midwest Political Science Association, Chicago, April 19, 1987).

28. John Morris, "Negro Delegates Drop Plans to Walk Out as a Demonstration Against Goldwater," *New York Times* (July 16, 1964).

29. Gerald M. Pomper, *Elections in America: Control and Influence in Democratic Politics*, revised ed. (New York, 1980).

30. Alan D. Monroe, "American Party Platforms and Public Opinion," *American Journal of Political Science* 27 (February 1983), p. 38.

31. Ibid., pp. 27–42.

32. Stanley Kelley, Jr., Richard E. Ayres, and William G. Bowen, "Registration and Voting: Putting First Things First," *American Political Science Review* 61 (June 1967), p. 362. More recent and equally comprehensive studies of this subject leading to similar results are found in Raymond E. Wolfinger and Steven J. Rosenstone, *Political Science Review* 72 (March 1978), pp. 22–48; and David Glass, Peverill Squire, and Raymond Wolfinger, "Voter Turnout: An

International Comparison," *Public Opinion* 6 (December/January 1984), pp. 55.

33. The general outline of this argument has been known in this country for at least fifty years. For example, in 1924, Harold G. Gosnell wrote, "In the European countries studied, a citizen who is entitled to vote does not, as a rule, have to make any effort to see that his name is on the list of eligible voters. The inconvenience of registering for voting in this country has caused many citizens to become non-voters." *Why Europe Votes* (Chicago, 1930), p. 185. See also Raymond E. Wolfinger and Steven J. Rosenstone, *Who Votes?* (New Haven, 1980).

34. In Richard A. Ayres, "Registration 1960: Key to Democratic Victory?" (unpublished senior thesis, Princeton University, 1964), cited in Kelley, Ayres, and Bowen, "Registration and Voting: Putting First Things First," p. 375, the author notes the correlation between convenience of registration and percent of the vote for the Democratic party as proof of the Daley machine's awareness of this phenomenon. By making registration extremely convenient, the state of Utah has succeeded in getting nearly total registration. See "Registration Procedures in the State of Utah," *Election Laws of the Fifty States and the District of Columbia* (Washington, D.C., June 1968), pp. 247–248. Similarly, Edmond Costantini and Willis Hawley estimate that turnout in California could be raised by more than 5 percent simply by keeping registration open until the last week before the election ("Increasing Participation in California Elections: The Need for Electoral Reform," *Public Affairs Report* 10, Bulletin of the Institute of Governmental Studies [June 1969]). A 1968 registration figure of 97.8 percent was attained by holding registrations open until the Wednesday before the election (when political interest, which would stimulate the voter to register and the party activists to get him registered, is highest) and by having publicized locations in every district.

35. Kelley, Ayres, and Bowen, "Registration and Voting: Putting First Things First," p. 373.

36. Some suggestions for a comprehensive program along these lines came from the Freedom to Vote Task Force of the Democratic National Committee, *That All May Vote* (Washington, D.C., 1969) and were embodied in House and Senate bills: The Universal Voter Enrollment Act of 1970 (House Resolution 19010 and Senate 4238). See the statement by Representative Morris Udall in the *Congressional Record* (August 13, 1970), pp. H8319–H8332.

37. See David Glass, Peverill Squire, and Raymond Wolfinger, "Voter Turnout: An International Comparison," *Public Opinion* 6 (December/January 1984), pp. 49–55.

38. Kelley, Ayres, and Bowen, "Registration and Voting: Putting First Things First," pp. 374–375.

39. See John R. Petrocik, "Voter Turnout and Electoral Preference: The Anomalous Reagan Elections," in Kay Lehman Schlozman, ed., *Elections in America* (Boston, 1987), pp. 261–292.

40. *Dunn* v. *Blumstein* 405 U.S. 330 (1972); and *Marston* v. *Lewis* 410 U.S. 759 (1973) and *Burn* v. *Forston* 410 U.S. 686 (1972).

41. Peverill Squire, Raymond E. Wolfinger, and David P. Glass, "Residential Mobility and Voter Turnout," *American Political Science Review* 81 (March 1987),

pp. 45–61. The quote is from p. 61. In an earlier study, Wolfinger and Rosenstone found that the effect of registration laws has been to depress voting turnout in national elections by approximately 9 percent.

Yet even if relaxation of voter registration restrictions brought about a corresponding expansion in the electorate, they conclude that the impact on electoral outcomes would be "wholly insignificant," since "the ideological composition of the expanded electorate would be virtually identical to the actual electorate in 1972." Rosenstone and Wolfinger, "The Effects of Registration Laws on Voter Turnout," p. 41; see also their response to a challenge to their conclusions in "Comment," *American Political Science Review,* 72 (December 1978), pp. 1361–1362.

42. On the other hand, California voters may now vote by mail for any reason, and increasingly are doing so; see Martha Walrath-Riley, "New Absentee and Mail-in Ballot Campaigns: The Winning Edge," *Campaigns and Elections* 5 (Spring 1984), pp. 20–30.

43. William G. Andrews, "American Voting Participation," *Western Political Quarterly* 19 (December 1966), p. 643.

44. Although we know of no effort to review the situation, there seems no compelling reason why felons—"ex-" or otherwise—should be denied the ballot. Voting may be a small way of maintaining their connection with society. Their ability to vote should make politicians more interested in their welfare, including the structure and management of penal institutions. The view that loss of the right to vote penalizes would-be felons and is, therefore, a deterrent to crime is hardly worth considering. If their having a vote constitutes a danger to society even after they are released from prison, then what is the rationale for letting them wander about at large where the rest of their behavior can also menace honest folk?

45. There were, of course, many other plans for "reform," involving almost all possible combinations of these three alternatives. For example, President Nixon at one point recommended that the 40 percent plurality plank which usually goes with the direct election proposal be applied instead to the present Electoral College setup (David S. Broder, "Mitchell Recommends Electoral Compromise," *Washington Post* [March 14, 1969]). A second example is the "federal system plan" of Senators Dole and Eagleton, which states

1. A president would be elected if he (a) won a plurality of the national vote and (b) won *either* pluralities in more than 50 percent of the states and D.C., or pluralities in states with 50 percent of the voters in the election.

2. If no candidate qualified, the election would go to an Electoral College where the states would be represented as they are today, and each candidate would automatically receive the electoral votes of the states he won.

3. In the unlikely event that no candidate received a majority of the electoral votes, the electoral votes of states that went for third-party candidates would be divided between the two leading national candidates in proportion to their share of the popular votes in those states (*Congressional Record* [March 5, 1970], p. S3026).

These plans have the following characteristics: (a) they are too complicated to solve any problems of public confusion or public perception that they are not "democratic," and (b) they have no significant body of congressional support.

46. This argument roughly corresponds to one of the main approaches to calculating

the strategic advantage of members of a coalition, pioneered by Irwin Mann and Lloyd Shapley. The argument proceeds as follows: "The Shapley value defines the power of actor A as the number of permutations (orderings) in which A occupies the pivotal position (that is, orderings in which A can cast the deciding vote) divided by the total number of possible permutations" (George Rabinowitz and Stuart MacDonald, "The Power of the States in U.S. Presidential Elections," *American Political Science Review* 80 [March 1986], p. 66). This approach shows the large states to be the winners. Their influence is more than proportional to their size. This model is often supplemented by an analysis that attempts to determine the influence of the average voter within each state. Along these lines, Lawrence Longley and James Dana, Jr. conclude that residents of California (the most advantaged state) have more than twice the "relative voting power" of the inhabitants of Arkansas (the least advantaged state). Lawrence D. Longley and James D. Dana, Jr., "New Empirical Estimates of the Biases of the Electoral College for the 1980s," *Western Political Quarterly*, 37 (March 1984), pp. 157–175.

Yet these calculations assume that all patterns of state voting are equally likely. This obviously is not a realistic assumption. Some states lean strongly toward one party; others are much more likely to occupy a pivotal "wing" position. Building on this insight, Rabinowitz and MacDonald utilize the results of recent elections to identify likely pivotal states and do their own calculation of relative voting power. Again, the large states are the winners. There are differences, however, from the results of the previous model. Most large states are even more influential but the power of those that lean strongly toward one party is diminished. Strongly Democratic Massachusetts is the biggest loser, dropping to a mere one-seventh of its influence as determined by the Shapley model.

Which model of state electoral power is more accurate? The second, which takes into account likely voting patterns, would appear more complete. Yet pivot patterns are an imperfect guide to future behavior. With Jimmy Carter at the head of the ticket in 1980, Georgia was one of the most strongly Democratic states in the nation. In 1984, Walter Mondale lost Georgia by an even larger margin than the nation as a whole. Predicting future swing states from past behavior may lead to serious errors.

One might also question the emphasis on the importance of swing states. Is a state that provides a loyal and consistent base of support for one party necessarily unimportant? Is not a solid base as important as more volatile swing states? In recent years, the Republicans have started presidential campaigns with a very strong position in the Mountain States. Since the outcome in these states has not been in doubt, neither campaign expends much effort on them. Thus it could be said that one-party states are less important. On the other hand, a safe base is valuable. The Republicans start ahead and are able to focus their resources on other areas. Democrats would love to have such a safe base of their own (besides D.C.). As we have seen, calculations of state influence depend heavily on the assumptions one begins with.

47. For example, Ed Gossett, original cosponsor of the district plan, asked, "Is it fair, is it honest, is it democratic, is it to the best interests of anyone in fact to place such a premium on a few thousand labor votes or Italian votes or Irish votes or Negro votes or Jewish votes or Polish votes, or Communist votes or big city machine votes, simply because they happen to be located in two or three industrial

pivotal states? Can anything but evil come from placing such temptation and power in the hands of political parties and political bosses? Both said groups and said politicians are computed as a nation suffers." Cited in David Brook, "Proposed Electoral College Reforms and Urban Minorities" (paper delivered at the 1969 Annual Meeting of the American Political Science Association, New York City, 1969), p. 6.

48. Eric R. A. N. Smith and Peverill Squire argue, following Shapley's logic, that the importance of states should be calculated according to the ease with which undecided voters can be influenced. While this method differs from ours, it also leads to the conclusion that southern states would gain in influence if the Electoral College was abolished. See Eric R. A. N. Smith and Peverill Squire, "Direct Election of the President and Power of the States," *Western Political Quarterly* 40 (March 1987), pp. 31–44.

49. In "The South Will Not Rise Again Through Direct Election of the President, Polsby and Wildavsky Notwithstanding," *Journal of Politics* 31 (August 1969), pp. 808–811, Professor Harvey Zeidenstein shows that the winner's margin of victory in eight large northern urban states—taken together—was greater than in the eleven states of the old Confederacy—taken together—in four of the six presidential elections between 1948 and 1968. From this he concludes that the influence of northern urban states, where the votes are, is likely to be very great under a system of direct elections. We agree, but we argue in the text that direct elections do improve the strategic position of one-party states (including some southern states), as compared with the Electoral College winner-take-all system. On this issue Zeidenstein is silent.

50. On September 18, 1969, by a vote of 339 to 70, a direct-election plan with a 40 percent plurality runoff provision was passed by the U.S. House of Representatives. See *Congressional Record* September 18, 1969), pp. H8142–8143; for the content of the bill, see *Congressional Record* (September 18, 1969), pp. H7745–H7746. For more recent discussion of proposed reforms, see "Hearings on the Electoral College and Direct Election," Committee on the Judiciary, U.S. Senate, 95th Congress (Washington, D.C., 1977).

51. The Michigan Survey Research Center finds that only 1.5 percent of the voters in 1968 had felt that Senator Eugene McCarthy was the best man for president in the spring and still felt that way after the election. If all participants in the system had known that he was not going to be defeated and disappear but would be a serious candidate at least through the first election, it is at least possible to conjecture that he could have picked up an additional 4 percent or 5 percent (Philip E. Converse, Warren E. Miller, Jerrold G. Rusk, and Arthur C. Wolfe, "Continuity and Change in American Politics: Parties and Issues in the 1968 Election," *American Political Science Review* 63 [December 1960], p. 1092). Cf. Richard N. Goodwin; "Reflections: Sources of the Public Unhappiness," *The New Yorker* (January 4, 1969), pp. 38–58.

52. The article that deals most clearly with the Electoral College in terms of its virtues of conciliation and broad coalition building is John Wildenthal, "Consensus after L.B.J.," *Southwest Review* 53 (Spring 1968), pp. 113–130. Wildenthal argues in part, "Rather than complain about being deprived of a choice when both parties wage 'me too' campaigns, the American people should be thankful that the interests of a wide variety of Americans can be reconciled by both parties with similar programs."

53. One summary of this position is given by Representative Thomas Kleppe of North Dakota in the *Congressional Record* (February 3, 1969), p. H648. An interesting sidelight is his citation of Senator John F. Kennedy, who said, "After all, the states came into the Union as units. Electoral votes are not given out on the basis of voting numbers, but on the basis of population. The electoral votes belong to each state. The way the system works now is that we carry on a campaign in fifty states, and the electoral votes of that state belong to that party which carries each state. If we are going to change that system, it seems to me it would strike a blow at states' rights in major proportions. It would probably end states' rights and make this country one great unit."

54. Roscoe Drummond, "Perils of the Electoral System," *Washington Post* (November 14, 1960). An argument in some ways parallel to our own is contained in Anthony Lewis, "The Case Against Electoral Reform," *The Reporter* (December 8, 1960), pp. 31–33. See also Allan P. Sindler, "Presidential Election Methods and Urban-Ethnic Interests," *Law and Contemporary Problems* 27 (Spring 1962), pp. 213–233.

55. See Estes Kefauver, "The Electoral College: Old Reforms Take a New Look," *Law and Contemporary Problems* 27 (Spring 1962), p. 197.

56. See Arthur Schlesinger, Jr., "A One-for-All Electoral College," *The Wall Street Journal* (August 19, 1988) p. 16.

57. Despite popular misconceptions, even the 1964 Republican platform, written by supporters of Barry Goldwater, contained explicit promises to preserve these programs.

58. See Kirk H. Porter and Donald Bruce Johnson, *National Party Platforms, 1840–1956* (Urbana, Ill., 1956). There are immense differences in both party platforms between 1932 and 1952. For example, the subheadings under domestic policy in the 1952 platforms deal with a range of topics entirely missing in 1932. The Democratic 1952 platform included subheadings on full employment, price supports, farm credit, crop insurance, rural electrification, the physically handicapped, migratory workers, river basin development, arid areas, wildlife, recreation, Social Security, unemployment insurance, public assistance, needs of our aging citizens, health, medical education, hospitals and health centers, costs of medical care, public housing, slum clearance, urban redevelopment, aid to education, school lunches, day-care facilities, specific steps under civil rights, and many other subjects completely absent in 1932. Most of these worthy causes were also supported in the 1952 Republican platform and were missing from the 1932 Republican platform. Nevertheless, there are differences between the parties in 1952 in regard to use of the public lands, public housing, labor legislation, farm legislation, public power, aid to education, and much more. In regard to education, for example, the 1952 Republican platform reads: "The tradition of popular education, tax-supported and free to all, is strong with our people. The responsibility for sustaining this system of popular education has always rested upon the local communities and the states. We subscribe fully to this principle." The corresponding Democratic plank reads in part: "Local, State, and Federal government have shared responsibility to contribute appropriately to the pressing needs of our education system. . . . We pledge immediate consideration for those school systems which need further legislation to provide Federal aid for new school construction, teachers' salaries and school maintenance and repair" (Porter and Johnson, pp. 485, 504).

See also Gerald M. Pomper, *Elections in America* (New York, 1968), pp. 149–178.

59. Anyone who thinks there are not serious and substantial differences between our national parties over a wide range of issues should consult the accompanying table, which outlines positions from the Republican and Democratic party platforms of 1988.

A Comparison of Democratic and Republican Platforms, 1988

Republican Platform Economic Policy	Democratic Platform Economic Policy
"More people are working than ever before; real family income has risen; inflation is tamed . . . Government didn't work this economic wonder. The people did. Republicans got government out of the way, off the back of households and entrepreneurs, so the people could take charge. . . . We want to reduce further the intrusion of government into the lives of our citizens. Let Democrats trust the federal bureaucracy. Republicans trust the creative energy of workers and investors in a free market."	"[T]he time has come for America to take charge once again of its economic future, to reverse seven years of 'voodoo economics,' 'trickle down' policies, fiscal irresponsibility, and economic violence against poor and working people that have converted this proud country into the world's largest debtor nation, mortgaged our children's future by tripling our national debt, placed home ownership out of reach for most young families, permitted the rise of poverty and homelessness on the streets of America, reduced the buying power of working men and women . . ."
National Security "Under Republican leadership, the United States will respond to requests from our Central American neighbors for security assistance to protect their emerging democracies against insurgencies sponsored by the Soviets, Cuba, or others."	*National Security* "Instead of the current emphasis on military solutions we will use negotiations and incentive to encourage free and fair elections and security for all nations in [Central America]."
Civil Rights "With its message of economic growth and opportunity, the GOP is the natural champion of blacks, minorities, women and ethnic Americans. A free economy helps defeat discrimination by fostering opportunity for all. That's why real income for Black families has risen 14 percent since 1982. It's why members of minority groups have been gaining jobs in the Republican recovery twice as fast as everyone else."	*Civil Rights* "[W]e honor our multicultural heritage by assuring equal access to government services, employment, housing, business enterprise and education, to every citizen regardless of race, sex, national origin, religion, age, handicapping condition or sexual orientation. . . . [T]hese rights are without exception too precious to be jeopardized by Federal Judges and Justice Department Officials chosen during the past seven years—by a political party increasingly monolithic both racially and culturally—more for their unenlightened ideological views than for their respect for the rule of law."

A Comparison of Democratic and Republican Platforms, 1988 (continued)

Republican Platform *Economic Policy*	*Democratic Platform* *Economic Policy*
Welfare "We are committed to assisting those in need. We are equally committed to addressing the root causes of poverty. Divorce, desertion, and illegitimacy have been responsible for almost all the increase in child poverty in the last 15 years. Because strong family life is the most remarkable anti-poverty force in history, Republicans will make the reinforcement of family rights and responsibilities an essential component of public policy."	*Welfare* "We believe that the strength of our families is enhanced by programs to prevent abuse and malnutrition among children, crime, dropouts and pregnancy among teenagers and violence in the family. . . . There are few better investments for this country than prenatal care, infant nutrition and preschool education, and there are few more successful programs than WIC, Head Start, and prenatal care."
Housing "The best housing policy is sound economic policy. Low interest rates, low inflation rates, and the availability of a job with a good paycheck that makes a mortgage affordable are the best housing programs of all."	*Housing* "[H]omelessness—a national shame—should be ended in America; . . . the supply of affordable housing should be expanded in order to avoid the projected shortfall; . . . the inventory of public and subsidized housing should be renovated, preserved and increased. . . ."
AIDS "AIDS education should emphasize that abstinence from drug abuse and sexual activity outside of marriage is the safest way to avoid infection with the AIDS virus."	*AIDS* "[T]he HIV/AIDS epidemic is an unprecedented public health emergency requiring increased support for accelerated research on, and expedited FDA approval of, treatments and vaccines, comprehensive education and prevention, compassionate patient care, . . . voluntary and confidential testing and counseling, and protection of the civil rights of those suffering from AIDS. . . ."
Drugs "We know the most powerful deterrent to drug abuse: strong, stable family life, along with the absolute approach summed up in 'Just Say No.' Nancy Reagan has made that phrase the battle-cry of the war against drugs, and it is echoed by more than 10,000 Just Say No clubs. We salute her for pointing the way to our nation's drug-free future."	*Drugs* "We believe that this effort should include comprehensive programs to educate our children at the earliest ages on the dangers of alcohol and drug abuse, readily available treatment counseling for those who seek to address their dependency, the strengthening of vital interdiction agencies, . . . a summit of Western Hemispheric nations to coordinate efforts . . ."

Excerpts from the Democratic and Republican party platforms, found in 44 *Congressional Quarterly Almanac 1988* (Washington, D.C., 1989), pp. 46-A-75-A and 87-A-90-A.

Chapter 6: American Parties and Democracy

1. This parallels in many respects an argument to be found in Robert A. Dahl, *A Preface to Democratic Theory* (Chicago, 1956).

2. Angus Campbell, Philip E. Converse, Warren E. Miller, and Donald E. Stokes, *The American Voter* (New York, 1960), pp. 525–527.

3. Richard A. Brody and Benjamin I. Page, "Policy Voting and the Electoral Process: The Vietnam War Issue," *American Political Science Review* 66 (September, 1971), p. 979. For the 1980 election, the evidence is clear that no special benefit with voters was conferred on Ronald Reagan by virtue of his conservatism. See William Schneider, "The November 4 Vote for President: What Did It Mean?" in Austin Ranney, ed., *The American Elections of 1980* (Washington, D.C., 1981), pp. 212–262; and Nelson W. Polsby, "Party Realignment in the 1980 Election," *The Yale Review* 72 (Autumn 1982), pp. 43–54.

4. See Dahl, *A Preface to Democratic Theory*, pp. 124–131.

5. See Nelson W. Polsby, *Consequences of Party Reform* (New York, 1983).

6. See Jack Dennis, "Trends in Public Support for the American Political Party System," *British Journal of Political Science* 5 (April 1975), pp. 187–230.

7. For the story on split-ticket voting and its effects, see Gary C. Jacobson, *The Electoral Origins of Divided Government*, (San Francisco, 1990).-

Index

Haggerty, Brian A., 62, 364*n*43
Hagstrom, Jerry, 390*n*68, 391*n*84
Haig, Alexander, 374*n*9
Halleck, Charles, 164
Hamilton, Alexander, 209
Hamilton, Bill, 221
Harding, Warren, 163, 165, 229
Harnsberger, Caroline T., 383*n*157
Harris, Fred, 106, 107
Harrison, Irwin "Tubby," 210, 211, 212, 213, 215
Harrison, William Henry, 228–29
Harris Poll, 188, 210, 212
Hart, Gary, 44, 53–54, 55, 58, 68, 80, 81, 99, 101, 109, 114, 116, 120, 127, 174, 210, 237, 293, 331, 373*n*8, 376*n*36
Hart, Peter D., 185, 210, 211, 396*n*187
Harwood, Richard, 380*n*93
Hatch Act, 89
Hawaii, 128, 199
Hawley, Willis, 402*n*34
Haynes, Paul R., 346*n*1
Hazlitt, Henry, 396*n*1
Heard, Alexander, 51, 360*n*3, 361*n*9
Hebert, Edward, 279
Heckling, 250
Helms, E. A., 372*n*2
Helms, Jesse, 59
Herring, E. Pendleton, 356*n*86, 357*n*90, 372*n*2, 399*n*5, 400*n*6
Herrnson, Paul S., 35, 357*n*100
Herzog, Arthur, 377*n*53
Hess, Stephen, 367*n*78, 395*n*167
Hidden vote theory, 188, 283
Highton, Ben, xvi, 355*n*62
Hispanic voters, 201, 203
Hodgson, Godfrey, 377*n*53
Hoffman, Nicholas von, 393*n*134
Hoffman, Paul J., 356*n*88, 381*n*116, 401*n*27
Holum, John, 224
Hoover, Herbert, xiii, 87, 189
Horton, Willie, 215, 218, 231, 232

Houston (Tex.), 134
Howe, Daniel Walker, 383*n*150
Hucker, Charles W., 360*n*8
Huckshorn, Robert J., 357*nn*93, 94
Hume, Ellen, 383*n*159
Humphrey, Hubert, 90, 130, 133, 141, 142, 143, 271, 358*n*111, 363*n*29, 365*n*52, 366*n*68
  in 1964 election, 166
  in 1968 election, 8–9, 51–52, 67, 94, 95, 100, 132, 161, 168, 180–81, 191, 244, 250, 280, 314
  in 1972 election, 123, 124
  in 1976 election, 55, 56
  personal style of, 240
Hunt, Albert R., 393*n*147, 394*n*161
Hunt Commission (1960–1988), 44, 126–27, 174
Huntington, Samuel P., 371*n*120
Huthmacher, J. Joseph, 350*n*14
Hyman, Herbert H., 350*n*19, 387*n*25
Hyman, Sidney, 363*n*29

Idaho, 190, 191, 199, 378*n*76
Idea mongers, 223–24
Ideology
  consultants and, 226
  of delegates, 152–58
  and party identification, 182–84
  polarization of, 203–4
  of voters, 6
Ifill, Gwen, 376*n*37
Illinois, 46, 163, 207, 228, 252, 310, 313
Income
  of delegates, 143
  voter turnout and, 24
Incumbency
  as a liability, 90–95
  media partisanship and, 75
  PAC contributions and, 65
  as resource, 86–89, 207
  television and, 207

Printed in the United States
By Bookmasters